THE NATIONAL GEOGRAPHIC TRAVELER
SPAIN

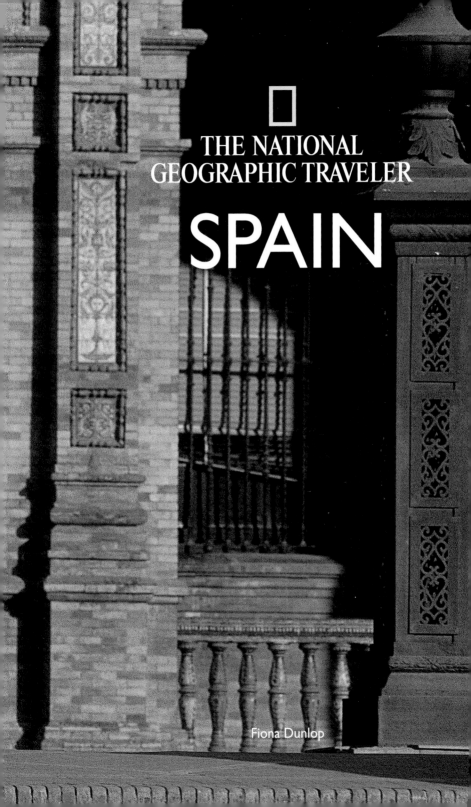

THE NATIONAL
GEOGRAPHIC TRAVELER

SPAIN

Fiona Dunlop

Contents

How to use this guide 6–7 About the author 8
The regions 53–340 Travelwise 341–90
Index 391–397 Credits 398–99

Page 1: Girl in traditional dress, Valencia
Pages 2–3: Junior flamenco dancer on the Plaza de España, Madrid
Left: Flamenco steps

How to use this guide

See back flap for keys to text and map symbols

The *National Geographic Traveler* brings you the best of Spain in text, pictures, and maps. Divided into three main sections, the guide begins with an overview of history and culture. Following are ten regional chapters with featured sites selected by the author for their particular interest. Each chapter opens with its own contents list for easy reference.

The regions, and sites within them, are arranged geographically. Some regions are further divided into smaller areas. A map introduces each region, highlighting the featured sites. Walks and drives, plotted on their own maps, suggest routes for discovering an area. Features and sidebars offer intriguing detail on history, culture, or contemporary life.

The final section, Travelwise, lists essential information for the traveler—pre-trip planning, communications, money matters, getting around, and emergencies—plus offers a selection of hotels, restaurants, shops, entertainment, and activities.

To the best of our knowledge, all information is accurate as of the press date. However, it is always advisable to call ahead when possible.

Place-names

In regions where dialect is spoken, for example Galicia, Euskadi (Basque country), Catalunya, Valencia, and the Balearic Islands, the dialect name is given first with the Castilian name in parentheses afterward.

Color coding

130

Each region is color coded for easy reference. Find the region you want on the map on the front flap, and look for the color flash at the top of the pages of the relevant chapter. Information in **Travelwise** is also color coded to each region.

Museu Picasso

🅰	155 E3
✉	Carrer de Montcada 15–23
☎	93 319 63 10
🕐	Closed Sun. p.m.
💲	$
🚇	Metro: Jaume I, Line 4

Visitor information

Practical information for most sites is given in the side column (see key to symbols on back flap). The map reference gives the page number of the map and grid reference. Other details are the site's address, telephone number, days closed, entrance charge in a range from $ (under $4) to $$$$$ (over $25), and public transportation. Other sites have visitor information in italics and parentheses in the text.

TRAVELWISE

CASTILLA Y LEÓN — Color-coded region name

SALAMANCA 37000 — Town name

🏨 **RECTOR** — Hotel name & price range
$$ ★★★★

PASEO RECTOR ESPERABE 10. — Address, telephone, & fax numbers
TEL 923 21 84 82
FAX 923 21 40 08

A grandiose 1940s building of Villamayor stone with elegant interiors and fabulous rooms. — Brief description of hotel

🛈 14 🅿 ⇄ 🄯 🆂 All major cards — Hotel facilities & credit card details

🍴 **CHEZ VICTOR** — Restaurant name & price range
$$

ESPOZ Y MINA 26 — Address & telephone number
TEL 923 21 31 23

Owner Victor Salvador offers creative French-Spanish cuisine at this Michelin starred restaurant. — Brief description of restaurant

🍽 50 🕐 Closed Sun. D, Mon. & Aug. 🄯 🆂 All major cards — Restaurant closures & credit card details

Hotel & restaurant prices

An explanation of the price ranges used in entries is given in the Hotels & Restaurants section (see p. 348).

REGIONAL MAPS

- A locator map accompanies each regional map and shows the location of that region in the country.
- Adjacent regions are shown, each with a page reference.

WALKING TOURS

- An information box gives the starting and finishing points, time and length of walk, and places not to be missed along the route.

DRIVING TOURS

- An information box provides details including starting and finishing points, time and length of drive, and places not to be missed along the route.

THE NATIONAL GEOGRAPHIC TRAVELER

SPAIN

About the author

Fiona Dunlop's peripatetic life has led her from the Australian beaches of her birth to an upbringing in London, university in Sussex, and subsequent jobs in Italy and Monte Carlo. During 15 years spent in Paris she was strongly involved in the arts, working in fashion and art galleries before immersing herself in journalism. She has written widely for numerous international art and interior design magazines and national newspapers (including the *Observer, Sunday Times, The Times, Art International, Elle Decoration, Interni,* and *Homes & Gardens,* among others). A taste for the tropics and ancient cultures has led Fiona to spend long research periods in developing countries. These have produced travel guides to India, Indonesia, Singapore & Malaysia, Vietnam, Mexico, Costa Rica, and southern Africa. Since 1980, in between her more exotic travels, she has regularly visited Andalucía to write articles and books in what she considers to be the optimum conditions, combining *sol y sombra* (sun and shade), not to mention tapas. Her main base is now in London.

Tomasina Wilson, a colleague of Fiona Dunlop's who lives and works in Alacant (Alicante), wrote the Travelwise chapter.

History & culture

Sevilla's Feria brings out the whole flamenco wardrobe.

Spain today

THE STEREOTYPICAL SPANIARD DISAPPEARED LONG AGO. BACK IN THE 19TH century, writers and artists wove images of a land inhabited by voluptuous, black-haired, fiery-eyed women and dubious-looking, mustachioed men in gaucho hats, who loitered in the shadows. Look for it today and you will be disappointed. Spain is firmly within the net of globalization and, superficially at least, its inhabitants resemble those of the rest of the Western world. Yet beneath the surface lies a web of regional differences and traditions that even mobile-phone-clutching young professionals have not forsaken.

Whether Catalan, Basque, Galician, Asturian, Cantabrian, Castilian, Aragonese, Extremaduran, Valencian, Manchegan, Murcian, Andalusian, or from the Balearics or the Canaries, the Spaniard of the 21st century clings adamantly to his or her roots, a habit illustrated in local fiestas and by language itself. After long suppression under the dictator General Franco, who died in 1975, regional identities have undergone an explosive revival, given impetus by the powers granted to the 17 autonomous communities set up in the new constitution of 1978. Separatism has reached extremes in Euskadi (Basque country), while Catalunya maintains a more pragmatic approach. Regional loyalty fragments further, from province to province, from town to town, and from village to village. There is no Spain or Spaniard as such. Instead, a passionately local spirit is cloaked in the dominant Castilian culture—and in a love of excess that fizzes in the action-packed calendar of fiestas.

If you stood a handpicked Spaniard, Sephardí, and North African side by side you would see little physical difference, as the blood of Spain is a cocktail of shifting cultures. You find Andalusians working in Catalunya, unemployed Castilian farmers migrating to Euskadi, and Madrid embracing incomers from every region. And still, deep in the rural countryside, unadulterated relics of distant invaders exist. Descendants of the Romans live in Asturias, and those of the Swabians on the borders of Extremadura and Castilla. Even more distinct and determinedly set apart from the mainstream is the 500-year-old Gypsy community, visible above all in Andalucía. Gypsies provoke waves of intolerance, and in the 1990s so did Spain's other highly visible minority—North African migrant workers.

Language is equally diverse. The language called "Spanish" is actually Castilian, from the central part of Spain. The Basque, Catalan, and Galician languages are utterly distinctive, as are regional accents. Each Canary island has its own accent, and the slurred tones of Andalusians are quite different from the crisp, machine-gun fire of Madrileños, the people of Madrid. This is something that you might not be aware of in Spain's anonymous coastal resorts, where signs are as likely to be in English and German as in Spanish. The onward march of tourism since the 1960s is creating another division of Spain, that between the Mediterranean *costas* (coasts) invaded by northern European retirees and summer sun-seekers, and the vast, underpopulated interior. It is in the latter that the reactionary heart of Spain beats, where rural inhabitants may barely know the next town and where population densities descend below 30 inhabitants per square mile. Catholicism rules in these areas—the two Castillas, Aragón, and Extremadura—and the bells peal daily.

In the big cities, it is another story entirely. Barcelona, capital of Catalunya, easily rivals the best of Europe's cultural hubs, and its inhabitants exude a prosperity, confidence, and sophistication seen nowhere else in Spain. Although they do not readily embrace foreigners, they exemplify the old adage: Once you get to know them, they are friends for life. Madrid, the capital and Spain's largest city (with a mere three million population), falls well behind in avant-gardism and style, however much its businesses bustle and art collections blossom. But its more tolerant and relaxed inhabitants have a talent for nocturnal intensity and living

Antoni Gaudí's Parc Güell in Barcelona epitomizes the architect's bent for fantasy.

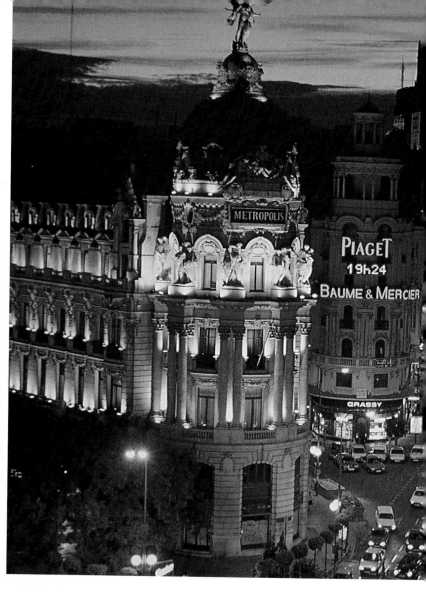

on the edge: They were the ones who spear-headed the *movida*, a cathartic surge of hedonism and creativity that seized Spain in the early 1980s. Sex, drugs, and rock and roll boomed, in tandem with a new wave of artists, filmmakers, and musicians. Spain's much underestimated third city is Valencia, whose people adeptly combine southern laissez-faire with a Catalan flair for business. Sevilla, Zaragoza, Málaga, and Bilbao follow, each with a distinct flavor, culture, and attitude, swinging from high southern exuberance to intelligent urbanism and industrial savvy.

Altogether, Spaniards number 40 million, but a significant sign of the times is demo-graphic aging. The forecast decline in birthrate of up to 24 percent over the next 50 years would make Spain home to the world's oldest population. Other problems are more pressing. An estimated 50 percent of house-holds are unable to afford a week's holiday away from home. Spain has the highest

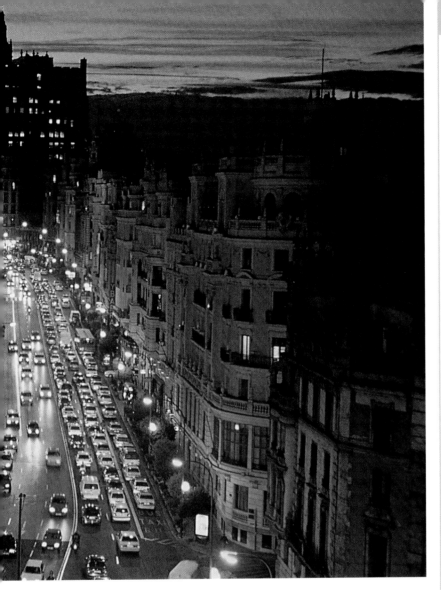

Bronze "Winged Victory" gazes over Madrid from atop the neoclassic Metropolis.

unemployment and second highest incidence of AIDS in the European Union (E.U.) It also has a poor environmental record. Yet Spain as a nation is undergoing a greater social, political, and economic transformation than any other Western European nation. And, somehow, despite drinking and smoking more than the people of any other European country,

Spaniards enjoy an exceptionally high life expectancy. The secret could well be that around 87 percent of the population declares itself happy—the key to Spanishness?

FESTIVALS

The fiesta of a village or town is the excuse for everyone to let their hair down. This is the zenith of the year, when normally dignified, well-mannered people (which means most Spaniards) take to the streets and dance the

night away. Tradition still pulls the heartstrings, despite the radical social upheavals of recent decades, and this is unlikely to change in the near future. Patron saints' days are the most common fiestas, but you also find a multitude of idiosyncratic celebrations stemming from seasonal, historic, or religious events, each one requiring costumed participants, food, drink, music, and dance. Stylized battles between Moors and Christians, wine-battles in Rioja, the running of the bulls in Iruña (Pamplona), bonfires and satirical figures in Valencia, towering human pyramids in Catalunya, horse-branding in Galicia, coffin races in La Mancha, men disguised in animal skins and masks in Mallorca, whip-brandishing bogeymen in Extremadura, and a hedonistic pilgrimage to Rocío, in Huelva province, of nearly one million people from all over Andalucía—all are permanent fixtures on the calendar.

Dominating the religious calendar is Semana Santa (Holy Week, see pp. 272–73), the week leading up to Easter. It is closely followed in importance by Corpus Christi a few weeks later, when devils, dance groups, dwarfs, giants, and mythological creatures form boisterous processions. Sometimes they follow a route of stunningly patterned carpets of flowers, salt, or sawdust. Medieval mystery plays are performed at this and other festivals. Christmas (Navidad), Los Mayos (a spring celebration of love and nature), San Juan (St. John, when pagan rites and bonfires celebrate the summer solstice), and September 8 (an autumn festival) feature among the other general celebrations. Carnival, which takes place in February or March before Lent, brings exceptional outbursts of color, costumes, and offbeat customs, above all in Cádiz, throughout Galicia, and in Santa Cruz de Tenerife, which approaches Rio de Janeiro's Carnival in scale and exuberance.

BULLFIGHTING

Bulls are the best known animal participants in Spain's festivals. Every town has a bullfighting season during its *feria* (annual fair)—look out for posters advertising the events—but

The Catalans are acrobatic experts at creating human pyramids (*castellers*), seen here in Tarragona.

matador prowess reaches a height in the bullrings of Madrid and Sevilla. *Encierros*—the running of the bulls, when bulls are let loose to charge through the streets—lie at the heart of local festivals from Peñafiel to Iruña (Pamplona) and beyond. Bullbaiting is still practiced by Basques. Devotees of bullfighting (primarily Andalusians) are called *aficionados,*

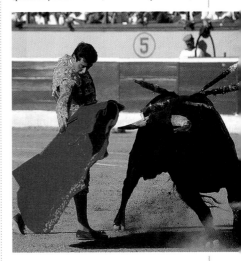

The national passion of bullfighting is considered art rather than sport.

and for them bullfighting is not a sport, but an art, both ritualistic and ceremonial, with primitive origins and echoes of Roman gladiatorial combat and medieval jousting.

The *corrida de toros* (bullfight) begins with a procession around the ring of the participants, accompanied by stirring music from the band. After testing how aggressive the bull is, the matador and his team on the ground leave center stage to the *picadores,* who ride out and encourage the bull to charge. The horses are padded to prevent serious injury, and their riders pierce the bull's neck and shoulders with their lances. Next, the *banderilleros* (bullfighters on foot, carrying *banderillas* or colored darts) enter and run at the bull trying to stick their banderillas into his shoulders. With the bull's energy depleted, the matador enters alone, to demonstrate his skill in making passes with his red cape and steering the bull expertly within inches of his body. Finally, he drives his sword in between the bull's shoulders for the kill.

Long reviled by sensitive foreigners and by many Spaniards, the bullfight is nonetheless the most perfect expression of Spanishness: pomp and ceremony, *sol y sombra* (sun and shade), a deep sense of drama, tragedy, and fatalism, all orchestrated by the fearless *furia española*—the legendary Spanish fury that made Spain's enemies tremble. Spaniards are not fazed by death, as history from the con-

quistadores and Inquisition to the Civil War ably demonstrates. Theatricality and pushing to the limit are enduring elements in the national psyche.

THE LAND

The third largest country of the continent of Europe (after Russia and France) is a vast, multifaceted expanse. From lush green valley to craggy granite rockface or barren scrub, the Spanish landscape always forms a powerful

Ubrique's whitewashed buildings and surrounding sierra characterize Andalucía.

absolute. No other European country can rival the splendor, wildness, and intensity of Spain's landscapes, whether shimmering in scorching heat, softened by drizzle, or swept by glacial winter winds. Space dominates, horizons seem infinite, towns are rare, and the climate revels in extremes. In January you can swim in the Canaries while Basques soak in *sirimiri* (misty drizzle), Castilians bend double against a blistering wind, Andalusians bask in gentle sunlight, and Catalans whiz down ski runs.

From the natural barrier of the Pyrenees and its westerly extension, the Sierra Cantábrica, 197,323 square miles (505,957 sq km) unfold southward through the central *meseta* (tableland) of Castilla to the peaks of the Sierra Nevada and the limestone desert of eastern Andalucía. Mountain ranges—*sierras*—zigzag across the peninsula: Spain's average altitude is second only to that of Switzerland among European countries. It has the continent's highest road and highest village, both in the Sierra Nevada. This predominance of often spectacular sierra is one of the reasons for the strength of tradition in Spain, as isolated mountain communities once had little contact with the sociocultural advances of the cities. Massive improvements in communications and infrastructure over the last 20 years have made most, though not all, of these hidden communities far more accessible.

Rainfall is notoriously sparse except in the far north. Water shortages and desertification are a major cause of concern in Andalucía. Only five large rivers course across this generous peninsula: the Ebro, Guadalquivir, Guadiana, Tagus, and Duero, each sprouting branches that end in pathetic trickles and may dry up completely. Yet, once again, Spain surprises, for it boasts one of Europe's most fertile regions: the rice fields and *huerta* (irrigated land) of Valencia. Verdant havens are found in the undulating meadows and orchards of Cantabria and Asturias, and lusher parts of the Costa del Sol, sprinkled with palm trees, jasmine, and bougainvillaea.

FLORA & FAUNA

An estimated 90 percent of Spain's prehistoric forests disappeared long ago. They gave way to wheat fields, vineyards, olive groves, and fruit orchards, but also to vast tracts of uncultivable scrub and barren shale where only cactuses dare to grow. The remaining pockets of forest harbor a high proportion of European species, including 368 native bird species. You are unlikely to encounter the wolves and the few brown bears that roam the mountains of the north and west, but you may glimpse chamois, deer, and possibly wild boars among the oak, beech, ash, and lime trees that cover the lower slopes before they give way to pine and fir at higher altitudes. Birds of prey also favor mountainous areas, and Spain is home to about 25 species, including red kites, griffon vultures, and the endangered imperial eagle. Southern Spain is a stopping point on migration routes between Europe, Africa, and Asia, and bird-watchers can spot the greatest number of species in the pine forests of the Sierra de Cazorla, near Úbeda, and in the sand dunes and marshes of

the Coto Doñana, southwest of Seville. On inland waters you may see migrating flamingoes and European cranes, while hoopoes, golden orioles, cuckoos, woodpeckers, and bee-eaters frequent the riverbanks and woods.

Flora is another outstanding attraction: Spain has about 8,000 species of which one tenth are endemic. Many of these are alpine varieties that thrive in the highest mountains. Much of the interior is carpeted in typical Mediterranean maquis—aromatic scrubby

Playa de la Frayata, in Sitges near Barcelona, offers the sun, sea, and sand that make Spain so popular with vacationers.

underbrush that is an absolute delight in early summer. Then there are the brilliant butterflies…the list is endless.

FOOD & DRINK

Although Spain is not traditionally a gastronome's destination, you may be pleasantly surprised. Cuisine is not treated as reverently as in France, but its ingredients are as rich and varied as the climate and terrain. An intimate knowledge of the quality of basic products—for example virgin olive oil, *jamón* (ham), ewe's cheese, anchovies, tomatoes, and lamb—is part of the traditional heritage that even city dwellers have not lost. Just as wine is leaping up the quality scale (see pp. 134–35), so cooking is fast developing from simple, hearty fare into far more sophisticated preparations. Leading this gastronomic revolution is a new generation of chefs from Euskadi and Catalunya—Spain's closest neighbors to France. As their influence spreads, every large town now has a few top-notch restaurants.

One of Spain's greatest contributions to international eating habits is the tradition of *tapas* (known in the north as *pinchos*), appetizers that you eat with glasses of beer, wine, or sherry at the end of the early evening *paseo* (stroll) or workday. Tapas let you sample regional specialties, and keep you going until dinner (which rarely occurs before 10 p.m.), or even replace it. They are served in small *porciones* and larger *raciones:* Typical tapas are *morcilla* (black pudding), *mojama* (air-dried tuna), broad beans cooked with bacon and mint, kidneys sautéed in sherry, gazpacho, simple skewers of grilled meat or seafood, and, most basic of all, *migas*—fried breadcrumbs. Tapas suit the Spanish character, as consumption is invariably linked to socializing in an

A paella of this size, made for a festival in L'Hospitalet de Llobregat, is exceptional.

impromptu, informal way. Some bars produce only one specialty, thus encouraging customers to move from bar to bar, eating, drinking, and chatting with groups of friends and family, often into the late hours.

Lunch is the most important meal of the day, starting after 2 p.m. and ending late in the afternoon. In restaurants the *menú del día* (menu of the day) is usually a good choice if you are on a budget, but daily specials have the freshest ingredients. Regional specialties include *cochinillo* (roast suckling pig) in Castilla, *rabo de toro* (ox tail) in Andalucía, *fabada* (pork and beans) in Asturias, paella in Valencia, and *pulpo a la Gallega* (octopus in sauce) in Galicia. From a basic peasant cuisine, the peninsula's food is evolving into an array of finely orchestrated gastronomic indulgences—all taken with an inimitable Spanish pinch of salt. ■

History of Spain

THE NAME IBERIA FIRST CROPPED UP IN THE SIXTH CENTURY B.C. WHEN A Greek writer referred to the people living along the River Ebre, or Ebro (Iberus). Spain's history goes back a lot further, to the time when early people first crossed the narrow Straits of Gibraltar from Africa.

Evidence has been found in Andalucía of human presence (and that of elephants and carnivorous mammals) more than one million years ago. By around 25,000 B.C., Paleolithic hunter-gatherers were creating cave paintings of bison and deer. The finest Paleolithic paintings known are in the caves of Altamira in Cantabria and date from around 15,000 B.C., long before the dolmens of Antequera (see p. 282) or the *talayot* of the Balearics (see p. 329) were built.

Settled culture appeared with the Iberians themselves, who are thought to have originated in North Africa. They were later joined by Celts to become Celtiberians. Galicia's *castros* (fortified hill villages) are relics of their advanced hybrid culture. Elsewhere, Spain had little sign of an ordered society other than the legendary Tartessos in Andalucía. This was the Biblical Tarshish, a sophisticated, hierarchic society between the lower Guadalquivir and Guadiana rivers, reported by Phoenician traders in the first millennium B.C.

PHOENICIANS, GREEKS, & CARTHAGINIANS

Change came in the first millennium B.C. through the trading network of more sophisticated peoples from the eastern Mediterranean—Phoenicians and Greeks. Spain's extensive mineral resources first attracted Phoenicians to Cádiz in the eighth century B.C. They were followed by Greeks, who spread inland from numerous points on the Mediterranean coast. The potter's wheel, currency, and iron technology were among Greek contributions to Iberian society. Spain's oldest works of art—La Dama de Elche and La Dama de Baza (both fifth to fourth century B.C.) display clear eastern Mediterranean influence.

When the sun set for the Phoenicians it rose in turn for their cousins, the Carthaginians (based at Carthage, in modern Tunisia). Rome and Carthage were at loggerheads over control of the Mediterranean, and the Iberian peninsula was a pawn in their game. Greek influence ended as the Carthaginians moved into Tartessos, but native Iberians continued to flourish, exporting wine, olive oil, grain, and their rich mineral deposits. During the Punic Wars (third century B.C.) between Rome and Carthage, Iberians were employed in Hannibal's army, which eventually crossed the Alps into Italy. The Roman response was to obliterate Carthage in 202 B.C. This announced Rome's long hold over Europe—including Hispania, as Roman Spain was known.

ROMAN SPAIN

For the next 500 years Rome imprinted its mark on Spain, still distinct today in straight-as-a-die roads, bridges, aqueducts, amphitheaters, urban layouts, and the Latin-based Spanish language. The towns of Córdoba (Corduba), Tarragona (Tarraco), and Mérida (Augusta Emerita) became capitals of the three Roman provinces of Baetica, Tarraconensis, and Lusitania. Numerous other urban settlements—Sevilla (Hispalis), León (Legio), Pamplona (Pompaelo), Zaragoza (Caesar Augusta)—are also Roman. Spain's mines continued to yield gold and silver in vast quantities, much of which was shipped back to Rome in an ironic reversal of Spain's own plundering of the New World more than a thousand years later. As Roman control strengthened, the process of colonization became Romanization. Waves of immigrant Romans settled permanently in Hispania and established their customs alongside those of the Iberians. Resistance to Romanization was strongest in the north and northwest, and Galicia's Celtiberians were allowed to preserve their traditions and names.

The ruins of a prehistoric Celtic-Roman *castro* (fortified village) at Monte Santa Tecla, in Galicia

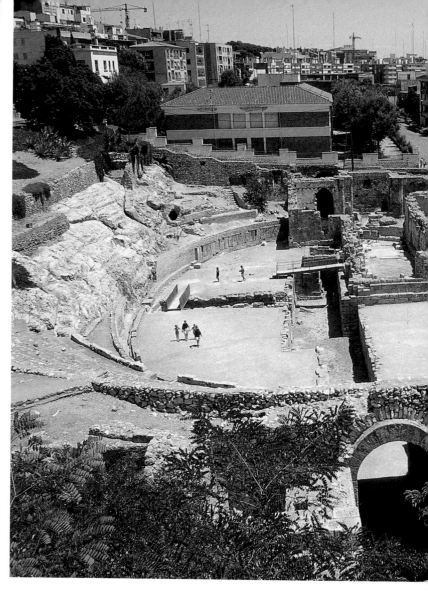

Under Roman rule, fish products (salted anchovies, spicy garum sauce) and fish (tuna, mackerel, and sardine) joined the Iberians' already prolific production. Culture blossomed: Hispania produced illustrious Roman emperors such as Trajan and Hadrian, scholars such as the Senecas (father and son), Martial, Quintilian, and the geographer Mela. Yet although born and bred in Hispania, they were all undoubtedly of Roman stock, for the Roman elite kept its distance from the Iberians. Stability and prosperity lasted almost three centuries, until, in the third century A.D., cracks began to appear in the Roman armor as the empire went into decline. Spain's weakness was exposed by roving northern tribes of Franks, Vandals, and, in the fifth century, Suebi (Swabians), and Visigoths. Through sporadic raids they gradually broke up the carefully constructed social and political fabric. The Roman Empire was in its death throes, and Hispania's economy disintegrated as defense

The amphitheater in Tarragona exemplifies the grandiose architecture undertaken during five centuries of Roman rule.

budgets spiraled. Finally in 409 the ruthless, nonliterate Visigoths moved in.

VISIGOTHS

For the next 300 years, the history of Spain became a complex series of regional and monarchic battles for supremacy, consolidated to a certain extent when the Visigothic kings established their capital in Toledo and the country was unified under King Leovigild in 584. In 654 King Recceswinth established a single code of law based on that of the Romans. Exceptions to this were the mountain people of the north (Cantabrians, Asturians, and Basques), who managed to retain their independence, and the south, which had a long period of Byzantine rule. Christianity had arrived in the late third century, and the emergence of church councils under the Visigoths established a link between Church and State that was crucial to Spain's subsequent history.

This was a dark period in Spain. The Roman system of huge estates *(latifundios)* owned by the aristocracy and worked by virtual slaves continued under the new invaders.

northern African Islamic province of the Caliphate of Damascus. Its Arab rulers sent a Berber army across the strait, and after a decisive victory over the Visigothic king Roderic, they took barely three years to complete their conquest. Berbers settled in arid areas that resembled their native Atlas Mountains and intermarried. By the ninth

Granada's Alhambra, with its backdrop of the snowcapped Sierra Nevada, is the most sophisticated and dreamlike of Spain's Moorish constructions.

Cities declined to become mere fortified clusters of churches and convents. Jewish people, who had emigrated to Spain under the Romans, were forced to convert or become slaves, a situation exacerbated by the Erwigian code of 681. This legalized anti-Jewish measures and enforced the return of slaves to their masters. Famine, dynastic disputes, and an absence of law and order created a fragile, easily exploitable situation. In 711 an army of Berbers (the indigenous people of North Africa) landed at Gibraltar. This was to be the beginning of a new era that lasted more than seven centuries.

MOORISH CONQUEST

Since the death of the prophet Mohammed (570–632), much of Arabia and northern Africa had come under the sway of Islam, a new, egalitarian religion. News of rich pickings in anarchic Spain—known as al-Andalus, meaning "isle of Vandals" —reached Ifriqiya, a

century, Arabic and the local Romance language had replaced Latin. This rapid success is not hard to explain, for Islam espoused religious tolerance, allowing Jews and Christians complete freedom of worship, and the end of Roman law brought liberty for Iberian slaves. Not least, Visigothic opponents of the Moors were embroiled in divisive conflicts that offered little to the average citizen but arbitrary bloodshed.

The one reversal in this astounding military advance was the battle of Covadonga in 718, when the Asturian prince Pelayo gave the army of the crescent its first whipping. This Moorish defeat was significant, as it left a chink of non-Muslim territory. Over the next century this expanded to cover all northern

Spain, from where it gradually spread south to culminate in the victory of the Catholic Monarchs (see pp. 31–33).

AL-ANDALUS & CÓRDOBA

The Arab conquerors and their Berber soldiers adopted an important Muslim ruler: Abd ar-Rahman of the Ummayad dynasty of Damascus, the successors of Mohammed himself. Fleeing the overthrow of his family, he arrived in Córdoba in 756 and established the emirate of al-Andalus, covering territory as far as the Pyrenees. Thus began the golden period of Islamic Spain, with Córdoba at its heart, seconded by Sevilla and Málaga. Agriculture diversified and prospered as sophisticated irrigation systems were installed. Rice, saffron, cotton, citrus fruits, figs, and dates were successfully introduced. Scholarly pursuits flourished among the philosophers, scientists, and writers who came to Córdoba from all over the Muslim world, and also among Jews, Christians (known as *Mozárabes)*, and local converts to Islam. This socioreligious tapestry was extended by thousands of slaves brought from eastern and northern Europe and the Sudan, who were able to take on important roles in the ruling classes if they converted to Islam. What could have been a hornets' nest actually fused to create one glorious civilization—that of al-Andalus.

In some respects this newly urbanized society was an embellished version of its Roman precursor. Roman foundations were used to rebuild towns that had crumbled under the Visigoths, but Islamic artistry went far beyond mere restoration. Palaces, fortresses, public baths, schools, mosques, fountains, and gardens of incredible beauty were created. At its zenith in the tenth century, when its population reached 100,000, Córdoba was rivaled only by Constantinople and Baghdad. Even today, the Great Mosque (Mezquita, see pp. 288–89) is unsurpassed in vision.

Not all was milk and honey in the land of al-Andalus. Sporadic raids were made on the infidels of the north in order to exact taxes and tributes under threat of death. Under the despotic rule of al-Hakem I (*R*.796–822), dissenters were decapitated, and violence spiraled. After an intervening period of cultural enrichment, unrest and revolts returned at the turn of the tenth century. Once again, a precarious situation was saved by an enlightened ruler—Abd ar-Rahman III (*R*.912–961), whose red hair and blue eyes were inherited from his Basque (or Frank) mother. Severing all ties with Baghdad, he assumed the title of Caliph in 929, took strategic points in north Africa (Melilla, Ceuta, and Tangiers) to preempt territorial threats, and reasserted his military strength against the Christian kingdoms of northern Spain. His palatial complex outside Córdoba, the Medina Azahara (see p. 291), became another of the glories of al-Andalus.

This great show of strength was followed by a period of dynastic weakness under Hisham II (*R*.976–1013), who relied on his Yemeni prime minister, ruthless Al-Mansur (*R*.938–1002), to such an extent that the latter even took the caliph's mother as his mistress. Al-Mansur's military ambition knew no bounds either, and León, Barcelona, and Santiago de Compostela all bowed temporarily to his might. By the early 11th century, after Al-Mansur's death, the caliphate had fallen prey to factional conflicts that led, in 1031, to its complete breakup into petty *taifas* (kingdoms). In the 300 years since its foundation al-Andalus had seen many peaks and troughs, and now a new wave of Muslim invaders, the Almoravids, appeared on the horizon.

The Almoravids were a fanatical group of Muslim Berbers who had established a kingdom stretching across North Africa from Morocco to Senegal. The taifa rulers invited them to Spain to help combat the increasingly successful Alfonso VI of Castilla y León, who conquered Toledo in 1085. The Almoravid leader, Yusuf, took a liking to al-Andalus. After defeating Alfonso in 1086, he decided to stay, so initiating the next Moorish dynasty.

Yet Moorish dominance over Spain was in decline, and for the next 400 years it was the Christians of the north who took the initiative. Raiding Muslim territory from their front lines of castles along the Ebro and Duero Rivers, they gradually extended Christian dominion southward. Christianity was strengthening its resolve, too, thanks to the Way of St. James pilgrimage route (see pp. 88–89), which brought a stream of foreign pilgrims to Spain. This stimulated a network of new churches and monasteries, and produced a unifying architectural style—the Romanesque.

CHRISTIAN SPAIN OF THE NORTH

A band of non-Muslim territories ran across northern Spain. The easternmost was Catalunya, which Charlemagne had established as an essential buffer zone against the

independent kingdom ruled by ambitious Fernando I, one of Sancho III's four sons. Castilla absorbed León, and Fernando enthroned one of his brothers as puppet-ruler of Navarra. He also made vassals of the Muslim kingdoms of Toledo and Zaragoza. In 1085, Alfonso VI of Castilla y León took the prestigious city of Toledo from the Moors and

Map showing the Christian reconquest of Spain from the Moors. Dates in bold and color shading show the Christian advance.

assumed the title Emperor of the Two Religions—a sign of things to come.

RECONQUEST

Moors at the turn of the ninth century. Its five counties were ruled by the Counts of Barcelona under a feudal system that concentrated property in the hands of civil and religious authorities. By the 12th century the Catalan identity had crystallized and its French-influenced language had taken root. Aragón, too, was developing under its own count, and in the early ninth century became linked with neighboring Navarra through marriage. Under Sancho III (*R*.1005–1035), Navarra attained political preeminence, but lost it after his death to Aragón and nascent Castilla. The latter was a newly created

As the Almoravids were settling comfortably into Andalusian ways, a revivalist Muslim movement led by the the Almohads, from the Atlas Mountains, started threatening their control. By the mid-12th century the Almohads had moved into al-Andalus, bringing a crusading spirit that recovered Extremadura from the Christians and temporarily halted the Christian advance. Christian forces were disorganized and fraught by dynastic crises, and military challenges to the Almohads were left to King Alfonso I of Aragón. He countered their religious zeal with his own, backed up by the newly introduced Knights Templar, an order of soldier-monks founded in 1118 during the First Crusade, and resolved to defeat Islam. Zaragoza was one of several Moorish towns to fall into his net, and when his daughter Petronila married Ramón Berenguer of Barcelona, a solid alliance was created.

remained of the taifas was Granada, a kingdom that stretched from Tarifa east to Almería.

This period, too, saw the Church peaking in strength and status, represented by the massive Gothic cathedrals of Burgos, Toledo, and León. Parallel to this ecclesiastical power came that of the Knights Templar and the Order of Santiago.

A major turning point in the Reconquest came in 1212 at the battle of Las Navas de Tolosa, when Castilla's Alfonso VIII trounced the Almohads with help from Aragón, Navarra, and France. Yet nothing was straightforward during this period of warlords, mercenaries, knightly orders, militant monks, and warring princes, and the Reconquest moved into its penultimate stages under three different Christian rulers. In the east, Jaume I of Aragón and Barcelona expanded his territory south to incorporate Valencia, Alicante, and the Balearics by 1238. Meanwhile, Fernando III led the armies of Castilla and León to capture Córdoba, Jaén, and Sevilla. Cádiz and Murcia were swept up by his son, Alfonso X (known as the Wise for his intellectual and poetic aptitude). Now all that

"The surrender of Granada" by Francisco Pradilla (1846–1921) depicts the final stage of the Reconquest by Fernando and Isabel.

In Granada the Almohads had been replaced in the 1240s by the Nazrids, an aristocratic Moorish family driven south from Zaragoza. They oversaw Granada's cultural zenith, epitomized by their palace at the Alhambra (see pp. 300–305). Cunning diplomacy ensured Castilla's protection for Granada, and until the mid-14th century most of the peninsula prospered, with Muslims, Jews, and Christians coexisting in a tolerant, cosmopolitan society. In eastern Spain, the *cortes* (chamber of representatives) of Catalunya, Aragón, and Valencia instigated a fair system of civil rights accorded by their

king in exchange for allegiance. Mozárabes (Christians from formerly Muslim territory) and Muslims were moved to repopulate newly conquered regions, sometimes provoking social tensions. Roman-style large-scale estates, or latifundios, were allocated to nobility or given as rewards to military orders and men from the ranks *(hidalgos)*, whose social code was exploited by Cervantes in *Don Quixote* (see pp. 238–39). The nefarious latifundio system, where large estates are often run by absentee landlords using low-paid laborers, still endures, mainly in Andalucía.

This was the period of Catalan expansion across the Mediterranean, bringing mercantile prosperity reflected in Barcelona's great 14th-century building boom. In 1348 bubonic plague struck, soon followed by famine. The combination drastically reduced Catalunya's population and, to a lesser extent, those of Aragón, Valencia, and the Balearics. By 1412 Castilla's hegemony was complete, and a branch of its ruling Trastámara family provided a new dynasty for eastern Spain.

Unrest continued into the 15th century. Dynastic wars resulted in outright civil war between supporters of Enrique IV's daughter, Juana, and his sister, Isabel, in 1474. Isabel's greatest ally was her husband, Fernando of Aragón. After winning the Battle of Toro in 1476, their collaborative rule transformed the face of Spain, culminating in the momentous events of 1492. That year saw Christopher Columbus landing in the New World, opening up a completely new chapter in Spanish history. Gold and silver were to pour into the national coffers for centuries, while the New World was taken over by Catholicism and the Spanish language. Equally important in 1492 was that after ten years of sieges and rural devastation, Muslim Granada was conquered by Fernando's army. Once Navarra had been annexed, Spain's unification was complete.

CATHOLIC MONARCHS

Fernando and Isabel's crusade against the Moors was heavily financed by the Church. In return they instigated a long period of reli-

Christopher Columbus's ornate tomb in Sevilla Cathedral shows the preeminent role this navigator played in Spanish history.

An engraving by John Pine portrays
Felipe II's Invincible Armada being
trounced by the English navy in 1588.

gious intolerance, first expelling Jewish people from Spain and soon after threatening the remaining Muslims. Both groups were offered the choice of conversion or exile, but converts could still suffer persecution. Muslim converts, known as *moriscos,* were moved into designated rural areas, and confiscated properties were handed out to nobility, military orders, and town councils. Mosques and synagogues were demolished and rebuilt as churches, and the Inquisition (introduced in 1478), became the central instrument of Catholic and monarchical power.

Fernando and Isabel also expanded their overseas territories. Naples fell to their greatest general, Gonzalo Fernández de Córdoba (known as El Gran Capitán), and Christopher Columbus's pioneering voyage across the Atlantic began to reap rich rewards. Although gold was the chief attraction of the Americas, the conversion of native peoples to Christianity earned Fernando and Isabel the title of *los Reyes Católicos* (the Catholic Monarchs) from the Pope himself, a Spaniard of the Borgia family. Apart from this spiritual justification, the Spaniards were also aided by the Castilian language in their expansionism: It had been codified into Europe's first vernacular grammar and became the lingua franca of the Americas. As the conquistadores extended their New World net, indigenous peoples fell before them—prey to Old World diseases and to the sword.

Isabel's death in 1504 announced a completely new twist in Spanish history. Fernando reigned as regent until his death in 1516, by which time his grandson, Carlos, was old enough to inherit the Crown. When Carlos I (*R.*1516–1556) arrived on Spanish soil in 1517, he faced a country wracked by disastrous harvests, plague, and widespread social discontent. Speaking no Castilian, this Habsburg king was far from ready to manage the complex and disorderly society he had inherited. Yet a new era had begun.

HABSBURGS & THE GOLDEN AGE

The Habsburg dynasty ruled Spain for nearly 200 years. Their monarchs presided over the arrival of untold amounts of bullion from the Americas, and ruled Europe's largest empire since that of Charlemagne, but the term "Golden Age" is questionable. Culturally Spain prospered, producing an impressive line of Renaissance artists and dramatists. Politically, however, it was another story. Two years after acceding to the Spanish throne, Carlos inherited the Holy Roman Empire through his father. As Carlos V (Charles V), he ruled a large part of northern Europe (the modern Netherlands, Belgium, Austria, and part of Germany), in addition to Spain and the

Americas—an unwieldy but unrivaled empire. His loyalties were divided, and regional *cortes* had to lobby intensely to obtain recognition and funds. Insurrections and revolts, notably those of the Castilian *comuneros* and Valencian and Mallorcan *agermanats* (brotherhoods), were brutally crushed by Carlos's German troops. He nonetheless dealt successfully with invasion by France, and his astute marriage to Isabel of Portugal brought further immense wealth to the Spanish Crown and an able replacement during his many absences abroad. Inevitably, the cost of his many wars mounted, so, weary of the worries of his vast empire, Carlos V abdicated in 1556 and retired to the monastery of Yuste, in Extremadura (see p. 249). He left a virtually bankrupt kingdom to his son.

Felipe II (Philip II, *R.*1556–1598), fanatically religious and highly cultivated, intensified the Inquisition's activities from his palace-monastery, El Escorial (see pp. 79–81). Protestants were killed in spectacular autos-da-fé (trial and execution ceremonies), and anyone "tainted" with Jewish blood was persecuted, as were moriscos. Felipe II won an important naval victory over the Turks in 1571, and in 1588 he sent the Invincible Armada to invade Protestant England. Instead the Spanish fleet suffered catastrophic losses, and lost international credibility.

Under Felipe III (*R.*1598–1621), the last 275,000 Moors were expelled from Valencia, a move that ruined local agriculture. This ruthlessness was echoed in Spain's New World activities, where indigenous populations were virtually wiped out by disease and slavery.

Inbreeding was a Habsburg habit, and as a result Felipe IV (*R.*1621–65) appeared only slightly more in control than his easily manipulated father. He was an astute patron of the arts, however. Despite his reformist tendencies, his reign saw increasing internal dissent, the loss of Portugal, and the defeats of the Thirty Years War, culminating in the independence of the Netherlands in 1648. Spain's loss of prestige was underlined in the reign of the last and most degenerate Habsburg king, Carlos II (*R.*1665–1700), whose 35-year rule saw further territorial losses. Spain became an economic wasteland: Once thriving and densely populated Castilla was a bankrupt desert. The only element still to prosper was the Church, and the heavily gilded baroque altarpieces of the time bear witness to its immense wealth.

WAR OF SPANISH SUCCESSION

Carlos II died childless, but he had appointed an heir: Philippe Bourbon, grandson of his sister María Teresa and the French king Louis XIV. Once again, Spain was faced with a foreign ruler, and in 1701 this French 17-year-old entered Madrid as Felipe V. However northern Europe and England supported his rival, the Austrian Archduke Charles, and joined Catalunya, Aragón, and Valencia in the 12-year-long War of Succession. England eventually accepted the Bourbon king when it was given the territorial concessions of Gibraltar (still a thorny point in Anglo-Spanish relations) and Menorca. Stimulated by childhood memories of Versailles, Felipe V (R.1701–1746) spent much of his long reign building sumptuous French-style palaces, a habit continued by more enlightened Carlos III (R.1759–1788).

Other than reveling in baroque artistry, Carlos III continued a centralizing tendency instigated by Felipe V. Steadily, Spain was regaining its lost prosperity, agriculture was recovering, coastal trading companies thrived, and the population expanded. A significant economic move was the Free Trade Act (1778) for the American colonies. Although bread riots ignited Spain in the 1760s, Carlos III found a scapegoat in the Jesuits, who were expelled in 1766. His great love for the arts was expressed by the building of the Prado Museum (see pp. 62–67), Palacio Real (see pp. 56–57), and San Ildefonso de la Granja (see p. 226), near Segovia, monuments to the final moments of an all-powerful monarchy.

WAR OF SPANISH INDEPENDENCE

Weak and indifferent Carlos IV (R.1788–1808) left governing to his wife, María Luisa, and her adviser Don Manuel Godoy. Spain soon found itself enmeshed in the aftermath of the French Revolution. Catapulted into war with Britain, France's arch rival, Spain tumbled into defeat at the Battle of Trafalgar (1805). On land, however, Napoleon was carrying the day. In 1808 he engineered the abdication of Carlos IV, and put his own brother Joseph (José I) on the throne. By now the people of Spain had had enough, and the Madrid uprising of May 2 was the spark that ignited Spain's five-year War of Independence against Napoleon.

The War of Independence produced Spain's first popular united front against a common enemy. Peasant guerrilla fighters played a major role, fragmenting the Napoleonic armies and their supply systems. Guerrillas also cooperated with Spain's former enemies, the British, led by the Duke of Wellington, whose many victories culminated in the Battle of Vitoria in 1813. As a result, José I fled back to France (taking with him considerable artistic booty). Church properties had been heavily targeted, and Spain's infrastructure lay in ruins, devastated by both French and British troops.

CARLIST WARS

In 1812 the cortes of Cádiz had worked out a new, liberal constitution, the Constitution of Cádiz, investing power in a democratically elected chamber. This was soon canceled when despotic Fernando VII (son of Carlos IV) took the throne. As Spain sank yet again under the whims of its king, its American colonies won independence. In 1820 the Constitution of Cádiz was temporarily revived, but a massive French army came to help the king suppress it. On his death in 1833, civil war broke out (the First Carlist War) between supporters of his conservative brother, Carlos, and the liberal promoters of his young daughter, the Infanta Isabel. Isabel's camp won, but her reign (1843–1868) was a troubled one, plagued by successive crises, including the Second Carlist War. In 1874, with Isabel's son Alfonso XII in the driver's seat, the army was assuming increasing power. As a result, Spain's oppressed workers began to organize themselves into trade unions. This was the germination of social conflicts that, around 60 years later, resulted in the rule of the dictator, General Franco.

SOCIAL TRANSFORMATIONS

In the late 19th century and early 20th century, Spain experienced a period of relative calm and prosperity. Yet in 1898 its last

The British fleet's triumph at the 1805 Battle of Trafalgar ran parallel to Napoleon's victories on land, leaving Spain caught between the two rival powers.

overseas possessions were lost to the United States, notably the Philippines and Cuba, and famines and disease wracked the south. Huge numbers emigrated: 1.5 million moved to Latin America between 1886 and 1913. The demographic face of the country was changing with a drift to the cities, although Catalunya, Euskadi, and Asturias were the only truly industrialized regions. Ideological differences became more marked, as did regional variations in wealth, and more than half the population was illiterate. Although the 20th century started with a dazzling cultural renaissance, this was limited to a tiny section of society—the majority languished in poverty.

Barcelona had seen workers' unrest in the mid-19th century, and by the 1880s both Andalucía and Castilla were home to widespread anarchist movements. Marxist-Socialism made advances in Madrid, where the PSOE (Socialist party) was born in 1888. After winning its first parliamentary seat in 1910, it widened its membership in the industrialized north. During World War I Spain remained neutral, and its industry profited for a while from exports to both sides, but in 1917 recession and a draining war in Morocco helped fuel a momentous general strike, which was violently repressed. In 1923 further social unrest caused General Miguel Primo de Rivera to stage a military coup, in cooperation with the king. This led to a military dictatorship until world depression precipitated the general's resignation in 1930. Within two years, anti-monarchist forces won a resounding success in municipal elections, and hapless Alfonso XIII went into exile.

SECOND REPUBLIC & CIVIL WAR

Euphoria greeted the establishment of the Second Republic on April 14, 1931. At last, Spain was falling into step with democratic movements elsewhere. A new Republican government led by Manuel Azaña soon introduced land reform and civil marriage among other sweeping changes, but political loyalties were becoming dangerously polarized between extreme Republicanism and extreme conservatism. The Church, army, and landowners still wielded enormous economic power. As Socialists, Anarchists, Radicals, and Marxists bickered among themselves, their opponents became organized around the Falange, a youth movement founded by José Antonio Primo de Rivera (son of the dictator). Elections in 1933 gave power to the Right— including the Falange and the Monarchists— who revealed their true nature the following year in the bloody suppression of a miners' strike in Asturias.

Decades of social unrest, unionization, and political movements preceded the tragic hostilities of Spain's civil war that broke out in 1936.

By 1936, Spain was spiraling into chaos with almost daily assassinations, riots, militia attacks on churches, strikes, and seizures of estates. When victory in the election was won by the leftist Popular Front, it took only five months for the army's response. In July 1936, the troops of General Francisco Franco were airlifted from their garrisons in Morocco by German transport planes and dropped into Spain. The Civil War had begun.

Spain's Civil War was the bloodiest, most tragic period that the country ever lived through, dividing families, devastating the countryside, ruining the infrastructure, and leaving half a million dead and millions starving. Helped by Moroccan mercenaries, Franco's Nationalist army rapidly won control

Communists within the Republican ranks. All this contributed to the capitulation of the north, and when Franco's offensive in southern Aragón reached the Mediterranean, the Republican forces in the east were divided in two. In early 1939 Barcelona fell, finally followed by Madrid and Valencia. The game was over, and the Generalísimo took up the reins of power on April 1.

GENERAL FRANCO

Social order and uncontested political authority were the priorities of Spain's new ruler. Franco used firing squads, labor camps, and civic ostracism to quell opposition, and the old adage of "convert or be exiled," used against Jews and Moors centuries before, was now reapplied to other sectors. Many intellectuals fled, about 7,000 teachers were executed, and schoolbooks were rewritten. At the end of World War II, during which Spain remained neutral, Franco was the only Fascist dictator left, ruling over a politically and economically isolated country. Any opposition was stamped upon, censorship was enforced, and the powers of the Catholic church were restored. Divorce became illegal, church weddings were obligatory, and the confessor was invoked as the ultimate adviser in reading matter.

Change came in the 1950s, when Franco received General Eisenhower and agreed to host American military bases in exchange for massive loans. This opened the floodgates, propelling Spain to the forefront of economic growth and into world institutions such as the United Nations (1955), so ending its former isolation. Franco invested in roads, electricity plants, apartment blocks for workers, and other infrastructure. Mass tourism arrived and a booming market economy developed, steered by a new breed of technocrats. Yet Spain's increased prosperity had a flipside: Andalusian peasants worked in miserable conditions, workers continued to flood from the land to the cities and abroad, and political and intellectual repression continued, above all in Catalunya and País Vasco. Clandestine groups and unions worked behind the scenes, and the Basque separatist group Euskadi Ta Askatasuna (ETA) emerged. In 1973 Franco's expected successor, Admiral Carrero Blanco, was blown sky-high by an ETA bomb.

of eastern Andalucía, Extremadura, and Castilla, but it was rebuffed by Madrid, the east, and the north, where Republican sympathies and forces were strongest. Proclaimed Generalísimo of the armed forces and head of state in Burgos, a city with well-entrenched conservative traditions, Franco soon received massive assistance from his Fascist allies in Europe—Germany, Italy, and Portugal. Meanwhile the Republicans received help only from the Soviet Union. Governments of western democracies such as Britain and France did nothing, although about 35,000 foreign volunteers, including George Orwell, Ernest Hemingway, André Malraux, and Willy Brandt, fought for the Republicans with the International Brigade. The Republicans could not compete with the size and resources of the opposing forces, epitomized by the merciless bombing of Gernika (Guernica) by German planes in 1937. Self-destructive rivalries also existed between Anarchists and

AFTER FRANCO

Franco, the wily old *Caudillo* (Chief), hung on for 40 years. When he died in 1975, a grandson of Alfonso XIII was crowned King Juan Carlos I. Franco had chosen him as successor partly because of his monarchist sympathies and partly because he thought that Juan Carlos was a malleable character. In this he

optimistic period when anything and everything seemed possible. The 1980s saw advances on every level, bringing stability, pride, and dynamism to a nation that had been thirsting for them. Spain's entry into the European Economic Community in 1986 brought European subsidies to build a much needed infrastructure and open up the country. In

was wrong, and the new king rapidly set about restoring democracy through his able Prime Minister, Adolfo Suárez. Political parties and trade unions were recognized, censorship was lifted, and the 1977 elections brought Suárez and his Christian-Democrat party, the UCD, to power. With a new, ultra-liberal Constitution, parliament set about undoing the knots of Castilian centralism and granting autonomy to the regions, starting with Catalunya and Euskadi, or País Vasco (Basque country), in 1979.

In 1981, the new government survived an attempted military coup that failed thanks to Juan Carlos's firm stand. The following year, Spain entered a new era with the electoral victory of the PSOE (Socialist Party). This brought the youthful and charismatic Felipe González to power and initiated a frenetically

A youthful King Juan Carlos I and Queen Sofia toured Andalucía in 1976, just one year after General Franco's death.

1992 (500 years after Columbus first set foot in the New World), the Olympics were held in Barcelona, Seville hosted Expo 92, and Madrid was designated cultural capital of Europe. Spain's fortunes seemed to be on a roll.

Nothing and nobody is perfect, however, and corruption finally brought down the Socialist government after 14 years in power. Although José María Aznar's Partido Popular (a merging of center-right parties) was elected in 1996 and reelected with a resounding majority in 2000, it is no less flawed. Spain still has hurdles to overcome: endemic corruption, Europe's highest unemployment rate, and ETA terrorism. Yet it has gained economic success, cultural dynamism, slick city centers, and a viable federal system. Spain has traversed light years in just a few decades. ∎

An anti-fascist propaganda poster from the civil war of 1936–39

The arts

SPAIN'S ART HISTORY GOES BACK TO THE EARLY STONE AGE WHEN HUNTERS started painting on the walls of their caves, but it was during the second millennium A.D. that a truly Hispanic style of art emerged. Among Spain's long roll call of great artists are Velázquez, Goya, Zurbarán, and Picasso. Architecture and film are the other major fields of Spanish creative genius.

PAINTING, SCULPTURE, & ARCHITECTURE

The earliest manifestations of Spanish art are mysterious, but probably had a ritualistic role for the Paleolithic hunter-gatherers who painted polychrome bison, wild boars, wolves, horses, and deer with amazing anatomical precision on the walls of their Cantabrian caves. These cave paintings, notably at Altamira, date from 15,000 to 8500 B.C. Later prehistoric art takes the form of copper idol plaques from the fortified settlement of Los Millares, near Almería. Spain's oldest constructions are the megaliths (huge stone monuments) of the Balearics and the dolmens (stone tombs) of Antequera (circa 2500 B.C.).

Iberian art

The growth of gold, silver, lead, and tin mines in the Andalusian kingdom of Tartessos, and the subsequent arrival of Phoenician and Greek traders, sparked the next stage in the peninsula's iconography. Sculpture (carved limestone and bronze figurines) is the only relic of the Iberian civilization in central and southern Spain, as the Punic Wars between Carthage and Rome devastated most architectural structures. The most outstanding work of art from those centuries is the Dama de Elche (sixth–fifth century B.C.), a beautiful bust of a serene, bejeweled lady. Important ceramics, too, have survived the ravages of time. Although influenced by the Greeks, Iberians found their own inventive style of abstract, zoomorphic, or anthropomorphic designs painted on crudely shaped vessels. In the north, Celtiberians produced the magnificent gold jewelry unearthed in Galicia's *castros* (fortified villages).

Roman classicism

Five hundred years of Roman rule steered Hispanic art and architecture into an entirely new phase. Urban design was paramount.

Towns centered on the forum (marketplace), around which stood the theater, amphitheater, and temples. The elite lived in magnificently decorated villas where mosaic panels, marble colonnades, and statues created dramatic backdrops for society. Busts of emperors, magistrates, and governors reflected a taste for realism rather than stylization. At this period in history, Spain was unique in Europe:

Nowhere else had such a wealth of distinctive cultures contributed to artistic development.

Visigoths

Christianity was the next major ingredient in the Hispanic mix. From the fifth century A.D., the Visigoths introduced their nomadic Scandinavian culture, while southern Spain underwent a century of Byzantine domination (522–621). Outstanding Visigothic craftsmanship is seen in gold- and silverwork of royal crowns and offerings in dignitaries' tombs.

Otherwise all that remains of their 300-year presence in the peninsula is the embryonic

Prehistoric paintings of animals and hunters cover the walls of the Tito Bustillo caves at Ribadesella.

structures of Christianity: The seventh-century hermitage of Quintanilla de las Viñas in northern Castilla has primitive, schematized reliefs in carved friezes, and capitals salvaged elsewhere show stylized figures and birds beside floral motifs. This was a far cry from the classical realism of the Romans, and decorative abstraction continued to dominate Spanish art until the flowering of the Romanesque period.

Pre-Romanesque architecture in Asturias, the only kingdom not conquered by the Muslim invaders, represents a more sophisticated bridging period before the Romanesque style was imported from France. Soaring barrel vaults, horseshoe arches, ashlar (square-cut stone facings), and illusionist murals were developed in a wide network of extraordinary, lavish churches.

Moorish style

Andalucía, above all, fell under the most con-centrated Islamic influence (see pp. 268–69). Fortresses (alcázabas), palaces (alcázares), and mosques (mezquitas) became the landmarks of al-Andalus, culminating in Granada's dream-like Alhambra (see pp. 300–305), which so perfectly catered to all the senses. Earlier Islamic legacies date from 8th- to 11th-century Córdoba. The Mezquita (Great Mosque, see pp. 288–89), representing par-adise and the holy city, and the Medina Azahara (the caliph's palace, see p. 291) incor-porated calligraphic stucco friezes, geometric patterns of brick, stone and marble, and intri-cately intertwined plant motifs. Since Islam forbade representation of humans, craftsmen channeled all their imaginative effort into

Colorful tiled walls surmounted by intricately carved stucco friezes are typical of the Moorish decorative style. These belong to the Alhambra in Granada.

these extensive and finely executed embellish-ments (although the rules were sometimes bent—even human figures appear in the dec-oration of the Medina Azahara).

Horseshoe arches, cupolas, blind arches, tracery, and artesonado (intricately carved ceilings) were the most lasting structural ele-ments, but art evolved considerably during the 700-year Moorish occupation. An early taste for decorative details came from Syria. The later Almoravids and Almohads were more conservative but nonetheless introduced multicolored azulejos (tiles) and the intricacies

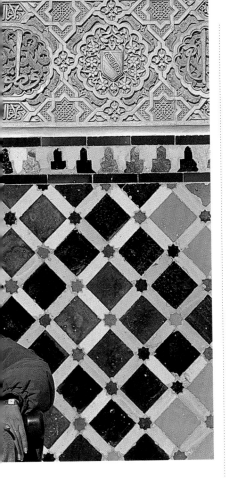

who brought Arab techniques and forms with them. Even after Moorish territories had been conquered and their mosques demolished, talented Moorish artisans continued to work for Christian masters. This was the origin of the Mudejar style, whose enduring influence on Hispanic art cannot be overestimated. Among its creations were Aragón's intricate brick and ceramic towers, Sevilla's Reales Alcázares (see pp. 266–67)—an indulgence of carved wood, stucco, and tilework—and the Gothic Mudejar of Toledo's towers and churches. Synagogues, too, were designed by Mudejar craftsmen, and the three that survive in Toledo and Córdoba are a unique conjunction of Hebrew calligraphy with Arab artistry. Mudejar was a profusely decorative style, and from it emerged an aversion to unadorned space that dominated Spanish art for the following centuries. In architecture, Mudejar forms continued in bullrings and railway stations right up to the beginning of the 20th century.

Romanesque

While the Moors were covering walls and arches in stucco and azulejos, Christian Spain was building its own masterpieces in the north: Romanesque structures designed to inspire every pilgrim who set foot on the long road to Santiago de Compostela (see pp. 90–93). From the mid-11th century, French and Italian religious orders set up monasteries and churches, and their artistic forms soon dominated northern Spain. Yet Spain, as usual, distinguished itself from the rest of Europe, as Visigothic, Pre-Romanesque, and Moorish influences all played their role. In Catalunya, the Lombards from Italy were another influence, introducing sobriety of form and lofty bell towers.

The cathedral of Santiago de Compostela (see pp. 90–93) retains its original Romanesque soaring nave, superb reliefs on the Puerta de las Platerías (circa 1100), and, above all, the sculptor Mateo's Romanesque masterpiece, the complex, high-relief statues of the Pórtico de la Gloria (1188). A few years earlier, an equally magnificent portal was created at the Catalan monastery of Ripoll as a visual bible for the illiterate. This teaching-through-pictures produced beautifully decorated capitals, cloisters, and portals: Wonderful examples

of artesonado. Palaces and houses were built around patios (courtyards), an intelligent response to the climate that continues today: Wealthier families escape the heat by living on the lower floors in the summer, and then they move to the upstairs in winter to catch all the available sun. Palace gardens had water and fragrant flowers and plants. In all this, the Alhambra represents the zenith of Moorish style, combining unparalleled decorative mastery with perspective and sensuality.

Mozarabic & Mudejar

As the Christians of the north extended their territory south during the period of the Reconquest (see pp. 28–31), their taste was influenced by Mozarabic emigrants— Christians who had lived under Arab rule and exist in Girona, Santo Domingo de los Silos, Tarragona, San Juan de la Peña, Sangüesa, Leyre, and Santillana del Mar. Altar sculpture was carved in wood and painted, a tradition that endures in the highly realist *pasos* (floats) of Holy Week processions (see pp. 272–73).

Other forms of Spanish Romanesque art are altarpieces and the dynamic, richly colored

Luis de Morales designed the main altarpiece in the Iglesia de la Asunción, in Cáceres.

frescoes in churches such as San Isidoro in León. Examples from Catalunya's remote parish churches are shown in the museums of Barcelona, Vic, and Jaca. Change came when reforming Cistercian monks brought a taste for austerity, and an end to richly carved capitals and portals groaning with apostles. Instead huge monastic complexes devoted to prayer

and work arose, such as Poblet (see pp. 191–92), Santes Creus (see p. 192), and Santa María de Huerta (see p. 151). Secular constructions of the time are the frontier castles of Castilla and towns with narrow winding streets, such as Besalú.

Gothic

By the 13th century, the Gothic was making inroads. This was not just an artistic fashion, but represented a new perception of life in which spirituality and culture were transferred from monastic complexes to medieval cities centered on their cathedrals. The three naves of the Romanesque period became one, and the use of stronger pointed arches rather than round ones meant that walls could rise to increasingly lofty ceilings and domes. Many cathedrals bridged these two major medieval styles, but the undisputed stars are the 13th-century cathedrals of León, Burgos, and Toledo, which has a marked Moorish influence.

By the following century the building craze had shifted eastward, producing the great cathedrals of Barcelona, Girona, Palma de Mallorca, and Valencia. As the 14th century gave way to the 15th, Gothic architecture acquired the often excessive flowery ornamentation known as Flamboyant Gothic. Two main schools developed. The first, in Toledo, was spearheaded by Juan Guas, who designed San Juan de los Reyes. The second, in Burgos, was led by Juan de Colonia and his son, Simón, who was responsible for the exuberant, lace-like façade of San Pablo in Valladolid. These examples of the Isabelline style crowned the 15th century, combining the height of Flamboyant Gothic with early Renaissance elements.

Sculpture and painting came into their own, their practitioners regarded as fully fledged artists instead of mere artisans. Major influences were absorbed from Italy and France, but by the late 15th century Spanish art had fallen under the sway of Flemish naturalism, a style of remarkably expressive precision. The Catalan Jaume Huguet (circa 1415–1492) was one of its greatest exponents. In sculpture, Gil de Siloé and Pere Joan respectively led the Castilian and Aragonese schools. *Retablos* (altarpieces) became towering painted panels with bas-reliefs, wooden sculptures, and heavily gilded frames—Spain's were the most elaborate of their kind in Europe.

Renaissance

When the Reconquest (see pp. 28–31) was complete, the door was definitively closed on medieval Spain and opened to a new philosophy of life—the Renaissance. Scientific discovery and voyages to the New World transformed ideas, and people turned to the classical ideals of ancient Greece and Rome for

such as gargoyles, pilasters, and medallions. Diego de Siloé in Burgos, Alonso de Covarrubias of Toledo, and Gil de Hontañón in Salamanca represented a transition to the more restrained Renaissance style that emerged in the 1520s, crowned by Pedro Machuca's palace of Carlos V (1526) in Granada, the purest Italianate building in

"San Hugo en el Refectorio de los Cartujos" (1633) by Francisco de Zurbarán

inspiration. Early Spanish Renaissance architecture, known as plateresque (meaning "resembling silversmith's work"), has delicate, filigree-like reliefs, best exemplified in Salamanca's superb university facade and Toledo's Santa Cruz hospice. Although related to the Isabelline style, plateresque makes greater use of Renaissance elements from Italy,

Spain. In the reconquered lands Renaissance mansions mushroomed, with large concentrations in Úbeda and Baeza.

The Italian aesthetic also came to dominate painting and sculpture. Pedro Berruguete (1450–1504), Juan de Borgoña (1470–1536), and Juan de Juanes (much influenced by Raphael) led the field in painting. In sculpture prolific Damián Forment (circa 1480–1540) bridged the Isabelline-Renaissance period with spectacular altarpieces. Alonso de

The *botafumeiro* dispenses incense in the cathedral of Santiago de Compostela.

Berruguete's obsession with dramatic realism anticipated the Baroque period, as did the Valladolid-based Frenchman, Juan de Juni (died 1577). One great difference between Italian and Spanish art of the Renaissance stems from simple economics. The Inquisition imposed a 10 percent tax on any work that did not contain a religious message, which partly explains the preponderance of saintly and monastic subjects in Spanish art before 1783.

By the late 16th century, Felipe II's patronage of the arts had brought many Italian and Flemish artists to Spain, and (despite the Inquisition) portraiture was becoming established. Domenikos Theotokopoulos, or El Greco—The Greek—arrived in Spain in 1577. His free brushstrokes did not meet with royal approval, forcing him to retreat to Toledo to work on ecclesiastical commissions. Architecture was dominated by Juan de Herrera (1530–97), whose austere masterpiece, El Escorial (see pp. 79–81), foreshadowed the next century.

Baroque & the Golden Age
The 17th century saw a profusion of civic building, such as Madrid's Plaza Mayor, but it took several decades for Spain to shake off Herreran influence and embrace baroque. Exuberant Spanish baroque architecture (Churrigueresque) was named after José de Churriguera (1665–1725) and his brothers, Joaquín and Alberto, although another major protagonist was Pedro de Ribera (1683–1742).

Andalucía has abundant Churrigueresque works, because it was the arrival point for the riches of the New World. During this Golden Age of Spanish art, the Granadino architect, sculptor, and painter Alonso Cano laid the foundation for a new school of three-dimensional work. His pupil Pedro de Mena (1628–1688) created that period's most emotionally expressive sculptures, and in Castilla, Gregorio Hernández (1566–1636) became the master of depicting pain and sorrow. Baroque gilding, salomonic columns (twisted and entwined), and inverted pilasters were created in a climax of creative delirium, fueled by the profits and optimism of the New World.

The greatest genius of the Golden Age was the painter Diego Velázquez (1599–1660), who emerged from the Sevillian school of Francisco Pacheco (1564–1654). After being appointed court painter by Felipe IV in Madrid, where he also met Peter Paul Rubens (1577–1640), he made two significant trips to Italy. From still lifes and genre paintings his work matured into courtly portraits and royal themes, before reaching its apogee with *Las Meninas* (The Maids of Honor) and *Las Hilanderas* (The Spinners). Master of optical illusions, color, and subtle psychological insights, Velázquez shared the limelight with his contemporaries the Extremaduran Francisco Zurbarán (1598–1664), and the Valencians Francisco Ribalta (1565–1628) and José de Ribera (1591–1652). Ribalta introduced tenebrism (contrasting light and shadow) to Spain, and Ribera took powerful realism to his adopted Naples. Zurbarán's portraits of monks are unsurpassed in their sobriety of composition, compelling the spectator to focus on the subjects' spiritual passion and personality. Sevilla's other great baroque painters were Juan Valdés Leal (1622–1690) and Bartolomé Esteban Murillo (1617–1682), who respectively produced images of the vanity of the world and diaphanous renderings of beatific Virgins surrounded by cherubim.

18th & 19th centuries

Frills and excessive ornamentation characterized the French rococo style that dominated the early 18th century, eminently seen in the palaces of the new Bourbon kings at La Granja, Aranjuez, and Madrid. In order to furnish them, decorative arts (porcelain, tapestries, and glass) were fostered in royal factories and workshops. Inevitably, reaction set in. Reason, order, and moderation soon became the ideals of the newly established Academia de Bellas Artes (1752), ushering in the more controlled neoclassic period. In architecture, this was exemplified by Ventura Rodríguez and by Juan de Villanueva, who designed the Prado. In painting, after a period of cold, elegant portraiture, it was Francisco de Goya (1746–1828) who was to make a lasting impact. Rebelling against neoclassic constraints, he developed a nonconformist style of expressive brushstrokes to depict character and emotions in earthy tones, whether in his series of "black paintings" stemming from personal depression, or in his vivid portraits and political commentaries.

Once the 19th century was in full swing, Goya's influence became apparent as the cult of reason was replaced by overt sensitivity and the notion of human freedom. With the secular replacing the religious, a stream of academic painters embraced the melodrama of Romanticism, producing scenes from Spanish history and, in the late 19th century, *costumbrismo* (depiction of local life and customs). It was only by the start of the 20th century that Spain was belatedly noticing French Impressionism.

20th-century modernism

The barriers of conservatism were finally shattered by Catalunya's *Modernista* movement, led by Antoni Gaudí (see pp. 172–75), Lluís Domènech i Montaner, Josep Maria Jujol, Juan Martorell, and Pere Dománech. Together they turned architectural tradition on its head with organically inspired structures, extensive use of decorative brickwork, and design "follies."

Spain was resistant to the revolution in art (modernism) that was sweeping Europe, despite being the source of some of its greatest protagonists. Pablo Picasso (1881–1973), a native of Málaga, but brought up in Barcelona before moving to Paris, was unquestionably the figurehead, and in later years he used early Spanish art as inspiration. Another Spanish cubist, Juan Gris (1887–1927) worked with Picasso in Paris. Joan Miró (1893–1983) remained faithful to Catalunya and Mallorca, despite international acclaim for his spontaneous, poetic abstraction. This derived from experiments with surrealism, but the latter movement's most faithful Hispanic representative was Salvador Dalí (see pp. 184–85). In both life and artifice, Dalí perfectly exemplified surrealism's obsession with the irrational. In contrast, sculptors such as Pablo Gargallo, Alberto Sánchez, and Julio González excelled in a more sober, abstract field.

For two decades after World War II, abstract expressionism dominated art in Spain. By the more prosperous 1960s, this was led by a rebellious artists' collective known as El Paso, out of which emerged the powerful

The Nativitat facade of Gaudí's Sagrada Família, in Barcelona, remains unfinished.

gestural works of Antonio Saura and the highly influential canvasses of Antoni Tàpies. Subtle color, geometric symbols, and the incorporation of other media (sand, wax) became the hallmarks of the Tàpies school. Its counterpoint was the pop art of Equipo Crónica and the bold narratives of Eduardo Arroyo. Today, Eduardo Chillida's purist geo-

Pablo Picasso painted this self-portrait in 1901.

metrical sculptures are virtually the "official" art of his native Basque country. The Mallorcan Miguel Barceló produces imaginative, mixed-media paintings that combine African references with metaphysical concerns. Susana Solano, José María Sicilia, Jaume Plensa, and Juan Muñoz have all acquired international profiles, and conceptual work flourishes among younger artists such as Txomin Badiola and Pep Agut.

In architecture, style nose-dived during the Franco era, but reemerged with Josep Luis Sert's modernist homages to Balearic antecedents and with Ricardo Bofill's 1980s postmodernism. At the start of the 21st century, Santiago Calatrava is feted for elegant feats of engineering, while Rafael Moneo is the uncontested star, creator of sensitive, functional, streamlined buildings that are the perfect symbols of a renovated Spain.

MUSIC

Perceived as the quintessential music of Spain, flamenco (see pp. 294–95), in fact, has Gypsy, Arab, and Jewish roots. Before this, Spanish music evolved from polyphonic chants of the early Middle Ages, and reached a high point during the Renaissance, when instruments such as the guitar *(vihuela,* with five strings rather than the modern six) proliferated. Spanish musicians also incorporated tonalities and instruments such as the lute, oboe, and tambourine from the Moors. This distinctive

Gypsy family gatherings in Andalucía inevitably break into spontaneous flamenco.

style faded as northern European music became more influential, but a present-day group of musicians called Mudejar have resurrected its unique sounds and instruments. For centuries, the main forms of homegrown music remained popular ballads and the *zarzuela,* a form of musical play invented by Pedro Calderón de la Barca in the 17th century. However, Spanish music rebounded under the aegis of composers such as Felipe Pedrell (1841–1922), Isaac Albeñiz (1860–1909), and Enrique Granados (1867–1916). Manuel de Falla (1876–1946) represented the psychological duality of Spain with *Nights in the Gardens of Spain:* introspection punctuated by violent outbursts. A still

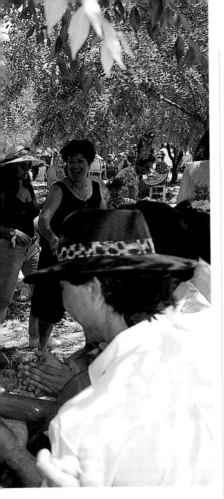

Any local fiesta is proof of this, and record shops display large sections devoted to local musicians, categorized, as always, by region.

THEATER & LITERATURE

Early playwrights Lope de Vega (1562–1635) and Calderón de la Barca (1600–1681) brilliantly mirrored the exploits and optimism of Spain's Golden Age, and Miguel de Cervantes created its universal protagonist, Don Quixote (see pp. 238–39). In theater, it is Catalunya that has always led the way. Barcelona's Teatre Principal was founded in 1603, and Frederic Soler created modern Catalan theater. More recently, an extreme participative form has been perfected by the Catalan company Fura dels Baus, whose acrobatic performances reveling in blood and guts (literally) shocked European audiences in the 1980s and '90s.

On a more contemplative note, Santa Teresa de Ávila (1515–1582) and Ignatius Loyola (1491–1556, the founder of the Jesuits) wrote mystic works about their spiritual quests. The 19th century saw Spanish literature evolving into the realism and satire of Pedro de Alarcón, Leopoldo Alas, and Benito Pérez Galdós. Galdós's epic *Torquemada* has been compared with the work of Balzac for its social realism and comment. Modern Spanish literature began at the end of the 19th century, when Spain's humiliation by the United States (see p. 35) led a group of intellectuals to explore the nature of individual and national identity. This was the Generation of '98, including the philosopher-essayists Miguel de Unamuno (1864–1936) and José Ortega y Gasset (1883–1955), playwrights Jacinto Benavente (1866–1954) and Ramón Maná del Valle-Inclán (1869–1936), and poets Antonio Machado (1875–1939) and Juan Ramón Jiménez (1881–1958). The following generation included the great poet Federico García Lorca (1898–1936) and Vicente Aleixandre (1898–1984), who was awarded the Nobel Prize for Literature in 1977. In the late 20th century, new registers of irony, drama, and psychology made up for 40 years of Francoist taboos and repression. Much innovative Hispanic writing came from Latin America; from Spain itself came the complex, postmodern novel of Julián Ríos *(Larva,* 1984), Camilo José Cela, winner of the Nobel Prize for Literature, and *nueva narrativa española* (new

more popular classic is Joaquín Rodrigo's (1901–1999) *Concierto de Aranjuez.*

Spain has produced some of the world's top guitar-players, including the classical performer Andrés Segovia and the flamenco artists Paco Peña and Paco de Lucía. The late Pablo Casals took cello playing to its zenith. Homegrown opera singers include Plácido Domingo, José Carreras, Teresa Braganza, Victoria de los Ángeles, Alfredo Kraus, and Montserrat Caballé. On a lighter note, Julio Iglesias is a household name. Spain has yet to produce rock bands of international standing, although flamenco-rock has blossomed (see pp. 294–95), and Galician-Celtic groups are popular. Hispanic rock culture thrives on its own territory, however, and lack of world status is due more to undeveloped marketing than to absence of talent.

"The Vermin of the Sewers" contributes to Spain's vibrant modern music scene.

Spanish narrative). Juan Madrid and Eduardo Mendoza, both popular thriller writers, and the intellectual fireworks of Juan Goytisolo, add to this inspiring spectrum of talent.

FILM

Spanish cinema saw its international genesis in two surrealist films by Luis Buñuel and Salvador Dalí, *Un chien Andalou* (1928) and *L'Age d'Or* (1930). Both are known better by their French titles than their Spanish ones, as they were filmed in Paris. With the glorious 1930s, when cinema excelled elsewhere, Spain had dived into a morass of sociopolitical upheaval, followed by decades of Franco's censorship. However a defiant new wave emerged in the 1950s and '60s. Luis García Berlanga (*Bienvenido, Mr. Marshall,* 1953, and *El Verdugo,* 1964), Juan Bardem (*Muerte de un Ciclista,* 1955), and Carlos Saura (*Los Golfos,* 1959, and *Cría Cuervos,* 1975) created films that artfully sidestepped censorship while maintaining integrity of vision. Buñuel, meanwhile, gravitated between Mexico, Hollywood, and France, writing and directing a succession of masterpieces, including *Viridiana* (1961), which was shot in Spain but also banned there, *The Exterminating Angel* (1962), *Belle de Jour* (1967), and the Oscar-winning *Discreet Charm of the Bourgeoisie* (1972). His eventful life covered the rise, fall, and incipient renewal of the Spanish film industry (he died in 1983).

The latest generation of filmmakers includes Fernando Trueba *(Belle Époque,* 1992, and *Two Much,* 1995, with heartthrob Antonio Banderas and Melanie Griffith); Juan Bigas Luna, whose outrageous *Jamón, Jamón* (1992) captivated audiences all over the world; Alejandro Amenabar *(Tesis,* 1995, and *Open Your Eyes,* 1997); and Pedro Almodóvar. If one person encapsulates the new Spain it is Almodóvar, taking up the torch from Buñuel, who once declared "In my own village...the Middle Ages lasted until World War I." Almodóvar, born in 1949 in La Mancha, produced his first feature film in 1980 when a new spirit was sweeping Madrid. From his first international box-office hit, *Women on the Verge of a Nervous Breakdown* (1988), he projected a quirky, frenetic, multicolor image of Spain onto world screens. His actors Victoria Abril, Carmen Maura, and Antonio Banderas shot to fame, while Almodóvar compounded his success with *Tie Me Up, Tie Me Down* (1990) and Oscar-winning *All About My Mother* (1999). Each one is a clever concoction of tragicomedy and high-decibel excess. In 1999, 70 films were made in Spain—we can only wait to see what dreams will be spun next. ∎

The sizzling nightlife of Madrid is counterbalanced by museums and art collections that create a visual marathon through some of the world's greatest paintings. It is also a city of gastronomic indulgence, good music, and fashion.

In & around Madrid

Kilometer Zero (the point from which all distances in Spain are measured) in Puerta del Sol, Madrid

Madrid

SPRAWLING OVER THE MESETA, THE PLATEAU OF CENTRAL SPAIN, MADRID is perfectly placed to play its coordinating role for the nation's 18 autonomous regions. It does not have a lengthy past—it has been Spain's capital only since 1561, when Felipe II moved his court from Toledo. Nor can it compete with the designer gloss of its rival, Barcelona. But Madrid makes up for this in every other way.

It is cosmopolitan, with wonderful food, art, and nightlife. Add to this a wide range of hotels and an excellent transportation system serving a compact group of sights, and you have the ingredients for a very pleasant few days. This is Europe's highest capital at 2,120 feet (646 m), and its mountain climate is best in spring or autumn. In winter, Madrid suffers

Madrid's emblematic bear and strawberry tree

from bitter winds straight off the Sierra de Guadarrama; in summer, it is scorchingly hot.

More than anything else, Madrid takes you on a compelling voyage through the history of art. Its oldest treasures are at the Museo Arqueológico, but the finest are at the Prado, which has thousands of paintings from the Middle Ages to the 19th century. The Thyssen-Bornemisza covers the same period and part of the 20th century, and the Reina Sofía takes you through the 20th century and into the 21st. Smaller collections include the wonderful Monasterio de las Descalzas Reales; contemporary art enthusiasts should enjoy Madrid's lively commercial galleries. Among the city's fine buildings, the best is the Palacio Real (Royal Palace)—an unforgettable confection of decorative whimsy and excess, overlooked by Madrid's first, and still barely completed, cathedral.

Chic designer shops line the 19th-century avenues north of Parque del Retiro. Throbbing clubs and tapas bars fill the narrow streets radiating from Plaza del Ángel. The old center has baroque churches. Northeast, modern office blocks rise on the Paseo de la Castellana, which links with Paseo del Prado to form the main north–south axis of the city. The main east–west axis is formed by the Gran Vía and Calle de Alcalá. The latter leads to the heart of Habsburg Madrid, the Plaza Mayor. Stay near any of these roads in order truly to enter the 24-hour spirit of the "city that never sleeps." ■

Palacio Real

IT IS NOT THE MOST HARMONIOUS OR TASTEFUL OF Spanish palaces, but the Palacio Real (Royal Palace) drips with regal opulence. Full of the decorative excesses of the 18th and 19th centuries, it reveals a lot about the royalty that commissioned them. The palace stands on the site of the Moorish ninth-century fortress. It became the royal residence in 1561, but was rebuilt after a calamitous fire in 1734. Three Italian architects and several French artists worked to complete the reconstruction, in 1764. The palace is very much a product of the Bourbon court (see p. 34), and the furnishing is almost all original 18th-century baroque and rococo. King Alfonso XIII lived here until he left Spain in 1931 when the Republicans took control. Today it is used only for state ceremonial purposes.

Palacio Real

🅰 54 B4

✉ Calle de Bailén

☎ 91 547 53 50 or
   91 542 00 59

🕐 Closed Sun. p.m. &
   for official
   ceremonies

💲 $$. Free on Wed.
   for E.U. citizens.
   Guided tours in
   English

🚇 Metro: Ópera

From the entrance in front of the cathedral (see p. 59), you go into a vast courtyard, at the back of which a grand staircase leads up to the royal apartments. White stone and granite from the Sierra de Guadarrama are the chief building materials, while inside, marble achieves an impressive acreage. The **Hall of Halberdiers** (royal guards), with its ceiling painting by Giovanni Battista Tiepolo (1696–1770), leads to the opulent **Hall of Columns,** where 17th-century Flemish tapestries adorn the walls, and sculptures symbolize the planets. The dictator General Franco lay in state in the hall in 1975, and in 1985, a formal signing ceremony took place here when Spain joined the European Economic Community. You then enter the most sumptuous hall, the Throne Room, where Tiepolo's ceiling painting **"Apotheosis of the Spanish Monarchy"** looks down on Neapolitan furniture, Venetian chandeliers, mirrors, and clocks from San Ildefonso de la Granja (see p. 226), and bronze lions by Benicelli.

You now move on to the **King's Rooms:** the Reception Room, Lunch Room, Dressing Room, and Bedroom, each one full of precious objects and furniture, much of it French. The paintings include portraits by Goya of Carlos IV and his wife, María Luisa. In the **Lunch Room** look out for the astonishing clock made of marble, bronze, and mahogany with a diamond-studded face. The Italian decorator Gasparini designed the rococo extravaganza of the **Dressing Room.** This riot of silk, gold, and silver wall hangings, an inlaid marble floor swirling with floral designs, and an ornately stuccoed ceiling created a fitting stage for the king to undergo the daily ceremony of being dressed in front of his courtiers. The **Bedroom,** now furnished as a sitting room with white-and-gold Empire furniture, has a ceiling painting by Vicente López containing numerous references to the religious and honorific order created by Carlos III.

Next, you see some of the more idiosyncratic rooms, starting with the **Porcelain Room,** a small chamber whose porcelain wall panels were designed for smokers of the time. The Buen Retiro workshop, founded by Carlos III, made the panels, which are decorated with grapes, garlands, and flowers. Next door is the **Yellow Room,** lined with fine tapestries, where ladies sat on marquetry chairs by Dugourc and ate chocolates, while the men puffed away in their adjacent smoking room.

Now comes the pièce de résistance, the vast, ornate **Ballroom,** created in 1879 by Alfonso XII out of three smaller rooms built for Carlos III's wife. On her premature death, Carlos closed them up, and so they remained for more than a century. Today the room is used as a banqueting hall seating 150 people, who can gaze at the ceiling painting of Christopher Columbus announcing his New World discoveries to Fernando and Isabel. The walls are lined with 16th-century Flemish tapestries and giant vases, both Chinese and French.

The **Music Room** has a rare and unusual collection of stringed instruments by the genius of violin-making, Antonio Stradivari (1644–1737). The instruments are occasionally used in private concerts organized by the present Queen Sofía, a great music-lover. Watch out, too, for the mother-of-pearl guitar dating from 1796. After the **Silver Room,** displaying a rather motley collection of silver, you reach the **Capilla Real** (Royal Chapel). Colossal marble columns sustain this neoclassic design, gleaming with gilt, by Ventura Rodríguez. The last four, smaller, rooms are the apartments of Queen María Luisa. These include a porcelain smoking room, a chinoiserie room, and an inspiring study with marble marquetry and painted silk ceiling panels. ■

The grand staircase leads to opulent reception rooms and the royal apartments.

Murals watch over the Plaza Mayor, a harmonious arcaded square at the heart of Madrid.

A walk around Plaza Mayor

This walk takes you to the heart of historical Madrid, where winding streets lead past churches and tapas bars, as well as give a glimpse of royal history. Follow the trail by day or night—the ambience changes radically.

Start your walk at the **Plaza Mayor ❶**, a majestic, porticoed square constructed in the early 17th century as the hub of Habsburg Madrid (see p. 33). The work took place under Felipe III, whose equestrian statue gazes over the square, and was directed by Juan Gómez de Mora. The most striking building is the gingerbread-style **Casa de la Panadería** (1672), home of the Bakers' Guild. Its incongruous murals by Carlos Franco are the third to have blanketed the facade. Opposite, the **Casa de la Carnicería** (Butchers' Guild) houses municipal offices and the tourist office. Gone are the weekday markets, bullfights, and autos-da-fé (trials and executions of heretics) that once filled the square: Today it is just a popular place to meet.

Leave the square through the arch in the northeast corner leading to Calle de Ciudad Rodrigo. On the left, you see the green wrought-iron facade of the **Mercado de San Miguel** (*Closed siestas, Sat. p.m. & Sun.*), an indoor fruit and vegetable market. It is a hive of activity inside. Turn left into the busy Calle Mayor and you soon reach the charming and historic **Plaza de la Villa ❷**. On the right flank of this sloping square stands the **Ayuntamiento** or Casa de la Villa (town hall) designed by Juan Gómez de Mora in 1640 to house the town council and prison.

🅰 See area map p. 54
▶ Plaza Mayor
↔ 1.2 miles (2.4 km)
⏱ 1.5 hours
▶ Plaza Mayor

NOT TO BE MISSED
- Plaza Mayor
- Ayuntamiento
- San Pedro
- San Francisco el Grande
- Calle de Cuchilleros

Facing you is the **Casa de Cisneros,** a reconstruction of a 16th-century palace that stood here, and on the left is the 15th-century **Torre de los Lujanes,** the birthplace in 1846 of the composer Federico Chueca and now part of the university. The tower has Mudejar (see p. 43) arches at its summit and, opening onto the narrow Calle del Codo, a horseshoe-arched doorway.

Retrace your steps to Calle Mayor, turn left and continue to the end. As you walk, you see the outskirts of Madrid receding in the distance, reminding you of the height of the city. The massive white forms of the **Catedral de Nuestra Señora de la Almudena** *(Tel 91 542 22 00)* soon appear ahead. It was built in 1985–1992, but the plans were first drawn up a century earlier. Cross the Calle de Bailén

if you want to see the interior—an odd mixture of pure white stone, garish ceiling paintings, and tasteless side chapels. Beside it stands the vast **Palacio Real** (see pp. 56–57). Return to the corner of Bailén and Mayor, and walk down the steps beside the Capitanía General, built as a palace in 1611 and now a military establishment. The city drops steeply here: You soon find yourself gazing back up at the lofty viaduct (1934) of Calle de Bailén. Circle around the back of the palace through the parking lot, and then turn right down Calle de la Villa to reach Calle de Segovia.

Looming opposite is the dome of the 16th-century **Capilla del Obispo** *(Plaza de la Paja, tel 91 365 48 71)*, Madrid's only Gothic chapel. Walk toward it up Costanilla de San Andrés to **Plaza de la Paja,** a pretty residential square with a few bars and restaurants. In the Middle Ages, this was the commercial heart of Madrid. Turn left into Calle Príncipe Anglona for a closer look at the church of **San Pedro** ❸ *(Tel 91 365 12 84)*. Its 14th-century Mudejar tower replaced the minaret of a mosque that once stood here. Return to Plaza

Shops and cafés line the arcades below the Casa de la Panadería, Plaza Mayor.

de la Paja, cross over it and turn into Calle Redondilla. This ends at Calle de Bailén, where you turn left to **San Francisco el Grande** ❹, a neoclassic basilica *(Tel 91 365 38 00, closed Sun.–Mon.)*. Built in 1762–1784, it has a Goya painting of San Bernardino and a lavishly painted cupola. The 16th-century choir stalls in the sacristy come from the Carthusian monastery of El Paular.

Walk along Carrera de San Francisco (away from the basilica), to Plaza de Puerta de Moros. Rising to your left is the baroque **Iglesia de San Isidro** *(Tel 91 369 20 37)* and the church of **San Andrés** *(Plaza de San Andrés, tel 91 365 48 71)*. Both overlook a peaceful square flanked by a contemporary trompe-l'oeil mural. Go past San Andrés to the tiny Plaza del Humilladero, and turn left down **Calle Cava Baja.** Stop for refreshments at one of the little restaurants and bars with wood-paneled facades that accompany you as far as Plaza de Puerta Cerrada. Or cross to lively **Calle de Cuchilleros** ❺, with more bars and cafés, before going up the arched steps leading into Plaza Mayor. ■

Coin- and stamp-collectors gather to trade in the Plaza Mayor on Sunday mornings.

Monasterio de las Descalzas Reales

THE ROYAL ORIGINS OF THIS FRANCISCAN CONVENT OF the Royal Barefoot Nuns lie in its conversion from a palace into a convent by Felipe II's sister Juana de Austria, who became a nun. Her sister María also lived in the convent, although without taking orders. Today 28 nuns of the order known as the Poor Clares live in seclusion here, and on your tour you may hear them singing and ringing bells. The magnificent late 15th- to early 16th-century building holds a mass of treasure.

Frescoes by various artists adorn the grand staircase that leads up from the cloisters. The dominant one shows Felipe IV and his family, and opposite is a Crucifixion scene. Off the first-floor cloisters, the remarkable side chapels contain original **Talavera tiled floors,** frescoes, coffered ceilings, and many paintings by anonymous artists. A beautiful recumbent **"Christ"** is the work of 16th-century sculptor Gaspar Becerra. Fra Angelico's masterful "Annunciation" hung here before being moved to the Prado (see pp. 62–67).

The anteroom to the main chapel is packed with silverware, Bohemian crystal crucifixes, and paintings. It leads to the **Choir,** used daily for Mass, where the marble tomb of María stands above that of her daughter, Marguerita. Notice the fabulously realistic and expressive **statue of Mary,** by Pedro de Mena (1628–1688). Back in the cloisters, the next side chapel is devoted to the Virgin of Guadalupe, celebrated in a riot of baroque gilt, with unusual paintings on mirrors. Farther along, look for the **"Madonna and Child"** painted by Bernardino Luini (circa 1480–1532).

From here you are taken upstairs to the vast Hall of Tapestries, lined with 17th-century Flemish tapestries based on cartoons by Peter Paul Rubens (1577–1640), and packed with other treasures—embroidered robes, silverware, and reliquaries (containers for relics of saints and other revered items). In the Chapterhouse overlooking the vegetable garden you'll see more works of art. Two of the more searing are Gregorio Fernández's **sculpture of Mary Magdalen** and Pedro de Mena's **"Ecce Homo."** The tour ends in splendor in a room hung with paintings by Zurbarán, Titian, Caravaggio, Bruegel the Elder, and Rubens. ■

Monasterio de las Descalzas Reales

🅰 54 C3
✉ Plaza de las Descalzas Reales 3
☎ 91 542 00 59
🕐 Closed Fri. & Sun. p.m., & Mon.
💲 $. Free on Wed. for E.U. citizens with passport. 50-minute guided tour in Spanish
🚇 Metro: Sol, Ópera, & Callao

Madrid's Monasterio de las Descalzas Reales, founded by Felipe II's sister, houses many Renaissance and baroque artworks.

Museo del Prado

Goya's "The Clothed Maja" and "The Naked Maja," painted around 1800, are displayed side by side in the Prado.

MADRID'S MOST FAMOUS MUSEUM MAY ARGUABLY HAVE the world's greatest collection of classical paintings, and for many people it is the main reason for visiting the capital. The vast collection is full of masterpieces, easier to absorb if you focus on a small number of artists or periods and make at least two visits. If you can manage only one, allow at least three hours, and avoid weekends when the museum is particularly crowded.

Zurbarán (see p. 47), the Prado has big collections of Italian (including Titian and Raphael) and Flemish artists. Many of the latter were collected by Felipe II, an astute art-lover whose taste was influenced by that of his Flemish aunt. Both he and his father, Carlos V, favored Titian (died 1576); Felipe IV chose Diego Velázquez (1599–1660) as court painter, and Carlos III appointed Francisco de Goya (1746–1828). In 1819, Fernando VII opened the collection to the public in this 18th-century building (designed by Juan de Villanueva, 1739–1811).

Museo del Prado

- ⓘ 55 E3
- ✉ Paseo del Prado
- ☎ 91 330 28 00
- 🕐 Closed Sun. p.m. & Mon.
- 💲 $
- Ⓜ Metro: Banco de España

Opposite: Peter Paul Rubens painted the powerful "Equestrian Portrait of the Duke of Lerma" in 1603, during his Italian period.

You can enter the Prado from either end of the building (but not the central entrance facing the Paseo). Locker and cloakroom space is very limited: Come lightly laden so you won't have to use it. Major redecoration and rehanging was completed in the summer of 1999, and plans are afoot to extend the galleries into the gardens, to a design by Rafael Moneo, the architect of the Thyssen-Bornemisza conversion (see pp. 68–71). Museums often change their displays, so the arrangement described below may have changed.

The source of this incredible body of works was the Spanish royal family, who, over the centuries, commissioned and collected art with passion. In addition to stars of Spanish painting such as Velázquez, Goya, Ribera, and

ROMANESQUE & EARLY ITALIAN ART

If you enter from the Puerta de Goya (the northern end) on the ground floor, look at **Rooms 51A** and **51B** off the rotunda, devoted to Romanesque art. Frescoes here show animals and hunting scenes from San Baudelio, near Soria. Continue to **Room 49** to see early Italian works, including a very delicately painted "Annunciation" (1425–28) by Fra Angelico (died 1455), and three panels by Sandro Botticelli (circa 1445–1510) telling the "Story of Nastagio degli Onesti" (1483). Among several paintings by Raphael (1483–1520) on religious themes, the most striking is his "Portrait of A Cardinal" (1510), with the cardinal in a brilliant red robe. Also in this room, you can see the evolution of Andrea del Sarto's

Goya's painting of the "Dos de Mayo" shows Spaniards being shot by French troops during the War of Independence.

work, from the beautifully expressive "Portrait of a Woman" (1514) to the more baroque "Sacrifice of Isaac" (1528–29).

FLEMISH & GERMAN PAINTING

Rooms 54 to **58A** hold 15th- to 16th-century Flemish works, among others. Strong commercial and marriage links between Spain and Flanders produced a style—Spanish but showing Flemish influence—evident in **Room 57**, while **Room 58** houses the "Descent from the Cross" by Rogier van der Weyden (1399– 1464). The faces are brilliantly executed and the whole composition leads the eye to the cross. In **Room 58A** look for

First floor

Ground floor

Puerta de Goya

Puerta de Velázquez

Hans Memling's "Adoration of the Kings" (circa 1470). **Room 56A** has works by Bruegel, Joachim Patinir, and Hieronymus Bosch (circa 1450–1516), whose weird "Garden of Delights" always draws a crowd. Bosch's imagination encompassed both bawdy pursuits and the more mystical. Albrecht Dürer's (1471–1528) magnificent "Self-portrait" (1498) in **Room 54,** another masterpiece, is flanked by his full-length paintings of "Adam" and "Eve" (1507). These were the first Renaissance-style paintings to emerge from northern Europe.

EARLY SPANISH WORKS
Room 55 has portraits by Antonio Moro (1519–1576), including one

of the English Queen Mary Tudor (1554), painted for Felipe II when he was considering marriage to Mary. **Room 56** contains fine portraits by Juan de Juanes (circa 1523–1579) and his "Last Supper." **Room 56B** shows Sebastiano de Piombo's luminous work—clear blue skies and dazzling white are his hallmarks.

VENETIAN SCHOOL
At this point you enter long **Room 75,** displaying Italian painters of the Venetian school, whose blending of color and light surpassed all other Renaissance schools. Painters include Paolo Veronese (circa 1528–1588), Jacopo Bassano (died 1592), and Jacopo Tintoretto (1518–1594). Take a good look at

GOYA

Goya (1746–1828) stands guard outside the Prado.

Italian painting

Spanish painting

Flemish painting

French painting

Romanesque painting

Sculpture

Special exhibitions

Close inspection of Velázquez's "The Surrender of Breda"

Puerta de Murillo

Inside one of the Museo del Prado's airy, uncluttered galleries

Tintoretto's "El Lavatorio," depicting Jesus washing the disciples' feet, a masterpiece of perspective. Titian (died 1576), who worked extensively for both Carlos V and Felipe II, is well represented in **Rooms 61, 61B,** and **63:** Look at his self-portrait, the superb horseback figure of "Carlos V at the Battle of Mühlberg" (1548), and the portrait of "Isabel of Portugal," painted after her death. Titian's fame during his life nearly matched that of Michelangelo, and it is said that Carlos V once did him the honor of picking up a paintbrush he had dropped.

EL GRECO & GOYA

El Greco dominates **Rooms 60A, 62A,** and **61A,** starting with early works and moving into his Spanish period when his figures lengthened and he adopted a very Spanish concern with the division between heaven and earth. Better works, however, are found in Toledo. Classical and Renaissance sculpture complete this floor, but this isn't a must. Instead, take the stairs to the next level where you are propelled into the world of Goya, whose diverse works fill seven rooms **(Rooms 32** and **34–39).** His huge political paintings "El Dos de Mayo" and "El Tres de Mayo" depict scenes from Spain's War of Independence in 1808—unusually for that time he was not working to commission, so the subject matter was his own choice. **Room 37** has the very strange "black paintings," produced in 1820–23, during a period of deep depression caused by the deaths of his wife and son, and by his own illness. Many of these paintings are grotesque; all are open to interpretation and their titles are conjectural. "Perro" seems completely modern in conception, with its extraordinary spatial arrangement of a dog's head against textured space. Some of the court paintings by Goya which are on display are just as idiosyncratic and often quite unflattering, with an emotional approach to the characterization of his subjects.

VELÁZQUEZ & OTHERS
The long hall off **Room 32** has 17th-century Spanish paintings, with works by Murillo, Ribera, and Zurbarán. **Rooms 12, 14, 15,** and **16** bring you to Velázquez. The Prado has his best pictures, and the greatest of them all, "Las Meninas" ("The Maids of Honor"), is in **Room 12.** It was cleaned in the late 1990s and is shown with its preparatory paintings. Look at it from a distance, and see Velázquez himself observing you from where he stands beside his easel in the picture. **Room 11** exhibits Peter Paul Rubens (1577–1640), with several paintings of hunting scenes brought from the royal hunting lodge at El Pardo. This floor ends with 17th-century French and Italian paintings. Upstairs, there are several rooms which are devoted to Goya (including selections from a range of his portraits, tapestries, and cartoons). Other rooms have 18th-century European art on display. ■

"Les Barrachos," or "The Drunkards" (1628-29), by Velázquez, one of the few Spanish painters to depict mythological scenes

Museo Thyssen-Bornemisza

Museo Thyssen-Bornemisza
www.museothyssen.org
🅰 55 E3
✉ Palacio de Villahermosa, Paseo del Prado 8
☎ 91 420 39 44
🕐 Closed Mon.
💲 $$
🚇 Metro: Banco de España

**Opposite:
"Swaying
Dancer" (1880)
by Edgar Degas
Below: The Museo
Thyssen-
Bornemisza
showcases
Western art of
the past 800 years.**

MADRID ACQUIRED THIS EXCEPTIONAL ART COLLECTION only in 1993, and its quality and coverage give it equal footing with the Prado across the road. The collection was built by two generations of the Thyssen-Bornemisza family, and it is now overseen by the Spanish Baroness Thyssen-Bornemisza. Critics initially sneered because of her youth and career as a fashion model, but she has turned out to be as astute a collector as her husband and late father-in-law. The collection, housed in a 19th-century neoclassic mansion converted by Rafael Moneo, represents the best of Western art from the last 800 years.

For a chronological tour, work your way down from the top floor. Begin in **Room 1** with the oldest paintings, the Italian primitives, among them "Christ and the Samaritan" by Duccio di Buoninsegna (1278–1319), the only artist known to have signed his work at this time. **Room 3** brings you to early Flemish paintings: Best of these are the black-and-white diptych of the "Annunciation" by Jan Van Eyck (1390–1441), which looks like carved stone, and the incredibly detailed

"Enthroned Madonna" by Rogier van der Weyden (1400–64). In **Room 5,** which has an exceptional display of Renaissance portraits, you touch on early examples of the modern cult of the personality: Look for Domenico Ghirlandaio's "Portrait of Giovanna Tornabuoni," a representation of perfection, and Hans Holbein's (1498–1543) masterful and much reproduced depiction of a self-satisfied Henry VIII of England. Next to it hangs a delightful portrait of a youthful Catherine of Aragón, Henry's first wife, the "Infanta" (circa 1496) by Juan de Flandes. The Villahermosa Gallery, adjoining, **(Room 6)** displays Raphael's (1483–1520) "Portrait of a Young Man" in a freer style. **Room 7** brings you to larger format Renaissance paintings. Bernardino Luini's (1486–1532) "Virgin and Child with the Infant St. John" shows wonderful delicacy in the Virgin's face, her veil, and the two babies. "Young Knight in a Landscape" by Vittore Carpaccio (1460–1525) is in a transitional style, part naturalistic, part stylized, and Gothic.

GERMAN & ITALIAN SCHOOLS

A more exaggerated, even caricatural, approach characterizes the paintings of the German school in **Rooms 8** and **9.** Albrecht Dürer's (1471–1528) "Jesus among the

Edward Hopper's "Hotel Room" (1931) is considered the most important representation of the American figurative school.

Doctors" is a compelling composition that draws the eye to the hands at the center. Next door, in **Room 10,** the "Reclining Nymph" by Lucas Cranach the Elder (1472–1553) has a superbly painted transparent veil.

Rooms 11 and **12** represent great artists of the Venetian school —Titian, Tintoretto, Bassano—and other Italians. El Greco appears here because he began his career in Italy, and José de Ribera (1591–1652) has a room to himself. This Spaniard, who worked and died in Italy, combines Spanish drama with Italian techniques, as well as displaying a startling realism.

BAROQUE
The early baroque section features anguished sculptures including, "San Sebastián" and "La Piedad" by Bernini (1598–1680); other highlights are Luca Giordano's (1634–1705) "Judgment of Solomon," Francisco de Zurbarán's (1598–1664) "Santa Casilda," and radiant views of Venice by Canaletto (1697–1768). Further Flemish and Dutch paintings are in **Rooms 19, 20,**

and **21:** Here you'll find superlative works by Van Dyck, Brueghel, and Rubens, especially his superb "Toilet of Venus." Don't miss Rembrandt's penetrating "Self-portrait."

Dutch 17th-century paintings fill a whole wing of the museum's middle level with beautifully observed and composed scenes of daily life, interiors, and landscapes. An unusual still life by William Claesz Heda (1593–1680) has a magnificent display of silverware and glass standing beside a half-eaten pie.

Rooms 28, 29, and **30** bring you to English and American artists such as Joshua Reynolds (1723–1792), Thomas Gainsborough (1727–1788), and Thomas Cole (1801–1848), an Englishman who emigrated to America and founded the American school. Apart from a rather fine "Portrait of the Duchess of Sutherland" by John Singer Sargent (1856–1925), this section is more interesting intellectually than artistically. After the Spanish, Flemish, and Dutch works, these portraits seem rather stilted and lifeless. Then comes the shock of

European Romanticism, with a wall of Goya, Géricault, and Delacroix in **Room 31,** followed by Courbet and Constable.

The Impressionists are in **Rooms 32** and **33:** Make sure you see Renoir's "Woman with Parasol" (1873), Berthe Morisot's "The Cheval-Glass" (1876), and Edgar Degas' "Swaying Dancer" (1880). Vincent van Gogh's "Les Vessenots" (1890), painted in thick impasto, may have been his last painting before his suicide.

MODERNISM

The modern art collection begins in **Room 34** with André Derain (1880–1954) and the other Fauves (wild beasts), so-called because they seemed to break all rules. However, the Thyssen-Bornemisza comes into its own with a superlative collection of German expressionists **(Rooms 35–40)**—Munch, Kokoschka, Nolde, Schiele, and Beckmann are all here, and Otto Kirchner (1880–1938) is especially well represented. Take a look at his radiating composition in "The Bay" (1914) and "Alpine Kitchen" (1918). Franz Marc (1880–1916) and Wassily Kandinsky (1866–1944) represent the Blaue Reiter group, and the last room has caricatural works by Georg Grosz (1893–1959).

Rooms 41–44 on the ground floor show parallel trends of early modernism, from cubism (Braque, Juan Gris, Picasso) to futurism, constructivism, dadaism and surrealism. The United States rules supreme in **Room 46,** with abstract expressionism by Rothko, O'Keeffe, and De Kooning. **Rooms 47** and **48** round things off with a general survey of postwar figurative work and pop art.

If any criticism can be made of this collection, it is in this last section, which gives a one-sided view of the 1960s and 1970s, completely missing out on the arrival of minimalism and conceptualism. For these two art movements, go to the Reina Sofía (see pp. 74–75). ∎

Venetian artist Giovanni Bellini, who painted "Nunc Dimittis" ("Presentation of Christ in the Temple"), helped make Venice an important center of the Italian Renaissance.

Parque del Retiro

MADRID IS NOT BY ANY MEANS A GREEN CITY, BUT IT DOES have a lovely breathing space in this 350-acre (142 ha) park. In the 17th century, the park surrounded Felipe IV's palace. Now it lies conveniently close to the capital's main cluster of museums, and it is the perfect place to recover from the physical and mental rigors of visiting them.

Parque del Retiro
- 55 F2
- Calle de Alfonso XII
- 91 588 86 80 (Departamento Parques y Jardines)
- Metro: Atocha, Retiro, & Ibiza

Real Jardín Botánico
- 55 E2
- Plaza de Murillo 2
- 91 420 30 17
- Metro: Atocha

The Conde-Duque de Olivares laid out the park in 1636, and its formal gardens, copses, fountains, statues, and paths remain. All that is left of the palace is the Casón del Buen Retiro, now an annex to the Prado, with a select display of 19th-century Spanish painting and sculpture *(Tel 91 330 28 00, closed Mon.; may be closed for renovation)*. It stands at the entrance to the park on Calle de Alfonso XII, just behind the Prado and Iglesia San Jerónimo el Real.

In the park itself, you can take a carriage ride, row a boat on the **Estanque Lake,** watch street theater, hear a concert, visit an exhibition, or just stroll. This is a popular meeting point for Madrileños, especially on Sundays. The **equestrian statue** by the lake portrays Alfonso XII (*R.*1874–1885), not Spain's most illustrious ruler but one of its youngest—he died at only 28. Jutting out south of the Prado in the far southwest corner of the park is the **Real Jardín Botánico** (Royal Botanic Garden), founded in 1774. It has about 30,000 plants, some of them exotic, and aging greenhouses designed by Juan de Villanueva (1739–1811). Also in the southern half are the **Palacio de Velázquez** *(Tel 91 573 62 45, closed Mon.)* and the soaring glass walls of the **Palacio de Cristal** *(Tel 91 574 66 14, closed Mon.)*. Both hold exhibitions of contemporary art. Nearby are a pool and grotto, and at the far southern end of the park there are rose gardens. ■

Museo Arqueológico Nacional

THIS MUSEUM OF ANCIENT ART WAS FOUNDED IN 1895 AND
is at the back of the grandiose Biblioteca Nacional (National Library)
building. The Spanish collection is very strong, but the museum also
covers ancient Egypt, Greece, Rome, and the Middle East. Some
exhibits are exceptional; others, especially some of the older ones,
seem less significant now than they did to their collectors.

The lower floor covers prehistory
and early humans. **Room 6** has the
most intriguing exhibits: the
Cuencos de Axtroki, hammered
gold vessels with circular designs
that suggest a cult of the sun in the
late Bronze Age. **Room 7** has beautiful gold torques (collars) from
northwest Spain, and **Room 9** has
Celtiberian silver, mainly from
southeast Spain. In the Egyptian
section **(Room 13)**, the sarcophagus of Amenemhat is beautifully
painted with religious scenes.
Rooms 14–16 display an exceptional collection of Greek pottery.

On the ground floor, start with
Iberian and Phoenician works in
Rooms 19–20 (next to the ticket
desk) and go around clockwise.
Pride of place goes to the limestone
bust called the Dama de Elche (late
fifth century B.C.). This rare example of Iberian art probably held
human ashes in the cavity in her
shoulder. It would once have been
brightly colored: A few traces of
polychrome paint remain, but you
get a better idea by looking at the
neighboring Dama de Baza (fifth
or fourth century B.C.), a seated
woman surrounded by the dowry
found in her tomb at Baza, near
Granada. Older still is another
female sculpture, the diminutive
Dama de Galera, a seventh-century
B.C. Phoenician artifact carved out
of alabaster. In **Room 19,** look for
the dazzling Tesoro de Javea (Javea

Treasure), a collection of Iberian
filigree jewelry. Rising in the
middle of these treasures is the
tomb from Pozo Moro, a stone
tower with traces of bas-reliefs
and sculpted lions.

Rooms 21–26 move on to
Roman art, including a fine bronze
"Apollo," a marble "Livia," swathed
in superbly carved draped clothes,
and huge mosaics, glass, bronze,
and pottery. The remaining rooms
are devoted to Visigothic and
Moorish pieces, including an ornate
gypsum archway from the Aljafería
palace in Zaragoza (see
p. 141). Temporary
exhibitions are on the
upper floor. ■

**Museo
Arqueológico
Nacional**

- 55 F4
- Calle de Serrano 13
- 91 577 79 12
- Closed p.m., Sun. &
  Mon.
- $. Free Sat. p.m. &
  Sun. a.m.
- Metro: Serrano
  (Line 4) & Retiro
  (Line 2)

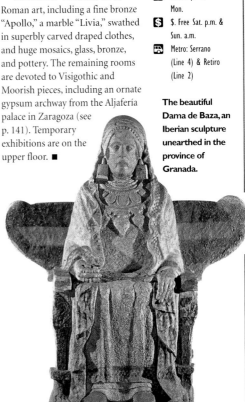

**The beautiful
Dama de Baza, an
Iberian sculpture
unearthed in the
province of
Granada.**

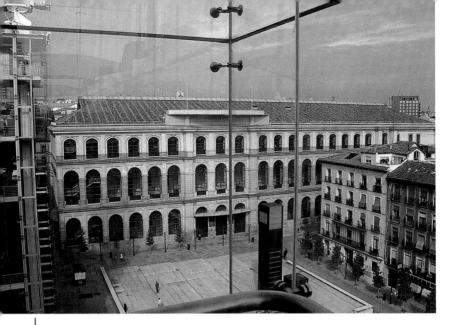

Museo Nacional Centro de Arte Reina Sofía

THE NATIONAL CONTEMPORARY ART CENTER AND MUSEUM stands out in a rather down-at-heel area on the southern side of central Madrid, opposite the grand old station of Atocha. Contemporary galleries have sprung up in the backstreets, but otherwise it is not the city's most enticing area. The Reina Sofía opened in 1986, in tune with Spain's frenetic *movida* spirit of personal and artistic freedom, and is home to Picasso's "Guernica" (see p. 125).

Museo Nacional Centro de Arte Reina Sofía
www.museoreinasofia.mcu.es

⒜ 55 E1
✉ Calle de Santa Isabel 52
☎ 91 467 50 62
🕐 Closed Sun. p.m. & Tues.
💲 $. Free Sat. p.m. & Sun. a.m.
🚇 Metro: Atocha

The permanent collection of 20th-century art is strong on Spanish art, but shows it in an international context, with plenty of work by prominent non-Spanish artists. The building is a converted 18th-century hospital, with immaculate white walls and transparent external elevator shafts. If you want to start at the beginning of modernism, go up to **Floor 2,** where 17 exhibition halls take you from the early 20th century up to the outbreak of World War II. At the turn of the century, the two main centers of artistic activity in Spain, Euskadi (the Basque country) and Catalunya, nurtured a clutch of artists including Ignacio

Zuloaga, Francisco Iturrino, Hermenegildo Anglada-Camarasa, and other Postimpressionists. Madrid produced the more experimental José Gutiérrez Solana, who has a room to himself.

Room 3 takes you through constructivism, cubism and dada: Keep an eye out for the strong colors of Robert Delaunay (1885–1941) and his wife Sonia, and the geometry of Joaquín Torres García (1875–1949). The world-famous names of the period are Juan Gris, Pablo Gargallo, Pablo Picasso, and Joan Miró, who are displayed in generous interconnecting rooms. This is where you will be confronted by the monumental canvas of Picasso's "Guernica" (1937), revealed in all its tortured, monochromatic splendor. It was painted in a white heat of outrage after German aircraft bombed the Basque town of Gernika (see p. 125). The spaces behind give a wonderful overview of Miró's career. They include numerous delightful sculptures such as "Pájaro Lunar" (1966), a huge black bronze of a horned creature. Sculpture dominates in the **Julio González Room,** and the early days of abstraction are reflected in **Room 9.**

SURREALISTS
Salvador Dalí's "Cenicitas" (1928) and "El Gran Masturbador" (1929), among other works, tell you unequivocally that you have reached the surrealists. **Room 12** is devoted to Spain's pioneering surrealist filmmaker Luis Buñuel (1900–1983), and shows his surrealist films. The rooms on Spanish art of the 1920s and '30s are missable, though neocubist Benjamín Palencia (1894–1980) is worth a look, he appears again in **Room 15,** with sculptures by Alberto Sánchez from the period just before World War II.

POSTWAR
Take the elevator to **Floor 4** to be plunged into postwar effervescence. **Rooms 18** and **19** display figurative work and early canvases by Antoni Tàpies (born 1923) beside geometrical abstraction by Serge Poliakoff and the more lyrical André Masson. The collection then focuses on the genesis of abstraction in Spain. International artists reappear in **Room 24** with powerful works by Francis Bacon, Henry Moore, Graham Sutherland, Pierre Alechinsky, and Asger Jorn, culminating in an excellent display of pieces by the brilliant French artist Yves Klein (1928–1962). His

Italian counterpart Lucio Fontana (1899–1968), the master of slashed and punctured canvases, has good coverage next door in **Room 26.**

The energetic brushstrokes of Antonio Saura (1930–1998) are prominent in **Room 29,** alongside international artists Jean Dubuffet, Yves Klein, and Mark Tobey. Sculpture returns in **Room 32** with Pablo Palazuelo's metal sheet works. The American abstract expressionist Robert Motherwell (1915–1991) appears in a large section on Tàpies, Spain's greatest living abstract-textural painter, in **Room 33. Rooms 38** and **39** juxtapose Eduardo Arroyo's bold narrative pictures with the issue-conscious pop art of the Equipo Crónica partnership and its Spanish contemporaries. The collection ends with American minimalism (Dan Flavin, Ellsworth Kelly, Barnett Newman, Bruce Nauman, Robert Mangold, and Donald Judd, represented by a compelling group of open-sided cubes), and the serene, organic sculptures of Basque sculptor Eduardo Chillida. ■

Picasso's famous "Guernica" (1937) is one of the star attractions here.

Museo de América

Museo de América

54 B5

Avenida Reyes Católicos 6

91 549 2641

Closed p.m., Sun. & Mon.

$. Free on Sun.

Metro: Moncloa (Line 3)

MADRID HAD NO PUBLIC MUSEUM ON SPAIN'S FORMER colonies in Latin America until the Museo de América opened in 1993, bringing together a huge array of scattered documents and exhibits under one roof. The presentation is slick, but you see the colonies just from the colonist's point of view. No mention is made of the atrocities and exploitation wrought by the Spanish, and indigenous peoples appear as mere exotic curiosities.

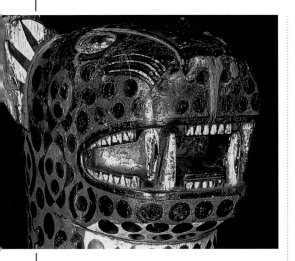

This carved and painted tiger's head typifies pre-Columbian Latin American art.

This said, the 2,500 exhibits are displayed in imaginative ways. The kernel of the collection came from the Royal Cabinet, but other items have been bought or donated: The Colombian government gave the fabulous Quimbayas treasure. **Room 1** is devoted to the voyages of discovery, Spanish chroniclers including Christopher Columbus, a reconstructed 18th-century scientific study room, and fascinating old maps. Also here are engravings, paintings, and stunning artifacts such as Amazonian feathered hats, the fantastic feathered Paracas cape, Costa Rican Diquís gold, and colonial antiques.

The main body of the pre-Hispanic collection fills half the first floor in **Rooms 2** and **3**. It is arranged in themes: birth and death,

ceremonies, body ornamentation, dwellings, and tools and implements. You see ceramic figures from Colima in Mexico, Mayan sculptures, Olmec jades, lovely pieces from Mexico's Gulf culture, Incan artifacts, Chilean textiles, ceramics from Ecuador, Colombian and Costa Rican gold ornaments, basketware by Hopi and Chumash Indians, and an enormous Amazonian canoe. Whimsical 18th-century Mexican paintings illustrate the Conquest, while Chinese inlaid furniture indicates maritime links with the Philippines, another Spanish colony.

The museum's most precious items concern the religious beliefs of America's pre-Hispanic societies, and are on the **upper floor** (sometimes closed to make way for temporary exhibitions). Here are the Mayan Stela of Madrid (incised stones), the Colombian gold Quimbayas treasure, the Tudela codex manuscript (1553) and, above all, the Trocortesiano codex (13th–16th century), one of only four Mayan manuscripts remaining in the world.

Outside the stately museum stands the surprising **Faro de Moncloa** (Moncloa Lighthouse, *Avenida Reyes Católicos, tel 91 722 04 00, closed Mon.*), a cylindrical steel tower rising 250 feet (76 m), designed by Salvador Pérez Arroyo in 1992. Take the elevator up to the observation platform for fantastic views over Madrid. ■

More places to visit in Madrid

MUSEO NACIONAL DE ARTES DECORATIVAS

This museum of Spanish decorative arts gives you a taste of the lavish interiors of Spain's many castles and palaces. There are six floors covering furniture, costumes, and objects from the 15th to the 20th century. The top floor houses a wonderful tiled Valencian kitchen.

55 F3   Calle de Montalbán 12
91 532 64 99   Closed Sun. p.m. & Mon.
$ Metro: Retiro

EL RASTRO

If you are in Madrid on Sunday morning, don't miss this vast flea market. Goods for sale vary from dusty, rusty bric-à-brac to high-quality antiques, in addition to the usual motley array of T-shirts, ethnic imports, cheap shoes, and bags. Stalls invade the streets of La Latina district, stretching from Plaza de Cascorro to the Puerta de Toledo. The best area for antiques and secondhand knickknacks is the Calle Mira el Río Baja and its offshoots. Old books are piled up in the Plaza del Campillo del Mundo Nuevo, and superior antiques are concentrated in the rather soulless Mercado Puerta de Toledo. A word of warning: As in any market, beware of pickpockets. The Rastro is notorious for them, although a greater police presence means things have improved a little in recent years.

54 C1   Metro: La Latina & Puerta de Toledo

REAL ACADEMIA DE BELLAS ARTES DE SAN FERNANDO

Despite its prime position on the stately Calle de Alcalá, this art museum is often overlooked by visitors intent on the art giants down the road (the Prado and Thyssen-Bornemisza, see pp. 62–71). Housed in the grandiose rooms of the former Palacio Goyeneche, the remarkable collection spans five centuries of Spanish painting, ending with 20 Picasso etchings. Look for Zurbarán's eight superb life-size **portraits of monks,** works by Alonso Cano (1601–1667), and Goya's **"Burial of the Sardine."** Other European artists include Paolo Veronese and Peter Paul Rubens. There are also displays of sculpture and porcelain.

54 D3   Calle de Alcalá 13
91 522 14 91   Closed p.m. Sat.–Mon.
$ Metro: Sol

REAL MONASTERIO DE LA ENCARNACIÓN

A few streets west of the Descalzas Reales (see p. 61), this Augustinian convent boasts a collection of religious paintings and sculpture

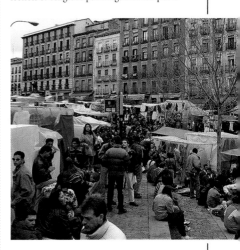

The Rastro flea market throngs with people every Sunday morning.

from the 16th to 18th centuries. Like the Descalzas Reales, it had a royal founder, in this case Margaret of Austria, wife of Felipe III. A passageway once connected the convent to the Alcázar (now the Palacio Real, see pp. 56–57), and the 17th-century decoration is by artists of the royal court. Look in particular for Ribera's **"John the Baptist"** and the impressive **sculpture of Christ** by Gregorio Hernández on the first floor. Best of all are the hundreds of reliquaries in the **Reliquary Room** attesting to the inspiration of countless artisans. You could combine a visit here with one to the nearby Palacio Real, and then relax in the **Jardines de Sabatini.**

54 B4   Plaza de la Encarnación 1
91 542 00 59   Closed Fri. & Sun. p.m., Mon. $. Free Wed. for E.U. nationals
Metro: Ópera ∎

Around Madrid

AFTER HOTFOOTING IT AROUND THE SIGHTS OF MADRID, if you feel you need some air, Aranjuez is the place to go. Strawberries and cream are a local specialty sold in season at every corner. Thirty miles (50 km) northwest of Madrid, you enter another world. Built for Felipe II on a site chosen by him, El Escorial is a summer palace, monastery, and mausoleum combined.

Fountains add a touch of French elegance to the Aranjuez Palace.

Aranjuez

78 B1

Visitor information

Plaza San Antonio

91 891 07 40

Closed Mon.

Palacio Real

Plaza de Parejas

91 542 00 59

Closed Mon.

$$ guided tour. Free Wed. for E.U. nationals

ARANJUEZ

This genteel royal town 30 miles (48 km) south of the capital has endless gardens, shady parks bordered by the Tajo and Jarama Rivers, a 200-year-old bullring, and two luxurious royal homes.

Aranjuez may remind you of the French royal palace of Versailles near Paris. The elegant grid pattern of the town, the lateral wings of the royal palace, and the delightful Casa del Labrador were all commissioned by the Bourbon kings of the late 18th century—the heyday of Versailles. Even the formal gardens and the vast park (Jardín del Príncipe, or Prince's Garden) were the work of a French landscape designer. If you don't want to walk, a visitor train *(Tel 925 14 22 74, closed Mon.)* makes regular circuits

of the town, starting from the Palacio Real (Royal Palace) and stopping at the main sights.

The **Palacio Real** was originally built for Felipe II by Juan Bautista de Toledo and Juan de Herrera. The grand staircase, the rococo Salón del Trono (Throne Room), the Sala de China (lined with whimsically decorated porcelain tiles), the Sala Árabe (inspired by the Alhambra in Granada, see pp. 300–305), and the Salón de los Espejos (Hall of Mirrors) are just some of the palace's wonders.

From here you can take a leisurely walk through the 370-acre (150 ha) **Jardín del Príncipe** to the **Casa del Labrador** (Laborer's House), a far more harmonious mansion built for Carlos IV by Isidro González Velázquez.

The most scintillating room is the **Gabinete del Platino** (Platinum Room), with walls encrusted with gold, platinum, and bronze.

EL ESCORIAL

Felipe II's palace-monastery, now a popular excursion from Madrid, looms over the little town of San Lorenzo de El Escorial. The king wanted the palace to reaffirm the glory of the Habsburg dynasty, but also to be a retreat where he could lead a more contemplative existence than was possible in Madrid.

The building was started by Juan Bautista de Toledo in 1563 and rapidly completed by his pupil, Juan de Herrera, in 1584, with constant input from the king himself. It is grandiose, but austere, and suits its bleak setting. The style was to Felipe's own taste, but reflects a wider reaction to the ornate fashions of Carlos V's reign.

If you visit in winter, snow may be on the ground, for you are at 3,370 feet (1,028 m). Whatever the season, the views from the 2,673 windows are sublime, sweeping over manicured hedges to the mountains beyond. The small town of San Lorenzo has a number of hotels and restaurants. You may be glad of these, as the Escorial is a vast labyrinth of patios, corridors, halls, staircases, and chapels, requiring at least three hours to visit.

You have to follow a set route around the building: It is well signed, and information panels give good descriptions in Spanish and English of the main features in each room. Your first sight on entering the palace is the series of tapestries called the **Golden Tapestry** (circa 1502), and also El Greco's massive **"Martyrdom of St. Matthew"** (1580–1582). From here you descend to the Museo de Arquitectura, which has a prodigious display of architectural drawings, plans, models, and examples of carpentry methods used for the turrets. Next is the **Museo de Pinturas** (Painting Museum), with Italian, Spanish, and Flemish masterpieces: Here are works by Titian, Tintoretto, Veronese, Van Dyck, and Rubens. Among them, look for the powerful light in Luca Cambiaso's (1527–

The Guadarrama mountains create a magnificent backdrop for the Escorial palace.

1585) **"Archangel St. Michael,"** and the **triptych** by Michel Coxcie (1499–1592). If you have been to the Prado, you may recognize Rogier van der Weyden's **"Descent from the Cross."** However, this is an inferior copy. Place of honor goes to van der Weyden's **"Calvary,"** which Felipe II inherited from his aunt, Mary of Hungary. Compare the original, with its extraordinary shadows and perspective, with the two Juan Fernández Navarrete (circa 1520–1579) copies flanking it. José Ribera (1591–1652), the great protagonist of tenebrism (depiction of shadows) is well represented by his dramatic and luminous **"St. Jerome Penitent"** and **"Aesop."**

Stairs lead up to Felipe II's palace, partly remodeled by Carlos

III. Here you glimpse the more intimate side of royal life, from Isabel Clara Eugenia's apartments to those of Felipe II himself, including the bedroom where he died in 1598. In between is the **Strolling Gallery,** an immense hall with windows on three sides, old maps, and countless paintings of 17th-century battle

confronted by a superb El Greco (1541–1614) painting: **"St. Peter,"** a perfect example of his free brushwork and extraordinary perspective. Here, too, are Titian's **"Last Supper"** and Hieronymus Bosch's **"Christ carrying the Cross"** and **"The Crown of Thorns."** The delicate ceiling paintings of these rooms date from the 1580s.

Next you reach the **cloister,** blanketed with fresh-colored **frescoes,** mainly the work of Pellegrino Tibaldi in the late 16th century, and housing the magnificent main staircase of the monastery. Above hovers a spectacular **ceiling fresco** by Luca Giordano (1632–1705), glorifying the Habsburg monarchy; on the walls are more Tibaldi frescoes. The cloister encloses the

Main entrance

College with four courtyards

Grand entrance

Tibaldi's ceiling frescoes crown the Royal Library.

scenes. The curious sundial inlaid in the floor by the south window is a "solar adjuster," a system for checking clocks made by Wendlingen and Baumgarten in 1755.

Pantheon Real

Ostentation soon returns. You now enter the baroque **Pantheon Real,** where a staircase lined with jasper and gilt leads to a circular chamber full of marble caskets. These contain the remains of nearly all the kings of Spain from Carlos V onward. A series of nine adjoining chambers contains the tombs of princes and princesses.

From the Pantheon, steps rise to the vast **Salas Capitulares** (chapterhouses), where you are

Evangelist Courtyard, with a temple (designed by Herrera) flanked by four pools.

Basilica & library

The basilica stands at the center of El Escorial and dazzles with its 45 side chapels, as well as a monumental marble **"Christ"** by Benvenuto Cellini (1500–1571). The choir stalls were designed by Juan de Herrera, and the beautiful ceiling frescoes are the work of Luca Giordano and Cambiasso. From the church you cross the Kings' Patio to ascend to the vast **royal library** (above the main entrance), with 45,000 books from the 15th and 16th centuries, and 5,000 Arab, Latin, and Castilian manuscripts. Don't miss the ceiling frescoes, again by Tibaldi. Felipe II's fascination for science and astronomy is well represented by various globes and the **Armillary Sphere,** made around 1582. This is an openwork celestial globe showing the solar system according to Ptolemy, the second-century Greek astronomer —a fitting end to what is a homage to one of Spain's most intellectual and concerned kings. ■

Basilica

Museo de Arquitectura

Pantheon Real (below church)

Museo de Pintura

Patio de Evangelistas

Salas Capitulares

Monastery with four arcaded courtyards

Patio de los Reyes

More places to visit around Madrid

ALCALÁ DE HENARES

The first planned university town in the world lies just 20 miles (33 km) east of Madrid, and is easy to reach by train, bus, or car. In its 16th-century heyday, the university produced the Complutensian Polyglot Bible with four original language texts side by side. Today, despite industrial areas, Alcalá remains a fascinating town, deserving of its World Heritage status accorded in 1998. Three monuments stand out: the **Monasterio de Religiosas Bernardas,** with its baroque extravaganza of a church; the illustrious **university,** centering on the fine plateresque (see p. 45) college of San Ildefonso; and, in contrast, the small **Museum of Miguel de Cervantes,** dedicated to Alcalá's most famous offspring (see pp. 238–39).

🅰 78 B1 **Visitor information** ✉ Callejón Santa María 1 ☎ 91 889 26 94

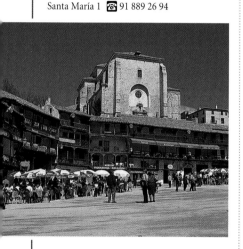

Chinchón's main square doubles up as a bullring during August festivities.

CHINCHÓN

Chinchón is a quaint, relaxing place, nestling on a hillside 28 miles (45 km) southeast of Madrid. Its only real sight, the **Plaza Mayor,** charms by its total irregularity, with three-story medieval houses rising above porticoes and the church of La Asunción at one end. In August, the square is transformed into a bull-ring, but otherwise life goes on quietly, despite the quantities of anise, gin, and other spirits brewed locally. In the 17th century, the Countess of Chinchón caught malaria in Peru, where her husband was viceroy, and cured herself using the bark of a tropical tree that she subsequently brought back to Spain. This was later named *chinchona* in her honor.
🅰 78 B1

VALLE DE LOS CAÍDOS

Only 7.5 miles (12 km) from El Escorial (see pp. 79–81) lies this spectacular valley of the Sierra de Guadarrama, chosen by General Franco as the site for his mausoleum. Madrileños come here on weekends for a breath of fresh air, but it has a grim history—Franco's political prisoners of the 1940s and '50s blasted the 804-foot-long (245 m) **basílica** out of the mountainside. A funicular takes you up to the 492-foot-high (150 m) stone cross (La Cruz), said to be the world's largest, above this gloomy church, which contains the tombs both of José Antonio Primo de Rivera, founder of the Falange (see p. 36), and of Franco. The remains of 40,000 soldiers and civilians who died during the Civil War lie in ossuaries beside countless statues of Spanish saints and soldiers. The whole place is a sober-ing reminder of Spain's dark days.
🅰 78 A2 ✉ Basílica and La Cruz ☎ 91 890 56 11 🕐 Closed Mon. 💲 $$ ∎

Guided tours from Madrid

To make life easier, you can visit Aranjuez, El Escorial, Valle de los Caídos, Toledo, Segovia, La Granja, and Ávila on a guided day trip from Madrid. Three companies offer comparable services and rates: **Juliatur** (Gran Vía 68, tel 91 559 96 05, Metro: Plaza de España), **Pullmantur** (Plaza de Oriente 8, tel 91 541 18 05, Metro: Ópera), and **Trapsatur** (Calle San Bernardo 23, tel 91 541 63 20, Metro: Santo Domingo). ∎

Wedged between the Atlantic and the Sierra Cantábrica are the regions of Galicia, Asturias, and Cantabria. Santiago de Compostela is the main magnet; others are prehistoric cave paintings, ancient churches, and exquisite seafood.

Northwest Spain

The ubiquitous scallop shell, the pilgrim's symbol

Atlantic
Ocean

Rías Altas

3▷

Cabo Ortegal Punta da Estaca de Bares

Cedeira • Ortigueira Burela

Cabo Prior Viveiro Foz Tapia de Casariego

Ferrol Foxas (Fene) As Pontes de García Rodríguez Ribadeo • Castropol Navia Luarca

A Coruña (La Coruña) Pontedeume Mondoñedo Vegadeo • Taramundi Tineo

Malpica Betanzos Villalba Meira • **Los Oscos** • Villanueva de Oscos

Laxe N634 Rábade Santa Eulalia • San Martín de Oscos

Cabo Vilán Camariñas • Carballo Guitiriz de Oscos Oscos

Muxía • Santa Comba Ordes A Fonsagrada Cangas del Narcea

Fisterra (Finisterre) • Corcubión A9 Friol **Lugo** Cordiller

Cabo Fisterra Negreira Melide NVI

Carnota • **Santiago de Compostela** NVI

2▷ Muros • Noia Padrón **GALICIA** Sarria Becerreá

Porto do Son • A Estrada Monterroso Pedrafita do Cebreiro

Santa Uxía de Ribeira Rianxo Lalín Embalse de Belesar

Cambados • Vilagarcía de Arousa Cerdedo Chantada

O Grove **Monasterio de Poio** O Carballiño Monforte de Lemos

Pontevedra

Marín A9 Ribadavia A52 **San Estevo** A Rúa • O Barco

1▷ Illas Cíes **VIGO** • Redondela **Ourense (Orense)** Parada do Sil **Castro Caldelas**

Baiona Ponteareas A Cañiza Allariz 1778m Viana do Bolo

Arrabal (Oia) Tui O Porriño Celanova Embalse das Portas

A Guarda (La Guardia) Miño Xinzo de Limia (Ginzo de Limia) A Gudiña

Santa Tegra Embalse das Conchas Verín A52

△ **A** △ **B** PORTUGAL △ **C** △ **D**

Northwest Spain

IF YOU REMEMBER JUST ONE IMAGE FROM TOURING SPAIN'S NORTHWEST, IT may be that of the humble scallop shell. Scallop shells appear on your plate, on pilgrims' staffs, and on roadside signs, pointing the way through history to Spain's greatest pilgrimage site and westernmost city, Santiago de Compostela. Santiago means "St. James," and pilgrims to his shrine adopted the scallop shell as their symbol. The city named for St. James is also the magnificent capital of Galicia. Once you have been to Santiago, you understand more about the rest of northern Spain and the spiritual fervor behind its Romanesque churches. You won't be alone either, as in the late 20th century the pilgrimage along the Camino de Santiago (Way of St. James) underwent an incredible revival.

For pilgrims of yesteryear, much of this part of Spain was quite simply inaccessible due to an awesome mountain chain, the Cordillera Cantábrica. These granite peaks helped protect the region from the Moorish advance, and today Asturias and Cantabria are the only part of Spain without any Muslim influence. The northwest does, however, have Paleolithic cave paintings, Celtic, Roman, and Visigothic remains, and a culture that may remind you of Cornwall in western England, Brittany in western France, or Ireland. Even the climate resembles that of its Celtic cousins: It is mild but often drizzly. Galicia occupies the northwest corner, and is swept by winds straight off the Atlantic.

Costa Verde

Cabo Vidio · Muros de Nalón · Luanco · Candás
Cudillero · Pravia · Avilés · Lastres · Gijón
Salas · Grado · Santianes · Villaviciosa · Pola de Siero
Oviedo · Cangas de Onís · Ribadesella
Langreo · Covadonga · Llanes
ASTURIAS · Mieres · Pola de Laviana · PARQUE NAC. DE LOS PICOS DE EUROPA · Picos de Europa 2648m
Los Beyos · Fuente Dé
Cantábrica · Puerto de San Glorio 1609m

Costa de Cantabria
Cuevas de Altamira · Santander · Ajo- Bareyo · Tregandín- Noja
Santillana del Mar · Santoña
San Vicente de la Barquera · Comillas · Torrelavega · Laredo · Castro-Urdiales
CANTABRIA · Los Corrales · Puente Viesgo · Ramales de la Victoria · Cuevas de Covalanas
Potes · Alto Cordillera Cantábrica · EUSKADI p. 111
Campoo · Fontibre · Reinosa
CASTILLA Y LEÓN p. 209 · Cervatos · Ebro

0 ————— 60 kilometers
0 ————— 40 miles

E   F   G   H

Madrid

Area of map detail

Weather apart, you can't fail to enjoy the green valleys, apple orchards, meadows, and healthy-looking cows of Asturias and Cantabria. Cider, rather than wine, is the local tipple in these two regions, and cheese is made in numerous shapes and flavors. The north-west is grain-growing country, and the grain (either corn, originally brought from America, or wheat) ends up in all sorts of dairy-based cakes. Throughout Galicia and Asturias you see picturesque *hórreos*—grain-stores on stilts to keep rodents at bay. For centuries Galicia was the poor cousin of the three, where people painstakingly gleaned a living from fishing or from tiny farms—even today, 70 percent are less than 2.5 acres (1 ha). Hardship prompted extensive emigration to Andalucía and to Latin America. Some emigrants returned once they had made money, and you can easily identify their more gracious houses by the symbolic pair of palm trees growing in front.

Spring wildflowers spangle the lush green foothills of the Picos de Europa.

The coast is one of high contrast. Galicia has 805 miles (1,289 km) of *rías* (long sea inlets) and rocky cliffs; Cantabria has long beaches, with the Picos de Europa mountains rising dramatically in the background. Fish, fish, and fish again is the main industry, although it is likely to suffer as a result of the reduction in European Union (E.U.) quotas announced in 2000.

Relaxed Santander and breezy, glass-balconied A Coruña are the only large coastal towns; otherwise the coast has just a string of fishing villages, low-key resorts, and a handful of industrial towns in Asturias. When touring this region, remember you cross and recross mountains. Journeys might take longer than you expect, but you go through breath-taking scenery. ■

Celtic bagpipes honor local Albarino wine in a festival at Pontevedra.

Galicia

Spain's most remote region is a wildly beautiful windswept land, squeezed into the peninsula north of Portugal and bordered by the Atlantic on two sides. Celtic culture arrived here around 1000 B.C. Bagpipes are the most obvious sign of Celtic influence, their strident wail still heard in every Galician festival. A deep sense of melancholy and mysticism, a love of poetry, but also a great joie de vivre are present.

Galicians have their own language, *gallego,* a combination of Spanish and Portuguese spoken by nearly 70 percent of the 2.7 million population. Street names, public information, and museum captions are often only in gallego, which makes this region even more distinctive. Nationalism raised its head in the late 19th century. It was thwarted by the outbreak of the Civil War in 1936, but still simmers today, just as it does in Euskadi (País Vasco) or Basque country and Catalunya.

For centuries Galicia was Spain's poorest region, whose rural inhabitants suffered frequent famines as they eked out a living, either farming on the harsh terrain, or fishing. As a result, Galicians were Spain's most enthusiastic emigrants to Latin America, where the term "Gallego" is interchangeable with "Spanish." Fidel Castro (whose surname derives from the Roman-Celtic word for "fortified village") is probably the most famous Latin American descendant of Galician stock. In the 1980s and '90s, Galicia greatly benefited from E.U. subsidies, and today it has a much more prosperous face, as people give up farms and settle in growing towns on the coast.

Galicia's capital city of Santiago de Compostela has been a magnet for European pilgrims since the Middle Ages. This is a city you must not miss, with its Romanesque architecture and unique atmosphere, but don't ignore charming smaller towns such as Pontevedra, Ourense, and Tui, or the sharply indented coastline and verdant inland hills. Here are remote hermitages, deserted beaches, and dramatic canyons, and all over Galicia you find the region's own wines and divinely fresh seafood. The regional newspaper devotes an entire page to maritime news and the price of 46 types of fish, so variety is assured. ∎

A Coruña (La Coruña)

GALICIA'S FORMER CAPITAL WAS DEMOTED IN 1982. IT NOW concentrates its energies on deep-sea fishing and cargo activities. Everything here evokes the sea: The city stands on a peninsula and has salty air, Atlantic beaches, and a Roman lighthouse (the city's emblem). The ill-fated Armada of 1588 set off from here, and its defeat by the English spelled the end of Spanish maritime power.

The most interesting part of the city starts at the well-defined neck of the peninsula, where La Coruña's nickname of "crystal city" originated. Street after street is lined with houses that have several stories of glassed-in balconies, to protect people from the wind while they enjoy the sun. From a distance this looks like modernist architecture of the 1960s, but at closer quarters you can see distinctive 19th-century styles. Here, too, is **Plaza de María Pita,** the arcaded main square, named for a local heroine who saved the town from an English invasion in 1589 by raising the alarm during the night.

Dominating one side of the square is the **Palacio Municipal,** an ornate late 19th-century building that also houses a small **museum of clocks** *(Plaza de María Pita, tel 981 18 42 00, closed a.m. & weekends).* Two blocks south lies the **marina,** and immediately east is the old quarter, which meets the waterfront at **Castillo de San Antón.** This castle is an archaeological museum with exhibits on Galicia's Roman culture, and beautiful Iberian and Celtic metalwork.

Nearby stands the church of **Santiago** *(Plaza de Azcárraga, tel 981 20 56 96, closed 1–6 p.m.),* part Romanesque and part Gothic. Two streets away is the harmonious collegiate church of **Santa María del Campo** *(Calle Damas, tel 981 20 31 86).* Built by the guild of seafarers, it has a beautiful carved Romanesque portal beneath its rose window. In front of the church is a

15th-century Calvary (representation of the Crucifixion). One mile north of this atmospheric area looms the **Torre de Hércules** (Hercules Tower, *Carretera de la Torre, tel 981 22 37 30),* built by the Romans in the second century A.D., but considerably remodeled in 1790. Said to be the world's oldest working lighthouse, it rises to a lofty 341 feet (104 m). You can climb to the top for the view. The ultramodern building across the cove below is **Domus** *(Ensenada del Orzán, tel 981 21 70 00),* an interactive museum of mankind designed in the 1990s by the Japanese architect Arata Isozaki. ∎

A Coruña (La Coruña)

🅜 84 B3

Visitor information

✉ Dársena de la Marina

☎ 981 22 18 22

Castillo de San Antón and Museo Arqueológico

✉ Paseo Maritimo del Parrote

☎ 981 20 59 94

🕐 Closed Sun. p.m. & Mon.

💲 $

A Coruña's penchant for glassed-in balconies is particularly visible along the seafront.

Way of St. James

For ten centuries pilgrims have been doggedly treading the long path to Santiago de Compostela in a protracted ritual of self-purification. Their goal is the immense cathedral built to house the remains of St. James (Santiago). The remains may or may not be there, but they have had immense symbolic significance for Spain. The apostle preached widely in Roman Spain before returning to Judea to face execution, after which his body was allegedly brought back by followers to Galicia. After long oblivion, its discovery in the ninth century inspired not just a cathedral and pilgrimage route (the Camino de Santiago, or Way of St. James), but also the infrastructure to serve it and the spread of Christian culture throughout northern Spain. In turn, this gave impetus to the fight against the Moors of al-Andalus, and later, a justification (proselytizing) for conquering the New World.

Originally just a simple monastic complex, the subsequent grandiose cathedral of Santiago rapidly became a magnet for pilgrims, bringing them along fixed routes lined with hospices, sanctuaries, and increasingly sophisticated cathedrals. From Tours, Vézélay, and Le Puy in France, pilgrims crossed the Pyrenees via Roncesvalles or Somport, meeting at Puente La Reina to continue together in 13-day stages along the "French Way." This became so popular that in the 12th century a type of pilgrim's guide (Book V of the Liber Sancti Iacobi, or Book of St. James) was written, detailing the characteristics of the regions and people en route. After giving the Basques and people of Navarra a poor press, it becomes more lyrical when describing Castilla and even more so with Galicia—"a land made pleasant by its rivers, meadows and marvelous orchards, its fine fruits and crystal springs.... Abundant too are gold and silver, textiles and furs and other riches, particularly Saracen treasures." With such worldly enticements, pilgrims flocked to Santiago from Portugal, Germany, the Low Countries, Italy, and, by maritime routes, England and Scandinavia. However, the French Way predominated, and it is still followed in today's revival of the medieval trail.

Along the route villages and towns grew up in characteristic ribbon mode. Bridges were built, and Romanesque and Gothic architecture blossomed. In addition to hospices and monasteries, pilgrims also needed protection from brigands, and this was provided by

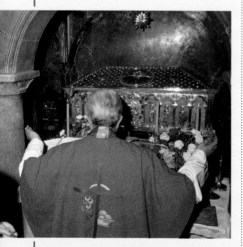

The casket at Santiago de Compostela is said to contain the relics of St. James.

0   300 kilometers
0   200 miles

A Coruña (La Coruña)

ASTURIAS   Oviedo

CORDILLERA

Cabo Fisterra

Santiago de Compostela   Cebreiro

GALICIA   Ponferrada

Pontevedra   Astorga

Vigo   Ourense (Orense)   **LEÓN**

PORTUGAL

Pilgrims cover a section of the long walk to Santiago de Compostela.

castles, forts, and military-religious orders such as the Knights of Santiago. Another offshoot was the proliferation of miracles and secondary cults associated with the Way of St. James.

To show their status, pilgrims adopted the scallop shell as a symbol. The Liber Sancti Iacobi explains this by a legend about St. James's arrival. A horseman plunged into the sea from the Portuguese coast at the precise moment when the boat transporting the apostle was sailing by. Miraculously, both steed and rider emerged from the depths, draped in scallop shells—hence the symbol that since 1987 has also been used as an official signpost for the Way of St. James. ■

Santiago de Compostela

SANTIAGO HAS BEEN DRAWING PILGRIMS FROM ALL OVER
Europe for more than a millennium. They wore scallop shells as proof
that they had completed their arduous journey. Shells which later
became a symbol for pilgrims in general. Today imitation shells sold
at street corners are evidence of a thriving tourism industry. Santiago
still exudes an inimitable atmosphere, with wonderful old buildings,
great seafood restaurants, and winding medieval streets.

Start your exploration at the
catedral, a massive edifice that
rises proudly between four squares.
Its ornate towers, intricately carved
doorways, and baroque facade are a
visual symphony of periods and
styles. The cathedral was first built
in Romanesque style in the 11th to
13th centuries, but much of it was
subsequently modified. Look at the
main western facade from the vast
Praza do Obradoiro, and you
see a baroque masterpiece (1750)
by Fernando Casas y Novoa. Climb
the steps to go in and you are faced
with the magnificent Romanesque
inner facade, the **Pórtico de la
Gloria,** which was the work of
Master Mateo in 1188. Pilgrims
touch the central pillar as they give
thanks for safe arrival, and over the
centuries their fingers have left
imprints. Above the triple-arched
doorway, the carvings of the central
tympanum show Christ in Majesty
flanked by the four evangelists with
the 24 Elders of the Apocalypse.
Above the central pillar is a seated
figure of Santiago (St. James);
crouched behind it is the **Santo
dos Croques,** meaning "saint of
the bumps," which may be a self-
portrait of Master Mateo himself. It
is said to impart wisdom to those
who knock their heads on it.

A long line grows at the **Puerta
Santa** (east facade door), which
gives direct access to the crypt containing the relics of St. James. To
avoid this, go around to the south
facade (on **Praza das Praterías),**
and enter the cathedral through the
equally stunning Puerta de las
Platerías. Its breathtakingly complex
low-relief sculptures (1103) illustrate biblical scenes from Adam and
Eve to the flagellation of Christ.

Despite the constant influx of
visitors, the **cathedral interior**
has a working atmosphere, with
numerous confession boxes and
side chapels in use. During major
celebrations the **botafumeiro,** a
gigantic incense burner, is suspended from the dome and swung
like a pendulum in front of the dazzling baroque high altar. Don't miss
the treasury, the 16th-century cloister, or the crypt museum: one ticket
gets you into all three. The **treasury** (off the south aisle, on the
right as you face the altar) has a
gold-plated bust (1332) of St. James
Alpheus, a lesser apostle, that contains his relics. You reach the 16th-
century plateresque cloisters from
the transept. The upper floors have
Flemish tapestries and give wonderful views. The **crypt museum**
has contemporary versions of the
zithers, fidulas, viols, and lutes
played by the Elders on the Pórtico
de la Gloria. Best of all is the reconstruction of the cathedral's original
choir structure, destroyed in 1603.

Next to the cathedral is the
Palacio Gelmírez (*Praza do
Obradoiro, tel 981 57 23 00, closed
Mon.*), the former archbishop's
palace, now used as an exhibition
space. Built in the 12th and 13th
centuries, it is a rare example of a

**Santiago de
Compostela**

🅰 84 B2

Visitor information

✉ Rúa do Vilar 43

☎ 981 58 40 81

Catedral

✉ Praza do Obradoiro

☎ 981 58 11 55

**Museos de la
Catedral**

☎ 981 58 11 55

💲 $ (Treasury, crypt, &
cloisters)

The baroque
facade of
Santiago's
cathedral towers
overshadows
the Praza do
Obradoiro.

Romanesque building that isn't a church. Austere on the outside, it contains an exceptional room, the **Salón Sinodal.** This vast hall, over 98 feet (30 m) long, has unusual rib-vaulting that ends in beautifully carved figures illustrating medieval domestic life. On the lively square outside, admire the imposing facades of the Colegio de San Jerónimo (1501) to the south, the Pazo Raxoi (1766) to the west, now home to the Galician government, and, to the north, the Antiguo Hospital Real, founded in the 16th century to care for sick pilgrims but now a luxury parador (state-run hotel).

High Altar

Entrance to crypt museum

Treasury

Puerta Das Praterias

West facade (1750) with Portico de la Glorie inside

Right: A gilded image of Saint James

Cloisters

At the back of the cathedral are two lovely old interconnecting squares. **Praza das Praterías** was the home of the silversmiths' guild, and **Praza da Quintana** used to be a cemetery. The setting is majestic, and you can enjoy it in several outdoor cafés: This is a wonderful spot from which to admire the cathedral entrance known variously as the **Puerta Santa** (Holy Door) or **Puerta del Perdón.** The doorway's lyrical sculptures are by Master Mateo and were transferred here from the old choir. Behind, rise the forbidding walls of the **Monasterio de San Paio de Antealtares** *(Praza da Quintana),* founded in the ninth century to house the tomb of St. James, and its church, dating from 1707. The church has a Roman altar stone used by early disciples, and a superb baroque altarpiece. The **Museo de Arte Sacro** *(Tel 981 57 11 67, closed Mon. & Oct.– March),* displays sculpture, paintings, gold, and silverwork.

One former monastery, now a museum, is the Convento de Santo Domingo de Bonaval, ten minutes' walk northeast of the center, now the **Museo do Pobo Gallego** (Museum of the Galicians, *Convento de Santo Domingo de Bonaval, Rúa Ramón del Valle-Inclán, tel 981 58 36 20, closed Sun.).* Set around verdant cloisters, the rooms are packed with traditional handicrafts, costumes, agricultural implements, and musical instruments. All captions are in gallego and some exhibits are dusty-looking, but the visit is worthwhile if only to climb the remarkable triple spiral staircase designed by Domingo de Andrade in the 17th century. Next door to the museum, in complete

Tapestry museum

Library

Rraza de Obradorio

contrast, stands Galicia's contemporary art center, **Centro Gallego de Arte Contemporáneo** *(Rúa Ramón del Valle-Inclán, tel 981 54 66 29, closed Mon.),* built in 1993 to a minimalist design by Portuguese architect Alvaro Siza.

The **Museo de las Peregrinaciones** *(Praza do San Miguel, tel 981 58 15 58, closed Sun. p.m. & Mon.)* sheds light on the fascinating story of the Santiago pilgrimage, and it is partly housed in a Gothic tower. Exhibits illustrate the history, traditions, and effects of the Way of St. James, and include jet jewelry, one of Santiago's traditional crafts. The main center was on nearby **Calle Azabachería** where you can still buy jet. A few yards downhill from the museum you will find the church of **San Martín Pinario** *(Plaza de la Inmaculada),* built in 1597, with gracefully curved steps leading down to its plateresque (see p. 45) facade. Inside are a breathtaking baroque altarpiece and finely carved 17th-century choir stalls. This church is part of the massive monastery of San Martín Pinario. ■

Drive: The hórreo trail from Santiago to Cabo Fisterra

This circuit takes you west to the wild reaches of Galicia's Atlantic coast. It encompasses the characteristic scenes of Spain's most remote province, from rural landscapes to empty beaches and historic fishing villages. You also see plenty of Galicia's *hórreos* (pitched-roof grain-stores on stilts), now more decorative than functional.

Leave Santiago de Compostela (see pp. 90–93) by following signs to Noia (C543), turning right at the unmarked traffic circle on the outskirts. At Bertamiráns, turn right to drive through eucalyptus and pine forests to Negreira, where you turn left toward Muxia (AC443). Rolling farmland, tiny hamlets, and hórreos are the recurring theme of this stretch. At Pereira, the road becomes AC441. On reaching a major junction at Berdoias, turn left on the C552 to Corcubión.

This takes you past the industrial town of Cée, then 1.8 miles (3 km) farther to

Corcubión ❶. This charming fishing village has fine emblazoned houses with glazed balconies. At low tide you see people collecting shellfish.

Continue by following signs to Fisterra (Finisterre), 9 miles (14 km) farther. On the way you round a headland with stunning views through pines to the Atlantic Ocean below, and you pass the half-moon beaches of Praia de Estorde, Praia de Langosteira, and Praia de Sardiñeiro. At **Fisterra ❷** itself, follow the sign marked Faro (lighthouse) through the town. Stop at the lovely 12th-

The end of the road
at Cabo Fisterra

century church of **Santa María des Areas** *(Closed in winter)*, on the main road at the edge of town, to see its much revered statue of Christ with a golden beard, before continuing to the lighthouse. It stands on Europe's westernmost point, **Cabo Fisterra ❸.** Magnificent panoramas open up over the rocky bay, and a path around the lighthouse gives vertiginous views of the surf below.

Retrace your route to Corcubión and Cée to turn right on the C550 towards Muros. After crossing the estuary of Ézaro you reach **O Pindo ❹,** another stunning beach, before passing the rock formations of the 2,063-foot (629 m) **Monte do Pindo,** also known as the Celtic Olympus. The next stop is **Carnota ❺,** which has Galicia's longest hórreo. On entering the village turn right at the main square, circle left around the church, and there it is—a grain-store of 1763 that stretches 78 feet (24 m) in length. Six miles (10 km) farther are Carnota's magnificent wild sand dunes and beach.

Traditional grain-stores or hórreos

Go back to the main road, and continue to **Muros ❻** *(Visitor information, Casa del Ayuntamiento, Curro de la Plaza, tel 981 76 21 48),* a surprisingly grand town with arcaded buildings facing the bay. In 1544, a French fleet was sunk offshore, and in 1809 French troops burned 185 houses in the town. Walk up through the labyrinth of picturesque lanes to see **Santa María do Campo** (1400), a blend of Romanesque and Gothic, then head for the **Pescadería Vella** to see a curious turtle-topped fount.

From Muros, the road snakes around forested promontories overlooking the bay, where you see platforms for collecting mussels. It then crosses a high bridge to make a dramatic arrival at the historic little port of **Noia ❼** *(Visitor information, Casa de la Cultura, Xardins Felipe de Castro, tel 981 82 41 69).* Noia's lovely Romanesque church of **Santa María a Nova** *(Carreiriña do E. Ferreiro, closed Sat. & Sun. p.m.)* was built in 1327 and has a unique collection of more than 300 tombstones from the 10th to the 16th centuries, each one carved with symbols of the deceased's trade. The **medieval quarter** radiates from the Praza do Tapal, dominated by the church of **San Martiño** (1434), an example of Galician Gothic with a magnificent carved portal. It may remind you of Master Mateo's work at Santiago, and Mateo was, in fact, a strong influence. Noia also has many fine old mansions that are well worth seeking out.

From Noia you can return 21 miles (34 km) to Santiago on the C543 or continue south to the Rías Baixas (see p. 97). ∎

- ⛰ See area map p. 84
- ▶ Santiago
- ↔ 125 miles (200 km)
- ⏱ 1 or 2 days
- ▶ Cabo Fisterra

NOT TO BE MISSED
- Cabo Fisterra
- Carnota
- Muros
- Santa María a Nova, Noia
- San Martiño, Noia

In & around Pontevedra

Pontevedra
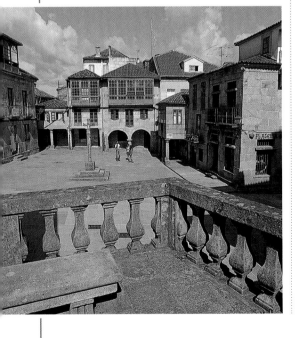 84 B2
Visitor information
✉ Calle General Mola 3
☎ 986 85 08 14

Museo de Pontevedra
✉ Pasanteria 10
☎ 986 85 14 55 or 986 84 32 38
🕐 Closed Sun. p.m. & Mon.
$ $. Free for E.U. nationals

Part of the Museo de Pontevedra faces Praza de Leña.

PONTEVEDRA IS ONE OF GALICIA'S MORE SEDUCTIVE small towns. According to legend it was founded by the Greek warrior Teucro, who fought at Troy. More prosaic history records that it prospered on sardine fishing until the mid-16th century, when its port silted up forever.

As a result of its former prosperity, Pontevedra has numerous fine old buildings of local granite, especially in the old town. This is now a lively pedestrianized zone. Pretty little squares such as **Praza do Teucro** and **Praza da Verdura** are still used by traditional specialist markets. The more grandiose **Praza da Herrería** has gardens overlooked by the 14th-century monastery and church of San Francisco. Opposite stands the unusual neoclassic church of the Virgen la Peregrina, built to an elliptical form to house a statue of the city's patron saint. To the west in the old fishermen's quarter stands the plateresque church of **Santa María la Mayor** *(Avenida Santa María 24, tel 986 86 61 85),* erected by the powerful seamen's guild in the 16th century. Low-relief biblical scenes adorn the western facade.

The excellent museum, **Museo de Pontevedra,** housed in five different sites, three of which face the delightful arcaded **Praza da Leña.** The 18th-century mansion of **Castro Monteagudo** displays magnificent Celtic jewelry from 800–700 B.C. and a collection of medieval and Renaissance Spanish, Italian, and Flemish paintings. The museum continues in the beautifully conserved neighboring house of **García Flórez,** with precious metalwork, religious statuary, and reconstructed period interiors, including one of a ship. Galician art and Spanish paintings of the 19th and 20th centuries are displayed in the Edificio Sarmiento and Edificio Fernández López. Don't miss the fifth section, however: This is the evocative Gothic ruin of **Santo Domingo,** next to the leafy gardens of the Alameda, where architectural fragments and sculptures are exhibited. The **Alameda** is a popular spot for the paseo.

Just 4 miles (6 km) west from Pontevedra is the Benedictine **Monasterio de Poio** *(Tel 986 77 00 00).* The monastery is medieval and rather forbidding, but the church is a fine example of late Galician classicism, completed in 1708. The 16th-century processional cloister was the work of Portuguese architect Mateo López. ∎

Rías Baixas

THE LONG, FJORDLIKE INLETS OF THE GALICIAN COAST are known as *rías*. Those between Noia and Vigo are called the Rías Baixas—the lower rías—to distinguish them from the Rías Altas on the more exposed northern coast that curves around to A Coruña. The Rías Baixas have a milder climate, and most of Galicia's tourism.

Fortified Roman-Celtic villages (*castros*) and dolmens (prehistoric slab tombs), *hórreos* (grain-stores), *pazos* (mansions), and Romanesque churches are plentiful. Some spots are overrated; including the island of Arousa, despite its bird sanctuary. The resort of O Grove, and the island of A Toxa have limited appeal.

Head instead for the delightful town of **Cambados.** Dominating the main square is the 16th-century **Pazo de Fefiñanes,** an L-shaped palace with a beautiful Renaissance facade carved with stone busts and heraldic arms, and an arched footbridge leading to the San Sadurniño tower. Across the square stands the church of **San Benedict.** Numbered flagstones help identify tombs in the nave. Vineyards around the town produce light,

slightly fruity and sparkling white Albariño wine. Bodegas (wine cellars) abound in the town, and good local bars face the Pazo de Fefiñanes.

The **Illas Cíes** are a cluster of uninhabited islands off the Ría de Vigo with white beaches, pine forests where rare seabirds nest, and Celtic remains. In summer, you can take a boat trip to this nature reserve from Vigo. The much industrialized fishing port of **Vigo** (Spain's largest) has pockets of interest around the harbor and a hilltop castle with wonderful views across the ría.

Baiona, the southernmost town of the Rías Baixas, has massive fortified walls of the **Castelo de Monte Real,** where the townspeople sheltered from pirate attacks in earlier centuries. ∎

In & around Ourense (Orense)

THIS INLAND TOWN RIMMED BY MOUNTAIN RANGES IS noticeably poorer than Galicia's prosperous seaboard, although Ourense is rich in natural resources. Here the Miño River, which crosses Ourense on its way south to the Portuguese border, creates an extensive, fertile valley, the heart of Ribeiro wine country.

Ourense (Orense)
- 🅰 84 C1

Visitor information
- ✉ Plaza de las Burgas 12
- ☎ 988 36 60 64

Museo Arqueológico
- ✉ Plaza Mayor
- ☎ 988 22 38 44
- 🕐 Closed Mon. & Sun. p.m.

The city of 100,000 inhabitants has a confrontational past: It was attacked by Romans, Visigoths, Swabians (who destroyed the town in A.D. 463), Moors, and Normans (responsible for further destruction in 970). Today, it proudly conserves a **Roman bridge,** rebuilt in the Middle Ages for pilgrims going to Santiago, and other monuments in the pedestrianized **casco viejo** (old town). The **catedral** *(Praza de Magdalena, tel 988 22 09 92),* originally Romanesque, has three exceptional portals. The best is the west-facing **Pórtico del Paraíso,** which is decorated with polychrome sculptures. The **interior** has carved choir stalls, suspended lanterns, gilded statues, and carved sarcophagi

set into niches, all combining to make a harmonious work of art. The high altar has a very ornate retable (1520).

Uphill from the cathedral, beyond lanes of tapas bars, the **Claustro de San Francisco** *(Emilia Pardo Bazán, tel 988 24 03 77, closed Mon.)* has elegant Gothic cloisters with finely decorated capitals on slender columns. Walk east of the cathedral to see the charming **Praza do Ferro,** lined with timbered medieval houses. Then walk down from the cathedral to the sloping, arcaded **Praza Maior.** On one corner, the excellent **Museo Arqueológico** is in a 12th-century archbishop's palace with an ornately emblazoned

Renaissance facade. The intelligently laid out collection (with fleeting views over internal patios) is strong on Gallic-Roman pieces, and has Romanesque and Gothic statuary. Notice the fine granite statue of a Roman warrior and the polychrome Romanesque figure of **Nuestra Señora del Refugio,** which shows a strong Byzantine influence.

Ourense's steaming thermal springs, known as **Las Burgas,** are on the square of the same name. The water (which heats up to 153°F/67°C) erupts into a neoclassic fountain and pools which are surrounded by contemporary sculptures.

It's an easy excursion 18 miles (30 km) west to **Ribadavia,** a pretty riverside town and the center of Ribeiro wine. In 1063, it was capital of the kingdom of Galicia. Old stone houses cluster around Praza Magdalena, once home to a large Jewish community that specialized in the wine trade. Among the town's six notable churches, 13th- to 14th-century Santo Domingo has a Romanesque-Gothic interior. Rising beside the road, the crumbling walls of the **Castillo de los Condes de Ribadavia** enclose tombs and towers.

CANYON DEL SIL

Venture 12 miles (20 km) northeast of Ourense and you could spend an entire day exploring the otherworldly canyon of the Río Sil, whose confluence with the Miño has been tapped to create two reservoirs. This wild, thickly forested region of oaks, pines, and ferns harbors unique historical sights. Hikers follow trails; the more indolent take two-hour boat trips across the river's dark green waters. Of the canyon's three monasteries, **San Estevo,** reachable only by car or on foot, is the most overwhelming in scale, style, and history. It was founded in the tenth century, but the earliest parts are the 13th-century **cloister** and **church** *(Closed except for Sun. Mass and festivals).* The other two cloisters date from the 16th and 17th centuries. This vast edifice is being extensively restored to turn it into a hotel.

The 9-mile (14 km) drive from Loureiro, 2.5 miles (4 km) east of the monastery, to the village of Parada do Sil gives the most spectacular views over the canyon. Teetering on the brink 3 miles (5 km) north of Parada is the **monastery of Santa Cristina,** which, like San Estevo, stands on the site of earlier wooden structures. What you see dates from the 12th and 13th centuries. Trails make this perfect hiking terrain.

Castro Caldelas is a ruined castle 25 miles (40 km) farther east. Medieval ramparts give huge views, and inside is an illuminating ethnographic museum. Don't miss the **Torre del Reloj** where you get a close view of a 1760 clock that functions with stone weights. ∎

Ribadavia

🅰 84 B1

Visitor information

✉ Praza Mayor

☎ 988 47 12 75

🕐 Closed Oct.–May

Boat trips along Sil canyon

☎ From Abeleda 982 25 45 45, from San Estevo 988 21 51 00

Canyon del Sil's striking topography has become a favorite with hikers, following in the footsteps of yesterday's monks.

More places to visit in Galicia

BETANZOS

The delightful and historic town of Betanzos, formerly a port (until it became silted up), lies 14 miles (23 km) southeast of A Coruña. By the 14th century the commercial talents of its inhabitants had earned them the nickname the "Genoese of Spain." They used their wealth to build the medieval streets and buildings you see today, including the pleasingly asymmetrical 14th- to 15th-century church of **Santa María del Azogue,** and the neighboring church of **San Francisco** (1387). This lovely Gothic structure has tombs in niches in the walls and sculptures of wild boar. Best of all is the tomb of the town's powerful 14th-century ruler and church founder, Count Fernán Pérez de Andrade. His extraordinary sarcophagus is raised on the backs of his heraldic animals, a boar and a bear. Betanzos holds fairs on the first and sixteenth day of every month, when you see crowds of locals selling and buying homemade

The cathedral of San Telmo dominates the atmospheric cobbled streets of Tui's medieval quarter.

baskets, cheese, tables, and all sorts of other things—even socks.
▲ 84 B3 **Visitor information** ✉ Praza Constitución 1 ☎ 981 77 29 08

A GUARDA (LA GUARDIA)

The local lobsters are excellent, but another reason to venture to this remote town on the Portuguese border is to see **Monte de Santa Tegra.** This legendary hill has the restored remains of a Celtic-Roman *castro* (fortified village) dating back to 600–200 B.C. The rebuilt circular stone dwellings occupy an impressive strategic location, and the *mirador* (viewpoint) that crowns the hill gives fantastic all-around views: The best are south across the Río Miño to Portugal and west across the Atlantic. Just below stands a small **museum** *(Tel 986 61 00 00)* with stone inscriptions, Roman amphorae, and other pieces found during excavations. From the castro, a path lined with stone crosses leads to the hermitage of Santa Tegra.
▲ 84 B1

TUI

The medieval quarter of this charming small town is clearly defined by a sharp rise in level along the elegant, tree-lined Rúa Ordoñez. Above lies a web of atmospheric cobbled streets enclosing nine religious structures, dominated by the **catedral San Telmo.** The cathedral dates from 1120 and looks like a fortress because its other role was to fend off attacks from Valença, in Portugal. It incorporates both Romanesque and Gothic styles, and the beautifully sculpted main portal is said to be the earliest example of Gothic in Spain. The **museum treasury** has fine liturgical objects and silverware. It leads to the **cloisters,** from which you reach the corner tower. Climb this to the ramparts for views to Portugal. Opposite the cathedral is the **Museo Diocesano** *(Tel 986 60 31 07, closed Oct.–May),* with exhibits from the Roman to baroque periods. At the **Convento de las Encerradas** (Convent of the Cloistered Nuns, *Rúa das Monxas),* barely visible nuns sell homebaked cookies through a swiveling counter in the wall.
▲ 84 B1 **Visitor information** ✉ Puente Tripes, Avenida de Portugal ☎ 986 60 17 89 ■

The Sierra Cantábrica rises in the distance behind Luarca in Asturias.

Asturias & Cantabria

Squeezed between some of Spain's highest mountain ranges and the Cantabrian Sea, these two regions are a seductive combination of magnificent landscapes richly spiked with history. If you are traveling by car, you are in for momentous driving, with vast vistas over emerald green valleys, precipitous ridges, and narrow, gushing ravines. Lush pastures, contented cattle, and solid stone houses are other hallmarks of Spain's most bucolic region, and it also has sandy beaches, fishing ports, and ski resorts.

About 12,000 years ago, Paleolithic (Old Stone Age) people occupied and painted the caves that riddle Cantabria's limestone terrain. The caves of Altamira are world famous and you have to reserve tickets far in advance, but at other sites you can gaze at this mysterious art more easily. Centuries later, the mountains that rear behind the Cantabrian coast protected the last Christian enclave in Spain: In 718, a Visigothic nobleman named Pelayo halted the Moorish advance north in a remote mountain valley of the Picos de Europa. These mountains now form Europe's largest national park.

Oviedo is the industrialized Asturian capital, with three beautiful pre-Romanesque churches. Throughout the region are Romanesque buildings: remote hermitages, monasteries, and well-frequented cathedrals. The undisputed star is at Santillana del Mar,

but Cantabrian roads are dotted with signs pointing travelers to lesser known structures. Santander, the Cantabrian capital, is a light-hearted 19th-century resort that makes a relaxing stopover. Westward from here, a string of small coastal resorts dish up generous portions of seafood and shellfish. Try large white beans *(fabes)* with clams and wash them down with Asturias' specialty: local cider.

The coast of Asturias is busy with industries based on its coal and iron mines. Move inland and you find age-old traditions such as clogmaking, and wild countryside still the haunt of bears and wolves. In Cantabria, 40 percent of the half million inhabitants live in rural communities where livestock farming predominates. You may even see mules loaded with delicious Cabrales cheeses stumbling down mountain paths to market towns. ■

Oviedo

Oviedo

85 E3

Visitor information

Plaza de Alfonso II 6

985 21 33 85

Catedral

Plaza de Alfonso II

Closed Sun. (Cámara Santa, Claustro, & Museo Diocesano)

$. Free Thurs.

985 20 31 17

Iglesias Prerrománicas de Monte Naranco

985 25 72 08

Closed Sun. & Mon. p.m.

$ (30-minute guided tour)

Outside Oviedo lies the church of Santa María del Naranco.

SET IN A BOWL OF LAND THAT IS OFTEN SMOTHERED BY low, misty cloud, Oviedo is not at first sight the most enticing of Spanish towns. Yet the modern capital of Asturias is Christian Spain's oldest city, and a good proportion of the 200,000 inhabitants keep the cider flowing nightly in the *sidrerías* of the old town.

Rising above the elegant **Plaza Alfonso II,** named after the ninth-century founder of the town, is the **catedral,** a sprawling edifice in Flamboyant Gothic style. It towers over the remains of the church of San Tirso (its ninth-century predecessor), the former monastery of San Vicente, now the **archaeological museum** *(Plaza Alfonso II, tel 985 21 54 05, closed Mon.),* and the Benedictine monastery of San Pelayo. Inside the cathedral is the vaulted **Cámara Santa,** which has remarkable statues, capitals, and precious objects. You reach it from the corner of the nave that also gives access to the 14th-century cloisters and the **Museo Diocesano.** This

has splendid processional crosses, chalices, and Romanesque statues.

A few steps from the cathedral, the **Museo de Bellas Artes** *(Palacio de Velarde, Santa Ana 1, tel 985 21 30 61, closed Mon.)* is richly stocked with art from the 16th to the 20th centuries. Emphasis is on Asturian and Spanish painting, but Flemish and Italian works are here, too, as are porcelain and glass. In the web of streets extending south from here baroque stone mansions are juxtaposed with Asturian timbered buildings with projecting first floors.

Just outside Oviedo are its most prized buildings: three rare pre-Romanesque churches. Closest to the center is ninth-century **San Julián de los Prados** *(Tel 985 28 25 18, closed Mon.).* Squeezed between the Gijón highway and suburban back streets near the Campus Universitario, it is a serene, brick-vaulted structure with well-restored frescoes and lattice windows. Venture 2.5 miles (4 km) northwest of Oviedo to Monte Naranco and you come to **Santa María,** built in A.D. 848 as the king's summer palace before being transformed into a church a century later. This beautifully proportioned two-story structure has open loggias and a vaulted crypt, originally built as a guardroom. Immediately uphill stands its contemporary, **San Miguel de Lillo.** The capitals and reliefs are very delicately sculpted. These two churches are called the **Iglesias Prerrománicas de Monte Naranco,** and visits are by guided tour only. ■

Los Oscos

SPANIARDS FROM FARTHER SOUTH VISIT ASTURIAS FOR one reason: to escape the unrelenting dryness elsewhere. Los Oscos, 60 miles (100 km) west of Oviedo, makes the classic destination. The valleys of these remote mountains have lush, untouched scenery, rivers, and waterfalls, strong folk traditions, and hearty food.

The warmhearted inhabitants who inherit their strong, dark features from Roman ancestors drawn here by gold. Rural tourism is taking off in the region, giving ample opportunities for hiking, horseback riding, and trout fishing, and encouraging traditional crafts. Accommodations are simple, but hospitable.

Three villages bear the name Oscos (Santa Eulalia, Villanueva, and San Martín), but **Taramundi** is the best place to start exploring. It was a center of knifemaking, as iron was worked in local forges using water power. Several old watermills show 18th-century technology, notably that of **Teixois,** a dizzy 20-minute drive southeast. From Taramundi the narrow, often potholed road winds southeast to the three Oscos, passing 3,330-foot

(1,015 m) Pico de Ouroso. **Santa Eulalia** is the most modernized of the three, but has exemplary 18th-century rural architecture and a stunning site. A road through pristine forest (where bears live) leads to **Villanueva,** with its partly ruined Benedictine monastery, where one barrel-vaulted room exhibits information on the region.

The last village, **San Martín,** has the most tortuous access roads, as it lies huddled between two sierra. Next to the church is an impeccable slate-and-thatch-roofed *hórreo* (grain-store), the best of the many in the region. The baroque archway leads to the former palace of the Guzmanes. A few miles on at **Mon** you will find the turreted, emblazoned 16th- to 18th-century palace of the Mon y Velarde family. ∎

Hórreo, or grain-store on stilts, typical of the Asturias region

Taramundi
🅰 84 D3
Visitor information
✉ Avenida de Galicia 33
☎ 985 64 68 77
🕐 Closed winter

Santa Eulalia de Oscos
🅰 84 D3
Visitor information
✉ Carretera General 33
☎ 985 62 12 61
🕐 Closed winter

San Martín de Oscos
🅰 84 D3
Visitor information
✉ Carretera General s/n
☎ 985 62 60 00
🕐 Closed winter

Costa Verde

THE "GREEN COAST" MEANS THE COASTLINE OF ASTURIAS,
from the Río Eo on the Galician border, to Llanes close to the border
with Cantabria, 125 miles (200 km) east. The coast is more dingy
than green in the industrial ports of Avilés and Gijón, but otherwise
it is characterized by low-key resorts, fishing villages, and sandy
beaches on a relatively straight coastline. Traditions remain strong
and the landscape is largely unspoiled.

Luarca

🔺 84 D3

Visitor information

✉ Olavarrieta 27

☎ 985 64 00 83

Cudillero

🔺 85 E3

Visitor information

✉ Plaza de San Pedro

☎ 985 59 01 18

Muros de Nalón

🔺 85 E3

Visitor information

✉ Parque del Palacio

☎ 985 58 34 85

Moving from west to east, **Luarca**
is the first resort of any importance.
This lively tuna-fishing port is
shaped by the sinuous Río Negro,
which winds through to the harbor
below the steep slopes of the old
town. Walk or drive up the hill at
the end of the harbor to the marine
cemetery and lighthouse for
wonderful views. Good clean
beaches are easily reached to the
west and farther east at Cabo Busto.

The lighthouse at **Cabo Vidio**
gives dramatic views in both directions before the next essential stop:
Cudillero, its tiny harbor sandwiched between cliffs in a cove
where the water is transparent and
crammed with fishing boats. A
cluster of outdoor restaurants

serves seafood and cider. The
beach, Playa de Aguilar, stretches to
a rocky headland. Immediately
beyond that is **Muros de Nalón,**
which has large elegant residences
of the 15th and 16th centuries. Six
miles (10 km) inland is the pre-
Romanesque church of **Santianes**
*(Keys from the Palacio de Salas next
door)*, with a rare example of a baptismal floor-pool.

The eastern part of the Costa
Verde has excellent secluded
beaches. **Lastres** is a picturesque
clam-fishing port, with the harbor
and noble mansions nestling
beneath a cliff. Three miles (5 km)
south of Lastres is the **Mirador
del Fito,** a lookout point with
sweeping views. ■

In & around
Santillana del Mar

IT IS SAID THAT THE NAME OF THIS NOBLE VILLAGE incorporates three lies. It is not saintly *(sant),* nor is it flat *(llana),* nor is it by the sea *(el mar),* which is 2 miles (3 km) away. But what does this matter when a village has a 1,200-year history and a unique, harmonious mix of architecture. Just 12 miles (20 km) west of Santander, Santillana attracts a lot of visitors. In summer they throng the narrow cobbled streets and local shops and restaurants.

The **Colegiata,** once a Benedictine monastery, was transformed in the 12th century into a Romanesque masterpiece. Its intricately sculpted main portal, interior friezes, and the 42 capitals of the magnificent cloisters depict lions, doves, snakes, pelicans, and plant motifs. The entrance to the **cloisters** is from the side—don't miss them, nor the beautifully carved stone **fount** at the back of the nave, nor the early 16th-century **altarpiece** honoring the relics of St. Juliana, whose tomb stands in the transept.

From the Colegiata, the main street runs through the village to the **Museo Diocesano,** in a converted convent by the road to Santander. The museum has a fine collection of medieval and baroque sculptures, silver, carved ivory, and enamelwork. Between the Colegiata and museum a web of delightful streets show off the best of civil design on the Gothic towers of Merino and Don Borja, houses in the Calle del Cantón, the Renaissance palace of Velarde behind the Colegiata, and many baroque mansions.

West of Santillana are Comillas and San Vicente de la Barquera. **Comillas** *(Visitor information Aldea 6, tel 942 72 07 68)* has the amazing neo-Gothic **Palacio de Sobrellano,** designed by Catalan *modernista* architect Joan Martorell. It stands on a hilltop (beside the marquis's chapel and a folly

designed in 1883 by the architect Gaudí, (see pp. 172–75), and it is now a restaurant. Comillas also has popular beaches.

San Vicente de la Barquera is an animated fishing port below a ruined castle *(Closed until 5 p.m.)* and 13th-century fortified church. The town attracts hordes of visitors in summer, and make sure you're among them—local restaurants serve spectacularly good seafood. One mile (1.6 km) south lie the world-famous caves of **Altamira** (see p. 109). ■

Santillana del Mar
🅰 85 G3
Visitor information
✉ Plaza Mayor
☎ 942 81 82 51

Colegiata, Claustro, & Museo Diocesano
☎ 942 81 80 04 or
942 20 43 41
🕐 Closed Wed. in winter
💲 $ (combined ticket)

San Vicente de la Barquera
🅰 85 G3
Visitor information
✉ Avenida del Generalisimo 20
☎ 942 71 07 97
🕐 Closed winter

A local wedding animates Santillana's Colegiata.

Picos de Europa

CANTABRIA'S IDYLLIC ROLLING PASTURES LEAD TO breathtaking mountains: the limestone massif of the Picos de Europa. They rise to more than 8,500 feet (2,600 m) just 15 miles (25 km) from the coast. Some 273 square miles (700 sq km) form a national park, paradise for hikers or climbers. Visitors share the mountains with bears, chamois, wild boar, wolves, vultures, and royal eagles.

Long isolated by its rim of peaks, the succession of valleys known as **Liébana** successfully repelled Romans, Arabs, and French. Cutting through it is the Río Deva, which has carved a spectacular gorge, the **Desfiladero de la Hermida.** Only one road (N621) runs into Liébana from the Cantabrian coast, and it follows the gorge, so be prepared for tortuous bends. Craggy, eroded pinnacles rise above, and

below is the boulder-strewn torrent of the Deva, teeming with salmon and trout. Two other roads lead into Liébana. The N621 comes from the province of León, south over the San Glorio Pass (5,278 feet/1,609 m). The C627 comes over the lower Piedrasluengas Pass southeast from Palencia. Both have incessant switchbacks and spectacular scenery.

Liébana has lovely churches and hermitages, above all **Nuestra**

Climbers in the Picos de Europa rise above the clouds.

Señora de Lebeña *(1.8 miles/3 km north of Cillorigo-Castro, tel 942 74 43 32, closed in winter)*, a tenth-century Mozarabic structure that nestles below rugged slopes. In the middle of Liébana at the crossroads of four valleys is the lively market town of **Potes,** which is sheltered and has a relatively mild climate, hence the outlying cherry orchards and grapevines. This center for climbers, mountain bikers, canoeists, and hikers has specialist equipment shops, and guides abound. The restaurants are warm and friendly, where sausages, cheeses, cheesecakes, and milk-based desserts are evidence of mountain gastronomy.

The road west out of Potes to Fuente Dé (12 miles/19 km) is worth taking. Just outside Potes, turn left at the signpost and go 2.5 miles (4 km) to the Franciscan **monastery of Santo Toribio de Liébana** *(Tel 942 73 05 50).* This place of pilgrimage is the most important religious site in the region. It began in the eighth century when a fragment of the True Cross (allegedly) was brought here from Jerusalem. A large gold-plated cross contains the holy relic, in the **Capilla del Lignum Crucis** (Chapel of the Wood of the Cross), reached from the north aisle of the restored church.

The main road runs on to the village of **Mogrovejo** (with a historic tower house) before coming to an abrupt end at the cluster of restaurants and a parador that form **Fuente Dé,** sitting at the base of a dramatic sheer rock face. A cable car takes you 2,460 feet (750 m) up to a lookout-point at 6,058 feet (1,847 m), with spectacular views. From the lookout, a 1.8-mile (3 km) path leads to the **Puerto de Aliva,** haunt of brown bear, chamois, and capercaillie (a large grouse)—and site of a small hotel.

On the Asturian (western) side of the mountains the most historic site is **Covadonga** (see p. 110), reached by a 7.5-mile (12 km) detour southeast from **Cangas de Onís** (see p. 110). Driving south on the main N625, you soon come to the gorge of **Los Beyos,** where multiple limestone strata rise on both sides. About 6 miles (10 km) farther south is the **Mirador de Oseja de Sajambre,** one of the region's panoramic lookout points. The road from here to Potes (via the LE 244 and N261) is for diehards only as it entails no fewer than four mountain passes: This is the highest and at times narrowest road of the whole national park. The highlight is the **Puerto de Pandetrave** (5,123 feet/1,562 m), which gives a panorama of three awesome mountain ranges. ∎

Fuente Dé

⚠ 85 F2

✉ Teleférico (cable car)

☎ 942 73 66 10

🕐 Closed Jan.–Feb.

$ $$

Santander

THE GENIAL CAPITAL OF CANTABRIA SWINGS AROUND A huge bay, and serves as both port and resort. Santander has its own charm, mixing stevedores, chic shoppers, shady bodegas, and stylish pavement cafés. The dominant architectural style in the central area is from the late 19th and early 20th centuries, and is typified by the wedding-cake casino overlooking the beaches.

The Península de la Magdalena separates the elegant resort area of **El Sardinero** from the bustling commercial town and port. It is crowned by the **Palacio Real** (late 19th century), built for King Alfonso XIII and his wife, Victoria Eugenia, by public donation from Santander's citizens, to encourage the king's pioneering habit of sea-bathing in their town. The palace is not open to the public, but the surrounding park is a popular promenade area with a small zoo and restaurants. It is accessible from the beaches on either side.

The **catedral** is in central Santander, and is in fact two buildings, one superimposed on the other. The lower church dates from the early 13th century, but within a few decades it was joined by the upper one. On one side of the old nave a transparent floor reveals archaeological **excavations** that in 1982–83 unearthed remains of Santander's original Roman settlement and remnants of earlier churches. The **baptismal font** may have had an earlier life as the ritual washing fountain of a mosque. External steps lead up to the upper, more ostentatious, new section. The outer cloister walls date from the 13th-century addition, but the cathedral church was rebuilt in the 17th century and again in 1941, after a house fire, spread by gale-force winds, devastated the old city. This destroyed part of Santander and led to extensive reconstruction.

Don't miss a breezy stroll along Santander's seafront avenue, which edges the pedestrianized shopping area. Note the ornate **Correos** (post office), **Palacete del Embarcadero** (Jetty Mansion) and **Museo Marítimo** (Maritime Museum). The **Museo de Prehistoria y Arqueólogia** (*Calle Casimiro Saínz 4, tel 942 20 71 05, closed Sun. p.m. & Mon.*) gives you an outline of Cantabria's extensive prehistoric past. The small collection includes a number of mysterious circular inscribed stones from the fourth to first centuries B.C. ∎

The beach at El Sardinero (above) and the floodlit casino (left)

Santander

🅰 85 G3

Visitor information

✉ Plaza Porticada 5

☎ 942 31 07 08 or
942 31 07 56

Catedral

✉ Plaza Obispo Eguino

☎ 942 22 60 24

Cantabria's prehistoric cave paintings

In 1991 archaeologists discovered Paleolithic paintings in the cave of **La Garma,** about 3 miles (5 km) inland from Santander. The cave seems to have been inhabited for thousands of years before being completely sealed up about 12,000 years ago.

Image of a bison, Altamira caves

(Apply at least three years in advance to Museo Altamira, 39330 Santillana del Mar, Cantabria, tel 942 81 80 05, fax 942 84 01 57, cave closed Mon. & p.m.).

The four caves of **Puente Viesgo** are less lyrical, but easier to see. They depict goats, cattle, and equestrian animals in

The first cave paintings found in Cantabria were those of **Altamira** (a mile/1.6 km inland from Santillana del Mar, see p. 105), in 1879. Altamira is still considered the Sistine Chapel of Paleolithic art, its roof covered with almost a hundred expressive renderings of bison, horses, deer, bulls, and wild boars. For conservation reasons, only 30 people a day are admitted various styles. Access is in small groups of visitors (no children under 10) with preference given to independent visitors reserving 24 hours in advance (Tel 942 59 84 25, closed Mon. in summer & Mon.–Tues. in winter). The caves are 17 miles (27 km) inland from Santander on the N623. There are more caves at **Covalanas** and near **Cangas de Onís** (see p. 110). ■

More places to visit in Asturias & Cantabria

CANGAS DE ONÍS

In the eighth century, Cangas was the capital of Christian Spain, and proclaimed Pelayo king after he defeated the Moors at Covadonga (see below). The **chapel of Santa Cruz** was built to mark the victory, but was rebuilt in the 15th century. It incorporates a Bronze Age dolmen (stone tomb). The town also has a hump backed medieval bridge. Three miles (5 km) east of Cangas at Cardes is the **Cueva del Buxu,** which has Paleolithic cave paintings. Just under 2 miles (3 km) north is the 12th-century Benedictine **monastery of San Pedro.** This abandoned building is destined to become a parador (state-run hotel).

🅰 85 F3   **Visitor information** ✉ Avenida de Covadonga 21 ☎ 985 84 80 05 or 985 84 80 43

COVADONGA

This is a picturesque mountain village on the northern flanks of the Picos de Europa is

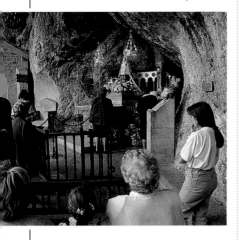

The shrine of the Asturian hero, Pelayo, in the Santa Cueva of Covadonga

where Pelayo started the Christian Reconquest (see pp. 28–31) by defeating a Moorish army in 722. A statue of the national hero stands in front of the 19th-century **basílica.** Inside the church, the **Museo de la Virgen** displays items given to the Virgin of Covadonga, including a priceless diamond-studded crown. Pelayo's sarcophagus is in the neighboring

cave, the **Santa Cueva,** where he retreated. Here, too, is the much venerated **statue of the Virgin,** patron saint of Asturias. From Covadonga a steep road twists 12 miles (20 km) up to a high limestone plateau and the beautiful lakes of Enol and Ercina, a good starting point for mountain hikes.

🅰 85 F3   **Visitor information** ✉ Explanada de la Basílica ☎ 985 84 60 35

CUEVAS DE COVALANAS

The cave paintings at Covalanas lie 1.8 miles (3 km) from Ramales de la Victoria and 42 miles (68 km) from Santander. The two painted caverns have masterful representations of deer, a horse, cattle, and possibly a stag. Visitors are limited to ten at a time and children under ten are not admitted.

🅰 85 H2   ✉ Ramales de la Victoria   ☎ 942 67 83 28 🕐 Closed Mon.–Tues. By appointment in winter

REINOSA

This lively market town on Santander's main road link with Castilla y León makes a good base, as it lies on the slopes of the Cantabrian Mountains. The ski resort of **Alto Campóo** is 16 miles (25 km) west, just beneath the towering peak of **Pico de Tres Mares** (7,136 feet/2,175 m). You can reach the summit by chairlift for magnificent views over the Picos de Europa.

On the C628 road to Alto Campóo, stop at **Fontibre** where a scenic footpath leads to the source of the Ebro River. This whole lush valley has great natural beauty and numerous dolmens (prehistoric stone tombs) lie hidden in remote corners. Immediately east of Reinosa is the immense **Embalse del Ebro,** a reservoir which attracts a wide variety of waterfowl (and bird-watchers). On its banks cows gently chew the cud. Four miles (7 km) south of Reinosa is **Cervatos,** which has a 12th-century Romanesque **collegiate church** *(Tel 942 75 10 36, keys next door).* It has wonderful carvings of lions and more unusual, blatantly erotic figures decorating the capitals of the apse.

🅰 85 G2   **Visitor information** ✉ Avenida Puente Carlos III   ☎ 942 75 52 15 ∎

From Basque fishing villages to remote farming communities, vast sweeps of vineyards, and the Pyrenees, this is one of Spain's most diverse regions. You can ski, hike, taste wine, visit monasteries, or enjoy contemporary art in Bilbo.

Northeast Spain

The medieval town of Ujne at dawn

Northeast Spain

THE MOUNTAIN BARRIER THAT separates Spain from France is nudged by four autonomous regions. They are Euskadi (Basque Country), Navarra, Aragón, and Catalunya (see pp. 180–98). Nestling south of the three is La Rioja. They present very different faces of the Spanish character. The Basques have a history of belligerence and share a language and culture with neighboring Navarra. Aragón has historically had closer links with Catalunya and Castilla. In between, the amiable Riojans produce excellent wine.

This region has never had as many foreign visitors as other parts of Spain, but it has immensely rewarding destinations. On the coast are the hip resort of Donostia (San Sebastián) and the burgeoning city of Bilbo (Bilbao), experiencing a tourist boom thanks to the Guggenheim Museum. Inland are the monasteries and sierra of La Rioja, Navarra, and Aragón, and the nature reserves of the Pyrenees. In Aragón especially, where the Moors held sway until the 12th century, you find tiny historic towns with elaborate Mudejar architecture, and open, rolling landscapes.

Unspoiled nature is never far away, although Euskadi has a lot of industry, which has contributed to its wealth and self-esteem. Be prepared for a new vocabulary, as the Basques, like the Catalans and Galicians, use their own language on every sign. This doesn't mean that they have a narrow outlook: Basques take pride in being a cultured and educated people. Explore the Basque coast between Donostia and Bilbo, but go into the hills to experience rural life and delightful small towns. The best wilderness areas in northeast Spain are in the Pyrenean foothills, and the most beautiful stretch of these is in Aragón's Parque Nacional de Ordesa y Monte Perdido—perfect for long treks.

Navarra has Iruña (Pamplona), world famous for bullrunning, but it also has some of the major stopping points on the Way of St. James (see pp. 88–89), hence the string of superb Romanesque constructions that continues through La Rioja. Royal palaces, castles, and other monuments are scattered through the region. San Juan de la Peña has a medieval royal pantheon and Zaragoza the magnificent Moorish palace used by Fernando and Isabel (see pp. 31–32). The fortifications at Gasteiz (Vitoria) were built by a 12th-century Navarrese king, and royal sarcophagi in Jaca and Huesca bear witness to the importance of these towns in Aragonese history. ∎

Area of map detail

of Biscay

Vasca
Zumaia
Getaria
Zarautz
Azkoitia
Azpeitia   Tolosa
A15
Peñas
de Aia   Lekunberri
1018m   (Larraun)

Hondarribia
(Fuenterrabía)
Irún
A8
Donostia (San Sebastián)

FRANCE

Bidasoa   Elizondo
(Baztan)

Orreaga
(Roncesvalles)

Puerto de
Somport

0   60 kilometers
0   40 miles

Sanctuario de
San Miguel de Excelsis

Iruña
(Pamplona)

Ansó   Hecho   Canfranc

Parque Nacional
de Ordesa y
Monte Perdido

Pico
Posets   Pico de
3371m   Aneto
3404m

Monasterio
de Iranzu

N A V A R R A

Estella
(Lizarra)

Monasterio
de Irache

Monasterio
de Leyre

Berdún

Torla   3355m
Monte
Perdido   Revilla

Bielsa

Benasque

Sangüesa
(Zangoza)
A15

Castillo
de Javier

Tafalla

Olite

Jaca

San Juan
de la Peña

Sabiñánigo

Gállego   Ainsa

Sos del
Rey Católico

Ebro

Uncastillo   Riglos

Castillo
de Loarre

Ara

Ésera

A68

Marcilla

Calahorra   Monasterio
de la Oliva

Sádaba

Ayerbe   Bolea

Alquézar

Graus

R I O J A
Arnedo
Arnedillo   Alfaro
Enciso   Corella   Fitero

Bardenas
Reales
Arguedas

Ejea de los
Caballeros

Huesca

Almudévar

Barbastro

Monzón

Binéfar

Cervera del
Río Alhama

Tudela

Ebro

Alcanadre

Cinca

Tarazona   Tauste   Zuera   Sariñena

2316m   Monasterio
de Veruela   A68

Sierra del
Moncayo

La Almunia de
Doña Godina

N II

Alagón
Utebo

ZARAGOZA

Jalón

Ebro

Los Monegros

A2

Fraga

A2

CATALUNYA (CATALUÑA)
p. 177

Bujaraloz

Quinto

Embalse de
Mequinenza

Calatayud

Ateca

Maluenda

A R A G Ó N

Fuendetodos

N330

Cariñena

Caspe

3   N II

Monasterio de
Santa María de Huerta

Monasterio
de Piedra

Daroca

Jiloca

Hijar

Andorra

Alcañiz

Calanda

Valderrobres

CASTILLA-
LA MANCHA
p. 233

Calamocha

Montalbán

Guadalope

2   N234   Monreal
del Campo

Villarluengo

Mirambel

E   F

Sierra de
Albarracín

Cella

Cantavieja

La Iglesuela
del Cid

Albarracín   Teruel

Mora de
Rubielos

VALENCIA
p. 177

Turia

Sarrión

Sierra de
Javalambre

C   D

Euskadi & Navarra

Euskadi (as the Basques call their country) and Navarra have long been linked by their common language, *euskera*, still widely spoken in varying dialects throughout the region. When Castilla wrested control from the kings of Navarra in the 13th century, the Basque identity and sense of civic rights strengthened, and seven centuries later, with grievances exacerbated by Franco's repression, this turned into a bitter separatist struggle that continues today. There is no threat to visitors, however, as targets are political.

The 2,800 square miles (7,200 sq km) of Euskadi are now divided into three historical territories: Vizcaya to the northwest, around Bilbo (Bilbao); Guipúzcoa to the northeast, with Donostia (San Sebastián) as its capital; and the inland region of Álava to the south, surrounding Gasteiz (Vitoria). The latter provinces share a border with Navarra, 4,056 square miles (10,400 sq km) of diverse landscapes, from Pyrenean peaks through green valleys to more arid southern plains.

You may find Euskadi's prosperous cities of Bilbo and Donostia more exciting than Iruña (Pamplona), the capital of Navarra. The Basque coast has a history of seamanship and fishing. Donostia and Hondarribia (Fuenterrabía) are established resorts; elsewhere are surfing beaches and low-key fishing villages strung along 125 miles (200 km) of rugged, sharply indented coastline.

Common to both Navarra and Euskadi are rolling green hills and valleys clad in beech, oak, and chestnut forests. Here are nature reserves, solid stone houses, pastoral scenes, and also a lot of history. This is where the Cantabrian Mountains meet the Pyrenees.

Navarra's 56,810 acres (23,000 ha) of vineyards have progressed by leaps and bounds since the late 20th century, and now produce highly regarded wines. Euskadi's *pintxos* (appetizers) and other innovative cuisine are as good as its traditionally excellent wines from the Rioja Alavesa (which neighbors La Rioja). Above all, a sense of renewal has infused this corner of Spain since the Guggenheim Museum opened in Bilbo. ■

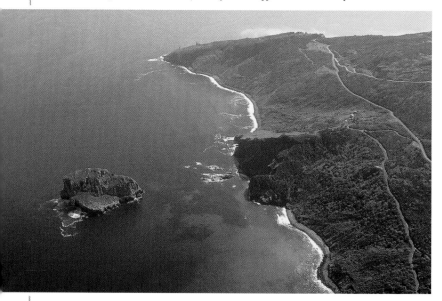

Dramatically indented coastline is typical of Vizcaya, the area around Bilbo (Bilbao).

Bilbo (Bilbao)

EVER SINCE THE MUSEO GUGGENHEIM OPENED IN LATE 1997, Bilbo has experienced a cultural renaissance and consequent surge in tourism. Half the population of Euskadi lives in greater Bilbo (1.2 million people), and the city is vital to the Spanish economy.

It was in 1300 that the city officially came into being. Its site on the navigable estuary of the Río Ibaizabal made it important for exporting Castilian goods, and its own wool, iron, and steel industries prospered. Today the old shipbuilding and dock area of **Abandoibarra** has been transformed into a new cultural hub. On the other side of Bilbo, the winding streets of the **casco viejo** (old town) around the **catedral** *(Closed for renovation)* have been injected with new life. The **Museo Vasco** *(Calle Cruz 4, tel 94 415 54 23, closed Sun. p.m., Mon., & public holidays)* gives good background information on the culture and economy of the Basque region. A few steps away is the lively **Plaza Nueva,** an arcaded square lined with cafés, restaurants, and shops. Behind rises the hill of **Artxanda,**

a leisure park reached by funicular railway. On the banks of the river, beside the Puente del Arenal, stands the majestic **Teatro Arriaga.** Most of the casco viejo is pedestrianized, with many tapas bars and small restaurants.

Between the casco viejo and the Guggenheim (see pp. 116–118) stretches Bilbo's stately **19th-century quarter,** and slicing across this is the Gran Vía, home to Bilbo's financial institutions and its more upscale shops. It ends in the west at the **Parque Doña Casilda de Iturriza,** a formal park next to the **Museo de Bellas Artes** *(Plaza del Museo 2, tel 94 439 60 60, closed Sun. p.m., Mon., & public holidays).* The museum has magnificent paintings by Zurbarán, Ribera, El Greco, van Dyck, Goya, Gauguin, Chillida, Tàpies, and Bacon. ■

The Nervion River twists through the heart of Bilbo; the Guggenheim stands on the right.

Bilbo (Bilbao)
🔼 112 B6
Visitor information
✉ Paseo del Arenal 1
☎ 94 479 57 60
🕐 Closed Sat. & Sun. p.m.

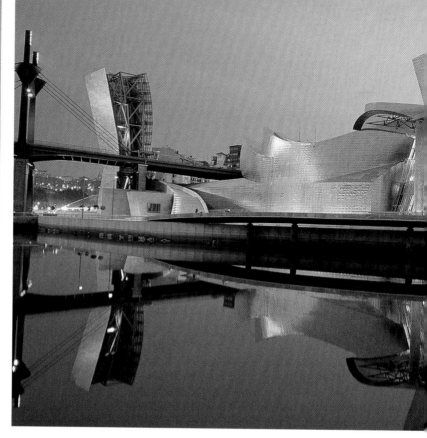

Museo Guggenheim

Museo Guggenheim

🅰 112 B6

✉ Abandoibarra Etorbidea 2

☎ 94 435 90 80

🕐 Closed Mon., Sept.–Jun.

💲 $$. Free guided tours in English daily at 4 p.m.

The bold steel planes of Frank O. Gehry's Guggenheim (above) and a vertiginous view of the interior

HOWEVER MANY PHOTOGRAPHS YOU MAY HAVE SEEN OF this building, the reality is still a visual shock. Its curved steel and titanium planes beside the Puente de la Salve reflect the hills, sky, and river of Bilbo in an endless play with light that defies all logic. Architect Frank O. Gehry's masterwork has put Bilbo firmly on the world cultural map and is one of the icons of the new Spain that is emerging at the turn of the millennium.

The idea of the museum arose in the late 1980s when the Basque government decided to diversify the city's economic base by redeveloping the old shipbuilding area. By 1992, the Solomon R. Guggenheim Foundation had been signed up to manage this important new institution, and in October 1997 the daring gamble with Gehry's innovative design paid off: The museum opened to world applause. The nucleus of Gehry's design is a soaring 164-foot-high (50 m) atrium, around which are interconnected blocks housing 19 galleries, an auditorium, a restaurant, and offices, in steel, glass, and limestone. Transparent elevator shafts, curving walkways, terraces, and internal balconies all add to the vertiginous sense of excitement in

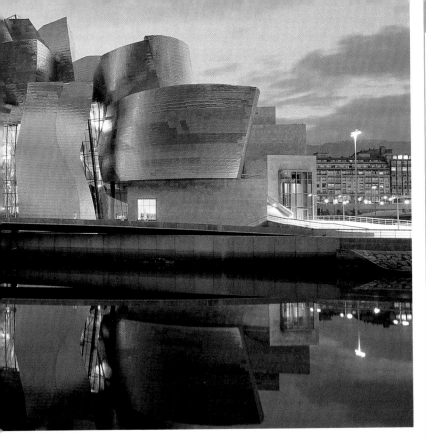

this rule-breaking building—an apt expression of Basque audacity.

The total floor area is 260,000 square feet (24,000 sq m), and just under half that is exhibition space, including the world's largest exhibition hall, a staggering 426 feet (130 m) in length. This is one of several halls designed for specially commissioned installations and site-specific works.

Along with its sister museums in New York and Venice (the Solomon R. Guggenheim Museum and the Peggy Guggenheim Collection), the Bilbo museum has access to an impressive sweep of 20th-century artworks that form a shared permanent collection. These are presented on a rotational basis, and offer contrasting perspectives on seminal movements and artists from the

American abstract expressionists and Pop artists, such as Robert Rauschenberg, Robert Motherwell, James Rosenquist, Clyfford Still, and Andy Warhol, can be seen in Galleries 103 and 105 on the third floor and also on the second floor.

Leading contemporary Spanish and Basque artists are also featured, and an exciting program of temporary exhibitions highlights current trends in Spanish art.

Much emphasis is placed on new forms of medium, bringing a Christian Boltanski installation together with a photo-montage by Gilbert & George and a painting by Julian Schnabel. Multimedia and site-specific commissions include Frrancesco Clemente, Sol LeWitt, Fujiko Nakaya, Richard Serra, and a witty LED installation by Jenny Holzer in a corner of the atrium. Another of the museum's aims is to build up in-depth representation of specific artists from the late 20th century, with Anselm Kiefer the most visible for the moment. ■

The world's largest exhibition hall (above), with a temporary show of works by Richard Serra; pop art (below)

U.S. and Europe. Early radicals, such as Vasily Kandinsky, Paul Cézanne, and Pablo Picasso, may appear beside Constantin Brancusi, Piet Mondrian, or Joseph Beuys. Works by Max Ernst, Man Ray, and Marcel Duchamp, and those of

Gasteiz (Vitoria)

THE STREETS OF THE OLD PART OF GASTEIZ RING THE hilltop cathedral, and their picturesque slopes have endless nooks and crannies to explore. The town was fortified in 1181 by Sancho III, king of Navarra, as a stronghold against Castilla, and flourished as a trading crossroads. Gasteiz is the old Basque name of the city.

Much of this capital of the small Basque province of Álava is pedestrianized, reinforcing the air of placid provincialism so evident in the formal gardens of the **Parque de la Florida** (1820) and stately **Plaza de España.** This square, **Los Arquillos,** and **Plaza del Machete** form an intriguing bridging area between the medieval hill town and the flat, largely 19th-century city below. Walk from Plaza del Machete along Calle de Santa María and you pass the **Palacio de Montehermoso** (1524), and, a block to the west, the **Palacio de Escoriaza-Esquivel,** which has a lovely plateresque doorway and staircase. At the end

stands the 14th-century **catedral of Santa María** *(Tel 945 25 55 67, currently closed for renovation),* and a cluster of medieval and Renaissance buildings.

This historic nucleus includes **El Portalón** (now a restaurant), built in timber and brick in the 15th century, the 15th-century **Torre de los Anda** (a fortified house), and the **Museo de Arqueología,** located in the 16th-century Casa Armera de los Godeo. The **Museo Fournier** *(Palacio de Bendaña, Calle de Cuchillería, tel 945 18 19 20, closed Mon. & p.m. Sat. & Sun.)* is devoted entirely to tarot and playing cards. It is located in a lovely palace, built in 1525. ∎

Gasteiz (Vitoria)
🅰 112 B5
Visitor information
✉ Parque de la Florida
☎ 945 13 13 21

Museo de Arqueología de Álava
✉ Casa Godeo-Guevara-San Juan, Correría 116
☎ 945 18 19 22
🕐 Closed Mon. & p.m. Sat. & Sun.

View over Gasteiz's rooftops toward the Plaza de Espana

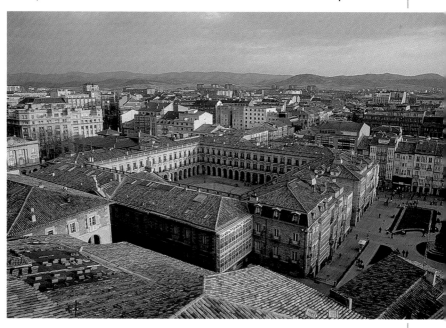

Basque identity

The mysterious origins of the Basques help to make Euskadi, as they call their country, one of Spain's most beguiling regions. Green valleys and a dramatically indented coastline do not, however, capture the headlines. Far more prominent is the Basque role as a thorn in the flesh of central government.

What is certain about their unique identity is that the Basque language predates Indo-European, and that it has significant links with Caucasian languages of Central Asia and with Berber, the language of the pre-Arab inhabitants of North Africa. Studies in diverse fields from blood groups to morphology eventually produced one common theory: the Basques have inhabited their remote, verdant valleys since the Stone Age, and they could well be the direct descendants of Cro-Magnon man.

Over the centuries, the Basques' fiercely independent nature kept Romans, Franks, and Visigoths mostly at bay, so protecting the last outpost of pagan beliefs in southwestern Europe. Basques converted to Christianity only in the ninth and tenth centuries, and were the last to adopt urban living—as late as the 14th century. Today this is hard to believe when you look at the burgeoning cities of Donostia (San Sebastián) and Bilbo (Bilbao), but the lack of towns did not stop the Basques forging ahead to establish personal liberties and elective assemblies in the provinces of Vizcaya and Guipúzcoa. Their ongoing battle with the central Spanish government dates from the days of the *fueros,* codes of traditional laws that were respected by the Catholic Monarchs and the Habsburgs, but were repeatedly revoked in the 19th century in order to create a more centralized Spain.

The man who catalyzed Basque resentment was Sabino de Arana Goiri (1865–1903), who fortuitously entered the stage at a time of increasing industrialization. After coining the word Euskadi to encompass the four Basque territories of Álava, Guipúzcoa, Vizcaya, and northern Navarra, where Basque is spoken, he founded the Basque National Party (PNV). By his death his avowed aim had swung from independence to autonomy, but a century later this region is still fraught with political unrest and conflicting goals. General Franco (dictator from 1939 to 1975) aroused intense bitterness: He colluded in the bombing of the Basque town of Gernika in 1937, and later repressed Basque identity and abolished all remaining fueros. In 1960 Basque separatists founded ETA (an acronym meaning Euskadi and Freedom), which started a campaign of terrorism against Madrid. Euskadi (País Vasco, or Basque Country) gained autonomy in 1979, but despite that, and despite the ever encroaching lifestyle, language, and immigrants of Castilian Spain, ETA bombs and assassinations continue to make headlines, goading the rest of Spain into massive demonstrations of outrage, except during a short-lived truce in 1998–99.

Politics aside, however, the Basques easily outpace their neighbors economically, with the notable exception of the Catalans. Having been an agrarian society housed in isolated *caseríos* (typical pitched-roof farmhouses accommodating extended families), Euskadi rapidly became Spain's most competitive industrialized region. Today the average Basque income is 10 percent higher than that of the rest of Spain, and 50 percent have at least secondary school education (compared with 30 per cent in Spain and 60 percent in Europe). Yet, like all Spaniards, they cling to their roots. Some of the most genuine expressions of Basqueness come from *bertsolaris,* poets who improvise in local competitions, *pelota* (a ball and bat game), and *hariketa,* a more primitive pastime of lifting massive stones of up to 660 pounds (300 kg). Closer to the outsider's heart is the renowned Basque gastronomy, which in the 1970s followed in the footsteps of French nouvelle cuisine to bring out the essence of fresh ingredients—particularly seafood. Despite its apparently inward-looking nature, Euskadi has also been a region of maritime explorers (Sebastián Elcano, Lope de Aguirre) and of spiritual philosophers (Ignatius de Loyola, Francis Xavier). Adventurous and introspective, radical and traditional, stone-hefters and gourmets—Basques may be the most paradoxical people of Spain. ∎

Symbols of Basque identity: pelota and traditional dance (above); red berets (below)

Donostia (San Sebastián)

THE QUEEN OF EUSKADI'S COAST, ALSO CALLED THE "PEARL of the ocean," is a dynamic, outgoing resort surrounding a stunning bay and spanning the estuary of the Río Urumea. A fishing village that grew into a port, it is now a prosperous resort town of 180,000 people. All of them seem to gravitate nightly to the streets of the old quarter, with allegedly the greatest concentration of bars in the world.

Donostia (San Sebastián)
www.paisvasco
.com/donostia
⚠ 113 C6
Visitor information
✉ Reina Regente 8
☎ 943 48 11 66

After surviving no fewer than 12 major fires from the 13th century onward, Donostia flourished in the 19th century. Queen Isabel II (R.1843–1868) was the catalyst, because she chose this spot when her doctor advised her to frequent the Cantabrian coast. For over 20 years she returned every summer, and in 1863 by agreeing to the demolition of the old town walls, she unleashed Donostia's expan-

sion. The result is the 19th-century city, a stately, harmonious grid of streets stretching south from the old quarter, east along the Bahía de la Concha and eventually west across the river. Donostia is relatively poor in monuments, but it has plenty of other good things, including excellent cuisine.

The coastline is punctuated by three hills, **Monte Igueldo** has an amusement park and is reached by cable car *(Tel 943 21 05 64, cars run every 15 minutes)* from the Plaza del Funicular. The old town grew at the foot of **Monte Urgull,** now a park, with a castle at the top. **Monte Ulía**'s whale lookout has fabulous views. Go by bus, car, or taxi from the old town to the base of the hill, then walk or drive about a mile up the hill. A 7-mile (12 km) waterfront promenade takes you the length of the city, and three city beaches give good swimming. Queen Isabel II's favored beach was the lively **Playa de la Concha,** where you can see her mock-English manorhouse, **Palacio de Miramar,** and visit its gardens.

In the old quarter, one of the nicest strolls is along Paseo del Muelle, at the back of the harbor. At the far end stands the **Aquarium** *(Plaza Carlos Blasco de Imaz, tel 943 44 00 99),* modernized in 1998, with a transparent tunnel for close views of sharks, manta rays, and other creatures of the deep. Packed into the atmospheric little harbor are fishing trawlers, tour boats, the fish market, local women selling egg cups filled with prawns, and a string of outdoor seafood restaurants. The **Museo Naval** *(Paseo del Muelle 24, tel 943 43 00 51, closed Mon. & p.m. Sun.)* has an 18th-century timbered interior and items from the city's seafaring past.

Penetrate the labyrinth of streets beside the harbor and you soon see the heavy baroque facade of the church of **Santa María** *(Calle 31 de Agosto).* The low vaults beneath the organ hold a sculpture by Eduardo Chillida, Euskadi's most prominent artist. On the same street is a side entrance to the **Museo San Telmo** *(Plaza Zuloaga 1, tel 943 42 49 70, closed Sun. p.m. & Mon.)* through a converted Dominican convent. Its highlight is 11 murals by the Catalan artist José María Sert

(1876–1945), depicting scenes of Guipúzcoa's history in sepia and gold on a red base. The museum also contains paintings from the Renaissance onward, including a room devoted to Antonio Ortiz Echagüe (1883–1942), a painter in the Postimpressionist style. Major renovations are underway here to create a museum for Basque culture. Also in this quarter, is the **Plaza de la Constitución,** site of a farmers' market and outdoor cafés. You'll see that the balconies are numbered—the square used to be a bullring, and the balconies were the seats for the spectators. ■

Tapas bars thrive in Donostia's back streets.

Film festival

Donostia has a flourishing cultural life, but the biggest event of the year is the international film festival in September. It was first held in 1952. Since 1999, screenings have been at Rafael Moneo's state-of-the-art congress hall, whose spectacular glass forms rise on the eastern tip of the estuary. The prize-giving ceremony still takes place at the lovely Teatro Victoria Eugenia, and no self-respecting star can stay anywhere but the regal-looking María Cristina hotel next door. ■

Donostia's buildings edge the regal sweep of the Bahía de la Concha, seen here from Monte Igueldo.

Costa Vasca

FROM THE PYRENEES AT THE FRENCH BORDER, A wonderful, often wild coastline of nearly 125 miles (200 km) stretches west to Bilbo. Most resorts are small, squeezed between rocky cliffs and the thundering surf of the Cantabrian Sea. Town outskirts may be marred by high-rises and light industry, but the coast has good opportunities for board sailing, surfing, scuba-diving, and sailing.

The prettiest resort by far is **Hondarribia (Fuenterrabía),** a picture-postcard town looking across the Bidasoa estuary to Hendaye in France. This strategic site was heavily fortified, and 15th-century ramparts still enclose the austere **Castillo de Carlos V,** now a parador. The steep narrow streets around it have several Baroque mansions. Down at the **Marina,** painted wooden balconies brimming with flowers overlook lively bars and outdoor restaurants. Toward sunset, drive west about 4 miles (7 km) to the *mirador* (lookout point) at **Jaizkibel,** for polychrome views.

West of Donostia, a string of resorts starts with **Zarautz,** which has this coastline's longest beach (2 miles/3 km), a favorite with surfers. The road in from the hills behind goes past modern buildings that do not augur well, but the old quarter has delightful places: 16th-century **Luzea tower, Palacio de Narros,** a Franciscan convent, and grand 19th-century villas.

From Zarautz the coast road (N634) twists around the indented shore to **Getaria,** *(Visitor information, Parque Aldamar 2, tel 943 14 09 57, closed winter)* a real charmer. The old quarter lies on a promontory ending at **Monte San Antón,** nicknamed the "mouse of Getaria." The Gothic church of San Salvador is worth visiting but the resort's main attraction is the seafood restaurants lining the lively port. This is the perfect place to sip a

glass of *txakoli* (local white wine) in honor of Getaria's most illustrious sons, fashion designer Cristobal Balenciaga (1892–1972), and Juan Sebastián Elcano, second-in-command to the Portuguese navigator Ferdinand Magellan on his great voyage round the world. Elcano completed the voyage in 1522 after Magellan was killed.

The corniche road soon comes to **Zumaia** *(Visitor information, Plaza Zuloaga, tel 943 14 33 96, closed winter),* a friendly town on an estuary, with a lovely medieval quarter and a breezy promenade. Zumaia has two good beaches, **Itzurun** and **Santiago;** surfers prefer the pounding surf at **San Telmo,** to the west. Ten miles (16 km) inland of Zumaia are the neighboring towns of Azpeitia and Azkoitia. On the outskirts of **Azpeitia** stands the sanctuary of St. Ignatius de Loyola, philosopher and founder of the Jesuits, and now a major pilgrimage spot. Next to his family's tower-house stands the **Basílica de Loyola** *(Tel 943 81 65 08),* designed by Carlo Fontana, a disciple of the Italian sculptor Bernini, with a striking baroque facade and 196-foot (60 m) cupola. Begun in the 17th century, it was completed only in the late 1800s.

Back on the coast, **Deba** is the next fishing port west of Zumaia, and also has a good beach. It lies at the mouth of the river of the same name and was important in the heyday of the Castilian wool trade—hence the surprisingly grandiose

Costa Vasca
- ▲ 113 C6

Hondarribia (Fuenterrabía)
- ▲ 113 C6
- **Visitor information**
- ✉ Javier Ugarte 6
- ☎ 943 64 54 58

Zarautz
- ▲ 113 C6
- ✉ Nafarroa Kalea
- ☎ 943 83 09 90

Deba
- ▲ 112 B6
- ✉ Portu Kalea 1
- ☎ 943 19 24 52

Lekeitio
- ▲ 112 B6
- ✉ Independentzia Enparantza
- ☎ 94 684 40 17

Gernika (Lumo)
- ▲ 112 B6
- ✉ Artekale 8
- ☎ 94 625 58 92

dimensions of the 16th-century church of **Santa María la Real.**

West of Deba, the coast road becomes increasingly scenic as it edges cliffs with plunging views over **Mutriku,** the rugged **Playa Saturraran,** and **Ondarroa.** A couple of lookout points let you stop to admire the scene in safety, before the road reaches **Lekeitio,** in its lovely bay setting. The protected beaches here have safe swimming and the seafood restaurants are predictably good.

Sixteen miles (25 km) to the west, houses at **Elantxobe**—the attractive marine extension of Ibarrangelu—seem to tumble down the steep hillside to the harbor and fishing boats. West of Elantxobe's rugged headland, **Cabo Ogoño,** are the area's two main sandy beaches, **Playa de Laida** and **Playa de Laga,** both at the mouth of the lovely Mundaka estuary. This was declared a biosphere reserve in 1984 and has a rich plant life and birdlife, beaches, and the prehistoric caves of Santimaiñe. The town of **Gernika (Lumo)** lies at the southern end of the estuary.

The name is immortalized in Picasso's painting "Guernica," and commemorated in Gernika's park with sculptures by Eduardo Chillida and British sculptor Henry Moore. Of vital symbolic importance for Basque political identity is the venerable oak tree under which the medieval Lords of Vizcaya (Biscay) would periodically vow to uphold Basque privileges. The original tree stands next to the neoclassic **Casa de Juntas** where, since 1979, Vizcaya representatives now meet once more. ■

"Guernica"

Picasso's painting "Guernica" hangs in Madrid's Reina Sofía (see pp. 74–75) after years at New York's Museum of Modern Art. It was inspired by the brutal bombing of the little town of Gernika on April 26, 1937. The three-hour raid was carried out on General Franco's orders by a German squadron and killed over 2,000 people, most of whom were in Gernika for the weekly market. ■

Elanxtobe's tiled roofs huddle high above the fishing harbor.

Valley towns

Bergara
🅰 112 B6
Visitor information
✉ Ayuntamiento, Plaza
San Martín de
Agirre
☎ 943 77 91 28

Oñati
🅰 112 B5
Visitor information
✉ Foruen
Enparantza 2
☎ 943 78 34 53

Estella (Lizarra)
🅰 113 C5
Visitor information
✉ Calle San Nicolás 1
☎ 948 55 40 11

Sangüesa
(Zangoza)
🅰 113 D5
Visitor information
✉ Alfonso el Batallador
20
☎ 948 87 03 29

DESPITE EUSKADI'S HIGH LEVEL OF INDUSTRIALIZATION, its green valleys encompass vast swaths of unadulterated nature and fascinating small towns. Northern Navarra has these, too, with the added bonus of Romanesque relics of the Way of St. James.

In the valley of the Deba River, 34 miles (54 km) southeast of Bilbo (Bilbao), **Bergara** has harmonious Renaissance buildings behind its industrialized outskirts. You may well arrive during one of its many music festivals.

The heart of Bergara is **Plaza San Martín Agirre,** where the arcaded baroque town hall faces the former royal Jesuit seminary. Also on the square are three Renaissance palaces with emblazoned facades. Immediately uphill, the church of **San Pedro de Ariznoa** has a 17th-century statue of Christ by Juan de Mesa and a painting by José Ribera. Don't leave Bergara without tasting the local *errellenoak* and *tostoiak* sweets.

Of the 20 hermitages that dot the surrounding countryside, the most venerated is that of **San Miguel de Aritzeta,** 1 mile (1.6 km) south of Bergara. From its site it gives wonderful views over this lush region.

Seven miles (12 km) south through the hills lies the noble town of **Oñati.** Its monuments make it the most historically rich town in the province of Guipúzcoa, and the calendar is studded with local fiestas that usually involve the populace parading in Basque costumes. **Sancti Spiritu university,** started in 1540, has a beautiful plateresque facade and a courtyard decorated in coffered Mudejar style. On the main square stands the church of **San Miguel Arcángel,** originally Gothic but with an 18th-century baroque-rococo tower, the work of Martin Carrera, who was also responsible for the rococo **Casa Consistorial** (Town Hall).

The monastery of Bidaurreta (1510) is on the southern edge of town. In the hills about 5 miles (9 km) on is Guipúzcoa's most important shrine—that of **Arantzazu** *(Tel 943 78 13 13)*, the region's patron saint. This modern building (1955) was a collaboration between architects Sainz de Oiza and Laorga, and sculptors Eduardo Chillida, Lucio Muñoz, and Jorge Oteiza.

Strong Basque traditions continue 27 miles (43 km) southwest of Iruña (Pamplona) at **Estella (Lizarra),** the 12th-century capital of the kings of Navarra. It became a center of the Carlists (see p. 34) seven centuries later. It flourished because it was on the Way of St. James (see pp. 88–89) and also enjoyed privileges granted by King Sancho Ramirez—hence its fine medieval buildings. The **Palacio de los Reyes de Navarra**—the royal palace—dates from the 12th century and is a rare example of civic Romanesque architecture. It is now the **Museo Gustavo de Maeztu.** Close by stands the 12th-century church of **San Pedro de la Rúa,** built in Cistercian style (see p. 151). Two sides of the cloisters were blown up in the 16th century, but what is left is very beautiful. Cross the Río Ega, by the Puente de la Cárcel, and you find an old quarter of winding medieval lanes, and the Romanesque church of **San Miguel,** with its intricately carved northern portal.

Outside town, in wild, bucolic surroundings, is the Cistercian **Monasterio de Irantzu** *(5.6 miles/9 km north of Lizarra on N120, tel 948 52 00 12),* now a college. The even older **Monasterio de Iratxe** *(1.8 miles/3 km southwest of Lizarra, tel 948 55 44 64)* is on the old pilgrimage route. It has magnificent, plateresque cloisters and a church combining Cistercian and Romanesque features. It houses the **Museo Julio Caro Baroja,** named for a Navarrese ethnographer (one who describes human cultures).

Less atmospheric than these, and in the much more arid area bordering Aragón, **Sangüesa (Zangoza)** has a remarkable church, **Santa María la Real** *(Guided visits only, arrange through visitor information),* which looms above the Aragón River. It was begun in the early 12th century, and final touches, such as the octagonal tower, the south portal, and spire, date from the middle of the 13th century. The highlight is the **south portal,** which contains an astonishing number of sculptures by the master of San Juan de la Peña (see p. 146) and Leodegarius. Close by in Calle Alfonso el Batallador is **Palacio de Vallesantoro,** with an unusual baroque facade: It has projecting carved eaves and elaborately carved columns inspired by Spanish colonial art in Latin America. ■

One of Oñati's many Basque festivals

Navarra's spiritual lookouts

Monasterio de Leyre
- 113 D5
- 4 miles (6 km) northeast of Yesa on the N240
- 948 88 41 00
- $

Castillo de Javier
- 113 D5
- 948 88 40 00

Sanctuario de San Miguel de Excelsis
- 113 C5
- 10 miles (18 km) southwest of Lekunberri
- 948 39 60 28

St. Francis Xavier's festival brings pilgrims to his birthplace.

NORTHERN SPAIN'S MONASTERIES AND OTHER HOLY SITES are often in remote and beautiful settings, and Navarra's are no exception. The three sites below have a long history as spiritual retreats, coupled with spectacular positions.

The **Monasterio de Leyre** stands in the rugged, pine-clad Sierra Errando, 31 miles (50 km) southeast of Iruña (Pamplona), and has sweeping views of the **Yesa Reservoir.** Benedictine monks returned here in 1954, and you should arrive early or stay late in order to hear their Gregorian chants *(daily at 7:30 a.m. and 7 p.m.)* in the serene Romanesque church of San Salvador. You can stay at the monastery, or visit from Sos del Rey Católico (see p. 152) or Iruña. The church entrance known as the **Porta Speciosa** has complex carvings; also in the church is the mausoleum of the kings of Navarra. You can visit the unique crypt (1057), where vaults and pillars spring from low, carved capitals of extraordinary dimensions—some are up to 1 yard in width.

A few miles southwest of Leyre, the much rebuilt **Castillo de Javier** was the birthplace of the great Jesuit missionary Saint Francis Xavier (1506–1552). He is Navarra's patron saint, and the castle is flanked by a basilica, a Jesuit retreat, and a mission. Inside the castle, exceptional exhibits include a Gothic sculpture of Christ carved in walnut, and a 15th-century wall painting of the Dance of Death (both in the Holy Christ Tower). From the crenellated walls on the terrace you look north toward Leyre and south to Aragón (see pp. 139–52). Javier itself has rather commercialized cafés and souvenir shops.

To reach the **Sanctuario de San Miguel de Excelsis,** you drive through lovely holm-oak and beech forests, up to wild heath. The area has dozens of dolmens—the largest concentration of Stone Age structures in northern Spain—and is popular with trekkers. Ask about trails at the **Casa Forestal** on the road to the sanctuary. The church is perched on a promontory with dizzying views over the Sierra de Aralar, about halfway between Donostia and Iruña. It has a Visigothic (ninth-century) apse, a pre-Romanesque (tenth-century) structure, and an enclosed Romanesque chapel. The fabulous gilded and enamel 12th-century altarfront, almost certainly from Limoges, was brought here from Iruña cathedral in 1765. ∎

Iruña (Pamplona)

IRUÑA, BETTER KNOWN AS PAMPLONA, IS FAMOUS FAR beyond Spain thanks to Ernest Hemingway. He wrote about the bull-running that takes place during Iruña's festival of Sanfermines, and the event now attracts hundreds of thousands of visitors.

At other times, Iruña is a quiet, even colorless little city, where life revolves placidly around the porticoed **Plaza del Castillo** on the edge of the old quarter. North of this are dark narrow lanes that date from when Iruña was the fortified capital of the kingdom of Navarra. Today they are lined with five-story houses and specialist shops. Close to the old city walls, the Gothic **catedral** has delicately structured cloisters. The old refectory and kitchen (1330) are now the **Museo Diocesano,** which displays religious objects. For an idea of Navarra's long and complex history, visit the **Museo de Navarra** (*Cuesta de Sto. Domingo, tel 948 42 64 92, closed Sun. p.m. & Mon.*),

housed in a 16th-century hospital with an impressive Renaissance frontage. It has Roman mosaics (Pamplona was founded by the Romans in 75 B.C. on the Basque settlement of Iruña), Romanesque capitals from the former cathedral, Renaissance paintings, and frescoes gathered together from all over the province.

The bullring lies immediately southwest of the old quarter on **Paseo Hemingway,** a lovely leafy promenade shaded by lofty plane and chestnut trees. Your next priority should be to follow the example of Hemingway himself and retire to the chandeliered 19th-century splendor of the **Café Iruña** on the Plaza del Castillo. ∎

Iruña (Pamplona)
www.cfnavarra
.es/turismonavarra
🅼 113 C5
Visitor information
✉ Calle Duque de
Ahumada 3
☎ 948 22 07 41

Catedral & Museo Diocesano
✉ Calle Dormitalería
☎ 948 21 08 27
🕐 Closed Sat. p.m. &
Sun.
💲 $

Hemingway eternalized Iruña's annual running of the bulls.

Sanfermines

The dates are fixed: Iruña's Sanfermines festival is always July 6–14. This is when the city has the debacle of bullrunning known as the *encierro*, immortalized by Hemingway in *The Sun Also Rises*. The encierro originated to honor Iruña's patron saint, but has since become a test for daredevil locals and visitors alike. It starts daily at 8 a.m., when bulls are let loose to charge along a fenced route through town on their way to the bullring. Hundreds of people run into the street to pit their wits and speed against those of the bulls. Bullfights take place every day and celebrations continue long into the night. ∎

More places to visit in Euskadi & Navarra

OLITE

Olite's castle is a massive affair with crenellated towers and battlements. It dates from 1407 and had numerous Moorish elements such as hanging gardens, *azulejos* (tiles), and stucco work, but much of this vanished during multiple renovations and a devastating fire in 1813. Part of the castle is now a parador. The neighboring 14th-century church of **Santa María la Real** has a Renaissance altarpiece and sculpted doorway. Olite's other medieval church, **San Pedro,** has been altered but still has a Romanesque doorway. From Olite, it's a 19-mile (30 km) drive to the **Monasterio de la Oliva** (*Tel 948 72 50 06*). This was one of the first monasteries built by French Cistercian monks (see p. 151) outside their country. The 12th- to 15th-century church and cloisters have a striking purity of style.

113 C5 **Visitor information** ✉ Galerías de la Plaza Carlos III el Noble, Olite ☎ 948 74 17 03

ORREAGA (RONCESVALLES)

This mountain pass in the Pyrenees has a special place in history and poetry: It was here that the Navarrese Basques unleashed their terror on the rearguard of Charlemagne's army in A.D. 778.

Over the centuries, thousands of pilgrims trudged through the pass on their way to Santiago de Compostela (see pp. 90–93). Landmarks include a 12th-century **hostelry,** the over-restored **collegiate church,** and its Gothic **chapterhouse,** which contains the tomb of Sancho VII (1154–1234) beside his queen. Don't miss the **museum** (*Tel 948 76 04 80*) in the old stables. Among other wonderful things it contains is an emerald from a Sultan's turban, worn during his last fatal battle against King Sancho at Navas de Tolosa in 1212, and a 14th-century enameled reliquary dubbed **"Charlemagne's chessboard"** because of its checkered design. From the village, you can walk up an easy trail to **Puerto Ibañeta,** the top of the pass (3,466 feet/1,057 m), for good views.

113 D5 **Visitor information** ✉ Antiguo Molino ☎ 948 76 03 01

TUDELA

Navarra's second largest city lies at the center of a fertile agricultural region, the source of Tudela's hearty vegetable soup and its robust red wine, la Ribera. Tudela was ruled by Moors for several centuries and developed intellectual and religious tolerance. The old Moorish quarter, the **Morería,** is an atmospheric labyrinth of winding lanes lined with Mudejar-style houses; also here is the 12th- to 13th-century **catedral,** built on the site of a mosque. Its carved **Portada del Juicio** (Last Judgment doorway) fronts a Romanesque-Gothic interior, and the lovely cloisters have columns carved with numerous biblical scenes. Tudela's patron saint, Santa Ana, is honored in an exuberantly decorated baroque side chapel.

Nine miles (15 km) northeast of Tudela is a desert-like region, the **Bardenas Reales,** where ocher-colored rocks have been eroded into extraordinary forms. The best way to see them is by following a hiking trail (GR13) from the hermitage of **Nuestra Señora del Yugo,** 1.8 miles (3 km) north of Arguedas on NA134.

113 C4 **Visitor information** ✉ Plaza Vieja 1, Tudela ☎ 948 84 80 58 ∎

The rolling landscapes of Navarra end at the Pyrenees.

Spain's Rioja wine tastes soft, full, and warm, with a hint of vanilla.

La Rioja

The word "Rioja" means one thing only to most non-Spaniards—Spain's most prestigious and internationally famous wine. But this small province of 1,950 square miles (5,000 sq km) sandwiched between Navarra and Castilla y León has a lot more. A combination of mountains, fertile farmland, and a mild climate has given rise to a cheerful, generous-hearted population and a rich, delicious cuisine. In between hearty Riojan meals you can explore historic monasteries, churches, and other religious sites.

The Ebro River marks the northern border with Euskadi (Basque Country), although vineyards continue in the Rioja Alavesa on the Basque side. An Ebro tributary, the Río Oja, gave the province its name, and it is along the Ebro's fertile banks that Rioja's main towns are sited: Logroño, the modern provincial capital, Calahorra, and Haro, the center of the wine industry. To the south loom Rioja's two mountain ranges, the Sierra de la Demanda and the Sierra de Cameros. This mountainous area is the Rioja Alta—Upper Rioja, as opposed to the flatter Rioja Baja in the northeast—with skiing, mountaineering, hunting (red and roe deer, wild boar), and fishing (river trout, crab, and carp). Low-key spas have grown up around the therapeutic springs at Arnedillo and Arnedo to the east on the bank of the Río Cidacos. The peaks have snow from late October until May and good hiking the rest of the year.

The Rioja Alta also has hermitages, churches, and monasteries. The Way of St. James (see pp. 88–89) runs north of the sierra (now the route of the N120), and sites here include the magnificent cathedral of Santo Domingo de la Calzada and the monastery of Nájera. As you climb south into the sierra, churches and monasteries multiply. So do the flocks of sheep and cattle—Rioja's cuisine is largely meat based, with succulent lamb the main specialty. Vegetarians won't go hungry: The Ebro valley produces abundant artichokes, asparagus, peppers, and beans, for the famous Riojan vegetable stew. The liveliest fiestas are Logroño's grape-picking festival in September, and Haro's Wine Battle every June 29, when the ammunition is Riojan wine. ∎

Sierra de la Demanda

Sierra de la Demanda
🅰 112 B5
Visitor information
✉ Calle Sagastia 1,
Ezcaray
☎ 941 35 46 79

Ezcaray
🅰 112 B4
Visitor information
✉ Calle Sagastia 1
☎ 941 35 46 79

**Santo Domingo de
la Calzada**
🅰 112 B5
Visitor information
✉ Calle Mayor 70
☎ 941 34 12 30

**San Millán de la
Cogolla**
🅰 112 B4
Visitor information
✉ Monasterio de Yuso
☎ 941 37 32 59

RISING TO OVER 6,500 FEET (2,000 M) IN WESTERN RIOJA and western Castilla y León, the Sierra de la Demanda is ruggedly beautiful. This is a place for hikers, and part of the western side is a nature reserve. The Way of St. James runs below the northern flanks.

Good walking trails on the Burgos (western) side start from the villages of **Pradoluengo, Pineda de la Sierra, Quintanar de la Sierra,** and **Neila.** The last gives access to the **Parque de las Lagunas Altas,** a series of high altitude lakes in stark, moody surroundings. The Riojan side is crowned by the pine forests of **San Lorenzo** (7,450 feet/2,271 m) and the ski-resort of **Ezcaray,** also a hub for Spanish hunters. The nature reserve of rivers and forest, which covers 200,800 acres (81,270 ha) has wolves, deer, mountain cats, eagles, and wild boars.

Beneath the northern flanks is the pilgrimage town of **Santo Domingo de la Calzada,** situated where a Riojan holy man, Domingo, built a hospice for pilgrims. The Romanesque catedral

was completed shortly before his death in 1109. The ornamental baroque steeple (1765) that rises 230 feet (70 m) above the cathedral is actually the third version. Inside the cathedral is its oddest feature, a late-Gothic **henhouse,** where a white cock and hen are kept to remind worshipers of a miracle that took place here: A roast chicken jumped up and crowed to prove the innocence of the pilgrim hanged for stealing it (the pilgrim was also revived).

Across the nave, look for the side chapel holding the stunning **main altarpiece,** moved in 1994 to uncover the Romanesque chapel that it concealed. The altarpiece is the last work of the prolific sculptor Damián Forment (circa 1480–1540), and is unique in its profuse depiction of mythological and fantastical figures. The sensitive polychrome painting of this 42-foot (13 m) masterpiece is by Andrés de Melgar. The restored early 14th-century cloisters and Sala Capitular are now a **museum** *(Closed Sun.)*, with treasures such as three Flemish triptychs and mid-17th century Mexican silver. In the Sala Capitular the coffered ceiling and **choir stalls** (1668) were carved by Santiago Allona and his son, Juan Baptista.

Southeast of Santo Domingo is **San Millán de la Cogolla,** named for the sixth-century Benedictine hermit whose legendary posthumous appearance on a white charger halted the Moorish advance against the Christians of this region. Pilgrims on their way to Santiago would make a detour into the hills between Nájera and Santo Domingo de la Calzada to pay homage to him at two monasteries 1.5 miles (2 km) apart. The tenth-century Mozarabic **monastery of Suso** is a pretty, tiered structure *(Tel 941 26 06 65,*

The monastery of la Valvanera sits in a high, wooded valley.

The festival of "100 maidens" at Santo Domingo

closed Mon.), built above the cave where San Millán had his retreat. It is now undergoing extensive restoration to its graceful horseshoe arches, Visigothic capitals, and the alabaster tomb of the saint himself.

In complete contrast, the much larger **monastery of Yuso** *(Tel 941 37 30 49, closed Mon., Oct.–May, guided visits only)* in the valley below, also inspired by San Millán, is a massive 16th- to 18th-century hulk, but it's a popular Sunday outing for Riojans, and the Benedictine monks are investing nearly two million dollars to convert part of the monastery into a hotel. The church itself is an unsuccessful mixture of styles from Renaissance to baroque, but the monastery **treasury** has exceptional pieces, including two carved ivory reliquaries and 12th-century processional crosses. The **library** contains one of Spain's best monasterial collections of medieval books.

Due south of here, over the sierra, lies the **Monasterio de la Valvanera** *(Tel 941 37 70 44, closed Dec. 20–Jan. 7).* Part of its attraction is the access along the winding LR113, which follows every bend of the Río Najerilla. A narrow turnoff snakes 3 miles (5 km) up through oak and beech forest to this peaceful monastery perched on the hillside with terraced vegetable gardens below. Dedicated to Santa María, the patron saint of Rioja, it was rebuilt in the 15th century after the original tenth-century structure burned down, but the lofty vaulted church still contains the precious 12th-century **sculpture of the Virgin Mary.** It is in Byzantine style and was allegedly carved out of an oak tree by a repentant thief. Climb upstairs behind the altar to see the back of the statue. Downhill is a little stone hermitage and the fountain of **Fuensanta.** ∎

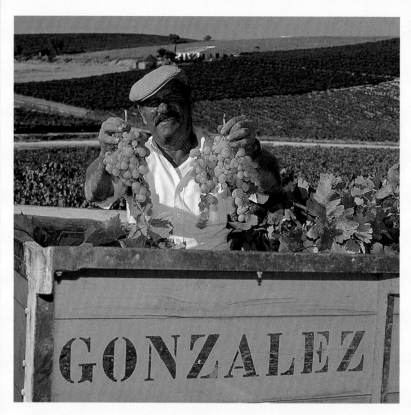

A Spanish wine renaissance

Spanish wines are undergoing huge changes. Winemakers are using innovative techniques to produce a delectable and highly diverse range that is causing concern among Europe's other big producers. About 1.5 million acres (600,000 ha) of vineyards make Spain the country with the largest productive area, and it is the world's third largest producer after France and Italy. From sparkling cava to smooth Riojan vintages, full-bodied Ribera del Duero, and light, fruity Galician whites, the choice seems endless. Spain now has more than 50 official wine-producing areas, each one a Denominación de Origen (D.O.) that may be further diversified by specially selected Reservas or Gran Reservas.

Spanish winemaking dates back to the Phoenicians in Cádiz and to the Romans' need to fuel their legions. According to Roman chroniclers Pliny and Martial, the wine of Tarragona vied with that of Sevilla as the finest wine of the Roman Empire. After centuries of Arab domination, production was revived by thirsty medieval monks and pilgrims on the Way of St. James and was subsequently boosted by English merchants in Galicia and Jerez. The biggest impetus came in the 19th century when Bordeaux vintners, after using Riojan wines to strengthen their own, were ruined by the grape scourges of oidium and phylloxera. They set up in Rioja instead, where many of their companies still figure among the elite of today's producers.

One of the fundamental differences between French and Spanish wines is the Spanish system of aging. Whereas in France the consumer takes the risk by choosing and investing in young wines, in Spain it is the vineyard that selects wines deemed most promising for aging. Crianzas must be at least two years old and have spent a minimum of six months in an oak cask. Reservas undergo a minimum of one year in an oak cask followed by two years in the bottle, and Gran Reservas require two years in oak casks followed by at least three years in the bottle. This long vigil in shady cellars at constant temperatures intensifies the character of each wine, as the wood adds aromatic qualities while its tannin is blended with that of the wine. For white and rosé wines aging periods are shorter, and oak is replaced by stainless steel vats.

Vintners are now experimenting with mixing native varieties of grapes such as Tempranillo, Garnacha, Cariñena, Palomino, and Albariño, with imported ones (Cabernet Sauvignon, Merlot, Pinot Noir, Chardonnay, Syrah), a system that was frowned upon until recently. A revolution in quality has swept Spanish vineyards since the 1980s, and greater

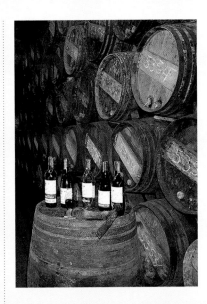

Grapevines are the mainstay of much of Spain's rural economy (left). Tourists taste wine at a bodega (below). A wine cellar in Haro, La Rioja's wine capital (above right)

use has been made of varieties that were once minorities—notably the Tempranillo grape. Although it has always been Spain's best-known variety outside the peninsula because of its primordial role in Riojan wines, it is no longer exclusive to that region. You now find it figuring in wines from Navarra to La Mancha and forming the basis for almost half Spain's Denominaciones de Origen. This has given rise to the following regional synonyms for cloned varieties adapted to local terrain: Cencibel, Tinto Fino, Tinta de Toro, Tinta del País, and Ull de Llebre. Although the grape is basically the same, wide variations in climate and soil produce quite different personalities.

An example of Spain's new wave wines is the denominación of Priorat, a region of Catalunya where winemaking dates from the 12th century. In the early 1980s, it was looking into an abyss of unproductive despair. Then a group of innovative young vintners came, attracted by the unique slate soil and steeply terraced terrain. For seasoned winemakers such as René Barbier, it provided a perfect combination of ancient Garnacha and Cariñena vines with soil that has no need of fertilizers or chemicals and that easily absorbs water. By introducing Cabernet Sauvignon, Syrah, and Merlot (and new French barrels), they were producing highly rated wines within a decade.

Other contenders in Spain's new wine stakes include Aragón's lesser known

Preparing barbecues for the feast cooked at Logroño's annual wine festival

Somontano. In the mid-1980s it was producing bulk wines for export, but it is now experimenting with international grape varieties that thrive in its relatively high terrain and cool night temperatures. Try an Enate label of the mid-1990s, and you are unlikely to be disappointed. Somontano's Chardonnays and Gewürztraminers are also gaining increasing recognition. Up-and-coming whites may be Rueda in Castilla, Penedés in Catalunya, and the fresh, crisp Albariño wine of Galicia's Rías Baixas. The latter, said to have originated in the Riesling grape brought by German monks in the 17th century, has reversed the previous reputation of Spanish white wines. ■

Laguardia

For aficionados of Riojan wines, one of the most atmospheric places to sample them is Laguardia. Although politically part of Euskadi (Basque Country), it produces Tempranillos flavored with Mazuelo and Graciano under the Rioja Alavesa label. Bodegas built into the walls of this fortified village give an atmospheric introduction to Spain's most internationally famous wine. ■

Logroño

THE PROSPEROUS RIVERSIDE CAPITAL OF LA RIOJA IS certainly not the most picturesque or historical town in the province, yet it has a dynamism and friendliness that make up for this.

Slicing through the center is the modern Gran Vía, which separates the new city to the south from the pedestrianized old quarter ending at the Ebro River. Just off the access road to the Puente de Hierro (iron bridge) you find Logroño's oldest church, **Santiago el Real** (*Barriocepo 6, closed except for Mass*), originally a Gothic structure but rebuilt in 1500. Look above the main portal for the **statue of St. James** astride a very chubby horse, slaying Moors. Opposite stands a 16th-century **pilgrims' fountain;** inside the single-naved church is a Renaissance **altarpiece.**

Logroño's cathedral looms a few steps away, **Santa María de la Redonda** (*Plaza del Mercado, closed p.m., may be closed for restoration*). The twin baroque towers, topped by storks' nests, can be admired from sidewalk cafés in front. The third church to see is **Santa María del Palacio** (*Calle Marqués de San Nicolás, 30, closed except for Mass*), remarkable above all for its soaring pyramidal spire, 146 feet (45 m) high. The old **pilgrims' hostel** stands close by on Ruavieja, Logroño's oldest street.

West of here, the **Museo de la Rioja** exhibits ecclesiastical art-work and 19th-and 20th-century paintings. Nobody should leave Logroño without touring the **Mercado San Blas** (*Plaza Espolón, corner of Calle de Sagasta*), a 1929 art deco market building that brims with La Rioja's finest and shiniest produce, which you can sample at restaurants and tapas bars in nearby Calle Laurel.

Logroño's grape-picking festival takes place in the second half of September, with bullfights, parades, and folklore. ∎

Logroño
🅜 112 B5
Visitor information
✉ Paseo del Espolón, Príncipe de Vergara 1
☎ 941 26 06 65

Museo de la Rioja
✉ Palacio del Espartero, Plaza de San Agustín
☎ 941 20 12 59
🕐 Closed Mon.
💲 $

More places to visit in La Rioja

CALAHORRA

The far east of Rioja province, known as Rioja Baja, is a fertile region of orchards, olive trees, and fields of vegetables watered by the Alhama and Cidacos Rivers. The Romans built a town and called it Calagurris, and by the fifth century A.D. it had gained episcopal status. The **catedral,** originally Gothic, has a neoclassic facade. The Renaissance cloisters now contain the **Museo Diocesano** *(Paseo de las Bolas 1, tel 941 13 00 98, closed p.m.).* The remains of the old Roman walls are most visible in the lower town near the church of San Andrés at the **Arco del Planillo,** the only surviving gateway. Go uphill from here on the Camino Bellavista for scenic views.

Rioja Baja also has Europe's largest number of **dinosaur footprints** *(ichnites).* The best place to see them is near the banks of the Cidacos at Enciso, about 22 miles (35 km) southwest of Calahorra.

113 C4 **Visitor information** ✉ Calle Angel Oliván 8 ☎ 941 14 63 98

HARO

Many of the world-famous crianza Riojan wines originate from the prestigious bodegas

The monastery of Santa María la Real in Nájera, a stop on the Way of St. James

of Haro, a strategic town on the banks of the Ebro, 22 miles (35 km) west of Logroño. Its economy blossomed with the growth of the wine industry in the late 19th century. Prosperity came fast and by 1890, Haro was the first town in Spain to install electric street-lighting. It has a few monuments: the flamboyant Gothic church of **Santo Tomás** *(Plaza Iglesia, tel 941 31 16 90, closed Sun. p.m.)* with its baroque altarpiece and plateresque facade, the elegant **Casa Consistorial** (1775) designed by Juan de Villanueva, architect of the Prado, and a former Augustinian convent (1741), now a hotel. The town makes an atmospheric setting for visiting bodegas, sampling Riojan cuisine, and enjoying the cafés and architecture of the sloping **Plaza de la Paz.** At the southern end of town, the **Museo del Vino** *(Calle Bretón de los Herreros 34, tel 941 31 05 47, closed Sun. p.m.),* has photographs and instruments to illustrate the latest processes of winemaking and aging. Captions are in Spanish, but an English translation is provided when necessary.

112 B5 **Visitor information** ✉ Plaza Monseñor Florentino Rodríguez, Haro ☎ 941 30 33 66

NÁJERA

This industrialized town was once the capital of the kings of Navarra and an important halt on the road to Santiago. The rather unattractive center conceals one architectural gem, the **monastery of Santa María la Real** *(Tel 941 36 36 50, closed Mon., Sept.–June, guided tours only).* Legend says it was founded in 1044 by King García Sánchez III after his falcon led him to a statue of the Virgin in a cave, but the present church dates from the mid-15th century. The **royal pantheon** is next to the cave and contains the tombs of kings of Navarra, Castilla, and León. The delicately carved sarcophagi of Doña Blanca de Navarra and Garcilaso de la Vega date from the 12th century. A 13th-century **statue of the Virgin** is at the center of the plateresque (see p. 45) altarpiece. Don't miss the masterly choir stalls (1495), or the lacelike stonework of the cloisters.

112 B5 **Visitor information** ✉ Calle Constantino Garran 8 ☎ 941 36 00 41 ■

Medieval lanes edged with half-timbered houses give old Albarracín a fairy-tale feel.

Aragón

Aragón has incredible diversity: the stark, snowcapped peaks of the Pyrenees in the north, rich green valleys, desolate sierra, and arid plains extending into the central meseta (plain). This vast area of 18,720 square miles (48,000 sq km), nearly one-tenth of Spain, harbors an abundance of artistic riches from Roman, Moorish, and medieval times, when the region reached its zenith.

Created in the 11th century and unified with Catalunya in 1150, the kingdom consolidated its power and influence under Jaime I (1213–1276), who drew even Naples, Sicily, and Sardinia into the Aragonese net. This lasted until 1469, when the marriage of King Fernando II of Aragón and Isabel of Castilla led to Spain's virtual unification.

One of Aragón's most outstanding characteristics is its high level of culture and tolerance, assets that led to a fruitful coexistence of Catholics, Jews, and Muslims until the days of the Inquisition. Out of this peaceful coexistence sprang the Mudejar architectural style (see p. 43). The province also has exceptional monasteries, just as diverse, from remote and rocky San Juan de la Peña to peaceful Cistercian-style Veruela. Even Zaragoza, the ungainly and industrialized provincial capital, has unique sights such as the Moorish Aljafería, two vast cathedrals, and several striking Mudejar towers.

The real magic of Aragón however lies in its small towns and villages, which may nestle in verdant valleys beside rushing streams, huddle in the shadow of a ruined castle, or look out over placid artificial lakes rimmed by sierra. Public transportation does not bring you easily to these places, so it is well worth renting a car and heading into the hills to explore the likes of the Sierra del Moncayo, south of Tarazona, the sleepy charms of Sos del Rey Católico, or the walled splendor of Daroca and Albarracín.

Aragón has excellent cross-country and alpine skiing from November to April, followed in the warmer months by canyoning (climbing up and down canyons), kayaking, and hiking. To finish off any day, the province also makes excellent wines. ■

Zaragoza

THE APPEARANCE OF THIS CITY OF MORE THAN 600,000 inhabitants is due to extensive reconstruction in the 19th century, after it was devastated by Napoleon's troops. Industry has played a major role, and unattractive outskirts sprawl over the Ebro River. Yet penetrate the center and you find wide boulevards and squares, a dynamic commercial life, and a large area of shady lanes.

Zaragoza
⚏ 113 D4
Visitor information
✉ Plaza del Pilar
☎ 976 20 12 00
Also information booths around city and tourist bus ($) making 14 stops along two different routes, July–Oct.

Zaragoza's history kicked off with the Romans, whose name for their settlement, Cesaraugusta, became today's Zaragoza. Remains from that time include the **Roman Forum** *(Plaza de la Seo, tel 976 39 97 52, closed Mon.)* in front of La Seo cathedral, and parts of the third-century A.D. wall on Avenida César Augusto. The next stage came in 714 when Zaragoza was conquered by the Moors, who remained here for four centuries. This period saw the city flourishing and becoming a cultural hub, of which the most outstanding monument is the beautiful Aljafería palace. Muslims, Jews, and Christians continued to coexist peaceably, leaving the skyline

spiked with Mudejar towers, until the Inquisition arrived (see p. 32). Zaragoza became capital of Aragón and continued to prosper, but half the population died in the Napoleonic siege of 1808–1809.

Zaragoza's two cathedrals rise over the vast, paved **Plaza del Pilar,** which lies between the old quarter and the river. The oldest and most interesting of the two, **La Seo,** dominates the eastern end. Its extraordinary mix of styles includes original 12th-century Gothic, later Mudejar, and finally 18th-century baroque of the ornate Spanish sort known as Churrigueresque. The gigantic edifice has been extensively restored and its interior gleams. The fantastic altarpiece was initially carved by the Catalan sculptor Pere Johan in 1434–1445, and 30 years later was reworked by Hans Piet d'Anso, a German sculptor who created the magnificent alabaster figures of the central panel. A Mudejar dome crowns the **Parroquieta,** a Gothic chapel in the chancel; also Mudejar is the northern brick facade inlaid with geometric ceramics, in high contrast to the 18th-century baroque of the main western facade.

At the back of La Seo is the entrance to the **Museo de Tapices** and **Museo Capitular** (Tel 976 29 12 31, closed Sun. p.m. & Mon.). This stunning collection of 60 tapestries, mainly 15th-century Flemish, is one of the best in the world. The huge, fine weavings measure up to 36 feet (11 m) in length, and are displayed beside beautiful antiques. Don't miss the **Arco del Dean** (Dean's Arch), four brick arches spanning the alleyway that were built in Mudejar style in the 16th century.

Dominating the northern flank of the Plaza del Pilar is the other cathedral, **Basílica de Nuestra Señora del Pilar** (Tel 976 29 12 31), a real hodgepodge of styles and materials built around a legendary pillar on which the Virgin Mary is said to have appeared to St. James in the year A.D. 40. This late 17th-century cathedral, crowned with incongruous tiled domes, has little of interest other than the huge **Capilla del Virgen** where the pillar and a statue of the Virgin are displayed in a niche. Her embroidered mantle is ceremoniously changed daily and she receives a constant stream of admirers, who kiss the pillar. Have a look, too, at the altarpiece carved by Damián Forment (circa 1480–1540) above the central high altar, and frescoes painted by the young Goya (see pp. 47–49) inside the cupolas.

Just east of the basilica and the 20th-century Town Hall stands one of Zaragoza's most important civic buildings, **La Lonja de Mercaderes** (Exchange Palace, tel 976 39 72 39, closed Mon.), a Renaissance building with Mudejar features that symbolized Zaragoza's influential economic role. Among Zaragoza's Moorish monuments, the jewel in the crown is the fully restored fortified **Palacio de la Aljafería,** which stands in isolation 2 miles (3 km) west of the old quarter. Originally built in the 9th century, it surrounds a central patio rich in carved stuccowork. The most exceptional sight is the **musallah,** an intimate mosque specially reserved for the emirs, which is a visual feast of Moorish fantasy and craftsmanship. After the Reconquest (see pp. 28–31), Fernando and Isabel could not resist using this stunning palace, and this is reflected in the decoration of the upper floor in Flamboyant Gothic style. ∎

La Seo
- ✉ Plaza de la Seo
- ☎ 976 39 38 56
- ⏱ Closed Mon. & Sun. p.m.

Palacio de la Aljafería
- ✉ Avenida Madrid
- ☎ 976 28 95 28
- ⏱ Closed Fri. a.m. & Thurs.
- 💲 $
- 🚌 Bus 23 from Plaza del Pilar

Zaragoza's prime attraction, the Palacio de la Aljafería has been used as a royal residence and as the seat of the Aragónese Inquisition.

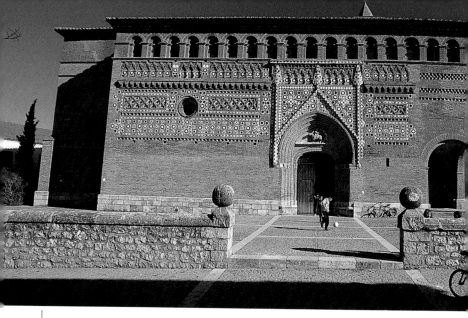

Mudejar towns

A UNIQUE FUSION OF ISLAMIC AND WESTERN STYLES developed in the wake of the 12th–16th-century Reconquest. This style was created by the remaining community of Arab craftsmen to meet the needs of Catholic Spain. Aragonese Mudejar is characterized by brickwork bell towers, decorated with glazed ceramic tiles.

Daroca
113 D3
Visitor information
Plaza de España 7
976 80 01 29

Tarazona
113 C4
Iglesias 5
976 64 00 74

Teruel
www.turismoaragon.com
113 D2
Tomás Nougués 1
978 60 22 79

The delightful little town of **Daroca** huddles beneath the roaring traffic on the N330 southwest of Zaragoza, but remnants of its Moorish origins are still very visible. It has an illustrious past: Symbolic of this is the ruined hilltop castle, originally an 11th-century Moorish fortress of which the keep, the **Torre del Homenaje,** remains, but subsequently much altered. Encircling the town below are 2 miles (4 km) of walls punctuated by towers and three surviving gateways *(puertas).* You can take a scenic three-hour walk around the walls starting at the **Puerta Alta,** climbing to the castle, then continuing round the northern and western perimeters to end at the crenellated and intricately worked **Puerta del Arrabal.** This walk gives wonder-

ful views over Daroca's pretty tiled roofs, pinkish stone houses, and verdant surrounding countryside.

Walk through the **Puerta Baja** to find atmospheric cobbled alleyways and graceful mansions. Also here is Aragón's first Mudejar tower, the belfry of **Santo Domingo.** The upper part was completed in the early 14th century by a Muslim mason, but when much of the church interior was destroyed by fire, the Gothic-Mudejar structure was replaced by 18th-century baroque. Next door is the **Museo Parroquial** *(Tel 976 80 07 61, closed Sun. p.m. & Mon.–Fri.),* displaying gold and silver plate made in Daroca beside other ecclesiastical objects. A few steps northeast is the stunning church of **San Juan,** begun in Romanesque style in the

12th century on the site of a mosque, and completed by Muslim craftsmen a century later with a flourish of Mudejar brick pilasters.

Northwest of Zaragoza lies **Tarazona,** the medieval home of the kings of Aragón. Between the 13th and 16th centuries Tarazona excelled in Mudejar craftsmanship, and numerous bell towers spike the clifftop site overlooking the Río Queiles. Of these, the one at the church of **La Magdalena** is particularly striking. The complex architecture of Tarazona's **cathedral** makes extensive use of brickwork and inlaid ceramic tiles beside its minaret-like belfry. Don't miss the **cloisters,** where niches are filled with delicate stucco tracery made in the 16th century. Tarazona's other curiosity is its arcaded old bullring, now transformed into a residential square, **Plaza de Toros Vieja.**

Southern Aragón's main town of **Teruel** has its own version of Mudejar towers: square in form, decorated with green and white glazed tiles, and sometimes incorporating a passageway at the base. Teruel stands on a high plateau, and its harmonious group is visible from miles around.

Teruel has five Mudejar towers, four of which are alongside equally exceptional churches. The most impressive are 13th-century **Torre de San Martín** (slightly leaning) and **Torre del Salvador,** both of which rise majestically over streets, leaving access through the arched base. The **catedral** *(Tel 978 60 22 75)* has a magnificent coffered ceiling painted with portraits, hunting scenes, and decorative patterns. The last tower of note, **Torre de San Pedro** is above the mausoleum of Teruel's star-crossed lovers, Diego de Marcilla and Isabel de Segura, the Aragonese Romeo and Juliet. Diego returned from his quest to make his fortune, to find Isabel had been forcibly married to someone else. He died of grief, and at his funeral Isabel kissed his lips and fell dead beside him. ∎

The square towers of Teruel's *parador* exemplify Mudejar architecture.

Huesca

Huesca

🅜 113 E4

Visitor information

✉ General Lasheras 5

☎ 974 22 57 78

Catedral

✉ Plaza de la Catedral

☎ 974 22 06 76

Iglesia de San Pedro El Viejo

✉ Plaza San Pedro

☎ 974 22 23 87

Huesca's cathedral mixes styles from the 13th to the 16th centuries.

THIS UNASSUMING TOWN IS IN FACT A MAJOR CROSSROADS of Aragón, the last of the plains before the momentous Sierra de Guara and the foothills of the Pyrenees. Called Osca by the Romans, Wasqa by the Arabs, and Vesca or Huesca in the local Iberian language, it reached its zenith in the Middle Ages when it was home to the royal court.

Particularly memorable was King Ramiro II (died 1137), formerly a monk, who, goaded by lack of support from his nobles, proceeded to decapitate them all. By 1354 Huesca had its own influential university, but decline followed and it was not until the late 19th century that its prosperity revived. Among its more illustrious recent sons are the artist Antonio Saura and the filmmaker Carlos Saura.

The **old town** lies on a hill at the center. Flanking the Plaza de la Catedral are the **Ayuntamiento** (Town Hall), a striking example of Aragonese Renaissance style, and the **catedral.** This towering 13th-

to 16th-century structure has an ornately carved **portal** (1302) sheltered by a wood and tiled gable that is typical of Aragón (added in 1574). The interior is Gothic and austere, but with an alabaster altarpiece (1533), intricately carved by Damián Forment (circa 1480–1540) with scenes of the Road to Calvary, the Crucifixion, and the Descent from the Cross. Another exceptional alabaster altarpiece is in the cathedral's **Museo Diocesano** *(Closed Sat. p.m. & Sun.);* this one, dating from 1512, is by Gil Morlanes el Viejo.

More poignant still is Huesca's oldest church, **San Pedro El Viejo,** a real marvel of Romanesque style with a beautifully restored cloister, where King Ramiro II spent his final years in retreat. Started in 1116 on the site of a Visigothic church, San Pedro has a fortresslike tower that was once much higher. Inside, it is severe and usually rather dark, but you can see beautifully restored late 13th-century **frescoes** and several impressive Renaissance **altarpieces.** The Romanesque capitals crowning the pillars of the cloisters are carved with themes ranging from the life of Christ to the conquest of Huesca, featuring apocalyptic monsters, devils, musicians, and dancers. Don't miss the **San Bartholomé chapel,** reached from Calle de Cuatro Reyes, where Ramiro II lies in a Romanesque alabaster sarcophagus opposite Alfonso I. ■

Jaca

LYING IN THE SHADOW OF THE PYRENEES AT AN ALTITUDE of 2,690 feet (820 m), the lively little town of Jaca is Aragón's prime base for winter skiers, with plenty of bars, hotels, and restaurants. If you come from the south, you notice a distinct change in architectural style, with timbered chalet-style interiors and high-gabled houses.

Jaca is well organized for outdoor pursuits, with mountain guides, adventure sports agencies, hunting and fishing equipment, and buses to ski resorts. The town was the first capital of the kingdom of Aragón, and the gateway for the French Romanesque style (see pp. 43–44) that was to spread across northern Spain to Santiago de Compostela. Aragón's first king, Ramiro I, commissioned the **catedral** *(Calle del Obispo, tel 974 35 51 30)*, built 1076–1130. Unusually, it is not easy to find as the low structure is tucked away in Jaca's narrow streets. The Romanesque portal, with its capitals and complex stone carving shaded by a carved wooden Aragonese overhang at the base of a squat stone tower, is obvious. Inside the Gothic style wins, sometimes rather florid, for example at the doorway to the cloisters. These have been transformed into the exceptional **Museo Diocesano,** with Romanesque and Gothic frescoes transferred for conservation from remote village churches. Some are breathtaking, above all those from Bagües, and, together with remarkable 12th-century wooden sculptures, form a rare collection.

The otherwise unexceptional church of **San Salvador y San Ginés** *(Calle Mayor, ask for key at adjoining Benedictine convent)* holds the exquisitely carved sarcophagus of the Infanta Doña Sancha, sister of Sancho Ramírez.

Jaca's pride and joy is the late 16th-century **Ciudadela** with its moated-and-walled exterior, the only one still standing in Spain. ∎

The cloisters at Jaca cathedral now function as a museum of frescoes collected from abandoned chapels in the Pyrenees.

Jaca
🅐 113 D5
Visitor information
✉ Avenida Regimiento de Galicia 2 (corner of Paseo de la Constitución)
☎ 974 36 00 98
🕐 Closed Sun. p.m.

Drive: Castles & eyries

Drive through wheatfields and pine forests to see stunningly sited relics of Aragonese history—both religious and royal—before ending at the influential monastery of San Juan de la Peña.

Leave **Huesca** by following signs to Iruña (Pamplona) (A132) as far as Esquedas, where a signed turnoff to the right leads across farmland to the hill village of **Bolea** ❶. Once under Muslim tutelage, it was reconquered by Pedro I of Aragón in 1101 and was important until the 18th century. Turn into the village and drive up to park on the main square. Walk up to the **Colegiata** (*Tel 974 27 23 77*), a Renaissance church built on the ruins of an Arab castle in 1556. Inside is a main altarpiece of 77 paintings by the anonymous "master of Bolea," with carvings and sculpture by Gil de Brabante. The altar of Santiago (1530) is attributed to the prolific Damián Forment (circa 1480–1540). Just downhill is the church of **San Tomás** (*Closed except Sat. p.m. & Sun. p.m.*), with an old covered fountain in the garden at the back.

Leave Bolea by the same road, then turn right at a junction below the village, following signs to Loarre. The road begins to wind through the hills, passing the occasional shepherd and his flock, fruit orchards, and wheatfields. After 5 miles (8 km) a signed turnoff to the right twists precipitously up to **Castillo de Loarre** ❷ (*Tel 974 38 26 27, closed Mon.*), a dramatic walled-and-turreted castle perched on a towering rock. Built on Roman walls in the 11th century by the king of Navarra, Sancho Ramírez, it may be the oldest castle in Spain, and was used both as a fortress and royal palace. Exploring it entails climbing narrow staircases in the three towers and crossing ruined ramparts, but it is well worth the effort. The beautiful **Romanesque chapel** is in excellent condition.

Drive back down to the village of Loarre, skirting around it to rejoin the main road (A1206) where you turn right. Continue 4 miles (6 km) to Ayerbe, where you turn right on the A132 (direction of Iruña/Pamplona). Soon, on your right, the intriguing sculptural forms of **Los Mallos** ❸ come into sight. These pink, eroded cylindrical rocks dominate the landscape for several miles. For a close view turn right to the village of Riglos, just after the village of Concilio, which nestles at the foot of these startling formations. Return to the A132, which runs through a gorge next to the torrential waters of the Río Gállego, passing the pretty village of Murillo de Gállego, before crossing a bridge over the **Embalse de la Peña** (reservoir). Immediately after, take a right turn marked San Juan de la Peña to embark on a long and winding road (A1205), which, after running parallel to the reservoir, soon starts climbing through beautiful wild pine forests. You may see falcons and eagles soaring above. After 21 miles (34 km), at the village of Bernués, turn left, again following signs to San Juan de la Peña. The road twists upward for 11 miles (18 km) until it finally reaches the grounds of the **Monasterio de San Juan de la Peña** ❹ (*Open May–Sept. & Easter Week*)

The grounds are a highly organized park with hiking trails, a small bar, and picnic tables in front of the partly ruined 18th-century monastery. It makes an ideal place to stop for lunch. You can walk or take a bus half a mile downhill to the much older original **monastery,** set under an enormous projecting rock reminiscent of Buddhist rock temples in India. Although only about a quarter of the original structure remains, this monastery (founded in 1025) has frescoes, an open-air **cloister** with superb capitals sheltered by the rock, the sarcophagi of Aragonese kings (the last, Pedro I, was buried here in 1104), a pantheon of nobles, and a vaulted **Romanesque church.** Much has been restored, but this has been done in a sympathetic way, and it remains an evocative and intriguing spot.

Leave the park by driving downhill past the old monastery (where parking is forbidden) and continuing 3 miles (5 km) to the N240 where you turn right to reach Jaca in 6 miles (10 km). ■

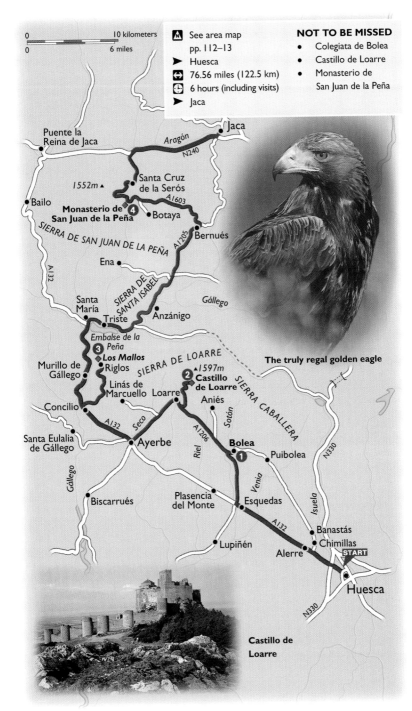

Symbol	Description
🔺	See area map pp. 112–13
►	Huesca
↔	76.56 miles (122.5 km)
🕐	6 hours (including visits)
►	Jaca

NOT TO BE MISSED
- Colegiata de Bolea
- Castillo de Loarre
- Monasterio de San Juan de la Peña

0   10 kilometers
0   6 miles

Puente la Reina de Jaca

Jaca

Aragón
N240

1552m ▲

Santa Cruz de la Serós
A1603

Bailo

Monasterio de San Juan de la Peña ④   ● Botaya

SIERRA DE SAN JUAN DE LA PEÑA

A1205

Bernués

Ena ●

A132

SIERRA DE SANTA ISABEL

Gállego

Santa María
Triste   Anzánigo

Embalse de la Peña

③ **Los Mallos**
Riglos

SIERRA DE LOARRE

The truly regal golden eagle

Murillo de Gállego

Linás de Marcuello   Loarre

▲1597m
② **Castillo de Loarre**

Aniés

SIERRA CABALLERA

Concilio

A132   Seco

Santa Eulalia de Gállego

Ayerbe

A1206

Riel   Sotón

Bolea ①   ● Puibolea

Gállego

Biscarrués

Plasencia del Monte

Venia

Esquedas

Isuela

N330

Lupiñén

A132

Banastás
Chimillas
START

Alerre

N330

Huesca

Castillo de Loarre

Pirineos (Pyrenees)

THIS IS THE PLACE TO COME TO ESCAPE ALL IMPRINTS OF modern civilization. The Pyrenees, and particularly the central section that lies in Aragón, have unadulterated wilderness beyond their tiny slate-roofed hamlets, spas, ski runs, and shepherds. This mountain range is Spain's natural barrier with France. Aragón has its highest peaks, the loftiest being Pico de Aneto (11,170 feet/ 3,404 m), and much harsher, more rugged landscapes than the Pyrenees in Navarra or Catalunya. Between the peaks lie wide valleys, lakes, gorges, sculptural limestone outcrops, and sparsely forested foothills. All these landscapes are encompassed by a national park, Parque Nacional de Ordesa y Monte Perdido. Its wild beauty is best in summer and fall. From October to May snow blocks the high roads and they are officially closed, leaving the terrain to climbers and cross-country skiers.

The lowland starting points for exploring these mountains are Jaca (see p. 145) in the west, Ainsa in the center, and Benasque, higher up in the east, near Parque Posets Maladeta. Outside the national park are villages where stone houses still have *cadieras* (wooden benches set around a cooking fire). The area used to be inaccessible, but tourism is making inroads.

PARQUE NACIONAL DE ORDESA Y MONTE PERDIDO

This 38,568-acre (15,608 ha) national park encompasses virtually every aspect of Pyrenean nature, and has unique species of flora and fauna. Rising over its northern perimeter is **Monte Perdido** (11,007 feet/3,355 m), a peak of sharply eroded limestone and glaciers. It overlooks the Ordesa valley, a canyon sliced by the Arazas River whose course is punctuated by waterfalls, notably **Cascada de Tamborrotera** and the 230-foot (70 m) **Cola de Caballo** (Horse's Tail). Beeches, maples, willows, and, higher up, silvester pines and firs are the dominant trees here. Eagles and vultures soar above and trout fill the water below.

This popular hiking area is easily reached by car from Ainsa via the pretty village of Torla. The road ends at Cascada de Tamborrotera, from where several hiking routes are laid out, the easiest along the river.

Parque Nacional de Ordesa y Monte Perdido
🅰 113 E5
Visitor information
✉ Plaza de la Catedral 1, Huesca
☎ 974 29 21 70

✉ Avenida Ordesa s/n, Torla
☎ 974 48 64 72

✉ Avenida Ordesa s/n, Broto
☎ 974 48 60 02

Aínsa
🅰 113 E5
Visitor information
✉ Avenida Pirenaica 1
☎ 974 50 01 27

Hikers' tips

Before embarking on any long hike, get reliable weather and geographical information from the nearest tourist office or visitor center. The Pyrenees are notorious for potentially dangerous storms and rising river levels. In a storm, do not stay on ridges or isolated outcrops, nor shelter under trees.

Be prepared for cooler temperatures as you rise in altitude, but remember that in summer the karstic (limestone) surrounds increase the aridity of the air, so take plenty of water. Start early, not only to catch the good morning light, but also to grab space at official parking lots. ∎

The region's loveliest town, Aínsa was the capital of the ancient kingdom of Sobrarbe.

Detailed route maps are available at the visitor center and cover more strenuous hikes such as the one to **Circo de Soaso,** a full-day trek with steep climbs and fantastic panoramas. Camping in small tents is allowed, but only at the four camping grounds. Refuge huts also provide for overnight treks.

To the east of this valley on the other side of the mountains is the **Cañon de Añisclo,** reached by car from Aínsa via Bielsa. This is a much narrower gorge than Ordesa, and has sheer cliffs striped with gray and red-ocher strata. The walk beside the Río Vellos (allow about five hours) is not difficult and takes you through woods of ilex and beech. Farther east still, on the edge of the park, is the **Valle de Escoaín,** best reached from Revilla

on a turnoff from the A138. You can follow a trail from Revilla down to the Río Yaga, and see the village of Escoaín across the river, high up on the flanks of Mt. Castillo Mayor.

From Bielsa it is also well worth driving beside the Río Cinca to the **Balcón de Pineta,** near the parador (state-run hotel) at the base of Monte Perdido. The views from here are quite spectacular. Beyond lie the French Pyrenees: You can reach them through the **Bielsa tunnel,** 7 miles (11 km) north of Bielsa.

AÍNSA & BENASQUE

The charming old town of **Aínsa** stands on a promontory at the meeting point of the Cinca and Ara Rivers, and of two main roads that twist up through the mountains—

Skiers revel in the slopes of the Pyrenees during the winter months (above). A golden eagle, one of Ordesa's specialties (below)

Benasque
🗺 113 F5
Visitor information
✉ Calle San Pedro
☎ 974 55 12 89

the A138 to France and the N260. The latter curves through stunning landscapes around the southern edge of Ordesa National Park. Aínsa's houses of golden stone, brimming with geraniums, surround the arcaded, cobbled Plaza Mayor, which is overlooked by the 12th-century church of **Santa María,** a lovely example of Aragonese Romanesque.

Benasque lies farther north and west, in a striking setting at 3,743 feet (1,138 m). The wide Benasque valley opens out at the base of the rugged Maladeta range that includes the Pyrenees' highest

peak, **Pico de Aneto,** with the popular ski resort of Cerler on its slopes. Benasque is a favorite hiking destination, but you should also take a stroll around the old quarter, which is lined with elegant mansions. Immediately west, trails lead into the **Parque Posets Maladeta,** surrounding the Pyrenees' second highest peak, **Pico de Posets** (11,060 feet/ 3,371 m). Lakes abound in this area. To the south, the Ésera River enters the dramatic **Congosto de Ventamillo,** 2 miles (3 km) of sheer limestone cliffs. ∎

Pyrenean wildlife

Parque Nacional de Ordesa y Monte Perdido has examples of all the wildlife that haunts these imposing rocky mountains. The rarest of them all, the Pyrenean ibex, once inhabited the higher slopes but was officially declared extinct in January 2000. You may still spot marmots, chamois (a goat-like antelope), foxes, and mink. The cold rivers have otters, trout, and

the Pyrenean newt. Among 65 species of birds nesting here are golden eagles, bearded vultures, lioned vultures, various sorts of falcon, and capercaillies (a large form of grouse). The 1,500 species of Pyrenean flora are a delight, especially in May and June when the snows have melted and brilliantly colored primulas, edelweiss, and gentians carpet the slopes. ∎

Cistercian monasteries

THE CISTERCIAN ORDER CAME TO NORTHERN SPAIN FROM
France in the mid-12th century to build a series of monasteries in iso-
lated sites. Cistercians devoted themselves to God and physical work.
Their architecture is suitably devoid of decoration.

One of Aragón's most beautiful
parks harbors the remains of the
Monasterio de Piedra, a
Cistercian abbey built with the
stones of a Moorish castle. It lies
near the village of Nuévalos about
75 miles (120 km) southwest of
Zaragoza. The monks remained in
this verdant oasis for 640 years,
until the closure of monasteries in
1835. Since then, Piedra has been
privately owned, and the monastery
has lost all sense of spirituality. It
has been converted into a hotel
with a motley assembly of wine
museum, restaurants, and carriage
collection. The vast **church ruins,**
open to the sky, are nonetheless
impressive, and the surrounding
park (well organized for visitors) is
a magnificent mixture of waterfalls,
lakes, grottoes, and woods.

The beautiful **Monasterio de
Santa María de Huerta** lies to
the west, just over the border of
Castilla y León, but it is best visited
together with other Aragonese
sights. Founded in 1162, it was
inhabited continuously by monks
until 1835, and was reestablished in
1930. The first sight as you enter is
the 16th-century **cloister,** now the
monks' quarters. Next are the older
Gothic cloister and, behind, the
refectory and enormous
kitchen. These two rooms give
you a wonderful picture of monastic daily life: You can imagine
monks eating in silence while lis-
tening to texts being read from the
carved stone pulpit, or cooking
communal meals in the central
oven of the kitchen. On the other
side of the cloister is the **church,**
whose original purity was enlivened
by frescoes (1580) by Bartolomé
de Matarana, and gilded baroque
altarpieces. The monks' shop sells
homemade cakes and liqueurs.

Ten miles (16 km) south of
Tarazona (see p. 143) in the verdant
Huecha Valley is the fortified
Cistercian **Monasterio de
Veruela** (1171–1224). The vast
Romanesque and early Gothic
church has an unusual green-and-
blue **tiled floor** beneath its massive pointed vaults, and the ornate
14th-century **cloisters** writhe
with carvings of gargoyles, plant
motifs, and human heads. The
chapterhouse, a more perfect
example of Cistercian sobriety, contains the tombs of early abbots. ∎

**Monasterio de
Piedra**
www.sta.es/monastpiedra
⊠ 113 C3
✉ Nuévalos
☎ 976 84 90 11
$ $ (monastery); $$
(monastery & park)

**Monasterio de
Santa María de
Huerta**
⊠ 113 C3
✉ Santa María de
Huerta (Soria)
☎ 975 32 70 02
$ $

**Monasterio de
Veruela**
⊠ 113 C4
✉ Vera de Moncayo
☎ 976 64 90 25
🕐 Closed Mon.
$ $

**Monasterio de Santa
María de Huerta**

More places to visit in Aragón

ALBARRACÍN

Lower Aragón's most spectacularly sited town lies 28 miles (45 km) west of Teruel in the arid Sierra de Albarracín overlooking the Guadalaviar River. If you are in Teruel, this is an essential detour. Albarracín has been declared a national monument, and restoration work has been sensitive. The ruined, turreted **ramparts** were originally built by the Moors in the tenth century. They are visible from miles away. In the center of the town, cobbled medieval streets twist up past pink, part-timbered houses with projecting upper stories and tiled roofs, then go through archways to eventually reach the Renaissance **cathedral** (*Tel 978 71 00 84, guided tours*). The cathedral museum has 16th-century Flemish tapestries and beautiful liturgical objects. Around Albarracín are pine forests with good walks, and you can see prehistoric

Albarracín's walls date from the 10th-century Moors.

rock paintings 3 miles (5 km) southeast of town toward Bezas.
◢ 113 C2 **Visitor information**
✉ Diputación 4 ☎ 978 71 02 51

ANSÓ

One of the prettiest Pyrenean towns lies in splendid isolation in northwestern Aragón, just 5 miles (7 km) from the border with Navarra. This remoteness led to Ansó's inhabitants developing their own dialect and traditions. The small **Museo Etnológico** (*Inside church, tel 974 37 00 22, closed Oct.–May*) tells you more. Ansó is in a valley between the equally attractive **Valle del Roncal,** to the west, and **Valle de Hecho,** to the east. **Hecho** (4 miles/7 km from Ansó) is a lovely town, though somewhat marred by its popularity, and from there you can take an easy short walk to the **monastery of San Pedro,** in Siresa, in the hills to the north. This entire area is ideal for hikes.
◢ 113 D5 **Visitor information** ✉ Calle Sta. Bárbara ☎ 974 37 02 25 🕐 Closed winter

SOS DEL REY CATÓLICO

This walled town studded with towering gateways acquired its name because it was the birthplace of King Fernando of Aragón (see pp. 31–32). Sos is in the rather bleak Sierra de la Peña of northwestern Aragón, and you could include it when visiting the Monasterio de Leyre (see p. 128) and Sangüesa (Zangoza) (see p. 127) in neighboring Navarra. The road from the reservoir Embalse de Yesa (A1601, the route from Jaca) has beautiful scenery.

Sos was a medieval stronghold against the kingdom of Navarra, and its shady lanes wind along a strategic hilltop between two promontories. Crowning the eastern end are the ruins of the **castle,** and just below is the 12th-century church of **Sant Esteban.** Inside are amazing things: the late-Renaissance **Capilla del Pilar** (with a stunning baroque altarpiece), Mudejar floor tiles, a 12th-century statue of a swarthy Christ, and an eighth-century font. For a small fee you can visit the **crypt,** which has unusual frescoes (13th to 14th century) in Byzantine style and beautifully carved capitals.

Sos also has fine Renaissance houses: the **Palacio de los Sada** where Fernando was born, and harmonious mansions linked by arches around the tiny Plaza Mayor. A few steps north of here, off the Calle Pérez de Biel, the medieval **corn exchange** has graceful pointed arches and a stone well.
◢ 113 D5 **Visitor information** ✉ Emilio Alfaro 7 ☎ 948 88 85 35 🕐 Closed winter ∎

This proud, self-sufficient city exudes style. Gothic and early 20th-century architecture combine with sleek contemporary work, enticing shops both old and new, innovative museums, and great restaurants.

Barcelona

Gaudí's Sagrada Família

Barcelona

CATALUNYA'S VIBRANT CAPITAL ROOTED ITSELF IN THE GLOBAL PSYCHE with its spectacular staging of the Olympic Games in 1992, and since then it has not looked back. Before that, during the long gray years of Franco's dictatorship (1939–1975), it was a city struggling to keep its own culture and politics alive despite vindictive repression from central government. Today Barcelona is at the forefront of Spanish business, theater, and design while simultaneously the Catalan thrust for a separate identity.

Barcelona's wide historical heritage ranges from Roman ruins to state-of-the-art contemporary architecture, with a good dose of Gothic and *modernista* (Catalan art nouveau) in between. Twentieth-century greats such as Pablo Picasso, Joan Miró, and Antoni Tàpies each have their dedicated museums. The Gran Teatre del Liceu and Rafael Moneo's

Intricate and elaborate sculpture adorns the top of the Monument a Colom.

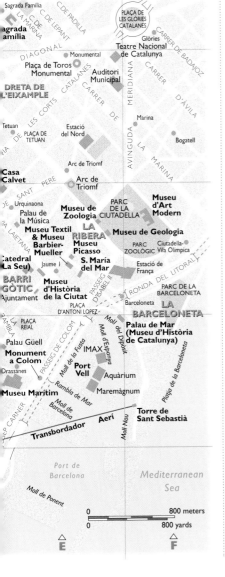

brand-new concert hall, the Auditori Municipal, stage memorable performances. For the visitor, the obvious place to start is the Barri Gòtic (Gothic quarter), where the cathedral, palaces, and museums all echo the zenith of Catalan trading prowess under Barcelona's powerful counts. In the 1990s the port area was transformed from a grimy, neglected network of streets into a glossy new window on culture and gastronomy overlooking the Mediterranean. The main artery in this area is La Rambla, a long avenue stretching from Plaça de Catalunya to the statue of Christopher Columbus on its column by the harbor.

West of the old town lies the grid of streets known as Eixample, developed in the late 19th century. Most of Barcelona's art nouveau monuments are here, standing beside the city's top designer shops and restaurants. This, too, is where you see the unmistakable spires of the Sagrada Família, Gaudí's masterwork, still under construction, and, farther inland, his fantastical Parc Güell. More of Barcelona's 40-odd museums lie in the lovely hilltop setting of Montjuïc, which you can reach via a breath-stopping cable car ride from the main harbor. Public transport, notably the metro, is very user friendly, restaurants are of high quality, and the surrounding hills and sea give a clear sense of the city's layout. Enjoy this culturally rich city and enter the heart of Catalan life. ∎

Catedral (La Seu)

Catedral (La Seu)

🅰 155 E3

✉ Plaza de la Seu

☎ 93 315 15 54

💲 $ (choir & elevator to rooftop); $ (chapterhouse museum)

🚇 Metro: Jaume I

THE IMPOSING FACADE AND SPIRE OF THIS MASSIVE cathedral may look Gothic, but they actually date from the 19th century when they were added to the existing 14th- to 15th-century structure. Luckily the original 1408 designs by Charles Galtès from Rouen were used, which ensured overall visual harmony. Before this Gothic edifice came into existence in 1298, the site was occupied by a Romanesque church, a mosque, and a Roman basilica.

Penetrate the interior and you are in a lofty single nave, whose vast space is broken midway by the elaborate choir. This, in turn, fronts stairs leading down to the **crypt.** Here in a low-vaulted chamber beneath the main altar stands the carved marble sarcophagus of Santa Eulalia, a locally born virgin martyr who was executed by the Romans in the fourth century and who subsequently became Barcelona's patron saint. From the sunken steps you have a magnificent view of the soaring vaulted ceiling supported by ribbed columns. The **choir** is among the cathedral's many masterpieces. Its white marble screen depicts Santa Eulalia's life (sculpted from designs by Bartolomé Ordóñez) and enclose beautifully carved Renaissance choir stalls. These were later decorated with the coats of arms of European kings.

No fewer than 29 side chapels line the nave and apse, nearly every one of them containing an altarpiece or sculpture of interest. On your immediate right as you enter the main doors is the large **Capella del Santíssim Sagrament,** whose 16th-century crucifix with its twisted Christ is alleged to have adorned the prow of Don Juan of Austria's flagship during the Battle of Lepanto (1571). In the opposite corner, a side chapel contains a huge marble font (1433) and a historic plaque recording the baptism of six Carib Indians brought back by Christopher Columbus in 1493.

At the back of the cathedral look at the first side chapel to the left of the altar to see the alabaster tomb of Ramon d'Escales, Count of Barcelona, sculpted by Antoni Canet in 1409. Farther around the ambulatory, **Chapel VI** contains a lovely 1390 painting of St. Gabriel on 18 panels, by Lluís Borrassa. Between these is the **Capella de Sant Benet,** dedicated to the Benedictine Order, which is celebrated by an altarpiece (1452) painted by Bernat Martorell. This corner of the apse also gives access to the elevator for the rooftop. Look for two surprisingly modest coffins attached to the transept wall that belong to Ramon Berenguer I (Count of Barcelona) and his wife.

Another surprise lies in store in the oasislike Gothic **cloister** (1498), which you can also enter directly from Carrer del Bistre through the Porta de Santa Eulalia: A gaggle of geese roams between a palm tree, potted plants, and a fountain mounted with a statue of Sant Jordi (St. George), Catalunya's patron saint. Huge vaulted chapels line the cloister, each dedicated to a saint, and the **chapterhouse** has a small museum. The purist font that stands in the lobby was salvaged from the original Romanesque cathedral. ∎

Recovering from history on the cathedral steps

Soaring rib vaulting leads the eye upward from the crypt.

Barri Gòtic walk

This walk takes you through the evocative narrow alleyways of Barcelona's oldest quarter, passing major monuments, such as the cathedral and medieval palace, while touching the pulse of the city.

Leave **Plaça Reial** by the northeast corner, Carrer del Vidre, and then cross Ferran to walk up the alley of Carrer d'en Quintana. Turn right into Boqueria and immediately left to emerge on Plaçeta del Pi. In front of you is the apse of **Santa María del Pi ❶** *(Open only for services)* and its 177-foot (54 m) octagonal tower. Walk around the church to the main plaza, backed by ornately decorated 18th-century houses, and admire the huge rose window. Turn into narrow, tile-studded **Carrer de Petritxol,** then right into Carrer Portaferrissa. Walk straight on to **Plaça Nova,** where the cathedral looms behind the Casa de l'Ardiaca (Archdeacon's house).

Turn right here, past remains of the Roman wall, into Carrer del Bisbe, where ahead of you is a surprising neo-Gothic **covered bridge** (1929) linking the medieval Casa dels Canonges (Canons' Residence) to the Palau de la Generalitat (Parliament Building). Turn right again into Carrer de Montjuïc del Bisbe to see the baroque church of **Sant Felip Neri ❷** on a delightful little square. In the

corner is the idiosyncratic **Museu del Calçat** (Shoe Museum, *tel 93 301 45 33, closed Mon.*), a must for shoe fanatics. Returning to Carrer del Bisbe, enter the **Catedral (La Seu) ❸** (see pp. 156–57) through the cloister doorway. Leaving the main door, turn right past the **Museu Diocesa** *(Tel 93 315 22 13, closed Mon.)* to walk beside a monumental section of the Roman wall and sections of the medieval royal palace that lead to impressive **Plaça Ramon Berenguer el Gran,** named after

> 🅼 See area map pp. 154–55
> ▶ Plaça Reial
> ↔ 1.25 miles (2 km)
> 🕘 1–2 hours (without visits)
> ▶ Plaça de Sant Jaume

NOT TO BE MISSED
- Catedral
- Museu d'Història de la Ciutat
- Museu Frederic Marès

A stamp and coin market adds to Plaça Reial's hubbub on Sundays.

the Catalan ruler who is honored by an equestrian statue. Turn right off the main avenue, Via Laietana, into Carrer Llibreteria, past a candlemakers' shop dating from 1761. Then turn right again into Carrer del Veguer, where you reach the **Museu d'Història de la Ciutat ❹** *(Plaça del Rei, tel 93 315 11 11, closed Sun. p.m., public holidays p.m., & Mon.).* This Museum of the History of the City overlooks the shadowy 14th- to 16th-century Plaça del Rei. Among the displays are Jewish and Arab artifacts, a large underground section showing Roman foundation walls and water channels, as well as Roman sculptures, the lovely 14th-century **Capella de Santa Àgata,** and, at the back of the square, the vast **Saló del Tinell,** a majestic construction of semicircular arches. Adjoining it is the five-story **Torre del Rei Martí:** Climb this for fine views of the entire Barri Gòtic.

On the left (southwest) of the square stands the Gothic-Renaissance palace used by Catalan viceroys. Walk around this to the back of the cathedral and turn right to reach Plaça de Sant Lu. In front is the **Museu Frederic Marès ❺** *(Plaça de Sant Lu, tel 93 310 58 00, closed Sun. p.m., public holidays p.m., & Mon.),* in the Romanesque-Gothic royal palace. This exceptional collection has Spanish sculpture from pre-Roman times to the 19th century. A section called the **Museu Sentimental** exhibits more everyday objects.

Return to Carrer Llibreteria and turn right to reach the administrative heart of Barcelona, the **Plaça de Sant Jaume ❻.** On the right is the **Palau de la Generalitat** *(Plaça de Sant Jaume, tel 93 402 46 00, open 2nd & 4th Sun. of month, & prearranged visits),* a 15th-century structure with a Renaissance facade, now home to the Catalan government. ∎

La Ribera & Carrer de Montcada

IF YOU ENJOY WANDERING THROUGH THE STREETS OF THE Gothic quarter, then neighboring La Ribera should prove equally fascinating. Through the district runs Carrer de Montcada, with wall-to-wall art galleries, craft shops, Gothic palaces, and museums.

La Ribera has been a residential quarter since medieval times. Any detour down its shady side streets takes you beneath balconies festooned with laundry, past neighborhood bars and Chinese-owned shops. Apart from Carrer de Montcada, it remains a blue-collar district. The entire port area used to look like this before it was transformed for the Olympic Games.

The **Museu Picasso** may not have the world's finest or most comprehensive collection of Picassos, but it certainly has the most illuminating. The richest sections here cover Picasso's burgeoning early years, his *Las Meninas* series, and his last burst of creativity, expressed in engravings. All this and more is displayed in the neighboring Gothic palaces of **Berenguer de Aguilar** and **Barón de Castellet.** Do not miss the vaulted arches linking the two palaces in front of the museum shop and café.

At the top of the beautiful courtyard staircase, the collection moves chronologically through Pablo Picasso's life (1881–1973), although unclear directions make backtracking inevitable. A long showcase displays his earliest work, including sketches he produced as a ten-year-old prodigy. Start at the far end and work back to see his lively imagination and academic prowess. Skillful life studies, portraits, and oil landscapes of A Coruña, painted when his family moved there from Málaga, demonstrate his early

application and humor (look for his self-portrait in a wig, 1897). These are followed by stylistic experiments, much influenced by a visit to Paris in 1900.

After a room devoted to his **Blue Period** (1901–1904), the collection leaps to 1917, when Picasso's artistic freedom was in full flower, then to his **Las Meninas series** (1957). These 57 oils, inspired by Velázquez's painting "Las Meninas" (see p. 67), are astounding in their deconstructed abandon. The last rooms on this floor display landscapes of Cannes and ceramics made at Mougins.

Upstairs is the masterpiece of Picasso's old age, **"Suite 156"** (1969–1972). A masterful series of engravings using every possible technique, this is the culmination of both his cultural inspirations and strong erotic impulses. The engravings are full of postmodern-style references to other artists (Degas, Rembrandt, Matisse, Ingres, Delacroix) while illustrating the voyeurism of the artist in front of his model.

Medieval Palau Nadal houses the **Museu Barbier-Mueller,** which has a choice collection of pre-Columbian art. Every exhibit is a masterpiece in perfect condition, and very well presented, so you have a real feast of the best of Latin America's indigenous cultures. Eight rooms on the first floor take you from Mesoamerica's mother culture, the Olmecs, through the classic period of Teotihuacán, the Aztec,

Museu Picasso
- 155 E3
- Carrer de Montcada 15–23
- 93 319 63 10
- Closed Sun. p.m.
- $
- Metro: Jaume 1, Line 4

Museu Barbier-Mueller
- 155 E3
- Carrer de Montcada 14
- 93 310 45 16
- Closed Sun.p.m., public holidays p.m., & Mon.
- $

Museo Textil i d'Indumentaria
- 155 E3
- Carrer de Montcada 12
- 93 310 45 16
- Closed Sun. p.m., public holidays, & Mon.
- $

The Museu Picasso in La Ribera district

feathered headdress, the fearsome, cross-eyed Maya mask of jade, and the strong geometry of Peruvian textiles.

In the adjoining Palau del Marquès de Lliό, the **Museu Textil i d'Indumentaria** grew out of several private collections of costumes and textiles, including that of the renowned couturier Cristόbal Balenciaga. Starting with Copt, Moorish, and Romanesque textiles, it ends with designs of the turn of the millennium.

At the end of Montcada you cannot miss the elegant Gothic church of **Santa María del Mar** *(Passeig del Born 1, tel 93 319 05 16),* funded by local sailors in the 14th century to rival the extravagance of the bourgeois cathedral. It has perfect proportions in its three soaring naves, the high altar separated by an open colonnade from the ambulatory with one statue spotlit on its pedestal. The 15th-century **rose window** above the western portal is a good example of Catalan Flamboyant Gothic. ■

Santa María del Mar, the seamen's favorite church

the Maya, as well as rare pieces from Costa Rica, Nicaragua, and Panama to South America. Chavin, Moche, Nazca, and Inca pieces represent Andean culture beside pottery from the Lower Amazon. Admire the complex Zapotec god in

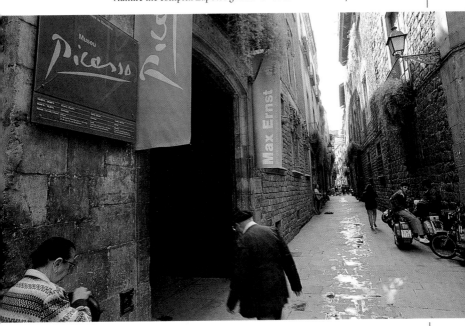

A walk down La Rambla

Soak up the many variations on Barcelona's 21st-century spirit by exploring the animated Rambla and its side streets. These harbor a wealth of historical and contemporary interest in an inspirational mix of styles.

With your back to the modern fountain **"Homenaje a Francesco Matia"** ❶ on the southwest corner of Plaça de Catalunya (*Visitor information, Plaça de Catalunya 17-S, tel 93 304 31 35*), cross to the central pedestrian walkway of **La Rambla.** This immediately gives you a taste of Barcelona's most famous avenue with sidewalk cafés, street performers, flower sellers, and people strolling. At the sign pointing to Anteneu, cross to the left and take a sharp left into the pedestrianized Carrer de Santa Anna. At No. 32, walk into the courtyard where the charming Romanesque church of **Santa Anna** ❷ (*Tel 93 301 35 76, open a.m. & 7-8.30 p.m.*) now stands jammed between 19th- and 20th-century buildings.

Retrace your steps to La Rambla. Cross to the other side, noting the ornate pharmacy, and walk down Calle d'Elisabets. This street crosses the Plaça del Bonsuccés before reaching a junction at Carrer dels Angels. Immediately visible on your right are the clean white contemporary forms of the **Museu d'Art Contemporani de Barcelona** or **MACBA** ❸ (*Plaça dels Angels 1, tel 93 412 08 10, closed Tues., www.macba.es*), a stone, glass, and metal-plated building designed by Richard Meier, which opened in 1995. The permanent collection starts in the late 1940s with artists such as Jean Dubuffet, Alexander Calder, and Marcel Broodthaers, and ends with contemporaries such as Christian Boltanski, Rosemary Trockel, Richard Long, and Jaume Plensa. Two floors are devoted to temporary exhibitions of the avant-garde.

From here, walk past the refurbished convent on the corner and turn right down tree-lined Carrer dels Angels until you come to Carrer del Carme. Opposite stands the massive Gothic-style **Hospital de Santa Creu,** which currently houses the **Biblioteca de Catalunya** ❹ (*Tel 93 317 07 78*). It is worth walking around to **Carrer de l'Hospital 56** to enter the courtyard and Gothic patio.

Continue across the pretty little square named for Alexander Fleming (the Scottish bacteriologist who discovered penicillin) and return to La Rambla. On your left is the rusticated baroque facade of the **Església de Betlem.** The interior of the church dates from a 1930s renovation after a fire and is of little interest. Turn right into the lively

View from the **Monument a Colom**

Rambla de Sant Josep, monopolized by a **bird market,** where caged parrots squawk beneath the chestnut trees.

You soon see on your right the imposing **Palau de la Virreina** ❺ (1778), whose baroque and rococo interior now hosts municipal exhibitions. Next comes the cornucopian **Mercat de la Boqueria** (also called Mercat de Sant Josep), where foodstuffs are sold beneath a wrought-iron and glass roof. Flower stands on La Rambla partly conceal a **Joan Miró design** on the central sidewalk as it widens into Plaça de la Boqueria. Look, too, at the tall, narrow building at **No. 77,** whose facade is decorated in art nouveau mosaics. Almost opposite is a kitsch example of the 1920s chinoiserie craze that bristles with dragons and parasols.

You have now reached **Rambla dels Caputxins.** On the right stands the **Gran Teatre del Liceu ❻,** Barcelona's most prestigious theater, reopened in 1999 after extensive renovation. After the Hotel Oriente turn right into Carrer Nou de la Rambla to see Gaudí's extraordinary **Palau Güell ❼** *(Carrer Nou de la Rambla 3, tel 93 317 39 74, closed Sun. & public holidays, guided visits only),* built 1885–1890. Back on La Rambla you pass the curved facade of the **Teatre Principal** (1847), opposite which stands a

statue of the founder of modern Catalunyan theater, Frederic Soler. You are now in the last stretch, **Rambla de Santa Mònica,** where the 17th-century **Convento de Santa Monica** hides behind the nondescript facade of a cultural center.

Cross over and walk back up La Rambla to No. 42 and enter a covered passageway crossed by a glassed-in bridge. This leads to the elegant mid-19th-century **Plaça Reial ❽,** where overpriced cafés overlook palm trees and lampposts designed by Gaudí. ■

Street performers on La Rambla captivate all ages.

🅜 See area map
pp. 154–55

► Plaça de Catalunya

🔁 1.75 miles (2.8 km)

🕐 1–2 hours (without visits)

► Plaça Reial

NOT TO BE MISSED
- Museu d'Art Contemporani de Barcelona
- Mercat de la Boqueria
- Palau Güell
- Plaça Reial

Waterfront

BARCELONA'S HARBOR WAS COMPLETELY TRANSFORMED in the 1990s and now bristles with marinas, leisure facilities, state-of-the-art museums, restaurants, and plenty of viewpoints. Alongside the spanking new is the illustrious old, nearly all of it connected with Barcelona's maritime history. The Aduana (Customs House), Capitania General (Naval Headquarters), and Gobierno Militar (Military Headquarters) line the harbor.

The Columbus Lookout or **Monument a Colom** *(Tel 93 302 52 24)* is no longer the tallest waterfront structure, but it is probably the most symbolic and makes a good starting point. Take the elevator up this 160-foot (50 m) iron column to join the statue of Christopher Columbus surveying the harbor. In front is the mooring for trimarans *(Las Golondrinas, tel 93 442 31 06)* that tour the harbor to the **Vila Olímpica.** You also look down on the world's largest **medieval shipyards,** a unique complex of 13th-century vaulted halls built around a central courtyard large enough to contain galleons. Luckily for Barcelona they were saved from demolition at the

last minute, and in their present spectacularly refurbished form they make a fitting background for the **Museu Marítim.** Model ships, paintings, prowheads, navigational instruments, maps, and charts illustrate Barcelona's maritime history and the Catalan sailing tradition. Exhibits also give a wider picture of the evolution of seafaring, ending with submarines before you are plunged into an aquatic virtual reality show. After this, you certainly need the café-restaurant, overlooking orange trees in the sunken entrance courtyard.

Another successful conversion houses the **Museu d'Història de Catalunya,** a lively chronological survey of Catalan history using

Museu Marítim

- 155 E2
- Avinguda de les Drassanes
- 93 318 32 45
- $
- Metro: Drassanes, Line 3

Museu d'Història de Catalunya

- 155 F2
- Palau de Mar, Plaça Pau Vila 3
- 93 225 47 00 or 93 225 47 26
- Closed Sun. p.m., public holidays p.m., & Mon.
- Metro: Barceloneta, Line 4

The panoramic view from the Mirador de Colom encompasses the modern marina.

interactive exhibits, information panels, charts, audiovisuals, photos, reconstructions, and models. Texts are in Catalan only, so most overseas visitors must borrow a translation brochure at the ticket desk. It is an illuminating display covering two remodeled floors of the 1900 **Palau de Mar,** the former main warehouses at the head of the Barceloneta wharf. The most interesting and complex section is on **Floor 2,** showing man's origins in Catalunya, the Iberians, and Romans. It also covers the short Moorish occupation and masses of information on medieval times and the Habsburg Empire. **Floor 3** moves into industrialization, urban growth, and the sociopolitical upheavals of the 20th century, ending with the new constitution of 1978. Don't miss **Floor 4,** where the café opens onto a terrace with fabulous port views.

A new boardwalk, **Rambla de Mar,** leads from the Monument a Colom across to **Port Vell** and the **Moll d'Espanya** (Jetty of Spain),

a large reclaimed area flanked by marinas and entirely devoted to entertainment and leisure. The Maremàgnum shopping mall and cinema complex jostle with the **IMAX theater** (Tel 93 225 11 11) and the **Aquàrium** (Tel 93 221 74 74), which has a special display of Mediterranean underwater life and a tunnel for viewing sharks.

La Barceloneta (Little Barcelona) lies between the main harbor and the Vila Olímpica, an 18th-century grid of streets that was traditionally the sailors' and fishermen's quarter. It has some very picturesque backstreets, and it's here that you'll find the beaches and cable car. On the seafront, 2.5 miles (4 km) of sandy beaches stretch northward. Beyond a few dilapidated harbor buildings to the south looms the rusty **Torre de Sant Sebastià** from where you can catch a cable car, **Transbordador Aeri** (Teleférico de Miramar, tel 93 430 47 16), over the harbor to Montjuïc (see pp. 168–69). ■

Catalan pride

At the heart of Catalunya lies Barcelona, "a city of merchants, conquerors and people of good upbringing, refined, well educated and luxurious…." Little has changed since these words were written in a 19th-century travel guide, and Catalunya still spearheads Spain's commercial development, culture, and cuisine. Pride is an integral part of the individualistic Catalan character, and it is manifest first in the language, which stirs Provençal French and Castilian Spanish into a unique cocktail peppered with the letter *x*, and secondly in a strong attachment to regional customs. Whether dancing the *sardana*, a slow-moving circular dance, or creating gravity-defying human pyramids (*castellers*), the six million or so Catalans have defied all attempts to quash their identity. Industrialized, hardworking, solidly white-collar, liberal, and anticlerical, they are very different from the fervent, fun-loving farmers of the south.

The Catalan flag flies high in Barcelona.

This individualism stems from the early ninth century when the French Holy Roman Emperor Charlemagne successfully besieged Barcelona, and then divided the surrounding land into feudal kingdoms ruled by counts. By the 12th century, Catalan had become a written language, and the word "Catalunya" was mentioned explicitly. For two centuries Catalunya remained at its zenith. Its seamen and merchants dominated trade in the Mediterranean, and citizens enjoyed a unique system of privileges. Although Catalan trading prominence was later usurped by Castilian and Andalusian monopolization of New World routes, Catalans never lost their strong sense of civil rights, something that has irritated every Madrid-based ruler since. The 19th and 20th centuries saw decades of industrial revolt and anarchism, and Catalunya was at its lowest ebb under General Franco's dictatorship (1939–1975), when the Catalan language itself was banned, as were books in Catalan and even the sardana.

Behind the scenes the radical spirit never died, and Catalan entrepreneurs now once more lead the way. Pragmatism (some would say mercantile obsession) is another enduring Catalan characteristic. Although one-third of Spanish wine is produced in Catalunya, it is textiles, chemicals, cars, and planes that form the backbone of the healthy economy.

Culturally, this region long dominated the Spanish avant-garde. Although Madrid and regional cities have caught up since the 1980s, Barcelona still boasts Spain's liveliest cultural calendar and a string of 20th-century luminaries. These examples have affected the activities of even the smallest Catalan towns. It is no surprise that Spain's greatest living writer, Juan Goytisolo, was born—where else?—in Barcelona.

Catalunya's geographical position has helped make it the most cosmopolitan of Spanish states. The proximity of France encourages high standards in gastronomy, art, and design, but French influence is tempered by habits that can only be termed Spanish, such as the relaxed post-meal chat (*sobretaula*), which can last several hours. On the table itself, refined, painstakingly prepared Mediterranean dishes are served with an elegant flourish, and restaurants may display audacious contemporary architecture and designer furniture. Innovation is an essential component in its identity. Catalan pride is seen as arrogance by some, but its record is nonetheless impressive. With six Catalan newspapers and three TV stations, it is unlikely to fade. ■

Gaudí's interpretation of the striped Catalan flag over the entrance to Palau Güell (above left); La Diada, the Catalan national holiday (above right); and dancing the Sardana (below)

Montjuïc

Montjuïc
 154 C1

**Museu Nacional
d'Art de Catalunya**
🅰 154 C1
✉ Palau Nacional, Parc
de Montjuïc
☎ 93 622 03 75 or
93 622 03 76
🕐 Closed Sun., public
holidays p.m., &
Mon.
💲 $
🚇 Metro: Espanya
Lines 1 & 3

**The core of the
Fundació Juan
Miró are the
artist's paintings,
textiles,
sculptures, and
drawings.**

EASILY ACCESSIBLE FROM THE CITY BELOW, MONTJUÏC (meaning "Mount of the Jews") is an essential destination for its cultural sites, pine trees, gardens, and panoramic views. This was the bucolic setting of the 1929 World's Fair, and in 1992 the stadium was remodeled for the Olympics.

You can reach Montjuïc by **cable car** from La Barceloneta (see p. 165) or by **funicular railway** (*weekends & public holidays only*) from Espanya metro station. Another cable car links the Montjuïc funicular station with the castle at the top of the hill, home to the **Museu Militar** (*Tel 93 329 8613*), with its displays of arms, uniforms, and suits of armor, and Montjuïc's best view.

Structures remaining from the 1929 World's Fair include the **Poble Espanyol** (*Avinguda Marquès de Comillas, tel 93 325 78 66*) with its lively nightspots and replicas of regional Spanish architecture, and the **Teatre Grec,** an open-air

theater used in the summer. The **Palau Nacional** was Spain's national pavilion. This extravagant building is now the **Museu Nacional d'Art de Catalunya,** which has the world's widest collection of Romanesque art, an equally impressive Gothic section, and the Cambó collection of Renaissance and baroque paintings.

Concentrate on the first two sections, respectively left and right of the entrance hall. The Romanesque part is largely composed of replicas of Catalan church interiors containing original frescoes and fragments that have been removed for conservation from the churches themselves. The exemplary display and multilingual explanations give clear indications of the location of each church or monastery and lead you around in chronological order. Also look for the late 12th century altar frontals, notably those from Avia and Baltarga. A diverse collection of capitals and sculptures completes this part.

The Gothic section, dazzling with gilt and multipaneled altar paintings, includes statues such as the graceful alabaster figure of Santa Elena and a row of lifesize saints by Pere Llobet (circa 1387). Look out for the fine double portrait of John the Baptist and St. Estève from Santa Maria de Puigcerdà (1445–1453), the room devoted to Bernat Martorell, and Jaume Huguet's magnificent paintings, including the St. Michael series from Barcelona's Santa Maria del Pi.

The Font Màgica performs a stunning display of color and light.

Pavelló Mies van der Rohe

www.miesbcn.com

- 154 C2
- Avinguda del Marquès de Comillas
- 93 423 40 16
- $
- Metro: Espanya Lines 1 & 3

Fundació Joan Miró

- 154 D1
- Parc de Montjuïc
- 93 329 19 08
- Closed Sun., public holidays p.m., & Mon.
- $
- Bus 50 or funicular

At the base of the wide steps to the Palau Nacional, beside the 1929 **Font Màgica** (Magic Fountain), stand the serene, purist forms of the **Pavelló Mies van der Rohe**—the pavilion designed by modernist architect Mies van der Rohe for the 1929 World's Fair. When the German government put it up for sale, no one reacted, so this masterpiece of international modernism was dismantled. In 1983 moves were made by the Mies van der Rohe Foundation to reconstruct it, and in 1986 the pavilion reappeared on its original site. Water is an essential element, and the inner pool comes to life with a copy of Georg Kolbe's sculpture "Morning." Inside are examples of the ubiquitous Barcelona chair.

Uphill to the east (nearer the cable car) from the Museu Nacional d'Art is the **Fundació Joan Miró.** One of the pleasures of this exhibition center is its architecture, the work of Josep Luis Sert in honor of his longstanding friendship with the Catalan artist Joan Miró (1893–1983). The foundation was set up by Miró himself in 1971 to conserve a body of his work for the public and to promote contemporary art. It retains its popularity thanks to excellent temporary exhibitions and a lovely setting overlooking the city. Sert's Mediterranean-style architecture creates free-flowing spaces with changing vistas and forms. The permanent collection is concentrated on the upper floor, leaving most of the ground floor for temporary exhibitions and services.

On entering, cross the courtyard to the back wing to see Alexander Calder's spellbinding **"Mercury Fountain,"** made in 1937 for the Paris World's Fair. Beside this are wonderful, playful Miró sculptures and a large room showing his early work from the 1930s and '40s, with the **"Constellations"** series. Take the ramp upstairs to see the main body of work from the 1950s to '60s. The last, equally revealing section is comprised of works donated by friends, from Henry Moore to Henri Matisse. Look for Arnold Newman's 1979 photograph of Miró, which spells out the intense humanity of this man. ∎

Gaudí's sculptural
chimneys on the
roof of La Pedrera

Eixample

THIS NEAT GRID OF STREETS, WHOSE NAME MEANS "NEW extension," dates from the late 19th century, when booming Barcelona expanded westward from the Barri Gòtic. It is the place to go for designer shopping, art galleries, and sophisticated dining.

Sagrada Família

🔺 155 E5

✉ Plaça de la Sagrada
Família

☎ 93 207 30 31

💲 $

🚇 Metro: Sagrada
Família, Line 2 & 5

**Casa Milà (Espai
Gaudí)**

🔺 154 D4

✉ Carrer de Provença
261–5

☎ 93 484 59 95

💲 $

🚇 Metro: Diagonal,
Lines 3 & 5

**Parc Güell & Casa-
Museu Gaudí**

🔺 154 D5

✉ Carrer d'Olot 7

☎ 93 424 38 09

💲 $

🚇 Metro: Lesseps,
Line 3

Chief among Eixample's architects is Antoni Gaudí (see pp. 173–75), and here you find his last and incomplete masterpiece, the unorthodox **Sagrada Família cathedral** (see pp. 174–75), and several other seminal buildings. The cathedral's multiple pinnacle steeples, permanently surrounded by cranes and a builders' site below, have become the emblem of Barcelona's individualism. Like it or not, the story behind the ambitious structure is one of an architect's total, and ultimately tragic, dedication to what he intended to be his greatest work.

Building started in 1882, but was interrupted by World War I. When Gaudí died in 1926, only the **Nativitat** (Nativity) **facade** was complete. Since then, work has continued sporadically, fraught by personality clashes, controversy, and,

above all, by a total absence of plans, as was Gaudí's modus operandi. In 1986 the **Passion** facade was commissioned from Josep Maria Subirachs, who added yet another thorny aesthetic issue with his stiff, unattractive sculptures.

Gaudí is buried in the **crypt,** where services are held, and a small museum relates the complexities of the cathedral's history and Gaudí's role. Best of all, for the moment, are the stunning views over the site and city from one of the steeples. An elevator takes you up.

Far more successful as a Gaudí memorial is **La Pedrera** (or **Casa Milà),** which lies ten blocks southwest in the heart of Eixample. This innovative block of flats was built in 1906–1912. On its vaulted top floor is the **Espai Gaudí,** a brilliantly conceived interactive display of Gaudí's designs, models, and inspiration. This gives access to the extraordinary and much photographed roof terrace crowned with organically shaped sculptures. The Caixa, the dynamic Catalan bank that runs the space, also organizes high-profile art exhibitions on the first floor (the adjoining gift shop and snack bar are excellent, too).

Other Gaudí designs that you can track down in the neighborhood are **Casa Batlló** (1906) at Passeig de Gràcia 43, **Casa Calvet** (1899) at Casp 48, the **Torre de Bellesguard** (1909) at Bellesguard 16–20, and **Casa Vicenç** (1888) at Carolines 24.

One of Gaudí's most colorful and expansive designs is **Parc Güell,** 1.5 miles (2.5 km) west of Sagrada Família at the foot of Mont Carmel, just outside Eixample. This massive project (1900–1914) was originally intended as a garden city for 60 houses, but when the plots did not sell, Count Eusebi Güell, the promoter who was also Gaudí's patron, allowed the architect to let his fantasies fly. The result is a labyrinth of textured viaducts, pavilions, stairways, fountains, benches, curved columns, and arches upon which he developed his characteristic use of randomly fragmented ceramics. The park structures are inspirational, but the **Casa-Museu Gaudí** (designed by Francesc Bereguer, and where Gaudí lived) is of less interest, displaying only limited furniture and drawings. Join a one-hour guided tour of the park at the ticket office to understand the concepts behind it all.

Antoni Tàpies (born 1923) is another Catalan artist with the status of a regional institution. He instigated the **Fundació Antoni Tàpies** (*Arago 255, tel 93 487 03 15, closed Mon.*) in 1984 to promote contemporary art, preserve

a representative body of his own work, and create an impressive reference library of modern and Oriental art. All this is installed in an extensively converted *modernista* building designed by Lluis Domènech i Montaner (1850–1923). ■

Casa Vicenç, by Gaudí

The Fundació Antoni Tàpies displays contemporary works in a modern setting.

Gaudí & modernism

Through his total dedication to organically inspired architecture, Antoni Gaudí (1852–1926) revolutionized architecture in Catalunya early in the 20th century. When art nouveau swept the Western world, the Catalan version, *modernismo,* became the most extreme form and Gaudí its most controversial and intuitively brilliant protagonist. He originated from Reus, near Tarragona, where he showed a precocious fascination with natural forms found in zoology, botany, geology, and anatomy. This, combined with a taste for craft techniques inherited from his father (a coppersmith), became the unifying thread running through his work. For Gaudí, structure was inseparable from form, color, and texture, a holistic approach inspired by the English Arts and Crafts movement. He transformed these ideas into reality with the assistance of architectural training and an enlightened backer.

Above: Ceiling boss from the Room of a Hundred Towers in the Parc Güell. Below: the magnificent towers of the Sagrada Familia

organic form and extensive use of fragmented ceramic tiles became the hallmarks of Gaudí's complex, playful style; other examples in Barcelona are in the Casa Batlló, nicknamed the "house of the emaciated tibia," and Casa Milà (La Pedrera), where chimney pots and access staircases on the roof were transformed into colorful, surrealistic sculptures. This rooftop fantasyland is still a popular meeting place for Barcelona's art-oriented youth.

Gaudí's approach to construction was equally unorthodox: He never used plans, instead depending on sketches, elevations, and models. This deliberate nonrationality may have predated the surrealists, but later produced insurmountable difficulties in completing Gaudí's last project, Barcelona's Sagrada Família cathedral, after his death. The architect intended this neo-Gothic church to synthesize his deepening sense of spirituality, developed in mystical theories of symbolic structure while he lived as a virtual recluse

Gaudí's early designs in the 1880s incorporated Mudejar and Gothic influences, using ornamental brickwork, ceramic tiling, parabolic arches, turrets, and domes. By the 1900s he had developed his inimitable, curvilinear style in ambitious, ground-breaking Parc Güell in Barcelona. This project was financed by Eusebi Güell, a local industrialist who became his faithful patron. Free-flowing,

Casa Batlló, with its lavish baroque face and sensuous ironwork, is a Gaudí redesign of a typical Eixample apartment block.

during the latter part of his life. His work on the Sagrada Família became so obsessional that when funds were low Gaudí even sold his possessions and begged money from friends. Finally, the life of this eccentric genius came to an end in a tragic, though fittingly unconventional way: When he was knocked over by a tram in 1926, Gaudí's appearance was so tramplike that nobody recognized him. Since then his star has risen, and the still incomplete Sagrada Família has become the architectural symbol of Barcelona. ■

Towers,
four on each facade
represent the 12
apostles

Nativity facade,
completed in 1904

Passion facade   Main entrance

Sagrada Familia

Begun by Francisco Villar in 1882, this project was taken over by Gaudí a year later. He planned to create a church in the form of the Latin Cross, with four towering spires over each of the three facades to represent the 12 Apostles and a central cluster of five more to symbolize Christ and the Evangelists. In medieval fashion, he worked without plans and remodeled as construction progressed. On his death, 40 years later, just one spire, the crypt, the apsidal walls, and the Nativity facade had been completed. Work on the church ceased temporarily, but it continues once more today. ■

How the finished church should look

Nave

View of the city from the rose window past the towers of the Passion facade

More places to visit in Barcelona

MONESTIR DE SANTA MARIA DE PEDRALBES

Come here to drift back into medieval times, and see a top-notch selection of paintings from the Thyssen-Bornemisza collection in Madrid (see pp. 68–71). The walled Gothic monastery was founded in 1326 by Elisenda de Montcada, the fourth wife of Jaume II. In the serene three-story cloister, a garden and fountains gave solace to the nuns in their tiny cells round the perimeter. Here, too, you enter a small, irregularly shaped chapel, **Capella de Sant Miquel,** faced in exquisite frescoes (1346) by Ferrer Bassá, a follower of Giotto.

From the cloister you reach the former dormitory and the Sala de la Reina (Queen's Room), where the 72 paintings from the **Thyssen-Bornemisza** collection hang. The jewel of medieval art and arguably of the entire collection is Fra Angelico's **"Virgin of**

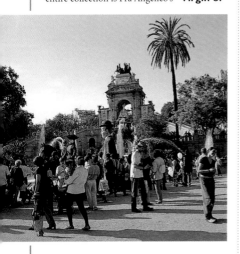

Giant festival figures dot the Parc de la Ciudatella

Humility," but the collection continues through the Renaissance to end with 18th-century baroque, and includes masterpieces by Tiepolo, Cranach, Tintoretto, Veronese, Canaletto, Zurbarán, Velázquez, and Rubens.
🅰 154 A4 ✉ Baixada del Monestir 9 ☎ 93 203 92 82 🕐 Closed Tues.–Sat. p.m. & Mon.
💲 $ 🚇 Metro: Maria Cristina, Lines 1 & 3

PALAU REIAL DE PEDRALBES

This palace was built for King Alfonso XIII in 1919–1929, courtesy of the Güell family. It is in the far southwestern corner of the city, within walking distance of the Monestir de Santa María de Pedralbes. Italian Renaissance style dominates, and the lavish interior flaunts Murano glass chandeliers beside antique furniture, tapestries, and a throne resting on golden lions. Visit the **Museu de Cerámica,** (Tel 93 280 16 21), with its rich display of Spanish ceramics, including 12th-century Mudejar work, 18th-century azulejos (tiles), and pieces by Miró, Picasso, and contemporary ceramicists. Here, too, is the **Museu de les Arts Decoratives,** (Tel 93 280 50 24), spanning the centuries from medieval days to the present. The surrounding classically designed gardens have plenty of shade. Use any remaining energy to walk around to the **Pavellons de la Finca Güell** (Avinguda de Pedralbes 7, closed Sat.– Sun.), near the crossroads with Passeig Manuel Girona, to see their decorative brickwork. Gaudí designed the buildings in 1887 as a porter's lodge and stables for the Güell estate.
🅰 154 A4 ✉ Avinguda Diagonal 686 ☎ 93 280 13 64 🕐 Closed p.m. & Mon. 💲 $
🚇 Metro: Palau Reial

PARC DE LA CIUTADELLA

Barcelona's largest park lies between the old town and the Olympic area on the site of a citadel developed for the 1888 World's Fair. Some of the original structures remain, such as the **Umbracle** (tropical plants greenhouse) and **Hivernacle** (glasshouse), and the elaborate restaurant building designed by Domènech i Montaner, now home to the **Museu de Zoologia** (Tel 93 319 69 12, closed Sun. p.m. & Mon.). Close by stands the **Museu de Geologia** (Tel 93 319 68 95, closed Sun. p.m. & Mon.). Paths lead through landscaped gardens to the **Museu d'Art Modern** (Tel 93 319 57 28, closed Sun. p.m. & Mon.), strong on Romanticism, 19th-century realism and the modernista period. Also in the park are the Catalan Parliament and the **Parc Zoològic.**
🅰 155 E3 🚇 Metros: Ciutadella-Vila Olímpica, Arc de Triomf, & Barceloneta ∎

S pain's prosperous eastern seaboard of Catalunya and Valencia has endless beaches, remote inland sierra, Roman Tarragona, and Spain's third city, Valencia. Juicy oranges, inventive rice dishes, and sparkling *cava* are part of the bargain.

Eastern Spain

Detail of a Roman mosaic

Some of Dalí's most notorious frolics took place at his summer home at Port Lligat.

Eastern Spain

FROM THE PYRENEES ON THE FRENCH BORDER SOUTH TO THE CAREFREE beach resorts of the Costa Blanca is a vast swath of land with one obvious trait—the Catalan language. Less obvious, but just as strong is left-wing Republicanism. During the Civil War of 1936–39, this part of Spain endured terrible hardship, resulting in simmering resentment throughout the four decades of General Franco's rule. In high contrast to these unifying factors, eastern Spain's landscapes vary from chilly Pyrenean villages with wandering goats, to mellow sandy beaches, rugged interior sierra, and valleys clad in almond and citrus trees. You can experience huge climatic variations in a day, but almost everywhere, with only a few exceptions, you also sense a burgeoning prosperity.

Of the cities, Barcelona (see pp. 153–76) has the highest profile, but Valencia, Spain's third largest city, is close on its heels. It is an increasingly strong cultural center, with plenty of spruced-up monuments. Between the two is Tarragona, giving an unparalleled vision of Roman Spain. The design-conscious town of Girona (Gerona) is to the north, and in the deep south the mirage of Alacant (Alicante) rises from arid hills over a generous bay. Seafaring is king, and it has been since the Greeks and then the Romans crossed the Mediterranean to colonize Spain. Charlemagne left his mark in the ninth century, creating the County of Barcelona and a feudal system that persisted

for several centuries. The Moors came and went fast from the north of this region, but more slowly from Valencia. By 1443, Catalunya, Aragón, Valencia, and the Balearic Islands had created one powerful kingdom including Sardinia, Sicily, and southern Italy and was soon united with Castilla. Many of the monuments remaining date from this Renaissance period, when prosperity soared and huge areas were repopulated by northerners to replace the victims of the Spanish Inquisition. Agriculture remains dominant in the economy—obviously so in Valencia's vast inland *huerta* (orchard, a nickname for its irrigated land), and more discreetly in Catalunya's sierra. The region is also highly industrialized. A major source of income is tourism, above all along the *costas*. The most venerable, the Costa Brava, saw its first waves of foreign visitors in the 1950s. The intense development of the 1960s and '70s now seems a terrible mistake. Vacationers continue to pour in and facilities continue to expand. Despite all this, you still see dramatic natural beauty. If you visit only one stretch of coast, the Costa Brava should be your choice. Farther south, the Costa Blanca, too, has pockets of outstanding scenery, and its specialty is that typical Spanish dish—*paella*, a fragrant blend (with variations) of rice, saffron, shellfish, meat, and lemon. ■

The Costa Brava, or "wild coast," is named for its rugged, rocky coastline.

Catalunya (Cataluña)

Together with the Madrid region and Euskadi (Basque Country), Catalunya is economically the most dynamic part of Spain and certainly stands on its own as the most avant-garde. Not only this, it clings jealously to its Catalan language and traditions, sometimes to the detriment of universal communication.

This clear sense of identity dates from the ninth century, when Charlemagne established Catalunya as a buffer zone. It has close linguistic and cultural links with southern France, although this did not protect it from destructive French troops during warfare between France and Spain in 1714 and in 1808. Geographic and cultural links continue today. However, for inhabitants of northern Catalunya, France is more easily accessible than the Spanish capital.

The Moorish occupation was short, enabling the counts of this feudal region to finally crystallize Catalan identity in the 12th century, crowned by the marriage of Count Ramon Berenguer IV with the Aragón heiress Petronila in 1137. This was the beginning of a golden age for Catalan merchants that peaked in the 14th century, when Catalunya and Aragón controlled a huge Mediterranean empire. Despite their alliance, each of these regions kept its traditional civic privileges, and the Catalans' proud sense of justice, expressed in strikes and industrial unrest, was one of the biggest thorns in Franco's side.

Catalunya has widely diverse interest, from gastronomy to history, wine to contemporary design, and volcanoes to sun-drenched beaches and crisp ski slopes. Highlights include historic monasteries in Pyrenean valleys and coastal sierra, spectacular Roman remains at Empuries and Tarragona, and Girona—Catalunya's most enjoyable, forward-looking town outside Barcelona. You can pick up the threads of Salvador Dalí's eccentricities in Cadaqués and Figueres, or take a half hour's drive into the hills to hike and taste wine and *cava* (the Spanish equivalent of champagne) before collapsing on a beach to digest it all. On the down side, Catalunya's greatest economic asset, its industry, does not always make for scenic landscapes. ∎

Costa Brava

FROM THE FRENCH BORDER AT PORTBOU SOUTH TO Blanes stretch 125 miles (200 km) of rugged coastline, coves, and beaches that still possess magic and beauty despite vigorous development in the 1960s and '70s. Dalí, Picasso, Chagall, and Man Ray were among the many artists captivated by the coast's fishing villages and limpid sky.

The Costa Brava has black spots such as the package vacation resort of **Lloret de Mar,** but its highlights include the inland medieval villages of **Pals** and **Peratallada,** the nature reserve of the **Les Medes** (islands reached by glass-bottomed boat from L'Estartit), and, in the south, the picturesque walled town of **Tossa de Mar.**

Empúries (Ampurias) was the site of a Greek and Roman settlement that held sway over the area for more than seven centuries from 600 B.C. Apart from its archaeological interest, the location encapsulates the original untouched beauty of this coast, with magnificent views across the Golf de Roses and a lovely beach that is accessible from the site. Wander through the Greek and Roman ruins in their landscaped park, look at the mosaics of the villas, then see the dramatic audiovisual show at the **Museu Arqueologia** (*L'Escala, tel 972 77 02 08*) to get a sense of Catalunya's long history. Even the anchovy industry at neighboring L'Escala dates back to the Romans.

One of the coast's most popular towns is **Cadaqués,** which, unlike more commercialized resorts, still has a distinctive atmosphere out of season. This whitewashed fishing port huddles in a cove at the end of a tortuous road across the hilly promontory and nature reserve of **Cap de Creus.** Seafood restaurants (*essential to make reservations in summer*) and art galleries are abundant, and Salvador Dalí's fascinating house, **Casa-Museu Salvador Dalí** (*Port Lligat, Cadaqués, tel 972 25 10 15, book in advance*), awaits over the hill.

The most exclusive resort is **Begur,** 30 miles (50 km) east of Girona. Crowned by castle ruins and backed by wooded hills, it lies within a couple of miles of idyllic sandy coves lapped by crystalline water. From here to the lighthouse of Llafranc is arguably the most beautiful stretch of the Costa Brava that you can explore on foot or by car before visiting delightfully well-preserved **Palafrugell,** preferably for its Sunday market. ■

Costa Brava
🗺 179 C5

Cadaqués
🗺 179 C5
Visitor information
✉ Carrer Cotxe 2A
☎ 972 25 83 15

Begur
🗺 179 C5
Visitor information
✉ Plaça de l'Església 8
☎ 972 62 40 20

Cadaqués has been a popular artists' getaway ever since Dalí spent his summers here.

The Onyar River flows past central Girona's colorful houses.

Girona (Gerona)

THE LOVELY OLD TOWN OF GIRONA IS UNDERGOING A minor boom and this, combined with its strategic location, makes it a stimulating base from which to explore the region. In some ways Girona is a mini-Barcelona, its characteristic river frontage replacing the Catalan capital's seafront. It even has its own equivalent of Gaudí, embodied in his contemporary, Rafael Maso (1880–1935), whose *modernista* buildings pepper the center.

Girona (Gerona)

🅰 179 C5

Visitor information

✉ Rambla de la Libertat 1

☎ 972 22 65 75

Iberians built Girona as a military fortress at the confluence of the Ter and Onyar Rivers. Romans, Jews, and Arabs all left their mark, and Charlemagne's army was not the only one to besiege it. The Onyar River clearly divides the medieval town from the 19th- and 20th-century quarter that spreads to the west, and the numerous footbridges give you lovely views of colorful old houses with laundry-draped balconies lining the banks. One of the best viewpoints is the **Pont de Peixateries Velles,** built in 1877 by Gustave Eiffel's company.

Back on the historic east bank, head for the social focal point, porticoed **Rambla de la Llibertat,** with a Saturday flower market, sidewalk cafés, and boutiques. From here it is a gentle uphill climb into the heart of medieval Girona, which culminates at the Roman walls and their highest point, the medieval **Torre Gironella,** where you have panoramic views and a rampart walk. Skirting around the walls you come to the magnificent **Roman north gate,** that opens onto a wide esplanade in front of 90 steps leading up to the **cathedral** *(Plaça de la Catedral).* The baroque facade conceals a Gothic interior of one single nave, an astonishing 94 feet wide (23 m), which caused controversy when it was designed in the 14th century.

The result is the world's widest Gothic nave, thick stone walls, and heavy buttresses. Penetrate the cloister and chapterhouse museum, to find the original, Romanesque section. In the intimate **cloister,** built in a trapezoidal shape to fit the Roman wall, look at the beautifully carved capitals and 11th-century bell tower. Visit the museum, the **Tresor Capitular** (*Tel 972 21 44 26, closed Sun. p.m. & Mon.*) to see the **Tapestry of the Creation,** a Romanesque masterpiece, alongside marvels of religious silverware, exquisite manuscripts (look for the Codex del Beatus), and sculptures.

Just outside the north gate stand the 12th-century **Banys Àrabs** (Arab Baths, *Carrer Ferranel Catòlic, tel 972 21 32 62, closed Sun. p.m.*), built in Moorish style but based on Roman design. The *frigidarium* (cold bath) has a colonnaded octagonal pool beneath a skylight. Immediately below this, you can't miss the unfinished Gothic bell tower of **Sant Feliu** church, which contains sarcophagi from the Roman and early Christian era, some from Italy. Here, too, is an unusual recumbent statue of Christ (1350) by Mestre Aloi, an example of Catalan Gothic sculpture.

Girona's newest jewel lies in the renovated Jewish quarter, **El Call,** just a few steps south of the cathedral square along Carrer de la Força. In the 15th century, the Jewish community that had lived there for six centuries was expelled, and part of this web of lanes was bricked up. Today, El Call is not only one of the most fashionable places to live, but is also home to the **Bonastruc Ça Porta** (*Carrer Sant Llorenc, tel 972 21 67 61, closed Sun. & public holidays p.m.*), a study center and museum. It has been rebuilt from a synagogue and named for Nahmánides, or Bonastruc de Porta, the 13th-century rabbi who symbolizes the importance of Girona's school of the Kabbalah (mystical Judaism). When it is completed, the Catalan museum of Jewish culture will provide essential insight on this community's role in Spanish history and on the religious tolerance that existed (most of the time) until the Inquisition.

A final glimpse of Girona's illustrious past can be had in Pujada de Sant Domenec at the **Palau dels Agullana.** The unusual oblique archway of this 14th- to 17th-century mansion flanks a picturesque stairway leading up to the seminary of Sant Martí Sacosta, and it is one of the city's most photographed corners. ■

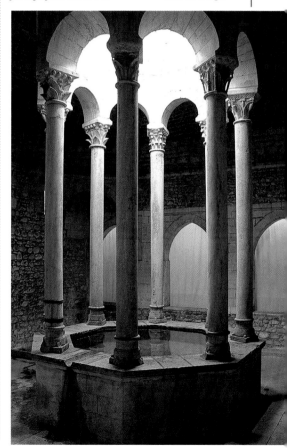

The graceful *frigidarium* of Girona's Arab baths were built to a Roman design.

Salvador Dalí

His image transcended nationality, as did his trademark moustache, dreamlike, liquid landscape paintings, and still unsurpassed megalomania. First and foremost, Salvador Dalí was seduced by fame, a status he expertly cultivated whether in his stage-set garden in Cadaqués, at the Hotel Meurice in Paris, or the St. Regis in New York. In 1958 he wrote, "It is difficult to hold the world's interest for more than half an hour at a time. I myself have done so successfully every day for twenty years." Andy Warhol predicted that everyone would be famous for 15 minutes, but Dalí made his fame last a lifetime, from the day he joined the surrealist movement in Paris in 1929, until his death in 1989. Nor did his cult end there, for Dalí's posthumous legacy was a minefield of unauthenticated works and question marks over his chosen burial place and will that provided headlines for years after.

Portrait of Salvador Dalí and Gala. Dalí sports his trademark moustache.

neuroses. From "Metamorphosis of Narcissus" (1936–37) to "Galarina" (1944–45), he showed off classical oil-painting techniques with mythological, sexual, and psychoanalytical references in a virtuoso body of work. Before that, his talents extended to collaborating with the filmmaker Luis Buñuel on two seminal surrealist films: *Un Chien Andalou* (1928) and *L'Âge d'Or* (1930).

At the center of Dalí's existence and of many of his paintings was his seductive, strong-willed Russian wife, Gala. From 1930 onward they led an unconventional existence between globetrotting winters and summers at their fisherman's cottage at Port Lligat, near Cadaqués. In 1970 Gala moved to a transformed castle ruin, Castell Pubol, to which Dalí was admitted only by written invitation. Here she entertained young lovers until her death in 1982, while Dalí dallied with the transsexual Amanda Lear. This arrangement is typical of their offbeat yet impassioned relationship. Dalí's last years were taken up with obsessional work on his museum at Figueres, where he was born. This converted theater was to be a monument to his life, creativity, and "paranoiac-critical" stance, surrealistically blurring the boundaries between fiction and reality. A coin-operated Cadillac that is sprayed by a fountain, articulated bronze sculptures, the Mae West room, a bed from a brothel, and facades studded with models of eggs and bread-rolls provide the context for hundreds of his works. Dalí's tomb is under the central stage, marked by a simple gravestone—unexpected for someone who once declared "I have always considered myself to be a genius." ∎

Dalí had a talent for drama, provocation, and exhibitionism, all held together by an unbridled imaginative genius. These qualities came at the perfect moment, propelling him to the forefront of the surrealist movement, although its founder, André Breton, later labeled him in disgust "Avida Dollars" (dollar greedy). Dalí's principles were questionable: He veered between anarchism, Marxism, monarchism, and Catholicism, and he did not hesitate to embrace Francoism when it suited him. Yet this extravagant opportunist was no empty bubble, and his earlier works, until the 1940s, reveal a consummate draughtsman and expert weaver of Freudian dreams and

The exterior of the Dalí Museum (above), constructed to the artist's own design, gives visitors a taste of what is to come inside (below).

Pirineos (Pyrenees)

THE PYRENEES IN CATALUNYA ARE DISTINCTLY MORE developed and prosperous than their counterparts in Aragón and Navarra, but you still find fortified medieval villages, remote monasteries and hermitages, and flocks of sheep and cattle grazing in meadows. Looming in the far west is the highest peak, Aneto (11,200 feet/3,408 m), and 83 miles (230 km) east the last bumps descend into the balmy Mediterranean at Portbou, on the French border.

The national park, **Parque Nacional d'Aigüestortes** *(Tel 973 62 40 36 or 973 69 61 89, visitor numbers restricted in summer),* covers 25,279 acres (10,230 ha) and is a perfect destination for hiking. The park, whose name means "winding waters," is a heady mountain mix of glacial lakes, waterfalls, and rushing streams, spiked by towering granite peaks with flanks clad in pine and fir forests. One of the most popular places is the **Estany de Sant Maurici** (Estany meaning "lake"), which you can reach by car from Espot (on the C147) in the east. Access from the west is from Boí (via Pont de Suert on the N230), and a trail connects

the two villages. Paths are well marked, and there are refuge huts for longer treks. Driving from the south, on the N260, you can't miss the spectacular **Estret de Collegats,** a narrow gorge gouged by the torrential Noguera River, where a rock face dripping with icy stalactites is named the **Roca de l'Argentaria.**

At the spa town of **Caldes de Boí,** on the western perimeter of Aigüestortes park, you can recover in hot springs. Then penetrate farther into the valley to admire its many 12th-century churches, where reproductions now replace unique frescoes that were painstakingly moved to Barcelona's Museu

Nacional d'Art de Catalunya (see pp. 168–69). If you are short of time, go straight to **Taüll,** where there are the lovely churches of **Santa Maria** and **Sant Climent,** both with multistory bell towers rising above slate roofs, in a setting of verdant meadows. In winter this area becomes the domain of skiers heading for the slopes of **Boí-Taüll,** which lie between 6,550 feet (2,000 m) and 8,060 feet (2,457 m).

The easternmost area of interest in the Pyrenees is the county of **Ripollès,** where peaks rising to 9,850 feet (3,000 m) dominate two valleys, **Camprodon** and **Ribes.** Their access point is **Ripoll,** a sleepy town at the confluence of two rivers that you will want to visit for its Romanesque monastery, **Monestir de Santa Maria** *(Plaça de l'Abat Oliba, Ripoll, tel 972 70 02 43, closed Mon.),* a landmark in Catalan history. Founded in A.D. 880 by Guifré "the Hairy," first Count of Barcelona, the monastery housed the royal pantheon until the focus moved to Barcelona in 1162. The monastery scriptorium produced illuminated masterpieces such as the Ripoll Bible (1015–1020), now housed in the Vatican. The library was said to be one of Europe's top four in the Middle Ages.

The monastery itself lost all charm during 19th-century alterations, but the **basilica** and **cloister** remain outstanding. Pick up a leaflet at the ticket office to identify countless fascinating details, and be sure to admire the basilica's structure from the garden at the back, where you can see the seven apses that end the single nave, four aisles, and transept. Santa Maria's masterpiece is the **front portal** (built around 1150), a monumental gateway sculpted with a multitude of scenes, figures, and symbols. Take

time to sit in the glassed-in lobby and follow its intricacies.

Guifré the Hairy was responsible for another remarkable monastery, **Sant Joan de les Abadesses** *(Plaça Abadesses, St. Joan de les Abadesses, tel 972 72 00 13),* only 6 miles (10 km) farther up the Ter River. His daughter Emma became its first abbess. A 15th-century earthquake caused the steeple to collapse, but the pure Romanesque interior remains a serene backdrop to rarities such as the **Santissim Misteri,** a 13th-century group of sculptures depicting Christ's removal from the cross. Visit the small **museum** *(Closed p.m. Mon.–Fri.)* at the entrance to see rock crystal crucifixes, Gothic silver maces, and antique textiles.

North of Ripoll, the mountain area of **Núria** has the Pyrenees' only rack railway (with a cogged rail between the bearing rails), the **Cremallera.** This lifts you 7.5 miles (12 km) from Ribes de Freser to Núria's ski station, **Estacio de Montanya Vall de Núria** *(Queralbs, tel 972 73 20 20),* 3,280 feet (1,000 m) higher up. ■

Volcanoes of Olot (Garrotxa)

Volcanoes of Olot (Garrotxa)
Visitor information & botanic garden
✉ Casal dels Volcans, Avinguda Santa Coloma, Olot
☎ 972 26 62 02

Olot
🗺 179 C5
Visitor information
✉ Mulleres 33, Plaça del Mercat
☎ 972 27 02 42

Now barely visible under vegetation, the volcanoes of Olot offer easy hiking.

SPAIN'S GREATEST VOLCANIC LANDSCAPE IS SOMEWHAT illusory: the 30 or so dormant volcanoes here are densely clad in forest. Ever since the last eruption took place, over 10,000 years ago, these 46 square miles (120 sq km) of valleys, plains, rivers, and volcanoes have been transformed into well-irrigated cropland and grazing pastures, and the produce reappears on local menus as volcanic food (food grown on volcanic soil). The craters are mostly visible from the volcano summits, and the walls of river valleys reveal spectacular basalt strata created by lava flows.

In 1985 the Garrotxa became a protected natural park, and visitor facilities make it a popular weekend hiking destination—to be avoided on Sundays. The starting point is the town of **Olot,** where you are within easy striking distance of the beech woods of **Jordà** and the neighboring volcanoes of **Croscat** and **Santa Margarita.** The latter, reached by an almost vertical path, has a hermitage that sits picturesquely in its crater. Croscat (17,000 years old) has a less strenuous trail past sections of fissured rock and lava blocks. Garrotxa's very diverse woodland provides habitats for an abundance of wildlife: beech marten, wildcats, genets, badgers, occasional wild boar, otters, and 143 bird species.

Three of the villages are exceptional. **Castellfollit de la Roca** perches dramatically on 197-foot (60 m) walls of basalt prisms and strata eroded by lava flows, with the Fluvia River at its feet. It is best seen from the N260, as the village itself holds little interest. Instead, head east to explore **Besalú** (*Visitor information, Plaça de la Llibertat 2, tel 972 59 12 40),* a stunning medieval village where a Romanesque bridge and four churches stand beside a Jewish quarter and baths. Hordes of visitors invade this village in summer, many boarding the tourist train that trundles 25 miles (40 km) up to a hilltop monastery. In **Santa Pau,** walk through cobbled medieval streets to the sloping main square bordered by Gothic arches (each one a different shape) where a cattle market was once held. Looming above the village is an 11th-century baron's castle that was used as a Dominican monastery before later being abandoned. A few steps more will bring you to the **Portal del Mar,** a gateway in the fortified walls giving panoramic views as far as Roses on the distant Costa Brava. ∎

Vic

AT FIRST SIGHT VIC IS A DARK, UNINVITING INDUSTRIAL town, not helped by an unhealthy climate of high rainfall and fog. Other Catalan towns may appear livelier, but don't be put off—the old town center is undergoing renovation to highlight numerous architectural jewels.

Vic has a long mercantile tradition (and tanning and sausagemaking industries), and the twice-weekly market *(Tues. & Sat.)* has been held on **Plaça Major** for centuries. This porticoed square lined with cafés exemplifies the historical continuity of the town: Gothic houses stand cheek by jowl with baroque and 1900s extravaganzas. The prize for true *modernista* excess must go to the **Casa Comella,** a neo-Gothic folly dominating the southwest corner. Walk in the narrow streets southeast of the square and you come to Vic's oldest building, a restored second-century **Roman temple** that stands beside the ruins of the **Palau dels Montcada.** For centuries this Romanesque palace concealed the temple in its interior patio.

Downhill from here stands the hulk of Vic's **catedral,** which again presents a mixture of styles from Romanesque to neoclassic due to progressive enlargements. What immediately strikes you inside are the theatrical **murals** in dark gold and red by Josep Maria Sert (1876–1945), painted twice over owing a devastating Civil War fire, and finally completed shortly before his death. Every surface of the vast nave writhes with Sert's powerful, symbolic figures illustrating both biblical subjects and the history of Catalunya. His modest tomb stands in the lovely Gothic **cloister** that surrounds the more ostentatious tomb of Vic's homegrown philosopher, Jaume Balmes (1810–1848).

Other unusual features are the beautiful 10th- to 11th-century capitals of the **crypt** (open the door on the left side of the ambulatory and switch on a light) and the main **altarpiece,** which now stands at the back of the apse—feed the light-meter a coin to illuminate Pere Oller's 1427 alabaster masterpiece, carved with scenes of the life of Christ and Mary. Other master-works from Vic's rich episcopal art collection are currently displayed at the **Hospital de la Santa Creu** *(Rambla de l'Hospital 52, tel 93 885 64 52, closed public holidays, Sun. p.m. in summer, & all p.m. in winter),* awaiting construction of a new museum beside the cathedral. ■

Vic
- 179 C5

Visitor information
- ✉ Carrer de la Ciutat 4
- ☎ 93 886 20 91

Catedral
- ✉ Plaça de la Catedral
- ☎ 93 886 01 18
- 🕐 Closed Mon.
- 💲 $

Vic's busy market adds to Plaça Major's hubbub.

Three monasteries

EASTERN CATALUNYA HAS MANY MONASTERIES, BUT three are outstanding. Montserrat is the most popular, Poblet the most beautiful, and Santes Creus the most informative, thanks to its audiovisual guided tour.

MONESTIR DE MONTSERRAT

Whatever way you choose to reach Montserrat (meaning "serrated mountain"), whether by road or cable car, the journey is absolutely unforgettable. For a thousand years pilgrims have been drawn to the spectacular pinnacles crowning the rugged sierra that is home to Catalunya's holiest site: the Benedictine monastery, chapels, and caves of Montserrat. About 80 monks live here, but don't expect a sense of deep spirituality. The entire complex has become heavily commercialized and it is thronged with crowds on Sundays and public holidays. That said, facilities are excellent, with funiculars to the caves of Sant Joan and Santa Cova, a museum, restaurants, two hotels, shops, and well-marked paths through the sierra.

The main priority is to see the carved wooden statue of the Virgin of Montserrat, popularly known as **La Moreneta** ("the dark one"),

Monestir de Montserrat
www.abadiamontserrat.net
🅜 179 C4
✉ Monistrol de Montserrat
☎ 93 877 77 01
⑤ $ (museum);
    $ (parking)

Refectory

Chapterhouse

Cloister

Nave of church

Sacristy

Romanesque church

due to her black face. Legend has it that the statue was carved by St. Luke and then miraculously found in 880 in Santa Cova, but more scientific testing has proved that it is 12th century. La Moreneta's status was enhanced in 1881 when she became patron saint of Catalunya. You can see her close-up by following a passage *(Closed 10:30 a.m.–noon)* to the right of the main doors to her jewel-studded eyrie behind the altar. The basilica itself was much transformed in the early 19th century following destruction by French troops, and the facade dates from 1901. Try to coincide your visit with **L'Escolania** *(Daily at 1 p.m. & 7:10 p.m.),* Europe's oldest boys' choir.

Beneath the esplanade in front of the basilica, the museum *(Tel 938 35 02 51)* displays a very mixed bunch of pieces ranging from a 4,000-year-old Egyptian mummy to classical paintings (look for Luca Giordano), Impressionists, and a touching collection of votive offerings to La Moreneta. Walkers can make the gentle climb to the shrine of **Sant Miquel,** or follow the longer **Way of the Rosary,** lined with *modernista* sculptures, to **Santa Cova.** Wilder in spirit but kinder to the leg muscles is the **Cami des Degotalls** that skirts around the mountain. All these paths command magnificent views of the Pyrenees.

The monastery of Montserrat sits in the cleft of the spectacular "serrated mountain."

Monks' dormitory

Library

SANTA MARIA DE POBLET
Named for the surrounding poplar trees, this tranquil, harmonious monastery (1151) lies near **Montblanc,** which is also worth seeing for its medieval walls and church. Poblet gives a wonderful sense of Cistercian purity (see

p. 44) within its walled precinct. Monks returned in 1940 after a century-long absence, and parts of the monastery are out of bounds, but you can, for instance, peer through the library doors to see these theologians working at computers. The library hall lies off the beautiful, contemplative Gothic **cloister** enclosing a pretty pavilion with a fountain, as do the kitchen, a vaulted refectory where monks eat and drink in silence, and the chapterhouse with its palm tree vaults and tombstones of past abbots. The cloister also leads to the Romanesque **church,** where attention focuses on the altar area. Look at the exceptional alabaster altarpiece carved by Damián Forment in 1527, and the elaborate royal tombs, dating from the 14th century but extensively restored in 1950. The stairs to the left of the altar lead up to the vast monks' dormitory—no longer in use—and out to the upper gallery of the cloister. The tour ends in the **wine cellars** below, a reminder of the Cistercians' involvement in viticulture and agriculture, which in medieval days gave a huge boost to the local economy.

SANTES CREUS

Founded shortly after Poblet by French Cistercians from Toulouse, Santes Creus has a similar layout to its sister monastery but is no longer in use. The austere **church,** on the other hand, never stopped functioning, and here you see a lovely rose window and royal tombs beneath elaborate Gothic canopies. There are two cloisters. The so-called "old cloister" was built in the 17th century on the site of the original one, and leads to the kitchen, refectory, wine cellars, and royal palace. The 14th-century **Gran Claustro** (Great Cloister) is lined with beautifully carved capitals and leads to the chapterhouse. Above this, the lofty dormitory is now used for summer concerts. An innovative audiovisual circuit guides you through the monastery, reconstructing its atmosphere and life. If you want the English version, make sure you arrive promptly at either 10 a.m. or 3 p.m. ∎

White-robed Cistercian monks inhabit Poblet, a much quieter monastery than Montserrat.

Santa María de Poblet
🅰 179 B4
✉ Poblet
☎ 977 87 00 89

Santes Creus
🅰 179 B4
✉ Santes Creus
☎ 977 63 83 29
🕐 Closed Mon.
💲 $. Free Sun.

Costa Daurada

THE FLAT COASTAL PLAIN OF THE COSTA DAURADA IS NOT one of Spain's most appealing coastlines, and a spate of low-cost constructions for sunworshipers has engulfed the original fishing villages. But it does have long golden *(daurada)* beaches, and a handful of unusual spots. Sitges is known as the gay beach resort of Spain, Port Aventura is a must for anyone with children, and the Ebre Delta is the largest in the Mediterranean after that of the Nile.

Sitges lies just half an hour's drive southwest of Barcelona airport, and crowds from all over Europe throng its bars and nudist beaches. It lies beside a beautiful stretch of high, rocky coastline. An outrageous February carnival continues the traditions of the heady past. The most enlightening windows on Sitges' history are the **Museu del Cau Ferrat,** once the home of the eccentric painter Santiago Rusinyol (1861–1931), where paintings and wrought ironwork are displayed, and the neighboring **Museu Maricel,** an old hospital that was lavishly refurbished for the American millionaire Charles Deering.

Barely 5 miles (8 km) south of Tarragona lies **Port Aventura** *(Avinguda Pere Molas, Vila-Seca, tel 900 40 44 40, closed Nov.–mid-March, www.portaventura.es),* Spain's largest theme park. Packed with high-adrenaline rides and entertainments, it is perfectly adapted to this balmy climate and ideal for anyone with children in tow.

The Costa Daurada's string of family resorts fades away in the south at the large, flat peninsula formed by the **Delta de l'Ebre** (Ebro Delta). These 124 square miles (320 sq km) of wetlands, partly protected as a reserve, come third only to France's Camargue and Andalucía's Parque Nacional de Doñana (see p. 274) for Mediterranean aquatic wildlife. Diverse ecosystems include inland rice fields, lagoons, salt marshes, and dunes, all much

favored by flamingoes and more than 300 other bird species that rest there while migrating, from April to late August and October to February. The best starting point is the village of **Deltebre** *(Visitor information, Plaça Vint de Maig, tel 977 48 93 09),* site of the **Eco-Museu,** or Ecological Museum *(Visitor information, Carrer Marti Buera 22, tel 977 48 96 79)* and horseback-riding activities. One mile (2 km) away is **La Cava** *(Visitor information, Plaça Vint de Maig, tel 977 48 93 09)* where you can rent traditional boats and canoes to tour the waterways. ∎

Sitges
🄰 179 C4
Visitor information
✉ Carrer Sinia Morera
☎ 93 894 42 51

Museu del Cau Ferrat & Museu Maricel
✉ Carrer Bernat de Fonollar 3
☎ 93 894 03 64
🕐 Closed Sun. p.m. & Mon.
🟦 $

One of Europe's most popular resorts, Sitges boasts a palm tree-lined seafront and a picturesque old quarter.

Tarragona

PRONOUNCED "THE MOST PLEASANT SPOT FOR RESTING" by the Roman poet Virgil (70–19 B.C.), Tarragona now has more than 100,000 inhabitants, whose livelihoods oscillate between the petrochemical industry and tourism. Spain's deepest port and Catalunya's most productive fishing harbor first attracted the Romans in the third century B.C. In another three centuries this city, known to the Romans as Tarraco, was capital of the vast Imperial *Hispania Tarraconensis.*

sandstone blocks once enclosed three terraced levels: a massive temple, the forum (marketplace), and vast **Circ Romans** (circus or chariot stadium), which could accommodate 30,000 of Tarraco's 40,000 inhabitants. The temple was replaced by a Romanesque cathedral, but much of the lower walls and structures were incorporated into houses and public buildings.

For the best view head straight for the **Pretori** (Praetorium), a stone tower and former palace of the counts of Barcelona that rises beside the circus at the base of the Rambla Vella. An elevator speeds you to the rooftop, where views open up over the entire seaside city. Roman remains lie at your feet, literally—beneath the tower, two of many vaulted tunnels have been excavated to reveal the sophistication of Roman engineering. Don't miss the model of Tarraco displayed here, and stop at the first floor to admire a superbly sculpted sarcophagus showing the legend of Hippolytus, salvaged from the sea. From the rooftop you also have a good aerial view of the scenic but much restored **amphitheater** (*Parc del Miracle, tel 977 24 25 79, closed Sun. p.m. & Mon.*), where gladiator fights were held.

Anyone bitten by the Roman bug should continue to the neighboring **Museo Arqueològic** (*Plaça del Rei 5, tel 977 23 62 09, closed Sun. p.m. & Mon.*), to see exceptional Roman artifacts. There is a fine

Contemporary Tarragona spreads west of the hilltop cathedral and Roman remains into a grid of 19th- and 20th-century streets. It is very much a provincial town, without the designer buzz of Barcelona or Girona. Archaeologists are still excavating numerous monuments that city authorities hope will give Tarragona world heritage status. A wonderfully mild climate, sandy beaches, and bountiful seafood are extras on this relaxed city's plate.

Once you climb to the third- to second-century B.C. walls and follow the **Passeig Arqueològic** (*Tel 977 24 57 96, closed Sun. p.m. & Mon.*) around their perimeter, you begin to understand the importance of the largest and oldest Roman settlement in Iberia. These fully restored, 40-foot-high (12 m)

Left: The soaring interior of La Concepción chapel in the cathedral

Tarragona
- ⬛ 179 B4
- **Visitor information**
- ✉ Carrer Major 39
- ☎ 977 24 52 03

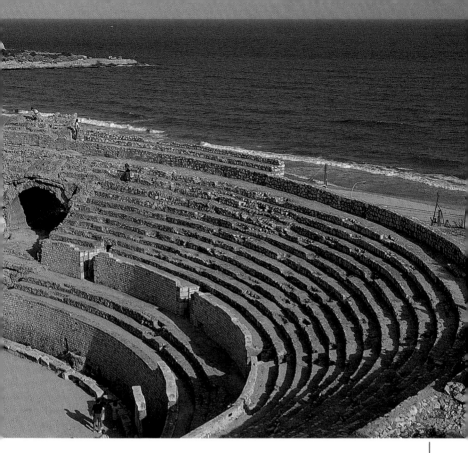

mosaic head of Medusa in Room 3 and, on the top floor, a copy of an articulated ivory doll whose original is exhibited at the **Necropolis** west of town. Tarragona's magnificent **aqueduct** can be seen only by making a dangerous turn marked off the A7 motorway, 3 miles (5 km) north of town.

Back at the summit, the **catedral** (*Plaça de la Seu, tel 977 23 86 85*) beckons, its curious facade combining Romanesque and Gothic portals beneath a huge rose window and two unfinished steeples. Enter through the **cloister,** where pointed Gothic arches enclose rounded Romanesque ones with Moorish-inspired tracery above. The museum and sacristy contain some interest, but keep your appreciation for the main **altarpiece** in the

cathedral itself. This 1430 masterpiece of alabaster and wood by Pere Joan illustrates in detail the life of Tarragona's patron saint, Santa Tecla. Look out for minutely carved animals and insects, and extremely realistic human expressions.

The 330-foot-long (100 m) nave has wonderful proportions, enhanced by suspended Flemish tapestries and light through the rose window. When you leave the cathedral, walk around the back to see the beautifully sculpted 12th- to 14th-century arches of the former **hospital of Santa Tecla,** and then go down the wide steps in front. At the bottom is **Carrer La Merceria.** Gothic market arcades that replaced the Roman forum colonnade are still used on Sunday mornings for an antique market. ■

Tarragona's elliptical Roman amphitheater held up to 14,000 spectators.

Pretori & Circ Romans
- ✉ Plaça del Rei, Rambla Vella
- ☎ 977 24 19 52
- 🕐 Closed Sun. p.m. & Mon.
- 💲 $ (combined ticket for Circ Romans, Museo Arqueológic, & amphitheater)

La Cartoixa, Escaladei

Castell de Miravet on the Ebre River

Drive: Priorat vineyards & Templars

This inland circuit takes you through rugged sierra ("serra" in Catalan) to a little-visited wine-producing region and to the impressive castle of Miravet. This was a stronghold of the Knights Templar, a religious military order of knighthood that was originally formed during the Crusades. The drive ends at Tortosa on the Ebre (Ebro) Delta.

Leave Tarragona on the N420 heading toward the airport and Reus, through a fairly uninter-esting, flat, semi-industrial area. Once you have entered Reus, turn right onto the beltway (Rondes), following signs to Montblanc, and then, farther on, to Falset and Alcañiz. You soon see the distant outline of the Serra de la Mussara with vineyards in the foreground. After climbing 1,800 feet (548 m), the road winds down through pine-clad limestone hills to **Falset** ① (*Visitor information, Avinguda Catalunya 6, tel 977 83 10 23*). Crowned by a

castle, the baroque church of Santa Maria, and arcaded Plaça Quartera, this pretty medieval town is a major wine-producing center. Its impressive **wine-cooperative building** was designed by Cesar Martinell, a disciple of Antoni Gaudí (see pp. 172–75). You can park your car down below the old town and walk uphill from there.

Leave Falset to tour the heart of the Priorat wine-producing area by following the contin-uation of the access road, now the T710, to Gratallops. Enjoy this good road while it lasts

DE LA MUSSARA

N420

Reus
Riudoms

A7
START

TARRAGONA

A7

Cap de Salou

⚑ See area map p. 179
► Tarragona
⟷ 90 miles (144 km)
🕐 Allow a day (including visits)
► Tortosa

NOT TO BE MISSED

- Falset old town
- Gratallops wineries
- La Cartoixa, Escaladei
- Castell de Miravet
- Tortosa cathedral

---

for the next 6 miles (10 km) and, when **Gratallops ❷** appears on its striking hilltop site, circle around the village to turn right at the sign Centre Urba. You enter Calle Piro, in the shadow of the church, where there are three wine cooperatives, at any of which you can taste and buy different varieties of wine and olive oil. Try the **Celler Cecilio** *(Carrer Piró 28, tel 977 83 91 81)*, which still uses time-honored methods. Continue your route on the T710, and then, after 1 mile (1.6 km), turn right onto the much narrower T711, toward Torroja del Priorat.

As the road twists through wild, semiarid landscapes where pine and olive trees grow, with glimpses of the lovely pink-ocher Serra de Montsant in the distance, you feel far from

civilization. Three miles (5 km) of bends farther you reach the picture-postcard vision of **Torroja del Priorat ❸**, perched high on an isolated hilltop. Cross the bridge to drive up behind the tiny village for a view over its tiled roofs and cobbled streets. It is inhabited by a population of only 140 people. Return to the T711 and turn right toward **Escaladei ❹**, 4 miles (7 km) ahead.

This beautiful village, also written "Scala Dei," is the historic and spiritual focal point of the whole Priorat area, because monks from the 12th-century Carthusian monastery here introduced the techniques of vine cultivation and wine-aging. Follow the sign beside the bridge (La Cartoixa) to drive half a mile (0.8 km) beyond the village to the picturesquely ruined and very extensive monastery of **La Cartoixa** *(Tel 977 82 70 06, closed Mon.).* Escaladei itself is an idyllic little stone village with two restaurants and a well-organized **winery** *(Cellers Scala Dei, Plaça Priorat 3, tel 977 82 70 27).* You can taste and buy wine, and don't miss the exquisite Siurana olive oil.

Spain's prehistoric inhabitants scratched then colored these cave paintings on rocks beside the Ebre River.

The ruined Templar castle of Miravet lords over the Ebré River.

There are further stunning landscapes to be seen by following the sign to La Morera de Montsant along a 3-mile (5 km) road. This route takes you up through the hills to the extraordinary village of **La Morera de Montsant** ⑤ (*Visitor information, Carrer Major 4, tel 977 82 72 73*), which nestles beneath the 3,660-foot (1,115 m) Seyalets peak. Though the Romanesque church and semideserted village are being renovated, the town is still a popular starting point for hiking and horseback riding in the Serra de Montsant. Return by the same road to Escaladei, where you turn right on the T702 to drive beside the scenic sierra to La Vilella Baixa. Rejoin the T710 back to Falset, 9 miles (15 km) away.

Drive through Falset, following signs for Móra d'Ebre on the N420, to follow a less dramatic but still pretty 20-mile (32 km) road through the agricultural plain. Pass by the unappealing town of Móra la Nova, cross over the Ebre River, and then, at a traffic circle, turn left to Miravet on the T324. On entering the village of **Miravet,** follow the signs to Castell that lead you uphill to the forbidding ruins of **Castell de Miravet** ⑥ (*Tel 977 40 73 68, closed Mon.*). This was the castle of the Knights Templar, an order of medieval soldier-monks (see p. 29). There are panoramic views from the castle over the river valley. From here you can either hike down a cliff path to the **Casc Antic** (old quarter), or drive back down, following signs to Casc Antic. Park on the shady, riverside square and walk through the old town, before continuing by car along the river to **Pas de Barca.** Here a simple ferry (*Closed 1–3 p.m. & in bad weather*), powered only by the swift-flowing current, takes up to three cars at a time across the Ebre. On the opposite bank you join the C230, a good road that for 20 miles (32 km) slices through forested sierra, follows the peaceful meanders of the river, and finally passes through extensive groves of orange trees to reach Tortosa.

In **Tortosa** ⑦, do not miss a visit to the spectacular Gothic **catedral** (*Tel 977 44 17 52*), built over a mosque. After this go for a well-deserved drink at the hilltop castle of **La Zuda,** now an impressive *parador* (state-run hotel). This magnificent building echoes with the ghosts of three former kings: Abd-ar-Rahman III, who ordered the *zuda* (well) to be built, Count Ramon Berenguer IV, who reclaimed Tortosa from the Moors in 1148; and Jaime I of Aragón, who used it as his royal residence. ■

Crates of Valencia's famed fruit, collected during the orange harvest and ready for shipment

Valencia

Valencia, kingdom of oranges and queen of the Levante (the East), has an indented coastline backed by hills and the inland *huerta,* said to be Europe's most fertile land. Contrary to what you might expect, this region is not particularly scenic. Agriculture is modern and intensive rather than picturesque, but you do see endless terraced orchards laden with oranges, lemons, and peaches, and rice fields stretching to the horizon. Rice reappears on your plate in countless guises: Paella is ubiquitous, and you also find a close cousin of Italy's more famous risotto. More striking still is the immense palm grove of Elx (Elche), an oasis in the increasingly arid terrain that borders Murcia to the south, and source of the symbolic palm fronds used in Holy Week processions.

For beach lovers the Costa Blanca has highlights at Dénia, Xàbia (Jávea), and Calp (Calpe). Best of all is the seaside capital of Valencia itself, where Renaissance and baroque buildings stand as testimony to the region's long history: Romans, Visigoths, and Moors were here before Valencia was drawn into the Aragonese net in 1238. This was the start of the kingdom of Valencia's golden age, and nurtured the independent streak that remains at its heart. Depression came in the 17th century when Valencia was forced by Madrid to expel its Jews and Moriscos—baptized Moors—who made up almost one-third of the population. This economic disaster was compounded by the War of Spanish Succession (see p. 34), when Valencia picked the losing side.

The Valencian language may only vary slightly from Catalan, but a quite different, easygoing character comes to the fore in the province's imaginative fiestas. It is here, after all, that a whole day is spent pelting friend and foe with tons of ripe tomatoes, producing one giant purée and a red-faced population. In case you are tempted, this takes place at Buñol, 25 miles (40 km) southwest of the capital on the last Wednesday of August. Nor does the capital rest in the wings, for it is here that pyromaniacs take over during Las Fallas, a fiesta of image-burning and fireworks every March. ■

Valencia city

Locally made lace trims the elaborate traditional dress of Valencian girls.

SPAIN'S THIRD LARGEST CITY IS NOT PARTICULARLY enticing at first sight, but once you penetrate the old center, you find a historically and culturally rich town that is too often overlooked by visitors. It shows stark contrasts between the new Spain and the old. Prosperous white-collar types pass down-and-outs, and narrow, dingy streets lead off wide avenues lined with upscale shops and palm trees. After the sun has set, the superb monuments are all spotlit, lending the city an evocative atmosphere. Spend the night there if you can. One-way systems make driving difficult, so if you are in a car, head for a downtown underground parking lot and then use your feet.

Valencia's history goes back to the Greeks, Carthaginians, Romans, Visigoths, and, in A.D. 714, the Arabs. Legendary El Cid conquered the city in 1094, but it was again taken by the Moors (the Almoravids), whose rule lasted until King Jaime I of Aragón's conquest in 1238. This was the start of a golden age during which Valencia became one of the strongest Mediterranean powers, prospering from trading links with possessions in Italy—the reason for its Italianate architecture. Hard times followed, culminating in the Civil War (1936–39), when Republican forces retreated to Valencia after Catalunya was taken by Franco. After much destruction, Valencia finally gave in to the Nationalists on March 30, 1939.

Today, Valencia's economy is equally based on agriculture, on industry (with Ford and IBM factories), and the service industry. Not wanting to be left behind by cities such as Barcelona and Bilbo, Valencia demonstrates a strong sense of art and design in the **IVAM** (Instituto Valenciano de Arte Moderno), a contemporary art center (see p. 203) and the

Valencia
179 A2
Visitor information
www.turisvalencia.es
Plaza del Ayuntamiento 1
96 351 04 17
Closed Sun. p.m.

glass-fronted **Palau de la Música y Congresos,** a congress center designed by British architect Norman Foster in 1997. Despite this dynamism, Valencians retain their traditions, notably the exuberant Fallas (March 12–19), when papier-mâché figures are set alight amid fireworks and festivities. Numerous shops sell ornate mantillas, hand-painted fans, hand-embroidered silk shawls, and ceramics from outlying Paterna. Paella is on every menu, for this is where it originated.

The main sights lie conveniently close to each other, within the area once enclosed by city walls that were demolished a century ago. Only two impressive gateways remain. North of this area are the **Jardines del Turia,** landscaped gardens in the old riverbed that offer a welcome splash of greenery to Valencia's 800,000 inhabitants. In the old center, the Gothic **catedral** *(Plaza de la Reina, tel 96 391 81 27)* is flanked by **El Miguelete,** an octagonal bell tower. Climb to the top of this for wonderful views over Valencia's glazed ceramic domes and labyrinthine streets. The main sight inside the cathedral is the **Capilla del Santo Cáliz**

In the main hall of the 15th-century Silk Exchange, a Latin inscription along the walls reads, "I am a famous building that took fifteen years to build."

(Chapel of the Holy Grail), a Flamboyant Gothic chapel with a superb alabaster altarpiece carved with biblical scenes by the Florentine sculptor Guiliano Poggibonsi. This enshrines the cathedral's marvel, a first-century agate goblet said to be the very one used by Christ at the Last Supper. Before reaching the cathedral in 1437, it transited via Rome, the monastery of San Juan de la Peña (see p. 146), and Zaragoza (see pp. 140–41). The chapel leads to the museum, which is full of treasures but may be closed for renovation.

In front of the cathedral, you can't miss the baroque bell tower of **Santa Catalina.** One block northeast lies the beautiful 13th- to 14th-century **Almudín** *(Plaza San Luis Bertran 1, tel 96 352 54 78, closed Sun. p.m. & Mon.),* the city's former granary, now used for temporary art exhibitions. It is worth taking a look at the sober stone interior enhanced by whimsical 17th-century wall paintings. Outside, a large archaeological site shows Roman and Moorish ruins. A few steps north of the cathedral is

the **Palacio Benicarló** *(Calle Santa Ana),* a striking Gothic structure of two arcaded stories that was once the residence of the Dukes of Gandia and is now the seat of the Valencian parliament.

For a vision of Valencian excess, head for the **Palacio del Marqués de Dos Aguas** *(Rinconada García Sanchís, tel 96 351 63 92, closed Sun. p.m. & Mon.),* now housing the national ceramics museum. It is a wedding cake of a building, with what is arguably Spain's most ornate domestic facade. The building dates from the 15th century, but was heavily restructured in 1740, and then again a century later. The lower two floors exhibit remarkable original furnishings and decoration: Don't miss the cupola painting by Hipolito Rovira (1693–1765), the Chinoiserie Room, the inlaid ivory and ebony furniture of the Smoking Room, the glittering ballroom, or the marquis's bedroom complete with carved marble bath.

On the top floor, the **Museo Nacional de Cerámica** gives an excellent overview of the development of ceramics in Spain, from early Arab pieces to the Moorish period, Mudejar, Catholic Spain (which still could not shake off Moorish influences), and on to the 18th century, when the Real Fabrica de Alcora created a delicate Spanish version of the famous French Sèvres porcelain. A re-created Valencian kitchen extends the use of ceramics even to the chandelier. The collection ends with six superb pieces by Picasso, and more contemporary pieces.

Valencia's **Mercado Central** (central market) occupies a vast *modernista* (see pp. 172–75) building, and is worth a morning visit to see the incredible wealth of produce from the *huerta*. A lovely church, the **Inglesia de los Santos Juanes,** is next to the market and **La Lonja,** the Silk Exchange building, *(Plaza del Mercado, tel 96 352 54 78, closed Sun. p.m.),* stands opposite. This was commissioned in the 15th century by the city's wealthy silk merchants. It is an exceptional Flamboyant Gothic building, from the imposing crenellated exterior to the vast interior hall of pillars, their twisted spiral structures rising to tracery high up in the vaults. Take the stairs from the orange-tree patio to the upper floor to admire a masterfully carved and gilded ceiling that has been resurrected from the old town hall.

In the 1980s Valencia's cultural riches were enhanced with the **Instituto Valenciano de Arte Moderno** or IVAM, split between the Centro del Carmen (a former Carmelite convent) and purpose-built modern galleries. Both are in the northwest corner of the old town. The permanent collection is devoted to the 20th-century sculptor Julio González. Neighboring exhibition halls and those of the Carmen regularly stage exhibitions of high-profile international artists.

The city's other main art collection is found at the **Museo de Bellas Artes,** on the far side of the old riverbed. This large and important collection has paintings that range from Valencian primitives, through the Renaissance, and up to the early 20th century. Watch for the Valencian painters Juan de Juanes (died 1579) and Francisco Ribalta (1565–1628), and for Hieronymus Bosch, Ribera, van Dyck, Murillo, Goya, and Velázquez (a wonderful self-portrait). The neighboring gardens, **Jardines del Real,** make a good place to relax afterward, with the added bonus of a zoo, sculptures, and fountains.

Valencia's palatial railway station, the **Estación del Norte,** *(Calle Xàtiva),* is an artistic treasure of a different sort—a fine example of the use of illustrative *azulejos* (tiles) and decorative woodwork in a purely functional building. It dates from 1910–17, the creative period that also produced the central market. ■

Instituto Valenciano de Arte Moderno (IVAM)

✉ Calle de Guillem de Castro 118

☎ 96 386 30 00

⊕ Closed Mon.

Museo de Bellas Artes

✉ Calle San Pio V

☎ 96 360 57 93

⊕ Closed Mon.

Valencia's Las Fallas celebrations feature enormous vats of paella.

The Costa Blanca's sugarloaf, the Peñon de Ifach, towers over the resort of Calp.

Costa Blanca

HALFWAY BETWEEN VALENCIA AND ALACANT ON THE MAP, the Costa Blanca still has immense natural drama. Moody mountains loom just a few miles inland, and the exceptionally mild climate nurtures lush vegetation. Many of the beaches are now full of high-rise hotels. Worst of all is Benidorm, give it a wide berth.

Costa Blanca

🗺 179 B1

Warning: Avoid driving along the coast road N332, as its many bends get choked with traffic. Stick to the Autovia and drive in to specific coastal spots from there. ■

Calp (Calpe) *(Visitor information, Plaça del Mosquit, tel 96 583 85 32, closed Sun p.m.)* has high-rises, but it also has a beautiful wide bay backed by sierra, a sandy beach, a working fishing harbor, and the **Peñón de Ifach,** rising 1,090 feet (332 m) above the Mediterranean. A **nature reserve** *(Tel 96 597 20 15, closed on rainy days)* here protects about 300 species of flora and a large number of seabirds that nest there in spring. Just inland is the hilltop **old town,** with the restored remains of a 16th-century castle.

North of Calp is the popular beach resort of Moraira. Far more scenic is **Xàbia (Jávea)** *(Visitor information, Plaça de l'Església 6, tel 96 579 43 56, closed Sun. p.m.),* on the north side of the Costa Blanca peninsula, near its point. El Arenal beach draws the sun lovers here. The attractive, partly walled old town was built inland around the fortified church of **San Bartolomé** for fear of pirates, and this is where you find its history explained at the small **Museo Arqueológico** *(Tel 96 579 10 98).* Today tourism has meant expansion, but the rocky capes and lovely beaches still hold their own. The same goes for **Dénia** *(Visitor information, Plaza Oculista Buigues 9, tel 96 642 23 67, www.communitat-valenciana.com),* 5 miles (8 km) northwest, a popular retirement area for northern Europeans. Its illustrious Greek and Roman past, is illustrated at the **Museo Arqueológico** *(Castillo de Dénia, tel 606 94 57 15, closed Mon.),* and the Moorish castle still stands. ■

Alacant (Alicante)

Set on a rocky peak, Alacant's old fortress offers a spectacular bird's-eye view of the city.

SPRAWLING AROUND A HUGE BAY, ALACANT IS A THRIVING, ever expanding port city with few historic sights other than its magnificent castle. You could spend a happy couple of hours exploring the backstreets of the old town, which burst into long nocturnal life on Friday and Saturday nights. Then head for one of the beaches.

In the **old town,** just behind the marina and beneath the hilltop castle, have a look at the 18th-century **Ayuntamiento,** with its beautiful baroque facade. Then head for the **Museo de la Asegurada** (*Plaza de Sta María 3, tel 96 514 07 68, closed Sun. p.m. & Mon.*), which inherited a large collection of contemporary art from local artist Eusebio Sempere (1923–1985), and shows it in rotation. Picasso, Miró, Rauschenberg, Tàpies, and Kandinsky are among the greats represented.

From here, take a stroll south along the **Explanada de España,** with its majestic banyan trees, past the marina to the early 20th-century **Lonja del Pescado** (*Tel 96 592 23 06, closed Mon. & a.m.*). This former fish market, designed in *modernista* neo-Mudejar style is used for temporary exhibitions.

For a magnificent view, take the elevator to the **Castillo de Santa Bárbara,** a fortress originally built by the Carthaginians. This is reached from the coastal highway via a 225-yard (208 m) tunnel. A large collection of 20th-century sculpture is dotted around the ramparts and in castle halls. The oldest buildings, dating from the Middle Ages, are found at the top of the elevator. Halfway down is the 16th-century section, and the lowest level is 17th century. Don't miss the vaulted exhibition hall, which illustrates the castle's long and momentous history. Walk down the access road, circle left along a path and go down steps that bring you back to the old quarter. ∎

Alacant (Alicante)
🅰 179 B1
Visitor information
✉ Rambla Méndez Núñez 23
☎ 96 520 00 00
🕐 Closed Sun.

Castillo de Santa Barbara
☎ 96 515 29 69
🕐 Exhibitions closed Sun. p.m. & Mon.
💲 $ (elevator)

Drive: Into Sierra via Guadalest

Leave the coastal crowds behind to head into the welcome emptiness of the sierra (called "serra" in Catalan). The Moors originally carved out the terraced hillsides, now covered in olive and almond trees, and orange and lemon groves. Guadalest attracts visitors from the coast because of its dramatic site, but it is worth visiting for the magnificent views over the surrounding mountains.

Leave the coastal resort of **Altea** on the Valencia road (N332) following the bay. Turn left toward Callosa d'en Sarrià (A150), and then left again onto C3313. The Serra de Guadalest looms ahead, with terraced orange and lemon groves in the foreground. You soon come to **Callosa d'en Sarrià ❶**, an agricultural town with a medieval arch and old walls around **Plaza del Castell.** As an antidote to the dry sierra, make a 2-mile (3.2 km) detour on the CV715 (direction Bolulla) to **Fonts de l'Algar ❷** *(Tel 96 597 21 29)*, an area of rushing springs with visitor facilities, environmental exhibits, and small restaurants.

From Callosa, follow signs to Guadalest (CV755) and drive 8 miles (12 km) through increasingly rugged limestone hills clad in pine trees and maquis. Your first sight of **Guadalest ❸** is extraordinary: Granite pinnacles topped by towers stand out of the valley, and in fact it was once accessible only through a tunnel. Drive into the village to the parking lot, and from there wander through narrow streets lined with souvenir shops to the tunnel that leads into the old part of Guadalest. (Follow signs to "Museo.") The castle ruins above are reached via 18th-century **Casa Orduña,** Guadalest's noble mansion, now the **Museo Municipal** *(Calle Iglesia 2, tel 96 588 53 93)*. This was built after a devastating earthquake in 1644 destroyed most of the original castle, and was subsequently rebuilt after being burnt down during the 1708 War of Succession. Inside, it retains the Orduña family's furnishings, paintings (look at the anonymous double-sided "Ecce Homo"), and vast library. From the garden, steps lead up to the ruins of **Sant Josep castle,** now partly a cemetery, which give fantastic panoramic views. Other sights in this popular village are the church and a small **ethnological museum** *(opposite church, tel 96 588 52 38, closed Mon.)*, with displays on Guadalest's chocolate-making industry.

Leave Guadalest on the same road, which winds around the flanks of the valley through terraced almond trees (a magnificent sight in February when the trees are covered in a mass of pink and white blossom) and tiny villages. When you reach the pretty village of **Confrides ❹** *(Visitor information, tel 96 588 58 04),* source of the Guadalest River, stop to enjoy the magnificent views and the monumental walnut tree on the main square.

Terraced almond groves

From here to Penàguila, the road winds through 6 miles (10 km) of rocky moor and over the 3,170-foot (966 m) pass. Turn left onto the CV781, and then make a stop at **Penàguila ⑤** to look at its medieval gateway and noble mansions.

Leave this village on the CV785 in the direction of Sella (14 miles/22 km), driving through the beautiful, densely forested **Serra de Aitana,** with the 4,626-foot (1,410 m) silhouette of Puig Campana a permanent companion. **Sella ⑥** has Roman ruins and the remains of a medieval castle at the top of the town, and is a good starting point for hikes. Keep going toward Finestrat, where you return to terraced agriculture and orchards. Stop in **Finestrat ⑦** (*Visitor information, Avenida Marina Baixa 21, tel 96 680 12 08*) to

walk up to the church and hermitage of the Remedio, built over a Moorish castle, which gives fine views toward the Mediterranean. The CV785 finally joins the busy CV70, from which you turn off on the N332 to **Alfaz del Pi.** The pretty beach at **Albir ⑧** is overlooked by the rocky outcrop of Serra Helada, another good spot for hiking, this time with a sea breeze. ■

🗺 See area map p. 179
▶ Altea
🔄 36.6 miles (58.5 km)
🕐 3 hours (5–6 hours with stops)
▶ Albir

NOT TO BE MISSED
- Fonts de l'Algar
- Guadalest
- Confrides
- Finestrat

More places to visit in Valencia

ELX (ELCHE)

Twenty-five miles (32 km) southwest of Alacant (Alicante) lies the small town of Elx, known for three things: the much reproduced Iberian sculpture, La Dama de Elche, found here and now displayed at Madrid's Museo Arqueológico Nacional (see p. 73); the medieval mystery play enacted every August 14–15; and, visible year-round, the immense and majestic **palm grove.** With more than 125,000 date palms, it is Europe's largest. It is thought to have been planted by Phoenicians who established trading posts along this coast for several centuries before the birth of Christ. Growing alongside canals of brackish water on the eastern side of the Vinalopo River, the palms reach heights of up to 78 feet (24 m). You see many with branches bound up to create the *ramilletes* (bleached fronds) that are used in Palm Sunday processions. You can get a closer look

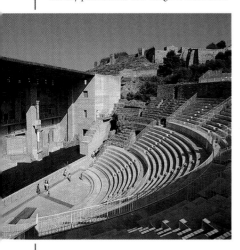

Sagunt's restored Roman amphitheater was built after Hannibal attacked the city.

at the **Huerto del Cura** (*Porta de la Morera, tel 96 545 19 36),* one of a series of separate, unenclosed plantations. Reigning supreme here among flowers and cactuses is the bizarre **Palmera Imperial,** which has seven secondary trunks.
🔼 179 A1 **Visitor information** ✉ Portell de Granyana, Parque Municipal ☎ 96 545 38 31

SAGUNT (SAGUNTO)

The story of Hannibal and his elephants crossing the Alps may be the one you know, but in Spain he is better known for his failure to defeat Rome, which led to Roman dominance of the peninsula. Sagunto, a Roman ally, put up an obstinate and heroic fight against Hannibal in 219 B.C. Later the town fell into decay, and by the time the Moors rolled up, it was renamed Murbiter, hardly inspiring as it meant "old walls." Today you can visit the imposing ruins of the old hilltop **fortress** *(Tel 96 266 55 81, closed Mon.),* added to by successive rulers. Remember, though, that the town is also engaged in heavy industry, so not every landscape is a delight. The best of the Roman remains is the heavily and controversially restored **amphitheater,** used as a venue during Sagunt's annual drama festival.
🔼 179 A2 **Visitor information** ✉ Plaza Cronista Chabret ☎ 96 266 22 13

XÀTIVA

About halfway between Valencia and Alacant on the inland route lies Xàtiva. A picturesque hill town among vineyards, it was one of Europe's first paper-manufacturing centers. The crenellated ramparts of a ruined 15th-century **castle** built on Moorish fortifications give sweeping views toward the sea. Just below, the Mozarabic church of **Sant Feliu** houses impressive Renaissance paintings. In the main historic center, head for **Plaza del Seo,** dominated by the bulky **Colegiata** (1596), standing opposite a more delicately decorated plateresque building, the former hospital. The most interesting spot is the **Museo del Almudín** (*Carrer de la Corretgeria 46, tel 96 227 65 97, closed Mon.),* housed in a former granary. Among excellent paintings, one portrait hangs upside down: This depicts Felipe V, who sacked most of the town in 1707. Xàtiva's spirit is also reflected in three remarkable emigrants to Italy: the great painter José de Ribera (1591–1652), and two notorious members of the Borja (Borgia) family who later became pope. One, the debauched Alexander VI, fathered infamous Cesare and Lucrezia Borgia.
🔼 179 A2 **Visitor information** ✉ Alameda Jaume I 50 ☎ 96 227 33 46 ∎

You can almost hear the Moorish and Christian armies thundering across the plains of this tableland punctuated by castles, super- lative cathedrals, numerous monasteries, and golden-stone Renaissance monuments.

Castilla y León

Corner turrets of Castillo de la Mota

Castilla y León

VAST, OFTEN HARSH, BUT ALWAYS MESMERIZING, THIS IS ARGUABLY THE quintessential region of northern Spain. Here you can explore secret villages, contemplate the serenity of Romanesque monasteries and churches, drive across endless plains of wheatfields, or clamber over the ramparts of medieval battlements. It is not all austerity: Salamanca and León are convivial and attractive cities to relax in.

Most of the nine provinces of Castilla y León are on the meseta, an arid, often barren plateau that lies between 2,300 feet (700 m) and 3,600 feet (1,100 m) above sea level. The climate is extreme, with mercilessly fierce summer temperatures and long harrowing winters. Each province is still touched by the Castilian spirit described by writer V.S. Pritchett in 1954 as "austere, frugal, and inhibited…puritan and grave." In between are tiny, simple farming villages where life and traditions have hardly changed in centuries.

Castilla y León is Old Castile, the original kingdom of Madrid. Castilla-La Mancha is New Castile, reconquered much later from the Moors. Dominating the landscape are the castles that gave the region its name in the ninth century, reminders of constant battles between Moors and Christians. In the towns are the emblazoned mansions of the ruling nobles, called *hidalgos,* meaning "free men." Catholicism is still deeply rooted. The Way of St. James (see pp. 88–89) pilgrimage route crossed the north of Old Castile, enriching the local population and resulting in the monumental cathedrals of Burgos and León. A string of monasteries and sanctuaries also lines the route.

The kingdoms of Castile and León were first united in 1037, a territorial marriage that was not fully consummated until the 13th century. Old Castile is the proud mother of the purest Castilian Spanish. The purest form of all is spoken in Burgos, seat of the first counts of Castile, and capital of Franco's provisional government

The castle at Arévalo

during the Civil War. This region was also the source of the Spanish culture that conquered the New World. Salamanca has some of Spain's finest Renaissance architecture and its first university. Ávila produced the feminist mystic, Santa Teresa. The legendary hero El Cid came from near Burgos, and Segovia has the archetypal, multiturreted royal castle.

Follow the course of the Duero River, from Zamora in the west to Peñafiel in the east, and you can sample Castilla y León's best wines (see pp. 134–36), organic sausages, cheese, and a wide variety of beans. Despite their haughty reputation, Castilians are welcoming to visitors. With city centers renovated and standards of living much improved since the 1980s, Castilians are proud of their heritage. ■

Map

Medina de Pomar
EUSKADI
P. 111
Oña
Frías
Castillo de Frías
Miranda de Ebro
Briviesca
A1
Belorado
Pradoluengo 2054m
Sierra de la Demanda
LA RIOJA
P. 111
Covarrubias
Salas de los Infantes
2228m
Santo Domingo de Silos
Sierra de Urbión
Duero
N111
Agreda
Peñaranda de Duero
◆ Numancia
Soria
Ólvega
El Burgo de Osma
San Esteban de Gormaz
Duero
Almazán
Sierra de Miñana
ARAGÓN
P. 111
Ayllón
Berlanga de Duero
Riaza
Santa María de Huerta
N11
Arcos de Jalón
Medinaceli
CASTILLA-LA MANCHA
p. 233
E   F

0   60 kilometers
0   40 miles

★ **Madrid**

Area of map detail

León

LIVELY AND ATTRACTIVE, LEÓN HAS AN EASILY NEGOTIATED
scale. Much of the old walled center—the **casco** *viejo*—is now pedestrianized, and ongoing renovation makes it a fabulous showpiece.
Historic buildings are being converted into apartments, and bars
and restaurants pack the Barrio Humédo quarter. The modern city
spreads westward along and over the banks of the Río Bernesga, but
still León's population barely tops 150,000.

León

🗺 210 C4

Visitor information

✉ Plaza de Regla 4

☎ 987 23 70 82

Catedral

✉ Plaza de Regla

☎ 987 87 57 70

🕐 Closed p.m.

The spires of the mighty **catedral,**
founded by Alfonso IX, are clearly
visible for a long way off, and for
centuries they have guided weary
pilgrims on their trek to Santiago
de Compostela (see pp. 88–93).
Little can prepare you for the
visual assault of entering this Gothic
masterpiece. It was built between the
mid-13th and late 14th centuries,
and has more than a hundred
stained-glass windows covering
an area of 19,375 square feet
(1,800 sq m). Painstaking restoration is almost complete. For searing
color, go late in the afternoon, when
sunlight pierces the rose window
above the magnificently sculpted
western portal. Other things to look

for are the Renaissance choir, with
four alabaster reliefs by Juan de
Badajoz, the Gothic tombs of the
ambulatory chapels; and the high
altar painting by Nicolás Francés
(died 1468).

The lofty vaults of the nave
are breathtaking in their scale
and simplicity, but they are easily
rivaled by the cloisters. You enter
through a plateresque (see p. 45)
doorway that doubles as the
entrance to the **museum** *(Closed
Sun.).* Frescoes by Nicolás Francés
and 16th-century keystone vaulting
in the galleries add to the impact
of this monumental courtyard.
Museum highlights include a textile
collection with fragments of

fourth- to seventh-century Coptic weavings, Chinese pieces, and a finely embroidered bishop's cape from the Philippines.

The **Basílica of San Isidoro** abuts the Roman ramparts at the northern perimeter of the old town. Although far less harmonious in style than the cathedral, as its construction ranged from the late 11th century through to a very baroque mid-18th century, it contains the remarkable **Panteón de los Reyes** (Kings' Pantheon) and a selective **museum** *(Tel 987 87 61 61, closed Sun. p.m., guided tours only).* Among other things here are 300 rare medieval books (in the library), the jewel-encrusted gold and agate chalice of Doña Urraca (11th century), and the silver reliquary of San Isidoro (whose bones, brought from Sevilla, inspired the building of the basilica). A spiral staircase goes down to the vaulted pantheon, which holds the sarcophagi of 23 kings and queens. Above are unique 12th-century frescoes covering every surface above the carved capitals of the columns. They illustrate not only the Last Supper and other biblical scenes, but also rural rites and life. The **cloisters** exhibit photos of Romanesque architecture throughout the region.

Forming the apex of a triangle between these two monuments, the **Palacio de los Guzmanes** *(Plaza de Santo Domingo, guided tours of upper floors on request)* is one of León's beautiful Renaissance mansions. Completed by the architect Rodrigo Gil de Hontañon in 1560, it has three floors around a typical arcaded patio, with gargoyles peering down from the roof, complex corner towers, and numerous carved coats of arms. It houses municipal offices. Immediately opposite stands the dreadful **Casa de Botines,** a mock-medieval

The regional government of Castilla y León is housed in this starkly modern building.

turreted castle designed by Antoni Gaudí (see pp. 172–75), and best left to its present occupier—a bank.

León's other major sight, the Renaissance **Convento de San Marcos,** lies west of the center on the banks of the Río Bernesga. The profusely decorated facade of this massive edifice extends over 109 yards (100 m). Behind are a *parador* (see p. 367), church, cloisters, and an archaeological museum, the **Museo de León** *(Convento de San Marcos, Plaza de San Marcos, tel 987 23 64 05, closed Sun p.m. & Mon.).* Among other dazzling exhibits in the museum, look for the beautiful Visigothic marble statue of Christ and a tenth-century jewel-encrusted cross.

Thirty miles (47 km) north of the city in a mountainous region of waterfalls and forests lie the cave formations of the **Cuevas de Valporquero** *(Tel 987 57 64 82, closed Oct.–Easter).* The vast subterranean spaces with stalactites and stalagmites have humidity at over 90 percent and a constant temperature of 45°F (7°C)—so be prepared, and take a sweater. ■

Zamora

Zamora

🅰 210 B2

Visitor information

✉ Calle Santa Clara 20

☎ 980 53 18 45

Catedral & Museo Catedralicio

✉ Plaza de la Catedral

☎ 980 53 06 44

🕐 Closed Mon.

💲 $

SOMETIMES CALLED A LIVING MUSEUM OF ROMANESQUE art, Zamora predates the Romanesque period. Its history goes back to the Celts and Romans who occupied this strategic hilltop site overlooking the Duero River. For most of the year, a charming, small-town atmosphere prevails, but in Holy Week Zamora's unique collection of *pasos* (sculpted floats) appears in fervent processions.

Zamora's Holy Week processions are renowned for their fervor.

Zamora's unusually squat 12th-century **catedral** has a beautiful dome clad in scalloped tiles and a Romanesque bell tower and south portal. Inside, look at the elaborately carved choir stalls and the anatomically perfect statue of Christ in the Capilla de San Bernardo. The 17th-century cloisters give access to the **museum,** which has remarkable silverware and exquisite 15th-century Flemish tapestries, including four illustrating the Trojan War. Behind the cathedral, peaceful gardens of the former castle abutting the old city walls give good views.

Zamora also has 16 Romanesque churches, each one different and many of them still functioning. All of the following are in the old town. At the beautifully proportioned **Santa María Magdalena** *(Rúa de los Francos, closed Mon.),* look at the delicately sculpted tomb of an unknown lady (1190) and intricate carvings in the southern portal. **San Cipriano** *(Plaza Claudio Moyano, closed Mon.)* has a purist interior: a single nave with ornamentation only in the carved capitals flanking the altar. Zamora's oldest church, **Santa María la Nueva** *(Calle Motín de la Trucha),* rebuilt in 1158, played an important role as both a refuge and a forum for nobles and their workforce.

Zamora's impressive civic architecture is later (16th century), notably the **Palacio de Los Momos** *(Plaza Zorilla)* with its exuberantly decorated Isabelline windows (now the Palace of Justice and not accessible to the public). The masterly Renaissance **Palacio del Cordón** houses the **Museo de Zamora** *(Palacio del Cordón, Plaza de Santa Lucia 2, tel 980 51 61 50, closed Mon.),* which has displays on local history and ethnography. ∎

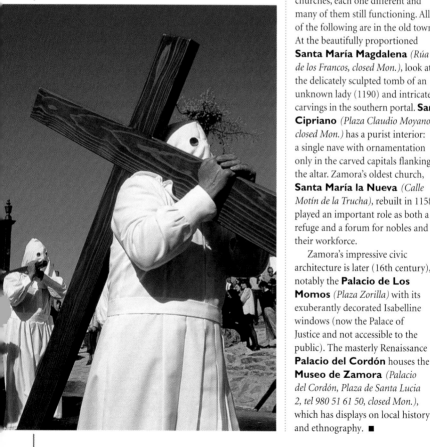

Valladolid

THE OVERTLY MODERN, FAST-GROWING CITY OF Valladolid plays a leading industrial role as Spain's chief car manufacturer but still has some intriguing secrets tucked away. With a population of 350,000, it is one of northern Spain's larger cities, but the partly pedestrianized center is easy to find your way around, and the shops are excellent. Valladolid was the residence of many early Castilian kings and is now the administrative capital of Castilla y León.

Valladolid
🅰 210 C3
Visitor information
✉ Calle Santiago 19
☎ 983 34 40 13

Museo Nacional de Escultura
✉ Colegio de San Gregorio, Calle Cadenas de San Gregorio 1
☎ 983 25 03 75 or 983 25 40 83

Its former status is symbolized by the **Plaza Mayor,** rebuilt in 1631 after a fire, and the dazzling sculpture collection of the **Museo Nacional de Escultura.** In the **Colegio de San Gregorio,** the magnificent setting of this museum is a remarkable example of Spanish Gothic dating from the late 15th century. The entrance gateway is a riot of sculpture inspired by plant forms. It is thought to be the work of Gil de Siloé, Simon of Cologne, and Juan Guas, and is rivaled in splendor by the patio, staircase, and funerary chapel of Fray Alonso. Sculptures on show, mainly in polychrome wood, cover the 13th to 18th centuries. In the 16th and 17th centuries, Valladolid was the uncontested master of this form. Some of the finest pieces are Alonso Berruguete's (circa 1488–1561) 16th-century altarpiece for San Benito, carved walnut choir stalls from the same church, and the "Burial of Christ" by Juan de Juni (died 1577). Adjoining the museum is the church of **San Pablo,** with a beautiful late Gothic facade by Simon of Cologne.

Valladolid's **catedral** is in a mixture of styles from the 16th to 19th centuries, but it has elaborate baroque decoration by the influential Alberto Churriguera (see p. 47), and a striking altarpiece by Juan de Juni. The **Museo Oriental** *(Paseo Filipinos 7, tel 983 30 68 00 or 983 30 69 00, closed Mon.–Sat. a.m. & Sun. p.m.),* housed in a neoclassic

Augustinian seminary, is an excellent antidote to a surfeit of Castilian religious art: It shows a priceless collection of sculpted ivory figures, embroidery, tribal pieces from the Philippines, and Chinese bronzes, porcelain, jade, calligraphy, and furniture. ■

The Gothic gateway to the Colegio de San Gregorio

The ship-shape, white stone castle of Peñafiel sits on a narrow ridge overlooking the Durero River.

Castles in Castilla y León

OLD CASTILE IS LIBERALLY STUDDED WITH CASTLES. Celtiberian fortified settlements were built over and multiplied by Roman military outposts. Moors built castles to defend their kingdom against the Christians of Asturias. As the Reconquest advanced south, Christian nobles rebuilt these and used them as bases for pushing farther south. Others were built completely afresh—nearly 90 survive today in Castilla y León. First the upper Ebré, and then the Duero was the front line between Christian kingdoms to the north and Moorish al-Andalus to the south. Castles proliferated on these demarcation lines, giving rise to the name of the kingdom of "Castilla." Most of these massive edifices are in magnificent sites.

Castillo de Coca

- 210 C2
- Coca, Segovia province
- 921 58 63 59
- Closed first Tues. of month
- $ (40-minute guided tour)

Castillo de Cuéllar

- 210 D2
- Cuéllar, Segovia province
- 921 14 22 03
- Closed weekdays in winter

Castillo de Frías

- 211 E4
- Frías, Burgos province
- 947 35 87 61

Castillo de Coca must be the ultimate in brick castles, with crenellated ramparts and polygonal turrets rising majestically from the plains about 30 miles (45 km) northwest of Segovia. It was built in Gothic Mudejar style for Alonso de Fonseca, archbishop of Sevilla, in 1453, and then given to the Marquis of Ayala and later the Duke of Alba (whose family still owns it, although it is used by a forestry training school). An outer square bailey encloses an inner one, both executed in decorative brickwork.

The **Pedro Mata Tower** has a circular room with a curious acoustic: Whisper a secret into a wall and it is heard on the opposite side. Here, too, the **dungeon** is a cruel reminder of those days when prisoners arrived through the ceiling, usually breaking their legs before enduring a long, slow death.

Set high on a citadel and incorporated into the town walls, **Castillo de Cuéllar** (mid-15th century) has been much lusted after. The original owner, Juan II, bequeathed the castle to his daughter

Isabel, but it was soon grabbed by her stepbrother Enrique IV, who then passed it to his favorite, Beltrán de la Cueva. Inside the castle is an extensive collection of antique arms.

Castillo de Frías is one of Castilla's most dramatically placed castles: It perches high on a craggy rock that towers over a charming medieval village. Although it is now mainly in ruins, you can climb up to the ramparts for stunning views north over the Ebré River. Construction spanned the 13th to 16th centuries, a period echoed in the church of **San Vicente** at the other end of the village. Below is a medieval fortified bridge.

Castillo La Mota is one of Castilla y León's greatest castles, with crenellated walls and a towering keep on a hilltop. Started by the Moors in the 13th century, it was much extended by Fernando and Isabel (see p. 31) in the 15th century. Their daughter, Juana the Mad, was another royal resident. It became a state prison, and Cesare Borgia was one of its political and military prisoners.

The austere 14th- to 16th-century **Castillo Pedraza de la Sierra** contrasts with one of Castilla's prettiest and best conserved medieval towns, its steep, narrow streets lined with atmospheric mansions, porticoes, and balconies. The castle belonged to the counts of Castile, the Fernández de Velasco family. Its present owners are the descendants of the painter Ignacio Zuloaga (1870–1945), some of whose works are exhibited beside antiques and engravings. The castle moat is cut into the rock, with circular and square towers rising above.

The elongated white stone **Castillo de Peñafiel** looms high above the plain and the charming wine-producing town at its feet. The castle was built in the 15th century, and the keep was remodeled in the following century for the Girón family, with walls 11 feet (3.5 m) thick and eight side-turrets. Visit the castle's **wine museum,** and don't miss the rest of this unusual town. **Plaza del Coso** is surrounded by timbered houses, and the church of **Santa María** has a museum of religious art. ∎

Castillo La Mota
- 210 C2
- Medina del Campo, Valladolid province
- 983 80 05 52
- Closed Sun. p.m.

Castillo Pedraza de la Sierra
- 210 D2
- Pedraza de la Sierra, Segovia province
- 921 50 98 25
- Closed Mon. & Tues., & when family is in residence

Castillo de Peñafiel
- 210 D3
- Peñafiel, Valladolid province
- 983 88 11 99
- Closed Mon.

Salamanca

SPEND A COUPLE OF DAYS IN SALAMANCA TO GET AN insight into Spain's earliest academic life and a complete picture of the evolution of Spanish architecture. Salamanca's university was opened in 1218. Over the centuries, this lively town has hardly stood still, and today its university population combines with a steady flow of visitors to create a dynamic, cosmopolitan atmosphere in which traditions are nonetheless respected.

The Romans founded Helmantica here and built a fine bridge that still spans the Tormes River. In 1102 the medieval city took root on the escarpment of its northern bank. Using a soft stone from nearby quarries whose high iron-ore content rusts into an inimitable golden color, the great men of Salamanca gradually constructed an architectural marvel. At its center is the **Plaza Mayor,** one of the most beautiful squares in Europe. This is where to start your exploration, sitting at a sidewalk café. Savor the majesty of the square, and pay homage to the Churriguera brothers (see pp. 46–47), who designed it in the 1720s. Look for the sculpted portraits of luminaries such as Christopher Columbus, El Cid, Cervantes, and a string of Spanish kings. At night the square becomes a stage set, invaded by wandering musicians and other street performers.

The main monuments lie west and south of here. The much photographed **Casa de las Conchas,** or House of Shells (*Calle Compañía, tel 923 26 93 17*), was once a palace and is now a public library. The stone Renaissance facade comes alive with 400 sculpted scallop shells, the symbol worn by pilgrims to Santiago de Compostela. Inside the courtyard are delicately carved balustrades and lions' heads. The pedestrianized Rúa Mayor is the most com-

mercial in Salamanca, as it leads straight to the cathedral, which dominates broad Plaza de Anaya. Turn down any side street, however, and you are projected back in time.

The massive cathedral is in fact two adjoining buildings: the Catedral Nueva (New Cathedral), which you enter first beneath the decorative Renaissance stonework of the west facade, and the Catedral Vieja (Old Cathedral). The **Catedral Nueva** dates from 1513, and additions over the next two centuries created a mixture of styles from late Gothic through Renaissance and plateresque to baroque. What is immediately striking is the immense scale. Visitors become antlike beside soaring carved arches, ribbed columns, and the ornately carved choir, another work of the Churriguera brothers. Here, too, you see one of Spain's most famous organs, the work of Pedro de Echevarría in 1745.

Go behind the main altar to see the much revered 11th-century figure of Christ set into an exuberant Churrigueresque altarpiece. And don't miss the **Patio Chico,** through a door in the south aisle, a terrace which gives an all-encompassing view of the old cathedral, cupola, and baroque tower of the new cathedral.

The entrance to the **Catedral Vieja** is also off the south aisle. As you step into its Romanesque serenity, the contrast could not be

Salamanca
🅰 210 B2
Visitor information
✉ Plaza Mayor 14
☎ 923 21 83 42

Catedral
✉ Plaza de Anaya
☎ 923 21 74 76
💲 $ (Catedral Vieja)

Convento de
las Úrsulas

LAS ÚRSULAS

PARQUE DE
SAN FRANCISCO

RAMÓN Y CAJAL

C. CONDES
DE CRESPO RASCÓN

Casa de las
Muertes

PLAZA
DE LOS
BANDOS

CALLE DE ZAMORA

CALLE DE TORO

AZAFRANAL

PLAZA
SANTA
EULALIA

GRAN VÍA

CUESTA DE
SANCTI SPIRITUS

PLAZA
MAYOR

PLAZA DEL
MERCADO

PLAZA SAN
CRISTÓBAL

CALLE PRIOR

DE LA

CALLE ANCHA

CALLE CERVANTES

CALLE DE LA COMPAÑÍA

Iglesia de
San Martín

PLAZA
ANGEL

CALLE SAN JUSTO

CALLE

Torre del
Clavero

CALLE MAYOR

CALLE DE SAN PABLO

PEDRO COJOS

SANTA CLARA

PASEO DE CANALEJAS

Casa de las
Conchas

Palacio de
Congresos

SERRANOS

Palacio de
Fonseca
(Diputación)

PLAZA
DE
COLÓN

Convento de
las Dueñas

MARQUESA DE ALMARZA

PATIO DE LAS
ESCUELAS

Hospital
del Estudio

Universidad

LIBREROS

RÚA MAYOR

Escuelas
Mayores

PLAZA
ANAYA

PLAZA
SANTA
DOMINGO

ROSARIO

Escuelas
Menores

Casa
Museo
Unamuno

Catedral
Nueva

Catedral
Vieja

Convento de
San Esteban

C. SAN
GREGORIO

PLAZA DEL
PUENTE

PASEO DEL

RECTOR

ESPERABÉ

PUENTE ROMANO

Tormes

AVE REYES
DE ESPAÑA

| 0 | | 200 meters |
| 0 | | 200 yards |

Lofty and
elegant,
Salamanca's
"new" cathedral
was built
between 1513
and 1733.

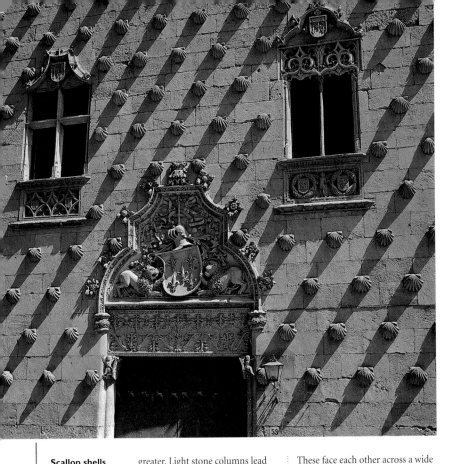

Scallop shells cover the extraordinary front of the Casa de las Conchas in ornate plateresque style.

greater. Light stone columns lead your eye to an early Renaissance **altarpiece** comprised of 53 exquisitely painted panels surrounding a bejeweled statue of the Virgin of the Vega, patron saint of Salamanca. This gilded sculpture dates from the late 12th century, as does the cathedral. Other outstanding features are the wall of frescoes (1262) by Antón Sánchez de Segovia, one of Europe's oldest works by a known artist, and the beautiful dome above the transept. You must also look at the part-Romanesque cloisters and **Capilla de Talavera,** with its Mudejar dome.

Back outside Salamanca's glowing edifices, head 200 yards (183 m) east to the church of San Esteban, attached to a Dominican monastery, and the convent of Las Dueñas.

These face each other across a wide street, but if you have time for only one, opt for the **Convento de San Esteban** *(Avenida Santo Domingo, tel 923 21 50 00).* The facade (1524–1610) is a stunning example of fine plateresque carving. Inside, the luminous single nave focuses on a fabulous Churrigueresque altarpiece, 98 feet (30 m) in height, that surrounds a painting of the martyrdom of St. Stephen (San Esteban). For an even better view, look from the elevated choir above the nave. You reach this through the **King's Cloister,** which blends Gothic, Renaissance, and plateresque details, and is notable for medallions depicting prophets. Climb the magnificent **grand staircase** to the upper gallery and the **biblioteca** (library), which exhibits lovely 17th-century ivory statues from the Philippines, and then continue to the choir viewpoint.

The **Convento de las Dueñas** *(Avenida Santo Domingo, tel 923 21 54 42)* is more intimate in scale, and its pretty Renaissance cloisters are the main point of interest. Dominican nuns still live in the convent and run a good business selling homemade cakes. The lattice screens of their cell windows are visible from the well-tended gardens of the cloisters. Go around the side of the convent to see the **Torre del Clavero,** an octagonal tower that is the only remnant of a medieval castle. It has traces of Mudejar decoration.

UNIVERSIDAD DE SALAMANCA

Salamanca's prestige was built upon its university, which opened in 1218 and is one of the world's oldest, a contemporary of the universities of Paris and Bologna. Its various buildings are clustered around Calle Serranos and Calle Libreros, immediately west of Rúa Mayor. The most spectacular facade is that of the **Escuelas Mayores,** a plateresque masterpiece completed in 1533 for the original Gothic university behind. Inside, the modernized patio (with a Mudejar wooden ceiling) is surrounded by the old lecture halls where literati such as the philosopher Miguel de Unamuno (see p. 51) once held sway. A beautiful carved stone staircase leads to the upper floor, where you can peer at the prodigious library through a glass vestibule. The shelves contain around 2,770 manuscripts, 483 incunabula (early books), and 62,000 pre-19th-century publications.

Flanking this building to the south is the **Casa Museo Unamuno,** the home of the writer Miguel de Unamuno, mostly of interest to

those who know his work. Opposite, overlooking a small square, are the **Hospital del Estudio** (Students' Hospice) and neighboring **Escuela Menores** (for pre-university studies). Here you discover a delightful Gothic patio and, in the **Museo Universitaria,** an extraordinary ceiling decoration, the Cielo de Salamanca (Salamanca Sky), transferred from the old library. Only a third of it is here, but it is enough to convey the finesse of Fernando Gallego's 1473 illustration of the cosmos and celestial beings. Other Renaissance exhibits include a collection of walnut sculptures by Felipe Bigarny, paintings, and dazzling silverwork. Next door, the curious **Sala de las Tortugas** (Tortoise Room) shows the world's second largest fossil collection. ■

Salamanca's Escuelas Mayores, built by order of Fernando and Isabel, bears their figures in its intricate plateresque facade.

Universidad de Salamanca

✉ Patio de Escuelas 1
☎ 923 29 44 00
🕐 Closed Sun. p.m.
💲 $

Ciudad-Rodrigo

Ciudad-Rodrigo
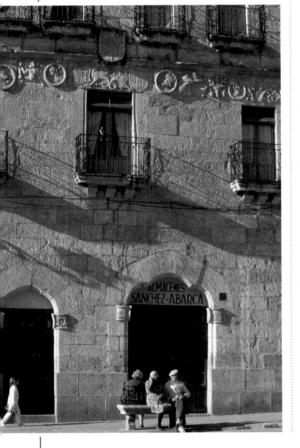
210 B1

Visitor information
Plaza de Amayuelas 5
923 46 05 61

Catedral
Plaza San Salvador
923 48 14 24
Closed during services
$ (cloisters)

Emblazoned facade of a mansion

OUT ON A LIMB IN LONELY COUNTRY TOWARD THE Portuguese border, the fortified hilltop town of Ciudad-Rodrigo is one of northern Spain's delightful secrets, redolent with history without being affected by mass tourism. It comes to life every year at the start of the bullfighting season, during Carnival in February, when the *encierro*—the running of the bulls—takes over the streets.

The surrounding agricultural region is by no means prosperous—you might guess this from Ciudad-Rodrigo's rather dubious speciality, *el farinato*, a sausage made from flour and lard, generally eaten with fried eggs. Years ago, this was surpassed by green lizard stew, but protected species status has taken it off local menus. The illustrious past is recalled by a string of elegant emblazoned palaces. The town was named for Count Rodrigo González Girón, who resettled it after driving out the Moors in the early 12th century. In 1812, the Duke of Wellington recaptured Ciudad Rodrigo from Napoleon's forces after a bloody siege and battle. Ciudad-Rodrigo's strategic position on the frontier is symbolized above all by its massive 12th-century ramparts. There are several stairways that follow the 1-mile (1.6 km) sentry path—to very good views.

Rising above the town is the 14th-century **castle of Enrique II de Trastámara,** now a *parador* (see p. 367). The austere stone walls bear traces of Roman foundations, and the crenellated towers are spectacularly illuminated at night. The **catedral,** has features from the 12th century in addition to a beautiful 13th-century portal, Portada de la Virgen, Isabelline choir stalls exuberantly carved by Rodrigo Alemán, an alabaster Renaissance altarpiece, and cloisters in a mix of architectural styles. Richly ornamented tombs of noblemen and women add to its interest.

Next door the more sober Capilla de Cerralbo is worth a visit for its altar-painting by José Ribero. Walk south to reach the town's main social gathering place, arcaded **Plaza del Buen Alcalde**—then sample a farinato. ■

Ávila

THE WALLED TOWN OF ÁVILA IS ONE OF SPAIN'S MOST spectacular urban sights, but within Spain it is more famous for just one person. The mystic Santa Teresa was born here in 1515, and convents and churches devoted to her grace its streets. It is a small town of 50,000 inhabitants perched on a spur above the Río Adaja at an altitude of over 3,700 ft (1,130 m). Winters are particularly harsh, but in any other season, it's pleasant to explore on foot.

Ávila's perfectly preserved walls date from the 11th century, when the 88 cylindrical towers and 9 gateways were built to fend off the Moors. You can walk 1.5 miles (2.5 km) beside the walls for panoramic views. Abutting the walls at the older, eastern end is the 12th- to 15th-century **cathedral.** Look for the tomb of El Tostado (a 15th-century bishop nicknamed "the toasted one" for his dark complexion). There are also finely carved plateresque choir stalls, two unusual wrought-iron pulpits, and a Renaissance altarpiece. Don't miss the 13th-century **sacristy** with its octagonal vaulted ceiling. Go through to the **museum,** where you find a gigantic silver monstrance (1571). The delicate Gothic **cloisters** lie next to the museum.

Turn right on leaving the cathedral to reach the Puerta de San Vicente and, just outside the walls, the **Basílica de San Vicente** *(Plaza San Vicente, tel 920 25 52 30, closed Mon.).* This Romanesque-Gothic construction has an exceptional sculpted west portal. Inside is the canopied **sarcophagus** of San Vicente and his sisters.

Santa Teresa, one of Spain's patron saints, was a great mystic, rebel, and writer, and founder of the barefoot Carmelite order. Her birthplace in Ávila is marked by the **Convento de Santa Teresa** *(Plaza de la Santa).* The **Convento de la Encarnación** *(Calle de la Encarnación, closed Tues.),* where she lived for 27 years, has a rather dull museum dedicated to her far-from-dull life. ■

Ávila's surrounding walls, restored in parts, look exactly as they did in the Middle Ages.

Ávila
- 🅰 210 C1
- **Visitor information**
- ✉ Plaza de la Catedral 4
- ☎ 920 21 13 87

Catedral
- ✉ Plaza de la Catedral
- ☎ 920 21 16 41
- 🕐 Closed public holidays
- 💲 $ (museum)

In & around Segovia

Segovia's Roman aqueduct, a masterpiece of 118 arches, brought water from the Frio River, several miles away.

LIKE A HUGE SHIP MOORED ON THE PLAIN OF OLD CASTILE, Segovia is one of northern Spain's most seductive towns. Depending on where you come from, your first sight may take in the Roman aqueduct, cathedral, and fantasy palace of the Alcázar, all clustered around the prominent limestone outcrop on which the old town stands. In addition to the monuments that have made it a world heritage city, Segovia has a healthy cultural life and a meat-and-game gastronomy produced in capacious brick ovens.

Segovia
🅰 210 D2
Visitor information
✉ Plaza Mayor 10
☎ 921 46 03 34

Catedral
✉ Plaza Mayor
☎ 921 46 22 05
💲 $ (cloisters, chapterhouse, museum)

In summer or winter you feel the climate change as you approach the city, for Segovia lies at 3,300 feet (1,000 m). The Romans were the first to recognize the site's attractions: The 95-foot-high (29 m) aqueduct spanning Plaza de Azoguejo still stands as proof of their superior engineering. After Visigothic and Moorish domination, Segovia came into its own in 1088 when the Castilian king Alfonso VI installed his court there and initiated a properous period represented by over 40 Romanesque churches. Segovia reached its zenith in 1474 when Isabel la Católica was proclaimed Queen of Castile in the

church of San Miguel. The town declined under the Habsburg kings (16th and 17th centuries), but enjoyed an 18th-century renaissance.

Segovia's old town is very much a place to explore, so arm yourself with a map from the visitor center and head for the backstreets, all of which contain notable churches, towers, and mansions enlivened by numerous storks. The hub of the old town is semiporticoed **Plaza Mayor,** lined with lively cafés and dominated by the huge, rhythmical hulk of the **catedral.** This Flamboyant Gothic extravaganza houses some rarities in its lofty interior, notably the baroque main altarpiece by Andrea Sabatini (circa 1480–1530) and the "Entombment" sculpture by Juan de Juni (died 1577) in a side chapel off the south aisle. The choir stalls and the cloisters were saved from the old cathedral, which was destroyed by fire during the Revolt of the Communeros (1520–1521) against Carlos V.

From the Plaza Mayor, follow Calle Infanta Isabel to reach Segovia's most striking square, **Plaza de San Martín.** This terraced area surrounds a statue of Juan Bravo, a local hero, in the shadow of the magnificent church of **San Martín.** Like most of Segovia's churches, this is open only for services, but you can admire the Mudejar tower and Romanesque capitals of the porch. Next door stands the elegant 17th-century **royal prison,** now a public library, and across the square looms a 14th-century tower, the **Torreón de Lozoya** *(Plaza de San Martín, tel 921 46 24 61, open from 7 p.m.),* now used for art exhibitions. A few steps farther bring you to the **Casa de los Picos** *(Calle Juan Bravo 33),* a 15th-century mansion with a remarkable facade of diamond-shaped granite studs. This is now the School of Applied Arts. You see plenty of facades decorated in plaster relief patterns *(esgrafiados)* throughout this quarter, including that of the **Alhóndiga,** meaning "public granary." This building is now home to the Municipal Archives. Both the Alhóndiga and the neighboring **Palacio de Aspiroz** *(Plaza Platero Oquendo).* are typical of 15th-century Segovian architecture.

Without a doubt, Segovia's greatest landmark is the **Alcázar,** the turreted castle that rises like a mirage at the western tip of the outcrop above the confluence of the Clamores and Eresma Rivers. The

Habsburg king Felipe II was responsible for the building of this unexpected sight. It was during his reign that major additions were made to the original medieval castle, and the roof bristles with slate-roofed turrets. But thank also the 1880s restorers who enhanced the castle's theatricality after a fire. It was then handed over to the Royal Artillery, who have a museum inside. Ask at the ticket office for a leaflet with detailed descriptions of the interior, although the itinerary tends to change. Arrows guide you through, from the medieval entrance hall with original mullioned windows to the elaborate throne room that dazzles with restored Mudejar decoration. Tapestries, antique furniture, paintings, beautiful coffered Mudejar ceilings (look in particular at the one in the chapel), and suits of armor accompany you throughout. Don't miss the panoramic views from the roof of the keep, reached by over 150 narrow steps in a tower beside the ticket office, and notice the half-formed turrets of its ramparts—truly theatrical!

The Torreón de Lozoya dominates the Plaza de San Martín in the heart of the old aristocratic quarter.

Alcázar

✉ Plaza de la Reina Victoria Eugenia

☎ 921 46 07 59

$ $. Free on Tues. for E.U. nationals

The whimsical Alcázar, built in Habsburg style, appears like a Germanic mirage in Segovia.

San Ildefonso de la Granja
- 🅰 210 D2
- ✉ Plaza de España San Ildefonso
- ☎ 921 47 00 19 or 921 47 00 20
- 🕐 Closed Sun. p.m., Mon., & public holidays
- 💲 $$. Free on Wed. for E.U. nationals

Real Palacio de Riofrío
- 🅰 210 D1
- ✉ Bosque de Riofrío
- ☎ 921 47 00 19 or 921 47 00 20
- 🕐 Closed Sun. p.m. & Mon.
- 💲 $$. Free on Wed. for E.U. nationals

ROYAL ENVIRONS

Segovia's environs are also replete with royal memorabilia. The finest is **San Ildefonso de la Granja,** 7 miles (11 km) southeast on the N601, in a stunning location at the foot of the Guadarrama Mountains. Begun in 1721, the palace reflects the nostalgia of the Bourbon king Felipe V for his grandfather's palace—Versailles in France. Several architects contributed to La Granja, producing a blend of Spanish baroque and French neo-classic styles. Marble, gilded stucco, and velvet surround predictably lavish furnishings such as beautiful 16th-century Flemish tapestries and scintillating chandeliers. The latter were made at the nearby glass factory, the **Real Fábrica de Cristales** *(Paseo del Pocillo, tel 921 47 17 12, closed Sun. p.m.in winter & Mon.),* where you can watch glassblowing and see a display of antique glass. The palace also has exceptional, extensive formal gardens, the work of French landscape gardeners, which, again like Versailles, are strewn with statues and fountains.

Felipe V's second wife, Isabella Farnese, was responsible for the royal retreat at **Riofrío,** 4 miles (7 km) south of Segovia off the N603. More a country mansion than a palace, it is surrounded by 1,700 acres (700 ha) of lovely holm-oak woods. The pink Italianate building houses valuable paintings (by Ribera, Velázquez, and Rubens), plus a museum of hunting.

SIERRA DE GUADARRAMA

Slicing across the border between Madrid and Castilla y León, this -62-mile (100 km) mountain range of granite outcrops, streams, and forests of oak and pine attracts hordes of overheated Madrileños in summer. With its highest peak, **Peñalara,** rising to 7,970 feet (2,429 m), the sierra is also a popular winter skiing destination, with low-key resorts at Navacerrada, Valcotos, Valdesqui, and La Pinilla. Hiking opportunities include the pine forest of **Valsaín,** 5 miles (8 km) south of La Granja, and the slopes around the forbidding fortress of **Manzanares el Real** higher up. ■

Soria

ALTHOUGH NOT THE MOST COMPELLING OF CASTILLA Y León's provincial capitals, Soria still holds some interest. Above all, it lies at the heart of some beautiful landscapes. This province is a region of transition wedged between Castilla, Aragón, and La Rioja. Northwest is the magnificent Sierra de Urbión, known for prolific game and trout. East is the dramatically rugged Sierra de Moncayo.

The red-tiled roofs of golden sandstone houses, much lauded by the poet Antonio Machado (1875-1939), slot into the narrow streets of a compact, albeit sleepy, town center. This stretches south from the formal **Parque Alameda de Cervantes** through squares and pedestrian streets to **Plaza Mayor,** the hub of the town. An interesting web of streets lies between, centering on **Calle Aduana Vieja.** Here, emblazoned Renaissance facades lead you to the Romanesque church of **Santo Domingo,** with statues of its founders flanking the richly carved portal, a rose window, and tiers of niches.

Other churches lie south, near the Duero River. The **cathedral of San Pedro** *(Obispo Agustín, tel 975 21 20 25, closed Sun. p.m. & Mon.)* dates mostly from the 16th century but has pure Romanesque cloisters. Across the Duero are the remains of the **Monasterio de San Juan de Duero** *(Camino Monte de las Ánimas, tel 975 22 13 97, closed Sun. p.m. & Mon.),* built with Moorish influence in the 13th century. From here you can see the **Parque del Castillo,** a landscaped hill topped by a *parador.*

The Romans rebuilt **Numancia** *(4 miles/7 km northeast of Soria)* in 133 B.C. The Roman ruins are of interest only for enthusiasts, but in town the **Museo Numantino** *(Paseo del Espolón 8, tel 975 22 13 97, closed Sun. p.m. & Mon.),* beside the Alameda de Cervantes park, has Roman artifacts. ∎

The atmospheric ruins of the Monasterio de San Juan de Duero include the curious remains of a Romanesque cloister.

Soria

🅰 211 E3

Visitor information

✉ Plaza Ramón y Cajal

☎ 975 21 20 52

Monks' graves on the hillside overlook Santo Domingo de los Silos.

Drive to Arlanza: Valley of Towers

From its source in the Sierra de Urbión, the Arlanza River meanders through a dramatic valley west to Lerma. This drive takes you through beautiful, often wild countryside, much of it ideal hiking territory. On the way visit jewel-like churches, each one in a different architectural style.

Leave Burgos on the N1/E6 in the direction of Madrid. After 22 miles (36 km), just after crossing the Arlanza River, turn off the high-way at the exit marked Lerma–Estacion. Follow the signs into **Lerma ❶,** and then drive through a stone arch, **Arco de la Cárcel.** This is all that remains of the medieval town walls, uphill to Plaza Mayor.

In front stands the **Palacio Ducal,** aus-tere symbol of the extensive political power of Francisco Gómez, Duke of Lerma, who virtu-ally ruled Spain from 1598 to 1618. The duke created Spain's best example of a 17th-century planned town. The old quarter, with many mansions and porticoes, lies downhill, and is best seen on foot. From the square, walk down Calle de la Audiencia past the former convent of Santa Teresa, now the town hall and tourist office *(Casa Consistorial, Calle de la Audiencia, tel 947 17 70 02, closed Mon. & Tues.).* The **Plaza de Santa Clara** is flanked by the

monastery of La Ascensión and a balcony with sweeping views. Lerma's most important ecclesiastical monument, the 1617 church of San Pedro, or **Colegiata** *(Closed Mon.),* just beyond, houses one of Spain's oldest organs.

Leave Lerma by continuing across the Plaza Mayor (following signs "Todas direcciones"),

---

- 🗺 See area map pp. 210–211
- ▶ Burgos
- ↔ 89 miles (142 km)
- 🕒 2.5 hours (excluding visits)
- ▶ Burgos

NOT TO BE MISSED
- Colegiata, Lerma
- Monasterio de Santo Domingo
- Colegiata, Covarrubias
- San Pedro de Arlanza
- Ermita Visigótica

Visigothic relief work, Quintanilla

and turn right downhill to take the left turnoff signed Santo Domingo de Silos. This local road (BU 900) winds gently through rolling hills and wheatfields, passing little stone villages typical of the Arlanza, such as **Castrillo de Solarana,** with a massive rocky outcrop rising to the south. Turn right at the next junction (signed Santo Domingo), and after 1 mile (2 km) turn right into Santibañez del Val. Follow signs for the Ermita Mozárabe, past the village church, and left at a junction to continue beyond the hamlet, parallel to the Ura River, for half a

mile. Cross a bridge to reach the charming little stone hermitage of **Santa Cecilia de Barriosuso ❷,** which dates from the 10th to 13th centuries. Below is a restored Roman bridge and a source of spring water *(fuente).*

Return to the BU900 to drive 3 miles (5 km) to **Santo Domingo de Silos.** This idyllic medieval village is the home of the **Monasterio de Santo Domingo de Silos ❸** *(Tel 947 39 00 68, closed Sun.–Mon. & public holidays until 4:30 p.m.).* As well as boasting one of the world's most beautiful monastery cloisters, it is more famous for the hugely successful recordings made by the monks. You can hear their melodic Gregorian chants during Mass *(Daily at 9 a.m., 7 p.m., & 9:40 p.m.)* in the 18th-century church. Take time to explore the cobbled streets of the village, and then visit the **cloisters.** The lower floor has carved 11th- to 12th-century capitals decorated with harpies, griffons, and other motifs on slender double columns. The ceiling is pure 14th-century Mudejar artistry, and the corner pillars have eight superb Romanesque bas-reliefs illustrating the life of Jesus. Of the many treasures in the **museum,** look for the 11th-century chalice of Santo Domingo, the Romanesque woman's head, the manuscript of the Mozarabic rite (tenth to eleventh century), and the old pharmacy with fine Talavera jars.

From Santo Domingo backtrack 4 miles (6 km) along the BU900, and then turn right to Covarrubias. For 7 miles (11 km) the road winds up through forested rocky hills, before descending to the village of **Covarrubias** ④

Exquisitely carved Romanesque capitals surround Santo Domingo's monastery cloisters in the old town of Santo Domingo.

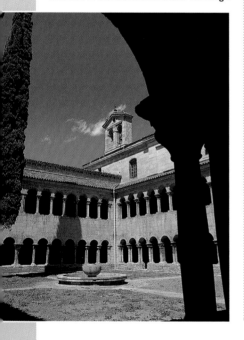

(Visitor information, tel 947 40 64 61, closed Jan. & Feb.), huddled at the base of the Sierra de las Mamblas. Wander through the streets past impeccably maintained medieval houses, admiring those of Doña Sancha and Doña Urraca that flank squares of the same names. The church of San Cosme y San Damián, or **Colegiata** *(Tel 947 40 63 11, closed Mon.–Tues., guided tour only)* is a harmonious white stone Gothic structure commenced in 1474. Numerous tombs include the sarcophagi of Fernán González, count of Castile, his wife Sancha, and three princesses. The 400-year-old organ still functions. The delicately carved cloisters, dating from 1528–1535, surround a lovely patio with a fountain and lead to the museum, a treasure trove of statues, papal bulls (documents), and 150 magnificent bishop's capes. The artworks include a painting by Jan van Eyck (circa 1390–1441) and a high relief triptych of the Adoration of the Magi by an unknown 16th-century artist.

Leave Covarrubias by following signs to San Pedro de Arlanza, 4 miles (6 km) away on the C110. Now an evocative ruin, **San Pedro de Arlanza** ⑤ *(Closed Sun. p.m., Mon., & last weekend of month)* was one of Castilla's largest Benedictine monasteries. The church structure dates from 1080 and the entire site is under renovation. The C110 continues through a delightful valley overshadowed by another towering escarpment, crisscrossing the Arlanza River before joining the N234 at Hortigüela. Turn left here and drive 4.4 miles (7 km) to a turnoff to the right marked Quintanilla de las Viñas. This narrow minor road twists through open wheatfields to reach the village of Quintanilla de las Viñas, where you take a right fork marked Ermita Visigótica. A few more bends and you come to the **Ermita Visigótica** ⑥ *(Closed Mon., first Tues., & last weekend of month),* the oldest religious structure of this region. It is a simple stone hermitage of the late seventh century, decorated with Visigothic carved friezes of grapes, birds, turkeys, and monograms. Similar whimsical carvings are inside.

Return to the N234, turn right and after 2.5 miles (4 km) pass the cave houses of **Cuevas de San Clemente** before returning to Burgos, reconnecting with the N1/E6 at Saldaña de Burgos. ■

Burgos

THIS PROSPEROUS AND ULTRACONSERVATIVE CITY ON THE Way of St. James has one of Spain's greatest Gothic cathedrals, and for this alone it is an essential stop in the barren *meseta* (plateau). Its other Gothic treasures are the monasteries of Las Huelgas and Miraflores, just outside town. Burgos also has the ghost of the heroic warrior and mercenary El Cid, whose legendary exploits ended in death at the hands of the Moors in 1099. His body was brought from the monastery of San Pedro de Cardeña, southeast of Burgos, to be entombed in the cathedral in 1921.

Burgos
- 🅰 210 D3

Visitor information
- ✉ Plaza Alonso Martínez 7
- ☎ 947 20 18 46

Catedral
- ✉ Plaza de Santa María
- ☎ 947 20 47 12
- ⏰ Closed Easter Thurs., Good Fri., & April 1–2
- 💲 $ (cloisters area & chapels)

Burgos is strung out on both banks of the Arlanza River, but the atmospheric old town lies to the north and can be easily toured on foot. Towering above everything are the lacelike steeples of the **catedral,** commenced in 1221 and extended over the next five centuries by some of Spain's most outstanding craftsmen. Audiophones, available for rent, are helpful for following the cathedral's complexities. Third in size after the cathedrals of Sevilla and Toledo, it presents an overwhelming display of Flamboyant Gothic design, sculpture, funerary art, carved Renaissance choir stalls, baroque wrought iron, and, despite considerable plundering by Napoleon's troops in 1809, a rich treasury. This is housed in the sacristy, the 14th-century **Capilla de Santa Catalina,** and the chapterhouse (with a beautiful coffered Mudejar ceiling), all of which lie off the cloisters. Admission to this area includes access to the main side chapels and the high altar. Look for the "Virgin and Child" by Hans Memling (circa 1430–1494), Diego de Siloé's "Christ at the Column," and stunning processional crosses made in Burgos.

Each of the side chapels is a work of art. In the **Capilla del Condestable,** designed by Simon of Cologne in 1482, note the star-shaped dome, heavily sculpted walls and altar, and the tombs of the Constable and his wife. The intricately sculpted back of the high altar illustrates the ascent to Calvary. West of the nave in the **Capilla de Santa Ana,** a massive Gothic altarpiece details events from the saint's life, and in the **Capilla de Santa Tecla,** there is a rococo ceiling sheltering an elaborate Churrigueresque (see pp. 46–47) altarpiece dedicated to this martyr. ■

Perched on the banks of the Arlanza River, Burgos has some of Spain's most spectacular medieval architecture.

More places to visit in Castilla y León

EL BURGO DE OSMA

This delightful old town has an air of faded grandeur, especially in the dilapidated medieval streets surrounding the Gothic **catedral** *(Plaza de la Catedral, closed Mon.)*. Originally built for the Cistercians, it acquired late Gothic cloisters and also has a baroque bell tower and ambulatory. The cloisters museum has interesting pieces, but the main attraction of Burgo de Osma is its placid streets, lined with 16th-century porticoes, and majestic emblazoned buildings such as the **Hospital de San Agustín** (1694) on Plaza Mayor. The hospital was built outside the town wall, but in the late 18th century it was incorporated into a new quarter. Today the building is used as an exhibition center. In the arcaded **Calle Mayor,** explore the specialist foodshops for local fare: cakes, pâté de foie gras, blood-pudding, and ewe's cheese, and then join bereted old men

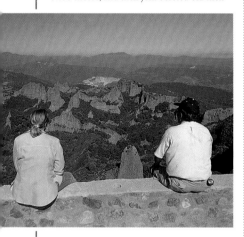

Surveying the view from Orellan over the red-ocher formations of Las Médulas

on the Plaza Mayor for a coffee.
🅰 211 E2 **Visitor information** ✉ Calle Mayor 6 ☎ 975 36 01 36

LAS MÉDULAS

Added to UNESCO's cultural heritage list in 1997, the Roman gold mines of Las Médulas are this region's most spectacular archaeological sight. These remnants of Roman excavations lie 14 miles (22 km) southwest of Ponferrada, close to the Galician border and the Sil River, and cover a vast, desertlike area, interrupted only by gnarled chestnut trees. The reddish ocher crags are most striking toward sundown, when their contours seem to catch fire. A visitor center explains the sophisticated system of hydraulics, tunnels, and channels set up by the Romans, and you can follow trails or drive effortlessly to a viewpoint at Orellan to admire this surreal landscape.
🅰 210 B4 **Aula Arqueológica de Las Médulas** www.bierzonet.es/ieb ☎ 987 40 19 54
🕐 Closed Mon. & Tues. a.m. (summer), Mon.–Fri. & Sun. p.m. (winter)

TORDESILLAS

Smack in the middle of the wine-growing region between Zamora and Valladolid, the friendly little town of Tordesillas stands at a busy intersection. It is notorious for the Treaty of Tordesillas, signed here in 1494, which carved up the New World between Spain and Portugal. The sight to head for is **Monasterio de Santa Clara** *(Tel 983 77 00 71, closed Sun. p.m. & Mon., guided tour),* built in 1350 as a royal palace. As the home of Pedro I's Andalucian mistress, it acquired extensive Moorish features, including Sevillian *azulejos* (tiles) and a stuccoed, arched patio. In 1373 a church was built and nuns were admitted; 13 *claustrados* (cloistered nuns) live there today. Outstanding features are the carved Mudejar ceiling (1430) of the church and the 43 paintings of saints, set off by Moorish stuccowork. A Gothic side chapel housed the tombs of the Catholic monarchs, Fernando and Isabel before they were moved to El Escorial and subsequently Granada, and it still has a superb gilded altarpiece by Nicolás Francés. A collection of unusual musical instruments includes a portable organ used by Juana the Mad. After the death of her husband, she was declared insane by Fernando (her father) and Carlos V (her son), and was shut away in Tordesillas for 46 years, from 1509–1555.
🅰 210 C2 **Visitor information** ✉ Calle del Tratado ☎ 983 77 10 67 ■

Out of the bleak plains of La Mancha spring surprises such as Cuenca and Toledo. Extremadura's bucolic hills and valleys lead to the historical Cáceres, Mérida, and Trujillo. This is a region for heading off the beaten track.

Castilla-La Mancha & Extremadura

Conquistador celebrations in Trujillo

Castilla-La Mancha & Extremadura

CASTILLA-LA MANCHA, THAT GREAT SWATH OF LAND THAT LIES BETWEEN Madrid and Andalucía, is not Spain's most compelling region. Flat, monotonous, and seemingly devoid of inhabitants, it seems drab compared with its neighboring regions on all sides—including Extremadura, which is a place of rural delights. For many people Extremadura represents the last bastion of old Spain, sidelined by the dynamism of the country's other autonomous communities, but still an enclave of tradition, Catholicism, and unspoiled countryside. Common to both regions are an audible population of storks, nesting on every available tower, and reminders of the medieval knights, half-monk and half-soldier, who fought so fiercely against the Moors.

Castilla-La Mancha does have two points of major interest: Toledo and Cuenca. Toledo, just south of Madrid, is one of Spain's great museum cities. Despite being entirely geared to tourism, it maintains an affable and still individualistic attitude. It was the center of multireligious learning during the Middle Ages, before a long period of intolerance, and is one of those places you simply have to see.

A long leap to the east is Cuenca, a much smaller town perched picturesquely on a cliff and edged by spectacular rock formations that resemble a ruined city. Exhilarating for its setting and for its fantastic museum of abstract art, it does, however, require a logistical effort to reach. The area north of Cuenca has beautiful landscapes and the charming town of Sigüenza. The central plains of the region are empty. Interest picks up again to the south at Almagro and at several smaller towns scattered through the Sierra de Alcaraz, which borders Andalucía. You should sample the local Manchego cheese,

a sharply flavored ewe's milk cheese, accompanied by robust Valdepeñas wine.

Over in Extremadura, the landscapes are another story entirely. Here you enter verdant valleys of cherry and olive trees (the locals are the champion pickers of Spain), rolling wheatfields, sheep pastures, and wooded hills, an intensely rural land that in the 16th century produced the conquerors of the New World. Two towns are especially redolent of the past: Cáceres, with its monumental upper town of silent Renaissance

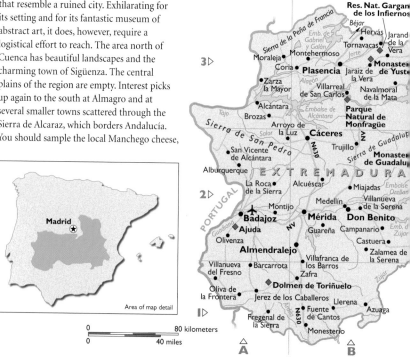

Area of map detail

0 — 80 kilometers
0 — 40 miles

mansions, and Mérida, once the heart of Roman Lusitania, whose Roman remains are quite exceptional. You can complete a triangular itinerary by also visiting Trujillo, a real charmer of a town where historic monuments are integrated into daily life. Extremadura's big religious center is the magnificent monastery of Guadalupe. Emperor Carlos V spent his last contemplative days in the monastery at Yuste, in the north of Extremadura. This is the most bucolic part, where fertile undulating terrain gives good hiking, and villages have unique rural architecture.

Extremadura is wetter and cooler than other regions of southern Spain, but the plains of La Mancha (whose name derives from the Arabic *manxa,* meaning "dry land") become a furnace in midsummer. Neither region is renowned for innovative gastronomy, but both have an honest cuisine of dishes such as goat or lamb stew, exquisite ham, fresh river trout, game, and La Mancha's vegetable *pisto.* Perhaps the most outstanding characteristic of this part of Spain is its unspoiled, undeveloped nature—here the visitor becomes a benign conquistador. ■ 4▷

A La Mancha windmill

2275m
Lobo

Sigüenza
Jadraque   Maranchón
Molina de Aragón
Brihuega
Guadalajara   Beteta

CASTILLA Y LEÓN
p. 209

MADRID
p. 53

Sacedón
Pastrana   Priego
Sayatón
Mar de Castilla
Garganta del Júcar-Ventana del Diablo
Ciudad Encantada

ARAGÓN
p. 111

Esquivias
Tarancón   **Cuenca**   Cañete
Talavera de la Reina
Torrijos
Ocaña   Villatobas   San Lorenzo de la Parrilla
Oropesa   Saelices   Carboneras de Guadazaón
Toledo
La Puebla de Montalbán   Corral de Almaguer   Quintanar de la Orden
Belvis de la Jara   Sonseca   Mora   Honrubia
Los Yébenes   Villacañas   El Toboso
Madridejos   **Alcázar de San Juan**   Belmonte   Motilla del Palancar   Minglanilla
Consuegra   Mota del Cuervo   A31
Campo de Criptana   San Clemente
Puerto Lápice
Herrera del Duque   Porzuna   Malagón   Socuéllamos   Villarrobledo   Tarazona de la Mancha
Parque Nacional de las Tablas de Daimiel   Argamasilla de Alba   Tomelloso   La Roda   Alcalá del Júcar
Daimiel   Barrax   La Gineta
Agudo   Manzanares   Munera   **Albacete**   N430
Peñalsordo   **Ciudad Real**   La Solana   Ossa de Montiel   Balazote   Chinchilla de Monte Aragón   Almansa
Almadén   Almagro   Caudete
Cabeza del Buey   Almodóvar del Campo   **Puertollano**   **Valdepeñas**   Villanueva de los Infantes   Alcaraz   Liétor   Tobarra
Calzada de Calatrava   Santa Cruz de Mudela   Hellín
Castillo de Calatrava   Viso del Marqués   Elche de la Sierra

ANDALUCÍA
p. 259

MURCIA
p. 259

C   D   E   F

Cuenca

◭ 235 E3

Visitor information

✉ Calle San Pedro 6

☎ 969 23 21 19

Museo de Arte
Abstracto Español

✉ Calle Canonigos

☎ 969 21 29 83

🕐 Closed Sun. p.m. &
Mon.

💲 $

Cuenca's
towering houses
cling to a rocky
precipice above
the gorge.

Cuenca

CUENCA IS CASTILLA-LA MANCHA'S GREATEST SURPRISE. IT
is set spectacularly on a cliff edge between the Huécar and Júcar
Rivers, northeast of the flat, central plains, where the Serranía de
Cuenca rises abruptly to become a natural frontier with Aragón. The
surroundings are equally exciting.

Virtually equidistant between
Madrid (165 km/103 miles) and
Valencia, Cuenca is famous for its
vertiginous **Casas Colgadas**
(hanging houses), best viewed from
the Puente de San Pablo. In these
14th-century houses you find the
Museo de Arte Abstracto
Español, where paintings by
important contemporary artists vie
with fantastic views. On the other
side of the bridge stands the
Monasterio de los Paúles,
partly a *parador* (see p. 370).

A few steps away looms the
beautiful Gothic-Norman and
Renaissance **catedral** *(Plaza
Mayor, tel 969 21 24 63, closed Sun.
p.m.).* Look for the carved walnut
door leading to the chapterhouse,
the work of Alonso de Berreguete
(see pp. 45–46), and the "Pieta" by
Juan de Mena. Next to the cathedral, the old Bishop's Palace houses
the **Museo Diocesano** *(Palacio
Episcopal, Plaza Mayor, tel 969 22 42
10, closed Sun. p.m. & Mon.),* where
exhibits include two paintings by El
Greco. Outside is the trapezoidal
Plaza Mayor, scene of Holy Week
processions, and the festival of San
Mateo (September 18–21).

Follow Ronda de Julián Romero
to descend steps to the pretty
Santuario de la Virgen de las
Angustias, on a peaceful square.
Beyond this are the church of San
Pedro and the castle ruins. In the
opposite direction, is the lofty
Torre de Mangana, a late 16th-
century watchtower.

Of the many beautiful spots in
the Serranía de Cuenca, the most
striking is the **Ciudad Encantada**
(Enchanted City), 15 miles (25 km)
northeast of Cuenca. You can
follow a marked path around this
surrealistic landscape of eroded
rocks. Three miles (5 km) north lies
the **Garganta del Júcar** (Júcar
Gorge), best seen through a rock
opening nicknamed the **Ventana
del Diablo** (Devil's Window). ■

Albacete

Dominated by a medieval castle and neoclassic church, Almansa lies between Albacete and Alacant.

ISOLATED ALBACETE, IN EASTERN LA MANCHA, HAS NO great monuments, but lies at a crossroads for routes between central Spain, Valencia on the east coast, and Andalucía. Its name refers to its flat setting, now the scene of intensive cultivation of vines, artichokes, and profitable saffron, introduced by the Arabs between the 8th and 13th centuries.

Arabs also brought the art of knife-making, and the quality of Albacete's steel knives and daggers has long been admired. Workshops use time-honored techniques to make knives in a wide variety of shapes and sizes, so this is the perfect place to restock your kitchen.

Albacete's modern **Museo Provincial** was built to house the wealth of finds from surrounding excavations. Prehistoric objects from the caves of Alpera range from an Iberian sphinx from Haches, to a lion from Bienservida, and count-less Roman artifacts. Many of the latter were uncovered at the fourth-century necropolis of Ontur.

Exploring Albacete province will take you off the beaten track. Drive 31 miles (50 km) northeast to **Alcalá del Júcar** to see a mini-Cuenca—a village built into a cliff, and dominated by a Moorish castle. South of Albacete is **Liétor,** another spectacularly sited village perched on a dolmitic crag above the Mundo River. Narrow medieval streets reflect the village's not-so-distant Moorish past, and the mountain views are superb. Don't miss **Chinchilla de Monte Aragón,** with its well-conserved medieval quarter, 15th-century cas-tle, noblemen's houses, and Arab baths. An important potterymaking center, it also has a ceramics museum. At any of these towns, sample the provincial specialities, notably game such as partridge, rabbit, and hare, which is prepared in about 30 different ways. ■

Albacete
⚐ 235 E2
Visitor information
✉ Calle Tinte 2
☎ 967 58 05 22

Museo Provincial de Albacete
✉ Parque de Abelardo Sánchez
☎ 967 22 83 07
🕐 Closed Sun. p.m. & Mon.
💲 $

Miguel de Cervantes & Don Quixote

Trotting across the plains of La Mancha are the ghosts of Don Quixote and his faithful squire, Sancho Panza, two comical but darkly allegorical figures created by Miguel de Cervantes (1547–1616). From its initial aim to be a parody of traditional romantic ballads and tales of knights errant, this book became a universally popular synthesis of the Renaissance. It is also a racy adventure story crammed with amusing, earthy characters. Superficially it paints a picture of the period in entertaining color, but beneath the surface lie a social critique and symbolism that enchanted Europe in the early 17th century.

Cervantes' own life was a picaresque adventure. Born in Alcalá de Henares, he started adult life as a soldier. He participated in the naval victory of Lepanto (1571) against the Ottoman Turks, where injuries left him with a crippled arm. He then ran into trouble when captured by pirates on his return to Spain in 1575. Enslaved for five years in Algiers, he made several unsuccessful attempts to escape before he was ransomed by his family and could start life again. Between periods of imprisonment for debt and mismanaged accounts, Cervantes led a disillusioned, outsider's life, not helped by an unhappy marriage or the menial jobs with which he made a living. He wrote when he was in prison, and from 1608 he was able to devote himself entirely to literary pursuits while living in Madrid. Little is known about the

Left: Dalí sketch of Don Quixote. Above: The familiar windmills that he perceived as giants

man himself except that he was reserved, cautious, and at times aggressive. He was 50 before he realized his own talent for narrative, first glimpsed in his unsuccessful pastoral novel, *La Galatea* (1585), and later in his short stories, *The Exemplary Novels* (1613).

The multiple dimensions of Don Quixote stretched Cervantes' imaginative powers to the fullest and brought him instant success. Publication of the first part of the book in 1605 was followed rapidly by pirate editions within just a few weeks, and made the public avid for more. This finally appeared ten years later, just one year before the author's death, and was a much deeper and more subtle text. Described at this point by a French visitor as "old, a soldier, a gentleman and poor," Cervantes nevertheless died knowing that his creation had become famous, with translations into French and English.

In Don Quixote's illusory, innocent world, the windmills of La Mancha become giants, and heroic misadventures are inspired by his parallel vision of reality. The knight's noble, eccentric generosity, set against the common-sensical, often skeptical attitudes of his faithful servant, Sancho Panza, becomes an allegory about human perception: Things can be real or ideal, feasible or fantastic, sane or insane. Don Quixote's descent into madness, accentuated by his awareness of it, is finally cured only by death. Ironically it is Sancho who has the hero's return. In the words of the English writer V.S. Pritchett, "The extreme strains of the Spanish nature are celebrated in these two characters: the passionate tendency to fantasy, the fatal reaction into skepticism, realism, and cynicism." Nearly 400 years after the publication of his masterpiece, Cervantes' analysis still holds true. ■

Toledo

TOLEDO'S PROXIMITY TO MADRID MAKES IT A CLASSIC DAY-trip destination (trains take 75 minutes), but its many monuments and eerie nocturnal atmosphere warrant an overnight stay. It is one of Spain's great historic cities, spectacularly sited on a hilltop and practically encircled by the Tajo River. The Greek painter El Greco lived and worked in Toledo until his death in 1614, and left an overwhelming pictorial legacy.

Toledo
- 235 C3

Visitor information
- ✉ Plaza Consistorial 1
- ☎ 925 25 40 30
- 🕐 Closed Mon. p.m.

Catedral
- ✉ Calle Cisneros
- ☎ 925 22 22 41
- 🕐 Closed Sun. a.m.
- 💲 $$ (museum, chapterhouse, treasury, & choir)

Toledo became the Visigothic capital in A.D. 554 and played a major role for the next eight centuries. It was a flourishing trading center under Moorish rule, when Jews, Muslims, and Christians worked side by side. After Toledo was captured by Alfonso VI of Castilla y León in 1085, the three communities continued to prosper peaceably under Christian rule until the mid-14th century, when persecution of the Jewish community began. From 1492, decline set in with the expulsion and repression of Jews and Muslims.

Modern Toledo depends above all on tourism, and you may become jaded at the sight of so many multilingual menus and tourist souvenir shops.

Plot your route carefully: Toledo is a labyrinth of steep cobbled streets. The extraordinary **catedral** is the obvious starting point, a symphony of Gothic spires and pinnacles rising over the Plaza del Ayuntamiento. Construction began in 1226, but it took over 250 years to complete, resulting in a bizarre convergence of styles and artists. Look at the **western portal,** consisting of three heavily sculpted doors (Hell, Pardon, and Judgment), the Flamboyant Gothic **spire** to the left, and to the right the Renaissance **dome** by the son of El Greco, Jorge Theotocópuli (who also designed the elegant town hall opposite). Access is from the side, in the Calle Cisneros,

where you should buy a ticket from the shop opposite to visit the cathedral's treasures.

Inside, between the lofty ribbed columns and 800 stained-glass windows, your first sight is the immense, elaborately sculpted choir. The **choir stalls** are masterpieces, especially the lower, 15th-century ones, carved by Rodrigo Alemán with mythical beasts and battle scenes of the conquest of Granada. Above are 16th-century alabaster seats (by Alonso Berruguete and Felipe Vigarny) separated by columns of jasper. Go around the outer walls of the choir (depicting Old Testament scenes) to the High Altar: the **altarpiece** is a gigantic Flamboyant Gothic polychrome carving of the Life of Christ. To your right is another outsize work, a 30-foot (9 m) mural depicting St. Christopher. Behind the altar is the cathedral's most remarkable architectural and artistic feature, the **Transparente** (1732). This baroque folly was designed by Narciso Tomé to allow light to penetrate from the ceiling and illuminate the tabernacle. It requires a real neck bend to admire the incredible feat of sculptures looking down from the painted dome, where the Virgin evaporates into a cloud of saints and angels.

To the right is the **sala capitular** (chapterhouse), where both the antechamber and main hall have magnificent coffered ceilings, the main one heavy with gold leaf (the work of Diego López de Arenas). Below are lovely frescoes by Juan de Borgoña, and a bottom row of portraits of Toledo's powerful archbishops—leaving space for those of the future. Look, too, at the delicately carved wardrobes in the antechamber. Your next surprise comes in the **sacristy and museum.** This is an art galley in itself, rich in El Grecos and work by Zurbarán, Juan de Borgoña, and Goya (note the light and expressions of his "Capture of Christ"). El Greco's dramatic **"El Expolio"** demands attention, but don't miss the exhibits flanking it: a superb Romanesque "Virgin and Child" in silver with a gold filigree crown, and to the right a beautiful 12th-century silver casket that contains the relics of St. Eugenio.

The vestry displays more masterpieces—Van Dyck, Velázquez, Titian, and Rubens—and leads to rooms filled with sumptuous clerical robes, altar dressings (look for the one of silver thread and coral), and embroidered Moorish banners from the 14th century.

If you have any powers of admiration left, visit the **treasury,** where you walk smack into the sight of a 10-foot-high (3 m) gold and silver monstrance made by Enrique de Arfe in the 1520s. Despite its immense weight of almost 400 pounds (180 kg), it is paraded through Toledo during Corpus Christi (May/June). Assorted items around it include the finely illustrated Bible of St. Louis (13th century) and a 15th-century calvary cross painted by Fra Angelico.

Long the spiritual capital of Spain, Toledo rises abruptly from the plain in an upsweep of gates, battlements, and church towers.

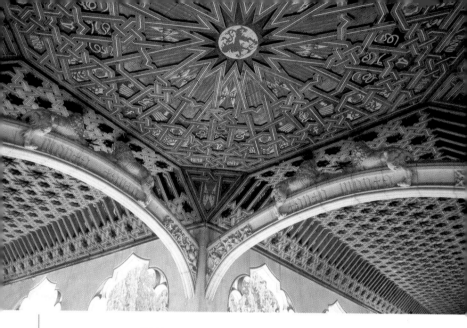

Intricate, delicate Mudejar designs grace the ceiling of the Monasterio de San Juan de los Reyes.

Hospital y Museo de Santa Cruz

✉ Miguel de Cervantes 3

☎ 925 22 10 36

💲 $

Upper floor under restoration and due to reopen in 2001

Monasterio de San Juan de los Reyes

✉ Calle de los Reyes Católicos 17

☎ 925 22 38 02

💲 $

EAST OF THE CATHEDRAL

Dominating Toledo's skyline, the **Alcázar** *(Cuesta Carlos V 2, tel 925 22 30 38, closed a.m. & Mon.)* is a massive fortress. It dates from the Middle Ages, but retains little of its original stucture. In the 16th century, both Carlos V and his son Felipe II extended it for use as a royal residence, but successive fires in the 18th and 19th centuries wrought havoc with the fabric. Even greater damage came during the Civil War (see pp. 36–37), when Franco's forces withstood a siege and bombardment for ten weeks. Since being rebuilt, the Alcázar has become the headquarters of military organizations, and its exhibits demand a keen interest in army history. If you venture to the basement to see the oven that baked 1,735 bread rolls daily during the siege, you pass through a Moorish arch, a relic from an even earlier structure, dated 970.

Just north of the Alcázar, pass through the horseshoe arch on the Plaza de Zocodover to reach Toledo's most beautiful Renaissance building, the **Hospital y Museo de Santa Cruz** (1524), a former orphanage. Its delicately carved facade, cloisters, and staircase are plateresque masterpieces by Alonso de Covarrubias, and the patio garden makes a wonderfully serene retreat. It is now Toledo's main museum of art and archaeology. The lower floor is worth visiting if only to see the giant tusks of a Paleolithic mammoth; also here are Roman mosaics and pottery. The upper floor has paintings by El Greco, Flemish tapestries, sculptures by Pedro de Mena, and decorative arts.

WEST OF THE CATHEDRAL

The west side of Toledo has a cluster of monuments that demonstrate the medieval coexistence of three cultures. The Franciscan **Monasterio de San Juan de los Reyes** is a Flamboyant Gothic construction by Juan Guas (died 1496), with a north portal by Covarrubias (1488–1570). Commissioned by the Catholic Monarchs (see pp. 31–33), it bears many traces of their royal patronage. The **cloisters** are superb, a harmonious mixture of ornate pinnacles, balustrades, and arches with a Mudejar ceiling on the upper gallery. The **church,** much rebuilt following a French attack in 1808, combines royal escutcheons with Gothic stone tracery.

Close by are two synagogue buildings, the only reminders of Toledo's once flourishing Jewish community and Jewish quarter, most of which was destroyed in 1491. The **Sinagoga del Tránsito** was commissioned in 1336–1357 by Samuel ha-Leví, a distinguished court adviser. It finally closed in 1494 after Jews were expelled from Spain. Subsequently it functioned as a hospital and a church, but is now the **Museo Sefardí** (Sephardic Museum). It has been completely restored to reveal its original use, with additional rooms illustrating Jewish traditions and the history of Sephardic Jews. The main worship hall, a sumptuous example of Mudejar artistry, incorporates Hebrew and Kufic inscriptions and heraldic shields. Look in particular at the spectacular cedarwood ceiling and intricate stuccowork around the *hejal* (Jewish altar). Above, in the women's gallery, numerous items from Tunisia, Morocco, France, and Italy illustrate the Sephardic culture, one that is alive today.

In contrast, the **Sinagoga de Santa María la Blanca** *(Calle de los Reyes Católicos 4, tel 925 22 72 57)* has an immaculately restored and whitewashed interior, almost devoid of any exhibits or furnishings. Five aisles are divided by rhythmical horseshoe arches (reminiscent of Córdoba's Great Mosque, see pp. 288–89) with identical capitals adorned with plant motifs. By 1405, the synagogue had been converted into a church and had acquired its present name. The three altars were decorated by Covarrubias.

Just opposite the Tránsito synagogue is the **Casa de El Greco** *(Calle Samuel Leví, tel 925 22 40 46, closed Sun. p.m. & Mon.)*. The artist never lived in this house, despite its name. Instead, it reflects the period and style of residence that he inhabited in Toledo and displays a good collection of his paintings. Look at the wonderful Mudejar ceiling of the chapel before embarking on the El Greco pilgrimage upstairs. Among the portraits of the apostles (whose free brushstrokes and expressive gestures become repetitive when seen together), the **"Tears of St. Peter"** is outstanding. The other masterpiece is the **"View and Map of Toledo"** (1614), an unusually conceptual approach for that period. Uphill from here, the church of **Santo Tomé** *(Plaza del Conde, tel 925 25 60 98)* houses El Greco's masterpiece, the **"Burial of the Count of Orgaz"** (1586). ∎

Museo Sefardí
- ✉ Calle Samuel Levi
- ☎ 925 22 36 65
- 🕐 Closed Sun. p.m. & Mon.
- 💲 $. Free Sat. p.m. & Sun.

The Casa de El Greco reconstructs the studio where the mannerist painter worked in the 16th century.

Toledo's center, with the cathedral straight ahead and the Archbishop's Palace to the left

A walk around Toledo

This walk takes you through the characteristically steep, high-walled streets of central Toledo, stopping at intriguing churches, convents, and even a mosque—a synopsis of this once spiritual city.

Start from the main door of the **Catedral ❶** and walk up the steps beside the **Palacio Arzobispal** (Archbishop's Palace) opposite. On the pretty Plaza Consistorial at the top, turn right and walk up Cuesta del Ordenal, where you turn right and then left into narrow Callejón de Jesus María. At the top turn right, where you will see the imposing baroque facade of **San Ildefonso.** Turn left beside the church into Calle de San Román, which leads to the church of **San Román ❷**; the entrance is around the corner in Calle San Clemente. San Román is Toledo's oldest church. Of Visigothic origin, it was later used as a mosque before being rebuilt in Mudejar style in the 13th century. Now it serves as a museum of Visigothic culture, the **Museo de los Concilios y de la Cultura Visigoda** (*Iglesia de San Román, Calle de San Román, tel 925 22 78 72, closed Sun. p.m. & Mon.*). The unusual interior combines Caliphal arches, Roman columns, Visigothic and Mozarabic

capitals, and, above all, wonderful frescoes that blanket nearly every wall and arch.

On leaving the church, walk down the street opposite and turn left at the bottom into Plaza de Padilla. Cross the square diagonally to descend the steps, and then turn right to skirt the convent and church of **Santo Domingo el Antiguo ❸** (*Tel 925 22 29 30, closed Sun. a.m.*). This was Toledo's first convent, founded in 1085 by Cistercians. Today it has about 14

🗺 See area map p. 235
▶ Plaza del Ayuntamiento
🔁 1.7 miles (2.7 km)
🕐 1–2 hours
▶ Mezquita del Cristo de la Luz

NOT TO BE MISSED
- San Román
- Santo Domingo el Antiguo
- Mezquita del Cristo de la Luz

nuns, whose work includes guiding tourists around their considerable treasures and selling homemade candies. The church is neoclassic inside and has three paintings by El Greco, as well as several copies. Two of the originals (depicting John the Baptist and San Bernard) are part of the altarpiece; the third is the exceptional **"Resurrection of Christ"** hanging to the right of this area. Switch on the lights to peer through a grille at the coffered ceiling of the chapterhouse and through the floor at El Greco's modest tomb in the crypt before being led through to the old choir. This magnificent room and adjoining antechamber are full of interest—the superb coffered ceiling, a carved head of John the Baptist by Pedro de Mena (see p. 47), a painting by Luca Giordano (1634–1705), richly embroidered altar dressings, and 12th- to 16th-century documents, including El Greco's contract with the convent, and others signed by King Sancho III (1154) and Alfonso VII (1150).

Walk down Calle de Santa Leocadia and turn right into Calle Real, passing the grandiose provincial council building before turning right and immediately left at the end through a typically narrow, high-sided lane, Calle Buzones. This brings you to the baroque facade of **Santo Domingo el Real,** one of several convents around this square. Walk through the *cobertizo* (a bridged-over passageway), turn right up another, and you come to the 13th-century Mudejar church of **San Vicente,** dominating a plaza. On your left is **Las Gaitanas,** a cloistered convent; beyond San Vicente is the neoclassic **Palacio de Lorenzana.** Turn left into Calle de los Alfileritos, and then take the third lane on your left, Calle del Cristo de la Luz. This brings you to the **Mezquita del Cristo de la Luz** ❹ (*Calle del Cristo de la Luz, tel 925 22 30 81, visits by appt. only*), a stunning intact mosque dating from A.D. 999, with a 12th-century Romanesque sanctuary. ∎

The Monasterio de Guadalupe's Gothic and Mudejar towers loom above the medieval town of Guadalupe.

Guadalupe

MEXICO'S MUCH REVERED PATRON SAINT, THE VIRGIN OF Guadalupe, and the Caribbean island named for her originated here, a village in the remote green hills of Extremadura, where a miraculous image of the Virgin was found seven centuries ago. This black-faced Virgin became the patron of "all Spains," the very essence of Spanishness, and her shrine continues to attract streams of pilgrims.

Guadalupe

🅰 234 B2

Visitor information

✉ Plaza Santa María de Guadalupe

☎ 927 15 41 28

Real Monasterio de Santa María

☎ 927 36 70 00

💲 $ (guided tours only)

A huge monastery and church dominate the pretty hillside village, where medieval streets lined with flower-filled balconies radiate from a wide plaza in front of the church. The 12th-century statue of the Virgin, allegedly carved by St. Luke, inspired the building of the **Hieronymite monastery** in 1340. It is now run by Franciscans, who have undertaken extensive restoration. There is a very pleasant guesthouse in the Gothic cloisters.

The golden-stone church facade rises between crenellated towers. In the church all attention is focused on the altarpiece and its diminutive, caped figure of the Virgin. You get a closer look in the Camarín above, a small, highly decorated 18th-century chapel. This is where

your guide spins the image around to face the crowd of expectant pilgrims. In the nearby **Relicario** are the Virgin's rich wardrobe and crown, reserved for processions.

The **Museo de Bordados** is an embroidery museum, with monks' needlework from the 15th to 19th centuries. In the **Museo de Pinturas y Esculturas** (paintings and sculptures), look for an ivory sculpture of Christ, said to be by Michelangelo, and the beautiful small portraits of monks by Zurbarán. The **chapterhouse** has a dazzling collection of illuminated psalmbooks. Structurally the most interesting section is the **Claustro Mudejar,** an unusually large, two-story cloister of horseshoe arches. ■

Sierra de la Peña de Francia

Looking toward La Alberca from the Sierra de la Peña de Francia

THIS RANGE IS PART OF THE RUGGED CORDILLERA CENTRAL that continues into the craggy Sierra de Gredos, and is a natural border between Castilla y León and Extremadura. The highest peak, Peña de Francia, rises to 5,682 feet (1,732 m), and its tortuous access road gives panoramic views west toward Portugal, east to the Sierra de Gredos, and north over the Castilian meseta.

The most interesting place to head is **La Alberca** in Castilla y León, a charming, restored mountain village of stone and half-timbered houses on cobbled streets. For centuries its remoteness preserved local traditions and religious zeal, but national monument status has resulted in a steady stream of visitors in summer. If you can, time your visit for August 15, when villagers don exuberantly embroidered costumes to enact a mystery play celebrating the triumph of the Virgin over the Devil.

Immediately south, over the Portillo pass, the dramatic road (SA201) descends into the bucolic valley of **Las Batuecas**—protected as a nature park. Rock formations in startling shapes harbor prehistoric cave paintings.

Las Batuecas is on the edge of **Las Hurdes,** a region brought to fame by Luis Buñuel in his 1932 film *Tierra Sin Pan* (Land Without Bread), which portrayed its extreme hardship and poverty. Today life has improved, but there remains a distinctive wildness in the landscape, and a time-warped atmosphere in the tiny whitewashed hamlets and stone farmhouses. Follow the C515 to see attractive **Miranda del Castañar** before reaching **Bejar,** a fortified hilltop town, and then go southeast to **Hervás**. This village preserves a remarkable old **Jewish quarter** among its leaning, half-timbered houses. The maze of narrow streets with a backdrop of snowcapped peaks makes a rewarding stroll. ∎

Sierra de la Peña de Francia
Bejar
🅰 234 B3
Visitor information
✉ Paseo Cervantes 6
☎ 923 40 30 05

Hervás
🅰 234 B3
Visitor information
✉ Calle Braulio Navas
☎ 927 47 36 18

In & around Plasencia

Almond orchards
near Plasencia

DRAMATICALLY SITED ON A HILLTOP ABOVE THE JERTE River, against a backdrop of jagged limestone outcrops, the "pearl of the Jerte" is a fine base for explorations of the beautiful Valle del Jerte. South are the rural delights of the Valle de la Vera, and the monastery to which Carlos V retired in 1556, exhausted from the burden of being Holy Roman Emperor.

Plasencia's star attraction is the **catedral,** which, like Salamanca's (see pp. 218–220), combines two distinct periods and buildings: the old Romanesque-Gothic cathedral, dating from the 13th and 14th centuries, and, linked to it by cloisters, the new cathedral. Completed in Renaissance style in the early 16th century by some of Spain's best architects of the time, the latter is Extremadura's most ornate church. Look in particular at the dome of the chapel of San Pablo, the beautiful plateresque north portal, the sculptures by Gregorio Fernández for the main altar (1634), and the carved choir stalls (1520).

Handsome mansions line the streets around the **Plaza Mayor,** where every Tuesday sees a bountiful food market dating from the Middle Ages. The Casa del Dean, Palacio Episcopal, and Casa de las Dos Torres are worth finding, and the **Museo la Etnográfico** *(Calle Marqués de la Puebla, tel 927 42 18 43, closed Sun. p.m., Mon., & Tues.)* gives insight into the area's rural traditions.

The beautiful **Valle del Jerte** is rich in oak trees, chestnut trees, and especially cherry trees: Over 30 varieties of cherry are grown here on an estimated one million trees. Imagine the blossom in spring, or, better still, be here to see it. If you are in the region in May, visit the village of **Valdastillas,** where you get a close-up on cherry-related activities: Families pick and sort them, and you can take guided tours

Plasencia
🅰 234 B3
Visitor information
✉ Plaza de la Catedral
☎ 927 42 38 43

Valle del Jerte
🅰 234 B3
Visitor information
✉ Paraje Virgen de Peñas Albas, Cabazuela del Valle
☎ 927 47 25 58

of the cooperatives where cherries are bottled and turned into liqueurs.

Near the village of Jerte is the **Reserva Natural Garganta de los Infiernos,** a stunning nature reserve of torrential waterfalls, that gives really scenic, though tough, hiking. Farther northeast along this valley, **Tornavacas** is the last village before the border with Castilla y León, 4 miles (6 km) away at the Puerto de Tornavacas mountain pass (4,183 feet/1,275 m). Slotted between the towering sierras of Gredos and Bejar, Tornavacas has only one main street, Calle Real. At **No. 23** is the inn where Carlos V spent the night on his way to the monastery at Yuste in 1556, in the fertile La Vera valley.

The **Valle de la Vera** is south of the Valle del Jerte. You can reach it on a twisting road from Valdastillas or, more easily, on the C501 from Plasencia. La Vera, riddled with streams, is a major producer of tobacco and vegetables. The main historical interest is at Jarandilla and Yuste, but you find traditional architecture at any of the rural villages, and the landscapes are wonderfully serene. One of the prettiest villages is **Cuacos,** from where you can walk or drive 1 mile (1.6 km) uphill to the monastery.

Carlos V, depressed with court life and political intrigues, chose to retire in 1556 to the simple Hieronymite **Monasterio de Yuste** (*Cuacos de Yuste, tel 927 17 21 30, guided tour only*). He stayed until his death two years later. Despite the apparent simplicity of the place (heavily restored after damage during the Peninsular War of the early 1800s), Carlos V did have a retinue of about a hundred servants, and had his bedroom built next to the chapel so that he could hear Mass from bed. (He had just retired from being the world's most powerful man, after all.) The

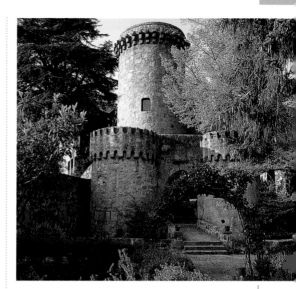

guided tour points out details such as the chair built specially for the gout-ridden emperor.

To complete this imperial tour, visit **Jarandilla,** just 3 miles (5 km) northeast of the monastery, where the magnificent 15th-century **castle** welcomed Carlos V while he awaited the completion of his quarters at Yuste. The **church of Jarandilla,** built by the Knights Templar, contains a baptismal font carved with the ancient Sanskrit sign of the swastika, and the castle stands on the ruins of the Templar fortress. Although austere from the outside, this Renaissance edifice conceals a gracious home centered on a verdant courtyard, and has become, not surprisingly, a *parador* (see p. 371).

Southeast of Plasencia lies the **Parque Natural de Monfragüe,** created to protect the rare flora and fauna of this region, notably Iberian lynxes, boars, badgers, imperial eagles, black storks, and numerous vultures. Head for the riverside village of **Villareal de San Carlos** where information on hiking trails is available. ■

Jarandilla's castle, once a Templar fortress, is now a luxurious parador (state-run hotel).

Parque Natural de Monfragüe
🅜 234 B3
Visitor information
✉ Villareal de San Carlos (on Plasencia-Trujillo road)
☎ 927 19 91 34

Cáceres

THIS IS STORK CITY, WHERE THE RATTLING OF BEAKS AND voluminous nests are part and parcel of the old town. White storks nest on towers, chimneys, and TV antennae in spring and summer. They are visible all over Extremadura and La Mancha. Cáceres displays its noble past in a walled hilltop quarter where emblazoned facades, lofty towers, archways, and winding cobbled streets create an inimitable atmosphere.

The only drawback today is that the historical center is barely inhabited. Most of its mansions are now municipal offices. To taste real life in this provincial capital you have to explore the **lower town,** which has an appealing, zesty atmosphere. It centers on a generous Plaza Mayor dominated by the town hall, where steps lead up to originally Moorish walls. Some of their rubble masonry towers are intact. Walk through **Arco de la Estrella,** an arch built by Manuel Lara de Churriguera in the 18th century. Here, beside the Ermita de la Paz, you enter the venerable old quarter at its heart, **Plaza de Santa María.** If the **catedral de Santa María** (*Plaza de Santa María, tel 927 21 53 13*) has reopened after renovation, go inside to admire the Gothic vaulting, serene proportions, and Renaissance details. Just behind is the **Palacio de Carvajal** (*Calle Amargura 1, tel 927 25 55 97, closed Sun. p.m.*), home of the local tourist board. Enter the lovely courtyard, walk out into the garden at the back, and don't miss the Moorish tower with fragments of 16th-century frescoes. In the lobby a model of old Cáceres gives you a clear idea of the various palaces, as every detail has been painstakingly crafted.

Facing the cathedral across the square there are three beautiful

Above: Steps from the Plaza Mayor lead up through the city walls into the immaculately preserved old town, a UNESCO World Heritage site.

Right: Palacio de los Golfines de Abajo on Plaza de San Jorge, with the cathedral in the background

Renaissance mansions, all of the honey and gray stone that is so typical of Cáceres: the **Palacio de Hernando de Ovando,** the **Palacio de Mayoralgo,** and the **Palacio Episcopal.** The first of these was built by the Ovando family. Nicolás Ovando was appointed governor of the Indies by the Catholic monarchs, taking over from Christopher Columbus and Francisco de Bobadilla. The palace now houses administrative offices and is closed to the public. Stepped back from the cathedral to the south is the magnificent **Palacio de los Golfines de Abajo,** whose tower, in turn, overlooks Plaza San Jorge. The facade combines late-Gothic and plateresque decoration of the 15th and 16th centuries: Look in particular at the rooftop balustrade of carved birds and the medieval tower. Looming above the souvenir shops of the little plaza is a very different style of building, the whitewashed Jesuit **church of San Francisco Javier** *(Plaza de San Jorge 8, tel 927 24 51 71),* dating from the 18th century. Check out the art and photography exhibitions that are regularly held here.

At the top of the wide steps flanking the church is another delightful square, **Plaza de las Veletas,** centering on the church of **San Mateo** *(Open only for Mass),* built on the site of a mosque. Next to it stands the crenellated tower of **Casa de las Cigüeñas** (House of Storks), the only tower in this quarter not to have been lopped off—a sign that its owner, Diego de Ovando, was a supporter of Isabel in the civil war of the 1470s (see p. 31). Opposite, on the south side of the square, is the elegant Casa de las Veletas, now the excellent **Museo de Cáceres.** Here you find a good collection of prehistoric and Roman artifacts, even a small incised menhir (an

upright prehistoric monumental stone) from the third millennium B.C., and regional ethnographic exhibits including beautiful weavings, lace, costumes, and ceramics. Downstairs is the star exhibit, an Arab *aljibe* (cistern) with perfectly conserved horseshoe arches. Across the garden a modernized annex displays fine art. Etchings by Picasso and Miró hang beside paintings by more recent Spanish artists; downstairs are 12th- to 19th-century works, a rather motley collection including "Jesus Salvador" by El Greco and an awkward "San Andres" by Luca Giordano (1634–1705).

Before leaving this square, notice the ivy-draped **Torre de los Plata,** behind San Mateo, then descend Calle Ancha past more emblazoned palaces to the *parador* (see p. 369), the former mansion of the Marquises of Torreorgaz. This is the perfect place to have a drink or a meal in a setting relevant to everything you have just seen. ∎

Trujillo

Trujillo
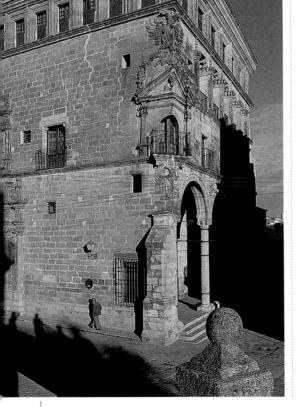 234 B2
Visitor information
✉ Plaza Mayor
☎ 927 32 26 77
🕓 Closed Sat. & Sun. p.m.

THIS DELIGHTFUL LITTLE TOWN IS A PLEASURE TO VISIT, with a network of fine old buildings, exuberant vegetation—cactuses, palms, olives, oranges, and magnolias—and plenty of life. Trujillo's renown, however, is due to one man: the conquistador Francisco Pizarro, who conquered the Incas of Peru. His statue (erected in 1927, and identical to one in Lima) reigns supreme over the Plaza Mayor, surrounded by palaces paid for with plunder from Latin America.

All Trujillo's narrow, winding streets eventually lead to this large, irregular square (actually more of a triangle). **Plaza Mayor** is the social hub of town, lined by sidewalk cafés, restaurants, and illustrious palaces. It is flanked by wide steps leading up to their porticoes, and the rather severe church of San Martín rises in the north corner.

Nuns now inhabit the 17th-century Palacio Carvajal-Vargas.

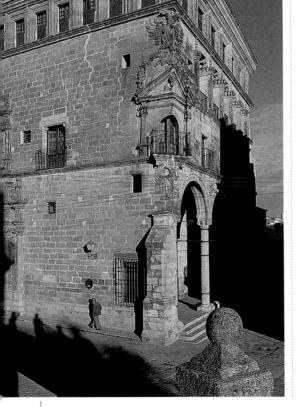

Opposite the church is the **Palacio Carvajal-Vargas** (or Palacio de Duques de San Carlos), a sober late Renaissance building. It was handed over to Hieronymite nuns (hermits of St. Jerome—a medieval religious order also called Jeronymite) in the 1960s, so public access is unfortunately restricted. Pull the bell chain in the entrance hall and a nun will open up, attempt to sell you cakes, and then wave you across the handsome patio toward the palace's most curious feature. The steps of this 17th-century staircase are not attached to the wall but held together by an interlocking structure, so earning it the name "flying."

At the other end of the square, the more ornate **Palacio del Marqués de la Conquista** was built by Hernando Pizarro, Francisco's brother. Its richly emblazoned corner, added in the 17th century, displays busts of the two brothers and their wives. From here you can walk up to explore the upper town by following the Cañon de la Cárcel, a passageway in the corner of the Palacio de la Justicia next to the Pizarro mansion. Go around the corner to your right and you come to the harmonious facade of the 16th-century **Palacio Orellana-Pizarro,** now a convent school. Francisco de Orellana was another of Trujillo's conquistadores, the first European to explore the Amazon. You can enter the beautiful patio for a small fee and look for the ghost of Miguel de Cervantes,

Francisco Pizarro

The actions of this illiterate, illegitimate son of a captain eventually led to the death of an estimated five million Incas. In 1513, Pizarro (ca 1478–1541) accompanied another Extremaduran explorer, Vasco Núñez de Balboa, on his expedition to the Pacific, and from 1524 began searching the coasts of Ecuador and Peru for the legendary Incan empire. He discovered it in 1532, had the Incan emperor Atahualpa treacherously killed in 1533, and founded Lima in 1535. Pizarro's ambition and ruthlessness eventually turned against him, when he was assassinated by the followers of Diego de Almagro, a fellow explorer whom Pizarro had double-crossed. ∎

author of *Don Quixote* (see pp. 238–39), who once stayed here.

By circling this mansion into the Cuesta de la Sangre, you pass another imposing Renaissance palace, before turning left through the archway of Santiago. This brings you to the charming **church of Santiago** *(Closed Mon.)*, where a Romanesque bell tower stands beside a basically Gothic structure. The scenic path beside the church takes you along the old town walls, built by the Moors in the 13th century to defend their 10th-century castle from Christian attacks. Views take in Trujillo's abundant stork population nesting on every available tower. The **castle** *(Closed Mon.)* stands above, an imposing sight of crenellated walls and sturdy towers. There is little inside, however, except the revered statue of the Virgen de la Victoria, the patron saint of Trujillo, who can easily be seen from outside in her glassed eyrie.

Take Calleja de los Martires to the left and you soon come to the **Casa-Museo Pizarro** *(Closed Mon.)*, a sturdy-looking 15th-century house where the conquistador was born. Inside, period furniture and conquistador memorabilia are shown with Inca artifacts. A few steps farther bring you to the Gothic **church of Santa María la Mayor** *(Closed Mon.)*, which holds the tombs of Trujillo's explorers. It also has a lovely main altarpiece painted by Fernando Gallegos. Climb the Romanesque bell tower for sweeping views over Trujillo's tiled roofs to the distant Sierra de Guadalupe. ∎

Despite his misdeeds, Francisco Pizarro remains Trujillo's local hero.

Mérida

WITH A STREET NAMED AFTER JOHN LENNON, MÉRIDA, capital of the Autonomous Community of Extremadura is not exactly buried in its Roman past. It is a lively town that has been developing on the eastern bank of the Guadiana River ever since its founding in 25 B.C., after which it became capital of the Roman province of Lusitania. It has more Roman remains than any other Spanish town except Tarragona, and since 1986, a superlative museum has displayed the best of its Roman artifacts.

The most impressive sights are the **Teatro Romano y Anfiteatro** (Roman theater and amphitheater), both built of blocks of granite. The majestic colonnaded levels of the theater facing the semicircular terraced seats are absolutely magnificent. Go there in July or August to watch Mérida's theater festival, when the entire structure returns to its original function. It holds 6,000 spectators. A few yards away is the vast amphitheater, with a capacity for 14,000 people. This was used for gladiator combats, chariot races, and mock sea battles, for which the arena was flooded. Close by, the **Casa del Anfiteatro** displays the ruins of a third- to fourth-century villa still being excavated. Note the mosaic floors. Another villa, **Casa de Mitreo** *(Calle Oviedo, tel 924 30 15 04)*, a five-minute walk southwest, displays the beautiful Mosaico Cosmológico, a lyrical mosaic rendering of the Roman gods. The **basilica of Santa Eulalia** dates from the 5th century and contains the relics of the martyr, Santa Eulalia. Since 1990, major excavations have revealed the successive stages of its long history. It stands east of the Plaza de España *(Calle Sta Eulalia, closed Sun)*.

The **Museo Nacional de Arte Romano** is opposite the

Mérida
🅰 234 B2
Visitor information
✉ Avenida José Alvarez Sáez de Buruaga
☎ 924 31 53 53
🕐 Closed Sat. & Sun. p.m.

Teatro Romano y Anfiteatro
✉ Avenida José Álvarez Sáez de Buruaga
☎ 924 31 25 30
💲 $ ($$ combined ticket includes Casa de Mitreo, Alcazaba, & Santa Eulalia excavations)

Museo Nacional de Arte Romano
✉ Calle José Ramón Mélida
☎ 924 31 16 90
🕐 Closed Sun. p.m. & Mon.
💲 $. Free Sat. p.m. & Sun.

Built in 24 B.C., Mérida's Roman theater is the best preserved in Spain.

theater and amphitheater. This brilliantly conceived design by Rafael Moneo evokes Roman architecture in a purist, sympathetic style. Captions are in Spanish, but ask for a leaflet in English at the ticket desk. The vast, skylit main hall exhibits superb sculptures, architectural details, and mosaics, with two mezzanine galleries rising to one side. The first mezzanine concentrates on daily objects (glass, pottery, lamps, coins, dice) and the second, not to be missed, has thematic displays, including an exceptional section of sculpted heads. Huge mosaic panels rising through the levels add to the general impact. In the main hall, don't miss the beautiful seated figure of Ceres, goddess of agriculture, or the trio of the imperial family (Augustus, Tiberius, and Drusus, in the end alcove). In Section IX, look especially for the torso of Thorocatus, with its remarkable depiction of movement in the tasseled strips of his uniform.

End your visit in the **crypt** below, where ruins of first- and second-century houses with murals and tombs were found during construction of the museum. From here, a tunnel leads directly into the amphitheater precinct.

From the museum, walk downhill (northwest) to the town center and turn left into Calle Sagasta. On your right you soon see the ruins of the **Forum** and then the magnificent **Temple of Diana.** Although named after the goddess of hunting, it was in fact dedicated to the cult of the emperor. Immediately behind is the Renaissance mansion of the counts of Corbos. Two blocks farther is the lovely **Plaza de España,** dotted with orange and palm trees. The **Town Hall** (1883) and the ceramic-faced folly of the **Palacio de la China** are particularly striking. The square has outdoor cafés, and is a good spot to relax before you visit the riverside **Alcazaba** *(Calle del Puente, tel 924 31 73 09),* a ninth-century Moorish fortress incorporating Roman and Visigothic details. It has a majestic cistern built into the rock. From the Alcazaba you get wonderful views of the **Roman bridge,** its 60 arches stretching 866 yards (792 m) across the river. ■

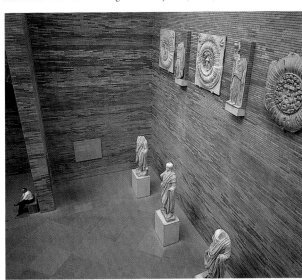

The Roman art museum's stately brick building, constructed in 1986, looks as if the Romans themselves had a hand in it.

Frontier towns

THE TOWNS OF OLIVENZA, JEREZ DE LOS CABALLEROS, and Zafra in southern Extremadura are close to two borders: that of Portugal across the Guadian River, and that of the vast sweep of Andalucía to the south. History here is inextricably linked to this strategic position and to the Christian Reconquest of Muslim land. As a result, this pastoral landscape, is dotted with fortresses.

OLIVENZA

Nudging the Portuguese border in a sea of olive groves, the fortified town of Olivenza was actually in Portuguese hands for six centuries. This has left it with an interesting dual character. The castle, with a mighty keep rising nearly 100 feet (30 m), was built by Juan II of Portugal in the 15th century; its royal bakery now houses the **Museo Etnográfico** *(Plaza de Santa María, tel 924 49 02 22, closed Mon.)*. The **church of Santa María Magdalena** is Spain's only example of 16th-century Manueline Gothic, a Portuguese style. The spiraling columns, slender rib-vaulting, *azulejos* (tiles), and genealogical tree of the Virgin crowning the altar are outstanding features. Close to the Puerta de los Angeles stands the Casa de la Misericordia, notable for a chapel faced in illustrative azulejos.

Seven miles (11 km) north of Olivenza stand the ruins of the 1,246-foot-long (380 m) **bridge of Ajuda** across the Olivenza River. Built by Manuel I of Portugal, it frequently became a battleground in the wars fought over this region.

The frontier towns display a distinct Portuguese flair, seen here at Jerez de los Caballeros.

JEREZ DE LOS CABALLEROS

About 50 miles (80 km) drive southeast, Jerez de los Caballeros became a stronghold of the Knights Templar after being captured from the Moors in 1230. In the hilltop town center, the sumptuously carved bell tower of San Miguel (1749) rises over the Plaza de España. Here, too, is the Templar castle, with Moorish remains still visible in the renovated structure. Other landmarks are the 1759 **church of San Bartolomé** *(Plaza de San Bartolomé)*, a dazzling combination of inlaid ceramic and gilt, and **Santa María** *(Llano de Santa María)*, both with ornate baroque towers. Keys for both churches are at the tourist office. The pretty whitewashed streets produced one of Extremadura's adventurers, Vasco Núñez de Balboa (1475–1517), the first European to cross the Central American isthmus and see the

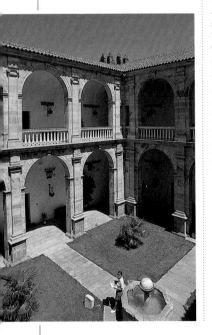

Left: Zafra's *parador*, **the former Alcázar, has a Renaissance patio by Juan de Herrera.**

Pacific. Jerez is famous for colorful celebrations during Semana Santa (Holy Week), and for its pork festival in May, when sausages and *jamón ibérico* (Iberian ham) abound.

Several dolmens (prehistoric stone tombs) are in the area. The most striking is the **Dolmen del Toriñuelo** *(5 miles/8 km northeast of town at La Granja).*

ZAFRA

About 30 miles (50 km) east of Jerez de los Caballeros is Zafra, which some people call a miniature Sevilla. Zafra has a wonderfully homogenous 18th-century center full of whitewashed houses, and larger, more elegant mansions, their architectural details picked out in saffron yellow.

The town's history started with the Moors, but fame and fortune came in the 1440s following construction of a massive stone castle, the **Alcázar,** by the Dukes of Feria. Although this is now a *parador* (see p. 372), you can visit the vast, graceful Renaissance patio (the work of Juan de Herrera, architect of El Escorial, see pp. 79–81). Ask to

see the superb gilded *artesonado* ceiling of the chapel, and have a drink beneath the more sober Mudejar ceiling of the bar. In front, the **Plaza Corazón de María** descends to a web of streets leading to the interconnecting **Plaza Grande** and **Plaza Chica.** These charming arcaded squares are the sleepy heart of Zafra. Palm trees dominate the former, and the old town hall (1750) the latter.

Rising above the roofs one block west is the unmistakable bell tower of the Renaissance **church of La Candelaria** *(Calle Tetuán, tel 924 55 01 28).* Inside are altarpieces by Francisco de Zurbarán (1598–1664), who was born nearby, and Juan Ramos Castro; also here is a small museum. Zafra's other architectural jewel, **Plaza del Pilar Redondo,** is dominated by the present **town hall** *(Tel 924 55 45 01),* which occupies a 16th-century Franciscan convent. Enter the patio to admire the arcaded structure, and then, for a contrast, look at No.14 on the square, an idiosyncratic art nouveau house completely faced in turquoise tiles. ∎

More places to visit in Castilla-La Mancha & Extremadura

ALMAGRO

Smack in the middle of Don Quixote country, Almagro is a small town with a long history. Mansions, monasteries, and churches surround the focal point of the **Plaza Mayor,** a beautiful arcaded rectangle. At No. 17 is Europe's oldest continuously used theater, the 16th-century **Corral de Comedias** (*Plaza Mayor 17, tel 926 86 15 39, closed Sun. p.m. & Mon.*). You can look inside, or, better still, see a play here during the festival of classical drama every July.

In the 13th century, Almagro became the base of the Knights of Calatrava, one of the military orders that fought for the Reconquest (see pp. 28–31). Their seat was the stunning castle of **Calatrava la Nueva** (*7 miles/11 km south of Almagro on Carretera de Calzada de Calatrava, tel 926 22 13 37, closed Mon.*).

Talavera de la Reina's blue and yellow *azulejos* (tiles) are justifiably famous, here put to decorative use in the park.

Extensive vineyards have replaced the battlefields of old, and red peppers, tomatoes, and eggplant are grown for the local specialty, *pisto manchego* (eggs, peppers, tomatoes, and eggplant fried together in La Mancha style).
🅝 235 D2 **Visitor information** ✉ Calle Bernardas 2 ☎ 926 86 07 17

SIGÜENZA

In the far north of Castilla-La Mancha, near the border with Aragón, this lovely hilltop town is dominated by its castle (now a hotel), and fortresslike Romanesque cathedral. The old town is a labyrinth, but if you keep going up you eventually reach the 16th-century Plaza Mayor and the **catedral.** Look for the poignant alabaster sculpture on the tomb of El Doncel, Isabel I's page, and the countless cherubim decorating the sacristy ceiling by Alonso de Covarrubias (1488–1570).
🅝 235 E4 **Visitor information** ✉ Hermita del Humilladero, Paseo de la Alamera ☎ 949 34 70 07

PARQUE NACIONAL DE LAS TABLAS DE DAIMIEL

Nineteen miles (30 km) northeast of the city of Ciudad Real is one of Spain's hidden gems, Tablas de Daimiel, an area of marshy wetlands formed by the Guaiana River. This ornithologists' paradise has breeding aquatic birds from April to July, and huge flocks of migrants from September to January. Depending on the time of year, you might see various species of duck, purple heron, and great crested grebes.
🅝 235 D2 **Visitor information** ✉ Parque Nacional de Daimiel, 11 miles (18 km) north of Daimiel ☎ 926 69 31 18

TALAVERA DE LA REINA

Talavera is renowned for one thing only: ceramics. Be prepared for the feast of color, above all in the form of the *cacharro* (drinking jar), now a souvenir stalwart. Talavera's production of handpainted glazed *azulejos* (tiles) blossomed in the 15th century, and Talaveran techniques were taken to Mexico by Spanish colonists. West of the center are ceramic workshops where you can buy both tiles and domestic ware. Other sights in the town include a Roman wall, extended during the Middle Ages, four Gothic-Mudejar churches, and the **Basílica de la Virgen del Prado** (*Tel 925 80 14 45*), where almost every surface is blanketed with azulejos.
🅝 235 C3 **Visitor information** ✉ Ronda de Cañillo ☎ 925 82 63 22 ∎

Sounds of flamenco and echoes of the Moors accompany you through the vast open spaces of Andalucía. Sevilla, Córdoba, and Granada synthesize the past, while the coast draws millions of sun worshipers.

Andalucía & Murcia

Decorative tile in Sevilla

Andalucía & Murcia

WILD, RUGGED SIERRA, VERDANT VALLEYS, ACRES OF OLIVE GROVES, SNOWY peaks, the blue Mediterranean, dazzling white hill villages, and a succession of Moorish castles and Renaissance mansions…these are the seductive ingredients of the vast swath of Andalucía. Together with neighboring Murcia, it covers 38,063 square miles (98,583 sq km), sweeping across from the Portuguese border and the Atlantic Ocean past the towering Sierra Nevada peaks to the lunar landscapes of southeastern Spain and the Mediterranean. Andalucía's southernmost tip is a mere 9 miles (14 km) from Africa, so it is not surprising that its history, climate, and topography have so many African influences.

This was the last part of Spain to be relinquished by the Moors when the Catholic Monarchs, Fernando and Isabel, swept southward. They finally united Spain in 1492 by conquering the Moors' last stronghold, Granada. Non-Christians were driven out of Spain, but the Moors did not all leave, and their skills gave rise to Andalucía's own form of Mudejar architecture.

Well before the first independent Arab kingdom emerged in Córdoba in 756, Phoenicians, Greeks, Romans, and Visigoths had joined the region's original Iberian and Tartassian inhabitants. Recent archaeological finds at Orce, in eastern Andalucía, have turned up a fragment of human skull dated at 1.5 to 1.2 million years old, the earliest evidence in Europe of humans who crossed the Strait of Gibraltar from North Africa.

Despite its rich and cultured past, Andalucía remains a laggard in Spain's economic tables, notching up a 30 percent rate of unemployment. This is most visible in the provinces of Cádiz and Almería. *Latifundios* (vast estates) are one reason, but climatic duress also contributes to the region's problems. In inland areas, July and August see temperatures over 105°F (40°C), and drought has reached dramatic proportions in recent years. The Andalusian personality plays a part. All the stereotypical images of Spain come from Andalucía: fiestas, siestas, flamenco, bullfights, and a relaxed approach to life—and there is some truth in them.

The flip side of an easy-going attitude is corruption, which in Andalucía has spawned Spain's worst coastal eyesores. Nonetheless, Andalucía has a string of unmissable cities: Sevilla, Córdoba, and Granada, each with spectacular (and well-maintained) monuments. Smaller towns, too, such as Málaga, Jerez de la Frontera, Ronda, Úbeda, Baeza, and Arcos de la Frontera, are all fantastic reflections of Spain's so-called Golden Age, when the booty of the New World was shipped back directly to Andalucía.

When you become monument weary, you can refresh your eyes in this region's virgin landscapes, from the vast marshes and dunes of Doñana to the Alpujarras (the lovely foothills of the Sierra Nevada), the green Sierra de Cazorla, and the desert of the southeast corner, home of spaghetti Westerns.

Lowland Andalucía divides into two halves, with Granada at its midpoint. To the west lies

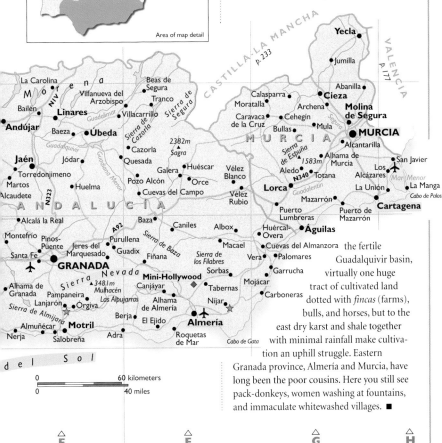

Area of map detail

the fertile Guadalquivir basin, virtually one huge tract of cultivated land dotted with *fincas* (farms), bulls, and horses, but to the east dry karst and shale together with minimal rainfall make cultivation an uphill struggle. Eastern Granada province, Almería and Murcia, have long been the poor cousins. Here you still see pack-donkeys, women washing at fountains, and immaculate whitewashed villages. ■

Sevilla (Seville)

SEVILLA IS A CITY OF 800,000 EXTROVERTS WHO REVEL IN flamenco, bullfighting, processions, fiestas, and tapas. The town center resembles a mosaic of stage sets, each plaza prettier than the next, with its colorful baroque church and orange trees. Discreet alcove shrines and shady tiled patios point to a more secret life, but the overwhelming characteristic is one of openness and conviviality.

Sevilla (Seville)

260 C3

Visitor information

Avenida de la Constitución 21b

95 422 14 04

Closed Sun. p.m.

The negative side of Sevilla's charm is the inevitable commercialization of the center. In the Barrio de Santa Cruz district (see p. 265), steer clear of the restaurants that most obviously cater to vacationers, and watch your wallets, bags, and cameras. That said, relax and take your time. Lose your way in the whitewashed streets and make your own discoveries. Enjoy the day-to-day life of specialist shops, markets, and bars that boom far into the night.

Sevilla's history began with the Romans. Extensive ruins of Itálica, where the emperors Hadrian and Trajan were born, lie 6 miles (10 km) northwest. Remnants of Hispalis, the Roman settlement of Sevilla itself, include the aqueduct (best seen in the Callejón del Agua,

in the Barrio de Santa Cruz), and the columns and statues of Hercules and Julius Caesar on the Alameda. Hercules was Sevilla's legendary founder; Julius Caesar was the real one. The Moors disembarked in 711. It took four centuries for Sevilla to reach its zenith. This came under the rule of the Almohad dynasty who left as a legacy not only the Giralda minaret, but also a lasting influence on architectural style, the Mudejar. From the sumptuous royal palace (Reales Alcázares) and the Casa de Pilatos to endless tiled walls, Sevilla is a dazzling window on an artistry still practiced today.

The end of this golden period came in 1248 when King Fernando III of Castile captured Sevilla from the Moors, but Sevilla soon prospered again following the European discovery of America in the 15th century. The Atlantic Ocean is only 56 miles (90 km) away down the Guadalquivir River, and Sevilla's port saw Ferdinand Magellan, Juan Sebastián Elcano, and Christopher Columbus set sail. Others followed, and the immense riches brought back in their holds financed many of the city's monuments. The 20th century had two high points: the 1929 Ibero-American Exhibition and the 1992 World's Fair. The first has survived best. The latter, a motley assembly of postmodern architecture on the Isla de la Cartuja, is best forgotten. ∎

Colorfully painted *azulejo* **tiles adorn Plaza de España, built for the 1929 Ibero-American Exhibition.**

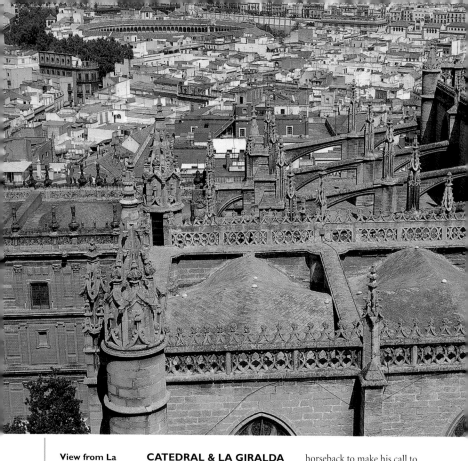

CATEDRAL & LA GIRALDA

The cathedral is outwardly ungainly but it has many treasures, not least being the Giralda tower rising majestically on one side. The Giralda, Sevilla's finest relic of the Almohad dynasty, served as the minaret for the Aljama, the mosque on the site of which the cathedral was built.

La Giralda was completed in 1198 by the architect Ali de Gomara. It suffered damage from an earthquake in 1365, then in the 16th century acquired a Renaissance belfry with 25 bells of differing ages, and finally the weather-vane, from which its name derives. Inside the 322-foot (98 m) tower is a ramp that enabled the *muezzin*, a Muslim crier whose job is the call to prayer, to go up on horseback to make his call to prayer. Lesser mortals must climb up on foot, but the effort is repaid by stupendous views over Sevilla.

You enter both La Giralda and cathedral through a large patio dotted with orange trees and edged by horseshoe arches on two sides, which is all that remains of the mosque. From here a double arch, one Arab and one Gothic, leads inside the world's third largest cathedral (after St. Peter's in Vatican City and St. Paul's in London), an overpoweringly scaled combination of late Gothic and Renaissance styles. It took more than a century to build, from 1403 to 1506. Start at the **high altar,** a staggering work of Flemish art incorporating 2.5 tons (2.4 tonnes) of gold from Mexico and Peru.

**Catedral de Sevilla
& La Giralda**

✉ Avenida de la
Constitución
(entrance at Plaza
Virgen de los Reyes)

☎ 95 421 49 71

🕐 Closed Sun. a.m.

💲 $. Free Sun. p.m.

This alone took 35 years to complete. The detailed carving is magnificent but difficult to see from a distance, so take binoculars. Behind you, the **choir** is another artistic feat, with beautifully carved 15th- and 16th-century choir stalls of Cuban mahogany. Look up into the transept dome to see ornate stonework dating from after the Lisbon earthquake of 1778, when this section collapsed and was rebuilt. The vivid stained-glass windows show that the building period spanned a change in style: The upper row is Gothic and the lower one Renaissance.

To the right of the transept stands the tomb of Christopher Columbus—or at least so the Spanish say. His remains may lie here or in the vast mausoleum of Santo Domingo, in the Dominican Republic, in which case this tomb contains his son Diego. In the sacristy rooms is the cathedral's dazzling **treasury.** You see paintings by Murillo, Zurbarán, and Goya (the only Goya in Sevilla), silver and gold chalices, reliquaries, and processional crosses laden with jewels, a beautiful 12th-century portable altar, and a massive monstrance. This later section of the cathedral has an oval **chapterhouse,** the first such construction in Europe. The cathedral's last surprise is the **Capilla Real,** entered separately from the plaza, which houses the much revered 12th-century statue of the Virgen de los Reyes, the patron saint of Sevilla.

BARRIO DE SANTA CRUZ

Immediately east of the cathedral lies a charming web of streets and little squares. The Barrio de Santa Cruz developed as the Jewish quarter from 1248, when Sevilla was taken from the Moors, and remained so until 1492, when Jews were expelled from Spain. Around 400 families lived here in a self-contained ghetto with their own judiciary and synagogue, although they still paid taxes to the Crown. Today, Santa Cruz has a very different image, firstly being a desirable residential quarter, as it has been since the 17th century, and secondly being heavily geared up for visitors.

It makes an attractive stroll though, and you pass typical flowery Sevillian patios on the way, particularly along the **Callejón del Agua.** Head for **Plaza de Santa Cruz,** the site of the main synagogue, which was later converted into a church and, in turn, destroyed by Napoleon's troops. Between this plaza and the cathedral is the impressive baroque **Hospital de los Venerables** *(Plaza de los Venerables, tel 95 456 26 96),* founded as an asylum for priests, with superb frescoes by Valdés Leal and his son Lucas in the church. The hospital is owned by the Focus cultural foundation and stages concerts and exhibitions.

All the world's a stage in Sevilla.

Pools were both extravagant and luxurious in Sevilla's hot, dry climate.

Reales Alcázares
- ✉ Plaza del Triunfo
- ☎ 95 450 23 23
- 🕐 Closed Sun. p.m. & Mon.
- 💲 $$

REALES ALCÁZARES

Sevilla's rulers did themselves proud, as this royal palace complex displays a masterful combination of Moorish techniques and Catholic symbols—the ultimate example of Mudejar architecture. One of Europe's oldest royal palaces, it is still used by the king of Spain.

The oldest surviving parts of the Alcázar were built by the Almohad dynasty, but long before that the Roman acropolis was here, then an early Christian basilica, and a Moorish castle. What you see today is essentially the work of Pedro I, who ordered its construction in 1362, about the same time as the Nazrid Palace was being built in Granada's Alhambra (see pp. 300–305). A century or so later Isabel I added a wing, and another century on Emperor Carlos V built an adjoining palace for his young Portuguese bride.

From the entrance (where it is advisable to rent audioguide headphones), your first sight is the **Patio de las Doncellas,** a beautiful arcaded patio of exquisite cedarwood marquetry, original *zelij* tiling, and intricate stucco. The upper story, now the king's official residence, and the adjacent **Salón de Carlos V,** with its beautiful mahogany *artesonado* (coffered Mudejar ceiling), are both 16th-century additions. Whenever you see red-and-gold paintwork, you are seeing 19th-century restoration. The Moorish and Mudejar palette was essentially blue and green.

The most masterfully worked rooms lie off the far side of the patio, a maze of interconnecting bedrooms and reception rooms. At their center is the stunning **Salón de Embajadores** (Ambassadors' Hall), topped by an exceptional cedarwood cupola with images of the Catholic Monarchs on the balconies. Horseshoe arches lead to a luminous dining room overlooking the garden: Note the more delicate decoration here, the work of Persian artists after the original hall burned down in a fire. Next is the delightful **Patio de las Muñecas** (Dolls' Patio—so-called for its diminutive size), also known as the Patio de la Reina (Queen's Patio) because it has pierced screens for court women to look through, just as harems did. The open upper gallery was for musicians. Off this lie the modest bedrooms of Fernando and Isabel and of their son, Don Juan.

From the tiled chapel flanking Pedro I's palace, you cross gardens to enter **Palacio de Carlos V,** a complete contrast in scale, with lifeless decoration dominated by tapestries (1740) of the Conquest of

Tunisia. Keep moving, however, and you enter the magnificent **Jardines del Alcázar** (gardens) beside Mercury's Pool, backed by decorative volcanic rock. This is the perfect place to wander, among the perfumes of aromatic plants, magnolias or orange trees in flower, and the sounds of trickling water.

PARQUE DE MARÍA LUISA
In 1893, María Luisa, Duchess of Montpensier, gave most of the vast grounds of Palacio San Telmo to the city. The 1929 Ibero-American Exhibition was staged here, so the 94-acre (38 ha) park is riddled with architectural curiosities.

Start at the **Palacio de San Telmo,** built in 1734 as the first nautical school in the world and later the palace of the Dukes of Montpensier. It is now home to the Andalusian government. Just beyond looms the imposing **Fábrica de Tabacos** (Tobacco Factory, now part of Sevilla University), the setting of Prosper Mérimée's story *Carmen* (1845), on which Bizet's opera was based.

The park is crisscrossed with roads and paths connecting the numerous structures that were built here for the 1929 Ibero-American Exhibition. Each building has found a subsequent function, whether as consulate, museum, art school, flamenco school, or police station (the Brazil pavilion). Spain's national pavilion reigns in splendor around the semicircular **Plaza de España.** Designed by Aníbal González, this outsized masterpiece of neo-Andalusian baroque uses brick and handpainted tiles (from Valencia, Toledo, and Sevilla) with generous abandon. Each Spanish province is represented in a tiled illustration of its historical highpoint, and three pretty bridges span the surrounding water channel. Don't miss the fabulous *artesonado*

Sevilla's favorite taxi service: a horse-drawn carriage

(marquetry) ceilings above the lateral staircases into the pavilion, and give the Gypsy fortune-tellers a wide berth.

Walk 300 yards (275 m) south to Plaza de América, site of two museums. The **Museo de Artes y Costumbres Populares** in the grandiose Mudejar Pavilion *(Plaza de América, tel 95 423 25 76, closed Sun. p.m.–Tues. a.m.)* is worthwhile for its ceramics exhibit on the lower floor, although the display of costumes and furniture above is rather dull. The **Museo Arqueológico** in the plateresque Pavilion *(Plaza de America, tel 95 423 24 01, closed Sun. p.m.–Tues. a.m.)* has a superb collection ranging from Phoenician statuary and the gold Carambolo Treasure through Roman works to Mudejar ceramics. ■

Moorish architecture

Although nearly all the mosques of the Moors were demolished after the Christian Reconquest, other structures such as palaces and bathhouses survived. The architectural elements they introduced to Spain became integrated into Hispanic architecture.

VAULTS & DOMES

Domes were a common feature in Moorish architecture, and they are best seen today in the remaining bathhouses. Developed in the Middle East in the eighth century, these single-story structures had domed and vaulted roofs perforated by star-shaped openings for ventilation and light. The most luxurious bathhouse in Spain is that of the Alhambra in Granada (see pp. 300–305), where white marble columns and floors combine with glazed wall tiles, plaster, and timber. Good examples of public baths can also be seen in Ronda, Girona, and Granada's Albaicín.

Ornate brickwork and blind arches face La Giralda in Sevilla.

HORSESHOE ARCHES

The quintessential Moorish arch is horseshoe-shaped, its most memorable example being in Córdoba's Mezquita. Although the Mezquita is based on the Great Mosque of Damascus, its superimposed tiered arches are said to have been inspired by Roman aqueducts. Builders recycled Visigothic and Roman columns and capitals, while creating a sensation of infinite space. Alternating bands of stone and red brick in the arch itself add even greater visual dynamism. Repetitive horseshoe arches can also be seen in Toledo's Santa María la Blanca synagogue, and blind horseshoe arches on facades were extensively used by Mudejar craftsmen. Later extensions brought other arch designs: the trefoil, multilobed, pointed horseshoe, and pointed arch.

MINARETS

The muezzin's call to prayer came from lofty minarets built next to mosques. Spain's most impressive remaining example is that of Sevilla, the main al-Andalus base for the orthodox Almohad dynasty. This was designed by Ahmed ibn Baso, who repeated its form at the Koutoubia Mosque in Marrakesh. The square tower, known as La Giralda, is faced in sebka brickwork, the repetition of small arch forms. The same use of brick patterning was multiplied by Mudejar craftsmen in the intricately faced towers of Teruel and at Zaragoza's La Seo cathedral.

STUCCO

The sculptural quality of plaster combined with powdered marble (stucco) produced acres of walls carved with arabesque and floral patterns, edged by bands of Kufic calligraphy. Stucco's fragility meant that it was applied only to upper walls, archways, and ceilings. The apogee of stucco complexity is found in the Nazrid Palace of the Alhambra, where *muqarnas* (resembling honeycomb and stalactites) dripping from star-shaped domes create a dazzling optical effect.

AZULEJOS

Glazed tiles were extensively used for surfacing dados (lower walls) in Moorish and Mudejar buildings. Their bold colors and geometric patterns create a strong visual contrast with the more delicate appearance of the stucco-faced upper walls. Geometry was one of the Arabs' greatest skills, and their talent for multiplying basic star forms can be seen in the incredible variations of their *azulejo* designs. Ceramics were also incorporated into Mudejar decorative brickwork. ■

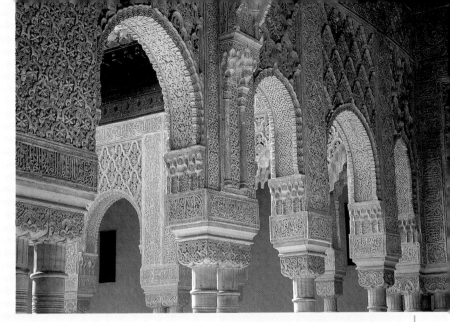

Superlative stuccowork on rhythmical arches (above) and intricate tile inlays (right) are examples of the zenith of Moorish decoration reached at the Alhambra. Below left: A typical horseshoe arch of cut stone surrounds a studded wooden door in Granada's Sacromonte. Below right: Stucco, tiles, and arches create a visual feast of receding perspectives.

The ground floor of the Casa de Pilatos showcases Mudejar artistry.

More places to visit in Sevilla

CASA DE PILATOS

Another fantastic example of Mudejar architecture, the intriguing Casa de Pilatos lies northeast of the Alcázar and cathedral. Built by the Marqués de Tarifa in the 15th to 16th centuries, it was erroneously thought to be a copy of Pontius Pilate's villa, hence the name.

The main patio presents an exceptionally harmonious combination of stuccowork, tiles, *artesonado* (coffered) ceilings, and marble and tiled floors. The same artistry continues in deserted rooms that lead to luxuriant gardens on both sides. In the garden to the left of the main patio, an incongruous Italian loggia is the wing of the palace where the 18th Duchess of Medinacelli and her family still live. Here and throughout the palace are numerous very fine Roman busts and statues, most of which were brought from Rome. The peaceful and well-tended garden to the right of the patio makes a wonderful spot for relaxing beside the fountain during Sevilla's long hot afternoons. Don't miss the gilded artesonado ceiling in the neighboring study, nor the spectacularly worked dome above the main staircase. On the upper floor (sometimes closed for private use), wait for a guide to walk you through a completely different universe, that of the Spanish Renaissance. Here, frescoes by Francisco Pacheco, heavy Spanish furniture, Flemish tapestries, and rather mediocre paintings set the tone. You are seeing how the Spanish nobility still live, and it is quite an eye-opener.

🗺 263 ✉ Plaza de Pilatos ☎ 95 422 52 98 💲 $$

HOSPITAL DE LA CARIDAD

The Hospital de la Caridad (Hospital of Charity) is a few steps west of the cathedral, behind the Teatro de la Maestranza, Spain's prestigious operatic and musical venue. The hospital started life as a burial ground for executed criminals and desperate drowned souls. Change came in 1625 when a repentant, formerly dissolute aristocrat, Miguel de Mañara, became head of the brotherhood of La Caridad and founded the hospital and church. Both are wonderful examples of Sevillian baroque.

In the church you can see the paintings Mañara commissioned: seven superb works by Murillo created for the site (four others were looted by Napoleon's troops), and Valdés

Leal's two compelling paintings of the "Triumph of Death."

 263 ✉ Calle Temprado 3 ☎ 95 422 32 32 🕐 Closed Sun. p.m. 💲 $. Free for Spanish nationals.

MONASTERIO DE LA CARTUJA

The Isla de la Cartuja, site of Expo '92, is of little interest other than for the vast and venerable Carthusian monastery that has stood here since 1428. Once a treasure trove of artworks that was visited by every Spanish monarch who came to Sevilla, it lost its function in 1836, like all Spain's monasteries, when Church property was seized by the state. An Englishman set up a porcelain factory on the site, the result being a line of chimney stacks connected to the kilns, which remained active until 1982. Since then, La Cartuja has become government property and extensive restoration has created a unique place. A pristine contemporary art center installed beside the orchards stages innovative shows, and the Mudejar church successfully displays contemporary paintings (José Manuel Broto, José María Sicilia) beside beautiful original features and the monks' quarters.

 263 ✉ Isla de la Cartuja ☎ 95 503 70 70 🕐 Closed Mon. year-round & Sun. in winter 💲 $

MUSEO DE BELLAS ARTES

The best display of Sevilla's great painters is at this museum, transformed from a 17th-century convent in 1841. It is a lovely building, laid out around three patios with two floors connected by a grandiose imperial staircase. The Aljibe cloister is particularly interesting for its central well and Sevillian tilework. Although the nucleus of the collection is the Sevillian school of painting that flourished in the 17th century, you can sidetrack to look at medieval art. Sevilla's 20th-century output is decidedly less interesting.

Rooms 3 and 4 on the lower floor are crucial—they hold mannerist works by Francisco Pacheco, who exerted such an influence on his students Diego Velázquez (1599–1660) and Alonso Cano (1601–1667). Cano's wonderful painting of the "Souls of Purgatory" and Velázquez's "La Casulla a San Ildefonso," in which the Virgin was modeled on Juana Pacheco, his wife and the daughter of his teacher, hang there also. Room 5 moves into the more baroque world of Murillo, perfectly represented in the reconstructed altar of the Convento de los Capuchinos, and the subtly executed "Virgen de la Servilleta" (Virgin of the Napkin, so-called because it was allegedly painted on Murillo's dinner napkin). You may tire of Murillo's sugary cherubim, so head for the upper floor to see the intense, colorful canvases of Juan de Valdés Leal (1622–1690) in Room 8, and the master of monks, Francisco de Zurbarán, represented in Room 10 by monastery altarpieces.

 263 ✉ Plaza del Museo 9 ☎ 95 422 07 90 🕐 Closed Sun. p.m.–Tues. a.m. 💲 $. Free for E.U. nationals. ∎

A patio in the Museo de Bellas Artes

Semana Santa

Spain's most important festival is not Christmas, but Holy Week (Semana Santa). The entire week from Palm Sunday to Easter Sunday is one long and spectacular demonstration of mourning, enacted with high Catholic color, fervor, and exoticism. In Andalucía you might encounter midnight processions with hooded, torch-bearing penitents, or, in brilliant sunlight, see crowds of villagers clutching palm fronds as a venerated statue of Christ is paraded by. *Pasos* (floats) of highly realistic sculpted figures in theatrical poses are the focal point, although in some places the week culminates in the ceremonial burning or exploding of an effigy of Judas.

In the words of the travel writer Jan Morris, "There are few spectacles on earth to match the holy parades of Malaga or Seville." The main protagonists are parish brotherhoods *(cofradías)*, whose penitential origins go back to the 15th century and who spend the preceding year preparing costumes and floats. The sculptures of the elaborate floats, usually focusing on a sorrowful Virgin Mary and a

Easter procession of penitents at Baeza, near Granada

tortured Christ, are life-size figures (some dating from the 16th and 17th centuries) dressed in embroidered robes and surrounded by flowers, palm fronds, and candles. Beneath them labor the cassocked *costaleros* (carriers), accompanied by hooded *nazarenos* (penitents) atoning for their year's errors.

Sevilla has 57 brotherhoods, 116 floats, and more than 50,000 nazarenos, who slowly advance in turn along a preset route from their *barrio* (quarter) to the cathedral. The weeklong commemoration reaches a climax early on Good Friday, when the most venerated statues of the Virgin Mary and of Christ are carried by six specific brotherhoods. With the penitents, worshipers and onlookers come the inevitable bands. Usually composed of wind and percussion instruments led by an obsessive drum beat, these bands are sometimes interrupted by the penetratingly deep wail of a *saeta*, a song that originates in flamenco. Traditionally, these agonized notes from the crowd impose an immediate silence and halt—signs both of respect for the vocalist and solidarity in his or her prayer. However, the saeta is often prearranged, giving the costaleros a break for a drink and cigarette. Although religious passions run deep, the Sevillian Semana Santa is also about enjoyment, a prelude to the hedonistic Feria that takes place two weeks later. ∎

Penitents

Although a royal decree in 1777 banned acts of medieval penitence and self-abasement, many have survived. In San Vicente de la Sonsierra (Rioja), you see penitents indulge in self-flagellation using strips of linen to beat their bare backs, pricked to facilitate bleeding and avoid blood congestion. Equally extreme are the acts of the *empalaos* in Valverde de la Vera (Extremadura) who cover their backs, torsos, and arms with thick rope before being bound to a cross-shaped plough and dragged through the stages of the Passion. ∎

Hooded penitents follow a *paso* (float), illuminated by candles, that bears a realistic statue of the crucified Christ (above), while other participants (below) take Holy Week in a lighter vein.

Parque Nacional de Doñana

TUCKED AWAY IN THE FAR SOUTHWEST CORNER OF Andalucía, this magnificent national park is Spain's largest and also a World Heritage site. Covering 195 square miles (500 sq km), it was created in 1969 to protect 360 species of birds that frequent these extensive wetlands edging the Guadalquivir River, as well as about a thousand groups of flora, including endemic species.

Aerial view of Doñana's endless expanse of dunes

Parque Nacional de Doñana
🅰 260 B2

El Acebuche
✉ Matalascañas
☎ 959 44 87 39 or 959 44 87 11

Fábrica de Hielo
✉ Avenida de Bajo de Guía, Sanlucar de Barrameda
☎ 956 38 16 35

Although Doñana is generally flat, it has higher areas of scrubland rich in wildflowers, 31 miles (50 km) of shifting coastal sand dunes, and riverbank pastures *(vera)* dotted with cork-oaks.

This diversity has nurtured one of Spain's richest wildlife populations. Unusual reptile species include the stripeless tree frog, sharp-ribbed salamanders, spur-thighed tortoise, and Lataste's viper. Top of the list of 37 mammals are the endangered Iberian lynx, mongooses, wild boar, and red deer. Doñana is a home of the very rare imperial eagle and numerous waterbirds. The park's other striking inhabitants are its bulls and wild horses. The latter are rounded up every year during the festival of Almonte. Spring and autumn bring huge flocks of birds migrating between Europe and Africa.

The park has five visitor centers where you can embark on a four-wheel-drive tour *(Cooperativa Marismas del Rocío, El Acebuche, tel 959 43 04 32)*. Or you can take a boat trip *(Real Fernando, Cristóbal Anillo, tel 956 36 38 13)* along the Guadalquivir River from the visitor center at Fábrica de Hielo. This is ideal for bird-watching. Or you can hire a row-boat in the vicinity of the Duna del Asperillo or, better still, tour the park on horseback *(Turismo a Caballo, tel 959 44 20 84)*. Hikers can follow trails from the visitor center at **Palacio de Acebrón** or at **El Acebuche,** the best place from which to explore the park. ■

Cádiz

CÁDIZ IS TRULY OUT ON A LIMB. IT SITS ON A NARROW
tongue of land curving northward on the Costa de la Luz—the coast
of light. Over the millennia, this seagirt site was much coveted by
Phoenicians, Greeks, Romans, Visigoths, and Arabs. Even today,
Cádiz has an end-of-the-world feel, enhanced by a constant wind
straight off the Atlantic.

**The old town of
Cádiz stretches
picturesquely
along the seawall
of a promontory.**

The Phoenicians founded Cádiz
around 1100 B.C., which makes it
Europe's oldest city. Its moment
came in the 18th century, when
Sevilla's port on the Guadalquivir
River silted up and left Cádiz as
Spain's main trading port with the
New World. In 1812, the city had its
moment as Spain's capital when a
republican constitution briefly saw
the light of day there.

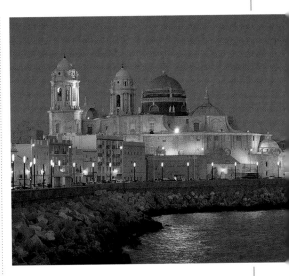

Once you have penetrated the
peripheral shell of modernity, you
find a harmonious old center of
baroque churches (stuffed with gilt
altarpieces) and elegant mansions,
many of them painted in delicate
pastel colors and sporting ornate
wrought-iron balconies.

Cádiz has no great monuments
or sights, but it makes a relaxed
stopover where traditions are still
strong. Artisans carve wooden furniture and gild baroque frames,
cafés align bottles of olive oil to
drizzle over morning toast, and in
the old part of the town, a network
of narrow alleyways reeks of Arab
urbanism. The silhouettes of ocean
liners moored in the port have a
certain romance too. In summer,
when the wind drops, head for the
beaches of fine white sand on the
west coast of the peninsula.

One place you should not miss
is the **Museo de Cádiz,** which
has an impressive collection of
archaeology and fine arts. Head
straight for **Room 2** to see a pair
of Phoenician marble sarcophagi
dating from the fifth century B.C.
These magnificent life-size tombs,

with distinct echoes of Egypt, were
unearthed almost a century apart.
They lie in serene splendor beside
sophisticated terra-cotta busts of
gods, amphorae, and Etruscan
pieces. Next door, bright, skylit
Room 4 exhibits fine Roman
statues including an imposing one
of the emperor Trajan, dating from
A.D. 98 to 117. In **Room 7**, look
for an unusual bronze torso in
military uniform. The painting
collection on the upper floors has
its marvels, too, above all Zurbarán's
series of portraits of monks, each
one expressing a different personality. Murillo, van Dyck, Rubens, and
a string of 20th-century artists
from Joan Miró to Chema Cobo
(born in 1952 in Tarifa) occupy the
other rooms of this grandiose
mid-19th-century building. ∎

Cádiz
- 🇦 260 B1
- **Visitor information**
- ✉ Plaza San Juan de
  Dios 11
- ☎ 956 24 10 01
- 🕐 Closed Sat.–Sun.
  (kiosk open daily)

Museo de Cádiz
- ✉ Plaza de Mina
- ☎ 956 21 22 81
- 🕐 Closed Sun. p.m. &
  Mon.
- 💲 $. Free for E.U.
  nationals.

Jerez de la Frontera

THIS ATTRACTIVE, LIVELY LITTLE TOWN MAY SMACK OF Sevilla (only 62 miles/100 km to the north), but it has its own raisons d'être: sherry, flamenco, horses, and bulls. No fewer than nine sherry bodegas are open for visits, the Royal Andalusian School of Equestrian Art is world famous for equestrian shows, and two Gypsy quarters (San Miguel and Bulería) perpetuate the traditions of the legendary flamenco dancer Lola Flores, a native of Jerez. In surrounding cattle farms, pampered bulls enjoy life—for a while. They are *toros bravos*, destined for the bullring.

These are the things that set Jerez apart, but it also has an impressive old **Alcázar,** containing a well-conserved mosque. This abuts the baroque **Villavicencia palace,** where you can climb up to a camera obscura projecting a bird's-eye view of the townscape below. The lovely Palacio Atalaya houses a clock museum, the **Museo de Relojes** *(Calle Cervantes 3, tel 956 18 21 00, closed Sat. & Sun. p.m. & Mon.),* where 302 17th- to 19th-century clocks and watches from Italy, Austria, France, and England strike in unison every noon. The surrounding gardens are an added pleasure, and certainly more peace-ful. Jerez has numerous beautiful baroque mansions and interesting old churches to discover as you roam. Among them, the **catedral** *(Calle Espiritu Santo, tel 956 34 84 82, closed except for Mass)* is a dignified combination of Renaissance and baroque styles.

Flamenco (see pp. 294–95) is nurtured at the **Centro Andaluz de Flamenco** *(Palacio Pemartín, Plaza San Juan 1, tel 956 34 92 65, closed Sat. & Sun.),* a dance school and museum where you can see videos of past flamenco stars and an excellent film (in Spanish) on this art form. Come to Jerez in September to catch the Feria de la

Bulería, Spain's greatest flamenco festival, with some of the most renowned practitioners.

Bulls and horses are part and parcel of the Jerez landscape. Jerez has a bull museum, **Museo Taurino** *(Calle Pozo del Olivar 6, tel 956 32 30 00, closed p.m. & Sun.),* but your priority should be the **Real Escuela Andaluza del Arte Ecuestre.** This equestrian academy was founded in 1973 to train dressage riders, all of whom use the Andalusian horse, the Cartujano, originally bred in the 18th century by Carthusian monks. You can watch morning training sessions on Mondays, Wednesdays, and Fridays (plus Tuesdays in winter), and then visit the stables and saddlery. Try to be here for the Thursday performance (also on Tuesdays in summer) of dancing horses mounted by riders in stunning 17th-century costumes. In May, Jerez has its Feria del Caballo (Horse Fair), with horse shows, dancing, and parades of horsedrawn carriages.

No one visits Jerez without investigating the process of sherrymaking. Andalucía takes great pride in sherry, as you might guess from the huge sherry barrels (each with with a capacity of 130 gallons/500 liters) sitting outside bars here and in Sevilla. Sherry drinkers already know the names Sandeman, Pedro Domecq, Harvey, and González Byass, all mainstays of Jerez's economy. A visit to a bodega is enlightening. One of the best to visit is **Bodega González Byass,** where you see a structure designed by Gustave Eiffel (designer of the Eiffel Tower in Paris), and barrels signed by the likes of Orson Welles, Winston Churchill, General Franco, Margaret Thatcher, Steven Spielberg, and the entire Spanish royal family. All visits are followed by a tasting. ■

Real Escuela Andaluza del Arte Ecuestre
www.realescuela.org
✉ Avenida Duque de Abrantes
☎ 956 31 80 08
🕐 Closed Sat.–Sun.
💲 $ (training); $$/$$$ (dressage show)

Bodega González Byass (Tio Pepe)
www.gonzalezbyass.es
✉ Calle Manuel M. González 12
☎ 956 35 70 16
🕐 Closed Sat. & Sun. p.m. in winter
💲 $$

Sherry

Sherry is a blended wine whose origins go back to the Phoenicians. Records show that it was produced by the Moors and exported to England in the 12th century. Although the Koran forbids alcohol, Arabs used it for medicinal purposes. The sherry trade blossomed in the 17th and 18th centuries, when London merchants became closely involved, as they have been ever since. Today, over 30 percent of Jerez's exports go to England. The next biggest markets are Holland and Germany, and lagging far behind is the United States.

Sherry is unique. It is made from palomino grapes that thrive on the chalky soil and local climate, and then aged in casks of American oak, in which old and young sherries are periodically mixed. The four main categories are: *fino,* the driest and lightest in color; *amontillado,* still dry but with greater body and more depth; *oloroso,* medium dry and a rich golden color; and *dulce,* the sweetest of all, whose color resembles a port. ■

Long golden
beaches define
Costa de la Luz,
Andalucía's
Atlantic coast
south of Cádiz.

Costa de la Luz

SOUTH OF CÁDIZ STRETCHES A COASTLINE OF POWDERY
golden beaches and dunes backed by pine forests and inland pastures.
However, the wind blows maddeningly and almost constantly.
Windsurfing is king here, and Tarifa at the southern tip is a venue for
the World Windsurfing Championships (see p. 322). Bird-watchers
enjoy the many waterbirds that inhabit the coast and inner lagoons.

Costa de la Luz
🅰 260 B2

**Conil de la
Frontera**
🅰 260 B1
Visitor information
✉ Calle Carretera
☎ 956 44 05 01

Barbate
🅰 260 C1
Visitor information
✉ Calle Ramón y Cajal
43
☎ 956 43 10 06

Wind aside, this coast has attractive
fishing villages and beautiful
scenery. **Conil de la Frontera,** a
traditional whitewashed village
with elegant baroque buildings,
stands beside 9 miles (14 km) of
unspoiled golden sand lapped by
calm, shallow water. Despite good
facilities, it remains pleasantly low
key and is mainly geared to families. A lighthouse 10 miles (16 km)
south marks **Cabo de Trafalgar**
(Cape Trafalgar), where British
admiral Horatio Nelson trounced
the French/Spanish fleet in 1805
and died in the battle. The nearby
clifftop village of **Los Caños de
Meca** is a base for windsurfers.

Between here and Barbate,
7.5 miles (12 km) to the east, is a
4,940-acre (2,000 ha) nature

reserve, the **Parque Natural
del Acantilado y Pinar de
Barbate,** with pines, junipers, and
scrub, much favored by gulls, rock
doves, kestrels, barn owls, and a
colony of cattle egrets. As the road
descends, you have lovely views
over the bay beside the old Roman
fishing port of **Barbate.** Tuna
fishing rules here, and you can buy
mojama (air-dried tuna) direct from
the producers. Another 6 miles (10
km) brings you to **Zahara de los
Atunes,** the most developed of all
these coastal villages thanks to its
beautiful beach. The road veers
inland here. You can either continue
19 miles (30 km) south to Tarifa
(see p. 322) or head northwest to the
region of the *pueblos blancos,* or
"white towns" (see pp. 280–81). ∎

Ronda

THIS IS ANDALUCÍA'S GREAT CLIFF-HANGER: RONDA straddles a gorge with a sheer 325-foot (100 m) drop down to the Guadalevín River. Over the gorge (known as El Tajo) stretches the Puente Nuevo, or "new bridge," connecting the old and new parts of town— "new" being only relative, as the latter quarter dates from the 18th century. Ronda is a popular town with extensive facilities for visitors, including numerous antique shops, yet it retains a powerful atmosphere if you avoid the crowded summer months.

The secret plazas and cobbled streets of **Old Ronda** are very evocative, and you can visit several mansions. One of the prettiest and most intimate is the **Palacio de Mondragón** *(Plaza de Mondragón, tel 95 287 84 50, closed Sat. & Sun. p.m.),* now housing a small museum. This was built in 1314 as the residence of the great Moorish king Abb el Malik. Fernando and Isabel stayed here in 1485, and the palace acquired its present facade in the 18th century. Of the many patios, the most outstanding is the Mudejar courtyard, rich in craftsmanship in brick, marble, tiles, and wood. From there a horseshoe arch leads to a charming garden. A few steps from the mansion is the stately **Parque Duquesa de Parcent,** overlooked by the church of **Santa María la Mayor** *(Tel 95 287 22 46),* which was built over a mosque, and the Renaissance **town hall,** with an impressive loggia.

Downhill (east) from here on the main road looms a Nazari-style minaret that now belongs to the church of San Sebastian. To the south stands a section of the old Arab walls with their double gateway: the Moorish **Puerta de Almocabar** and the Renaissance **Puerta de Carlos V.** At the bottom of the hill to the east lie the restored **Baños Árabes** (Arab Baths). If you walk down to them on Calle Santo Domingo, you pass the beautiful facade of the **Palacio del Marqués de Salvatierra** with its curious sculptures of naked children, thought to be pre-Columbian figures.

In the new town, don't miss the venerated bullring, the **Plaza de Toros,** where man has been pitting his wits against bulls since 1785. On display inside, in the **Museo Taurino,** are dazzling toreadors' jackets and capes encrusted with beading, sequins, and braids, beside photos of historic matadors, fights, deaths, and aficionados such as Orson Welles. ∎

Ronda

🗺 260 C2

Visitor information

✉ Plaza de España 1

☎ 95 287 12 72

🕐 Closed Sun. p.m.

Baños Árabes

✉ Calle San Miguel

☎ 95 287 38 89

🕐 Closed Wed.–Sat. p.m., Sun.–Mon.

Plaza de Toros & Museo Taurino

✉ Calle Virgen de la Paz

☎ 95 287 41 32

💲 $

Drawn by Ronda's secure position, Andalusian bandits held court here from the early 18th to 20th centuries.

A drive through *pueblos blancos*

This drive takes you through the dramatic Sierra de Grazalema Natural Park from west to east, stopping at typical white villages (pueblos blancos) before arriving at Ronda, the most inviting of them all.

Arcos de la Frontera ❶ *(Visitor information, Plaza del Cabildo, tel 956 70 22 64)*, first settled by the Romans, is the western gateway to this region, with roads radiating in all directions from its spectacular clifftop site. Negotiating the narrow, winding streets of Arcos by car is an art in itself, so allow time to climb up on foot to the main square. On one side is the **church of Santa María,** a beautiful Gothic-Mudejar building with plateresque details; on the other is a *mirador* (lookout point) with views over orchards and olive groves. Here, too, are the Moorish walls of the **Castillo de los Duques** and numerous baroque and Renaissance facades.

Leave Arcos on the beltway by following signs for the A372 to El Bosque, 17 miles (27 km) away. You go through densely farmed land of vegetables, olive groves, and horse ranches, and eventually the Sierra de Grazalema comes into view. Scenery becomes increasingly spectacular as you arrive at

El Bosque ❷, huddled at the base of the mountains. This center for hikers, rock climbers, trout fishers, and hang gliders consists of a handful of cafés and a waterwheel grouped around a bridge over El Bosque River. Cross this and turn right after the bar to reach the parking lot from where you can walk to the visitor center of the **Parque Natural de la Sierra de Grazalema** *(Oficina del Parque Natural de la Sierra de Grazalema, tel 956 72 70 29)*.

Leave El Bosque on the A372 and after 1 mile (1.6 km) watch for a turnoff on the left to Grazalema. From here the road climbs immediately through eucalyptus and pine trees, and the soil becomes chalkier. You soon see the village of **Benamahoma ❸** on your left. Views open up over the valley, and forests alternate with rock. Views of the stark, granite-capped peak of **Monte Simancón** (5,134 feet/1,565 m) accompany you to the pass, the **Puerto del Boyar ❹** (3,618 feet/1,103 m),

Arcos de la Frontera, set on a crag above the Guadalete River

where you can park to admire the superb perspective of mountain ridges receding to the west and buy honey from local vendors. This is classic territory for roe deer, mountain goats, Griffon vultures, and eagles. Also here is the Spanish fir (pinsapo), a rare species that grows only above 3,280 feet (1,000 m) and is a survivor from the forests of the Tertiary era.

As the road snakes down, you catch sight of **Grazalema** ❺ (Visitor information, Plaza de España 11, tel 956 13 22 25), a dazzling sight of whitewashed houses, tiled roofs, and church towers wedged between the sierras of El Pinar and El Endrinal. Opposite is the rocky outcrop of El Reloj (The Clock). Drive down into the village, cross the main square, and turn right at the church into the parking lot (invaded by a market on Tuesday mornings). Then start exploring this immaculate village, its houses thick with layers of whitewash and its streets well endowed with bars, restaurants, and churches. The neoclassic **church of La Aurora** is the one with the octagonal tower; the other churches are the **Encarnación** and **San José,** which was once a Carmelite monastery and is built over a mosque.

Leave Grazalema by continuing on the A372 marked Ronda (20 miles/33 km). After

1 mile (1.6 km) a turnoff to the left, signed to **Zahara,** is a worthwhile detour if you can face more than an hour of truly tortuous bends. Otherwise continue on the A372 down through a rock-strewn valley with striking views of Grazalema perched high above. Cork- and holm-oak forests line the road as you cross into the province of Málaga, and views gradually open up to farmland dotted with white fincas (farms). Turn right toward Ronda when you reach the first junction, and then turn right again onto the A376. As this twists rapidly downwards past steep granite cliffs on the right, **Ronda** (see p. 279), set dramatically over a gorge, appears on the horizon. ∎

▲ See area map pp. 260–61
► Arcos de la Frontera
⇄ 47 miles (76 km)
⏱ 3 hours (with short visits)
► Ronda

NOT TO BE MISSED
- Arcos de la Frontera
- El Bosque
- Puerto del Boyar
- Grazalema

Ronda, from the bridge across the ravine

Antequera

IT SEEMS APT THAT THE TOWN AT THE GEOGRAPHICAL heart of Andalucía also claims the greatest number of churches of any town in Spain. Antequera also lies in an exceptionally beautiful spot, with the spectacular rock formation of El Torcal to the south.

Antequera

🄰 260 D2

Visitor information

✉ Plaza San Sebastián 7

☎ 95 270 25 05

🕓 Closed Sun. p.m.

El Torcal

🄰 260 D2

Visitor information

✉ Centro de Interpretación

☎ 95 203 13 89

Crowned by the **Alcazaba,** or Moorish castle, the white houses of Antequera spill down the hillside, their tiled roofs spiked with some 30 church steeples. The one you must see is the **church of El Carmen** (Plaza del Carmen, tel 95

Eroded limestone shapes at El Torcal create a surreal landscape for hiking.

270 25 05, closed Sun. p.m.), which has delicate 16th- to 17th-century wall paintings, polychrome statues, a Mudejar coffered ceiling, and, best of all, a masterfully carved main altarpiece, one of Andalucía's finest baroque works. Walk uphill, through the 16th-century **Arco de los Gigantes,** to the **Colegiata de Santa María** (Closed p.m. & Mon.), an early example of Andalusian Renaissance architecture, with another impressive Mudejar ceiling. From here you can walk up through the landscaped gardens of the Alcazaba to the tower, **Torre del Homenaje** (Closed Mon.) for wonderful views.

Back in the center of town, don't miss the graceful Palacio de Nájera, one of many noble mansions, now converted into the **Museo Municipal** (Plaza Coso Viejo, tel 95 270 40 51, closed Sun. p.m. & Mon.). The main exhibit is a superb first-century Roman bronze statue of a boy. Take the Málaga road out of town to three dolmens (stone tombs). The **Cueva de Menga** and **Cueva de Viera** (Carretera de Málaga, closed Mon., Tues. p.m.), the most impressive, date from about 2500 B.C. One mile (1.6 km) farther on is the slightly younger **Romeral** (Closed Mon. & Tues., & p.m. Wed.–Sun.), dating from about 1800 B.C.

Older than all of these is **El Torcal,** 8 miles (13 km) south, where 6.5 square miles (17 sq km) of calcareous rock have been eroded into extraordinary shapes. Well-marked hiking trails lead through this fantasy landscape. ∎

Málaga

Views from
the castle of
Gibralfaro take
in Málaga town
and harbor.

THIS CITY OF OVER HALF A MILLION PEOPLE HAS AN
animation and atmosphere of its own, and Malagueños are known
for their exuberance. The port was frequented by Phoenicians,
Romans, and Moors. Today, cargo ships and ferries still dock there.

Crowning a hilltop in the center of
town is the Moorish **Alcazaba.** Its
many towers and walls enclose the
former palace, which is now the
Museo Arqueológico. Enjoy the
views but don't forget to go inside
to see the Mudejar-style carved and
painted ceilings, fine Roman
pottery, mosaics, and Arab ceramics, appropriate echoes of the mixed
architectural elements of the
fortress. At the entrance below is a
Roman theater—a venue for
summer concerts. Higher still than
the Alcazaba, the 14th-century
castle of **Gibralfaro** gives
sweeping views over the Alcazaba
and the harbor. Part of it is now
a *parador* with an inviting
panoramic terrace.

Much of Málaga's attraction lies
in its easy, breezy walking areas,
from the **Paseo Marítimo** on
the seafront to the luxuriant gardens, tiled benches, and duck ponds
of the **Paseo del Parque** leading
to the leafy **Alameda.** As pony
carts trot by, flower vendors set up
their stands under towering centen-
nial trees in front of elegant 19th-
century buildings. Running north
from the Alameda is the marble-
paved shopping street, **Marqués
de Larios,** which ends at the Plaza
de la Constitución. The web of
narrow streets east toward the
cathedral bristle with little restaurants, bars, and small stores selling
books, clothes, and antiques. Three
blocks west of Marqués de Larios,
the bustling mock-Mudejar market,
Mercado de Atarazanas, has
wonderful fresh produce and a real
curiosity: a 14th-century stone

Málaga
🅰 260 D2
Visitor information
✉ Pasaje de Chinitas 4
☎ 95 221 34 45
🕐 Closed Sat. & Sun.
    p.m.

**Alcazaba & Museo
Arqueológico**
✉ Calle Alcazabilla
☎ 95 222 00 43
🕐 Closed Tues.
💲 $

arch, all that survives of the Moorish arsenal.

The **catedral** *(Calle Molina Larios, tel 95 221 59 17, closed Sun.)* is a must. Although its second tower was never built (the bishop of the time apparently siphoned the funds to aid the American Revolution), the cool late Renaissance interior has great harmony. Subtly carved cupolas crown the three naves, with spectacular choir stalls carved by Pedro de Mena. Side chapels house an abundance of artworks, although these are difficult to see in the gloom. The most visible are in the chapel directly behind the altar, where dazzling white marble sculptures by Juan de Salazar vie with those of the retrochoir (facing the main doors), the work in 1802 of the brothers Pissani. To the right of Juan de Salazar's sculptures another chapel contains a striking Gothic altarpiece, the "Mass of Saint Gregory" by Fernando de Coca. Don't miss the delightful **gardens** at the back, where the church of **El Sagrario** houses a magnificent plateresque altarpiece by Juan

Balmaseda and has an ornate Isabelline-Gothic portal.

Málaga still awaits completion of a Picasso museum in the lovely Palacio de Buenavista *(Calle San Agustín)* to honor its most famous son, Pablo Picasso (1881–1973). In the meantime you can visit his birthplace, **Casa Natal de Picasso** *(Plaza de la Merced, tel 95 221 50 05, closed Sun. p.m.)*, an elegant house on a rather scruffy square. The pristine, renovated interior tells you nothing about his life, but displays wonderful ceramics, enlarged photos, and small-scale works (exhibited in rotation). The lower floor is used for art exhibitions.

Four miles (7 km) north of Málaga is a botanical garden, **Finca de la Concepción** *(Carretera de las Pedrizas Km 166, tel 95 225 21 48, closed Mon.)*, a collection of palms and exotic plants that was started in the 1850s and has flourished in the mild, humid climate. Pools and Roman statues add to the charm, and a *mirador* (lookout point) gives views across the city to the Mediterranean. ■

Costa del Sol

STRETCHING FROM GIBRALTAR EASTWARD TO ALMERÍA, this much visited coast has its highs and its lows. The coast west of Málaga has been intensely developed but still has interesting corners, and even glamour at the jet-set resort of Marbella.

East of Málaga, the coast is less built up, but still has eyesores. One major exception is **Nerja,** *(Visitor information, Puerta del Mar 2, tel 95 252 15 31)* an attractive resort town 3 miles (4.5 km) from Málaga, with a cave complex, **Cuevas de Nerja** *(Carretera de Maro, tel 95 252 95 20).* The chambers, with their stalactites and stalagmites, stretch for 2,625 feet (800 m). Background music, spotlights, and a cave restaurant dispel the mystery somewhat, but you can see Paleolithic rock paintings in the upper chamber, and the small museum has prehistoric items.

Southwest of Málaga is **Torremolinos,** a jumble of high-rises packed with bars, shops, discos, and other facilities for vacationers. **Fuengirola** has more of the same, but it also has the ruins of a Moorish castle and nearly 4 miles (6 km) of beach. If you like water sports, this is a good place to be. Five miles (8 km) inland is the beautiful and well-preserved hill village of **Mijas,** once a haunt of artists but now suffering from a tidal wave of visitors from the coast. Sights include the remains of Arab walls and the 17th-century hermitage of the Virgen de la Peña, but the chief attractions are the town's picturesque corners, geranium-laden balconies, craft shops, and wonderful views—all easily seen by donkey taxi.

Next stop west along the coastal highway is **Marbella,** the most glitzy and upscale resort in Spain. A steady flow of top-of-the-range cars cruises past endless bars and restau-rants. The old and pretty center radiates from the Plaza de la Constitución, with a 16th-century town hall and fountain, and a castle, **Castillo de Madera.** Its nightlife is the hottest on the costa, and the gastronomy is highly rated.

San Pedro de Alcántara was the ancient Roman colony of Silniana, destroyed by an earthquake in A.D. 365. You can see well-restored structures and a sixth-century **Visigothic basilica** here. San Pedro also has a lovely beach and several golf courses, and it is the start of the long, tortuous, but magnificent drive of 31 miles (50 km) through rocky landscapes, woods, ravines, and isolated villages up into the Serranía de Ronda. ∎

Fuengirola
 260 D1
Visitor information
✉ Avenida Jesús Santos Rein 6
☎ 95 246 74 57

Marbella
 260 D1
Visitor information
✉ Glorieta de la Fontanilla
☎ 95 277 14 42

San Pedro de Alcántara
 260 D1
Visitor information
✉ Avenida Marqués del Duero 69
☎ 95 278 52 52

The Sierra de Tejeda looms behind Nerja, one of the Costa del Sol's most attractive resorts.

Córdoba

THERE IS SOMETHING SPECIAL ABOUT CÓRDOBA, SLIGHTLY off the tourism trail between the Sierra Morena to the north and the Campiña agricultural plains to the south. You see a plethora of souvenir shops around the Mezquita, Córdoba's greatest monument. Head through the twisting alleys and strike out into surrounding districts and you find the true spirit of Andalusian life.

Córdoba
🔺 260 D3
Visitor information
✉ Plaza Judá Leví
☎ 957 20 05 22
🕐 Closed Sun. p.m.

With a population of little more than 300,000, Córdoba is a small city. It was the capital of Roman Spain and of a Moorish kingdom, but ruins of Roman and Moorish structures remain unexploited due to lack of funds. The city endures baking temperatures in July and August, when shady patios become essential oases. This climatic adversity has not prevented a string of festivities. During Holy Week (see pp. 272–73) processions invade the narrow streets. In May, the Feria (festival) takes place, and the entire population seems to be involved in crucifix-decorating, patio contests, and pilgrimages. Córdoba's legendary bullfighters and flamenco dancers spring into action. The sultry summer months bring long evenings of flamenco music in various gardens of the city.

The Romans founded the town in 169 B.C., but it was under Islamic dominance that Córdoba reached its zenith. In 756, Abd ar-Rahman I founded Córdoba as capital of Moorish Spain. By 929, when Abd-ar-Rahman III declared himself caliph, it had become the envy of Europe. About 1,000 mosques, 600 public baths, public street lighting, and a renowned university graced the city, where philosophers, poets, mathematicians, and doctors (including the great Jewish thinker, Maimónides) created an intellectual ferment. Decline came in the 11th century after the skillful but ruthless reign of Al-Mansur. Al-Andalus fragmented into petty _taifas_ (kingdoms), although intellectual life continued until 1236, when Córdoba was conquered by Fernando III.

From then on it was a steady downward slide. Ingenious Moorish waterworks were abandoned and every mosque except the Mezquita was replaced by a church. In the 16th and 17th centuries, Córdoba's artisans of embossed leather and silver were much sought after, but plague decimated the population in the 17th century.

It is an easy city in which to orient yourself, although you may get lost in the Judería, the old Jewish quarter. Bordered to the south by the Guadalquivir River, Córdoba radiates from the Mezquita and the labyrinthine Judería. Few sights lie outside this area, but it is worth exploring the barrios to the east: Their modest houses have produced famous bullfighters and flamenco artists. Outside town is the Medina Azahara, epicenter of Córdoba's golden age.

A much rebuilt Roman bridge spans the Guadalquivir River, with the Mezquita and cathedral rising beyond.

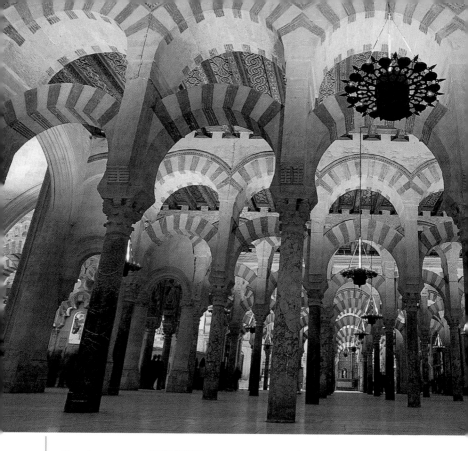

Mezquita

✉ Calle Torrijos

☎ 957 47 05 12

🕐 Closed Sun. a.m.

💲 $$

Alcázar de los Reyes Cristianos

✉ Calle Caballerizas Reales

☎ 957 42 01 51

🕐 Closed Sun. p.m. & Mon.

💲 $. Free on Fri.

MEZQUITA

The jewel in Córdoba's crown is still called by its Arabic name, Mezquita, meaning "mosque," despite the extraordinary intrusion of a Catholic cathedral in its midst. It is the only mosque left from medieval Spain, and it is one of the largest in the world.

The vast, walled Mezquita covers 258,330 square feet (24,000 sq m). Building started in 785, it was extended in 848 and 961, then almost doubled in size in 987. Your first sight is from the **Puerta del Perdón,** an immense gateway beside the baroque belfry that encloses the old minaret. In front is the beautiful **Patio de los Naranjos,** dotted with orange trees whose fragrant blossoms in April are unforgettable. Once you enter the oldest part of the mosque, you understand why Charles V ordered that the building be saved, despite immense pressure from the Church to demolish it. It is a visual masterpiece of rhythmical horseshoe arches that somehow gives the sense of infinity that underlies Islamic belief. Each of the 824 columns is different, as are their capitals, since they were mostly salvaged from previous Roman and Visigothic structures. The two-tiered arch was copied from Roman aqueducts for structural purposes and to increase the light. Notice the alternating bands of red brick and white stone, and their painted imitations in the later, northern section, built with inferior materials under the aegis of power-crazy Prime Minister Al-Mansur.

Penetrate the interior, passing the cathedral on your left, and you come to the end wall, the **Kibla,** which should face Mecca (southeast of Córdoba) but actually faces due south. The Mezquita's most stunning piece of craftsmanship is here, the **mihrab,** or prayer niche, from which the imam (Muslim prayer-leader) would lead worshipers in prayer. Look carefully at the exquisite mosaics and dome decorated by Byzantine craftsmen, and the entire *maqsura,* the marble-flagged space that was once reserved for the caliph and his courtiers. Koranic texts are engraved into marble cornices, and you can see Spain's earliest stucco tracery—later to become a major feature of Nazrid and Mudejar architecture.

From here you move to the **Tesoro,** a comparatively heavy baroque chapel containing Córdoba's massive silver and gold monstrance, made by Enrique de Arfe in 1516. It weighs 270 pounds (122 kg), and since 1518 has had an annual airing at Corpus Christi. Turn around from here to see the 14th-century **Capilla Real** (Royal Chapel), built under Alfonso X and sympathetically decorated in Mudejar-style stucco. Then you get to the carbuncle of the Mezquita, the Renaissance-baroque **catedral** (1523–1617) that was plunked down in the center of the mosque, thus destroying much of its unique harmony. The only real interest here lies in the beautifully carved **choir stalls** (1750). On leaving, take time to look at the exquisitely carved outer doorways on Calle de Torrijos (by the Mezquita's western wall), where an elevated walkway once joined the caliph's palace.

A few steps southwest of the Mezquita lies the **Alcázar de los Reyes Cristianos** (Fort of the Christian Kings), which was built in 1328 after the Christian Reconquest

(see p. 32)

of Córdoba. Fernando and Isabel used this fortified palace as their base in 1491–92 while plotting their attack on Granada, the last Moorish stronghold of Andalucía. After that its functions became less glorious: It was the Court of the Inquisition (see p. 32) until the early 19th century and then a prison. Today, the interior has a few interesting features—including Roman mosaics, an ornately carved Roman sarcophagus, and a Gothic chapel in the tower—and the **water gardens** are superb. They were re-created in Moorish style in the 1960s, and every July are the setting for Córdoba's guitar festival.

Cross the Roman bridge from here to reach the **Torre de la Calahorra** (*Puente Romano, tel 957 29 39 29*), originally an Arab tower that replaced a Roman gateway and was itself rebuilt in 1369. From the roof you have spectacular views of Córdoba across the river; inside is an audiovisual display on Moorish culture that you can follow with headsets. Some rooms are simplistic, but the commentary gives easily accessible information.

**Above left:
The Mezquita's rhythmic interior was designed over a thousand years ago to create a spatial sense of infinity.**

**Above right:
A service at Córdoba's cathedral, built within the walls of the mosque**

**Museo
Arqueológico**

✉ Plaza de Jerónimo
Páez 7

☎ 957 47 10 76

🕐 Closed Sun.
p.m.–Tues. a.m.

💲 $. Free for E.U.
citizens

The short-lived
Medina Azahara
once boasted
fantastic whims
such as curtains
of water, domes
of crystal, and
African
menageries.

MUSEUMS & PALACES

Two blocks northeast of the
Mezquita, on one of Córdoba's
most delightful squares, the
Museo Arqueológico is as
interesting for its setting as for its
collection. The collection is
imaginatively distributed throughout the four patios and galleries of
a lovely Renaissance mansion with
a magnificent sculpted gateway.
Patio II has a superb Roman
statue of a crouching Aphrodite,
copied from a Greek piece. In
Patio III the remains of Roman
steps face a mosaic panel of the Nile
River. Fragments of stone inscriptions, columns, and capitals in
Room V lead you to a model of
the Roman temple standing on
Calle Claudio Marcelo and a superb
statue of Hermaphrodite.

As you climb the Renaissance
staircase examine the carved *artesonado* ceiling before moving clockwise around the upper galleries
devoted to Moorish artifacts.
Among them are a lovely capital

sculpted with four figures of
musicians and, in **Room VII,** the
incised bronze of a fawn: This and
the surrounding glass and ceramic
all came from Medina Azahara.
Also outstanding is the rare
collection of terra-cotta wells.

Just northwest of the Mezquita,
the **Museo Taurino** (*Plaza de
Maimónides, tel 957 20 10 56, closed
Sun. p.m. & Mon.*), a museum of
bullfighting, is in a traditional
16th-century house in the Judería.
It has a fine collection of paintings
and posters, and sections devoted
to Córdoba's four caliphs, its top
four matadors—Lagartijo,
Guerrita, Machaquito, and the legendary Manolete. All have their
tributes of memorabilia, implements, glittering costumes, and
action photos. Just beside the
museum is the **Zoco,** or souk,
a small artisans' market where
some of Córdoba's many silversmiths and ceramicists practice
their trade. Opposite, don't miss
the tiny **Sinagoga** (*Calle Judíos,*

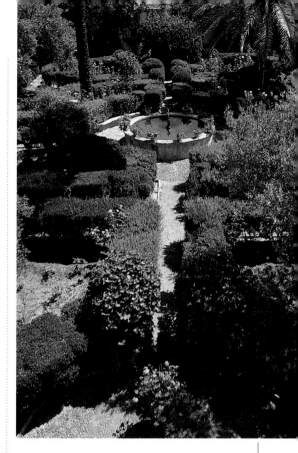

tel 957 20 29 28, closed Mon.), built in 1315, one of only two major synagogues that survive in Spain today.

Well outside the Judería but still within walking distance, the **Palacio de Viana** *(Plaza de Don Gome 2, tel 957 48 01 34, closed Sat. p.m. & Sun.)* is a fine and substantial aristocratic mansion. The one-hour guided tour (in Spanish but with an explanatory leaflet in English) whisks you through a labyrinth of halls and rooms, all stuffed with valuable antiques, chandeliers, paintings, and tapestries. Their provenance varies, but they are mainly European with a few Oriental additions. Like the Casa de Pilatos in Sevilla (see p. 270), it makes a fascinating eye-opener on the lifestyle and means of the Spanish nobility. You are left on your own to explore the twelve stunning patios and one garden that surround the mansion, each one perfumed by aromatic plants. If you miss Córdoba's Festival of Patios, held in May, this makes an excellent substitute.

MEDINA AZAHARA

Medina Azahara is one of Spain's most important archaeological sites, and it is a must on your Andalusian journey. It lies 7 miles (11 km) west of Córdoba off the C431. The extensive ruins in front of you are the vast tenth-century palace of Caliph Abd ar-Rahman III, of the Ummayad dynasty. The palace was built in pink, blue, and white marble and decorated with ebony, ivory, and precious stones. It is said that 10,000 workers, 1,500 mules, and 400 camels were employed on the site to build this homage to the Caliph's favorite wife, Al-Zahra ("orange blossom"). The Medina became both the seat of government and a palatial residence, but it stood for only 70 years before it was destroyed by North African Berbers in 1010.

Of the surviving structures, the most impressive are the army barracks and the marble-carved **Salón Rico** (Rich Room), a restored hall of the reconstructed palace. Here you see the relaxed attitude of the Ummayads to representation: Trees, animals, and even human figures appear in the decoration, in a less rigid style than the strict geometry of the Almohads and Almoravids of Granada and Sevilla. Below, the ruins of the mosque are correctly oriented towards Mecca, unlike the Mezquita in Córdoba. The terraced site, with its sweeping view, cypress trees, palms, and wild cactuses, evokes a sense of the power and majesty of Córdoba's caliphate. ∎

The Palacio de Viana is known as the Museum of Patios, for its twelve distinctly different patio gardens.

Medina Azahara
- ✉ Carretera de Palma del Rio (C431)
- ☎ 957 32 91 30
- 🕑 Closed Sun. p.m. & Mon.
- 💲 $. Free for E.U. nationals.

Úbeda

JUST 5 MILES (8 KM) APART, ÚBEDA AND BAEZA ARE TWO
jewels of Renaissance architecture in the province of Jaén. Úbeda
was founded as Ubbadat al-Arab and was one of the most important
towns of the Moorish region of al-Andalus.

Úbeda
📍 261 E3
Visitor information
✉ Palacio del Marqués
de Contadero, Calle
Baja del Marqués
☎ 953 75 08 97
🕐 Closed p.m. & Sun.

After Fernando III captured the
town in 1234, it became a base for
the struggle against the Muslims. At
the peak of its fortunes in the 16th
century, gold from America was
pouring into Spain. The result is a
cluster of Renaissance buildings in
the **old town,** untouched by the
hurly-burly of modern life. Sit on a
bench by the esplanade of **Plaza
de Vázquez de Molina,** looking
at the church of El Salvador ahead
of you, the town hall to the left,
and, to your right, Santa María, the
Palacio del Marqués de Mancero,
and the old granary. **El Salvador**
*(Calle Baja del Salvador, tel 953 75
81 50)* has an extravagant baroque
altarpiece with a sculpture of
Christ by Alonso Berruguete, but
better still is the inner lobby of the
main portal—a masterwork of
carved wood.

Úbeda has long been known for
complex ceramics finished in a
deep green glaze. Take a quick look
at the pottery museum, **Museo de
Alfareria** *(Plaza Vásquez de
Molina, tel 953 75 04 40, closed Sun.
p.m. & Mon.)* before heading for
Calle Valencia, just north of the
Puerta del Losal, one of the old city
gates. Here in a string of ceramics
workshops you can watch craftsmen at work. On your way, stop to
admire the lovely **church of San
Pablo** *(Plaza del 1° de Mayo)* on
the old market square, an early
Gothic church with beautifully
carved portals. A few steps from
here is the small **Museo
Arqueológico** *(Casa Mudéjar,
Calle Cervantes 6, tel 953 75 37 02,
closed Sun. p.m. & Mon.),* attrac-
tively set out in a 14th-century
Mudejar house. ■

Baeza

THE SLIGHTLY POORER COUSIN OF ÚBEDA HAS A SIMILAR inheritance of Renaissance structures, more civic than domestic, and all built in a lovely golden stone. Baeza's monuments are more integrated into the modern town than Úbeda's, which makes it less of a museum and more enjoyable.

In the 13th century Baeza became capital of the High Guadalquivir before Jaén was conquered. Like Úbeda, it reached its zenith in the 16th and 17th centuries, when the university was founded and the cathedral was transformed. The **catedral** dominates high ground to the east of the center, and is a good starting point for a walk. Inside, climb the bell tower for wonderful views over the town and countryside. Don't miss the Mudejar cloisters with their four chapels inscribed in Arabic, echoes of the mosque that once stood on this site. Outside, stop to admire the oldest elements of the cathedral, the 13th-century Puerta de la Luna and the Gothic rose window. In front is the pretty fountain of Santa María, built in the 16th century by Ginés Martínez, who also designed Baeza's water conduits.

A few steps west on the Plaza Santa Cruz stands Baeza's most exceptional building, the **Palacio de Jabalquinto.** The facade is a masterpiece of delicate Flamboyant Gothic stonecarving, incorporating diamond-shaped studs. It was commissioned by Juan Alfonso de Benavides, a cousin of Fernando V of Aragón. Restoration work will prevent you from visiting the inner patio, but try and get a peep at the sumptuous baroque staircase in one corner. Across the square, enter the charming little **church of Santa Cruz** (Plaza de Santa Cruz, closed Sun. p.m.), built in 1227 in late Romanesque style. Among the traces of frescoes, look inside the arch to the left of the altar for the one of San Sebastián, still looking saintly despite the cascading arrows. The other impressive building on this square is the old university, founded in 1538.

Baeza's social focus is oval **Plaza de la Constitución,** just downhill. Other Renaissance buildings lie to the north on Calle de San Pablo; another attractive cluster is on **Plaza de los Leones** (Lions' Square). It is named for the fountain at the center, thought to have come from the Roman town of Cantulo. On one side is the distinctive double arch of the **Puerta de Jaén** and **Arco de Villalar.** ∎

Baeza
🅰 261 E3
Visitor information
✉ Plaza del Pópulo
☎ 953 74 04 44
🕐 Closed p.m. & Sun.

The fountain of Santa María stands outside Baeza's imposing cathedral.

Flamenco

Flamenco is a form of song, guitar playing, and dance that epitomizes the complex soul of Andalucía. Arab, Oriental, and Gypsy influences mingled to produce this extraordinarily characteristic sound, which in its rawest, most authentic state is a spontaneous outburst late at night in a backstreet bar. The frills, flounces, castanets, and syncopated hand-clapping of the dancers are more easily accessible to foreigners, but often produce disappointingly mechanical shows laid on for tourists on the *costas*. Nonetheless, true flamenco is alive, well, and, since the 1980s, reinventing itself.

Joaquin Cortés, one of the young, innovative flamenco dancers

expression of loss, grief, or injustice is considered more important than tonal clarity, and is often performed a cappella.

Solo guitar playing evolved from providing the singers with a break to becoming an art in itself. Guitarists such as Paco Peña, Paco de Lucía, and Tomatito have become world famous, more so than their singing companions, whose harsh voices are less easily appreciated. The total performing art of song, music, and dance came together in the late 19th century and was crowned by Manuel de Falla's flamenco ballet, El Amor Brujo, in 1915. Since the 1950s, the spread of *tablaos* (specialized flamenco bars) has encouraged exponents of all three elements to test their abilities in front of aficionados.

Most experts believe that the roots of flamenco lie in the 15th century, when Gypsies arrived from north India via Egypt and eastern Europe, and fused their music with that of the Moors and Jews in Andalucía. The word "flamenco" probably derives from the Arabic "felag mengu," meaning "fugitive peasant"—a reference to Gypsies and perhaps also Moriscos (baptized Moors). Since then it has evolved into several branches, notably the *soleá* of Sevilla's Triana district, the *bulería* of Jerez de la Frontera, and the *cantes festeros* (festive styles) of Cádiz. These three towns were the homes of Spain's first flamenco schools. The different styles, or *palos*, have a common rhythmical cycle of 12, like the blues, but differ in key and harmonic progression.

For all its variations, the bottom line of flamenco is to attain *duende*, an intense, interactive communication with the audience, which participates with interjected cries of appreciation. As a nonwritten, oral tradition, flamenco song can be modified according to need and context. The *cante jondo* (deep song), reserved for virtuosos, is the oldest form, in which the singer's emotional

In dance, it is mesmerizing footwork that is primordial, hence the flounced, long-trained dresses cut high at the front. In the 1970s, the Sevillian dancer Manuela Carrasco carried this technique to its greatest heights. Anyone who has seen Carlos Saura's film *Carmen* (1983) must remember the fabulous footwork of Cristina Hoyos dancing with Antonio Gades. Their generation may be on the wane, but the torch is carried forward by young blood such as Joaquin Cortés and, younger still, Isaac de los Reyes. In music itself, flamenco still has traditional interpreters, most of whom are Gypsies. With women singers such as Aurora Vargas entering the fray, and the impetus of *nuevo flamenco* (new flamenco) groups such as Ketama, Pata Negra, and Radio Tarifa (fusing flamenco with Arab music), flamenco is gaining wider audiences and, again, evolv-

A flamenco group usually includes a guitarist, singer, and hand-clapper, as well as the dancers, both male and female.

**The exquisite
Alhambra palace
and gardens
exemplify the
apex of Muslim
architecture in
Spain.**

Granada

IT WAS IN THE 19TH CENTURY THAT THE IMAGE OF Granada as the quintessential Oriental town first floated into the Western imagination. This was in part thanks to the American writer Washington Irving, whose *Tales of the Alhambra* inspired a succession of writers and artists to try to capture the wonders of Granada's palace, the Alhambra. Today the Alhambra is the number one sight for visitors to Spain. You are never alone beside the fountains of its cool patios and verdant gardens, though you can always find a relatively secluded corner in which to muse on the past. The rest of Granada is also very rich in monuments and has a lively cultural program, partly because of its burgeoning population of 50,000 students. Behind the city loom the snowcapped peaks of the Sierra Nevada, creating an ethereal atmosphere.

Granada
🅰 261 E2
Visitor information
www.dipgra.es
✉ Plaza Mariana
   Pineda 10
☎ 958 22 66 88
🕐 Closed Sat. p.m. &
   Sun.

You can divide your sight-seeing neatly into three areas: first, the hilltop Alhambra; second, the steep, rambling lanes of the Albaicín opposite (packed with restaurants that give huge views); and third, the "new" town that sprawls and bustles below. The heart of modern Granada beats here, and is far from lacking in interest between specialist shops, graceful avenues, and a good sprinkling of historical musts. A possible fourth area is Sacromonte, the Gypsy cave dwellers' quarter that stretches north from the Albaicín. Flamenco clubs abound, but they are not authentic. Don't take valuables, or leave anything in your car—better still, leave the car itself in a downtown parking lot, using your feet or local minibuses to get you uphill.

Granada was ruled by Moors from 731, but it came into its own in 1031, with the collapse of the Córdoban caliphate. Out of centuries of obscurity emerged a kingdom of splendor, wealth, and poetry, ruled by the Almoravids, then by the Almohads, and, from 1238, the Nazrids. Arts and sciences flourished side by side, in an era of brilliance and religious tolerance that drew together thinkers from Europe, North Africa, and the Middle East. The magnificent buildings of the Alhambra arose, culminating in the magical Nazrid palace. During this time, however, the Christian Reconquest (see pp. 28–31) was pushing southward. Granada held out longer than any other Muslim city in Spain.

However, in January 1492, after a six-month siege of the city, the Catholic Monarchs Fernando and Isabel finally rode in victorious. The boy-king Boabdil fled with his mother into exile, famously shedding a last tear as he looked back at Granada from the mountain pass now called El Suspiro del Moro ("the moor's last sigh"—used by English novelist Salman Rushdie as the title of a book published in 1995). Nearly eight centuries of Muslim rule in Andalucía were over, although it was not until the expulsion of the Moriscos (baptized Moors) in 1570 that Granada wholly lost its true creators.

Granada continued to flourish in the Renaissance: Monuments from this time include the massive cathedral, monastery of San Jerónimo, and Hospital Real (Royal

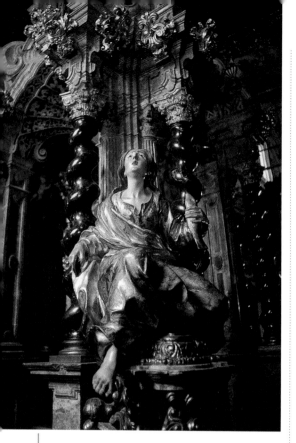

Lavish baroque carving decorates the tabernacle at La Cartuja monastery.

The heart of downtown is **Plaza de Isabel la Católica,** a little square with the cathedral and other sights clustered around it.

The grandiose **catedral** dominates the southwest corner of Granada. The main building is a Renaissance masterpiece, begun under Diego de Siloé (1495–1563) in 1528, with a facade by Alonso Cano, completed in 1667, the year of his death. The most impresssive part of it, however, is the earlier **Capilla Real** (Royal Chapel) abutting its southern flank. You enter it through the **Lonja** (Exchange). Commissioned by the Catholic Monarchs to house their tombs, the Capilla Real was built in just 15 years, and the result is a harmonious profusion of Isabelline Gothic, fittingly lavish for its royal encumbents. The superb tombs of Fernando and Isabel are by the Florentine sculptor Domenico Fancelli (1469–1519). Bartolomé Ordóñez (circa 1485–1520) was responsible for those of their daughter Juana ("the Mad") and her husband Felipe. The tombs lie beneath a soaring rib-vaulted ceiling, while their lead coffins lie in the crypt below. Look, too, at the gilded, wrought-iron screen in front, another masterpiece, this one by Maestro Bartolomé de Jaén. The **sacristy museum** dazzles you with chalices, processional crosses, reliquaries, the crown and scepter of Isabel herself, Fernando's sword, and banners carried during the conquest of Granada. Here, too, is Isabel's impressive collection of Flemish and Italian paintings, including works by Memling, van der Weyden, and Botticelli.

In contrast, the main cathedral seems rather a soulless affair, despite its airiness and height. In the **Capilla Mayor** look for Pedro de Mena's praying figures of Fernando and Isabel. You see

Hospital). In the 17th century the monastery of La Cartuja was built, and the city produced artists such as Alonso Cano (1601–1667) and Pedro de Mena (1628–1688). Later the city wove its spell over Eugène Delacroix, the French 19th-century Romantic painter, and on musicians such as Manuel de Falla and Andrés Segovia. Granada's greatest 20th-century writer was the poet Federico García Lorca (1899–1936), shot by Franco's troops in the Civil War. Today, this is a sophisticated, vibrant, city, redolent of the past but not buried in it. However, an expanding Moroccan community is bringing Islam back to the city.

DOWNTOWN GRANADA
The Gran Vía de Colón is the main artery through downtown Granada.

Alonso Cano's works throughout. The cathedral was built on the site of the demolished Great Mosque, the last remnant of which is **La Madraza** *(Closed Sat.–Sun., & Aug.)*, opposite the Capilla Real. This was a 14th-century Islamic college, rebuilt in baroque style and now part of Granada University, but it still has a superb prayer hall. You can drop in to admire its magnificent stuccowork. Another relic of this period, tucked away behind Calle de los Reyes Catolicos, is the **Corral del Carbón** *(Calle Mariana Pineda, tel 958 22 59 90, closed p.m. Sat. & Sun.)*, an unusually sober courtyard building that functioned as a storehouse and merchants' inn. Between this and the cathedral lies the old Arab souk, the **Alcaicería,** completely rebuilt following a fire and now full of overpriced souvenirs.

West of the cathedral, follow Calle San Jerónimo to the 16th-century **Monasterio de San Jerónimo** *(Calle Rector López Argüeta, tel 958 27 93 37)*. This jewel of Spanish Renaissance architecture has a wonderful two-tiered cloister, the work of Diego de Siloé, architect of the cathedral. In the church are beautiful 18th-century frescoes, and the tomb of the Catholic Monarchs' general, Gonzalo Fernández de Córdoba, known as El Gran Capitán. Nuns still live here: You can buy their cakes and jams at the entrance, and occasionally you hear them singing.

Now take bus No. 18 or Linea C from Gran Vía to the Carthusian monastery of **La Cartuja** *(Paseo de Cartuja, tel 958 16 19 32)*, by far the greatest baroque monument in Granada. The Carthusians lived austerely but ornamented lavishly, and this monastery takes the cake. Gold leaf, mirrors, stuccowork, marble, Venetian glass, mural paintings, marquetry, and a

profusion of sculpted cherubim, flowers, and vines set the tone—and that's just in the church **sanctuary.** This exercise in excess was created by Francisco Hurtado Izquierdo from 1704 to 1720 and is rivaled only by the **sacristy,** which he designed later. Here you find a sculpture of St. Bruno by José de Mora, Alonso Cano's "Inmaculada," and cupola frescoes by Tomás Ferrer. The church glitters with the gilt of Churrigueresque altarpieces, doors inlaid with mother-of-pearl, ivory, ebony, and tortoiseshell—the work of a monk, José Manuel Vázquez. Recover from this visual assault in the peaceful **cloisters.**

Poet Federico García Lorca is honored at his family's former summer house, the **Huerta de San Vicente** *(Calle Virgen Blanca,*

Designed by Hurtado Izquierdo, the sacristy of La Cartuja dates from 1727 to 1764.

Catedral
- ✉ Gran Vía de Colón
- ☎ 958 22 29 59
- 🕐 Closed Sun. a.m.
- 💲 $

Capilla Real
- ✉ Calle Officios 3
- ☎ 958 22 78 48
- 💲 $

Patio del Cuarto Dorado in the Nazrid Palace

Alhambra & Generalife

- ✉ Avenida de los Alixare
- ☎ 958 22 75 25 or 958 22 26 27
- 🕐 Open for night visits Fri. & Sat. (winter); Tues., Thurs., & Sat. (summer).
- 💲 $$. Book your visit to Nazrid Palace at 902 22 44 60 or at any branch of BBV bank in Spain.

Opposite: The Patio de los Leones, named for the 12 lions bedecking its fountain, embodies the archetypal image of Granada.

tel 958 25 84 66, closed Mon., www.huertagarcialorca.org). He did much of his writing here; at that time the house stood in an orchard, but it has been swallowed up by suburbs. You see original furnishings, drawings by friends such as Salvador Dalí, manuscripts, and photos. Reserve a place on the guided tour in advance, as numbers are limited.

ALHAMBRA

It is visible from all over the city, reigning in splendor from its hilltop, the simple crenellated towers and walls rising above a cloud of greenery that extends to the white structures of the Generalife beyond. You can walk up the steep incline of Cuesta de Gomérez, through shady pine trees, or ride in a tomato red minibus that drops you near the main entrance. If you are driving, plenty of signs point the way from the center of town. Another, little-used route for walkers is to approach from the Darro riverbank up Cuesta del Rey Chico, where a path brings you to the Generalife.

The Alhambra encompasses four sections: the military fortress of the Alcazaba (the oldest part); the exquisite Nazrid Palace (the ultimate flowering of Moorish architecture); the summer palace of the Generalife; and the Renaissance Palace of Carlos V. Between them lies a labyrinthine garden of paradise, or at least a good earthly semblance of heavenly bliss. Every sense is ignited by the subtle combination of light, color, sound, and smell created by trickling fountains, reflective ponds, high hedges, and an abundance of fragrant flowers— roses, plumbago, honeysuckle, jasmine, and bougainvillea.

The color of the walls, built from a durable mixture of red earth and stone, gave the Alhambra its name, derived from the Arabic word for "red." The walls once enclosed a self-contained town with four gateways, 23 towers, seven palaces, workers' houses, workshops, baths, a *madrasa* (Islamic school), and mosques. Many of these buildings have disappeared, but the surviving palaces continue to exert their magic, just as they did

Washington Irving

He was not the first or last person to be enamored of the Alhambra, but Washington Irving was the first writer to describe in so humane a fashion the tales and legends of this rambling fairy-tale palace, bringing to life its silent towers and chambers. It was in 1829 that he installed himself in the governor's apartments overlooking the orange trees and fountains of the garden of Daraxa, and over the next few weeks, penned his tribute to the palace's inhabitants, *Tales of the Alhambra*. You can buy it everywhere in Granada. ∎

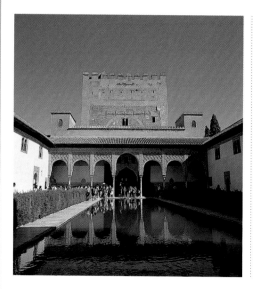

on Carlos V: He built his own imperial palace here but used it only for ceremonial functions, preferring to live with his family in the more congenial Moorish palaces.

The Alhambra's overwhelming popularity means that in peak season you have to dodge large guided parties. Ideally, make time for a second daytime visit, and also come back at night when subtle lighting brings to the fore elements that you might have missed by day. For the Nazrid Palace you have to book to visit within a given half-hour (try late in the afternoon when crowds have thinned), but you can soak up the sensual atmosphere of the rest of the Alhambra for as long as you want.

Clipped myrtle hedges surround a long goldfish pond in the Patio de los Arrayanes (Court of the Myrtles).

Patio de los Arrayanes

Mexuar (council chamber)

Palacio de Carlos V

Sala de los Abencerrejes

Alcazaba

This is a good place to start. You can climb to the roof of the Torre de la Vela for a fantastic panoramic view of the entire site, and of the rest of Granada, the Sierra Nevada, and the endless *vega* (plain) to the west. Dating from the ninth century, the Alcazaba was Granada's first major Moorish structure, though the front two towers were built four centuries later. An often deserted garden on the southern side makes a meditative oasis.

Palacios Nazaríes (Nazrid Palace)

Called an earthly paradise by the French poet Théophile Gautier, the palace was built for Yusuf I and

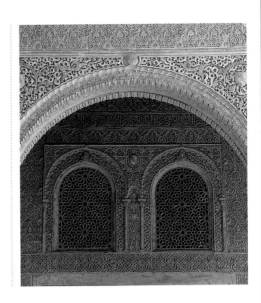

Painted and carved stucco frames an archway of the Nazrid Palace.

Salon de los Embajadores

Palacio del Partal

Salon de las Dos Hermanas

Sala de los Reyes

Patio de los Leones

Mohammed V in the 1300s, and its two patios, intricately carved stucco ceilings, friezes, capitals and archways, geometric mosaics, fountains, and infinite perspectives constitute the zenith of Moorish style in Spain.

From the beautifully tiled **Mexuar** (Council Chamber) you

enter the Patio del Cuarto Dorado, then the overwhelming **Salón de los Embajadores** (Hall of Ambassadors, inside the Comares Tower). Its complex domed marquetry ceiling is said to consist of more than 8,000 polygonal pieces of cedarwood, and the stuccowork of the walls is masterful. Look at the beautiful *muqarnas* (honeycomb stuccowork used in ceiling, archways, and domes), then admire the wonderful views from the windows. Outside, the **Patio de los Arrayanes** (Court of Myrtles) presents one of the finest perspectives in the Alhambra, accentuated by the myrtle hedges flanking the pool.

From here, a passage leads to the **Sala de los Mozárabes,** an anteroom that opens onto the much photographed **Patio de los Leones** (Court of Lions). This rhythmical, colonnaded courtyard is divided into four sections, in traditional Islamic style, accentuating the fountain and water channels, symbols of the four rivers of life. You have to imagine this patio planted with cypresses, palms, orange trees, pomegranates and flowers. Twelve stone lions hold the fountain basin, whose rim is carved with a poem extolling the beauty of the court, the garden, and the play of water. Written by Ibn Zamrak, Mohammed V's chief minister, it is one of many that are inscribed in the Alhambra's surfaces.

Around the patio are three halls, each one a jewel of delicate craftwork. The most breathtaking is the **Sala de las Dos Hermanas,** (to the left as you enter the patio) where the domed octagonal ceiling has finely worked muqarnas resembling stalactites, lit by natural light filtered through the tracery of windows just below.

Opposite, linked to the Sala de las Dos Hermanas by a water channel, is the **Sala de los Abencerrajes,** with its high domed ceiling and stalactite vaulting. The third hall, the **Sala de los Reyes,** lies behind the main cluster of arches. The ceiling paintings here may be the work of Christian painters commissioned by Mohammed V. North of the Sala de las Dos Hermanas, another hall leads to the **Mirador de Daraxa,** overlooking a lovely garden patio.

Outside the main palace, you come to the **Palacio del Partal,** which was probably the first part to be built. Its arched gallery leads to the Torre de las Damas (Ladies' Tower), reflected in the mirrorlike surface of a large pool. Beyond this, the **gardens** take you through their different levels to cross a bridge to the Generalife.

Left: **Running water refreshes the Generalife's luxuriant, shaded gardens. Standing on the Cerro del Sol (Hill of the Sun), the Generalife was the ancient palace of the Nazrid kings.**

Generalife

Built on a higher level than the Alhambra, the Generalife is a summer palace that celebrates the outdoors. Its central attraction is an oblong pool edged by fountain jets in the **Patio de la Acequia;** also here are terraced gardens, pergolas, bowers, and cypress trees, providing refreshing shade even at the height of summer. There is little to see in the royal apartments except stupendous views: Don't miss the **Mirador de la Sultana** view-point at the very top. In late June, some of the performances in Granada's music and dance festival are held in the Generalife gardens.

Palacio de Carlos V

Carlos V's palace was designed by Pedro Machuca, a disciple of Michelangelo. The vast circular courtyard represents the Universal Empire (the globe) and is unlike anything else in the Alhambra, although it is stunning in its own right. Inside are the **Museo de Bellas Artes** *(Tel 958 22 48 43, closed Sun. p.m., Mon., & Tues a.m.)* and the **Museo de la Alhambra** *(Tel 958 22 91 05 or 958 22 62 79, closed p.m., Sun.–Mon.).* The latter has beautiful Hispano-Muslim exhibits, including ceramics, carved screens, and fragments of sculpted stucco. Upstairs, the Bellas Artes has a good display of Granadino artists (Diego de Siloé, Alonso Cano, Pedro de Mena, Diego and José de Mora), but it is hard to do them justice after the very different artistry of the Moorish palaces and gardens. ■

The Renaissance palace of Carlos V is an intruder in the midst of an Arabian Nights setting.

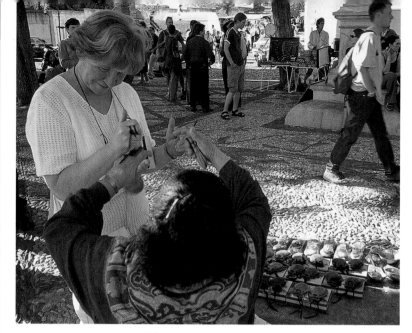

Gypsies practice their mercantile charm at the Mirador de San Nicolas in the Albaicín.

A stroll in the Albaicín

The Albaicín district flanks the hill opposite the Alhambra and was the site of the first Arab fortress. This walk leads you through its steep, picturesque lanes, with stupendous views at every turn.

Start from the **Plaza Nueva** and walk north past the pretty church of Santa Ana, following the Darro riverbed. On your left you soon come to **El Bañuelo ❶** *(Carrera del Darro 31, tel 958 22 23 39, closed p.m. & Sun.),* 11th-century Arab baths with colonnaded rooms, some with star-shaped ceiling openings. A little farther on stands the **Casa de Castril,** a Renaissance mansion housing the **Museo Arqueológico ❷** *(Carrera del Darro 41, tel 958 22 56 40, closed Sun. p.m., Mon., & Tues. a.m.),* with impressive Moorish exhibits in Room 7. Continue past the Convento de Santa Catalina with the walls and towers of the Alhambra looming high above to the right. You come to a large esplanade, **Paseo del Padre Manjón,** packed with bars and cafés. Turn left up Cuesta de la Victoria, left again into Calle San Juan de los Reyes, and then right up steps that plunge you into the Albaicín. Here, many *cármenes* (large walled villas) stand in lush, gardens. Climb to the top,

turn left then right up Calle Carrillo, and then take a sharp left into Carril de San Agustín.

Follow it to the top, passing the 17th-century Convento de las Tomasas, and circle around the church, **Colegiata del Salvador ❸** *(Plaza del Salvador, tel 958 27 86 44, closed Sun.),* to reach its entrance. El Salvador was built in 1501 on the foundations of the Albaicín's largest mosque, and has a magnificent Almohad patio of horseshoe arches. The small museum has beautiful religious paintings and sculptures, and the church itself a reconstructed Moorish ceiling. Outside, you could stop for a drink on Plaza del Aliatar, then continue by turning right into Calle Panaderos, which leads to shady Plaza Larga. Cross the square diagonally to admire the restored Arab house on the corner, now an ice-cream parlor, and the beginning of the Arab walls, which are being renovated.

Retrace your steps along Calle Panaderos, then go right on a dogleg turn to reach charming **Plaza Charca,** encircled by typical, geranium-laden houses. Walk up steps opposite, then down an alley to emerge at **Plaza San Nicolás** ❹ with its white-washed brick 16th-century church *(Open only for Mass).* In front is the quintessential view of the hilltop Alhambra with the peaks of the Sierra Nevada behind. This spot is a favorite with guitar-strumming students and castanet-clicking Gypsies. Behind San Nicolás is Granada's brand new **mosque.**

Walk down the steps beside the viewing terrace to Camino Nuevo de San Nicolás, turn right, and stop to see the **Carmen-Museo Max Moreau** ❺ *(Camino Nuevo de San Nicolás 12, tel 958 29 33 10, closed Sun.–Mon.).* This house belonged to the Belgian painter Max Moreau (1902–1992) and his wife Felice. His studio and their home are full of items from their extensive travels. After leaving, turn left down Calle Gumiel to Placeta del Nevot and keep walking down Cuesta San Gregorio to finally take a sharp left into Placeta de

Porras. The **Casa de Porras** ❻ *(Placeta de Porras, tel 958 22 44 25, closed Sun.)* is a magnificent example of Renaissance-Mudejar wooden architecture and now belongs to Granada University. Return to San Gregorio, turn left, and walk down **Calderería Nueva,** the most Arab part of the Albaicín, full of Moroccan pastry shops. At the bottom, turn left to return to Plaza Nueva. ■

🗺 See area map pp. 260–61
▶ Plaza Nueva
⟳ 2 miles (3 km)
⏱ 1.5 hours
▶ Plaza Nueva

NOT TO BE MISSED

- El Bañuelo
- Museo Arqueológico
- Colegiata del Salvador
- Carmen-Museo Max Moreau
- Casa de Porras

Troglodyte towns

Guadix

🅰 261 E2

Visitor information

✉ Avenida Mariana
Pineda s/n

☎ 958 66 26 65

🕒 Closed p.m. &
Sat.–Sun.

Baza

🅰 261 F2

Visitor information

✉ Calle Arco de la
Magdalena

☎ 958 70 06 91

🕒 Closed Sat.–Sun.

**Guadix's cave
district features
some 2,000 caves
carved out of soft
limestone hills. Far
from being holes
in the wall, they
are quite cozy.**

THE ARID LIMESTONE LANDSCAPE OF ALMERÍA AND
eastern Granada provinces was one of Europe's earliest inhabited
areas: People were here more than a million years ago. It is still a land
of cave dwellers—troglodytes—but today they have TV aerials, satellite dishes, and even burglar alarms sprouting from their pristine,
ever expanding houses.

The distinctive whitewashed
chimneys of cave dwellings stud the
landscape around Guadix, 34 miles
(54 km) northeast of Granada.
They extend north and east to the
Sierra de Baza, to Orce, and beyond
to Cuevas de Almanzora. **Guadix**
is the most accessible of these
towns, but be wary of inhabitants
who do not always take kindly to
ogling tourists. Keep an eye on your
wallet, too. Crowned by a dramatic
Moorish castle, Guadix has a generous sprinkling of 16th- and 17th-
century buildings, but is otherwise
pretty ramshackle. You'll find the
Ermita Nueva, or cave zone,
beyond the whitewashed church of

Santiago. On your way, stop at the
Museo de Alfarería *(Calle San
Miguel, tel 958 66 47 67, closed Sun.
p.m.),* a pottery museum in a renovated cave dwelling. Continue to
the **Cueva Museo** *(Plaza del
Padre Poveda, closed Sun. p.m.),* a
charming reconstruction of a traditional cave dwelling complete with
furniture, antiques, and farming
implements. Then wander around
this extensive troglodyte area to
admire the increasing sophistication of today's dwellings.

Purullena, 4 miles (6 km) west
of Guadix, has numerous cave
houses, their smooth white
chimneys punctuating the outskirts
of town. Pottery shops line the
main road selling typical
Granadino green-and-blue ware.

Baza lies 27 miles (44 km)
northeast of Guadix across a stark
landscape of hillocks and esparto
grass. The sculpture known as the
"Dama de Baza," now in Madrid's
archaeological museum (see p. 73),
was found here. Historical sights
include the crumbling **Alcazaba,**
tenth-century **Arab baths**
(Spain's oldest), and the lovely
16th-century church of **Santa
María de la Encarnación.** The
church was designed by Alonso de
Covarrubias and built under the
supervision of Diego de Siloé.

Baza's cave district is on the
eastern side of town. About 25
miles (40 km) northeast is **Galera,**
an Iberian necropolis and an entire
valley of cave dwellings at the back
of town. ■

Sierra Nevada

THIS SPECTACULAR MASSIF, INCORPORATING SPAIN'S newest national park (1999), is a challenge throughout the year, whether you are traveling on foot, skis, or by car. The tortuous road that runs from Granada into the sierra is Europe's highest and defies even the hardiest drivers.

Whatever the season, the Sierra Nevada is awesome, and for most of the year it is snowcapped. With Mulhacén peak rising to 11,420 feet (3,481 m) and neighboring Veleta to 11,128 feet (3,392 m), it is the highest massif in Western Europe after the Alps. It is also the continent's southernmost ski resort—barely 25 miles (40 km) from the balmy coast.

The mountains have glacier lakes such as Laguna Altera around the 10,000-foot (3,000 m) mark and stark tundra landscapes favored by agile mountain goats. Lower down are pine forests where badgers, beech marten, and wild mountain lions roam. Among more than 2,000 botanical species are the Sierra Nevada violet, gentian, aconite, royal camomile, and a rampant honeysuckle. Butterflies include the rare Nevada blue and Glandon blue. Hoopoes whoop and show their flashy plumage, and numerous birds of prey soar overhead. The main visitor center for the national park is at Pampaneira in Las Alpujarras (see pp. 310–12).

Skiers can whiz down the slopes of the ski resort of **Solynieve** from November right into May. However, the resort is a truly uninspiring 1970s design. Buses from Granada stop here, and there is a parking lot at the Albergue Universitario. The road beyond, which crosses the national park to the Alpujarras, is only accessible on foot or by bicycle. You can hike to the summit of **Veleta** in about three hours, allowing two hours for the descent, for a predictably stupendous panorama south to the Mediterranean and north across the sierra. Experienced mountaineers take three to four days to cross the Sierra Nevada, starting in Jerez del Marquesado on the north flank and ending in Lanjarón, in the Alpujarras.

The light in the Sierra Nevada is incredibly clear, and an observatory, **Observatorio Astronómico** (*Central de Reservas Sierra Nevada, Plaza de Andalucía, Monachil, tel 958 24 91 11, www.cetursa.es*), lies on the slopes at 9,348 feet (2,850 m). In summer, groups of up to five people can observe the night sky. ∎

Sierra Nevada
🅜 261 E2
Visitor information
✉ Plaza Mariana Pineda 10, Granada
☎ 958 22 66 88

Centro de Visitantes El Dornajo
✉ Carretera de Sierra Nevada, Km 23,
☎ 958 34 06 25

Parque Natural de la Sierra Nevada
Visitor information
🅜 310–311
✉ Plaza de la Libertad, Pampaneira
☎ 958 76 31 27
🕐 Closed Sun. & Mon. p.m. in winter

Après-ski at the ski resort of La Veleta

A drive in Las Alpujarras

This drive makes a circular route through the Alpujarras, the southern foothills of the Sierra Nevada. It passes few specific sights, but the scenery is beautiful, and you may want to allow time for a hike to enjoy the clear air and spectacular views and to get a close look at the wildflowers.

Start your drive in **Lanjarón ❶**, a popular spa town and source of a renowned mineral water. It was a Roman town, but is more famous for the Moorish population's heroic stand against the troops of Fernando and Isabel of Aragón in March 1500. The Moorish castle, downhill from the main road, has been left to slowly crumble, but the scenic view over the valley is special.

Drive out on the C332 toward Órgiva, and you start to enter the dramatic mountain scenery of the Alpujarras. In the market town of **Órgiva ❷** stop at the main junction to look at the twin-towered baroque church and rather dilapidated Mudejar mansion across the road. The castle of the counts of Sástago stands here, but it has been left to deteriorate.

On Thursday Órgiva's **weekly market** draws northern European expatriates who live in the hills. The large alternative community has spawned a few health-food shops and vegetarian restaurants to join pack mules as part of the townscape. Return to the entrance to Órgiva and turn right onto the GR421 in the direction of Trevélez (21 miles/34 km).

Switchbacks immediately take you uphill into an extraordinary landscape of chasms and glowering mountains with tiny white villages clinging to the slopes. A surprising number of people live here. On this northern side of the valley the road passes numerous isolated houses and *fincas* (farms), many of which are now foreign owned, and the hamlets of Soportújar and Carataunas. As the road

Almond blossoms festoon the Alpujarras.

swings north, you enter the **Barranco del Poqueira ③,** a deep canyon created by the Poqueira River.

At **Pampaneira ④,** park the car and walk into the main square behind the church. This pretty, well-conserved village is a major crafts center, and its shops are draped with hand-woven rugs. Ceramics and jewelry are the other chief attractions. The **Parque Nacional de la Sierra Nevada** (see p. 309) has its main visitor center in the village, and you can pick up detailed trekking maps here—this is one of the best hiking areas. Wander around the pretty streets and enjoy a drink on the little square with its old fountain before continuing. The road now climbs to dizzying heights as you come to a turnoff to the left for **Bubión ⑤** (2 miles/3.2 km) and **Capileira** (3 miles/4.8 km). These spectacularly sited villages cater to visitors with abundant craftshops and other facilities. The Sierra Nevada's highest peaks rise behind them, and Capileira is a well-trodden meeting point for mountaineers descending from the heights.

Filling water bottles at the local spring

Return to the GR421 and turn left toward Trevélez. Three miles (4.8 km) farther, take a turnoff down to the right to visit the traditional villages of **Mecina Fondales ⑥, Ferreirola,** and **Busquistar.** Lying 1 to 2 miles (2–3 km) away from the main road, they still have unspoiled Alpujarras architecture: thick stone walls, often whitewashed, flat roofs, and a few covered bridges between the upper stories. Return to the main road to drive through Pitres and Pórtugos, enjoying the views of stark mountains studded with white hamlets, occasional meadows, oaks, chestnuts, and poplars.

The road then turns north into another deep gorge with a reservoir far below. This is wilder country, favored by goats and free-

See area map pp. 260–61
► Lanjarón
⮂ 70 miles (110 km)
⏱ 3 hours (excluding stops)
► Órgiva or Motril

NOT TO BE MISSED
- Lanjarón
- Órgiva
- Pampaneira
- Bubión

A typical Alpujarras village with terraced farmland

roaming pigs—which turn up on your plate at **Trevélez** ❼, the local capital of *jamón serrano* (cured ham). In the Renaissance the town was famous for silk made by Moriscos expelled from Granada. Here you are among mountain pine trees, at a height of 4,820 feet (1,470 m), with the village spilling down the cleft of the mountain to the Trevélez River. The lower part of the village is not particularly picturesque, but it has plenty of watering holes. Walk uphill to see traditional buildings. Trails from here lead up into the mountains or across to Juviles.

The road that you arrived on now backtracks along the opposite side of the gorge, then curves back into the main valley skirting the peak of **Peñabón** (8,310 feet/2,533 m). Ignore turnoffs and follow signs to Bérchules and Ugijar until you come to the attractive village of **Juviles** ❽, also a major silk producer in Renaissance times. This peaceful place is worth another stop before you make the last push to the neighboring villages of Bérchules and Alcútar, through increasingly barren moor dotted with olive trees. As you reach Alcútar you see the road snaking ahead of you across the Guadalfeo River and up again to give more vertiginous views.

Follow signs to Cádiar, then on to Órgiva

(24 miles/39 km), as you turn right down into the valley. **Cádiar** ❾ has become one of the Alpujarras' largest towns because of its strategic setting. Life revolves around the main square dominated by a 16th-century church. The slopes of the Sierra de Contraviesa rising to the south are blanketed in terraced almond trees, with clouds of pink and white blossom in February. Drive out of Cádiar, continue following signs for Órgiva, and after 2 miles (3.2 km), at a small sign for Alquería de Morayma, turn right up a dirt road, which brings you to a magical spot overlooking the valley—perfect for a snack or lunch.

Continue on the A348, which skirts the Sierra de Contraviesa. This is a less tortuous road, with continuous views across the valley of the region you have just driven through. Despite its beauty, this north-facing flank is not much inhabited, and for the next 35 miles you see very few houses. Torvizcón, the only village, is an attractive place clustered around a church tower. From then on, as Órgiva comes into view, the road straightens out considerably and soon brings you down to the bridge with a turnoff to Órgiva (1.5 miles/2.4 km). Alternatively drive straight on through the tunnel towards Motril (18 miles/29 km) on the Costa del Sol. ■

Almería

SEEN FROM THE EYRIE OF THE IMMENSE ALCAZABA, Almería resembles North Africa, with a background of yellow ocher desert and a hodgepodge of traditional flat-roofed houses and concrete high-rise apartment blocks. From the harbor car ferries leave for Melilla, one of Spain's remaining possessions in Moroccan territory.

Soak up the atmosphere in the seafront **Parque Nicolás Salmerón,** with its palm trees, fountains, and gardens. Moroccans clad in *djellabas* (loose robes) come here to sip mint tea. Almería's large Moroccan immigrant population is mainly employed in the fruit and vegetable fields around the city. In February 2000 racial tension produced vicious attacks on the immigrants at El Ejido, 19 miles (30 km) to the west, but government initiatives have since calmed the situation. You find a more European face to the city in **Paseo de Almería,** the main shopping and social hub. Take a peek at No. 35, the ornate **Círculo Mercantil,** or Traders' Guild, *(Tel 950 23 11 22).* In the streets to the west is the fortified **catedral**

(Plaza de la Catedral, tel 950 23 50 10, closed except for Mass), built in the 17th century.

Don't miss the **Alcazaba** (Arab citadel), its crenellated walls and towers dominating the town. Built in 955 to crown Muslim Spain's most prosperous port, it fell to the forces of the Catholic Monarchs in 1490. Today, little remains within its walls, but wander through three enclosures, partly landscaped with aromatic plants and water channels. Climb the **Torre de Pólvora** at the far end, and admire the **Muralla de la Hoya,** a fortified wall that dips into the valley and rises to St. Christopher's Hill opposite. Plans are afoot to open up the underground dungeons and tunnels that riddle the soft limestone. ∎

Dominating the town from its hilltop perch, the Alcazaba, or fortress, is a reminder of Almería's Moorish past.

Almería
🅐 261 F2
Visitor information
www.almeria-turismo.org
✉ Parque Nicolás Salmarón, corner of Calle Martínez Campos
☎ 950 27 43 55
🕐 Closed Sat. & Sun. p.m.

Alcazaba
✉ Plaza Joaquín Santiesteban
☎ 950 22 50 58
💲 $. Free for E.U. nationals

Desert places

THE PROVINCE OF ALMERÍA HAS THE LOWEST RAINFALL IN Spain, barely 16 inches (400 mm) annually. Dryness combines with 3,000 hours of sunshine to create the steppelike semidesert of the province. This torrid climate is exploited at Spain's largest solar-energy installation, which lies between Tabernas and Sorbas.

Sorbas
🅰 261 F2
Visitor information
✉ Calle Terraplén 9
☎ 950 36 44 76

Mini-Hollywood
🅰 261 F2
✉ Carretera Nacional 340, Km 138, Desierto de Tabernas
☎ 950 36 52 36
🕐 Shows at noon & 5 p.m.
💲 $$

You find spectacular scenery in the **Desierto de Tabernas,** 19 miles (30 km) northeast of Almería, where an undulating lunar landscape is alleviated only by the odd palm tree and cactus. Dramatic hills and canyons, crystalline light, and low production costs have lured many a filmmaker to the area. David Lean made *Lawrence of Arabia* here, and Sergio Leone filmed a string of spaghetti Westerns, including A *Fistful of Dollars* and *The Good, The Bad, and The Ugly.* You can visit old film sets of this Spanish Wild West at **Mini-Hollywood.** Then continue to the village of **Tabernas,** dominated by the ruins of a Moorish castle.

From Tabernas it is 15 miles (25 km) east to **Sorbas,** a dramatically sited village hanging over a dry gorge. This characteristic little village has long been renowned for its pottery, particularly simple glazed terra-cotta ovenware. Follow signs for *Alfarería* (Pottery) to see potters at work and buy their wares. Around it is the **Parque Natural de Karst en Yesos,** an eerily white landscape that is the world's largest gypsum karst. Huge subterranean caves with stalactites and stalagmites can be visited on tours *(Tel 950 36 44 81, www.cuevasdesorbas.com),* which you must reserve in advance. Tours last about two hours and lighted helmets are provided. Alternatively you can walk or drive eastward to **Los Molinos del Río Aguas** for panoramic views. ∎

A drive around Cabo de Gata

This route takes you from a village renowned for crafts, through arid and rugged landscapes typical of eastern Andalucía. It includes stops at pretty fishing villages and a succession of wonderful sea and mountain views. Most of this area lies in the Parque Natural de Cabo de Gata-Níjar.

Allow an hour or so to look at crafts in **Níjar** ① (*Visitor information, Calle Correos, tel 950 38 02 99, closed p.m. & weekdays in winter*), a typical Almerian village of whitewashed houses huddled against the slopes of the Sierra de Alhamilla. Leave the car at the top of the village, dominated by a 15th-century church with a fine Mudejar ceiling. Then you can walk to the **Plaza del Mercado,** or descend to the main street lined with shops selling *jarapas* (woven cotton rugs and blankets), ceramics, and baskets made of coarse esparto grass. Most of the items are made in Níjar.

- See area map 261 F2
- ► Níjar
- ⟷ 70 miles (110 km)
- ⏱ 2.5 hours (without stops)
- ► Mojácar

NOT TO BE MISSED
- Níjar
- Isleta del Moro
- Rodalquilar gold mine

Back in the car, leave Níjar on the main street, turning right at the bottom, then left following signs to Almería and San Isidro. Don't turn onto the highway but drive straight on through an underpass to emerge into an unappealing plain of *plásticos* (plastic greenhouses) under which tomatoes, asparagus, avocadoes, and tropical fruits are cultivated. This lasts for 8 miles (12 km) before the scenic landscapes of the **Parque Natural de Cabo de Gata-Níjar** (*Visitor information tel 950 16 04 35*) begin. Follow signs to San José as the road winds over low sierra through

The Morrón de los Genoveses etches the coastline in Parque Natural de Cabo de Gata-Níjar.

sparse vegetation, mainly yuccas, aloes, prickly pears, and olive trees. As you drive through **Boca de los Frailes,** look for the igloo-shaped stone oven (formerly used for baking bread) on your left. At **Pozo de los Frailes,** stop to look at the mill and old *noria* (water wheel), one of 95 in the park, on your right. When you finally enter San José, turn right at a fork in the road following signs to Playa de los Genoveses.

Drive uphill and circle around the headland. The road soon becomes an easily negotiated dirt road, passing an old windmill on the left before descending to a sea of prickly pear cactuses and other more unusual flora. Turn off to enjoy **Playa de los Genoveses ❷** or continue 2.5 miles (4 km) to **Playa de Monsul,** signaled by an enormous sand dune on the left. Both beaches are of fine yellow sand, and Monsul has a great view south to the Cabo de Gata lighthouse (*faro*) at Spain's extreme southeast-

ern point. These beaches have been locations for numerous films, including *Indiana Jones and the Last Crusade* (1989) and *The Last Adventures of Baron Münchhausen* (1989). They become packed in high summer.

Retrace your tracks to the largest tourist resort in the area, **San José,** where you can stop for a drink on the beach. Better still, continue to more authentic villages where local farmers and fishermen live in traditional cousin subsequently kills the ex-lover. Turn off into **Rodalquilar** ❹ village and drive up to the back, where you can look at the ruined remains of an old gold mine and maybe find a nugget, then return to the main road. You pass a turnoff to El Playazo, a secluded little beach between volcanic gullies, before reaching a junction. Turn right to the fishing village of **Las Negras** ❺ and drive straight down to the beach where you can stop for a drink and enjoy the lovely sea view. A walk along a path to the left brings you to **Cala de San Pedro,** a cove containing the only freshwater spring in the entire nature reserve.

Return up the main road and drive straight on to Fernán Pérez, passing herds of goats as you rise into the sierra. In the village itself, watch for a sign on the right to Agua Amarga. This takes you onto a severely rutted dirt road that soon becomes easier. You drive right through farmland, past almond trees, goats, prickly pears, and derelict houses before entering an area of powdered lime mounds, quarried from the surrounding hills. As you emerge, the sea reappears in the distance beyond the stark, rocky hills. Ignore any side roads and keep going until you reach a junction with a paved road. Turn right and drive down past scattered white houses to eventually reach the fishing village of **Agua Amarga** ❻ nestling in its bay, a pleasant stop, with beach restaurants and a few craftshops.

Leave Agua Amarga by returning to the main road and turning right up into the hills. As you descend, you are confronted by huge cementworks that introduce the little resort of **Carboneras** with its long palm-lined beach and marina. Follow signs for Mojácar (16 miles/26 km) that take you around the village and up into the hills. As you round the headland, the road skirts the beautiful **Playa la Galera** ❼, backed by dramatic clefts of high sierra. Spectacular switchbacks lead to a lookout point, where you can take in the stupendous coastal views north and south. Descending through rugged mountains, the road traverses the pretty village of **Sopalmo,** and soon passes the fort of Macenas. One more headland brings you to the long, developed sweep of **Mojácar Playa,** and another 5 miles (8 km) leads to the turnoff up to the hill village of Mojácar (see p. 321). ∎

houses. Follow the same main road out for 2.5 miles (4 km) as far as Pozo de los Frailes, where you turn right at a sign for Rodalquilar and Isleta del Moro (5 miles/7 km) into yucca- and palm-studded hills. After passing the 18th-century coastal fort of **Los Escullos** (built to fend off pirates) and capriciously eroded cliffs nearby, watch for a turnoff to your right down to the promontory and islet of **Isleta del Moro** ❸. This tiny fishing village makes a relaxing spot for lunch.

From here continue north, stopping at the **Mirador de la Amatista** for sweeping views, before arriving in the lovely valley of Rodalquilar. Lost in the hills to the west is the farmhouse of Cortijo de los Frailes, scene of the crime of passion that inspired Federico García Lorca's *Blood Wedding,* the story of a bride-to-be kidnapped by her ex-lover on the eve of her wedding. The groom's outraged

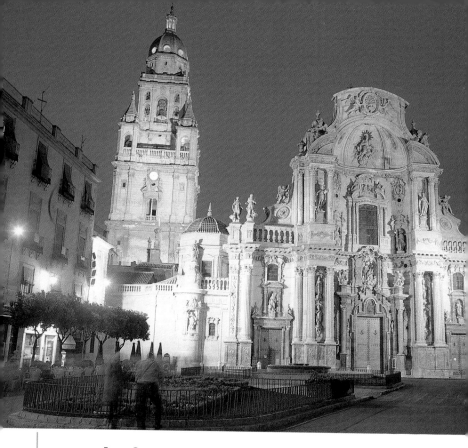

In & around Murcia

IT IS EASY TO OVERLOOK THE SMALL AUTONOMOUS community of Murcia, sandwiched between vast Andalucía and the coastal region of Valencia, but it does have points of interest. To the north lies the prolific wine-growing region of Jumilla. In the arid south is the attractive old market town of Lorca. If you are lucky enough to be there during Semana Santa (Holy Week), you can see one of Spain's finest and most traditional commemorations. Give the rather flat, overdeveloped coastline a miss: It is not comparable to beaches farther north or south.

Murcia has long flourished on oranges, mining, and industry. Its inhabitants have a proud, independent spirit that dates from its ninth-century status in the kingdom of al-Andalus: The name derives from the Arabic "Murshiya." Other Spaniards think Murcianos are inward-looking. During the Civil War Murcia backed General Franco's Nationalist forces, which did little for neighborly relations with anarchist Almería or republican Valencia. The city of Murcia, the prosperous modern capital, still has a distinctive feel. It shows little

Murcia's striking cathedral is an eclectic mix of styles, ranging from its Churrigueresque facade to its Gothic Los Vélez chapel.

Murcia
🔼 261 G3
Visitor information
www.ayto-murcia
.es/turismo
✉ Palacio Almudí,
Plano de San
Francisco s/n
☎ 968 35 87 20
🕐 Closed Sun. p.m.

concern for the needs of visitors, but stop there anyway for a long lunch, as it is a renowned gastronomical center.

At the heart of the pedestrianized **old quarter** spreading north from the Segura River stands the **Catedral de Santa María** *(Plaza de la Cruz, tel 968 21 63 44, closed Sun. p.m.)*, notable for the lavish plateresque **Capilla de los Vélez** and exhibits of Gothic paintings, woodcarvings, and church silver in the museum. Follow Calle de Trapería north of here to the idiosyncratic **Casino,** now partly a restaurant. It is a 19th-century remake of Moorish style. To the west lies Murcia's main commercial street, **Gran Vía Escultor Salzillo,** named for the Murcian sculptor Francisco Salzillo (1707–1783). The **Museo Salzillo** *(Plaza San Agustín 1, tel 968 29 18 93, closed Sun. p.m. & Mon.)* displays his carved wooden figures for the Semana Santa *pasos* (Holy Week floats), carried on the shoulders of penitents during Murcia's spectacular though somber processions.

Thirty-four miles (55 km) southeast of Murcia, the port of **Cartagena** was named for the Carthaginians from North Africa who captured it in 223 B.C. Their fortifications still look down on Spain's largest naval base. The diminutive submarine displayed in the old town center is an early prototype designed by Isaac Peral in 1888. The **Museo Nacional de Arqueología Marítima** *(Tel 968 50 84 15, closed Sun p.m. & Mon.)* has Punic (Carthaginian), Phoenician, and Roman artifacts collected from the seabed, with models of boats. Cartagena is between Murcia's main beach resorts of Mazarrón and La Manga and has become a popular summer venue for concerts of contemporary music, well worth checking out.

Right: Mudejar interior of Murcia's unusual casino

Lorca
⚑ 261 G3
Visitor information
www.lorca.net
✉ Calle Lope Gisbert 12
☎ 968 46 61 57
🕐 Closed Sun. p.m.

Alhama de Murcia
⚑ 261 G3
✉ Plaza de la Constitución 10
☎ 968 63 35 12
🕐 Closed p.m.

LORCA

The coastal highway misses Lorca, by tunneling through the chalky hill crowned by the ruins of a Moorish castle. Follow the turnoff signs to Lorca to see some fine baroque mansions. Head uphill from the main street to Plaza de

España, dominated by the **Colegiata de San Patricio** *(Plaza de España, tel 968 46 99 66, closed Sat. & Sun. p.m.)*, built of pink stone between 1534 and 1780. The west facade teems with cherubim. Opposite, look at the former Casa del Corregidor with its corner carvings (1750) by Juan de Uzeta.

Downhill, next to visitor information, don't miss the wonderful **Casa de los Guevara** *(Calle Lope Gisbert)*, Lorca's most impressive example of domestic baroque architecture with a wonderful entrance and salomonic (twisted and entwined) columns. Inside, richly carved marble columns create the arcades of the patio, around which a number of reconstructed rooms include a well-stocked, woodpaneled 19th-century

Murcianos enjoy good hiking in the hills of the Sierra de Espuña.

Sierra de Espuña
🅐 261 G3
Visitor information
✉ Casa Forestal, Huerta Espuña
☎ 968 43 14 30

silk and gold thread. Its rival, the White Brotherhood, has a similar display in the church of **Santo Domingo** *(Calle Santo Domingo, tel 689 78 25 04, closed Sat. p.m. & Sun.–Mon.).*

SIERRA DE ESPUÑA

Rising abruptly from Murcia's plain, this sierra is best reached from **Alhama de Murcia,** an 11th-century Moorish town with hilltop castle ruins and remains of Arab baths beside the church of San Lorenzo. From here the road twists through the sierra to end at Aledo and Totana, on the N340. The mountain range is named after its highest peak, Espuña (5,193 feet/1,583 m), and represents a miracle of repopulation and refor-

pharmacy, and an 18th-century ballroom with Venetian furniture. Close by, the **Centro Regional para la Artesanía** *(Closed Sat.– Sun.)* is housed in a starkly modern building by the Murcian architect Juan Antonio Molina. Traditional local materials (clay, wood, glass, ceramics, bamboo) are used for a wide variety of handicrafts, all of which are for sale.

If you can't be here for Lorca's sensational Semana Santa processions, you can get an idea of them at the **Museo de Bordados del Paso Azul** *(Casa de las Cariátides, Calle Nogalte, tel 968 47 20 77, closed Sat p.m. & Sun.).* It is situated beside the church of San Francisco, which is itself worth a look for its dazzling baroque interior, full of gilded altarpieces. This restored late 19th-century house is the base of the Blue Brotherhood, one of the two organizations that vie with each other in the splendor of their processions. Upstairs is an embroidery workshop; also here are photos showing the evolution of the procession and a selection of the most finely worked costumes in

estation in what had become an arid desert by the 18th century, due to over-logging of the native oak forest. Today, a century after extensive replanting, the cool flanks of the hills harbor a wide variety of pine trees, and the 61,780-acre (25,000 ha) hunting area has become the lungs of Murcia. A winding road takes you up past the Fuente del Hilo to the slopes of Espuña, from where hiking trails lead to the Sierra's wonderful **pozos de la nieve** (snow wells). An example of real peasant ingenuity, these 16th-century domed brick structures were built to store snow during the winter months; this was subsequently hammered into crushed ice, and then transported on horseback at night, to keep it cool, to villages below. Snow wells became obsolete in the 1920s, and only two of the original 26 wells remain in good condition. Just outside Aledo, look for the hermitage of **Santa Eulalia,** a tiny Mudejar chapel dedicated to Totana's patron saint and entirely covered in 17th-century frescoes by Juan de Ibáñez, a local artist. ■

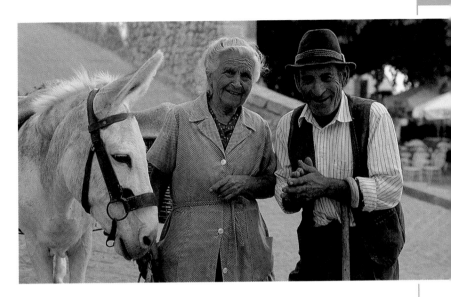

Donkeys are still used for transport in Andalucía's more remote villages.

More places to visit in Andalucía & Murcia

MOJÁCAR

Once one of Andalucía's prettiest coastal resorts, Mojácar has succumbed to developers and lost much of its charm. Nothing, however, can detract from its spectacular site, high in the shadow of the Sierra Cabrera overlooking the Mediterranean. One mile (1.6 km) separates the pueblo from the *playa* (beach), the latter an unbroken white strip of low-rise development. In the village itself, cubelike white houses pile up the slopes to a main square with numerous craft shops and, just uphill, the sturdy, much restored church of Santa María. You can wander up and down cobbled streets, pass through the bougainvillea-shrouded Moorish arch, and from the mirador at the very top admire the view of Mojácar's curious, pyramidal hillocks in the plain below. Sixteen miles (25 km) south is the Parque Naturel de Cabo de Gata (see pp. 315–317).

🅰 261 G2 **Visitor information** ✉ Calle Glorieta 1, Edificio Servicios Multiples, Mojácar Pueblo ☎ 950 61 50 25

OSUNA

Osuna is one of Andalucía's many surprises, lost in agricultural plains north of the Serranía de Ronda. When you penetrate the old center, you enter a Renaissance and baroque world of elegant mansions, convents, and churches that seem utterly incongruous in Osuna's rural location. The town's aristocratic character stems from it having been made a ducal seat in 1562—the Dukes of Osuna were subsequently among Spain's most powerful nobility. High above the town and overlooking it are the old **university** and the interesting 16th-century **Colegiata,** which you can visit on a guided tour. It is a treasure trove of plateresque decoration and fine art works, including the "Expiración de Cristo" by José de Ribera (1591–1652) and a superb crucifixion by Juan de Mesa (1583–1627). Best of all is the lavish underground pantheon housing the tombs of the illustrious Dukes of Osuna.

🅰 260 C2 **Visitor information** ✉ Plaza Mayor ☎ 95 582 14 00 🕐 Closed p.m. & Sun.

SIERRA DE CAZORLA

The craggy mountains of the Sierra de Cazorla are the source of three major rivers: the Guadalquivir, the Segura, and the Borosa, their waters gushing through vast forests of pine, holm-oak, and ash to create lakes and reservoirs. The very beautiful biosphere reserve **Parque Natural de las Sierras de Segura y Cazorla** lies in the northwest of the province of Jaén near the border with Murcia. It was created in 1986 to protect the countryside and wildlife of the region. You can use several places as a base to visit the park. One of the nicest is the town of **Cazorla,** a picture-postcard white village nestling in the shadow of a Moorish castle on the western side. From there you can take a stunning but dizzying road up to the **Puerto de las Palomas,** then drive north 25 miles (40 km) to Tranco, where you have a choice of onward routes. In between are hiking trails: Cazorla has 2,300 species of plants, and you might get a glimpse of wild deer, foxes, or stone marten. Overhead, look for birds of prey, including the royal eagle.

🅰 261 F3 **Visitor information** ✉ Paseo de Santo Cristo 17, Cazorla ☎ 953 72 00 29

Olive groves blanket much of eastern Andalucía's interior.

TARIFA

The southernmost point of peninsular Spain is Tarifa, a town with a distinctive taste of North Africa, just 9 miles (14 km) away. In 711 Tarifa became the first Arab settlement in Spain, and the old walled town, Castillo de Guzmán el Bueno, and Puerta de Jerez all stand as testament to long Moorish rule. Its recent prosperity comes from its optimum, year-round conditions for windsurfing. Tarifa is a venue for the World Windsurfing Championships, and the windsurfers who flock here give it a lively, cosmopolitan atmosphere. Divers, too, are discovering Tarifa's transparent waters. Numerous beaches line the coast, and the fertile pastures inland are grazed by fighting bulls and horses.

🅰 260 C1 **Visitor information** ✉ Paseo de la Alameda ☎ 956 68 09 93

VEJER DE LA FRONTERA

It is a precipitous drive up to the medieval village of Vejer, 10 miles (16 km) inland from the Costa de la Luz (see p. 278), but every invader from the Phoenicians to the Moors coveted its strategic hilltop site. Steep cobbled streets and immaculate whitewashed houses surround the old castle (now a hostel) and the attractive church of **San Salvador,** which combines Romanesque, Gothic, and Mudéjar styles. A well-preserved Jewish quarter is on **Calle Cobijadas,** by the walls. Relax on delightful Plaza de España, and admire the ornate fountain faced in 19th-century Sevillian ceramic.

🅰 260 C1 **Visitor information** ✉ Calle Marqués de Tamarón ☎ 956 45 01 91

VÉLEZ BLANCO

The picturesque village of Vélez Blanco lies in the rocky, semiforested Sierra de Maria, wonderful hiking territory west of Lorca (see p. 319). The towering castle was built for the local marquis in 1515, but to see its main patio (complete with Carrara marble columns) you must visit New York's Metropolitan Museum of Art. It emigrated in 1903 courtesy of George Blumenthal, an American millionaire who bailed out the bankrupt marquis by buying the whole thing through a French antiques dealer. Other sights are the fine **Convento de San Luis,** on the opposite side of the village, and the nearby **Cueva de los Letreros.** This prehistoric cave contains barely visible paintings, including one known as the *indalo*—a stick figure holding a rainbow, adopted as the region's symbol.

🅰 261 F3 **Visitor information** ✉ Almacén del Trigo, Avenida del Marqués de los Vélez ☎ 950 41 25 60 ∎

Artists have long favored the gentle Mediterranean climate and landscapes of the Balearics. Today high summer sees floods of tourists but go off-season to discover a world of prehistoric structures and stunning coves.

Balearic Islands

Another charter flight arrives.

Yachts and local fishing boats share the marina of Ciutadella in Menorca.

Balearic Islands

TAKE A FERRY FROM BARCELONA OR VALENCIA, A DOMESTIC FLIGHT FROM Madrid, Barcelona, Valencia, or Alicante, or a charter flight from almost any European capital, and you reach this jewel-like cluster of islands scattered over the Mediterranean azure. Mallorca, in particular, has been pulling in the package crowds since the 1960s, and Ibiza, formerly an artists' hideaway, is now the summer nightlife capital of Europe. Mellow Menorca, after a long, sleepy existence on the fringe, is being discovered by more discerning travelers, while tiny, rocky Formentera welcomes visitors who return regularly.

Although widely perceived as a simple sun-and-sea destination, the Balearics have great beauty, and (especially Mallorca) a rich history set against an idyllic, rural interior. The islands' background is linked with Catalunya's, and its language is a close cousin of Catalan, although Castilian Spanish is also spoken. Carthaginians, Romans, Vandals, Moors, French, and British were all attracted to these indented shores strategically located on Mediterranean trade routes, and they left contrasting historical imprints on the various islands. Mallorca is the most developed, but it is also the largest island and the one with the most varied landscapes and history. In recent years German investment has soared, and the result is a string of residential villas dotting the beautiful coves of the east coast and countless German banks and estate agents. The island still retains

extraordinary beauty and unique points of historical interest, not least megalithic structures, also a feature of other islands. Crafts have abounded on all the islands since the 1950s, when people came to the Balearics for alternative lifestyles. Eivissa-Ibiza became the hippie capital of Europe in the 1960s and '70s, and hippie-style crafts such as pottery and basket-making continue to flourish today, despite the islands' popularity and rising prices. One of the main traditional industries in the Balearics is leatherware, from shoes to bags and belts, and it is a good place to stock up.

Artists have left major legacies, especially on Mallorca, which has the foundations of Joan and Pilar Miró, Miguel Barceló (Spain's leading contemporary artist, who was born in Felanitx), and Joan March. Military history is explored at length in Menorca, and Eivissa has an excellent archaeological museum. But most visitors come for the great outdoors. The mild Mediterranean climate makes for wonderful hiking and cycling year-round. Swimming and other water sports are popular from May to October. Sailing and scuba-diving are widely available (the latter above all in Ibiza). Golf is another major attraction. The peak season for vacationers is July and August, when beaches are packed with roasting bodies and waters off the big resorts of Mallorca become polluted. Try to come outside this time, when the islands are less crowded and wildlife is more visible. Finally, food: It tends to be good, as the long cosmopolitan history of these islands has injected unusual influences that are combined with traditional Catalan refinement. ■

La Seu's Gothic spires, and its clearly visible rose window, command Palma's harbor.

Mallorca (Majorca)

MULTI-FACETED MALLORCA IS NO SECRET TO MILLIONS OF vacationers. Here you can switch your focus from rugged mountains to coves of crystalline water, white-sand beaches, underground caves, or lively Palma. Mallorca's popularity in summer extends even to the Spanish royal family, so an off-season visit is the best option.

Palma de Mallorca

325 C3

Visitor information

Carrer Sant Domingo 11

971 72 40 90

PALMA DE MALLORCA

The Balearic capital is an attractive, upbeat town with a lively cultural scene. Half Mallorca's population of 700,000 lives here. Waterfront palm trees and elegant Renaissance and 18th-century mansions create an grand backdrop, and pedestrianized streets around Plaça Major hum with life.

Scenically built around the secluded curve of the bay, Palma was founded by the Romans in 123 B.C., captured by the Moors in A.D. 903, and entered the Catalan net in 1229. Dominating the port is the **Almudaina** *(Carrer Palau Reial, tel 971 72 71 45, closed Sat. p.m. & Sun.)*, the Moorish citadel. It acquired Gothic extensions as the palace of Jaume II, and it is still an official royal residence and military headquarters. You reach it by steps from the breezy **Parc de la Mar,** an elongated lake set in gardens, with sculptures and a Miró mural.

Inside are precious Flemish tapestries and furnishings fit for a king and the part-Romanesque church of **Santa Ana.**

Opposite stands the cathedral, **La Seu,** a wonderful Gothic edifice topped by numerous spires and a towering belfry. The ornate southern portal, the **Portada del Mirador,** gives fine sea views. Vast proportions continue in the massive, sober nave overlooked by **rose windows** designed by Antoni Gaudí (see pp. 172–75); he also designed the wrought-iron baldachin that protects the Renaissance choir stalls in the royal chapel. Kings Jaume II and Jaume III are buried in the lovely Mudejar chapel of **La Trinitat.**

Immediately to the east of the cathedral lies the **Museo de Mallorca** (*Carrer Portella 5, tel 971 71 75 40, closed Sun. p.m. & Mon.*), where archaeological exhibits and medieval artworks are displayed in a lovely 17th-century mansion. Just behind are the tenth-century **Baños Árabes** (*Arab Baths, Calle Serra 7, tel 971 72 15 49*), Palma's only complete relic of Moorish presence. To the north lie Palma's oldest church, **Santa Eulalia** (13th century), and the baroque **town hall,** distinguished by a prominent overhanging eave. From here, Calle de Morey brings you into the heart of old Palma, epitomized by a Roman arch and the **Calle Platería,** once a thriving Jewish quarter.

NORTHWESTERN MALLORCA

Avoid Mallorca's concentrated resort area, west of Palma between Magaluf and Santa Ponça, but don't miss the island's dramatic coastline to the north. Here, the coast is backed by the Serra de Tramuntana and edged by a tortuous clifftop road (C710) with vertiginous views.

Even when the granite sierra is blanketed in glowering clouds, the mountain villages and rocky cliffs are spectacular.

Just inland from the picturesque **Port d'Andratx,** a fishing harbor invaded by luxury yachts in summer, is **Andratx** itself, dominated by a fort. From here a secondary road leads down to the extreme southwestern cove of **Sant Telm,** where boat tours take you past the island nature reserve of **Sa Dragonera.** The next place to stop is the Carthusian **monastery of Valldemossa** (*Tel 971 61 21 06, closed Sun. p.m.*), nestling in the flanks of 3,490-foot-high (1,064 m) Tex. This atmospheric monastery has never forgotten the winter of 1838–39, when the French writer Georges Sand and her lover, Frédéric Chopin, stayed there—their romance is recalled by hourly piano concerts.

The beautiful hilltop village of **Deiá,** discovered decades ago by writers and artists (including Robert Graves, 1895–1985, British author of *I, Claudius*), makes a colorful stop as much for its bucolic surroundings as for its hip bars, galleries, and typical Mallorcan architecture. Farther north, the market town of **Sóller** is connected by a little train with a bay below that has expanded into a burgeoning resort. Boat tours go along the magnificent coast. It is worth making the detour from Sóller through the hills to see the lush **Jardines de Alfàbia** (*Carretera Palma-Sóller, tel 971 61 31 23*), which surround a stately mansion. Inside you can visit the library and admire an *artesonado* (carved coffered ceiling), saved from the original Moorish building. Far more seductive, however, are the lush gardens of palm trees, oleanders, bougainvillea, and bamboo—a cool summer retreat.

La Seu & Museo de Mallorca

- ✉ Carrer Palau Reial 29
- ☎ 971 72 31 30
- 🕐 Closed Sat. p.m., Sun., & p.m. in winter
- 💲 $

Sóller

- 🅰 325 C3

Visitor information

- ✉ Plaça de sa Constitució 1
- ☎ 971 63 02 00

The northern stretch of this road wiggles inland to finally reach **Pollença,** wedged between two hills. Down below is a sheltered bay, **Bahía de Pollença,** whose waters are perfect for waterskiing (but may be too polluted for swimmers). At the very end of the promontory, **Cap de Formentor,** a lighthouse is perched above a sheer 650-foot (200 m) drop down to the waves. From here, sweeping views take in the island of **Formentor** in the bay below. To reach its white-sand beaches, take a half-hour boat ride from the Bahía de Pollença. Overlooking the bay from the east is the charming walled town of **Alcúdia.** The interesting **Museo de Pollentia** *(Carrer Sant Jaume 30, tel 971 54 70 04, closed Sat. & Sun. p.m. & Mon.)* is devoted to the outlying Roman site of Pollentia, dating from the second century.

SOUTHEASTERN MALLORCA

The much flatter southeastern side of Mallorca unfolds in idyllic, pastoral splendor toward a string of coves, creeks, and breathtaking caves indenting the eastern coast. Beaches are fewer in the south, where salt flats and marshes give good bird-watching, and monasteries and megalithic sites dot the interior.

In the easternmost corner, just 9 miles (15 km) apart, Capdepera and Artà make a good starting point for exploring the nearby cave networks of Coves d'Artà. **Capdepera** is a striking hill town topped by a 13th-century fortress, **Castillo de Capdepera** *(Tel 971 81 87 46),* looking down on its marina. You can visit the castle though there is little to see other than sweeping views. **Artà,** too, rises in medieval fortified splendor from a high rock crowned by the church of **San Salvador.** Both towns have megalithic settlements on their outskirts.

Due east of Capdepera, **Cala Rajada** *(Visitor information, Plaça dels Pins, tel 971 56 30 33)* is notable for the imposing **Casa March** *(Tel 971 56 30 33 for guided tour appt.)* overlooking the harbor. Don't miss this impressive collection of contemporary sculpture, including work by Henry Moore, Barbara Hepworth, and also Arman and Eduardo Chillida.

Mallorcan scenic drama returns in the island's 800 limestone caves. Just beyond the **Canyamel,** a landmark 12th-century tower, the magnificent **Coves d'Artà** lie on the seashore. This cavernous underworld dripping with stalactites is spotlit to highlight the extraordinary formations and scale: The so-called **Sala de las Banderas** (Hall of Flags) soars to an inspiring 148 feet (45 m). If your appetite is whetted, continue south to the fishing village of **Porto Cristo** *(Visitor information, Calle Gual 31, tel 971 82 09 31, closed in winter)* to reach the mile-long (1.6 km) chambers of the **Coves del Drac.** A tour of this awesome geological sight includes a boat ride across **Lago Martel,** the largest subterranean lake in the world, extending to 1 mile (1.6 km) and named for the French speleologist who stumbled across it in 1896. To add to its otherworldliness, boatloads of musicians play classical music in this eerie natural theater set.

South of here is pretty **Felanitx,** an important ceramics center dotted with kiln chimneys and overlooked by windmills on the ridge above. The **main square** is a lovely place to relax and admire the unusually rich church, which mixes Gothic, Renaissance, and baroque decoration. Just south of town, a road switchbacks up through pine trees to the stunningly sited **Santuari de San Salvador** *(Tel 971 82 72 82),* which has panoramic

Alcúdia
🅜 325 D4
Visitor information
✉ Carrer Mariners, Port d'Alcúdia
☎ 971 54 72 57
🕐 Closed winter

Coves d'Artà
🅜 325 E3
☎ 971 84 12 93
💲 $$

Coves del Drac
🅜 325 E3
☎ 971 82 07 53
💲 $$

views and intriguing shrines. Together with Campos and Santanyí, Felanitx creates a golden triangle of delightful pastoral scenes where dry-stone walls edge fields of wheat, citrus orchards, and olive groves. **Campos** is the market town for this fertile land and has traditional Mallorcan architecture, as does **Santanyí.** Look for the *talayot* **of Son Danus,** a megalithic watchtower that stands on the outskirts.

The coastline east of this triangle is a succession of stunning creeks of transparent water edged by white sand, with wooded hills rising above. **Cala d'Or** is one of the most developed resorts but remains low key in comparison with those of the west coast. **Cala Figuera** still has the atmosphere of a fishing village. Top in the beauty stakes comes

Cala Mondragó, declared a nature reserve. Off the south coast resort of Colònia Sant Jordi lies the archipelago of **Cabrera** *(Tel 971 65 60 73, visit by permit only),* a national park with rich underwater life and good bird-watching. A last leap 28 miles (45 km) inland from the nudist beach of Es Trenc brings you north of Llucmajor to the **Santuari de Cura** *(Tel 971 12 02 60),* which in many ways encapsulates Mallorca—this modernized Franciscan medieval monastery has nonetheless conserved its 17th-century church, grammar school, and museum related to its didactic role. From the hilltop site you have magnificent views west toward Palma, the bay, and moody Serra de Tramuntana, and north toward the lighthouse of Formentor. ■

Eivissa (Ibiza) & Formentera

Turquoise waters surround the island of Formentera, a popular day-trip from Eivissa.

EIVISSA IS HOT IN TEMPERATURE AND MOOD. IT ATTRACTS planeloads of hip young things who come here purely for the nightlife. If clubs and street fashion are not your scene, then avoid July and August. Or head for quieter Formentera. Both islands are much drier and rockier than Mallorca, lacking its fertile meadows but basking under clear blue skies virtually all year-round.

Eivissa (Ibiza)
▲ 324 A1
Visitor information
✉ Vara del Rey 13
☎ 971 30 19 00

The old capital of Eivissa, **Dalt Vila,** is perched on a promontory dominating the harbor of Eivissa town and defined by the silhouettes of the cathedral and castle. Spectacular 16th-century ramparts, steep stone steps, and elegant mansions testify to its history, but this is engulfed by the countless bars, restaurants, and boutiques that line the narrow streets. To get an idea of the island's ancient past, look at the Carthaginian and other artifacts at the **Museo Arqueológico de Ibiza i Formentera** *(Plaça de la Catedral 3, tel 971 30 12 31, closed Sun. p.m. & Mon.)* in the old University and chapel of San Salvador. Then take off into the interior of the island.

The traditional rural house of Eivissa is a simple, south-facing *casament*, a composition of white-washed cubes around a central, communal room, with verandas for storing crops. Beside these very North African-looking houses are simple, fortified churches where inhabitants used to shelter from pirate attacks. **Sant Jordi, Sant Antoni de Portmany,** and **Sant Joan de Labritja** are all good examples.

Eivissa's 56 beaches have trans-parent warm waters, and some remain unspoiled. **Cala Salada,** near Sant Antoni, is one of the few more tranquil beaches in this devel-oped area and has both sandy and rocky areas. Less accessible Sant Joan in the north of the island has **Cala d'en Serra** and **S'Illot des Rencli** along its vertiginous coastline. This wilder end of the island is where best to escape crowds, apart from Cala de Sant Vicent. Santa Eulària des Riu is a booming high-rise resort, but if you head south to the nature reserve of **Ses Salines** you find surprising landscapes, extensive salt flats, and endless water sports.

FORMENTERA

The tiny little island of Formentera may seem a mere hiccup in the Balearics: Its 5,000 inhabitants occupy an area of just 31 square miles (80 sq km). But for faithful visitors it represents the last bastion of unadulterated tranquillity in the Mediterranean. Only 11 miles (18 km) from Eivissa it is easily reached by ferry. Cyclists and hikers revel in Formentera's untouched landscapes and well-marked trails; swimmers like the sandy beaches edged by crystalline water.

The Romans grew wheat extensively on Formentera, but constant pirate attacks made it uninhabitable in the Middle Ages,

and it recovered only in the late 17th century. If you are looking for culture, you are in the wrong place. The capital, **Sant Francesc de Formentera,** is not much more than an 18th-century fortified **church,** a small ethnological **museum** *(Tel 971 32 26 40)*, and a

Rave time at the Club Amnesia in Eivissa

cluster of hippy-style craft shops. Both Sant Francesc and the main tourist center, **Es Pujols,** lie on the shores of **Estany Pudent,** a large lagoon that attracts flocks of migrating birds and leads to a skinny promontory of land edged by beaches. To the west is **Estany des Peix,** a smaller lagoon pro-tected as a nature reserve. On the northern bank stands the striking megalithic monument of **Ca na Costa.** The stone slabs are thought to be a prehistoric burial ground, dating from 4,000 years ago. At the eastern point of Formentera is **La Mola,** a lookout point with a light-house and a monument to Jules Verne (1828–1905), the French writer who wove the magic of this beautiful spot into a book. Views reach right across the island. ■

Formentera

🗺 324 B1

Visitor information

✉ Port de la Sabina

☎ 971 32 20 57

Menorca (Minorca)

LONG OUTSHONE BY THE MORE OBVIOUS ATTRACTIONS of Mallorca and Eivissa, this peaceful, 274-square-mile (702 sq km) island is slowly gaining in popularity. Declared a biosphere reserve in 1993, it has a gently undulating landscape. A long history of occupation by a series of invaders, including a century of intermittent British rule, has given it a very distinctive flavor and gastronomy. North African couscous meets British puddings here, and Maó (Mahón) is the place where mayonnaise was first created.

Outdoor seafood restaurants line Ciutadella's harbor.

Menorca (Minorca)
⚠ 325 E4
Maó (Mahón)
Visitor information
✉ Plaça Esplanada 40, Maó
☎ 971 36 37 90

Menorca's only drawback is the wind—so be prepared. **Maó (Mahón),** the capital, lies at the end of a 3-mile (5 km) inlet and is one of the safest harbors in the Mediterranean. Life revolves around the cafés and restaurants of **Plaza del Ejercito,** and shops are concentrated in the streets between here and Plaza de España. Signs of sporadic British occupation from 1713 to 1802 are evident in older houses. In the town of Es Castell, 2 miles (3 km) along the inlet, well-conserved **Fort Marlborough** (*Cala Sant Esteve, Es Castell, tel 971 36 04 62*) gives you a picture of the period.

Far more memorable are the 500 **megalithic monuments** dotted over the island. Three main types of monument are *talayots* (conical stone mounds), *taules* (T-shaped structures), and *navetes* (upturned troughs resembling boats). They date from the second millennium B.C. and probably served as altars and funerary monuments. Two sites are outstanding: the settlement of **Trepucó** with its 16-foot-high taula, just outside Maó, and the **Naveta des Tudons,** 3 miles (5 km) east of **Ciutadella** (*Visitor information, Plaça Catedral 5, tel 971 38 26 93*).

The north coast beaches are pebbles and red-ocher sand backed by windy heath. Beaches of finer sand line the south coast creeks attracting the majority of visitors, but you can still find solitude at **Son Saura, Cala en Turqueta, Es Talaier,** and **Macarella,** all accessible from Ciutadella. ∎

Closer to Africa than to Spain, these islands have year-round sun and are firm favorites for package vacations. Leave the high-rise resorts and you find volcanic landscapes, unique flora and fauna, and picturesque local architecture.

Canary Islands

Spain...or Africa?

The dramatic volcanic cone of Taburient lords over the island of La Palma.

Canary Islands

CLUSTERED IN THE ATLANTIC OCEAN 620 MILES (1,000 KM) SOUTH OF mainland Spain, just below the Tropic of Cancer, these stark, volcanic islands are only 71 miles (115 km) from the African coast. The Spanish troops of Fernando and Isabel conquered the native Guanches in 1496 and quickly destroyed Europe's last Stone Age culture, but the archipelago's unique geological and biological features have proved more resilient. Today the Canaries' reputation as a budget sun-and-sea destination for northern Europeans tends to eclipse their other charms, but visitors with a bit of initiative find endless corners of astounding beauty and wonderful hiking territory.

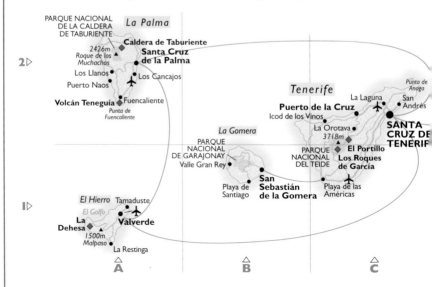

Seven main islands make up this archipelago. They all belong to one autonomous community, but there is considerable rivalry between the islands, and each one has a separate identity. The main bulk of tourists spills out onto the sands of Tenerife, the largest of the archipelago, dominated by the snow-covered peak of Teide. It is closely followed in popularity by Gran Canaria, the most populated island and the one with the greatest scenic diversity. La Palma has the greenest landscapes, in total contrast to Lanzarote's extraordinary lunar horizons of lava flows or Fuerteventura's desertlike dryness. Idyllic La Gomera has subtropical vegetation of laurel forest and palms, and tiny Hierro's abrupt, windswept slopes end in twisted juniper trees.

Much of the appeal of the Canaries lies in their mild, sunny climate. Temperatures hover between 66°F (19°C) in winter and 77°F (25°C) in summer. The other magnet is the sea. Deep-cobalt waters wash 930 miles (1,500 km) of coastline edged by dramatic cliffs and beaches. Huge high-rise resorts monopolize most of the beaches of Tenerife and Gran Canaria. If you want to escape the hordes, head out to the smaller islands. ■

Flora & fauna

The ancient Greeks and Romans knew of the Canary Islands, but no outsiders settled there before the 15th century. This long isolation preserved an exceptional flora and fauna: Only Hawaii and the Galápagos islands have a comparable wealth of native species. The most famous is the chirping yellow canary itself, but the name of the islands probably stems from the fierce Verdino dog (from the Latin *canis,* meaning "dog"). Endangered species include the giant lizard, the hourbara bustard, the long-toed pigeon, and the blue chaffinch of Teide. Of the 2,000 species of flora, 600 are endemic. Evergreen laurel forests *(laurisilva)* that disappeared several millennia ago from the rest of the planet still thrive here. Laurisilva depend on specific conditions of humidity, temperature, and altitude, and can best be seen in Tenerife's Anaga highlands, at El Cedro in Gomera, and in La Palma's national park. ■

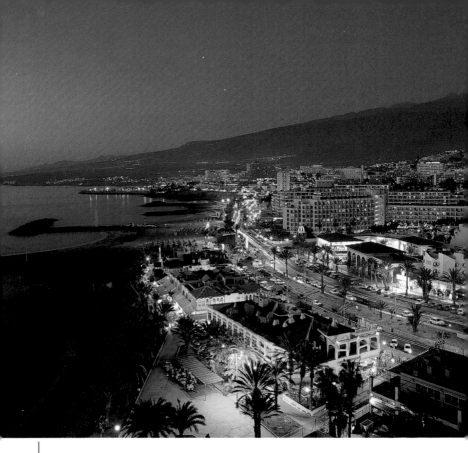

Tenerife

THIS MOUNTAINOUS, 780-SQUARE-MILE (2,000 SQ KM) island divides into the highly developed southern coast with its drier climate and golden beaches, and the more humid, windier northern coast, where black-sand beaches beneath sheer cliffs remind you of Tenerife's volcanic origins. Between these areas is Spain's highest peak, permanently snowcapped Teide, rising 12,192 feet (3,718 m).

The capital and main port, **Santa Cruz de Tenerife,** lies in the southeastern corner of the island in a dramatic bay setting. Its February carnival is Spain's most exuberant. Five miles (8 km) northeast is **Playa de Las Teresitas,** a pretty curve of golden sand from the Sahara, with good seafood at the fishing port of **San Andrés.** For historical interest, head inland to

La Laguna, Tenerife's first capital and now the university town, with several museums and fine 16th- and 17th-century mansions.

More upbeat in tone is verdant **Puerto de la Cruz,** Tenerife's oldest resort. It has mushroomed into a high-rise mirage built on black lava-stone rocks—no beach!—but in recompense every seafront hotel has a rock-built pool.

The popular beach resort of Playa de las Americas, in Tenerife

Santa Cruz de Tenerife
- 334 C2

Visitor information
- Palacio Insular, Plaza de España
- 922 23 95 92

Better still is **Lago Martiánez,** a series of large saltwater pools dreamed up by the Lanzarote artist César Manrique (see p. 339) to harmonize with the lush vegetation and volcanic rock. You can enjoy subtropical plants even more at the town's **Jardín de Aclimatación de Orotava** (*Urbanización La Paz, tel 922 38 35 72*), a botanical garden created in the 18th century. The **Loro Parque** (*Carretera Punta Brava, tel 922 37 38 41*) has the world's largest collection of parrots and a dolphinarium.

La Cruz's magnificent surroundings include the **Valle de la Orotava,** a luxuriant cleft cutting down to the water's edge from Teide. A dizzying 17-mile (27 km) drive up to the lookout point, **Mirador de Humboldt** (named after the German naturalist Alexander Humboldt) gives you stunning views over banana groves to the sea. The nearby town of **La Orotava** is a jewel of traditional timber houses with intricate latticework balconies and leafy patios. Don't miss the baroque church of **La Concepción** or the beautiful **Casa de los Balcones,** actually two 17th-century mansions built of tea (a local pinewood) that now house the craft museum, **Museo de Artesanía Iberoamericana** (*Calle de San Francisco, La Orotava, tel 922 33 06 29, closed Sun. p.m.*).

Twenty-six miles (42 km) southwest from La Orotava, the road winds up to the **Parque Nacional del Teide,** where you enter another world. The immense Cañadas de Teide are a volcanic plateau and former crater of 50 miles (80 km) circumference. Here the vagaries of mineralogy have left luminous strata of turquoise iron oxide. Natural lava-stone sculptures, **Los Roques de García,** stand near the park's only building, the parador (hotel, see p. 000). You

can take a cable car from beside the C821 up to the peak, from which views sweep across the entire archipelago on clear days. This is classic hiking territory, and you may see unique sights such as the Teide violet, the Teide marguerite, and the conspicuous Teide bluetit. Join daily treks from the visitor center at the pass of **El Portillo** (*Tel 922 29 01 29, treks start at 9 a.m. & 1:30 p.m.*), or obtain information from the other center in the parador.

Fourteen miles (22 km) west of Puerto de la Cruz on the north coast is **Icod de los Vinos,** once famous for the production of Malvasía wine, which is being successfully revived after centuries of oblivion. The town also has traditional architecture, baroque churches, lush vegetation, and a drago tree (dragon tree—named for its gnarled, monstrous appearance) that is thousands of years old. Sloth-like growth and a penchant for wild locations make it extremely rare—long may it survive. ■

Parque Nacional del Teide

🅰 334 C1

Visitor information

✉ El Portillo

☎ 922 29 01 29

🕐 Closed Sat.–Sun.

Everything stops in Santa Cruz for the May festival procession.

Gran Canaria

TOURISM HAS A HIGH PROFILE ON THE MOST POPULATED island of the Canaries. This is partly due to 31 miles (50 km) of beaches, but another reason is its incredibly diverse landscapes.

Gran Canaria
🔺 335 D1

Las Palmas
🔺 335 D1

Visitor information
✉ Parque de Santa Catalina
☎ 928 26 46 23

Peaks cradle the village of Tejeda, in the center of the island.

Volcanic formations dominate the interior, making the cliff-edged north coast wetter, cloudier, and perfect for banana plantations. In contrast the most popular beaches fringe the almost desertlike terrain of the south coast. Canyons dominate the west, and the ravines of the central plateau vary from pine forests to stark volcanic rock.

An extensive network of hiking trails runs through these diverse landscapes. Naturalists head for the **Parque Rural del Nublo** on the flanks of Pico de las Nieves (6,393 feet/1,949 m), which has the largest number of endemic species of the archipelago.

Gran Canaria's biggest draw is the immense 5-mile-long (8 km) beach shared by three resorts: **San Agustín, Playa del Inglés,** and **Maspalomas.** Innumerable facilities include water sports and hot nightlife but the greatest sight is the area of undulating sand dunes and oases of palm trees at Maspalomas. Smaller resorts are on the west coast, including the attractive fishing port of **Puerto de Mogán** (with good seafood) and secluded **Playa de Güigüi.**

Las Palmas de Gran Canaria, the sprawling capital and largest city of the Canaries, developed on a spit of land that gives sea access on both sides. This major Atlantic port was founded in 1478 by Isabel la Católica, and the historic **Vegueta** district survives among towering modern apartment blocks. Here you find the twin-towered **cathedral** and the lovely Renaissance **Casa de Colón** (*Calle Colón 1, tel 928 31 23 84, closed Sat. & Sun. p.m.*), which has exhibits on Colombus's four stopovers on the island and on the importance of the Canaries in the early voyages to America. At the **Museo Canario** (*Calle Doctor Chil 25, tel 928 33 68 00, closed Sat. & Sun. p.m.*) you get a picture of the indigenous Guanche culture. The **Centro de Arte Moderno** (*Calle Los Balcones 11, tel 928 31 18 24, closed Sat.–Sun.; closed Sun. p.m.–Mon. during exhibitions*) exhibits contemporary Spanish art in a converted 18th-century building. Overlooking the port is the **Castillo de La Luz,** built in the 16th century to fend off pirates and now an occasional exhibition venue. **Playa de las Canteras** is the buzzing city beach. ∎

Lanzarote

DROMEDARIES, ARCHITECTURE THAT IS SENSITIVE TO the environment, and blinding white beaches are just some of the attractions of this 323-square-mile (836 sq km) island, all of which is a biosphere reserve. Lanzarote is special for its otherworldly volcanic cover, the result of momentous eruptions in 1730–36 and 1824 that buried towns and fertile valleys under lava flows.

These events produced the awesome landscapes of the **Parque Nacional de Timanfaya** or **Montañas del Fuego o de Timanfaya,** which include 300 volcanic cones. Don't pass up on a bumpy dromedary-ride through this extraordinary national park, where the volcanoes still simmer.

The main port and town is **Arrecife,** named for the outlying reefs of this south coast and defended by the 16th-century **Castillo del San Gabriel.** This houses the **Museo Arqueológico y Etnográfico** *(Tel 928 81 19 50, closed Sat. p.m. & Sun.).* Arrecife's other guardian, **Castillo de San José,** has been converted into the **Museo Internacional de Arte Contemporáneo** *(Tel 928 81 23 21, castle closed p.m.).* The latter was the brainchild of Lanzarote's greatest artist, César Manrique (1920–1992), who was almost solely responsible for the islanders' admirable attitude to their architecture and environment. You can enjoy more of Manrique's work at the **Jameos del Agua** (a saltwater lagoon in a volcanic cave) and the breathtaking, clifftop **Mirador del Río,** both in the north of the island, and at the **Fundación César Manrique** *(Taro de Tahíche, Teguise, tel 928 84 31 38, closed Sun. p.m.).* This intriguing lava-top house was built by Manrique in 1968 to exemplify affinities between art and nature, and it houses a good collection of contemporary Spanish art.

On the southern edge of the park lies **El Golfo.** This spectacular emerald-green crater lake is at the base of volcanic cliffs and creates a startling contrast with the black-sand beach. More tormented rockscapes characterize **Los Hervideros,** farther south on this western coast, before the road reaches the **Salinas de Janubio.** This natural phenomenon is formed out of dazzling white salt mounds and salt pans within a crater. Some of Lanzarote's best beaches are the white sandy coves of **Papagayo** and the resort of **Playa Blanca,** both on the south coast. ■

Lanzarote
🗺 335 F3

Parque Nacional de Timanfaya
🗺 335 F3
Visitor information
✉ Calle Laguneta 64, Pinajo
☎ 928 84 02 38
928 84 02 40

Arrecife
Visitor information
✉ Parque José Ramírez Cerdá
☎ 928 80 15 17 or 928 81 18 60

A fiery photo opportunity in Lanzarote's national park

Other islands

LA GOMERA

For decades most visitors who came to this round island with its rugged terrain were seeking to escape the rat race. The 40-minute hydrofoil ride from Santa Cruz de Tenerife has changed that, yet Gomera's deep ravines and bad roads have preserved its charms for hikers and cyclists. Terraced farming, date palms, and banana plantations surround the central plateau characterized by its ancient laurel forest, which is often shrouded in mist. This is the **Parque Nacional de Garajonay,** where you find around 400 native species of flora that became extinct in Africa and Europe millions of years ago. There are well-marked trails, and guided treks are available. Accommodations are concentrated in the capital of **San Sebastián de la Gomera** (where Columbus prepared to cross to America), **Playa de Santiago,** and idyllic **Valle Gran Rey.**

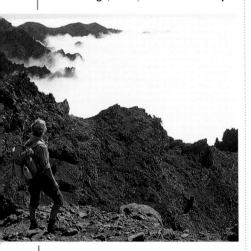

Standing above the clouds on the edge of Caldera de Taburiente, La Palma

🗺 334 B1 **Visitor information** www.gomera-island.com ✉ Calle Real 4, San Sebastián de La Gomera ☎ 922 14 15 12

EL HIERRO

This somewhat bleak bump in the Atlantic Ocean has inspired numerous legends. As the westernmost island in the archipelago for Europeans it was the end of the known world—in fact it was used by geographers as zero meridian until this was relocated to run through Greenwich in London. Fishing, sheep, goats, pineapples, and vineyards are the islanders' main resources, and tourism is mainly limited to **Valverde,** the capital, and neighboring **Tamaduste** with its tranquil lava pool. **El Golfo,** a 15-mile (25 km) crescent-shaped depression of the north coast, is backed by a sheer rock face rising to 3,280 feet (1,000 m). The rest of the island slopes dramatically down from the peak of **Malpaso,** ending in curious rock formations and cliffs.

🗺 334 A1 **Visitor information** ✉ Licenciado Bueno 1, Valverde ☎ 922 55 03 02

LA PALMA

Claiming to be the highest island in the world, and home to the Northern Hemisphere's largest astrophysical observatory on the summit of **Roque de los Muchachos** (7,957 feet/2,426 m), La Palma has a mellow, low-key atmosphere with an increasing accent on rural pursuits. This lush, well-irrigated island of only 80,000 inhabitants has two small resorts: **Los Cancajos,** near the capital on the east coast, and the black-sand beach of **Puerto Naos** on the sunnier west coast. Another center is at **Los Llanos,** close to the impressive **Caldera de Taburiente** and national park. This gigantic volcanic crater (6 miles/10 km in diameter) is best seen from lookout points or explored on foot. La Palma's spine of volcanic cones and craters ends at the southernmost **Volcán Teneguía,** scene of the island's last eruption in 1971.

The capital, **Santa Cruz de la Palma,** was once a major port and preserves a delightful **seafront quarter** of Renaissance buildings and picturesque houses with typical fretwork balconies. See the lovely church of **El Salvador** (Tel 922 41 32 50), then stroll uphill to charming **Plaza Santo Domingo.** Don't miss out on La Palma's handmade cigars, silk, embroidery, and basketwork, and taste its tea (pinewood) wine.

🗺 334 A2 **Visitor information** www .la-palma-tur.org ✉ o'Dally 22 ☎ 922 41 19 57 or 922 41 21 06 ∎

Travelwise

**Round the volcanic bend in
Tenerife**

TRAVELWISE INFORMATION

PLANNING YOUR TRIP

WHEN TO GO

Unless you wish to bask on the busy summer beaches or ski in the Pyrenees or Sierra Nevada in winter, the time to visit Spain is during spring or fall (March to mid-June, mid-September to November). Spring is perhaps the finest season, when the wild flowers burst into colorful life and the naturally social and gregarious locals return to the streets after the short and, in places, severe winter. Fall sees Spain return to life as scorching temperatures drop to a pleasant level and rain ends the summer drought. Although winter can be cold in some areas of the country, the Mediterranean coast, particularly near Valencia, has some of the highest winter temperatures in Europe. On the other hand, Spain also has some of the highest summer tempera-tures on the continent, resulting in an exodus from the cities to the coast. In August virtually the entire country is on vacation. Combined with the arrival of millions of (mostly European) foreign visitors, this makes the coasts, particularly the Mediterr-anean, terribly overcrowded.

CLIMATE

The geographical and geological diversity of the regions means that the climate varies greatly. The north coast is battered by the Atlantic over the winter, suffering cold, rain, and mist, but has hot summers marked by thunderstorms. The Mediterr-anean coast ranges from the deserts of Almería (Europe's lowest rainfall) to a subtropical climate in Granada to the pine-covered hills of Catalunya. To the north, the Pyrenees are perman-ently snowcapped. The center of the country is occupied by the high meseta, "the plain of Spain," that ranges in height from 1,310 feet (400 m) to 3,280 feet (1,000

m). This region bakes in the summer and is swept by freezing winds in the winter. To the west, the meseta stretches to Extremadura and then on to the border with Portugal. In this verdant area of rivers and oak forests, moss and lichen thrive in the damp air.

Average temperatures (from the Spanish Meteorological Office):

Barcelona
Jan. 43°F/6°C–56°F/13°C
Aug. 70°F/21°C–83°F/28°C
Madrid
Jan. 34°F/1°C–49°F/9°C.
Aug. 63°F/17°C–88°F/31°C
Málaga
Jan. 49°F/9°C–63°F/17°C
Aug. 72°F/22°C–86°F/30°C

MAIN EVENTS

Spain has an enormous number of festivals and fiestas. Probably the best known of these is **San Fermín,** the running of the bulls in Iruña (Pamplona), July 6–14. Holy Week or **Semana Santa** (the week before Easter) is marked by spectacular processions in many towns, but most famously in Sevilla. If it's a party you want, then visit Valencia for **Las Fallas de San José** (March 12–19). More sedate are the fiestas of Madrid. During **San Isidro** (two weeks from May 15), many operas, concerts and ballets are performed. Other festivals are listed on pp. 388–89.

WHAT TO TAKE

You should be able to buy most things that you need in Spain. Clothing depends on the time of year and your destination. Spaniards tend to dress quite formally except at the coastal resorts during the summer months. Casual clothing and footwear (such as trainers) are quite acceptable during the day,

but you should dress up when going out at night.

Bring any essential prescribed medication; for other medicines, Spanish pharmacy staff are helpful and knowledgeable, and dispense many drugs that in other countries might need prescriptions.

INSURANCE

Make sure you have adequate travel and medical coverage for treatment and expenses, including repatriation, baggage, and money loss. Keep all receipts for expenses. Report losses or thefts to the police and obtain a signed statement (una denuncia) from a police station to help with insurance claims.

FURTHER READING

Publishers are not included as many of these books have been reprinted by different companies.

For Whom the Bell Tolls by Ernest Hemingway. Perhaps the most famous book written on Spain and the Civil War.
The Sun Also Rises by Ernest Hemingway. This book put the San Fermín festival in Iruña (Pamplona) on the map.
South From Granada by Gerald Brenan. A fascinating account of life in rural southern Spain between the two World Wars.
The Spanish Temper by V.S. Pritchett. Perceptive portrait of Spain's people, landscape, history, and myth.
Homage to Barcelona by Colm Toibin. Firsthand account of modern life in Barcelona.
Voices of the Old Sea by Norman Lewis. The author looks back at the fishing village he knew in his youth from the unrecognizable place it has become today.
Spain by Jan Morris. A good general book on the country.
Our Lady of the Sewers by Paul Richardson. Pieces about "the ancient, perverse and eccentric" side of Spain that is becoming increasingly hard to find.

HOW TO GET TO SPAIN

ENTRY FORMALITIES

U.S., Canadian, and E.U. citizens may enter Spain without a visa and remain there for up to 90 days. It is advisable to keep your identity card or passport on you at all times.

AIRLINES

The national carrier, Iberia, has regular direct flights from several North American destinations to Madrid. Onward internal flights bought in conjunction with the international flight are often very good value. U.S. airlines such as Delta also offer direct flights. Several other European carriers have services to Spain, including British Airways and Air France.

Useful numbers & internet addresses
In Spain:
Iberia, tel 902 40 05 00
Air Europa, tel 902 24 00 42
American Airlines, tel 902 11 55 70
British Airways, tel 902 11 13 33
Delta Airlines, tel 91 749 66 30

In the U.S. and Canada:
Air Europa, tel 888-238-7672
www.air-europa.com/
Iberia (U.S.), tel 800/772-4642
Iberia (Canada), tel 800/423-7241
www.iberia.com
British Airways (U.S.),
tel 800/247-9297
British Airways (Canada),
tel 800/668-1059
www.britishairways.com
American Airlines, tel 800/433-7300
www.americanair.com
Delta Airlines, tel 800/241-4141
www.delta-air.com

ARRIVAL

AIR
Most intercontinental flights touch down at Barajas airport, Madrid. The airport is 10 miles (15 km) from downtown Madrid, a 20-minute taxi ride

costing roughly 2,500 ptas. Buses run every 20 minutes to Plaza Colón, between 4:45 a.m. and 1:15 a.m. Tickets cost 380 ptas. The underground train is much slower and harder to use than the bus. If you arrive in Barcelona, a taxi ride into the center takes roughly 20 minutes and costs 2,500 ptas. Buses leave about every 30 minutes between 5:30 a.m. and 10 p.m., and cost 485 ptas. A train service operates from 6:15 a.m. to 10:13 p.m., and charges 350 ptas.

BY TRAIN
You can go by train to Spain from the U.K. via the Channel Tunnel, changing trains in Paris and passing the night on board on a *trenhotel*. The Madrid sleeper leaves Paris Austerlitz train station at 7:47 p.m. and arrives at Madrid Chamartín at 8:58 a.m. The train for Barcelona leaves at 8:47 p.m. and arrives at 9:30 a.m. the following morning.

BY CAR
Arriving by car, you have to choose between the Atlantic or Mediterranean coasts if you wish to travel on the motorways. Smaller roads cross the Pyrenees, but they may be blocked by snow in winter. The exception is the road through Andorra; it is closed only during extreme conditions.

SEA
Several ferries sail from the U.K. and France to the northern ports of Santander and Bilbao. Timetables change depending on the season. Useful numbers in the U.K.:
Brittany Ferries
Tel 0990 360 360
www.brittany-ferries.com
P&O European Ferries
Tel 0990 980 555
www.poef.com/portsmouth/

HEALTH

No vaccinations are required. Tap water is safe to drink although it may have a strong taste of chlorine. Plastic 1-liter

bottles of water are available in most bars and restaurants. The primary health concerns are sunburn and dehydration. If you are out in the hot sun make sure you wear suitable clothing and put on sunscreen. During the hottest parts of the day in the summer you will notice few locals about on the streets.

GETTING AROUND

BY AIRPLANE

Most major cities in Spain have an airport for internal and international flights. The national airline Iberia (Tel 902 40 05 00) has the most frequent internal flights. Other airlines are Air Europa (Tel 902 24 00 42) and Spanair (Tel 902 13 14 15).

BY TRAIN

RENFE (Red Nacional de los Ferrocarriles Españoles) is the mainline national rail network. Outside the main holiday periods (summer and Easter Week), traveling by train is recommended, particularly on the Talgos (Tren Articulado Ligero Goicoechea Oriol) and the high speed AVEs (Alta Velocidad Español). Despite being relaxed and reminiscent of an earlier age of train travel, Talgos are fast, comfortable, and reliable, and usually have a well-equipped snack bar. AVEs have telephones and other facilities.

Tickets can be bought at the station up to 15 minutes before the train departs; it is unwise to leave it so late as long lines form. Travel agents that display a RENFE sticker sell rail tickets, and RENFE also has offices in downtown areas in many cities, where you can purchase your ticket. If you are planning a long-distance rail journey, especially in the high season, book well in advance through your travel agent in your home country.

Trains are generally divided into 1st and 2nd class, but standards vary between the type of train and also between the trains themselves. You can often get a 20 percent reduction on the purchase of a round-trip ticket. There are special rates for those over 60 and children under 11, and for travelers with disabilities.

Inter Rail and Eurail passes are valid in Spain as they are elsewhere in Europe. The Flexipass, available for North American citizens, offers three days unlimited rail travel over a two-month period. For U.K. and Irish residents, the Spanish EuroDomino Pass allows five to ten days travel in a month. RENFE issues a Tarjeta Joven for those under 26, valid for three to ten days.

RENFE has a comprehensive website with up to the minute details of prices and timetables in both Spanish and English. You can also have a virtual look at the AVE: www.renfe.es/

BY CAR

Getting around by car is a good option, allowing you to get to out-of-the-way places that otherwise would be difficult to reach. Driving in the countryside is often a relaxing experience if you are used to the congested roads of northern Europe, but driving in the cities can be quite the reverse. Dual lane *autopistas* and the *autovías* link many provincial capitals and, outside of major cities and holidays, are relatively free of traffic. Tolls are paid in cash or with credit cards on exiting the autopista or, on short stretches, on entering. National roads, or *Nacionales,* marked in red on the road maps, were the old main roads, now superseded by the motorways. They are still in constant use, although mostly by local traffic. Smaller roads marked in yellow are *comarcales,* regional roads, and are often picturesque and quiet, as are the smaller local roads (white and often without any names or numbers). The

roads marked in green have been singled out as especially scenic.

Motoring information

European, U.S., and Canadian driving permits are valid in Spain. It is compulsory to carry two warning triangles, spare light bulbs, fuses, and a spare tire. The minimum legal age for drivers is 18. If entering Spain in your own car, make sure that you have appropriate insurance, including the green card, available from your insurers.

On-the-spot-fines Fines of up to 50,000 ptas for nonresidents are issued on the spot. The fine for failing to wear your seat belt can range from 25,000 ptas to 50,000 ptas. Exceeding the speed limit results in a fine of between 50,000 ptas and 100,000 ptas.

Drunk-driving The alcohol limit for drivers is 50 mg of alcohol per 100 ml of blood. The fine for exceeding this starts at 50,000 ptas.

Speed limits The speed limits are: motorways 75 mph (120 kph); dual carriageways 62.5 mph (100 kph); other roads outside built-up areas 56 mph (90 kph); towns and built-up areas 31 mph (50 kph).

Fuel Fuel prices are controlled by the government and are slightly cheaper than in the U.K. but nearly twice those of the U.S. The types of fuel available are: Super (4 Star), Normal (3 Star), Sin plomo (Unleaded), and Gasoleo (Diesel).

Breakdown assistance Motorways have emergency telephones at intervals. A tow truck from the nearest garage will be sent to help you. You must place a a warning triangle behind your vehicle. If you belong to an automobile club such as the AAA, CAA, or AA you can get help from RACE, the Spanish motoring organization, tel 900 11 22 22.

Traffic circles Vehicles already on a traffic circle have right of way unless it is clearly marked otherwise.

Seat belts Wearing seat belts is compulsory in the front seats and also in the back if the car is fitted with them.

Distances All distances in Spain are marked in kilometers (1 km=0.62 mile).

Parking A yellow line on the road or along the pavement means no parking. Sometimes a sign indicates that you can park along yellow lines after a certain time. Blue lines denote pay parking. Look for ticket-dispensing machines marked by a sign of a coin being pushed into a slot, and display the ticket in your car. If your car has disappeared, look for an orange sticker on the pavement where you parked. If it has been towed away, the sticker will give details of your car, the time it was taken, and the number to call.

RENTING A CAR

Renting a car in Spain is straight forward and relatively cheap. There are many small local companies, and international ones such as Hertz and Avis. It is worth looking into fly-and-drive deals when booking your trip. **Avis,** tel 902 13 55 31 **Hertz,** tel 901 10 10 01 **Europcar,** tel 901 10 20 20 If you start in Madrid, bear in mind that road signs as you leave the city give numbers rather than destinations. If you are heading for Granada, for example, on the Andalucía autovía, look for signs that say IV, not Granada or Sevilla.

TRANSPORTATION IN MADRID

TAXIS

Downtown Madrid teems with taxis (white, with a red stripe along their sides), and you rarely have to wait long before one appears. Madrid is quite a compact city, and taxis are not very expensive, which makes them an ideal mode of transport. A supplement is charged for each piece of luggage and for passing beyond the city limits.

METRO
The subway system is the most efficient and rapid mode of public transport. The distances between stops are short, so you tend to be near your destination when you exit the station. There is a flat rate of 130 ptas per trip, but you can buy ten tickets, an *abono*, for 670 ptas. Lines are color coded and the train's direction is indicated by the stations at the end of the line. Hold on to your ticket until exiting the system: Inspectors on the trains and platforms check for fare dodgers.

BUS
Madrid's bus network is extensive but confusing. On a short stay in the capital it may not be worth mastering. The price of a journey is the same as on the metro, and you can use tickets from your abono if you have one. If not, pay the driver, using small change rather than a note. Punch your ticket in the machine near the driver.

TRANSPORTATION IN BARCELONA

Barcelona has buses, cable cars, and overground and underground trains. If you plan to stay for more than a few days, buy one of the various *targetes* (similar to *abonos* in Madrid), blocks of tickets that can be used on various local transport systems. Pick up a Guia del Transport Public de Barcelona at a visitor information center; it has a good explanation of the various modes of transport.

TAXIS
Like Madrid, Barcelona abounds in taxis, only here they are a very distinctive black and yellow. They offer a quick (depending

on the traffic!) and reasonably cost-effective way of getting around the city. There is a minimum charge of 300 ptas.

METRO
Again, the quickest way of getting around the city is the metro. Smaller than the system in Madrid, just five lines, it is open between 5 a.m. and 11 p.m.

BUSES
Much easier to use than Madrid's, the buses in Barcelona are color coded: red buses for the city center, yellow for cross-city, green for those that head out to the suburbs, and blue for the night buses.

PRACTICAL ADVICE

COMMUNICATIONS

POST OFFICES
To send a letter or postcard of less than 20 g costs 70 ptas within the E.U. and 115 ptas to North America. Registered mail, *certificado*, costs an extra 175 ptas. Stamps are available at post offices or at government-sponsored tobacconists known as *estancos* and recognizable by their "Tabacos" signs. Post offices are open from 8:30 a.m. until 8 p.m.; estancos are open both mornings and afternoons. American Express will hold mail sent to you in Spain as will the post office where it should be addressed Lista de Correos (poste restante).

TELEPHONES
The country code for Spain is 34 and all provincial codes start with a 9. You must always include the provincial code when making a call, even for local calls to the province you are in. Codes to some of the larger provinces are: Madrid (91), Barcelona (93), Valencia (96), Sevilla (95), and Vizcaya (94). Many provinces have three-digit codes, for example Navarra (948), Granada (958). Call boxes usually allow you to pay in cash or with a card

(tarjeta telefónica). Cards often work when the coin slot is jammed or damaged. Tarjetas are sold at post offices and estancos, and come in 1,000 and 2,000 ptas denominations. The access code to make an international call is 00. The international lines may be busy and you get a recorded message. This rarely lasts long. To speak to the operator dial 1009. For national directory inquiries dial 1003, for international 025.

E-MAIL
Spain has not been slow in jumping on the internet band-wagon and there should be no problem in finding an internet café in any large city.

Madrid
Cibercafé Matrix Cardenal Silíceo 37, tel 91 510 23 80, nearest Metro Cartagena (open noon–1 a.m., Sun. 6 p.m–1 a.m.)
Cibercafé Xnet San Bernardo 81, tel 91 444 40 35, nearest metro San Bernardo (open 10 a.m.–2 a.m., weekends 11 a.m–3.30 a.m.)

Barcelona
El Ciber Mundo Bergara 3, tel 933 17 71 42 (open 9 a.m.–1 a.m.)
Inetcorner Plaza Ramón Verenguer el Grande 2, tel 932 68 73 55 (open daily, except Sun., 10 a.m.–10 p.m.)

Sevilla
Cibercenter Julio César 8, tel 95 422 88 99; ww.cibercenter.es (open 9 a.m.–9 p.m.)

CONVERSIONS

1 kilo = 2.2 pounds
1 liter = 0.2642 U.S. gallons
1 kilometer = 0.62 mile
1 meter = 1.093 yards

Women's clothing
U.S.	8	10	12	14	16	18
Spanish	36	38	40	42	44	46

Men's clothing
U.S.	36	38	40	42	44	46
Spanish	46	48	50	52	54	56

PRACTICAL ADVICE

Women's shoes

U.S.	6–6½	7–7½	8–8½	9–9½
Spanish	38	39	40–41	42

Men's shoes

U.S.	8	8½	9½	10½	11½	12
Spanish	41	42	43	44	45	46

ELECTRICITY

The electricity voltage is 220 or 225 AC. Occasionally you might come across a building that is still 125 volts. Plugs are two pin. U.S. appliances need adaptors.

HOLIDAYS

Spain has national, regional, and local holidays. It is not possible to keep track of all of them as each city, town, and village celebrates its own saint's day, and since all the days of the week have saints there is always a fiesta or festival going on somewhere. Most regions have at least seven others, but the main national holidays are:
January 1 & 6 (Epiphany)
Good Friday
Easter Sunday
Easter Monday
May 1 (May Day)
October 12 (National Day)
November 1 (All Saints)
December 6 (Constitution),
8 (Immaculate Conception),
& 25 (Christmas)

MEDIA

NEWSPAPERS
The three most popular daily newspapers are El País, El Mundo, and ABC. The left-leaning El País has the best international coverage. There are regional English language papers such as Sur, which is distributed along the Mediterranean coast. In the larger cities you find the day's copy of the Herald Tribune and the Guardian newspapers, and the Observer on Sundays.

RADIO
The airwaves are full of local and national radio stations. The state-run Radio Nacional de España has four stations

covering sport, pop, and classical music, current affairs, which are on the whole better than local stations. The Voice of America is broadcast on short-wave, but moves around according to the time of day: Try 9.700, 15.205, and 15.255 MHz. The same applies to the BBC World Service: Try 3.955, 7.150, 9.410, 15.070, and 15.400.

TELEVISION
Spanish television has good news coverage but otherwise tends to be a mess of game, quiz, and audience participation shows, and Latin American soaps. Spaniards love their televisions and have them on constantly, in bars and even restaurants, but often no one is actually watching them.

There are two state-run channels, TVE1 and TVE2, and two independents, Antena 3 and Tele 5. The superior Canal Plus is a pay channel. Most hotels are equipped with satellite, cable, or digital television, giving the international channels such as CNN, BBC World, and Sky.

MONEY MATTERS

Take a combination of traveler's checks and credit or debit cards that you can use to extract cash from the plentiful ATMs. Major credit cards are accepted in many establishments and all gas stations. Traveler's checks are a secure way to hold money (keep a list of their numbers separate from the checks) and can be changed in banks and exchange offices. Banks give you a better exchange rate but exchange offices are open longer hours.

Until the Euro coin is introduced on January 1, 2002, Spain's currency remains the peseta. After this date both currencies will be in circulation until July 1, when the peseta will cease to be a legal tender. The peseta is permanently fixed against the Euro at 166.386 ptas which means when you change money you are in fact changing it into Euros, which are then converted

into pesetas. The peseta comes in coins of one, 5, 10, 25, 50, 100, 200 and 500 ptas, and notes are divided into 1000, 2000, 5000, and 10,000 ptas. Five pesetas are known as a duro and it is not unusual to be given the price of something in duros, so that something costing 100 ptas is veinte duros (twenty duros).

OPENING TIMES

Banks open 8:30 a.m to 2 p.m. (1 p.m. on Sat.).

Post offices in large towns open 8:30 a.m. to 8 p.m. In villages they close at 2 p.m. Museums open 9 a.m. to 7 p.m. Virtually all close on Monday.

Shops, including pharmacies, open 9:30 a.m. to 2 p.m, and reopen between 4:30 p.m. and 5 p.m., closing again at 8 p.m. Restaurants open around midday, close around 5 p.m., reopen around 7 p.m. and often serve food until past midnight.

Bars are open virtually 24 hours. Cafés open from 7 a.m. onward. Music bars open until between 3 a.m. and 5 a.m.

PLACES OF WORSHIP

When visiting churches, remember that they are not tourist attractions, but places of worship. It is not necessary to dress formally, but be aware of where you are and act accordingly.

REST ROOMS

Public toilets are rare outside the most obvious tourism areas. Luckily, you are never far from a bar in Spain and it would be unusual if the owner did not let you use the toilet. Carry toilet paper with you, as this, too, is often in short supply.

TIME DIFFERENCES

Spain runs on CET (Central European Time), one hour ahead

of Greenwich Mean Time, six hours ahead of Eastern Standard Time except for the Canary Islands, which run on CET minus one. Noon in Spain is 6 a.m. in New York.

TRAVELERS WITH DISABILITIES

Only in recent years has Spain begun to cater for the needs of people with disabilities. Newer buildings are more accessible than older ones, but there may still be problems. Check with hotels and restaurants before booking. Advice is available from: **RADAR** (Royal Association for Disability and Rehabilitation) 12 City Forum, 250 City Road, London EC1V 8AF, U.K., tel 020-7250 3222
Mobility International Rue de Manchester 25, Brussels 1070, Belgium, tel 32 2 201 5711, E-mail mobint@products.be
Mobility International U.S.A. P.O. Box 10767, Eugene, Oregon, U.S.A., tel 541/343-1284
Twin Peaks Press Box 129, Vancouver, WA 98666, Canada, tel 604-694-2462

ETIQUETTE & LOCAL CUSTOMS

The Spanish siesta is not a myth. Almost everything closes from 2 p.m. to 5 p.m., particularly in summer. It is unusual to begin lunch, which is the main meal of the day, before 2 p.m., and often it lasts until 5 p.m. Sunday lunch can go on even longer. Dinner is a lighter affair, as it is considered unhealthy to eat large quantities before going to bed.

TIPPING

Service is included in all restaurant bills, so there is no need to tip if you do not wish to. However, the Spanish service industry is poorly paid and waiting is considered a profession; a tip for good service would not be amiss. The Spanish themselves often leave their small change when paying for a drink and tip about 5 percent at restaurants.

Tip taxi drivers and porters 100–200 ptas, depending on the distance and amount of luggage.

EMERGENCIES

EMBASSIES

Embassies are in Madrid, but larger cities have consulates.
United States Callede Serrano 75, tel 91 587 22 00
Canada Calle de Núñez de Balboa 35, tel 91 423 32 50
United Kingdom Callede de Fernando Santo 16, tel 91 700 82 00

Spanish embassies
United States 2375 Pennsylvania Ave. N.W., Washington, DC 20037, tel 202/728-4568
Canada 74 Stanley Ave., Ottawa, Ontario K1M 1P4, tel 613/747-2252
United Kingdom 39 Chesham Place, London SW1X 8SB, tel 020-7235 5555

EMERGENCY PHONE NUMBERS

The central number for police, fire, and ambulance is 112.

POLICE

Spain has three distinct police forces. The Policía Local (or Municipal) are controlled by the local town hall and deal with minor matters such as traffic infringements. The Policía Nacional are the main crime-fighting force in the cities, and the Guardia Civil tend to operate in the countryside and on highways, in addition to controlling borders and prisons.

LOSS OF CREDIT CARDS

American Express España, tel 915 72 03 03 (24 hrs.)
Diners Club Español, tel 91 701 59 00

Mastercard, tel 900 97 12 31
VISA Internacional, tel 900 97 44 45

WHAT TO DO IN A CAR ACCIDENT

The Guardia Civil operates special units designed to deal quickly and effectively with anything other than minor accidents. If involved in an accident you should mark the position of your vehicle as accurately as possible, then move it to a safe place on the hard shoulder or nearest pull-off and wait for the police. If it is a minor accident with no injuries but involving another vehicle, there is no need to call the police as long as both parties agree how it occurred and where the blame lies. If this happens simply fill out the insurance details.

HEALTH

Make sure that your health insurance covers you during your visit to Spain. E.U. citizens should complete and carry the E111 form available from main post offices. Doctors are listed in the telephone directory, but in an emergency go to the nearest *urgencia,* call an ambulance on 112, or call the number for the nearest Red Cross (Cruz Roja). A hospital stay can be expensive, so make sure your insurance is valid and up to date.

International Association for Medical Assistance to Travellers (IAMAT) is a nonprofit organization that anyone can join free of charge. Members receive a directory of English speaking IAMAT doctors on call 24 hours a day, and are entitled to services at a set rate.
United States 417 Center St., Lewiston, New York 14092, tel 716/754-4883
Canada 1287 St. Claire Ave., W. Toronto M6E 1B9, tel 416/652-0137

HOTELS & RESTAURANTS

Spain has a wide variety of accommodations, ranging from the humblest of *fondas* or *casas de huéspedes* (guesthouses) to luxurious five-star hotels. A new interest in the countryside is reflected in the number of *casas rurales* (country houses) that have opened their doors in recent years. Located in some of the most beautiful and wild spots in Spain, they may be farm houses, country cottages, or restored palaces, and offer outdoor activities such as horseback riding, hiking, and bicycling. Facilities are reflected in prices, and in cheaper hotels you may not have a private bath. If in doubt check when making your reservation.

HOTELS

A number of hotels offer *media pensión* (includes breakfast and dinner) or *pensión completa* (includes lunch as well) at a competitive price. Inquire upon reservation or arrival. Spain is a noisy country and peace and quiet can be hard to come by. When reserving a room, mention that you would like one away from likely noise.

Paradors

Unique to Spain are the paradors, the nationally owned chain of hotels, some in historic and beautiful buildings, often in national parks or other places of scenic interest.

Grading system

Spanish hotels are officially graded according to a star system of one to five, five being top of the range. *Hostales* or *pensiones* have a different system of one to three stars. Standards may vary somewhat from region to region as the autonomous governments are responsible for their own classifications.

Some of the hotels in this guide fall out of the star rating system—this includes the *casa rurales* and *posadas*.

The following is a selection of hotels throughout the country, listed by location, price, then in alphabetical order. Hotels that are historically, architecturally, or aesthetically interesting have been chosen wherever possible. Note that unless otherwise stated:
• Breakfast is not included in the price.
• The hotel has a restaurant. If the hotel restaurant is

particularly good, a description is included.
• All hotels allow smoking in rooms and communal areas. Non-smoking areas are very rare in hotels and restaurants.
• Price categories are given only as guidance and do not take into account seasonal variations.
• The 7 percent I.V.A (Value Added Tax) is not included in the price categories.
• Prices are for a double room.

In high season always try to book in advance. You may be asked for a deposit or credit card number.

Credit & debit cards

Many hotels accept all major cards. Smaller ones may only accept some, as shown in their entry. Abbreviations used are: AE (American Express), DC (Diners Club), MC (Mastercard), and V (Visa).

Hotel chains & groups

www.solmelia.es (reservations: 00 34 902 14 44 44)
www.parador.es (reservations: 00 34 91 516 66 66)
www.nh-hoteles.es (reservations: 00 34 902 11 51 16)
www.husa.es (reservations: 00 34 902 10 07 10)

Hotel groups or chains often have special offers, for example five nights in selected paradors at a fixed price that works out one-third cheaper than the normal price. Ask your travel agent or the hotels themselves.

RESTAURANTS

By law, all restaurants have to provide a *menú del día* (starter,

main course, dessert, and a drink), an economical option that is popular but it is usually offered only for lunch. More upscale restaurants may have a *menú degustación* (taster menu) that allows you to try small portions of several courses, including desserts. The price categories in the guide are for a meal à la carte, excluding wine. Some restaurants close on public holidays. Check before you go.

CAFÉS & BARS

Bars and cafés play a central role in Spanish social life. They open early in the morning and close late at night. It is common to have a *tapa* (a snack that can be anything from a small plate of olives or almonds to a tiny bowl of stew) with your beer or wine.
L= lunch D = dinner

IN & AROUND MADRID

🏨 PALACE
$$$$$ ★★★★★
PLAZA DE LAS CORTES 7
TEL 91 360 80 00
FAX 91 360 81 00
Inaugurated by King Alfonso XIII in 1912, the Palace has sumptuous reception and

main rooms, with period furniture, chandeliers, and tapestries. An enormous stained-glass cupola in one of the French-style salons is a distinguished feature of this palace-hotel. Bedrooms are small, but interior furnishings and bathrooms are impressive.

🛏 440 🅿 ⇄ ❄ 🏋
💳 All major cards

🏨 RITZ
$$$$$ ★★★★★
PLAZA DE LA LEALTAD 5
TEL 91 521 28 57
FAX 91 532 87 76
E-MAIL reservas@ritz.es
Purpose-built in 1910 by King Alfonso XIII, who on the brink of his marriage to Queen Victoria's granddaughter realized that there wasn't a hotel in Madrid grand enough for his guests. The hotel is crammed full of beautiful antiques and elegant chand-eliers, and is surrounded by luscious gardens.

🛏 158 🅿 ⇄ ❄ 🏋
💳 All major cards

🏨 VILLA MAGNA
🍴 **$$$$$** ★★★★★
PASEO CASTELLANA 22
TEL 91 587 12 34
FAX 91 431 22 86
The modern facade contrasts with the Charles IV-style interiors and 18th-century antiques. The rooms are beautifully decorated with plants in the bathrooms. It also has two fine restaurants. The walnut-paneled Berceo specializes in fish. The Tse-Yang serves the highest quality Chinese cuisine (Chinese mushrooms tossed in oyster sauce, Peking-style duck) in the capital, in an elegant room. The hotel is surrounded by wonderful gardens and there is a terrace to dine on in summer.

🛏 164 🚇 Núñez de Balboa
🅿 ⇄ ❄ 🏋 💳 All major cards

🏨 SANTO MAURO
🍴
Going to the island of A Toxa uilt in neoclassic style by the Duke of Santo Mauro in 1894, this palace has interiors by Josep Joanpere, combining the original cornices and Italian marble fireplaces with contem-porary furniture and textiles. No two rooms are the same. An intriguing feature is the amazing basement pool with columns and vaulted ceilings. Belagua, the hotel's restaurant occupies the old library, still lined with books. A modern, Basque-Navarrese influenced cuisine produces dishes such as scallop and spider crab carpaccio with vegetable tempura, monkfish with cuttle-fish and mango tagliatelle, and for dessert, chocolate mousse with caramelized banana.

$$$$ ★★★★★
ZURBANO 36
TEL 91 319 69 00
FAX 91 308 54 77
E-MAIL santomauro@itelco.es

🛏 37 🍴 56 🚇 Gregorio Marañón 🅿 ⇄ ❄
🏋 💳 AE, DC, V

🏨 VILLA REAL
A modern hotel in an ideal location, built to blend in with its older surroundings, Inside, the reception, salons and bedrooms are all exquisitely decorated, in the French style. Wonderful modern and antique sculptures, paintings, tapestries, and other art, include a collection of third-century Roman mosaics. Rooms have sitting areas, mahogany furniture, and bathrooms with Carrara marble. Suites have balconies, spa-baths, and individual saunas.

$$$$ ★★★★★
PLAZA DE LAS CORTES 10
TEL 91 420 37 67
FAX 91 420 25 47
E-MAIL info@derbyhotels.es
www.derbyhotels.es

🛏 120 🅿 ⇄ ❄ 💳 All major cards

🏨 SUECIA
$$$ ★★★★
MARQUÉS DE CASA RIERA 4
TEL 91 531 69 00
FAX 91 521 71 41
E-MAIL hotelsuecia@genio.infor.es
Right next door to the stylish and old-fashioned Círculo de Bellas Artes, this hotel is a modern building with airy rooms and modern art on the walls. Two restaurants.

🛏 128 ⇄ ❄ 💳 All major cards

🏨 TRYP AMBASSADOR
$$$ ★★★★
CUESTA DE SANTO DOMINGO 5
TEL 91 541 67 00
FAX 91 559 10 40
A 19th-century palace that became a hotel in 1991. Right in the heart of historic Madrid, near the Royal Palace, it retains some of the original features, such as the sweeping staircase and front door. The elegant rooms are spacious with mahogany furniture.

🛏 159 🅿 ⇄ ❄ 💳 All major cards

🏨 INGLES
$$ ★★★
ECHEGARAY 8
TEL 91 4 29 65 51
FAX 91 420 24 23
Virginia Woolf and other writers and artists of her time stayed at this hotel. No frills but very well situated near Plaza Santa Ana and Puerta del Sol. No restaurant.

🛏 58 🅿 ⇄ 💳 All major cards

🏨 LIABENY
$$ ★★★★
SALUD 3
TEL 91 531 90 00 OR
91 531 46 09
FAX 91 532 74 21
E-MAIL liabeny@apunte.es
Large and modern, the Liabeny is situated two minutes from Puerta del Sol and Gran Vía. It has marble bathrooms and all the facilities of a four-star hotel.

HOTELS & RESTAURANTS

[i] 222 [P] [elevator] [S] [S]All major cards

🏨 PARIS
$$ ★★
ALCALÁ 2
TEL 91 521 64 96
FAX 91 531 01 88
A charming, old-fashioned establishment, with a dark wooden-paneled reception, right on the corner of Puerta del Sol. The rooms are spacious and airy. Good value.
[i] 120 [elevator] [S]All major cards

🏨 REGINA
$$ ★★★
ALCALÁ 19
TEL 91 521 47 25
FAX 91 522 40 88
An unassuming historical building within walking distance of many of Madrid's sights. Spacious rooms for the tired sightseer. No restaurant.
[i] 142 [elevator] [S] [S]All major cards

🏨 LA RESIDENCIA DE EL VISO
$$ ★★★
NERVIÓN 8
TEL 91 564 03 70
FAX 91 564 19 65
E-MAIL elviso@estanciases.es
A very small, intimate hotel in a smart part of town. It occupies a 1930s mansion house and the best rooms look onto a lovely interior courtyard. Colorful rooms. Very personalized service.
[i] 12 [elevator] [S] [S]All major cards

🏨 TRYP REINA VICTORIA
$$ ★★★★
PLAZA DE SANTA ANA 14
TEL 91 531 45 00
FAX 91 522 03 07
Once home to Count Teba, this central hotel has a spectacular facade. It was at one time popular with bullfighters and writers, including Ernest Hemingway. Since renovation the hotel has gone upscale. The best rooms look onto the Plaza Santa Ana.

[i] 195 [P] [elevator] [S] [S]All major cards

🏨 CARLOS V
$ ★★★
MAESTRO VITORIA 5
TEL 91 531 41 00
FAX 91 531 37 61
E-MAIL recepcion@hotelcarlosv.com
www.hotelcarlosv.com
On one of the pedestrian streets, two minutes walk from the Puerta del Sol, the Carlos V has an unusual art nouveau entrance. Rooms are large and simply decorated with stucco ceilings. Ask for one with a balcony. The guest lounge also has stucco ceilings and crystal chandeliers. No restaurant.
[i] 67 [P] [elevator] [S] [S]All major cards

🍴 JOCKEY
$$$$$
AMADOR DE LOS RÍOS 6
TEL 91 319 10 03
Among the top restaurants in Spain, Jockey has elegant, old fashioned decor of wooden paneling and racing prints. Start with the house aperitif, Gin Jockey. Specialties at this one-Michelin-star establishment include the excellent *langostinos crudos al caviar con crema fresca* (thinly sliced prawns, marinated and served with caviar, cream, and dill), *filetes de lenguado Cortés* (sole poached in white wine), beef fillets filled with spinach, and fresh cheese with homemade tagliatelle. Excellent selection of wines and ports.
[seats] 100 [metro] Colón [P] [S] [S]All major cards

🍴 EL AMPARO
$$$
PUIGCERDÁ 8
TEL 91 431 64 56
A charming restaurant offering interesting and adventurous modern cuisine. Dishes that justify the one Michelin star include puff pastry layered with apple, smoked fish, and foie gras;

and prawns tossed with creamy corn-filled ravioli. Exquisite desserts. Excellent wine cellar.
[seats] 80 [metro] Serrano [closed] Closed Sat. L, Sun., Easter, & 1 week Aug. [S] [S]AE, MC, V

🍴 PRÍNCIPE DE VIANA
$$$
MANUEL DE FALLA 5
TEL 91 457 15 49
An old favorite offering Basque-Navarrese cuisine. Try these specialties: *menestra de verduras de Tudela* (asparagus stewed with other vegetables); monkfish with clams in a green sauce. The ham croquettes are famous. Reservations essential at this one-Michelin-star restaurant.
[seats] 80 [metro] Lima [P] [closed] Closed Sat. L, Sun., Easter, & Aug. [S] [S]All major cards

🍴 LA TERRAZA (CASINO DE MADRID)
$$$
ALCALÁ 15
TEL 91 521 87 00
A successful recent addition to Madrid's gastronomical stage with grand dining rooms and a fantastic summer terrace. The modern Mediterranean cuisine is a superb combination of aromas and textures. Dishes include: turron soup with artichokes and cèpes, and rabbit with courgette flowers, mascarpone cheese, and mango.
[seats] 65 [metro] Sevilla [P] [closed] Closed Sat. L & Sun. [S]All major cards

🍴 ZALACAÍN
$$$
ÁLVAREZ DE BAENA 4
TEL 91 561 48 40
Twenty years ago nouvelle cuisine came to Spain here. Some dishes are Zalacaín classics, others are more recent innovations. Specialties include cold cream of pumpkin with profiteroles, scallops and leeks in Albariño

wine, and grilled sea bass with green olive vinaigrette. The desserts are exquisite. One of Spain's top restaurants. Two Michelin stars. Reservations are essential.

🍴 100 🚇 Gregorio Marañón 🅿 🕐 Closed Sat. L, Sun., Easter, & Aug. ❄
🔺 All major cards

🍴 BOTÍN
$$
CUCHILLEROS 17
TEL 91 366 42 17
Reputed to be the oldest restaurant in the world—1725—and, according to Hemingway, the best. Takes up four floors of an old building. Recommended are traditional roast suckling pig and also the roast lamb.

🍴 260 🚇 Sol ❄ 🔺 All major cards

🍴 CASA LUCIO
$$
CAVA BAJA 35
TEL 91 365 32 52
Casa Lucio keeps the dishes simple and focuses on high quality ingredients. Try the Lucío potatoes, Madrid-style stewed tripe, and the rice pudding. The decor is in line with the traditional Castilian houses in the area.

🍴 120 🚇 La Latina 🕐 Closed Sat. L, & Aug. ❄
🔺 All major cards

🍴 ENTRE SUSPIRO Y SUSPIRO
$$
CAÑOS DEL PERAL 3
TEL 91 542 06 44
Good Mexican food is hard to find in Spain, but this small restaurant, cheerfully decorated in pinks and oranges, is a must for aficionados of Mexican cuisine. The corn quesadillas filled with *cuitlacoche* (corn mushrooms) and jalapeño chilies are very tasty, as is the *ensalada mandinga* (prawn, mango, onion, and coriander salad). Choose from the four hundred different tequilas.

🍴 65 🚇 Santo Domingo 🅿 🕐 Closed Sat. L. & Sun. ❄ 🔺 All major cards

🍴 NODO
$$
VELÁZQUEZ 150
TEL 91 564 40 44
The Japanese-Mediterranean cuisine here is so popular that you have to reserve weeks in advance. The red tuna is excellent. Try the tuna *tataki* with garlic, or to sample various dishes go for the "bandeja nodo-box."

🍴 130 🚇 República Argentina 🔺 All major cards

🍴 EL OLIVO
$$
GENERAL GALLEGOS 1
TEL 91 359 15 35
The French chef at this one-Michelin-star restaurant vigorously defends olive oil and Mediterranean cuisine. Various olive oils are served, and these are also sold at the shop next door, La Oleoteca. Specialties include marinated sardines on a bed of aubergine caviar, and warm lobster salad with herb vinaigrette. Outstanding desserts.

🍴 80 🚇 Cuzco 🕐 Closed Sun., Mon., & 2 weeks Aug. ❄ 🔺 All major cards

🍴 TEATRIZ
$$
HERMOSILLA 15
TEL 91 577 53 79
E-MAIL bgarcia@mail.vips.es
An old theater remodeled by architect and designer Philippe Stark, this is an unusual place to dine with lots of decorative features. Try the fettuccine with prawns and artichoke sauce, or just go for a drink at the bar.

🍴 70 🚇 Serrano 🅿 🕐 Closed Aug. ❄ 🔺 All major cards

🍴 TERRAZA EL SUEÑO
$$
MUSEO THYSSEN-BORNEMISZA
PASEO DEL PRADO 8

TEL 91 429 27 32
In summer the museum's garden-terrace full of palms and magnolias becomes a restaurant. Minimum lighting and lots of candles provide an enchanting setting. Excellent modern Mediterranean cuisine: lobster-filled ravioli with truffle puree; fresh tuna with cauliflower cream. Dinner gives you free entry to the current temporary exhibition open until midnight. Reservations are essential.

🍴 30 🚇 Banco de España 🕐 Closed Oct.–May & Sun.–Mon. June–Sept. 🔺 All major cards

🍴 LA TRAINERA
$$
LAGASCA 60
TEL 91 576 05 75
A long-established informal establishment with the best seafood in Madrid, recognized by one Michelin star. Dishes are kept simple, generally either grilled or cooked on the hotplate. Many order the *salpicón de marisco* (various types of shellfish to share). You could also have delicious grilled turbot or sole. Ham is the only meat on the menu. Wines include Albariño.

🍴 240 🚇 Serrano 🅿 🕐 Closed Sun. & Aug. ❄ 🔺 All major cards

🍴 LA BIOTIKA
$
AMOR DE DIOS 3
TEL 91 429 07 80
A cozy vegetarian place that makes delicious salads, soups and tofu-based dishes. Near Plaza Santa Ana.

🍴 25 🚇 Antón Martin 🔺 No credit cards

🍴 CASA MINGO
$
PASEO DE LA FLORIDA 34
TEL 91 547 79 18
A large tavern-style restaurant beneath the Príncipe Pio train station, with long wooden tables where everyone sits together—a noisy affair. Three

things are on the menu: roast chicken, salad, and sausages, and plenty of cider. Tables are set up outside in summer. No reservations so arrive early.
🍴 100 🚇 Príncipe Pío ♿

🍴 "CUANDO SALÍ DE CUBA"
$
TERNERA 4
TEL 91 522 93 18
Hemingway's favorite place in the late fifties (when it was El Callejon). Serves good, unpretentious Cuban food and offers a very reasonable lunch menu.
🍴 40 🚇 Callao 🅿
🕐 Closed Sun. D, & Mon.
♿ 💳 MC, V

🍴 LA PAMPA
$
AMPARO 61
TEL 91 528 04 49
Rustic style decor at this Argentine restaurant in the rather run-down area of Lavapies. Offers Argentine cuts of meat and pasta dishes. The house special is *bife La Pampa* (a large steak, fried eggs, tomatoes, and peas). On weekends you can tango after dinner.
🍴 30 🚇 Lavapies
🕐 Closed Sun. ♿ 💳 All major cards

🍴 REINA SOFÍA
$
SANTA ISABEL 52
TEL 91 467 50 62
Basement coffee bar and restaurant but with windows and natural light. Unusually, the restaurant is non-smoking.
🍴 45 🚇 Atocha 🕐 same hours as museum ♿

🍴 SAMARKANDA
$
GLORIETA DE CARLOS V
TERMINAL DEL AVE
TEL 91 530 97 46
Come here for the amazing location in the old Atocha train station, transformed into a tropical garden. The international cuisine includes

caramelized duck crepes. You could also just go for a coffee break between museums.
🍴 45 🚇 Atocha–Renfe 🅿
💳 AE, MC, V

🍴 TABERNA CARMENCITA
$
LIBERTAD 16
TEL 91 531 66 12
This attractive *taberna* opened in 1850 and García Lorca, Dalí, and Buñuel have all come here. The decor is probably still much the same. Good cooking using quality produce and very reasonable prices. Baby broad beans and clams (in season) are delicious.
🍴 40 🚇 Chueca
🕐 Closed Sat. L & Sun. ♿
💳 All major cards

🍴 THYSSEN-BORNEMISZA
$
PASEO DEL PRADO 8
TEL 91 369 01 51
The coffee bar is in the basement but it's more modern and appealing than the Prado's gloomy one.
🍴 40 🚇 Banco de España
🕐 Closed Mondays (Open Sat. & Sun.) ♿

🍴 LA VACA VERÓNICA
$
MORATÍN 38
TEL 91 429 78 27
A small informal place with antique chandeliers and bright yellow walls covered with vivid art work. Short menu of salads, pastas, meats, and fish—the spinach, mushroom, and pancetta salad is worth trying. Tasty homemade desserts such as white chocolate tart with fresh raspberries. Reservations.
🍴 30 🚇 Banco de España
🕐 Closed Sat. L & Sun. ♿
💳 All major cards

ARANJUEZ 28300

🍴 CASA JOSÉ
$$
ABASTOS 32

TEL 918 91 14 88
A small cozy restaurant with imaginative and seasonally based cuisine that has won it one Michelin star. Specials include artichoke hearts glazed with sea urchin eggs, and roe deer chops in a cinnamon and caraway batter.
🍴 50 🕐 Closed Sun. D, Mon., 1 week July, & 3 weeks Aug. ♿ 💳 All major cards

🍴 PALACIO DE OSUNA
$$
PRÍNCIPE 21
TEL 918 92 42 15
In a wing of the Duke of Osuna's old palace down by the river, an unpretentious place. Choose from lamb or suckling pig roasted in a wood fired oven, and don't miss the Aranjuez asparagus in season.
🍴 350 🅿 🕐 Closed Sun. D ♿ 💳 All major cards

CHINCHÓN 28370

🏨 PARADOR DE CHINCHÓN
$$ ★★★★
AVENIDA GENERALÍSIMO 1
TEL 918 94 08 36
FAX 918 94 09 08
E-MAIL chinchon@parador.es
A 17th-century monastery

founded by Augustinian monks, very close to the Plaza Mayor. The cloister encloses a pretty landscaped garden with cypresses and hedges. Rooms are decorated in the traditional Castilian style of dark wood and tiles; some have Renaissance murals.

🛏 38 P 🟦 🟦 🟦
🟦 All major cards

🍴 MESÓN DE LA VIRREINA
$$
PLAZA MAYOR 28
TEL 918 94 00 15
One of several restaurants on a picturesque plaza that doubles as a bullring. Staples are filling Castilian dishes such as roast lamb or suckling pig. Try the local anise for which Chinchón is famous. Reserve if you want a table on one of the wooden balconies overlooking the plaza.

🍽 50 P No parking on weekends 🟦 🟦 All major cards

SAN LORENZO DE EL ESCORIAL 28200

🏨 BOTÁNICO
$ $ ★★★
TIMOTEO PADRÓS 16
TEL 918 90 78 79
FAX 918 90 81 58
E-MAIL botanico@itelco.es
A beautifully restored old stately mansion set in gardens away from the bustle of the town. A peaceful place to spend the night.

🛏 20 P 🟦 🟦 🟦 All major cards

🏨 MIRANDA SUIZO
$ ★★★
FLORIDABLANCA 18
TEL 918 90 47 11
FAX 918 90 43 58
One of many Victorian buildings in the town. The interiors are functional and well kept You can have meals in the hotel's wonderful *modernista* café.

🛏 52 🟦 🟦 🟦 All major cards

NORTHWEST SPAIN

GALICIA

CAMBADOS 36630

🏨🍴 PARADOR DE CAMBADOS
$ ★★★
PASEO DE LA CALZADA S/N
TEL 986 54 22 50
FAX 986 54 20 68
E-MAIL cambados@parador.es
Built as a fortress in the 14th century with some exquisite Mudejar carving. Beautifully decorated rooms have views of the pretty interior patio and garden or out across the countryside. The restaurant serves local dishes such as *empanada de berberechos* (cockle pie); try the local Albariño wine. Tennis.

🛏 63 🍽 130 P 🟦 🟦
🟦 All major cards

A CORUÑA (LA CORUÑA) 15000

🏨🍴 ATLÁNTICO
$$ ★★★★
JARDINES DE MÉNDEZ NÚÑEZ
TEL 981 22 65 00
FAX 981 20 10 71
E-MAIL nh@nh-hoteles.es
A renovated 1960s building in the heart of the old town with views onto the port. Spacious rooms. The hotel has no restaurant, but the adjacent casino (free entry for guests) does. Recommended dishes include crepes filled with crab and hake with baby eel cooked in the local white wine.

🛏 198 P 🟦 🟦 🟦 All major cards
Casino del Atlántico 🍽 100
🕐 Closed Sun. 🟦 🟦 V

🏨 FINISTERRE
$$ ★★★★
PASEO DEL PARROTE 2
TEL 981 20 54 00/04
FAX 981 20 84 62
A distinguished building, situated on the edge of the old town on the port. Wonderful views and a large

---

sports complex with four heated seawater swimming pools, tennis, table tennis, basketball courts, and a gym.

🛏 127 P 🟦 🟦 🟦 🟥
🟦 All major cards

🍴 CASA PARDO
$$
NOVOA SANTOS 15
TEL 981 28 00 21
Near the port, this impeccably decorated restaurant has wooden furnishings. It chooses ingredients carefully as befits its one-Michelin-star status. Try the *rape a la ajada gallega* (monkfish with a Galician sauce made by beating garlic, paprika, and oil together), scallops with ham and onion sauce, and game in season.

🍽 60 P 🕐 Closed Sun. & 2 weeks June 🟦 🟦 All major cards

🍴 LA PENELA
$
PLAZA MARÍA PITA 12
TEL 981 20 92 00
Housed in one of the finest *modernista* buildings in La Coruña, this elegantly decorated place offers traditional Galician dishes with a touch of class. Try the stuffed mussels, roast beef, or monkfish stew. Excellent value.

🍽 110 🕐 Closed Sun. 🟦
🟦 AE, MC, V

NOIA (NOYA) 15200

🍴 CEBOLEIRO
$$
RÚA GALICIA 15
TEL 981 82 44 97
Good home-style cooking in a quiet, friendly atmosphere at this restaurant with rooms (14 bedrooms).

🍽 60 🟦 🟦 All major cards

OURENSE (ORENSE) 32000

🏨 ARNOIA
$ ★★★
VILA TERMAL 1
ARNOIA (2 MILES/3 KM FROM

RIBADAVIA, 19 MILES/30 KM W.
OF OURENSE)
TEL 988 49 24 00
FAX 988 49 24 22
A spa hotel in one of the
prettiest spots along the Miño
River. All types of health
treatments are available, along
with outdoor sports including
sailing and tennis.
🛏 30 🅿 🛗 🏊 🍸
🃏 All major cards

🏨 BARCELONA
$ ★
AVENIDA PONTEVEDRA 11
TEL 988 22 08 00
FAX 988 22 08 00
This restored historic building
faces a lovely treelined square
in the heart of the old town.
The rooms have high ceilings
and double windows with
balconies. Ask for a room with
a bathroom. No restaurant.
🛏 35 🅿 🛗 🃏 MC, V

🏨 ZARAMPALLO
🍽 $ ★
HERMANOS VILLAR 19
TEL/FAX 988 23 08 19 OR
988 23 00 08
An old house that has been
completely modernized inside
and decorated very elegantly.
All the rooms look onto
pedestrianized streets. The
restaurant's contemporary
Galician cuisine pays particular
attention to vegetables.
🛏 14 🍴 50 🕐 Closed Sun.
D 🛗 🃏 All major cards

🍽 RESTAURANTE
MARTÍN FIERRO
$
SÁENZ DÍEZ 17
TEL 988 37 26 43
The owner lived many years
in Argentina before returning
to Ourense to set up this
restaurant. The menu offers
chargrilled Argentine cuts of
meat and Galician seafood.
Specialties include monkfish in
asparagus sauce, beef entrecôte cooked in Ribeiro wine,
and chestnut tart for dessert.
🍴 70 🅿 🕐 Closed Sun.
🛗 🃏 All major cards

PONTEVEDRA 36000

🏨 PARADOR DE
🍽 PONTEVEDRA
$ ★★★
BARÓN 19
TEL 986 85 58 00
FAX 986 85 21 95
E-MAIL pontevedra@parador.es
A 16th-century renaissance
palace in the historic heart of
Pontevedra. The elegant
interior complements the
grand stone facade with
antiques and a hand carved
stone staircase. Bedrooms
look onto a tranquil rose
garden. The dining room has
large antique mirrors, candel-
abras, and beautiful drapes.
🛏 47 🍴 140 🅿 🛗
🃏 All major cards

🏨 RUAS
$ ★★
PADRE SARMIENTO 20
TEL 986 84 64 16
FAX 986 84 64 11
Most of Pontevedra's hotels
are in the commercial part of
the town, but Ruas is an
exception. It has simple quiet
rooms looking onto a lovely
old square (may be noisy on
weekends), opposite the
museum. No restaurant.
🛏 18 🅿 🛗 🃏 All major
cards

🍽 CASA SOLLA
$$
AVENIDA SINEIRO 7
SAN SALVADOR DE POYO (ON
ROAD TO LA TOJA: 2 KM)
TEL 986 87 28 84
A mile or so outside Ponte-
vedra this garden restaurant
boasts one Michelin star.
Typical dishes are hake with
rosemary, pisto, and small red
peppers; filet mignon in red
wine; and hot apple tart with
black pepper ice cream.
🍴 200 🅿 🕐 Closed
Thurs. & Sun. evenings & 2
weeks Christmas 🛗 🃏 All
major cards

🍽 DOÑA ANTONIA
$$
SOPORTALES DE LA HERRERÍA

4, 1ST FLOOR
TEL 986 84 72 74
Galician cuisine using the
freshest regional produce. The
dining room looks onto the
lovely Plaza de la Herrería.
🍴 35 🕐 Closed Sun. 🛗
🃏 All major cards

SANTIAGO DE
COMPOSTELA 15700

SOMETHING
SPECIAL

🏨 PARADOR HOSTAL
🍽 DE LOS REYES
CATÓLICOS
Standing on Santiago's most
impressive square by the
cathedral, this parador is one of
the great hotels of the world. In
1499 Ferdinand and Isabella
built it as a hostel for pilgrims to
the shrine of St. James. It still
boasts an exquisite carved doorway, huge reception areas
looking into the four superb
courtyards, and a Gothic chapel.
Rooms, many with canopied
beds, have tapestries and
antiques. Terrace looking onto
the cathedral. Reserve well ahead.
$$$ ★★★★★
PLAZA DEL OBRADOIRO 1
TEL 981 58 22 00
FAX 981 56 30 94
E-MAIL santiago@parador.es
🛏 126 🅿 🛗 🃏 All
major cards

🏨 MELIÁ ARAGUANEY
$$$ ★★★★★
ALFREDO BRAÑAS 5
TEL 981 59 59 00
FAX 981 59 02 87
E-MAIL melia@araguaney.com
A modern building in the
commercial area of Santiago,
ten minutes walk from the
cathedral. The hotel has a
disco, a tavern, and a shopping
center.
🛏 80 🅿 🛗 🛗 🏊 🍸
🃏 All major cards

🏨 COMPOSTELA
$$ ★★★★
HÓRREO 1
TEL 981 58 57 00
FAX 981 58 52 90

Reproduction antiques adorn the spacious rooms in this historic building. On the corner of two main roads, so be sure to ask for one of the quieter rooms. No restaurant.
🛈 99 ⇄ 🚭 All major cards

🏨 VIRXE DA CERCA
$$ ★★★
VIRXE DA CERCA 27
TEL 981 56 93 50
FAX 981 58 69 25
E-MAIL pousadas@.jet.es
This renovated 18th-century building opened as a hotel in July 1999. Rooms in the old wing have rustic furniture, and sitting areas. The modern wing has more spacious rooms. Both wings look onto the garden. Breakfast included.
🛈 37 🅿 🚭 🚭 All major cards

🍴 ANEXO VILAS
$$
AVENIDA DE VILLAGARCÍA 21
TEL 981 59 86 37
The owner, Moncho Vilas, is keen to promote Galician fare and selects quality local produce. His traditional dishes include grilled sea bass with clams, fillet steak cooked in Oporto sherry, and hake a al gallega (with a paprika sauce).
🍽 80 🚭 🚭 All major cards

🍴 DON GAIFEROS
$$
RÚA NOVA 23
TEL 981 58 38 94
An old-fashioned restaurant in the heart of Santiago offering traditional Galician cuisine and international dishes. Try the griddled scallops, veal a la gallega (with a paprika sauce), and a hot chocolate ice cream for dessert.
🍽 48 🕐 Closed Sun. & Christmas–New Year 🚭 All major cards

🍴 TOÑI VICENTE
$$
ROSALÍA DE CASTRO 24
TEL 981 59 41 00

Toñi Vicente has won critical acclaim and one Michelin star for his cuisine. The innovative menu has a Galician flavor. Recommended are sea bass salad, grilled tuna on a bed of black olives and tomatoes.
🍽 50 🕐 Closed Sun., 3 weeks Jan., & 1 week Aug.
🚭 🚭 All major cards

🍴 LA TACITA D'JUAN
$
HÓRREO 31
TEL 981 56 20 41
This is the busiest place in town, providing hearty Galician food and a good selection of wines of the region. Specials include seafood filled crepes, conger eel pie, and ox entrecôte.
🍽 80 🕐 Closed Sun. & 2 weeks Aug. 🅿 🚭 🚭 AE, MC, V

A TOXA (ISLA DE LA TOJA-O GROVE) 36991

SOMETHING SPECIAL

🏨 GRAN HOTEL LA
🍴 TOJA
Going to the island of A Toxa (La Toja) is like going back in time. The original hotel building was constructed in 1907, and is still a busy place in summer though somewhat dated. This is a very luxurious hotel right on the waterfront and with lavishly decorated interiors. The hotel has access to a sports complex with tennis courts, golf course (9 holes), thermal baths, riding, and sailing.
$$$ ★★★★★
TEL 986 73 00 25
FAX 986 73 00 26
🛈 198 🍽 500 🅿 ⇄
🏊 🏋 🚭 All major cards

🏨 HOTEL LOUXO
🍴 $ ★★★★
TEL 986 73 02 00
FAX 986 73 27 91
Also on the waterfront, but less spectacular than the Gran, the Louxo is next to

the casino. Sumptuous rooms. Tennis courts, golf course (9 holes), and sailing.
🛈 112 🍽 350 🅿 ⇄
🏊 🚭 All major cards

TUI 36700

🍴 O CABALO FURADO
$
PLAZA GENERALÍSIMO S/N
TEL 986 60 12 15
This restaurant serves excellent fresh fish and shellfish in its simply decorated dining room or, in summer, a small patio. Try the mixed fish cooked on a hot plate, and for dessert, a walnut and chocolate cake. (The tapas bar of the same name is run by the owner's brother).
🍽 60 🕐 Closed Sun. July–Oct., Sun. D, & Mon. Nov.–June, Christmas–early Jan., & 2 weeks June 🚭 AE, MC, V

ASTURIAS & CANTABRIA

CASTRO-URDIALES 39700

🍴 MESÓN EL MARINERO
$$
CORRERÍA 23 - BAJO
TEL 942 86 00 05
With a fantastic array of tapas and an upstairs dining room overlooking the little port, this restaurant is a find. Choose from the selection of fresh fish cooked in the oven or in salt.
🍽 140 🚭 🚭 MC, V

COSTA VERDE

🏨 AULTRE NARAY
$ ★★★
PERUYES 33547
(OFF CTRA N-634, KM 335)
TEL 985 84 08 08
FAX 985 84 08 48
E-MAIL aultre@hpr2.es
A large 19th-century house in a beautiful spot looking out onto the mountains. The decor combines traditional and modern styles.
🛈 14 🅿 🚭 All major cards

🏨 CASA CONSUELO
🍴 $ ★★

CTRA. N-634, KM 511
OTUR (5 KM FROM LUARCA)
TEL 985 47 07 67
FAX 985 64 16 42

A family-run hotel that is particularly known for its restaurant. The traditional Asturian dishes depend on seasonal produce. Very fresh fish and great desserts.

🛏 36 🪑 50 🅿 🕐 Closed Mon. except July & Aug 🛗
🔲 All major cards

🏨 LA CASONA DE PIO
🍴 $ ★★

RIOFRIO 3, CUDILLERO 33150
TEL 985 59 15 12
FAX 985 59 15 19

Right in the town center in a restored stone house, this hotel offers a comfortable stay in rustic style rooms. The restaurant serves locally caught fish including the Cudillero specialty, *curadillo* (dogfish).

🛏 11 🪑 50 🔲 MC, V
🛏 127 🅿 🛗 🕐 🌊 🔳
🔲 All major cards

LOS OSCOS

🏨 CASA DE ALDEA "CABEZA DA VILA"
$

SAN MARTIN DE OSCOS 33777
TEL 985 62 60 19
FAX 985 62 61 34

An atmospheric 17th-century farmhouse restored by descendants of the original owners, and almost like a museum. Large rooms furnished with antiques. No television in rooms.

🛏 5 🅿 🔲 V

🏨 CASA RODIL
🍴 $ ★

LAS POCEIRAS
2 KM FROM SANTA EULALIA DE OSCOS 33776 (CRTA. VEGADEO)
TEL 985 62 61 85

Surrounded by green fields and mountains this idyllically sited hotel has simple rooms with large bathrooms. Delicious down-to-earth

cooking uses locally produced ingredients. No television.

🛏 4 🅿 🔲 MC, V

🏨 LA RECTORAL
🍴 $ ★★★★

TARAMUNDI 33775
TEL 985 64 67 60/7
FAX 985 64 67 77

Typical of Spain's new wave of rural tourism, this hotel is set in beautiful countryside and offers lots of activities. The building is an 18th-century rectory with mountain views.

🛏 18 🪑 40 🅿 🔳 🌊
🔳 🔲 AE, MC, V

OVIEDO 33000

🏨 DE LA RECONQUISTA
$$$ ★★★★★

GIL DE JAZ 16
TEL 985 24 11 00
FAX 985 24 11 66
E-MAIL reconquista@hoteldelareconquista.com

Originally built as an orphanage in the 18th century, this elegant building has an arcaded courtyard. Spacious, modern rooms.

🛏 142 🅿 🛗 🔳 🔲 All major cards

🍴 GATO NEGRO
$

MON, 5–TRASCORRALES 22
TEL 985 21 70 86

Watch the ritual pouring of cider from a great height at this *siderías* and enjoy a cider at the bar with a few *raciónes*, or have a meal of *cochinillo al horno* (suckling pig) or hake cooked in cider.

🪑 90 🕐 Closed Mon. 🔲
🔳 🍴 AE, V

PICOS DE EUROPA

🏨 HOTEL DEL OSO
🍴 $ ★★

COSGAYA 39539
CARRETERA DE POTES A FUENTE DÉ, KM 14
TEL 942 73 30 18
FAX 942 73 30 36
E-MAIL hoteldeloso@ wwwdivia.es

A hotel in the heart of the Picos de Europa beside the

Deva River. Warm and cozy rooms have wooden balconies. Hearty regional fare such as river trout and stews.

🛏 36 🪑 90 🅿 🕐 Closed 3 weeks Jan. & 2 weeks Feb.
🌊 🔲 D, MC, V

SANTANDER 39000

🏨 REAL
🍴

This imposing French style château was built by the Botín family for their royal guests. In a superb position overlooking the bay, the Real is surrounded by gardens. A vaulted ceiling graces the huge Royal Suite The restaurant, El Puntal, offers modern cuisine in distinguished rooms. Try lobster salad with avocado and mango, and grilled duck's liver with ginger and vodka.

$$$$ ★★★★★

PASEO DE PÉREZ GALDÓS 28
TEL 942 27 25 50
FAX 942 27 45 73
E-MAIL realsantander@husa.es
🛏 123 🪑 40 🅿 🛗 🔳
🔲 All major cards

🏨 RHIN
🍴 $$ ★★★★

AVENIDA REINA VICTORIA153
TEL 942 27 43 00
FAX 942 27 86 53
E-MAIL rhin@gruporhin.com

A classic hotel situated on El Sardinero beach. The rooms are light and spacious with traditional furnishings. The restaurant, La Cúpula, promotes modern Cantabrian cuisine: for example crystalized hake on crunchy skinned tomatoes, and black olive pâté. Elaborate desserts.

🛏 89 🪑 70 🛗 🔳
🔲 All major cards

🏨 CENTRAL
$ ★★★

GENERAL MOLA 5
TEL 942 22 24 00
FAX 942 36 38 29

Everything is blue from the facade to the beds in this central, family-run hotel. No restaurant.
🛏 41 🔁 ❄ 🏧 All major cards

🍴 DEL PUERTO
$$
HERNÁN CORTÉS 63
TEL 942 21 30 01
This traditional and reliable restaurant maintains a high standard and serves the best shellfish in Santander. The service is impeccable, and the bar has a wonderful selection of *raciónes* (similar to *tapas*, but larger portions).
🍽 150 ❄ 🏧 All major cards

SANTILLANA DEL MAR 39330

🏨 PARADOR DE SANTILLANA DEL MAR
$$ ★★★
PLAZA RAMÓN PELAYO 11
TEL 942 81 80 00
FAX 942 81 83 91
E-MAIL santillana@parador.es
An 18th-century mansion in the center of the town furnished with dark wooden pieces and floors, in a similar style to its original decor. The *parador* has expanded to include a new building across the plaza.
🛏 54 🅿 🔁 🏧 All major cards

🏨 ALTAMIRA
🍴 $ ★★★
CANTÓN 1
TEL 942 81 80 25
FAX 942 84 01 36
A former palace reconstructed in the 19th century and since extended into the next door building. Rooms are different shapes and sizes, all with wooden floors and exposed stone walls. The restaurant has a growing reputation for its game, cod, and rice dishes.
🛏 32 🍽 120 ❄ Restaurant only 🏧 All major cards

NORTHEAST SPAIN

EUSKADI & NAVARRA

BERGARA 20570

🏨 ORMAZABAL
$ ★★
BARRENKALE 11
TEL /FAX 94 376 36 50
In the center of Bergara, this 17th-century stone house is full of period furniture. Cheerful rooms have rather creaky floorboards. No restaurant.
🛏 16 🅿 🔁 🏧 All major cards

BILBO (BILBAO) 48000

🏨 LOPEZ DE HARO
🍴 $$$ ★★★★★
OBISPO ORUETA 2
TEL 94 423 55 00
FAX 94 423 45 00
Only five minutes walk from the Guggenheim, this remodeled 19th-century building has a classical English feel to its decor. Rooms are luxurious and quiet, and the hotel is unusual in having non-smoking ones. The restaurant, Club Naútico, serves both modern and classical cuisine. Sample the prawn tails tossed with artichokes. Wide choice of desserts.
🛏 49 🍽 60 🅿 🔁 ❄ 🏧 All major cards

🏨 CARLTON
$$ ★★★★
PLAZA FEDERICO MOYÚA 2
TEL 94 416 22 00
FAX 94 416 46 28
On one of the prettiest plazas, this elegant old hotel has hosted bullfighters and artists such as Hemingway and Orson Welles. It was the seat of the Republican Basque government during the Civil War. The hotel retains its charm despite renovations.
🛏 141 🅿 🔁 ❄ 🏧 All major cards

🏨 ITURRIENEA
$ ★★
SANTA MARÍA 14
TEL 94 416 15 00
FAX 94 415 89 29
In Bilbao's historic town, this old pension has appealing interior decor that matches the original facade colors. The rooms have large beds and artwork by local artists.
🛏 21 🏧 DC, MC, V

🍴 GORROTXA
$$
ALAMEDA URQUIJO 30
TEL 94 443 49 37
A Bilbao classic, with superb haute cuisine and traditional Basque recipes. Try the wild mushrooms with prawns and the beef carpaccio with a truffle vinaigrette.
🍽 85 🕐 Closed Sun., Easter, 1 week Aug., & 2 weeks Sept. ❄ 🏧 All major cards

🍴 GUGGENHEIM
$$
ABANDOIBARRA ETORBIDEA 2
TEL 94 423 93 33
Inside the museum itself. Try the *arroz de chipirones* (tiny squid cooked in their ink with rice) or one of the taster menus. Must reserve.
🍽 100 🅿 🕐 Closed Sun. & Mon. ❄ 🏧 AE, V

🍴 ZORTZIKO
$$
ALAMEDA DE MAZARREDO 17
TEL 94 423 97 43
E-MAIL zortziko@comunet.es
www.zortziko.es
Daniel García is one of the Basque region's top chefs. His extremely modern cuisine contrasts with this historic early 20th-century villa. Dishes include prawns with wild mushroom risotto and pigeon roasted in muscatel grape juice. Great wine list. This one-Michelin-star restaurant is close to the Guggenheim Museum.
🍽 120 🕐 Closed Sun., Mon., 1 week Aug., & 1 week Sept. ❄ 🏧 All major cards

---

🔲 Air-conditioning 🏊 Indoor/🏊 Outdoor swimming pool 🏋 Health club 🏧 Credit cards   KEY

HOTELS & RESTAURANTS

DONOSTIA (SAN SEBASTIÁN) 20000

SOMETHING SPECIAL

🏨 MARÍA CRISTINA

🍴 An old-fashioned, luxurious hotel, named after Queen María Cristina who opened it in 1912, now restored to its belle epoque glory. The bedrooms and salons overlook the Urúmea River and the sea, and have Oriental rugs, Carrara marble columns, and plants. The restaurant, Easo, is on the way up.

$$$$$ ★★★★★
OQUENDO I
TEL 94 342 49 00
FAX 94 342 39 14
E-MAIL hmc@sheraton.com
ⓘ 136 🅿 ⬍ 🄢 🄐 All major cards

🏨 DE LONDRES Y DE INGLATERRA

$$ ★★★★
ZUBIETA 2
TEL 94 342 69 89
FAX 94 342 00 31
E-MAIL hotellondres@nauta.es
Right opposite the Playa de la Concha this central belle epoque hotel has superb sea views. The casino is in the same building.
ⓘ 144 🅿 ⬍ 🄢 🄐 All major cards

SOMETHING SPECIAL

🍴 ARZAK

Possibly the best restaurant in Spain (three Michelin stars). Chef Juan Mari Arzak produces innovative cuisine that never loses sight of traditional Basque recipes. The entire menu is superb: for example prawns with pistachios and almonds. Reserve.

$$$$
ALTO DE MIRACRUZ 21
TEL 94 327 84 65
E-MAIL arzak@jet.es
🔲 80 🅿 🕐 Closed Sun. D, Mon., 2 weeks June, & 3 weeks Nov. 🄢 🄐 All major cards

🍴 UREPEL

$$
PASEO DE SALAMANCA 3
TEL 94 342 40 40
Very popular with San Sebastián's upper crust, this one-Michelin-star restaurant combines classic dishes with modern in a stylish way. Mainly fish, such as smoked cod with roasted vegetables.
🔲 60 🕐 Closed Sun., Tues. D, Easter, & 3 weeks July 🄐 All major cards

🍴 BODEGÓN ALEJANDRO

$
FERMÍN CALBETÓN 4
TEL 94 342 71 58
Modern cuisine using simple ingredients. You choose your own fixed-price, three-course menu for 2,900 pesetas.
🔲 75 🕐 Closed Sun., D, Mon., I week Dec. & I week Jan. 🄢 🄐 All major cards

🍴 RAMÓN ROTETA

$$
IRÚN I, VILLA AINARA
TEL 94 364 16 93
The Mediterranean cuisine here rates one Michelin star. Try the shellfish salad and the sea bass with pistachios.
🔲 350 🕐 Closed Sun. D, & Tues. (except summer) 🄐 All major cards

GASTEIZ (VITORIA) 01000

🏨 CIUDAD DE VITORIA

$$ ★★★★
PORTAL DE CASTILLA 8
TEL 94 514 11 00
FAX 94 514 36 16
E-MAIL
vitoria@hoteles-silken.com
Opened in 1993, the building looks like a 19th-century French hotel, but the modern interiors lack character. The bedrooms are spacious, and well protected from outside noise.
ⓘ 148 🅿 ⬍ 🄢 🄦 🄐 All major cards

🏨🍴 PARADOR DE ARGÓMANIZ

$$ ★★★
CARRETERA N-1, KM 363
TEL 94 529 32 00
FAX 94 529 32 87
E-MAIL argomaniz@parador.es
This old stone Renaissance palace is only 7.5 miles (12 km) from Vitoria and worth the trip if you want a peaceful, restful sleep. Spacious and light rooms with pine floorboards and balconies. Beautiful dining room.
ⓘ 53 🅿 ⬍ 🄢 🄐 All major cards

🍴 IKEA

$$
PORTAL DE CASTILLA 27
TEL 94 514 47 47
Traditional cuisine with innovative twists and a varied menu in a late Victorian mansion. Recommended dishes include prawn carpaccio with truffle oil and flakes of salt, and crispy pigs' trotters with Biscayan sauce.
🔲 80 🅿 🕐 Closed Sun. D, Mon., & 3 weeks Aug.–early Sept. 🄢 🄐 All major cards

---

KEY   🏨 Hotel   🍴 Restaurant   ⓘ No. of bedrooms   🔲 No. of seats   🄜 Metro   🅿 Parking   🕐 Closed   ⬍ Elevator

HONDARRIBIA (FUENTERRABÍA) 20280

PARADOR DE HONDARRIBIA
$$ ★★
PLAZA DE ARMAS 14
TEL 94 364 55 00
FAX 94 364 21 53
E-MAIL hondarribia@parador.es
In the old town, this fortified castle was built in the tenth century by the Navarrese King Sancho Abarca. The parador has made the most of its wonderful building, leaving the beautiful thick stone walls exposed, even in the bedrooms. Some rooms have terraces overlooking the sea and there is a medieval feel throughout. No restaurant.
36 P All major cards

IRUÑA (PAMPLONA) 31000

IRUÑA PALACE TRES REYES
$$$$ ★★★★
JARDINES DE LA TACONERA S/N
TEL 948 22 66 00
FAX 948 22 29 30
Luxurious surroundings in the center of town offering spa-baths, saunas, a hairdresser, squash courts, and golf.
170 P All major cards

MAISONNAVE
$$$ ★★★
NUEVA 20
TEL 948 22 26 00
FAX 948 22 01 66
E-MAIL informacion@hotelmaisonnave.es
www.hotelmaisonnave.es
The French founded this hotel 100 years ago and since then personalities such as Hemingway, Valle-Inclán, and Ava Gardner have stayed here. Art exhibitions and musical recitals in the salons.
138 P All major cards

JOSETXO
$$
PLAZA PRINCÍPE DE VIANA 1
TEL 948 22 20 97
FAX 948 22 41 57
A sober dining room is the setting for this classic one-Michelin-star establishment. Bull's meat is served here at the San Fermín festival. Try the warm goat's cheese salad and monkfish, clams, and prawn stew. Notable wine list.
125 Closed Sun. (except May) & Aug. All major cards

ORREAGO (RONCESVALLES) 31650

LA POSADA
$
CARRETERA DE FRANCIA, S/N
TEL/FAX 948 76 02 25
This restored 17th-century inn has been declared a historic monument. Simple, rooms and delicious home-style cooking.
18 P Closed Nov. DC, MC, V

TUDELA 31500

RESTAURANTE 33
$$
CAPUCHINOS 7
TEL 948 82 76 06
Traditional cuisine using an abundance of vegetables. Specials include artichokes filled with foie gras and bull's tail stuffed with vegetables.
130 Closed Sun. & 3 weeks Aug. AE, MC, V

LA RIOJA

HARO 26200

HOSPEDERÍA SEÑORÍO DE BRIÑAS
$ ★★★
TRAVESÍA DE LA CALLE REAL 3, BRIÑAS (3 MILES/5 KM FROM HARO)
TEL 941 30 39 84
FAX 941 30 43 45
E-MAIL hsbrinas@arrakis.es
Set among vineyards, this

grand 18th-century mansion is a lovely place. The interiors have been restored with flare, using frescoes and antiques. No restaurant.
14 Closed 2 weeks Dec.–Jan. MC, V

LOS AGUSTINOS
$ ★★★★
SAN AGUSTÍN 2
TEL 941 31 13 08
FAX 941 30 31 48
In a 14th-century monastery in the town center, this hotel has been beautifully restored.
60 P Closed Sun. All major cards

TERETE
$
LUCRECIA ARANA 17
TEL 941 31 00 23
A family-run establishment providing typical Riojan fare. The oven dates back to 1877 and specials include roast kid and vegetable stew.
40 Closed Sun. D, Mon., 2 weeks July, & 2 weeks Oct. V

LAGUARDIA 01300

CASTILLO EL COLLADO
$ ★★
PASEO EL COLLADO 1
TEL 941 12 12 00
FAX 941 60 08 78
This small castle dating from 1920 with an 18th-century chapel makes an enchanting little hotel. Imaginatively decorated bedrooms. The restaurant serves refined Riojan cuisine. Be sure to try the good desserts.
8 70 Closed Christmas–New Year All major cards

POSADA MAYOR DE MIGUELOA
$ ★★★
MAYOR 20
TEL 941 12 11 75
FAX 941 12 10 22
A charming hotel in a mansion built in 1640. Interiors follow Spanish 17th-

century style. All rooms are different and full of decorative details. Regional cooking includes homemade foie gras and delicious desserts.
🛈 8 🛏 105 🕒 Closed 10 days Dec. & 3 weeks Jan.
🆑 All major cards

LOGROÑO 26000

🏨 CARLTON RIOJA
$ ★★★★
GRAN VÍA DEL REY JUAN CARLOS I, 5
TEL 941 24 21 00
FAX 941 24 35 02
E-MAIL hotels@pretur.es
A modern building with a glass facade, central but not in the old town. Spacious rooms.
🛈 116 🅿 🛗 🆑 🆑 All major cards

SAN MILLÁN DE LA COGOLLA 26226

🏨 HOSTERÍA DEL MONASTERIO DE SAN MILLÁN
$ ★★★★
MONASTERIO DE YUSO S/N
TEL 941 37 32 77
FAX 941 37 32 66
E-MAIL hosteria@sanmillan.com
www.sanmillan.com
Restored wing of the Yuso Monastery with inviting and warm rooms.
🛈 22 🅿 🛗 🆑 AE, MC, V

SANTO DOMINGO DE LA CALZADA 26250

🏨 PARADOR DE SANTO 🍴 DOMINGO DE LA CALZADA
$ ★★★★
PLAZA DEL SANTO 3
TEL 941 34 03 00
FAX 941 34 03 25
E-MAIL sto.domingo@parador.es
Part of the parador is in the 12th-century pilgrims hospital, next to the cathedral, built by Santo Domingo. In the restaurant try Riojan style cod with local wines. Sauna, golf.
🛏 100 🛈 61 🅿 🛗
🆑 All major cards

ALBARRACÍN 44100

🏨 CASA DE SANTIAGO
$ ★★
SUBIDA A LAS TORRES 11
TEL 978 70 03 16
A charming little hotel in a 16th-century building set in the old walled town. Colorful rooms with cane furniture and traditional baked clay floors. No television.
🛈 9 🆑 MC, V

DAROCA 50360

🏨 POSADA DEL ALMUDI 🍴 $
GRAJERA 5–9
TEL 976 80 06 06
FAX 976 80 11 41
Intimate, central hotel in a renovated 15th-century mansion. Warm yellows and patterned textiles enliven the rooms and there is a beautiful Renaissance courtyard. Try the local fare in the restaurant. Price includes breakfast.
🛈 13 🅿 🛗 🆑 All major cards

HUESCA 22000

🏨 HOSPEDERÍA DE LOARRE
$ ★★★
PLAZA MAYOR S/N, LOARRE (30 KM FROM HUESCA)
TEL 974 38 27 06
FAX 974 38 27 13
A 16th-century palace in the center of the village looking onto the church tower.
🛈 12 🅿 🛗 🆑 MC, V

🍴 LILLAS PASTIA
$$
PLAZA DE NAVARRA 4
TEL 974 21 16 91
Situated in the old casino, the dining room is modernist and the one-Michelin-star cuisine modern Aragonese.
🛏 170 🕒 Closed Sun. D, Tues., 1 week Oct., & 3 weeks Nov. 🛗 🆑 All major cards

---

JACA 22700

🏨 GRAN HOTEL
$ ★★★
PASEO DE LA CONSTITUCIÓN 1
TEL 974 36 09 00
FAX 974 36 40 61
Located in the center, this is the town's most popular hotel. The wood, stone, and glass exterior conceals simple warm rooms.
🛈 165 🅿 🛗 🛗 🚉
🆑 All major cards

🍴 LA COCINA ARAGONESA
$$
CERVANTES 5
TEL 974 36 10 50
Regional cuisine with Basque influences in a typical Aragonese room. Game specialties in season. Try the artichoke hearts with foie gras or the stuffed partridge.
🛏 150 🛗 🆑 All major cards

SOS DEL REY CATÓLICO 50680

🏨 PARADOR DE SOS DEL REY CATÓLICO
$ ★★★
SAINZ DE VICUÑA 1
TEL 948 88 80 11
FAX 948 88 81 00
E-MAIL sos@parador.es
Set in the historic area of the town, this parador is in the characteristic Aragonese style. Spacious, light rooms have views of the countryside.
🛈 65 🅿 🛗 🛗 🆑 All major cards

TARAZONA 50500

🏨 ITURI-ASSO 🍴 $ ★★★
VIRGEN DEL RÍO 3
TEL 976 64 31 96
FAX 976 64 04 66
A simple hotel in the heart of the old town. The restaurant offers regional cuisine.
🛈 17 🅿 🕒 Closed Dec. 24 🛗 🛗 🆑 All major cards

TERUEL 44000

REINA CRISTINA
$$ ★★★
PASEO DEL ÓVALO 1
TEL 978 60 68 60
FAX 978 60 53 63
On the edge of the old town, this hotel has balconies with views. Corner rooms are the most spacious and have the best views.
🛏81 P 🔄 🆑 All major cards

ZARAGOZA 50000

BOSTON
$$ ★★★★
AVENIDA DE LAS TORRES 28
TEL 976 59 91 92
FAX 976 59 74 10
A large ultramodern hotel opened in 1992. The lobby and panoramic lift are positively futuristic and the rooms comfortable.
🛏314 P 🔄 🆑 🎽 All major cards

GRAN HOTEL
🍴 **$$ ★★★★**
JOAQUIN COSTA 5
TEL 976 22 19 01
FAX 976 23 67 13
E-MAIL nh@nh-hoteles.es
Celebrities stay in this most classical and elegant of all the hotels in Zaragoza. Its restaurant is the renowned La Ontina, where modern Mediterranean cuisine conjures up dishes such as monkfish with partridge vinaigrette, and cuttlefish and mango spaghetti.
🛏141 🍽500 P 🔄 🆑 🎽 All major cards

BARCELONA

ARTS BARCELONA
🍴 **$$$$ ★★★★★**
MARINA 19–21
TEL 93 221 10 00
FAX 93 221 10 70
E-MAIL info@harts.es
Occupying one of the two Olympic towers in the Puerto Olímpico, one of Barcelona's

most impressive buildings and Spain's tallest (44 floors). Superb views of the sea and city from the incredibly luxurious rooms. A little removed from the sights.
🛏455 🍽45 P 🔄 🆑 🎽 🎽 All major cards

CLARIS
$$$$ ★★★★★
PAU CLARIS 150
TEL 93 4 87 62 62
FAX 93 215 79 70
E-MAIL claris@derbyhotels.es
A sumptuous hotel in a former palace with over 400 works of art and archaeological artifacts in the rooms, plus a delightful Japanese garden.
🛏120 P 🔄 🆑 🎽 🎽 All major cards

LE MERIDIEN
$$$$ ★★★★
LA RAMBLA 111
TEL 93 318 62 00
FAX 93 301 77 76
The top hotel on La Rambla where stars such as Madonna, Sting, and Julio Iglesias stay. It is a 1900s building with a neo-classic facade and modernized interiors that have been decorated with fabrics by the designer Kenzo.
🛏205 P 🔄 🆑 All major cards

REY JUAN CARLOS I
$$$$ ★★★★★
AVENIDA DIAGONAL 661–671
TEL 93 364 40 40
FAX 93 364 42 64
E-MAIL reservas@hrjuancarlos.com
Built for the 1992 Olympics, and impressively designed in the shape of a ship's bow, this hotel won the National Architectural Prize for that year. The elegant rooms are fully equipped.
🛏412 P 🔄 🆑 🎽 🎽 All major cards

RITZ
$$$$ ★★★★★
GRAN VIA DE LES CORTS
CATALANES 668

TEL 93 318 52 00
FAX 93 318 01 48
Still Barcelona's classic grand hotel offering all possible elegance and luxury. Since it opened in 1919, many famous guests have stayed here including Dalí. The 34 suites have marble roman baths and Sevilla mosaics.
🛏161 P 🔄 🆑 🆑 All major cards

AVENIDA PALACE
$$$ ★★★★
GRAN VIA DE LES CORTS
CATALANES 605
TEL 93 301 96 00
FAX 93 318 12 34
E-MAIL avpalace@husa.es
A distinguished hotel with old-fashioned elegance situated in the business area. Rooms are in art deco style.
🛏160 P 🔄 🆑 🆑 All major cards

CONDES DE BARCELONA
$$$ ★★★★
PASSEIG DE GRÀCIA 73–75
TEL 93 488 22 00
FAX 93 467 47 81
In the center of the business district, this is one of Barcelona's best hotels. It has two magnificent separate buildings (built in 1872 and 1890s) facing each other across Carrer de Mallorca. The light, modernized rooms retain many art deco details.
🛏183 P 🔄 🆑 🎽 All major cards

GAUDÍ
$$ ★★★
NOU DE LA RAMBLA 12
TEL 93 317 90 32
FAX 93 412 26 36
E-MAIL gaudi@hotelgaudi.es
Modern rooms with views of the Palau Güell roof. No restaurant but a café.
🛏73 P 🔄 🆑 🎽 All major cards

RIALTO
$$ ★★★
FERRÁN 40-42
TEL 93 318 52 12

HOTELS & RESTAURANTS

FAX 93 318 53 12

The painter, Joan Miró, was born here, right in the heart of the Barrio Gótico. Simple rooms have pine floors and dark wood furniture. Rooms looking onto the interior are quieter. No restaurant.

🛈 163 🛗 🅢 🅐 All major cards

🏨 ESPANYA
$ ★★

SANT PAU 9–11

TEL 93 318 17 58

FAX 93 317 11 34

This hotel is famous for its *modernista* dining rooms designed by Lluis Domenech i Montaner. One has a sculpted hearth by Eusebi Arnau and sea life murals by Ramón Casas. Rooms that look onto the interior patio are quieter.

🛈 69 🛗 🅢 🅐 All major cards

🏨 GRAN VIA
$ ★★★

GRAN VIA DE LES CORTS CATALANES 642

TEL 93 318 19 00

FAX 93 318 99 97

For old-fashioned charm and elegance, this 19th-century town house with an elaborate *modernista* staircase and incredibly high ceilings is a good option. Spacious rooms, athough some that overlook Gran Via don't have double glazing. Roof terrace.

🛈 51 🅿 🛗 🅢 🅐 All major cards

🍴 GAIG
$$$

PASSEIG DE MARAGALL 402

TEL 93 429 10 17

This classic restaurant (one Michelin star) has been run by four generations of the Gaig family. Carlos Gaig has developed a modern approach to the traditional family recipes. Try the truffle cannelloni with truffle cream. Fantastic desserts and wine list.

🪑 65 🚇 Vilapicina 🅿 🕐 Closed Mon., Easter, & Aug. 🅢 🅐 All major cards

🍴 JEAN LUC FIGUERAS
$$$

SANTA TERESA 10

TEL 93 415 28 77

In a lovely town house in Gràcia that was once the designer Cristóbal Balenciaga's studio, Chef Jean Luc Figueras prepares an imaginative modern Mediterranean cuisine that has gained one Michelin star. Must reserve.

🪑 50 🚇 Diagonal 🅿 🕐 Closed Sat. L, Sun., Easter, & 2 weeks Aug. 🅢 🅐 All major cards

🍴 NEICHEL
$$$

BELTRAN I RÓZPIDE 16 BIS

TEL 93 203 84 08

One of the top restaurants in Barcelona, serving modern Catalan-French haute cuisine in a stylishly modern dining room. French chef Jean Louis Neichel uses very fresh ingredients. Desserts and cheese are superb. Two Michelin stars. Reservations essential.

🪑 60 🚇 Maria Cristina 🅿 🕐 Closed Sat. L, Sun., Easter, & Aug. 🅢 🅐 All major cards

🍴 VIA VENETO
$$$

GANDUXER 10

TEL 93 200 72 44

www.adam.es/viaveneto/

A classic restaurant noted for its elegance and awarded one Michelin star. Try the monkfish tail cooked in the oven with sesame seeds, and crunchy chick peas with balsamic vinegar. Own large bodega.

🪑 94 🚇 La Bonanova 🅿 🕐 Closed Sat. L, Sun., & 3 weeks Aug. 🅢 🅐 All major cards

🍴 CA L'ISIDRE
$$

LES FLORS 12

TEL 93 441 11 39

This charming restaurant serves traditional Catalan recipes using local ingredients.

Popular with artists; the many pictures on the walls include Dalí originals.

🪑 35 🚇 Parallel 🕐 Closed Sun., last week July, & 3 weeks Aug. 🅢 🅐 AE, MC, V

🍴 LA DAMA
$$

AVENIDA DIAGONAL 423

TEL 93 202 06 86

Modern Catalan cuisine (one Michelin star) in a wonderful *modernista* building in the Eixample. Leave space for dessert; the pastries made here are excellent.

🪑 80 🚇 Diagonal 🅿 🅢 🅐 All major cards

🍴 JAUME DE PROVENÇA
$$

PROVENÇA 88

TEL 93 430 00 29

Chef Jaume Bargués has won a Michelin star for his Catalan–French haute cuisine, such as salted cod salad with pickled vegetables and beetroot vinaigrette, and rabbit stuffed with prunes and thyme mustard. Remarkable wine list. Reservations essential.

🪑 60 🚇 Hospital Clinic 🅿 🕐 Closed Sun. D, Mon., Easter, Aug., & 4 days Christmas 🅢 🅐 All major cards

🍴 OT
$$$

TORRES 25

TEL 93 284 77 52

Despite the modest setting this restaurant is worth a visit. A set five-course menu offers variations of traditional Catalan recipes such as cream of artichokes with lime, and Palamos shrimp ice cream. Reservations necessary.

🪑 20 🚇 Verdaguer 🕐 Closed Sat. L, Sun., 2 weeks Dec.–Jan., 2 weeks Aug. 🅢 🅐 DC, MC, V

🍴 EL RACO D'EN FREIXA
$$

SANT ELIES 22

TEL 93 209 75 59

Young chef, Ramón Freixa, executes adventurous cuisine at this restaurant north of the Diagonal. Try the grilled crêpes with poached egg, maize, and sweet wine, and the *San Pedro* (St. Peter's fish) with baby octopus and aniseed sauce. Excellent bread, desserts, and Spanish cheeses. One Michelin star. Must reserve.

🛏 50 🚇 Lesseps 🅿
🕐 Closed Mon., Easter, & Aug. 🆂 🅰 All major cards

🍴 IL BELLINI
$
MUNTANER 101
TEL 93 454 31 25
One of Barcelona's best Italian restaurants in a small cozy dining room. From October to January the Italian chef prepares dishes with white truffles.

🛏 34 🚇 Hospital Clinic
🕐 Closed Sun. & 2 weeks Aug. 🆂 🅰 All major cards

🍴 BIOCENTER
$
PINTOR FORTUNY 25
TEL 93 301 45 83
For vegetarians this is a good option offering tasty hot dishes and a salad bar.

🛏 70 🚇 Liceu 🕐 Closed Sun. 🅰 No credit cards

🍴 SET PORTES
$
PASSEIG ISABEL II, 14
TEL 93 319 30 33
This early 19th-century high-ceilinged establishment near the waterfront serves generous portions of traditional Catalan cuisine.

🛏 300 🚇 Barceloneta 🆂
🅰 All major cards

EASTERN SPAIN

CATALUNYA

COSTA BRAVA

🏨 MAS DE TORRENT
🍴 $$$$ ★★★★★

FINCA MAS DEL REI
TORRENT 17123
TEL 972 30 32 92
FAX 972 30 32 93
E-MAIL mtorrent@intercom.es
This spectacular 18th-century farmhouse has fantastic views of the coastline from its balconies. The decor is a mix of sophisticated Catalan and rustic elements. The very good restaurant offers traditionally prepared food such as asapragus tossed with artichokes and foie gras. Notable wine list. Activities includ tennis, bicycling, and horseback riding.

🛈 30 🅿 🔀 🆂 🏊
🅰 All major cards

🏨 DURÁN
🍴 $ ★★★
LASAUCA 5
FIGUERAS 17600
TEL 972 50 12 50
FAX 972 50 26 09
E-MAIL hotelduran@sol10.es
This hotel was Dalí's Figueras base; the owner was a friend. Low-key and central, it is good value and has a reputable restaurant.

🛈 65 🅿 🔀 🆂 🅰 All major cards

🏨 DIANA
$ ★★
PLAÇA D'ESPANYA 6,
TOSSA DE MAR 17320
TEL 972 34 18 86
FAX 972 34 11 03
E-MAIL diana@estanciases.es
Curious early 20th-century building by Antoni de Falguera with a maritime facade. Views of the sea and Platja Gran. No restaurant.

🛈 21 🔀 🅰 All major cards

🏨 PORT LLIGAT
$ ★★
PLATJA DE PORT-LLIGAT
SALVADOR DALÍ S/N,
CADAQUÉS 17488
TEL 972 25 81 62
FAX 972 25 86 43
E-MAIL ubald@hgintercom.es
Next door to Dalí's last home. Some rooms have terraces

and views of the sea. The mixture of furnishings adds to the general charm.

🛈 29 🅿 🏊 🅰 MC, V

SOMETHING SPECIAL

🍴 EL BULLI
This is among the absolute top restaurants in Spain and has three Michelin stars. Chef Ferrán Adriá has created his own Mediterranean cuisine, best sampled in the 12-course taster menu, an unforgettable experience. The bodega matches the cuisine.
$$$$
CALA MONTJOI (6 KM FROM ROSAS), ROSAS 17480
TEL 972 15 04 57
E-MAIL bulli@grn.es
www.elbulli.com

🛏 45 🅿 🕐 Closed Mon. & Tues. (except July–Sept.)
🆂 🅰 All major cards

GIRONA (GERONA) 17000

🏨 CARLEMANY
$$ ★★★★
PLAÇA MIQUEL SANTALÓ S/N
TEL 972 21 12 12
FAX 972 21 49 94
E-MAIL carlemany@grn.es
Very good-value modern hotel with large rooms in the new part of town, but only five minutes' walk from the old.

🛈 90 🅿 🔀 🆂 🅰 All major cards

🏨 COSTABELLA
$$ ★★★
AVENIDA DE FRANCIA 61
TEL 972 20 25 24
FAX 972 20 22 03
E-MAIL costabella@es
Five minutes from the old town, this new hotel has non-smoking rooms and serves superior breakfasts.

🛈 46 🅿 🔀 🆂 🅰 All major cards

🍴 EL CELLER DE CAN ROCA
$$
CARRETERA TAIALÀ 40

HOTELS & RESTAURANTS

TEL 972 22 21 57
Joan Roca, one of the top Catalan chefs, has won a Michelin star here. Dishes include scallops with artichokes, honey, and ginge. Outstanding wines.
🍴 45 🅿 🕐 Closed Sun., Mon., 2 weeks July, & 2 weeks Dec.–Jan. 🔲 All major cards

MONTBLANC 43400

🏨 DUCAL
$ ★★
FRANCESC MACIÀ 11
TEL 977 86 00 25
FAX 977 86 21 31
On the outskirts of the old medieval town and not far from Poblet monastery, this is a warm and agreeable hotel.
🛏 41 🅿 🔲 All major cards

SANT CELONI 08470

🍴 EL RACÓ DE CAN FABES
$$$$$
SANT JOAN 6
TEL 93 867 28 51
FAX 93 867 38 61
E-MAIL racocanfabes@troc.es
Top restaurant in an old stone farmhouse. Sample Santi Santamaría's exquisite cuisine, which has won three Michelin stars, with the taster menu.
🍴 50 🅿 🕐 Closed Sun. D, Mon., 2 weeks Feb., & 2 weeks June–early July 🔲 All major cards

SITGES 08870

🏨 CELIMAR
$ ★★★
PASSEIG DE LA RIBERA 20
TEL 93 811 01 70
FAX 93 811 04 03
Modernista hotel right on the seafront. No restaurant.
🛏 26 🅿 🔲 🔲 All major cards

TARRAGONA 43000

🏨 FARISTOL
🍴 $ ★★

SANT MARTI 5, ALTAFULLA 43893 (7 MILES/11 KM FROM TARRAGONA)
TEL 977 65 00 77
FAX 977 65 07 70
E-MAIL amarti@tinet.fut.es
www.faristol.jazztel.es
The few rooms in this 17th-century mansion have been carefully furnished with period furniture. The restaurant serves grilled meats in its cool interior courtyard.
🛏 5 🔲 DC, MC, V

🏨 IMPERIAL TARRACO
$$ ★★★★
PASSEIG DE LES PALMERES
TEL 977 23 30 40
FAX 977 21 65 66
E-MAIL imperial@tinet.fut.es
The semicircle of this large white 1960s block reflects the remains of the Roman amphitheater. Rooms have balconies, but ask for a sea view. Tennis.
🛏 155 🅿 🔲 🔲 All major cards

🍴 MERLOT
$$
CAVALLERS 6
TEL 977 22 06 52
Occupying three floors of a marvelously restored modernista building in the old town. The Mediterranean cuisine is based on regional products including fish. Try the fresh goat cheese and tasty anchovy salad with a green olive vinaigrette.
🍴 65 🔲 AE, V

TORTOSA 43500

🏨 PARADOR DE TORTOSA
$ ★★★★
CASTILLO DE LA ZUDA S/N
TEL 977 44 44 50
FAX 977 44 44 58
E-MAIL tortosa@parador.es
An impressive tenth-century fortress above Tortosa with views of the Ebro plains and Beceite Mountains, furnished in keeping with its history.
🛏 75 🅿 🔲 🔲 All major cards

PRICES

HOTELS
An indication of the cost of a double room without breakfast is given by $ signs.

$$$$$	Over $300
$$$$	$220–$300
$$$	$160–$220
$$	$80–$160
$	Under $80

RESTAURANTS
An indication of the cost of a three-course dinner without drinks is given by $ signs.

$$$$$	Over $80
$$$$	$50–$80
$$$	$35–$50
$$	$20–$35
$	Under $20

VIC 08500

🏨 PARADOR DE VIC
$ ★★★★
PARATGE BAC DE SAU
(14 KM FROM VIC)
TEL 93 812 23 23
FAX 93 812 23 68
E-MAIL vic@parador.es
This parador on the edge of the Sau Reservoir resembles a Catalan masia (farmhouse). Some rooms have terraces looking onto the reservoir and mountains. Traditional decor except for the interior patio covered in multicolored panes of glass. Fantastically situated outdoor pool. Tennis.
🛏 36 🅿 🔲 🔲 All major cards

🍴 JORDI PARRAMON
$$
CARDONA 7, VIC
TEL 93 886 38 15
One Michelin star. Charmingly restored old building, with carefully thought-out cuisine. Try the oysters in melon soup and the orange duck. Spectacular wine list. Good value.
🍴 28 🕐 Closed Sun. D, Mon., 2 weeks Feb.–early March, & 2 weeks Sept. 🔲 DC, MC, V

VALENCIA

ALACANT (ALICANTE) 03000

🏨 **MELIÁ ALICANTE**
$$ ★★★★
PLAYA DEL POSTIGUET S/N
TEL 96 520 50 00
FAX 96 520 47 56
E-MAIL meliaAlacant@solmelia.es
An enormous, plain hotel built
in the 1970s and stretching
along the port. The decor is
outdated but the rooms all
have balconies and sea views.
🛏 545 🅿 ⇄ ❄ 🏊
❄ All major cards

🏨 **TRYP GRAN SOL**
$$ ★★★★
RAMBLA MÉNDEZ NÚÑEZ 3
TEL 96 520 30 00
FAX 96 521 14 39
E-MAIL hotel@tryp.es
The only high-rise in the
center of Alacant near the
sea, with great views.
🛏 123 🅿 ⇄ ❄ ❄ All
major cards

🍴 **DÁRSENA**
$
MARINA DEPORTIVA
MUELLE DE LEVANTE 6
TEL 96 520 75 89
Popular restaurant on the
new marina serving 70 rice
dishes. The warm monkfish
and squid salad, and the black
rice with broad beans and
mushrooms are
recommended.
🪑 200 🅿 🕐 Closed Sun.
& Mon. D ❄ ❄ All major
cards

🍴 **NOU MANOLÍN**
$
VILLEGAS 3
TEL 96 520 03 68
Eat at the bar or in the dining
room. The *montaditos*,
particular to Alacant, are mini
sandwiches with fillings of
your choice. A plate of
vegetables a *la plancha*
(grilled) is delicious, as are the
jamón ibérico and the prawns.
🪑 160 🅿 ❄ ❄ All
major cards

ALCOI (ALCOY) 03803

🏨 **MAS DE PAU**
$ ★★★
CARRETERA ALCOY-
PENAGUILA, KM 9
TEL 96 551 31 11
FAX 96 551 31 09
Sheltered between mountains
in the Penaguila Valley, this
18th-century farmhouse is a
quiet retreat among the olive
and almond groves. Fine views
from the terrace. Bedrooms
are somewhat cramped.
Tennis and sauna.
🛏 18 🅿 🏊 ❄ All major
cards

ALTEA 03590

🍴 **MONTE MOLAR**
$$$
PARTIDA MONTE MOLAR 38
TEL 96 584 15 81
Set in a villa with a spectacular
terrace, the Monte Molar has
won one Michelin star for its
fashionable cuisine. Try the
braised lamb in red wine with
green beans.
🪑 60 🅿 🕐 Closed Wed.
(except July and Aug.) & 3
weeks Jan.–March ❄
❄ All major cards

CALP (CALPE) 03710

🏨 **VENTA LA CHATA**
$ ★★
CARRETERA N 332 ALICANTE-
VALENCIA, KM 172
TEL/FAX 96 583 03 08
Old-fashioned country house
with rustic furniture and a
garden. Spacious rooms with
views of Calpe.
🛏 17 🅿 ❄ ❄ All major
cards

GUADALEST 03517

🍴 **CASA PATRICIO**
$
ARRIBA 37
TEL 96 588 53 10
A modest restaurant that
offers good local cuisine such
as roast lamb.
🪑 55 🕐 Closed Sun. D ❄
❄ MC, V

POLOP 03520

🏨 **DEVACHAN**
$$$ ★★★★
SAN FRANCISCO 13
TEL 96 689 56 40
FAX 96 689 62 33
www.parador.es
A magical little hotel in an
18th-century seignorial house
up in the mountain village of
Polop. Sunny rooms in rustic
style with a mix of furniture
and great attention to detail.
🛏 5 🪑 30 ❄ ❄ AE,
MC, V

VALENCIA 46000

🏨 **MELIÁ VALENCIA
PALACE**
$$$ ★★★★★
PASEO DE LA ALAMEDA 32
TEL 96 337 50 37
FAX 96 337 55 32
Opposite the Palau de la
Música and next to the Turia
gardens, the modern facade of
this hotel in black and pink
marble encloses state of the
art design interiors.
🛏 183 🅿 ⇄ ❄ ❄
�: ❄ All major cards

🏨 **REINA VICTORIA**
$$ ★★★★
BARCAS 4
TEL 96 352 04 87
FAX 96 352 27 21
Still the most elegant hotel in
Valencia despite its rather
faded decor. The rooms are
classically decorated and
comfortable. Queen Victoria
is said to have stayed here.
🛏 94 🅿 ⇄ ❄ ❄ All
major cards

🏨 **AD HOC**
🍴 **$ ★★★**
BOIX 4
TEL 96 391 91 40
FAX 96 391 36 67
E-MAIL adhoc@nexo.net
A beautiful 19th-century
house in the old town. The
owner, an antiquarian, has
combined modern design
with antiques. The restaurant
serves Mediterranean cuisine
at reasonable prices.

❄ Air-conditioning 🏊 Indoor/🏊 Outdoor swimming pool 💪 Health club ❄ Credit cards   **KEY**

🛏 45 🚪 28 ♿ 🔲
♦ All major cards

🍴 ALBACAR
$$
SORNÍ 35
TEL 96 395 10 05
The very modern setting provides the right atmosphere for pioneering cuisine. Oysters come with herring, celery, and tomato caviar, and red mullet with crispy smoked pancetta. Subtle flavors.
🪑 50 🕐 Closed Sat. L, Sun., Easter, 3 weeks Aug., & 1 week Sept. 🔲 ♦ All major cards

🍴 ÓSCAR TORRIJOS
$$
DOCTOR SUMSI 4
TEL 96 373 29 49
One of Valencia's top restaurants gaining one Michelin star. Feature dishes include: *arroz con pintada y alcachofas* (rice with guinea fowl and artichokes), and warm salad with wild mushrooms and scallops.
🪑 56 🕐 Closed Sun., 15 Aug.–15 Sept. 🔲 ♦ All major cards

🍴 RÍAS GALLEGAS
$$
CIRILO AMORÓS 4
TEL 96 352 51 11
E-MAIL riasgallegas@vlc
.servicom.es
www.servicom.es/riasgallegas
This one-Michelin-star restaurant has its ingredients sent from Galicia. Sample the scallops and the Galician style turbot. Galician wines, too.
🛏 80 🅿 🕐 Closed Sun. & 3 weeks Aug. 🔲 ♦ All major cards

XÀBIA (JÁVEA) 03730

🏨 VILLA MEDITERRANEA
$$$$ ★★★★★
LEÓN 5
TEL 96 579 52 33
FAX 96 579 45 81
E-MAIL hotelvillamed@ctv.es
www.hotelvillamed.com
An exclusive and luxurious villa looking down onto Javea,

the Mediterranean, and on clear days even to Ibiza. Two suites are available on the top floor. Sauna.
🚪 7 🅿 🔲 🏊 🏊 🛗
♦ All major cards

XÁTIVA (JÁTIVA) 46800

🏨 HOSTERÍA DE MONTSANT
$$ ★★
SUBIDA AL CASTILLO S/N
TEL 96 227 50 81
FAX 96 228 19 05
E-MAIL rusticae@edigital.es
This restored Cistercian monastery dating back to 1320 has simple elegant rooms and is surrounded by a huge garden. Sauna and cycling. Breakfast included.
🚪 7 🅿 🔲 🏊 🛗
♦ All major cards

CASTILLA Y LEÓN

ÁVILA 05000

🏨 PALACIO DE LOS VELADA
$$ ★★★★
PLAZA DE LA CATEDRAL 10
TEL 920 25 51 00
FAX 920 25 49 00
E-MAIL palacio@isid.es
A restored 16th-century palace opposite the cathedral. The rooms are airy, spacious, and attractively decorated. Amazing interior courtyard.
🚪 84 🅿 ♿ 🔲 ♦ All major cards

🏨 HOSTERÍA DE BRACAMONTE
$ ★★
BRACAMONTE 6
TEL 920 25 12 80
E-MAIL bracamonte@
estanciases .es
Practically on the Plaza del Ayuntamiento and very close to the cathedral, this 16th-century mansion is a charming place to stay in a distinguished Castilian dining room. Lamb roasted in a wood-burning

oven is a specialty.
🚪 20 🛏 200 🅿 ♦ MC, V

🍴 EL ALMACÉN
$
CARRETERA DE SALAMANCA 6
TEL 920 25 44 55
On the outskirts of town with views of the Adaja River, this restaurant probably serves the most refined cuisine in Ávila. Try the gilt-head bream fillet with mussels *al pil-pil* (sizzling oil with garlic and chili) or the taster menu.
🪑 75 🔲 🅿 🕐 Closed Sun. D, Mon., & Sept. ♦ All major cards

BURGOS 09000

🏨 LANDA PALACE
🍴 $$$ ★★★★★
CARRETERA MADRID-IRÚN, KM 235
TEL 947 20 63 43
FAX 947 26 46 76
E-MAIL landapalace@itelco.es
www.itelco.es/landapalace
For luxury and the best food in Burgos, stay in this former palace with its Gothic tower. The restaurant serves seasonal specialties and particularly good rice dishes. Delicious desserts shouldn't be missed.
🚪 36 🅿 ♿ 🔲 🏊
♦ All major cards

🏨 LA POSADA
$
LANDELINO TARDAJOS 3, CASTROJERIZ 09110 (25 MILES/40 KM FROM BURGOS)
TEL 947 37 86 10
FAX 947 37 86 11
A restored 16th-century inn on the Camino de Santiago, this offers a quiet alternative to staying in Burgos itself. Filled with rustic furniture and ornaments the posada also has medieval bodegas and a glass-covered patio (now a sitting area). Tennis, horseback riding, bicycles, and fishing.
🚪 21 🅿 ♿ 🏊 ♦ All major cards

CIUDAD-RODRIGO

37500

🏨 PARADOR DE CIUDAD-RODRIGO
$ ★★★
PLAZA CASTILLO 1
TEL 923 46 01 50
FAX 923 46 04 04
E-MAIL ciudadrodrigo@
parador.es
A 14th-century castle on the
banks of the Águeda river
surrounded by well-kept
gardens. The rooms have a
sombre medieval look, and
some have fantastic views.
One is circular with a domed
ceiling. Ask for the key to the
tower to admire the views.
🛏 27 🅿 🔧 ❄ 🖪 All major
cards

🍴 LA BRASA
$
AVENIDA DE SALAMANCA 32
TEL 923 46 07 93
A straightforward restaurant
for quality meats grilled over
an open fire, homemade
sausages, and other Castilian
recipes such as *huevos con
farinato*. Exceptional wine list,
and reasonable prices. Terrace
in summer.
🍽 100 🕐 Closed Mon. &
Nov. ❄ 🖪 All major cards

LEÓN 24000

🏨 PARADOR "HOSTAL
🍴 SAN MARCOS"
$$ ★★★★★
PLAZA SAN MARCOS 7
TEL 987 23 73 00
FAX 987 23 34 58
E-MAIL leon@parador.es
This stunning *parador*, built by
King Ferdinand in the 16th
century for pilgrims, has an
ornate plateresque facade and
is filled with antiques and
works of art. Ask for a room
in the medieval part not the
new wing. A splendid dining
room where regional dishes
such as frog legs, river eel
stewed with potatoes, and
cecina (dried beef) are served.
🛏 200 🅿 ❄ 🖪 All
major cards

🏨 LA POSADA REGÍA

🍴 $ ★★★
REGIDORES 9–11
TEL 987 21 31 73
FAX 987 21 30 31
E-MAIL regialeon@bornet.es
www.si-santamonica.es/regialeon/
A small hotel in a town house
that dates back to 1370.
Rooms in rustic fashion are in
reds and blues with wooden
floors and beamed ceilings.
The restaurant, Bodega Regía,
serves regional cuisine.
🛏 20 🍽 80 🖪 All major
cards

🍴 VIVALDI
$$
PLATERÍAS 4
TEL 987 26 07 60
Creative modern cuisine using
the local produce. Rustic
decor. Specials include grilled
turbot with tarragon sauce
and courgette puree.
🍽 115 🕐 Closed Sun. D,
Mon., & 2 weeks July ❄
🖪 All major cards

SALAMANCA 37000

🏨 PALACIO DE
CASTELLANOS
$$ ★★★★
SAN PABLO 58–64
TEL 923 26 18 18
FAX 923 26 18 19
E-MAIL: nh@nh-hoteles.es
The most stylish place to stay
in Salamanca, and right in the
old town near the Plaza
Mayor. The original cloister,
now a sitting area, is a fantastic
example of Hispanic-Flemish
architecture.
🛏 62 🅿 ❄ 🔧 🖪 All
major cards

🏨 RECTOR
$$ ★★★★
PASEO RECTOR ESPERABE 10
TEL 923 21 84 82
FAX 923 21 40 08
A grandiose 1940s building of
Villamayor stone with elegant
interiors and fabulous bedrooms. Excellent breakfast but
no restaurant.
🛏 14 🅿 ❄ 🔧 🖪 All
major cards

🏨 SAN POLO

$ ★★★
ARROYO DE SANTO
DOMINGO 1–3
TEL 923 21 11 77
FAX 923 21 11 77
A modern designer hotel built
amongst the 11th-century
Romanesque ruins of the
San Polo church. Many rooms
look out over the old town.
🛏 37 🅿 ❄ 🔧 🖪 All
major cards

🍴 CHEZ VICTOR
$$
ESPOZ Y MINA 26
TEL 923 21 31 23
Owner Victor Salvador offers
creative French-Spanish
cuisine at this Michelin starred
restaurant. The goat cheese
charlotte is delicious and
desserts are phenomenal—a
menu just for chocolate ones.
🍽 50 🕐 Closed Sun. D,
Mon., & Aug. ❄ 🖪 All
major cards

🍴 EL BARDO
$
COMPAÑIA 8
TEL 923 21 90 89
Just off the Calle Mayor, this
small place has a lively tapas
bar on the ground floor and a
dining room on the first
Recommended dishes include
lamb chops with vegetables
and the *arroz negro* (squid
with rice cooked in its ink).
🍽 50 🕐 Closed Sun. &
Aug. ❄ 🖪 MC, V

SEGOVIA 40000

🏨 PARADOR DE SEGOVIA
🍴 $$ ★★★★
CARRETERA DE VALLADOLID
S/N
TEL 921 44 37 37
FAX 921 43 73 62
E-MAIL segovia@parador.es
One of the modern paradors
filled with contemporary
works of art and designer
furniture. The views onto
Segovia are stunning, but the
distance from the center is a
disadvantage. The restaurant
serves some of the best roast
suckling pig in Segovia and

---

other more imaginative dishes.
🛏 114 🅿 ⬍ 🅢 ☒
☒   🅢 All major cards

🏨 LOS LINAJES
$ ★★★
DOCTOR VELASCO 9
TEL 921 46 04 75
FAX 921 46 04 79
Within the city walls in a
narrow, quiet street, this hotel
occupies part of the medieval
palace of the Falconi family,
the Casa de los Linajes. Some
of the older rooms have
views of the Eresma Valley.
No restaurant.
🛏 55 🅿 ⬍ 🅢 🅣
🅢 All major cards

🍴 MARACAIBO–CASA SILVANO
$$
PASEO EZEQUIEL GONZÁLEZ 25
TEL 921 46 15 45
An establishment that
eschews traditional recipes
and large portions to
concentrate on new, subtle
flavors. The *carpacio con
hongos* (carpaccio with wild
mushrooms) and the chicken
are good. Impresive wine list.
🪑 70 🅢   🅢 All major
cards

🍴 MESÓN DE CÁNDIDO
$$
PLAZA AZOGUEJO 5
TEL 921 42 59 11
E-MAIL candido@seis.es
Right under the *aquéduct,*
these quaint dining rooms
have functioned since 1786
and are now a national
monument. The cuisine is
traditional Castilian, with roast
suckling pig and also good
trout.
🪑 300 🅢   🅢 All major
cards

SORIA 42000

🏨 PARADOR DE SORIA
🍴 **$$ ★★★**
PARQUE DEL CASTILLO S/N
TEL 975 24 08 00
FAX 975 24 08 03
E-MAIL soria@parador.es

A modern *parador* in the '
park dedicated to the poet
Antonio Machado, who often
stayed there. Wooden floors
and furnishings give the place
a warm feel. Ask for a room
overlooking Soria and the
Duero River. The restaurant
offers good Soria-style garlic
soup and beans.
🛏 34 🅿   🅢 All major
cards

TORDESILLAS 47100

🏨 LOS TOREROS
$ ★
AVENIDA VALLADOLID 26
TEL 983 77 19 00
FAX 983 77 19 54
A family-run hotel in a former
country house with small but
cozy rooms.
🛏 27 🅿   🅢 All major
cards

TORO 49800

🏨 JUAN II
$ ★★★
PASEO DEL ESPOLÓN 1
TEL 980 69 03 00
FAX 980 69 23 76
A very good value hotel right
next to the Colegiata with
views over the plains of
Zamora. The rooms are
spacious with tiled floors and
rustic decor.
🛏 42 🅿 🅢 ☒   🅢 All
major cards

VALLADOLID 47000

🏨 MOZART
$$ ★★★
MENÉNDEZ PELAYO 7
TEL 983 29 77 77
FAX 983 29 21 90
E-MAIL hotelmozart@vites.es
In a house right in the city
center, dating from 1872, this
hotel has attractive wooden
balconies. The rooms are of
ample size and functionally
equipped. Ask for one with a
balcony. No restaurant.
🛏 42 🅿 ⬍ 🅢 🅢 AE,
MC, V

🍴 MESÓN PANERO

$
MARINA ESCOBAR 1
TEL 983 30 16 73
Traditional Castilian cuisine.
The best dishes are stews,
game, and roasts. A select
wine menu, mainly regional.
🪑 60 🕐 Closed Sun. D, also
Sun. L except summer 🅢
🅢 All major cards

ZAMORA 49000

🏨 HOSTERÍA REAL DE ZAMORA
$ ★★★
CUESTA PIZARRO 7
TEL 980 53 45 45
FAX 980 53 45 22
This delightful hotel occupies
the Palacio de la Inquisición, a
historic monument, on a quiet
street with a terrace and
walled garden. The smallish
rooms open onto the 16th-
century interior patio.
🛏 15 🅢   🅢 All major
cards

🍴 LA POSADA
$$
BENAVENTE 2
TEL 980 51 64 74
The *menú turístico* is a good
choice at this classically
decorated restaurant.
🪑 50 🕐 Closed Sun. D & 2

weeks July 🌀 🌊 All major cards

ALARCÓN

🏨 PARADOR DE 🍴 ALARCÓN
$$ ★★★★
AVENIDA AMIGOS DE LOS CASTILLOS 3
TEL 969 33 03 15
FAX 969 33 03 03
E-MAIL alarcon@parador.es
A fortified medieval castle with only 14 rooms. Turret rooms have narrow slits for windows; some rooms have four-poster beds. Dine in a high-arched hall with a huge fireplace on typical local fare including *morteruelo* (a hash of mixed meats including game and liver) or leg of lamb.
🛏14 🍴80 P 🔁 🌀
🌊 All major cards

ALMAGRO 13270

🏨 PARADOR DE ALMAGRO
This 16th-century Franciscan convent is built around 14 courtyards. It is a peaceful place, decorated with naive paintings and beautiful old tiles. Rooms were monks' cells but are well arranged. The restaurant serves traditional Manchegan fare such as *mojete*, (cold roasted onions and peppers), and *tiznao* (cod).
$$ ★★★★
RONDA SAN FRANCISCO 31
TEL 926 86 01 00
FAX 926 86 01 50
E-MAIL almagro@parador.es
🛏54 P 🌀 🌊 🌊All major cards

🍴 EL CORREGIDOR
$
PLAZA FRAY FERNANDO FERNÁNDEZ DE CÓRDOBA 2
TEL 926 86 06 48
A delightful restaurant in an old house with rustic decor

and original tiling. The food is modern Manchegan, such as red pepper mousse *al pil pil* with slithers of marinated cod.
🍴130 P 🕐 Closed Mon.
🌀 🌊 All major cards

BADAJOZ 06000

🏨 MONASTERIO DE ROCAMADOR
Built by Franciscan monks in the 16th century. No two rooms are the same in decor or size, and some are even built into the rock. Basque-Extremaduran cuisine is served in the former chapel.
$$ ★★★★
CARRETERA BADAJOZ-HUELVA, KM 41.1, ALMENDRAL
TEL 924 48 90 00
FAX 924 48 90 01
E-MAIL mail@rocamador.com
🛏25 P 🌊 🌊MC, V

🏨 GRAN HOTEL ZURBARÁN
$$ ★★★★
PASEO CASTELAR S/N
TEL 924 22 37 41
FAX 924 22 01 42
Attentive service though slightly dated decor at this hotel overlooking both the Castelar Park and the Guadiana River.
🛏215 P 🔁 🌀 🌊
🌊 All major cards

🍴 ALDEBARÁN
$
AVENIDA ELVAS S/N URBANIZACIÓN GUADIANA
TEL 924 27 42 61
Elegant and charming, this is the best restaurant in the province and has gained one Michelin star. Fernando Bárcena uses the freshest of local produce to create the Basque-influenced menu of Extremaduran haute cuisine. Recommended dishes include marinated cod with black olives, *solomillo de cerdo ibérico* (Iberian pork fillet steak) with truffle purée, and Casar

cheese salad.
🍴70 P 🕐 Closed Sun.
🌀 🌊AE, DC, V

🍴 LA TOJA
$
CARRETERA PORTUGAL 22
TEL 924 27 34 77
On the outskirts of town, this classy restaurant provides Galician seafood: *chipirones en su tinta* (tiny squid in their own ink), *merluza a la gallega* (hake stewed with potatoes, parsley, and paprika), and sorbets. Paella on Sundays.
🍴60 P 🕐 Closed Sun. D
🌀

CÁCERES 10000

🏨 MELIÁ CÁCERES
$$ ★★★★
PLAZA DE SAN JUAN 11
TEL 927 21 58 00
FAX 927 21 40 70
In a renovated 16th-century palace in the old town, next to Cáceres' commercial center. The rooms are spacious with modern decor. The restaurant, bar, and some bedrooms have beautiful brick-vaulted ceilings.
🛏86 P 🔁 🌀 🌊All major cards

🏨 PARADOR DE 🍴 CÁCERES
$$ ★★★★
ANCHA 6
TEL 927 21 17 59
FAX 927 21 17 29
E-MAIL caceres@parador.es
The Torreorgaz family built this 14th-century palace in the heart of medieval Cáceres. A small, pretty interior patio leads to the reception and bedrooms. The restaurant Torreorgaz offers fine local fare including: *migas* (fried bread crumbs) with quail eggs and venison with Casar cheese.
🛏31 P 🔁 🌀 🌊All major cards

🍴 ATRIO
$$
AVENIDA DE ESPAÑA 30
TEL 927 24 29 28

HOTELS & RESTAURANTS

FAX 927 22 11 11
A charming, elegant restaurant serving classical and modern cuisine, which has one Michelin star. Recommended dishes include truffles in lasagna with goose liver, apple puree and a scented sauce, partridge *al modo de Alcántara* (cooked with truffles), and caramelized banana tart with nutmeg.
🏨 60 🕐 Closed Sun. D ⚡
⚡ DC, MC, V

🍴 CHEZ MANOU
$
One of the few restaurants in the historic walled town, near the museum. A small cozy place specializing in French cuisine and regional dishes.
🏨 50 🕐 Closed Sun. D & Mon. ⚡ ⚡ MC, V

CUENCA 16000

🏨 PARADOR DE CUENCA
🍴 $$ ★★★★
PASEO HOZ DEL HUÉCAR S/N
TEL 969 23 23 20
FAX 969 23 25 34
E-MAIL cuenca@parador.es
In the beautifully restored 16th-century monastery of San Pablo, the *parador* sits in the Hoz del Huécar gorge looking up to the Casas Colgadas (hanging houses). The restaurant in the old refectory has an interesting modern menu: Ravioli filled with shellfish and *chanterelles*; and *mero* (grouper) grilled with Swiss chard and tiny squid are recommended.
ℹ 61 🏨 150 🅿 ⚡ ⚡
🚇 ⚡ All major cards

🏨 LEONOR DE AQUITANIA
$ ★★★
SAN PEDRO 60
TEL 969 23 10 00
FAX 969 23 10 04
E-MAIL hogar@globalnet.es
A hanging house overlooking the gorge, one of two hotels in the old town. It combines traditional design with contemporary decor. No restaurant.

ℹ 46 ⚡ ⚡ All major cards

SOMETHING SPECIAL

🏨 POSADA DE SAN JOSÉ
In the heart of the old town, this posada in a hanging house was home to Velázquez's daughter-in-law. The rambling 17th-century six-floor building is filled with antiques. Simple rooms; none have televisions or telephones, and not all have bathrooms. A bar-dining area for breakfast and tapas has a spectacular view. No restaurant. Reserve well in advance.
$ ★★
JULIÁN ROMERO 4
TEL 969 21 13 00
FAX 969 23 03 65
E-MAIL psanjose@arrakis.es
ℹ 21 ⚡ All major cards

🍴 MESÓN CASAS COLGADAS
$$
CANÓNIGOS S/N
TEL 969 22 35 09
In one of the hanging houses next to the Museum of Abstract Art. Enjoy the magnificent panorama as you dine on game and Manchegan specialties. Well worth sampling are *ajo arriero* (a paste made from salted cod, garlic, parsley, and paprika, served with toasted bread), venison, and roast suckling pig.
🏨 100 🕐 Closed Mon. ⚡
⚡ All major cards

🍴 FIGÓN DE PEDRO
$
CERVANTES 13
TEL 969 22 68 21
A modest but lively restaurant in the business district owned by Pedro Torres, who also runs the Mesón Casas Colgadas (see above). The menus are almost identical but the prices here are lower. Specials include a Moorish sweet called *alaju* (made with honey, almonds, and orange water).
🏨 55 🕐 Closed Sun. D ⚡

PRICES

HOTELS
An indication of the cost of a double room without breakfast is given by $ signs.
$$$$$ Over $300
$$$$ $220–$300
$$$ $160–$220
$$ $80–$160
$ Under $80

RESTAURANTS
An indication of the cost of a three-course dinner without drinks is given by $ signs.
$$$$$ Over $80
$$$$ $50–$80
$$$ $35–$50
$$ $20–$35
$ Under $20

⚡ All major cards

GUADALUPE 10140

🏨 HOSPEDERIA DEL
🍴 REAL MONASTERIO
$ ★★
PLAZA DE JUAN CARLOS I S/N
TEL 927 36 70 00
FAX 927 36 71 77
An imposing 13th-century monastery that incorporates many styles: Gothic, Renaissance, and Baroque. Part of the building is still used by Franciscan monks who also run the hospederia. Simple but comfortable rooms surround a three-story Gothic cloister. The restaurant serves hearty fare such as tomato soup, goat *caldereta* (stew), and meatballs *a la monasterio*. For weekends reserve two months ahead.
ℹ 47 🅿 🕐 Closed 4 weeks Jan.–Feb. ⚡ ⚡
⚡ MC, V

🏨 PARADOR DE GUADALUPE
$ ★★★★
MARQUÉS DE LA ROMANA 12
TEL 927 36 70 75
FAX 927 36 70 76
E-MAIL guadalupe@parador.es
Built in the 15th century, the

---

parador was originally the pilgrims' hospital and a noted medical school. Orange and lemon trees in the courtyard, enhance the Moorish atmosphere of this elegant Mudejar-style building. Renovated in 1965, the rooms open up to the courtyards. Tennis.

🛈 42 🅿 🔄 ❄ 🌊
🅲 All major cards

JARANDILLA DE LA VERA 10450

🏨 PARADOR DE 🍴 JARANDILLA DE LA VERA
$$ ★★★★
AVENIDA GARCÍA PRIETO 1
TEL 927 56 01 17
FAX 927 56 00 88
E-MAIL jarandilla@parador.es
The Counts of Oropesa and the Marquises of Jarandilla built this fortified summer palace in the 15th century, a perfectly proportioned and elegant building. Good selection of typical Extremeduran dishes. Tennis.

🛈 53 🍴 50 🅿 ❄ 🌊
🅲 All major cards

JEREZ DE LOS CABALLEROS 06380

🏨 LOS TEMPLARIOS
$ ★★★
CARRETERA DE VILLANUEVA S/N
TEL 924 73 16 36
FAX 924 75 03 38
A simple three-star hotel in a town with little choice of accommodations.

🛈 49 🅿 🔄 ❄ 🌊
🅲 All major cards

MÉRIDA 06800

🏨 PARADOR DE MÉRIDA
🍴 **$$ ★★★★**
PLAZA CONSTITUCIÓN 3
TEL 924 31 38 00
FAX 924 31 92 08
E-MAIL merida@parador.es
Founded by Franciscan monks in the 18th century, this elegant building is in the heart of Mérida. Some of the rooms

give onto a pretty interior courtyard and there are also Mozarab gardens. Bedrooms have terra-cotta tiled floors and vaulted ceilings with comfortable furnishings. The restaurant provides reliable regional gastronomy: *gazpacho extremeño* (chilled soup), *caldereta extremeña* (stewed lamb with red peppers, fried bread crumbs and the regional sausage), and truffles.

🛈 82 🅿 🔄 ❄ 🌊 🌿
🅲 All major cards

🏨 NOVA ROMA
$ ★★★
SUÁREZ SOMONTE 42
TEL 924 31 12 61 /31 12 01
FAX 924 30 01 60
E-MAIL novaroma@extremadura .net
Only two minutes walk from the Roman ruins and the museum, this modern, four-story red brick building has a white marble reception area and cafeteria. The rooms have large beds and armchairs. Breakfast is expensive.

🛈 55 🅿 🔄 ❄ 🅲 AE, MC, V

🍴 RUFINO
$
PLAZA DE SANTA CLARA 2
TEL 924 31 20 01
A wide selection of tapas and solid Extremaduran fare such as partridge stew and roast kid. In summer you can eat outside on the terrace.

🍴 45 🕐 Closed Sun. & 3 weeks Sept. ❄ 🅲 All major cards

SIGÜENZA 19250

🏨 MOLINO DE ALCUNEZA
$ ★★★
CARRETERA DE ALBORECA, KM 0.5 ALCUNEZA
TEL 949 39 15 01
FAX 949 34 70 04
E-MAIL rusticae@edigital.es
A 15th-century flour mill on the banks of the Henares River has been converted into a comfortable hotel. Bicycling and horseback riding.

🛈 11 🅿 ❄ 🅲 All major cards

TOLEDO 45000

🏨 ALFONSO VI
$$ ★★★★
GENERAL MOSCARDÓ
TEL 925 22 26 00
FAX 925 21 44 58
E-MAIL alfonsovi@macom.es
www.alfonsovi.macom.es
Probably the most luxurious hotel in Toledo, the Alfonso is situated opposite the Alcazar. Slick, modern rooms have Castilian decor

🛈 83 🅿 🔄 ❄ 🅲 All major cards

🏨 PARADOR DE TOLEDO
$$ ★★★★
CERRO DEL EMPERADOR S/N
TEL 925 22 18 50
FAX 925 22 51 66
E-MAIL toledo@parador.es
A fine example of a *cigarral*—a Toledan country home built beside the Tajo River. Rooms are spacious and some have magnificent views of the city.

🛈 76 🅿 🔄 ❄ 🌊
🅲 All major cards

SOMETHING SPECIAL

🏨 HOSTAL DEL 🍴 CARDENAL

This beautiful hotel was built as a summer palace for Cardinal Lorenzana in the 18th century. Rooms are decorated in Castilian style with dark wooden headboards, big old mirrors, and hand-painted bathroom tiles. Book well in advance. Mainly local dishes such as oven-baked sea bass and lamb stew.

$ ★★★
PASEO DE RECAREDO 24
TEL 925 22 49 00
FAX 925 22 29 91
E-MAIL cardenal@macom.es
🛈 29 🍴 200 ❄ 🅲 All major cards

🏨 PINTOR EL GRECO
$ ★★★
ALAMILLOS DEL TRÁNSITO 13
TEL 925 21 42 50

FAX 925 21 58 19
E-MAIL elgreco@estanciases.es
Right in the heart of the old
Jewish quarter next to the
synagogues and El Greco's
house-museum, this pretty
17th-century bakery became
a hotel in 1989. The interior
courtyard and facade are well
preserved, as are brick arches
in some rooms. Airy rooms
off the three galleries have
ironwork, tiles, and lanterns.
[i] 33 [P] [⇄] [◻] [◈]All
major cards

🍴 ADOLFO
$$
LA GRANADA 6
TEL 925 22 73 21
A classic establishment in a
beautiful building with intri-
cate Mudejar workmanship. It
offers both innovative cuisine
and traditional Toledan dishes.
Try the fresh prawn salad with
vegetables, and the courgette
flowers in tempura on a bed
of pisto manchego with
saffron scented olive oil. An
excellent wine cellar has a
variety of new wines.
[🍴] 100 [🕐] Closed Sun. D
[◻] [◈] All major cards

🍴 HIERBABUENA
$$
CRISTO DE LA LUZ 9
TEL 925 22 34 63
FAX 925 22 39 24
Good-value food served in a
covered Moorish patio with
lots of natural light. The menu
is seasonal; artichokes filled
with seafood are delicious, as
is the dorada a la sal (bream
baked in salt).
[🍴] 80 [🕐] Closed Sun. D
[◈] All major cards

🍴 LA LUMBRE
$$
REAL DEL ARRABAL 3
TEL 925 22 03 73
E-MAIL lalumbre@macom.es
Regional and national dishes:
Try sautéed baby broad beans
with leeks and jamón iberico,
or deer steak from the
Toledan Mountains.
[🍴] 40 [🕐] Closed Sun. & July

[◻] [◈] All major cards

🍴 MILLE GRAZIE
$
CADENAS 2
TEL 925 25 42 70
Italian brothers own this
restaurant and it makes an
enjoyable change from
Toledan dishes. Excellent
pizzas and pasta dishes. Veer
away from the familiar and
you will be pleasantly
surprised: crepes Talaggio,
lenguado a la parmigiana (sole
with parmesan), risottos.
[🍴] 72 [🕐] Closed Sun. D &
Mon. [◻] [◈] All major cards

TRUJILLO 10200

🏨 FINCA SANTA MARTA
$
CARRETERA TRUJILLO-
GUADALUPE, KM 89
TEL/FAX 927 31 92 03
E-MAIL henri@interia.es
This tranquil rustic-style hotel
on the Trujillo-Guadalupe
road was an olive farm and is
still surrounded by acres of
olive, cherry, and almond
trees. Rustic feel with wooden
beams and stone floors.
Order meals in advance.
[i] 12 [P] [🚇] [◈] MC, V

🏨 PARADOR DE
TRUJILLO
$ ★★★★
SANTA BEATRIZ DE SILVA 1
TEL 927 32 13 50
FAX 927 32 13 66
E-MAIL trujillo@parador.es
The only hotel in the old
town, the parador occupies
the 16th-century convent of
Santa Clara. The rooms lead
onto the Renaissance cloister
(now glassed in) and the
courtyard. Recommended
dishes in the restaurant
include wild boar.
[i] 46 [P] [◻] [◈] All major
cards

🍴 MESÓN LA TROYA
$
PLAZA MAYOR 10
TEL 927 32 13 64

Huge portions and low prices
so very popular. You can have
tapas at the long bar, which
leads to several dining areas.
The chaotic noisy atmosphere
and the eccentric old lady
owner are reason enough to
dine here—you will be served
a tortilla (potato omelette) to
start the meal whether you
ordered one or not!
[🍴] 200 [P] [◻] [◈] MC, V

ZAFRA 06300

🏨 HUERTA HONDA
[🍴] $ ★★★
LÓPEZ ASME 30
TEL 924 55 41 00
FAX 924 55 25 04
Rooms in this hotel next to
the parador are decorated
with different colors and
textiles, resulting in a country
manor style. The restaurant
serves regional and national
cuisine with a strong Basque
influence. Delicious specials
include artichokes filled with
salmon, fresh goats' cheese
with a sherry vinaigrette, and
roast suckling pig with a fruit
sauce.
[i] 40 [🍴] 40 [P] [⇄] [◻]
[◈] AE, MC, V

🏨 PARADOR DE ZAFRA
$ ★★★★
PLAZA CORAZÓN DE MARÍA 7
TEL 924 55 45 40
FAX 924 55 10 18
E-MAIL zafra@parador.es
This castle, built by Arab
stonemasons in the 15th
century, has nine towers, one
of which is more than 98 feet
(30 m) high. Hernán Cortés
stayed here before setting out
for Mexico. All the rooms are
off the central white marble
courtyard, and are rather
sombre, but the marble
bathrooms are luxurious.
[i] 45 [P] [⇄] [◻] [🚇]
[◈] All major cards

🍴 LA CABAÑA
$
RECINTO FERIAL S/N, ZAFRA
06300

TEL 924 55 21 06
Straightforward cooking of
fresh produce, either meat or
fish, grilled, fried, or roasted.
Try sea bass or partridge.
🍴 30 🕐 Closed Wed.
💳 MC, V

ANDALUCÍA & MURCIA

ALMERÍA 04000

🏨 TORRELUZ IV
$$ ★★★★
PLAZA FLORES 5
TEL 950 23 49 99
FAX 950 23 47 99
The most comfortable place
to stay in Almería. Roof
terrace with pool and
wonderful views of the sea.
On this same plaza, are two
other Torreluz hotels, one has
two stars and the other three.
🛏 100 P 🔄 ❄ ⛱
💳 All major cards

🍴 MARTÍN FIERRO
$
CARRETERA DE RONDA S/N
TEL 950 27 68 53
Right next to the train station
this Argentinian restaurant
serves delicious grilled steaks,
empanadas (pastry with
various fillings), and *ravioles
con tuco* (raviolis with tomato
and onion sauce). Desserts
include a pancake filled with
caramel sauce).
🍴 80 P ❄ 💳 All major
cards

ALPUJARRAS

🏨 CENTRO AGRO-
🍴 TURÍSTICO
$ ★★
CADIAR 18440
TEL 958 34 32 21
Nice rustic bedrooms in a
wonderful setting with
fantastic views. The restaurant
serves local food and you can
sit outside.
🛏 10 P 💳 V

ANTEQUERA 29200

🏨 CASTILLA
$ ★★

INFANTE DON FERNANDO 40
TEL/FAX 95 284 30 90
Right in the historic center,
this is a new hotel in a
restored building.
🛏 18 ❄ 💳 All major
cards

🏨 PARADOR DE ANTEQUERA
$ ★★★
PASEO GARCÍA DEL OLMO, S/N
TEL 95 284 02 61
FAX 95 284 13 12
E-MAIL antequera@parador.es
A modern *parador*: ample,
luminous rooms with wooden
floors and ceilings, and leather
furnishings. Quiet and
surrounded by green gardens.
🛏 55 P ❄ ⛱ 💳 All
major cards

🍴 EL ANGELOTE
$
PLAZA COSO VIEJO S/N
TEL 95 270 34 65
Traditional cooking in a
restored 17th-century
building with an interior
courtyard opposite the
Nájera Palace.
🍴 90 ❄ 💳 MC, V

BAEZA 23440

🍴 LOS LUCAS
$
PORTALES TUNDIDORES 17
One of the oldest bars on the
plaza, this business has passed
down through three
generations opening first as an
ice-cream parlor and then
extending to tapas and
seafood. Tables outside.
🍴 25 🕐 Closed Sun.
💳 No credit cards

CABO DE GATA 04150

🏨 CORTIJO EL SOTILLO
$ ★★★★
CARRETERA DE SAN JOSÉ S/N
TEL 950 61 11 00
FAX 950 61 11 05
A ranch-style building with
large rooms and cool marble
floors, which was used in the
film, *A Fistful of Dollars*. Tennis,
bicycles, and horseback riding.

🛏 20 P ❄ ⛱ 💳 All
major cards

🍴 LA OLA
$
ISLETA DEL MORO
TEL 950 38 97 58
A very simple restaurant, with
a terrace over the water
where you can dine all year-
round. Limited menu depend-
ing on the catch of the day.
🍴 35 P 🕐 Closed Sun.
💳 No credit cards

CÁDIZ 11000

🏨 PARADOR "HOTEL ATLÁNTICO"
$ ★★★★
AVENIDA DUQUE DE NÁJERA 9
TEL 956 22 69 05
FAX 956 21 45 82
E-MAIL cadiz@parador.es
One of the modern paradors
and not particularly attractive,
but all rooms have views of
the Atlantic. In the old town
opposite the Santa Catalina
castle. Sauna and golf.
🛏 150 P 🔄 ❄ ⛱
💳 All major cards

🍴 EL FARO
$
SAN FELIX 15
TEL 956 21 10 68
Specializes in seafood. A
fantastic spread of *raciónes*
at the bar.
🍴 215 ❄ 💳 All major
cards

CARMONA 41410

🏨 CASA DE CARMONA
$$$ ★★★★★
PLAZA DE LASSO 1
TEL 95 419 1000
FAX 95 419 0189
E-MAIL reservations@
casadecarmona.com
This elegant 16th- to 17th-
century house is a fine
example of Mudejar archi-
tecture. It has three interior
arcaded courtyards and a
couple of regal sitting rooms.
Rooms have antiques.
🛏 29 P 🔄 ❄ 💳 All
major cards

HOTELS & RESTAURANTS

🏨 PARADOR DE CARMONA
$$ ★★★★
ALCÁZAR S/N
TEL 95 414 1010
FAX 95 414 1712
E-MAIL carmona@parador.es
Built within the 14th-century Moorish fortress walls, this *parador* has spectacular views of the Corbones plains. Spacious rooms, some with wooden balconies, others with huge windows looking down onto the plains. The medieval refectory makes an impressive dining room.
🛏 63 🅿 ⬍ 🆒 ⛱
🆎 All major cards

🍴 SAN FERNANDO
$$
SACRAMENTO 3
TEL 95 414 3556
In a grand house on one of Carmona's plazas. The duck with blue cheese is very good, as is the *menú degustación*. Game in season. 🍴 60
🕐 Closed Sun. D Mon., & Aug. 🆒 🆎 All major cards

CÓRDOBA 14000

🏨 AMISTAD CÓRDOBA
$$$ ★★★★
PLAZA DE MAIMÓNIDES 3
TEL 957 42 03 35
FAX 957 42 03 65
Córdoba's most stylish hotel is in the heart of the Judería, and backs onto the Arab city walls. Two beautifully restored mansions plus the annex across the square all date back to the 18th century.
🛏 84 🅿 ⬍ 🆒 🆎 All major cards

🏨 MACÍA ALFAROS
$$ ★★★★
ALFAROS 18
TEL 957 49 19 20
FAX 957 49 22 10
E-MAIL alfaros@maciahoteles.com
www.maciahoteles.com
A quiet modern hotel built over a convent in the heart of old Córdoba. Modern rooms,

some of which have terraces and look onto the patio and pool. Easy to reach by car.
🛏 133 🅿 ⬍ 🆒 ⛱
🆎 All major cards

🏨 ALBUCASIS
$ ★★
BUEN PASTOR 11
TEL 957 47 86 25
This hotel off a quiet street centers on a pretty courtyard. Simple rooms and spacious tiled bathrooms.
🛏 15 🅿 🆒 🆎 DC, MC, V

🏨 MEZQUITA
$ ★★
PLAZA SANTA CATALINA 1
TEL 957 47 55 85
FAX 957 47 62 19
Just opposite the mosque, this mansion has two patios, one of which is cool and leafy. The rooms and halls have antique furniture and paintings. Each is different, but all are spacious with white-marble floors.
🛏 21 🆒 🆎 All major cards

> ### SOMETHING SPECIAL

🍴 ALMUDAINA
A beautiful 15th-century house that originally belonged to Bishop Don Leopoldo de Austria and is now Córdoba's top restaurant. Several elegant dining rooms lead off the covered interior patio. The cuisine puts a modern twist on local recipes: smoked salmon, crab and melon salad, sea bass with a sauce of asparagus, and wild mushroom and tiny squid. If you are up to it try the *rabo de toro* (bull's tail).
$$
JARDINES DE LOS SANTOS MÁRTIRES 1
TEL 957 47 43 42
🍴 220 🕐 Closed Sun. D & Sun. mid-June–Aug. 🆒
🆎 All major cards

🍴 BODEGAS CAMPOS
$$
CALLE DE LOS LINEROS 32

TEL 957 49 76 43
www.alcavia.net/bodegascampos/
This rambling collection of old houses and typical Córdoba courtyards was founded as a bodega in 1908. Superb collection of fair posters and rows of oak barrels signed by famous visitors, including British Prime Minister Tony Blair. Rustic decor and lovely leafy patios for dining in summer. Traditional local cuisine with modern touches.
🍴 600 🅿 🕐 Closed Sun. D 🆒 🆎 All major cards

GRANADA 18000

🏨 PARADOR DE GRANADA
$$$ ★★★★
REAL DE LA ALHAMBRA S/N
TEL 958 22 14 40
FAX 958 22 22 64
E-MAIL granada@parador.es
An exquisite *parador* in a 15th-century Franciscan monastery built by the Catholic Monarchs in the Alhambra gardens, with privileged access to these and views of the city and the Sierra Nevada. The old wing has rooms with antiques and rugs; the new wing is simpler. A popular place, so you need to reserve a year in advance.
🛏 36 🅿 🆒 🆎 All major cards

🏨 ALHAMBRA PALACE
$$ ★★★★
PEÑA PARTIDA 2
TEL 958 22 14 68
FAX 958 22 64 04
E-MAIL reservas@alhambrapalace.es
A rather over-the-top imitation of the Alhambra. Most rooms have fine views over the Alhambra, the city, and out over the countryside to the Sierra Nevada.
🛏 122 🅿 ⬍ 🆒 🆎 All major cards

🏨 PALACIO DE SANTA INÉS
$$ ★★★
CUESTA DE SANTA INÉS 9

TEL 958 22 23 62
FAX 958 22 24 65
www.eel.es/granada/hotels/sines/si
nes.htm
A small 16th-century palace in
the Albaicín with a plateresque facade and only 11
rooms, all off an interior patio.
Ask for a room with views of
the Alhambra. No restaurant.
🚹 11 🅿 🕃 🏧 All major
cards

🏨 AMÉRICA
$ ★
REAL DE LA ALHAMBRA 53
TEL 958 22 74 71
FAX 958 22 74 70
E-MAIL bamerica@moebius.es
An old house with a pretty
Andalusian patio and simple
rooms set within the
Alhambra precincts. Book
months in advance. Meals are
served on the shady patio.
🚹 11 🕒 Closed Dec.–Feb.
🕃 🏧 All major cards

🏨 CARMEN DE SANTA INÉS
$ ★★★
PLACETA DE PORRAS 7
TEL 958 22 63 80
FAX 958 22 44 04
Also in the Albaicín and run
by the same family as the
Palacio de Santa Inés, this old
Arab house on the Alcazaba
wall has tastefully decorated
rooms filled with antiques,
and views of the Alhambra.
Quiet. No restaurant.
🚹 9 🅿 🕃 🏧 All major
cards

🏨 REINA CRISTINA
🍴 **$** ★★★
TABLAS 4
TEL 958 25 32 11
FAX 958 25 57 28
E-MAIL reinacri@lander.es
This was the poet Luís
Rosales' home, and García
Lorca spent his last night here
before being arrested on
August 16, 1936. It is a grand
19th-century town house
with an elegant reception and
traces of an interior patio—
fountain, columns, and plants.
Simple rooms. Try the

restaurant for local and
innovative dishes, and the café
for delicious cakes.
🚹 43 🛏 50 🅿 🔌 🕃
🏧 All major cards

🍴 CUNINI
$
PLAZA DE LA PESCADERÍA 14
TEL 958 25 07 77
By the cathedral, and popular
for the superb spread of
seafood at the tapas bar. Very
good fish stew. Outdoor
terrace. Must reserve.
🛏 45 🕒 Closed Mon. 🕃
🏧 All major cards

🍴 HORNO DE SANTIAGO
$
PLAZA DE LOS CAMPOS 8
TEL 958 22 34 76
Modern cuisine based on
regional recipes and market
availability. Warm chick pea
and prawn salad is a good
option. Excellent wine list.
🛏 120 🕒 Closed Sun. D &
Aug. 🕃 🏧 All major cards

🍴 RINCÓN DE LA VIRGEN
$
ANCHA DE LA VIRGEN 4
TEL 958 22 10 39
Next to the Basílica de las
Angustias, this restaurant
serves creative cuisine in a
brick-decorated basement,
and also has a bar with a large
selection of good tapas.
🛏 40 🕒 Closed Mon., 2
weeks Aug., & 2 weeks Sept.
🕃 🏧 All major cards

🍴 SEVILLA
$
OFICIOS 12
TEL 958 22 12 23
Open since 1930, this cheerful
restaurant was frequented by
García Lorca and fellow poets
and intellectuals. It has real
character with a wonderful
tapas bar, four dining rooms,
and a terrace. Local dishes.
🛏 40 🕒 Closed Sun. D 🕃
🏧 MC, V

<table>
<tr><td colspan="2" align="center">**PRICES**</td></tr>
<tr><td colspan="2">**HOTELS**</td></tr>
<tr><td colspan="2">An indication of the cost of a double room without breakfast is given by **$** signs.</td></tr>
<tr><td>**$$$$$**</td><td>Over $200</td></tr>
<tr><td>**$$$$**</td><td>$150–$200</td></tr>
<tr><td>**$$$**</td><td>$100–$150</td></tr>
<tr><td>**$$**</td><td>$75–$100</td></tr>
<tr><td>**$**</td><td>Under $75</td></tr>
<tr><td colspan="2">**RESTAURANTS**</td></tr>
<tr><td colspan="2">An indication of the cost of a three-course dinner without drinks is given by **$** signs.</td></tr>
<tr><td>**$$$$$**</td><td>Over $75</td></tr>
<tr><td>**$$$$**</td><td>$50–$75</td></tr>
<tr><td>**$$$**</td><td>$35–$50</td></tr>
<tr><td>**$$**</td><td>$20–$35</td></tr>
<tr><td>**$**</td><td>Under $20</td></tr>
</table>

GUADIX 18500

🏨 HOTEL COMERCIO
🍴 **$** ★★★
MIRA DE AMEZCUA 3
TEL 958 66 05 00
FAX 958 66 50 72
E-MAIL hotelcomercio@
moebius .es
www.moebius.es/hotelcomercio
A surprisingly sophisticated
hotel for Guadix, with simple,
comfortable rooms and big
bathrooms. Prize-winning
restaurant serves regional
dishes: Try the roast lamb with
honey, raisins, and pine nuts.
Jazz bar.
🚹 24 🅿 🔌 🕃 🏧 All
major cards

JAÉN 23001

🏨 PARADOR DE JAÉN
$$ ★★★★
CASTILLO DE SANTA
CATALINA
TEL 953 23 00 00
FAX 953 23 09 30
E-MAIL jaen@parador.es
Next to the 13th-century
Arab fortress, and built in the
same style. The rooms have
fantastic views, and one salon
has amazing high-crossed
arches. The restaurant serves
local dishes such as lamb with

HOTELS & RESTAURANTS

rosemary. Try the local red wine, Duque de Bailén.

🛏 45 🅿 🔄 🔲 ⛵
🃏 All major cards

JEREZ DE LA FRONTERA 11400

🏨 **JEREZ**
$$ ★★★★
AVENIDA ALCALDE ÁLVARO DOMECQ 35
TEL 956 30 06 00
FAX 956 30 50 01
E-MAIL jerez@travelcom.es
www.travelcom.es/jerez
One of Jerez's few hotels, set on a wide avenue near the Real Escuela Andaluza de l'Arte Ecuestre. The unusual garden is tropical. Tennis.

🛏 116 🅿 🔄 🔲 ⛵
🃏 All major cards

🍴 **LA MESA REDONDA**
$
MANUEL DE LA QUINTANA 3
TEL 956 34 00 69
Decorated with antiques and works of art. Traditional Andalusian specialties and game in season. Try the gilt-head bream fillets cooked in Jerez Fino. Reservations essential.

🍽 40 🅿 🕐 Closed Sun., Easter, 1 week July & 3 weeks Aug. 🔲 🃏 All major cards

MÁLAGA 29000

🏨 **PARADOR DE MÁLAGA GIBRALFARO**
$$ ★★★★
CASTILLO DE GIBRALFARO S/N
TEL 95 222 19 02
FAX 95 222 19 04
E-MAIL gibralfaro@parador.es
The best accommodations to be found in Málaga are undoubtedly the *parador*, a modern building with a unique view of Málaga and the bay. It is up on the Gibralfaro hill near the castle. Ask for a room with views. Reserve well ahead.

🛏 38 🅿 🔄 🔲 ⛵
🃏 All major cards

🏨 **MOLINO DE SANTILLÁN**
$
CARRETERA DE MACHARAVIAYA, KM 3, RINCÓN DE LA VICTORIA 29730 (11 MILES/18 KM FROM MÁLAGA)
TEL 902 12 02 40
FAX 95 240 09 50
E-MAIL msantillan@spa.es
You reach this idyllic spot via a dirt road from the coast. The colonial-style villa nestled in the hills is surrounded by gardens and avocados, custard apples, and other subtropical plants. Although small the rooms are comfortable and very quiet. Cycling and riding.

🛏 10 🅿 ⛵ 🃏 All major cards

🍴 **MONTE SANCHA**
$$
MONTE DE SANCHA 16
TEL 95 260 31 76
A very young chef and maître d' run this up-and-coming restaurant in an old restored house in the smart part of Málaga. Try the monkfish with long clams, lemon juice, and hot chili oil.

🍽 50 🕐 Closed Sun. 🔲
🃏 AE, MC, V

SOMETHING SPECIAL

🍴 **ANTIGUA CASA GUARDIA**

Málaga's oldest bar probably hasn't changed much since 1840. Packed with locals, it is a very lively place to try Málaga wines, made from muscatel grapes and dispensed from large wooden barrels stacked in rows along one wall of the bar. The Seco Añejo (matured for a year) is less sweet than the new season Pedriot, accompanied by a plate of ice cold prawns. No tables, standing only.

$
ALAMEDA 18 (CORNER OF CALLE PASTORA)
🕐 Closed Sun. 🃏 No credit cards

MOJÁCAR 04638

🏨 **MAMABEL'S**
🍴 **$ ★★**
EMBAJADORES 5
TEL/FAX 950 47 24 48
A charming little hotel up in the village with fantastic sea views and agreeable rooms. Good restaurant. Don't miss out on the lemon pie.

🛏 9 🃏 MC, V

MURCIA 30000

🏨 **HISPANO II**
🍴 **$ ★★★**
RADIO MURCIA 3
TEL 968 21 61 52
FAX 968 21 68 59
Functional and central with very reasonable prices. Well-known restaurant on the ground floor.

🛏 35 🅿 🔄 🔲 🃏 All major cards

🍴 **MORALES**
$
AVENIDA DE LA CONSTITUCIÓN S/N
TEL 968 23 10 26
A popular intimate dining room serving typical Murcian fare. Try the *verduras de la huerta murciana* (Murcian vegetables).

🍽 60 🕐 Closed Sat. D, Sun., & 2 weeks Aug. 🔲
🃏 All major cards

RONDA 29400

🏨 **PARADOR DE RONDA**
$$ ★★★★
PLAZA DE ESPAÑA S/N
TEL 95 287 75 00
FAX 95 287 81 88
E-MAIL ronda@parador.es
Once the town hall and located in a stunning position, on the edge of the gorge. Modern interiors. Ask for a room overlooking the gorge.

🛏 78 🅿 🔄 🔲 ⛵
🃏 All major cards

🏨 **DON MIGUEL**
🍴 **$ ★★★**
PLAZA DE ESPAÑA S/N
TEL 95 287 77 22

FAX 95 287 83 77
Opposite the *parador* and on
the edge of the gorge, with
spectacular views, particularly
from the restaurant. Local
dishes such as suckling pig.
① 28 **🛏** 100 **P**
🕐 Closed Jan. 11–25 **🔼**
⑤ **🅂** All major cards

🏨 SEVILLA (SEVILLE)
41000

🏨 ALFONSO XIII
$$$$$ ★★★★★
SAN FERNANDO 2
TEL 95 422 28 50
FAX 95 421 60 33
The grandest place to stay in
Sevilla was inaugurated in
1929 by King Alfonso XIII. It is
a splendid neo-Mudejar
palace built around a large,
leafy interior courtyard. The
salons are ornately decorated
with Moorish lamps and
Sevilla tiles.
① 149 **P** **🔼** **⑤** **🏊**
🅂 All major cards

🏨 CASA IMPERIAL
$$$ ★★★★★
IMPERIAL 29
TEL 95 450 03 00
FAX 95 450 03 30
E-MAIL casaimperial@
casaimperial.com
www.casaimperial.com
This beautifully restored 16th-
century palace adjoins the
Casa de Pilatos. The hotel is
arranged around three tiled
courtyards painted in Sevilla
white and yellow. All the
suites are different: some have
king-size beds. No restaurant.
Bicycling and horseback riding.
① 24 **P** **🔼** **⑤** **🅂** All
major cards

🏨 DOÑA MARÍA
$$$ ★★★★
DON REMONDO 19
TEL 95 422 49 90
FAX 95 421 95 46
Opposite the Giralda and the
cathedral, this is a large stately
mansion filled with reproduction antiques. All the rooms
have a different decor: some
have four-poster beds.

Fantastic top floor terrace
with a pool. No restaurant.
① 68 **🔼** **⑤** **🏊** **🅂** All
major cards

**SOMETHING
SPECIAL**

🏨🍴 TABERNA DEL
ALABARDERO
The poet Antonio Cavestany
was born and died in this
early 20th-century house, a pure
Andalusian building around a
central patio. The elegant
restaurant is popular, and has
one Michelin star for its modern
Mediterranean cuisine. Try
Sanlucar prawn carpaccio and
Alabardero style partridge.
$$$ ★★★★
ZARAGOZA 20
TEL 95 456 06 37
FAX 95 456 36 66
E-MAIL alabardero@estanciases.es
① 7 **🛏** 80 **P** **🕐** Closed
Aug. **🔼** **⑤** **🅂** All major
cards

🏨 PLAZA DE ARMAS
$$$ ★★★
AVENIDA DEL MARQUÉS DE
PARADAS S/N
TEL 95 490 19 92
FAX 95 490 12 32
www.nh-hoteles.es
A very modern structure of
steel and glass contains
functional rooms. Beware of
the breakfasts—they can be
disappointing.
① 262 **P** **🔼** **⑤** **🏊**
🅂 All major cards

🏨🍴 LOS SEISES
$$$ ★★★★
SEGOVIAS 6
TEL 95 422 94 95
FAX 95 422 43 34
A 16th-century palace has
become a smart, stylish hotel
incorporating the Roman
mosaics, Renaissance paneling,
and Moorish tiling, arches, and
columns discovered during
restoration. Airy, rooms. Roof
terrace and pool. The rest-
aurant serves creative cuisine
with an Arabic influence.
① 43 **🛏** 150 **P** **🔼** **⑤**
🏊 **🅂** All major cards

🏨 LAS CASAS DE LA
JUDERÍA
$$ ★★★
CALLEJÓN DO HERMANAS 7
TEL 95 441 51 50
FAX 95 442 21 70
In the heart of the Barrio de
Santa Cruz, this magical hotel
occupies three palaces, each
with an inner courtyard full
of plants. The rooms are
spacious, minimalist, and quiet.
① 56 **P** **🔼** **⑤** **🅂** All
major cards

🍴 EGAÑA ORIZA
$$$
SAN FERNANDO 41
TEL 95 422 72 11
This simple, elegant restaurant
backs on to the old city walls
and boasts one Michelin star..
Basque-influenced recipes
include game in season.
Recommended dishes are
smoked eel with asparagus,
and hake with clams in green
sauce. Must reserve.
🛏 200 **🕐** Closed Sat. L,
Sun., & Aug. **⑤** **🅂** All major
cards

🍴 LA ALBAHACA
$$
PLAZA SANTA CRUZ 12
TEL 95 422 07 14
Right in the center of the
Barrio de Santa Cruz, this
restaurant occupies a lovely
old Andalusian house built by
the architect Juan Talavera.
🛏 60 **🕐** Closed Sun. **⑤**
🅂 All major cards

🏨 SIERRA NEVADA
18196

🏨 EL LODGE
$$$
MARIBEL 8
TEL 958 48 06 00
FAX 958 48 05 06
Log cabin interiors with cozy,
warm rooms entirely covered
in Finnish pine; ski room for
keeping skis, boots etc. In the
winter season guests can ski
to the hotel itself.
① 20 **P** **🏋** **🅂** All major
cards

---

⑤ Air-conditioning **🏊** Indoor/**🏊** Outdoor swimming pool **🏋** Health club **🅂** Credit cards **KEY**

HOTELS & RESTAURANTS

TARIFA 11380

🏨 HURRICANE HOTEL 🍴

Close to Tarifa the Hurricane stands in a luscious garden with palm trees. The modern building has a design in keeping with the traditional local architecture. Interiors are minimalist with big potted plants and earthy tones, and the laid-back atmosphere is popular with windsurfers in summer. The candlelit restaurant is popular for its modern cuisine with eastern influences. Ask for the fish of the day with basmati rice and rocket from the garden. Windsurfing school, horses, and sauna. Breakfast included.

$$ ★★
CARRETERA N-340 CÁDIZ-MÁLAGA, KM 78
TEL 956 68 49 19
FAX 956 68 03 29
www.hotelhurricane.com
🛏 33 🅿 🏊 🖥 🌐 All major cards

ÚBEDA 23400

🏨 PARADOR DE ÚBEDA
$$ ★★★★
PLAZA DE VÁZQUEZ MOLINA S/N
TEL 953 75 03 45
FAX 953 75 12 59
E-MAIL ubeda@parador.es
A grand 16th- to 17th-century Renaissance palace. Around the two interior patios are rooms with high beamed ceilings.
🛏 36 🅿 🐾 🌐 All major cards

🏨 ALVAR FAÑEZ
$ ★★★★
JUAN PASQUAU 5
TEL/FAX 953 79 60 43
In the heart of the historic center. A pretty covered interior courtyard leads to rooms with wooden floors. Roof terrace.
🛏 11 🅿 🐾 🌐 All major cards

🏨 PALACIO DE LA RAMBLA

This exclusive and peaceful hotel in the center of Úbeda is a 16th-century palace with a Renaissance cloister. The interior courtyard is draped in ivy and other vegetation. Each of the eight rooms has palatial dimensions; some have four-poster beds and all contain interesting antiques. No restaurant. Breakfast included.

$ ★★
PLAZA DEL MARQUÉS 1
TEL 953 75 01 96
FAX 953 75 02 67
E-MAIL rusticae@edigital.es
🛏 8 🅿 🕒 Closed 2 weeks July & 2 weeks Aug.
🌐 AE, V

VEJER DE LA FRONTERA 11150

🏨 CONVENTO DE SAN FRANCISCO 🍴
$ ★★★
LA PLAZUELA S/N
TEL 956 45 10 01/02
FAX 956 45 10 04
In the middle of the village this recently opened hotel was originally a 17th-century convent. Tranquil and simply decorated with pine furniture and bare stone walls. Good restaurant; try the delicious fish soup.
🛏 25 🔄 🐾 🌐 All major cards

🍴 TRAFALGAR
$
PLAZA DE ESPAÑA 31
TEL 956 44 76 38
A rather sophisticated establishment for Vejer with a dining room painted in warm colors, a wooden bar and lovely old floor tiles. Modern cuisine using fresh local produce.
🍽 45 🕒 Closed Mon. 🐾 🌐 All major cards

PALMA DE MALLORCA 07000

🏨 SAN LORENZO
$$ ★★★★
SAN LORENZO 14
TEL 971 72 82 00
FAX 971 71 19 01
E-MAIL sanlorenzo@fehm.es
A 17th-century mansion with each room decorated differently. There is no parking near to the hotel.
🛏 6 🐾 🏊 🌐 All major cards

🏨 HOTEL BORN
$ ★★
SANT JAUME 3
TEL 971 71 29 42
FAX 971 71 86 18
In the center of the city, this 16th-century palace has spacious, elegant rooms with a classical Palma-style patio.
🛏 35 🐾 🌐 All major cards

🍴 KOLDO ROYO
$$
AVENIDA INGENIERO GABRIEL ROCA 3
PASEO MARÍTIMO
TEL 971 73 24 35
www.koldoroyo.es
Modern Mediterranean cuisine with Mallorcan influences is served in this warm intimate dining room looking out over the bay. Good taster menu and superb desserts. One Michelin star.
🍽 80 🕒 Closed Sat. L, Sun., 2 weeks Jan., & 2 weeks June 🐾 🌐 AE, MC, V

🍴 PARLAMENT
$
CONQUISTADOR 11
TEL 971 72 60 26
Next to Palma's parliament building, this is an old-fashioned establishment with high ceilings. Mainly fish and rice dishes.

🛏 105 🕐 Closed Sun. & Aug. 🈁 🈶 No credit cards

🍴 RESTAURANT CELLER SA PREMSA
$
PLAÇA DEL BISBE BERENGUER DE PALOU 8
A tavern full of old wooden wine barrels and walls covered in old faded *feria* posters. Great setting, and filling, but quite basic food.
ℹ 14 🛏 45 🈁 DC, MC, V

NORTHWESTERN MALLORCA

🏨 L'HERMITAGE
$$$
ORIENT
CARRETERA ALARO-BUNYOLA, KM 8
TEL 971 18 03 03
FAX 971 18 04 11
A peaceful 17th-century convent with a grand tower and baroque cloister that encloses orange and lemon trees, in the wilderness of the Tramuntana. Four rooms in the convent itself; others are in an adjacent building with terraces and rustic decor. Sauna, tennis, and cycling.
ℹ 24 🅿 🏊 🈁 All major cards

NORTHEASTERN MALLORCA

🏨 PETIT HOTEL CASES DE PULA
$$$
SON SERVERA, CARRETERA SON SERVERA-CAPDEPERA, KM 3
TEL 971 56 74 92
FAX 971 56 72 71
Warm and full of character, this little hotel occupies the Finca de Pula (1581). The rooms have been modernized and each has an internet connection. Suites are spacious with Italian marble floors and rustic decor. Golf.
ℹ 10 🅿 🈁 🏊 🈁 All major cards

🏨 EL CORSARIO
🍴 $$ ★★
PONIENTE 5
TEL 971 30 12 48
FAX 971 39 19 53
E-MAIL elcorsario@ctv.es
www.ibizahotels.com/corsario
At the highest point of the old town inside the city walls, this lovely hotel occupies a 17th-century building. The best rooms have views overlooking the town and harbor, although not all are equipped with air-conditioning. The restaurant, under the French chef Alexander Bulle, offers a short and expensive menu. The food is superb and includes such specialties as cold tomato soup with monkfish.
ℹ 14 🛏 45 🈁 DC, MC, V

🏨 LA VENTANA
$$
PLAZA SA CARROSSA 13
TEL 971 39 08 57
FAX 971 39 01 45
This small hotel has simple rooms, each of them different. For a quiet night ask for a room as far from the terrace as possible. When reserving, you are asked for a 50 percent deposit on a credit card.
ℹ 14 🈁 🈁 AE, MC, V

MAÓ (MAHÓN) 07700

🏨 PÓRT MAHÓN
$$ ★★★★
FORT DE L'EAU 13
TEL 971 36 26 00
FAX 971 35 10 50
E-MAIL portmahon@infotelecom .es
A colonial-style building decorated with reproduction furnishings and a terrace looking on to the sea. Quiet, well-equipped rooms.
ℹ 82 🈁 🈁 🏊 🈁 All major cards

🍴 PILAR
$
FORN 61
TEL 971 36 68 17
Imaginative, modern Mediterranean creations served in a charming setting. Try the mussels and tomato tossed with black pasta, and the chicken stuffed with figs in a moscatel and orange sauce.
🛏 45 🕐 Closed Sun. D, Sun. (in July), Mon. (in winter), & Jan.–Feb. 🈁 V

🍴 LA RUEDA
$
SAN LUIS 30, SAN LUIS, 2.5 KM FROM MAHÓN
TEL 971 15 11 84
Traditional cuisine in an establishment that has been going for 50 years. Popular among the islanders.
🛏 60 🅿 🈁 🈁 AE, MC, V

PARQUE NACIONAL DE LAS CAÑADAS DEL TEIDE

🏨 PARADOR DE CAÑADAS DEL TEIDE
$$ ★★★★
LAS CAÑADAS DEL TEIDE
TEL 922 38 64 15
FAX 922 38 23 52
E-MAIL canadas@parador.es
The only place to stay within the Parque Nacional de las Cañadas del Teide, which covers a huge old volcanic crater. The *parador* stands at 6,500 feet (2,000 m) above sea level and has stunning views of the Pico del Teide and the Montaña Blanca. It is not a particularly attractive building, but the rooms have fine views and some have balconies. Sauna and golf.
ℹ 37 🅿 🈁 🈁 🈁 All major cards

HOTELS & RESTAURANTS

PUERTO DE LA CRUZ 38400

🏨 MONOPOL
$ ★★
QUINTANA 15
TEL 922 38 46 11
FAX 922 37 03 10
A long-established elegant hotel in a building dating back to 1742, it has impressive stylish rooms and a leafy Canarian courtyard.
ⓘ 100 🔲 🔲 🔲 🔲 All major cards

SANTA CRUZ DE TENERIFE 38000

🏨 MENCEY
$$$ ★★★★★
AVENIDA DOCTOR JOSÉ NAVEIRAS 38
TEL 922 27 67 00
FAX 922 28 00 17
E-MAIL mencey@ctv.es
www.sheraton.com
The most expensive hotel in town occupies a grandiose marble and stucco building in a quiet residential area. Colonial-style interiors with crystal chandeliers, and wonderful gardens. Tennis.
ⓘ 285 🅿 🔲 🔲 🔲 🔲 All major cards

🍽 EL COTO DE ANTONIO
$$
GENERAL GODED 13
TEL 922 27 21 05
FAX 922 29 09 22
Recommended for Canarian cuisine with modern influences using local produce. Try a seafood stew with yams, potatoes, and cheese.
🔲 42 🕑 Closed Sun. & 3 weeks Aug. 🔲 🔲 All major cards

🍽 MESÓN DEL DUQUE
$
TEOBALDO 15
TEL 922 27 49 09
Tasty *raciones* at the old wooden bar with wine barrels for tables, or go through to the restaurant for local fare.
🔲 40 🕑 Closed Sun. & Aug. 🔲 🔲 MC, V

LAS PALMAS 35000

🏨 SANTA CATALINA
$$ ★★★★★
LEÓN Y CASTILLO 227
TEL 928 24 30 40
FAX 928 24 27 64
E-MAIL aferrer@entorno.es
www.hotelsantacatalina.com
This is Las Palmas' classiest hotel in a local-style building with the air of another era, set in the middle of the palm park. The casino is in the same building.
ⓘ 187 🅿 🔲 🔲 🔲 🔲 All major cards

🏨 APARTAMENTOS PLAYA DORADA
$
LUIS MOROTE 61
TEL 928 26 51 00
There are no middle-of-the-range hotels in Las Palmas, but these apartments are a good alternative. They each include a sitting room, balcony, and minibar.
🔲 MC, V

🏨 EL REFUGIO
$
CRUZ DE TEJEDA S/N (SAN MATEO)
TEL 928 66 65 13
FAX 928 66 65 20
E-MAIL tesve@mira-studio.com
At the foot of volcanic rocks this homely hotel is built in Canarian style with stone and red-tiled roofs. Views of the pine trees native to Gran Canaria. Cozy rooms and delicious homemade bread is served for breakfast. Sauna, bicycling.
ⓘ 10 🅿 🔲 🔲 🔲 All major cards

🍽 CASA JULIO
$
LA NAVAL 132
TEL 928 46 01 39
FAX 928 46 60 02
Excellent fresh fish and seafood, Canarian soup or stew prepared daily. Try the *cherne* (sea bass) in a white wine clam sauce. The small dining room is interestingly decorated like the inside of a boat.
🔲 75 🕑 Closed Sun. 🔲 All major cards

🍽 EL CUCHARÓN
$
RELOJ 2
TEL 928 33 32 96
Typical Canarian cuisine with modern touches is served in this simple restaurant. It's worth the visit to try local fare.
🔲 50 🕑 Closed Sat. L, Sun., 2 weeks Aug., & 1 week Sept. 🔲 🔲 All major cards

🏨 FINCA DE LA FLORIDA
$
A rural hotel just outside San Bartolomé that attracts a mainly German clientele. Traditional whitewashed farmhouse surrounded by an attractive garden: simple but comfortable rooms. Ask for directions when reserving. Tennis, bicycling, horseback riding, and sauna. Breakfast is included.
ⓘ 21 🅿 🔲 🔲 🔲 All major cards

🏨 FINCA DE LAS SALINAS
$
LA CUESTA 17, YAIZA 35570
CARRETERA YAIZA-ARRECIFE
TEL 928 83 03 25
FAX 928 83 03 29
E-MAIL fsalina@santandersupermet.com
Beautifully restored grand 18th-century mansion with elegant and spacious interior areas and quiet bedrooms. Activities include tennis, riding, bicycling, and sauna. Breakfast is included.
ⓘ 19 🅿 🔲 🔲 🔲 All major cards

KEY 🏨 Hotel 🍽 Restaurant ⓘ No. of bedrooms 🔲 No. of places 🚇 Métro 🅿 Parking 🕑 Closed 🔲 Elevator

SHOPPING

A number of goods are particularly associated with Spain, such as leather (shoes, handbags, wallets, belts), ceramics, emboidery, fans, and certain foods including olives, almonds, hams, olive oil, honey, wines, and sherry. You come across these items all over Spain, though more so in their place of origin, where often prices are lower and the quality is higher. Spain is still full of those fantastic old-fashioned shops with service to match that are disappearing fast from the rest of Europe. Some of the most beautifully laid out are those that sell everything from cheese to apple liquor to dish detergent. However, the chain stores are encroaching. You find the same names in northern Spain and another set in the south. The department store that you'll find in all the major cities is El Corte Inglés. It is a very comprehensive store that carries absolutely everything. Big hypermarkets like Pryca on the outskirts of the towns and cities, are useful for bulk shopping including good wines, cheeses, bread, clothes, newspapers, and film; they also have gas stations. Smaller shops are in town centers, which are often pedestrianized. Hardware stores (ferreterías) are packed with interesting kitchen utensils and other unusual items.

MARKETS

Everywhere, from the smallest village to the largest city, there's at least one weekly market where you can find everything from clothes to pottery and food. Markets usually start early in the morning and last until around 1 p.m. For the pick of the produce go early, although you won't find it really bustling until around 10 a.m. Often there will be a stand where you can buy freshly made churros (fritters) accompanied by coffee for breakfast. A lot of the produce on sale is locally grown and you can recognize local farmers by the woven baskets they use for weighing produce. Buy things that are in season and that are more expensive at home, such as almonds, strawberries, avocados, and wonderful red and green tomatoes. Look also for local delicacies like cheeses, honey, olives, dried peppers and tomatoes, hams, and herbs. When buying cheeses it is quite acceptable to ask to taste a small portion first.

Spain has few secondhand markets (rastros) or flea markets (mercadillos) and you are more likely to come across them, apart from Madrid and Barcelona, in places where there are communities of other nationalities, for instance on the Costa Blanca and Costa del Sol.

OPENING HOURS

Apart from bakeries (panaderías) that open at 8 a.m., other shops open at 9:30 a.m. or 10 a.m. They close for lunch between 1:30 p.m and 4 p.m or 5 p.m., and then stay open until 8 p.m. or 8:30 p.m. Supermarkets and stores like El Corte Inglés stay open all day, often until later than 8:30 p.m. Some shops close on Mondays, and bakers are open on Sunday mornings.

PAYMENT

Supermarkets, El Corte Inglés, and other chains accept credit cards, but smaller shops do not. Check the signs on the door before you go in and always ask before paying.

EXPORTS

VAT (value-added tax), known as IVA (impuesto sobre el valor añadido), is 16 percent, usually included in the price of most retail goods. Check by asking, "¿Está incluido el IVA?" ("Is IVA included?"). Visitors from outside the E.U. are entitled to claim back the 16 percent IVA if they have spent more than 15,000 pesetas in any one shop and will be taking the goods out of the E.U. within three months. Ask the shop for an invoice (factura) showing the price and the IVA paid for each item and identifying the vendor and the purchaser (you have to show your passport). When you leave Spain, present the invoice to the IVA booth in the airport for customs to stamp, then hand it in at a Banco Exterior (there's one at Madrid's Barajas airport), or mail it back to the vendor. The vendor will then mail the refund to you.

RETURNS

If you have any complaints about a purchase, return it to the shop as soon as possible with the receipt as proof of purchase. Anything bought in a sale is usually not refundable.

IN & AROUND MADRID

CAKE SHOPS & DELI

Casa Mira Carrera de San Jerónimo 30, tel 91 429 88 95. Excellent handmade turrones, marzipans, and other pastries. Open since 1842.
LHardy Carrera de San Jerónimo 8, tel 91 521 33 85. Open since 1839. You can buy pastries, cakes, cold meats, and cheeses. Also has a restaurant.
La Mallorquina Puerta del Sol 8, tel 91 521 12 01. Incredible selection of delicious cakes to take away, or eat at tables upstairs with a coffee.

CIGARS

Cava de Puros Barquillo Barquillo 22, tel 91 522 02 22. Excellent selection of cigars.

CLOTHES & SHOES

Ágatha Goya 6-8, tel 91 577 63 11. Contemporary jewelry.
Camper Gran Vía 54, tel 91 547 52 23. Trendy shoes for men and women.
El Corte Inglés Preciados 3; Plaza Callao 2; Goya 76 & 87; Raimundo Fernández Villaverde 79; Princesa 42; Serrano 47. Madrid's largest department store, found all over the country.
Purificación García Serrano 28, tel 91 435 80 13. Designer clothes for women.
Zara Serrano 61, tel 91 575 63 34. Very good clothes and

accessories chain with reasonable prices. All over Spain.

EMBROIDERY
Gil Carrera de San Jerónimo 2, tel 91 521 25 49. Beautifully embroidered silk shawls and fans, plus flamenco dresses and accessories. Open since 1880.
Reyes Preciados 11, tel 91 531 81 48. Embroidered shawls, sheets, and tablecloths.

HATS & UMBRELLAS
Casa de Diego Puerta del Sol 12, tel/fax 91 522 66 43. Opened in 1858, this shop specializes in umbrellas of every design.
Casa Yustas Plaza Mayor 30, tel 91 366 50 84. Specializes in hats.

MARKETS
In Madrid:
El Rastro Ribera de Curtidores, Sun.
El Rastrillo Marqués de Viana, Sun.
Mercado Filatélico de la Plaza Mayor Plaza Mayor, Sun.
Mercado de San Miguel Plaza de San Miguel, Permanent covered food market. Mon.–Sat.

Around Madrid:
Alcalá de Henares Mon.
Aranjuez Sat.

NORTHWEST SPAIN

CHEESES
La Casa de los Quesos Artesanos Rúa Fuenterrabía 10, Santiago de Compostela. All types of Galician cheeses: Arzua-Ulloa, Tetilla, Cebreiro, and San Simón.
La Masera Párroco Camino 29, Luarca, tel 98 564 09 83. Cheeses from the region, and vacuum-packed ingredients for making the famous *fabada* (Asturian bean stew).
Viuda de Macrino Suárez Párroco Camino 4, Luarca, tel 98 564 02 84. Combination of food and hardware store.

CHOCOLATE AND CANDY
Chocolatería Raposo Rúa das Orfas 15, Santiago de

Compostela. Chocolates and cookies, plus a selection of different honeys from the region, and Galician liqueurs.

JEWELRY
Marín & Durán Huérfanos 11, Santiago de Compostela, tel/fax 981 58 17 83. Jewelry made from silver and jet stone.
Regueira Rúa da Azevachería 9, Santiago de Compostela. Jewelry made from jet stone.

LACE & EMBROIDERY
Bolillos Rúa Nova 40, Santiago de Compostela, tel 981 58 97 76. Handmade lace and embroidery made by several women in the shop, using traditional methods.
Tejidos Lévy Calle Huérfanos 6, Santiago de Compostela, tel 981 58 52 05. Handmade lace and very good quality sheets, tablecloths, cushion covers, etc. Also hand-embroidered shawls.

MARKETS
Cudillero	Fri.
A Coruña (La Coruña)	Tues. & Sat.
Luarca	Daily
Noia (Noya)	Thurs. & Fri.
Ourense (Orense)	7th & 17th each month
Oviedo	Thurs. & Sun.
Pontevedra	1st, 8th, 15th, 23rd each month
Santander	Daily
Santiago	Wed. & Mon.–Fri.

POTTERY & CERAMICS
A Mouga Rúa Xelmírez 26, Santiago de Compostela, tel 981 56 07 96. Locally made handicraft including traditional Galician pottery.
Arte Moreira Antigüedades Plaza de la Leña 2, Pontevedra, tel 986 85 88 15. Silver and pottery antiques.
Sargadelos Rúa Nova 16, Santiago de Compostela, tel 981 58 19 05. Modern designs and variations on the traditional blue-and-white pottery.
Toural Praza do Toural 1, Santiago de Compostela, tel 981 55 88 39.

NORTHEAST SPAIN

ANTIQUES
Eduardo Borrás Barriocep 44, Logroño, tel 941 20 10 83/689 58 96 80.
Roberto Iturrióz Portales 7–1, Logroño, tel 941 25 33 63.

FOOD
Aitor Lasa Aldamar 12, Donostia (San Sebastián), tel 94 343 03 54. Specializes in cheeses and all varieties of mushrooms (fresh, dried, and frozen). Also walnuts and Tolosa beans.
Caídos del Cielo Plaza de Irún 6, Centro Comercial ARCCO Amara (top floor), Donostia, tel 94 345 31 86. Cakes, pastries, and ice creams made by Martin Berasategui. Also pâtés and jams, and a coffee bar.

MARKETS
Bilbo (Bilbao)	Sat.
Calahorra	Thurs.
Daroca	Thurs.
Haro	Tues. & Sat.
Huesca	Mon. & Tues. clothes market; Thurs. flower market
Hondarribia (Fuenterrabía)	Daily fish market
Jaca	Fri.
Laguardia	Tues. & Fri.
Logroño	Tues. & Fri.
Nájera	Thurs.
Oñati (Oñate)	Sat.
Iruña (Pamplona)	Sun. & first Sat. each month (secondhand)
Donostia (San Sebastián)	Wed. & Sat.
Santo Domingo de la Calzada	Sat.
Sos del Rey	Fri.
Teruel	Thurs.
Gasteiz (Vitoria)	Thurs. & Sat., first Sat. each month furniture market
Zaragoza	Wed. & Sun

POTTERY
Arte y Artesanos, León XIII 18, Zaragoza, tel 976 21 20 51. Pottery from all over Spain.

WINE

Bodegas Hergabía Blanca de Navarra 1, Murchante (2.5 miles/4 km from Tudela). Wines from Navarra.

Bodega Nuestra Señora del Romero Carretera Tarazona 33, Cascante (4.5 miles/7 km from Tudela). Wines from Navarra.

Bodega Vinícola Real Santiago Aldaz s/n Albelda de Iregua, Logroño, tel 941 44 42 33. Regional wines and foods. Also functions as a 12-room hostel.

C.V.N.E. (Compañía Vinícola del Norte de España) Avenida Costa del Vino 21, Haro, tel 941 30 48 00. Rioja wines.

Mi Bodega Santo Tomás 13, Haro, tel 941 30 40 03. Rioja wines and other regional products.

Vinacoteca Ezkerra Beato Tomás de Zumarraga 27 bajo, Gasteiz Vitoria. A wide selection of Rioja wines, and their own wine from Leza.

BARCELONA

CAKES & PASTRIES

Farga Diagonal 391, tel 93 416 01 12. Delicious homemade pastries that you can sample in the tearoom.

CHOCOLATES

Petit Plaisir Ganduxer 33, tel 93 414 41 93. Belgian chocolate. **Xocoa** Petritxol 11. Swiss chocolates and homemade candies.

FOOD

Bacallarines Pairó L'Illa Diagonal 557, tel 93 444 02 16. Mainly cod (bacalao).

Feria del Colectivo de Artesanos de la Alimentación Plaça del Pi 1. First Fri. and Sat. of each month 10 a.m. to 10 p.m. Homemade cheeses, pâtés, and various candies with honey and almonds.

La Cansaladería Alsina Canalejas 29. Open since 1880. All types of cold meats.

Il Capriccio del Caffe Comte Borrel 51. In a colonial-style café with a long wooden bar. Try and then buy coffees from more than 80 countries.

Semon Ganduxer 31, tel 93 240 30 88. Excellent smoked fish, caviar, and pâtés.

GADGETS

Beardsley Petritxol 12. Kitchen utensils, gadgets, and cook books.

El Corte Inglés Plaça de Catalunya 14 / Diagonal, 617/ Plaça Francesc Macià, 20

Konema Consell de Cent 296, tel 93 488 33 25. Designer gadgets for the kitchen.

Vinçon Passeig de Gràcia 98. Sophisticated designer store, from sofas to kitchen knives.

JEWELRY

Puíg Doria Avenida Diagonal 612, tel 93 201 29 11.

MARKETS

Feria del Grabado Avenida Pau Casals 1. Second Sun. of each month, 11 a.m.–3 p.m. Watercolor exhibition and sale.

Feria Nova Artesanía Rambla Santa Mónica 1. Sat. & Sun. all day. Arts and crafts.

Mercadillos de Anticuarios de la Catedral All day Thurs. Antiques in the square opposite the cathedral.

Mercado de Antigüedades Plaça del Pi 1. All day Thurs. Antique show and sale at reasonable prices.

Mercado de San José Rambla de San José. A spectacular array of food.

Mercat de les Encants Plaça de las Glories. Mon., Wed., Fri., & Sat., 8 a.m.–7 p.m. Secondhand and sometimes antique market, and new stuff. Anything from furniture to fabrics.

Mercat de San Antoni Mon., Wed., Fri., & Sat., 8 a.m.–7 p.m. Flea market. Old books, collector cards, movie posters, and records on Sun. a.m.

WINE

Celler de Gelida Vallespir 65, tel 93 339 26 41. A wide selection of Catalan wines and

cavas, Rioja, Rueda, armagnacs, and more.

Lafuente Juan Sebastián Bach 20, tel 93 201 25 21. Wines from all over Spain including rare Reservas.

Viniteca Agullers 7, tel 93 268 32 27. An outstanding collection of Spanish wines, also wines from France, and port from Portugal.

EASTERN SPAIN

FOOD

La Garriga Espalter 9, Sitges. Hams and other meats.

La Granadina Girona (Gerona) 7, Alacant (Alicante), tel 96 521 11 51. A selecton of bout 70 cheeses, hams, pâtés, and caviar.

MARKETS

Alcoi (Alcoy)	Wed., Thurs., & Sat.
Alacant (Alicante)	Thurs. & Sat.
Altea	Tues.
Bégur	Wed. & Sun.
Cadaqués	Mon.
Calp (Calpe)	Sat.
Dénia	Mon.
Elx (Elche)	Mon. & Sat.
Girona (Gerona)	Tues. & Sat.
Xàtiva	Tues. & Fri.
Montblanc	Tues. & Fri.
Palafrugell	Sat. & Sun.
Ripoll	Sat.
Sagunt (Sagunto)	Wed., Thurs., & Sat.
Sitges	Sat.
Tarragona	Tues., Thurs., & Sun.
Tortosa	Mon.
Tossa de Mar	Thurs.
Valencia	Sun.

CASTILLA Y LEÓN

BASKETWORK & ANTIQUES

Antiquaria Rúa Mayor 47, Salamanca, tel 923 26 72 99. Antiques and reproductions.

Carlos Antonio Trinidad Avenida Yurramendi s/n, Ciudad Rodrigo, tel 923 48 09 26. Basketwork.

SHOPPING

FOOD
Artesa Ordoño II 27, León, tel 987 25 18 55. Regional products such as meats, sausages, Bierzo wines, cheeses, and chocolates from Astorga.
La Casa de los Quesos Plegarias 14, León. Cheeses from Spain and abroad.
La Despensa Ramos Carrión 6, Zamora, tel 980 53 68 16. Local products.
La Quesería Alcalde Miguel Castaño 1, León. Spanish cheeses including some produced by the shop; particularly appetizing is the Campo de Oro.

LEATHER GOODS
Artesanos de Mogarraz Rúa Mayor 30, Salamanca. Leather goods including traditional wine bladders.
Calzados San Luis Plaza Mayor 5, Ciudad Rodrigo, tel 923 46 03 65. Make and sell leather wine bottles.
Salón Campero Plaza Corrillo 5, Salamanca. Traditional leather shop, selling everything from wallets to boots.

MARKETS
Ávila	Fri.
Burgos	Thurs.
Ciudad-Rodrigo	Tues.
El Burgo de Osma	Sat.
León	Sat.
Peñafiel	Thurs.
Salamanca	Mon. & Fri.
Segovia	Thurs.
Soria	Daily
Tordesillas	Tues.
Valladolid	Sun.
Zamora	Tues.; livestock market on the 12th of each month

POTTERY
Bazar Prieto Prolongación Amargura 29, Zamora, tel 980 51 71 65. A good variety of pottery and ceramics.
Luisa Pérez Carretera Fermoselle 79, Zamora, tel 980 53 06 02. A traditional pottery workshop.
MJ Cerámica Balborraz 13 Zamora, tel 980 53 44 45. Traditional pottery with interesting modern influences.

CAKE & CANDY
Convento de las Dueñas In fron of Iglesia San Esteban, Salamanca. Cakes and marzipan made by the nuns.
Convento de Santa Teresa Plaza Santa, Ávila. Spain's best *yemas* (yellow cakes, named after the egg yolks used to make them and which they resemble).

WINES
Bodegas Farina Camino del Palo s/n, Toro. Toro wines. Guided tour of the bodegas, wine tasting, and wines for sale, including their own Gran Colegiata.
Bodegas Protos Avenida General Sanjurjo 64, tel 983 88 11 58. Wines from the Ribera del Duero region.
Hijo de C. Revilla Puerta Nueva 4, Toro, Tel 983 69 01 46. An entire warehouse full of excellent maturing cheeses and Toro wines.
Pecados Originales Pasaje Gutierrez 6, Valladolid, tel 983 39 23 26, e-mail vinos@pecadosoriginalesvinos.com. Regional, national, and international wines.

CASTILLA-LA MANCHA & EXTREMADURA

EMBROIDERY & ANTIQUES
Carlos A Marcos Plaza de San Juan s/n, Cáceres. Antiques.
Carmen Manzano Dominicas 26, Almagro. Lace embroidery using traditional methods. Sheets, tablecloths, etc.

FOOD
Casa Telesforo Plaza Zocodover 17. Cakes and delicious marzipan.
Gabriel Mostazo San Antón 6, Cáceres, tel 927 24 28 81. Regional products and Extremaduran wines, including those from the Monasterio de Tentudia.
La Almazara Plaza Mayor 4, Trujillo, tel 927 32 24 05. Regional products such as hams, wine, cheeses, honey, and oil.

KNIVES
Arcos La Feria 30, Albacete. Excellent place to buy all sorts of knives.
Mañas Mayor 6, Albacete. Another good place for knives both practical and ornamental.

MARKETS
Belmonte	Mon.
Cáceres	Wed.
Cuenca	Thurs.
Mérida	Tues.
Plasencia	Tues.
Sigüenza	Sat.
Toledo	Tues.
Trujillo	Thurs.
Zafra	Thurs.

POTTERY
Centro de Artesanía Iglesia Santa Cruz Santa Catalina s/n, Cuenca. Very good arts and crafts.
Cerámica Extremeña Plaza Corazón de María 8, Zafra. Extremaduran pottery, opposite the parador.
DAM—Diseño—Decoración Adarve del Padre Rosalio 14, Cáceres, tel 927 24 46 92. Furniture, pottery.

ANDALUCÍA & MURCIA

BOOKS & ANTIQUES
Antigüedades Juan Ruíz González 26, Úbeda. All sorts of antiques.
Librería Atlántida Via de Colón 9, Granada. Bookshop that stocks books in English.

CARPETS & ARTS & CRAFTS
Lorca Artesana Río Guadalentín 9, Lorca, tel 968 46 61 97. Traditional carpets and rugs from Lorca.
ACA Zoco—Artesanía Cordobesa Judíos s/n, Córdoba, tel 957 20 40 33, e-mail asociación@aca-zoco.com. Jewelry, leather crafts, and ceramics all made by local artisans.

FOOD & WINE
Convento de Santa Paula Santa Paula 11, Sevilla (Seville),

tel 95 442 13 07. These nuns make delicious jams and maramlades using Sevilla oranges, plus other sweetmeats and candies.

COVAP Barqueros 2, Córdoba, tel 957 49 85 05. Modern shop selling legs of ham, sausages, cheeses, and vacuum-packed packages of ham, etc. Ideal for taking home.

Galería de Vinos Cerón 12, Jaén, tel 953 23 59 99. A wide selection of wines, including the very good Duque de Bailén from Jaén.

La Flor de Toranzo Jimios 1, Sevilla, tel 95 422 93 15. Very good quality cheeses, ham, and cod. This is also a popular bar, offering traditional tapas for a tasty light lunch.

Las Campanas Plaza del Socorro, Ronda. *Yemas* (small sweet yellow cakes made with egg yolks).

Vinos Baumar Avenida de Murcia 33, Jumilla. Local and national wines.

HATS

El Sombrero de Tres Picos Plaza de Cuba 8, Sevilla, tel 95 428 34 58. Specializes in sombreros—wide brimmed, felt, five stars—as well as a variety of bags and belts.

Sombreros Padilla Crespo Avenida de la Constitución 2, Sevilla, tel 95 422 24 55. The proprietors have been making hats here since 1935 and have very stylish selection of Sevilla sombreros.

LEATHER GOODS

Arcab Paseo Cristóbal Colón 18, Sevilla, tel 95 421 81 30. Everything to do with horses and horseback riding, from saddles to boots.

Curtidos Varo Alfaros 5 and González Francés 7 (opposite the mosque), Córdoba, tel/fax 957 47 87 03 or 957 47 40 05. Leather goods, including boots made to measure and everything to do with horeseback riding and hunting. This fascinating old-fashioned shop has been open since 1917.

MARKETS

Almería	Sat.
Antequera	Daily except Sun., Tues. flea market.
Baeza	Tues.
Carmona	Mon. & Thurs.
Granada	Wed. & Sat., Sun. flea market.
Guadix	Sat.
Jerez de la Frontera	Sun. flea market, except in summer.
Lorca	Thurs.
Málaga	Sun. flea market.
Mojácar	Wed.
Murcia	Thurs.
Níjar	Wed.
Sevilla	Arts & crafts daily; antiques & paintings Thurs.; general Fri. & Sat.; secondhand & antiques Sun.

OLIVE OIL

La Tienda del Aceite Avenida de Castro del Río 66, Baena, tel 957 69 20 31, www.aceitebaena .com. Olive oils from the region in bottles and tins. Balsamic vinegar.

POTTERY & TILES

Alfarería Melchor Tito Valencia 44, Fuenteseca 17, tel 953 75 33 65. Pottery.

Azulejos Santa Isabel Alfarería 12, Sevilla, tel 95 434 46 08. Hand-painted tiles.

Cerámica Fajalauza Fajalauza 2, tel/fax 958 20 06 15. Famous Granada pottery.

Cerámica Tera Alfarería 45, Sevilla, tel 95 434 43 70. Handmade pottery and ceramics. You can visit the workshop during shopping hours to watch the potters at work.

Diego Lozano Jiménez Arco de las Escuelas 2, Baeza. Pottery including the green designs particular to Baeza. The owner in his spare time has also obsessively sculpted all of Baeza's monuments in miniature in marble. Ask to see them and make a small contribution.

Hermanos Almarza Valencia 8, Úbeda. Pottery.

La Tienda de los Milagros Lavadero 2, Nijar, tel 950 52 57 51. Pottery with very colorful and original designs, each one

different. Higher prices but better quality than many.

SHERRY BODEGAS

Domecq San Ildefonso 3, Jerez de la Frontera, tel 956 15 15 00. Reserve in advance for a tour.

González Byass Manuel María González 12, Jerez de la Frontera, tel 956 35 70 00. Call ahead for a tour and tasting.

BALEARIC ISLANDS

Ca's Corder Andén Poniente 61, Mao (Mahón). Local pottery and basketwork made from esparto grass.

Colmado de la Montaña Jaime II 27, Palma de Mallorca, tel 971 71 25 95. Good local cheeses and the popular *sobrasada* (soft, raw, red pork sausage with paprika and a lot of fat).

Masupta Piel Calvo Sotelo 26, Mao. Leather goods and shoes made to measure.

MARKETS

Eivissa (Ibiza Town)	Daily
Maó (Mahon)	Tues. & Sat.
Palma	Mon., Fri., & Sat. arts & crafts; Sat. flea market

CANARY ISLANDS

El Rincón del Fumador Albareda 48, Las Palmas, tel 928 27 82 15, fax 928 22 46 10, www.step.es/rincon. An immense selection of tobacco and cigars from the Canaries, Cuba, and the Philippines; pipes, and other smoking accessories.

Mercado de Nuestra Señora de África Plaza Mercado, Tenerife. Cheeses from all the islands and other food.

Pabellón de Ventas del Cabildo Insular Plaza de España, Tenerife, tel 922 29 15 23. Goods made by local artisans.

MARKET

Santa Cruz de Tenerife Secondhand market Sun.

ENTERTAINMENT

Madrid and Barcelona are packed with bars, cafés, and things to do in the evenings. Madrileños tend to stay up the latest, often until sunrise, and really know how to enjoy themselves. Barcelona is very good for classical music and avant-garde theater and designer bars. The weekly *Guia del Ocio* in Madrid and Barcelona is an excellent guide to what is on. In these and other places you can also pick up information on entertainment and events from visitor information centers, and this is often in English.

MADRID

For tickets for the theater, cinema, concerts, bullfights, and football, and phone reservations:
Localidades La Central tel 91 521 12 13
El Corte Inglés tel 91 432 93 00, 91 532 81 00 or 91 542 48 00
Localidades Galicia Plaza del Carmen, 1, tel 91 531 27 32
Servi-Caixa tel 902 33 22 11 Pay by credit card.

FLAMENCO
Café de Chinitas Torija 7, tel 91 559 51 35, 9:30 p.m.–2 a.m. A flamenco show with dinner in a palace Geared to vacationers. Métro Santo Domingo.
Corral de la Morería Morería 17, tel 91 365 84 46. Flamenco from 9:30 p.m.. Métro Ópera.
La Soleá Cava Baja 34, tel 91 365 52 64, Mon.–Sat. 10 p.m. until late. The last of the genuine flamenco bars. Entrance fee includes a drink. Métro La Latina.
Taberna Casa Patas Cañizares 10, tel 91 369 04 96/91 429 72 89, e-mail cpataS@teleline.es Flamenco 10:30 p.m., Fri. & Sat. midnight. Top flamenco singers, dancers, and guitarists. Must reserve. Métro Antón Martín.

THEATER
Madrid's Theater Festival, from late October to the end of November features all forms of theater including dance.
Teatro de Bellas Artes Marqués de Casa Riera 2, tel 91 532 44 37. Classical theater.
Teatro de la Comedia Príncipe 14, tel 91 532 15 31. A beautiful old theater where the Compañía Nacional de Teatro Clásico performs classic drama.

OPERA & CLASSICAL MUSIC
Auditorio Nacional de Música Príncipe de Vergara 146, tel 91 337 01 40, Métro Cruz de Rayo. Classical music.
Teatro la Zarzuela Jovellanos 4, tel 91 524 54 00, Métro Banco de España. Spanish genre of classical music and dance, *la zarzuela.*
Teatro Monumental Atocha 65, tel 91 429 81 19, Métro Antón Martín.
Teatro Real Plaza de Oriente, s/n, tel 91 516 06 60, Métro Ópera. The grandest theater in Madrid for opera and ballet. Phone reservations through Caja de Madrid, tel 902 24 48 22 or from abroad tel 34 91 558 87 87 or 34 902 48 84 88.

POP & JAZZ
Buy tickets in advance at Madrid Rock, Gran Vía 25 and Calle Mayor 38, and the FNAC store, Calle de Preciados. Cash only. Live concert venues include:
Café Central Plaza del Ángel 10, tel 91 369 41 43, Métro Sol & Antón Martín. 10 a.m.–midnight. Live jazz.
Clamores Jazz Club Alburquerque 14, tel 91 445 79 38, Métro Bilbao. 6 p.m.–3 a.m. Live jazz performances start at 10:30 p.m.
Palacio de Congresos y Exposiciones Paseo de la Castellana 99, tel 91 337 81 00, Métro Santiago Bernabeu.
Palacio de Gaviria Arenal 9, tel 91 526 60 69, Métro Sol & Ópera.
Mon.–Sat. 10:30 p.m. until late, Sun. from 8 p.m. Ballroom dancing, Mon. & Sun.; salsa, Tues.; tango and buffet, Wed. A beautiful old palace in the center of Madrid with Louis IV-style furniture.

Populart Las Huertas 22, tel 91 429 84 07, Métro Sevilla & Antón Martín. From 6 p.m.–2:30 a.m. (3:30 a.m. at weekends). Have a drink and hear live jazz.

CINEMA
These central cinemas show films in their original language:
Alphaville Martín de los Heros, 14, tel 91 559 38 36, Métro Ventura Rodríguez y Plaza de España.
Cine Doré (Filmoteca Nacional) Santa Isabel 3, tel 91 369 11 25, Métro Antón Martín. Old and new films.
Ideal Doctor Cortezo 6, tel 91 369 25 18, Métro Sol.
Princesa Princesa 3, tel 91 547 67 42, Métro Plaza de España.
Renoir Cuatro Caminos Raimundo Fernández Villaverde 10, tel 91 534 60 18, Métro Cuatro Caminos.
Renoir Plaza de España Martín de los Heros, tel 91 541 39 14, Métro Plaza de España.

CASINO
Casino Gran Madrid Carretera de La Coruña, km 29, tel 91 856 11 00, open 4 p.m.–5 a.m. Playing rooms, restaurant, buffet, disco, and live acts. Passport or driver's license required to get in.

BULLFIGHTING
Plaza de Toros Monumental de las Ventas Calle de Alcalá 237, tel 91 356 22 00, Métro Ventas.
The biggest bullring in Spain. The main season starts in mid-May for the San Isidro feria. Must reserve for this; best seats are in the shade. Tickets from the bullring or at the central ticket office: Localidades La Alicantina, Plaza de Santo Domingo.

CAFÉS & BARS
All kinds of cafés and bars are found in Madrid, and you won't have any problem in discovering them. However, here is a short list of some worth visiting:

Café de las Extrellas Martín de los Heros 5, tel 91 542 16 30,

Métro Plaza de España. Ideal for a coffee or drink, before or after the cinema. Cozy atmosphere.
Café de Oriente Plaza de Oriente 2, tel 91 541 39 74, Métro Ópera. An elegant old-fashioned café-bar opposite the royal palace.
Café Gijon Paseo de Recoletos 21, tel 91 521 54 25, Métro Banco de España & Colón. An old-fashioned café where you can eat good regional fare in style.
Círculo de Bellas Artes Marqués de Casa Riera 2, tel 91 531 85 03, Métro Banco de España. Elegant surroundings.
La Venencia Echegaray 7, tel 91 429 73 13, Métro Sevilla. A dusty old bar with six different sherrys.
Los Gabrieles Echegaray 17, tel 91 429 62 61, Métro Sevilla. Covered in beautiful tiles; you can have tapas with your drink.
Viva Madrid Manuel Fernández y González 7, tel 91 429 36 40, Métro Sevilla. Covered in tiles both inside and out; Lively place for a drink, but go early as it gets very crowded.

BARCELONA

THEATER
Barcelona is full of theaters and stages a lot of avant-garde shows, mainly in Catalan and sometimes in Spanish. Check in the Guía del Ocio. Some groups mix miming, special effects, and modern theater such as La Fura dels Baus, Els Joglars, and Els Comediants. The following show modern work unless other details are given. Phone reservations through Caixa Catalunya, tel 902 10 12 12, or on the internet at www.telentrada.com.
Barcelona City Hall Rambla Catalunya 2–4, tel 93 317 21 77 Métro Catalunya. Cabaret.
Mercat de les Flors Lleida 59, tel 93 426 18 75, Métro Poble Sec. At the foot of Montjuïc, this popular venue stages drama, music, and concerts.

Teatre El Molino Vila i Vila 99, tel 93 215 00 69, Métro Paral.lel. Musical cabaret.
Teatre Llantiol Riereta 7, tel 93 329 90 09 Métro Paral.lel. Music hall-cabaret. Good option if you don't speak Spanish or Catalan.
Teatre Lliure Montseny 47, Gràcia, tel 93 218 92 51, Métro Fontana.
Teatre Poliorama dels La Rambla dels Estudis 115, tel 93 317 75 99, Métro Catalunya.
Teatre Romea Hospital 51, tel 93 317 71 89, Métro Liceu.
Teatre Tivoli Casp 10, tel 93 412 20 63, Métro Catalunya.
Teatre Victoria Paral.lel 67, tel 93 443 29 29, Métro Paral.lel. Often ballet and contemporary dance.

OPERA & CLASSICAL MUSIC
The monthly Informatiú Musical leaflet from tourist offices has listings of classical music.
Gran Teatre del Liceu La Rambla 65, tel 93 485 99 13, Métro Liceu. The Liceu that burned down in 1994, reopened 1999. Opera and dance.
Palau de la Música Catalana Sant Francesc de Paula 2, tel 93 295 72 00, Métro Urquinaona. Classical and choral music.

POP & JAZZ
Barcelona Pipa Club Plaça Reial 3, tel 93 302 47 32, Métro Liceu. Thurs.–Sat. 10 p.m.–2 a.m. Jazz, playing starts at midnight. Ring bell to get in. Price includes a drink.
Harlem Jazz Club Comtessa Sobradiel 8, tel 93 310 07 55, Métro Jaume I. Every night (except Mon.) 8 p.m. –2 a.m. Usually jazz.
Jamboree-Jazz & Dance Club Plaça Reial 17, tel 93 301 75 64, Métro Liceu. Jazz and funk every night starting at 11 p.m. The admission price includes drink.
La Boite Diagonal 477, tel 93 419 59 50, Métro Verdaguer. Jazz or blues jam sessions usually start around midnight.

CINEMA
The following cinemas show films in their original language with Spanish subtitles (V.O.— versión original):
Casablanca Passeig de Gràcia 115, tel 93 237 32 92, Métro Fontana.
Filmoteca De La Generalitat Cine Aquitania, Avinguda de Sarrià 33, tel 93 410 75 90 Métro Hospital Clinic. Old and new films.
Icaria Yelmo Salvador Espriu 61, tel 93 221 79 12, Métro Carlos I.
Malda Carrer Pi 5, tel 93 317 85 29, Métro Liceu.
Renoir Les Corts Eugeni D'Ors 12, tel 93 490 43 05, Métro Les Corts.
Verdi Verdi 32, Gràcia, tel 93 238 79 90, Métro Fontana.
Verdi Park Torrijos 49, tel 93 238 79 90, Métro Fontana.

CASINO
Gran Casino de Barcelona Carrer de La Marina 19–21, Marina-Village, tel 93 225 78 78. 1 p.m.–5 a.m. Gaming room and machines. Restaurant. Passport or driver's licence to get in.

CAFÉS & BARS
Bar Pastis Santa Mónica 4, Métro Drassanes. Old bar with a French cabaret theme.
Café de l'Ópera La Rambla 74, Métro Liceu. One of Barcelona's classiest cafés.
Café Salambo Torrijos, 51, An unpretentious designer bar.
El Paraigua Pas de L'Ensenyança 2, Métro Jaume I. Classical music with your drinks.
El Xampanyet Montcada 22, Métro Jaume I. Cava and French champagne. Good tapas.
La Cava del Palau Verdaguer I Callis 10, Métro Uriquinaona. Cava bar and tapas.
Languedoc Roussillon Pau Claris 77, Métro Uriquinaona. Cava and oyster bar.
The Quiet Man Marqués de Barbera 11, Métro Liceu. Irish pub. Live music some nights.
Zsa Zsa Rossello 156, Métro Provença. Professional cocktails in elegant surroundings.

ACTIVITIES

Spain is a large mountainous country with huge tracts of land turned in to national parks that are available to all. It also has thousands of miles of coastline—everything from rugged and spectacular cliffs to the gentle beaches that have proved so popular with vacationers. Consequently, it is a delight to anyone seeking outdoor activities, whether skiing, climbing, diving, golf, or walking. The Canary Islands offer excellent diving and hiking all year, the golf courses on the Costa del Sol are among the finest in the world, the Doñana National Park, despite problems, is among the most fascinating in Europe, and the endless mountains on the peninsula have some of the wildest countryside in Europe for hiking.

Below are telephone numbers and addresses for various central federations and some individual venues for a variety of activities, but it is by no means a complete list. For comprehensive information on local activities and events, tourist offices should be able to provide you with additional sources.

GOLF
Real Federación Española de Golf (Royal Spanish Golf Federation), tel 91 555 26 82

POLO
Real Federación Española de Polo, tel 91 531 01 94

MOUNTAINEERING
Federación Española de Montañísmo (Spanish Mountaineering Federation), tel 93 462 42 67

SAILING
Federación Española de Vela (Spanish Sailing Federation), tel 91 519 50 08

SCUBA DIVING
Scuba Schools International, tel 96 152 22 97, fax 96 153 74 09, e-mail ssispain@jet.es

THERMAL SPRINGS
La Asociación de Estaciones Termales, tel 91 549 03 00

MADRID

CLIMBING
Club de Montaña Culmen, tel 91 369 1652

HIKING
Espacio Acción, tel 91 473 93 16, www. espacioaccion.com

HORSEBACK RIDING
Club de Real Sitio, El Escorial, Madrid, tel 91 853 42 29

PARAGLIDING
De Madrid al Cielo Escuela de Parapente, tel 91 552 84 33

NORTHWEST SPAIN

FESTIVALS
Feast of St. James, July 25, Santiago de Compostela. Huge festival with incredible fireworks and mock burning of the cathedral facade.

GENERAL
Samsara, Luarca, Asturias, tel 98 547 09 90, e-mail freixas@ozu.es
Outdoor sports and activities are available, including mountain biking, scuba diving, canoeing, and rafting.

GOLF
Club de Golf de La Coruña, A Coruña (La Coruña), tel 981 28 52 00, fax 981 28 03 32
Real Golf de Pedreña, Santander, tel 942 50 00 01, fax 942 50 01 36

HORSEBACK RIDING
Valdomedio, Luarca, Asturias, tel 98 597 71 07, www. cyberastur.es/dpf

SCUBA DIVING
Buceo Galicia, A Coruña, tel 981 21 22 06, e-mail buceogalicia@hotmail.com

NORTHEAST SPAIN

FESTIVALS
Festival de Cine, (film) second half of September.
Festival Internacional de Santander, All July and August. Music from across the board.
Fiesta de San Fermínes, July 6–14. The running of the bulls festival in Iruña (Pamplona).
Fiesta de San Mateo, September 21. Logrono Grape crushing.
International Jazz Festival, July in Donostia (San Sebastián).

GOLF
Club de Golf Larrabea, Legutiano, Álava, tel 94 546 58 44, fax 94 546 57 25

HORSEBACK RIDING
Club Hípico del Zaldiaran, Armentia, Gasteiz (Vitoria), tel 94 514 53 87
El Rancho de Boca la Roca, Benabarre, Huesca, tel 974 54 35 65

KAYAKING & CLIMBING
TT Aventura, Ainsa, Huesca, tel 974 51 00 24, e-mail tete@ pirineo.com

SCUBA DIVING
Buceo Euskadi, Donostia, tel 94 331 23 13, e-mail buceo@ buceoeuskadi.com

WHITE-WATER RAFTING
Aguas Blancas, Aínsa, Huesca, tel 974 51 00 08, e-mail aguasblancas@pirineo.com

BARCELONA

CLIMBING
Travessa, Barcelona, tel 93 339 34 58, fax 93 339 34 58

GOLF
Club de Golf La Mola, Barcelona, tel 93 730 05 16, fax 93 730 01 56, e-mail golflamola@golflamola.com

TREKKING
Sport i Aventura, Barcelona, tel 93 415 58 38. Also mountain biking, archery, horseback riding.

EASTERN SPAIN

FESTIVAL
Las Fallas de San José, Valencia March 12–19. Incredible mix of fireworks and music.

GOLF
Club de Golf de Girona, Girona (Gerona), tel 972 17 16 41, fax 972 17 16 82

HIKING
Oasis Adventure, Benidorm, Alacant (Alicante), tel 96 586 24 04

HORSEBACK RIDING
Club Hípico Lloret, Lloret de Mar, tel 972 36 86 15

RAFTING & KAYAKING
Deportur Val D'Aran Les, Lleida (Lérida), tel 973 64 70 45, fax 973 64 80 47

PARACHUTING
Centro de Paracaidismo Costa Brava, Empuriabrava, Girona, tel 972 45 01 11

SCUBA DIVING
Montgo-Sub, L'Escala, Girona, tel 972 77 13 07, fax 972 77 49 49
Sotamar, Cadaqués, Girona, tel/fax 972 25 88 76

SKIING
Estación Baquiera-Beret, Vielha, Lleida, tel 973 64 44 55

CASTILLA Y LEÓN

GOLF
Club de Golf Villar de Olalla, Cuenca, tel/fax 969 26 71 98

CASTILLA-LA MANCHA & EXTREMADURA

FESTIVALS
WOMAD (World of Music and Dance), Spanish version staged in Cáceres at beginning of May. International bands, reggae to Indian.
Festival de Teatro Clásico, Mérida, Badajoz in July. Greek and Roman classics staged at the Roman theater.

GOLF
Norba Club de Golf, Cáceres, tel 927 23 14 41, fax 927 23 14 80

PARAGLIDING
Parapente Extremadura, Cáceres, tel 927 23 84 71

ANDALUCÍA & MURCIA

TurAc, Úbeda, tel 953 79 25 12, e-mail turac@turac.com. www .turac.com. For outdoor activities in the province of Jaén, including the Sierra Cazorla.
Nevadensis Guías de Montaña, tel 958 76 31 27, fax 958 76 33 01, www.nevadensis .com. For a wide selection of activities in the Sierra Nevada, from horseback riding and skiing to paragliding.

FESTIVALS
Carnaval in Cádiz, a month before Easter.
Feria del Caballo, (Horse Fair) April or May, Jerez de la Frontera, Cádiz. One of Andalucía's biggest festivals. Expect crowds.
Festival Internacional de Guitarra, late May/early June, Córdoba. Guitar concerts.
Corridas Goyescas, early September, Ronda, Málaga. Top matadors fight in 19th-century costumes, as seen in Goya's famous paintings of Ronda bullfights.
Semana Santa, Easter processions in Sevilla (Seville) and elsewhere.

GOLF
Club de Golf de Mijas, Mijas, Málaga, tel 95 247 68 43, fax 95 246 79 43
La Manga Club, La Manga, Murcia, tel 968 17 50 00, fax 968 17 52 58
Real Club de Golf Sotogrande, Sotogrande, Cádiz, tel 956 78 50 14, fax 956 79 50 29
Real Club de Golf Las Brisas, Marbella, Málaga, tel 95 281 08 75, fax 95 281 55 18

HORSEBACK RIDING
Club Hípico, Córdoba, tel/fax 957 27 16 28
Club Hípico de Benalmádena, Benalmádena, Málaga, tel 95 256 84 84, fax 95 256 82 00

SCUBA DIVING
Granada Sub, La Herradura, Granada, tel 958 64 02 81, fax 958 64 02 96
La Trucha, Málaga, tel/fax 95 221 22 03

BALEARIC ISLANDS

GOLF
Golf Club de Ibiza, Eivissa (Ibiza), tel 971 19 60 52, fax 971 19 60 51

HORSEBACK RIDING
Mallorca Riding School, Palma, tel 971 61 31 57

SCUBA DIVING
Ibiza Diving, Eivissa, tel 971 33 29 49, www.ibiza-diving.com

CANARY ISLANDS

GOLF
Golf Costa Teguise, Lanzarote, tel 928 59 05 12, fax 928 59 04 90
Real Club de Golf Las Palmas, Las Palmas, tel 928 35 10 50, fax 928 35 01 10. Also has horses.

HORSEBACK RIDING
Club Hípico La Atalaya, Santa Cruz, Tenerife, tel 922 25 57 39

SCUBA DIVING
Aquanauta, Santa Cruz de Tenerife, tel/fax 922 86 72 17

LANGUAGE GUIDE

USEFUL WORDS & PHRASES

Excuse me *Perdón*
Hello *Hola*
Goodbye *Adiós*
Please *Por favor*
Thank you *Gracias*
You're welcome *De nada*
Good morning *Buenas días*
Good afternoon/evening *Buenas tardes*
Good night *Buenos noches*
today *hoy*
yesterday *ayer*
tomorrow *mañana*
now *ahora*
later *más tarde*
this morning *esta mañana*
this afternoon/this evening *esta tarde*
Do you speak English? *¿Hablas inglés?*
I am American *Yo soy americano*
I don't understand *No entiendo*
Where is...? *¿Dónde está...?*
I don't know *no lo sé*
At what time? *¿a qué hora?*
when? *¿cuando?*

Do you have...? *¿tienes un...*
a single room *una habitación sencilla?*
a double room (double bed) *una habitación matrimonio?*
a double room (twin beds) *una habitación con dos camas?*
for one night *para una noche?*

I need a doctor/dentist *Necesito un médico/dentista*
Can you help me? *¿Me puedes ayudar?*
hospital *hospital*
police station *comisaría de policía?*

I'd like *Me gustaria*
How much is it? *¿Cúanto es?*
Do you accept credit cards? *¿Puedo pagar con tarjeta de crédito?*
cheap *barato*
expensive *caro*
post office *el correo*
visitor information center *la oficina de turismo*
open *abierto*
closed *cerrado*
every day *todos los días*

MENU READER

breakfast *el desayuno*
lunch *el almuerzo/la comida*
dinner *la cena*
I'd like to order *Me gustaría pedir*
Is service included? *¿Está incluido el servicio?*

la carta menu
menú del día fixed priced three-course meal including a drink
a la carta ordering anything other than *menú del día*
lista de vinos wine list
la cuenta check

tapa small snack taken with a drink
ración portion, helping
a la parrilla grilled
a la plancha grilled on a hotplate
crudo raw
ahumado smoked
estofado stew
frito fried
horno oven
empanada savory pastry
tortilla Spanish omelet made with potatoes and often served cold

un agua mineral mineral water *sin gas* (still) *con gas* (sparkling)
el azúcar sugar
un café americano large black coffee
un café con leche large white coffee
un café descafeinado decaffeinated coffee
un café solo short black/ espresso
una cerveza beer
cubiertos knives and forks
la leche milk
el pan bread
la sal salt
un té tea
un vino tinto red wine
un vino blanco white wine
vino de la casa house wine
un zumo de naranja fresh orange juice

cabra goat
callos tripe
cerdo pork
chorizo spicy sausage
conejo rabbit
cordero lamb
hígado liver
jamón ham
lomo loin (usually of pork)
pato duck

pavo turkey
pollo chicken
perdiz partridge
riñones kidneys
salchichas sausages
ternera beef

atún tuna
caballa mackerel
chanquetes whitebait
dorada bream
lenguado sole
lubina sea bass
merluza hake
pescadilla whiting
rape monkfish
salmonete red mullet

almejas clams
calamares squid
camarón shrimp
cangrejo crab
chipirones small squid
gambas prawns
langosta lobster
mejillones mussels
ostra oyster
pulpo octopus
vieira scallop

alcachofa artichoke
arroz rice
berenjena eggplant
calabacín zucchini
cebolla onion
champiñones mushrooms
col cabbage
espárragos asparagus
espinacas spinach
guisantes peas
habas broad beans
judías beans
lechuga lettuce
patatas fritas french fries
pepino cucumber
puerro leek
seta wild mushroom
zanahoria carrot

albaricoque apricot
cereza cherry
ciruela plum
frambuesa raspberry
fresa strawberry
limón lemon
mandarina tangerine
manzana apple
melocotón peach
naranja orange
sandía watermelon
uva grape

CREDITS

ILLUSTRATIONS CREDITS

Abbreviations for terms appearing below: (t) top; (b) bottom; (l) left; (r) right

Cover (tl), M. L. Stephenson/Corbis UK Ltd. (tr), Stock Market Photo Agency Inc. (bl), Gettyone/ Stone. (br), Diaf/Y. Travert. (spine), M. L. Stephenson/Corbis UK Ltd. 1, M. Chaplow/Andalucia Slide Lib. 2/3, AA Photo Library/A. Molyneux. 4, M. Chaplow/Andalucia Slide Lib. 9, P. Thompson/Eye Ubiquitous. 11, M. Chaplow/Andalucia Slide Lib. 12/13, Steve McCurry. 14, N. Egerton/Travel Ink. 15, G. Azumendi/ Vision Photo. 16/17, A. Guinart/ Vision Photo. 18/19, G. M. Azumendi/Vision Photo. 20/21, Index Fototeca. 23, Age Fotostock. 24/25, R. Duaso/Fototext. 26, M. Chaplow/ Andalucia Slide Lib. 29, Index Fototeca. 30/31, Age Fotostock. 32/33, Godo-Foto. 35, Index Fototeca. 36, Bettmann/Corbis UK Ltd. 38, Age Fotostock. 39, Index Fototeca. 40/41, Index Fototeca. 42/43, Vision Photo. 44, Index Fototeca. 45, Index Fototeca. 46/47, H. Gruyaert/ Magnum Photos. 48, AA Photo Lib./ S. Day. 49, Pablo Picasso, self portrait, 1901, © Succession Picasso/DACS 2001, Musee Picasso, Paris, France/ Bridgeman Art Library, London. 50/51, M. Chaplow/Andalucia Slide Lib. 52, Rex Features. 53, AA Photo Lib./R. Strange. 55, AA Photo Lib./ J. Edmanson. 56, J. Lawrence/Travel Ink. 57, R. Roberts/Impact Photos. 58, M. Chaplow/Andalucia Slide Lib. 60t, M. Chaplow/Andalucia Slide Lib. 60b, P. Enticknap/Travel Ink. 61, M. Chaplow/Andalucia Slide Lib. 62, Age Fotostock. 63, Prado, Madrid, Spain/ Bridgeman Art Lib., London. 64, Age Fotostock. 65t, G. Wright/Axiom. 65b, S. Black/Travel Lib. 66, S. Black/ Travel Lib. 67, Godo-Foto. 68, B. Ducke/Incolor. 69, Thyssen-Bornemisza Museum/AKG - London. 70, M. Chaplow/Andalucia Slide Lib. 71, Thyssen-Bornemisza Museum/ AKG - London. 72, AA Photo Lib./J. Edmanson. 73, Godo-Foto. 74, M. Chaplow/Andalucia Slide Lib. 75, M. Chaplow/Andalucia Slide Lib. 76, Museo de America, Madrid, Spain/Index/Bridgeman Art Lib., London. 77, R. Duaso/Vision Photo. 78, A Guinart/Vision Photo. 79, H Schmidt/Travel Lib. 80, A Guinart/ Vision Photo. 82, R. Duaso/Vision Photo. 83, Age Fotostock. 85, Eye Ubiquitous. 86, Age Fotostock. 87, G. Azumendi/Vision Photo. 88, D. Cumming; Eye Ubiquitous/Corbis UK Ltd. 89t, M. Alavedra/Fototext. 89b, A Guinart/Vision Photo. 91, Age Fotostock. 93, A Guinart/Vision Photo. 94, Age Fotostock. 95, Index Fotostock. 96, Age Fotostock. 97, Age Fotostock. 98, Age Fotostock. 99, F. Dunlop. 100, Age Fotostock. 101, Travel Lib. 102, Index Fototeca. 103, M. Alavedra/Fototext. 104, Age Fotostock. 105, G. M. Azumendi/ Vision Photo. 106/107, P. Enticknap/ Travel

Lib. 107, M. Alavedra/ Foto-text. 108, G. M. Azumendi/ Vision Photo. 108/109, G. M. Azumendi/ Vision Photo. 109, M. Holford. 110, G. M. Azumendi/Vision Photo. 111, Gettyone/ Stone. 114, Age Fotostock. 115, G. M. Azumendi/Vision Photo. 116/117, E. Barahona Ede/Museo Guggenheim Bilbao. 117, E. Barahona Ede/Museo Guggenheim Bilbao. 118t, E. Barahona Ede/Museo Guggenheim Bilbao. 118b, G. M. Azumendi/Vision Photo. 119, Age Fotostock. 121tl, G. M. Azumendi/Vision Photo. 121tr, A. Arzoz/Axiom. 121b, Age Fotostock. 122/123, Index Fototeca. 123, G. M. Azumendi/Vision Photo. 124/125, Age Fotostock. 126, Age Fotostock. 127, F. Dunlop. 128, G. M. Azumendi/ Vision Photo. 129, Godo-Foto. 130, M. Alavedra/Fototext. 131, G. M. Azumendi/Vision Photo. 132/133, Age Fotostock. 133, G. M. Azumendi/ Vision Photo. 134, M. Chaplow/ Andalucia Slide Lib. 135t, Age Fotostock. 135b, C. O'Rear/Corbis UK Ltd. 136, C. Bowman/Robert Harding Picture Lib. 137, K. Gillham/ Robert Harding Picture Lib. 138, Age Fotostock. 139, A. Guinart/Vision Photo. 140, F. A. Lopez/Vision Photo. 141, A. Guinart/Vision Photo. 142/143, A. Guinart/Vision Photo. 143, Vision Photo. 144, G. M. Azumendi/Vision Photo. 145, G. M. Azumendi/Vision Photo. 147t, M. Hamblin/Oxford Scientific Films. 147b, Vision Photo. 148, Age Fotostock. 150t, G. M. Azumendi/Vision Photo. 150b, H. Reinhard/Bruce Coleman. 151, Age Fotostock. 152, A. Guinart/Vision Photo. 153, Gettyone/Stone. 155, K. Russell. 156, Age Fotostock. 157, A. Blomqvist/The Seeing Eye. 159, AA Photo Lib./S. Day. 161t, R. Duaso/ Fototext. 161b, L. Artus/Vision Photo. 162, AA Photo Lib./S. Day. 163, Zooid Pictures. 164, AA Photo Lib./M. Jourdan. 164/165, AA Photo Lib./M. Jourdan. 166, S. Black/Travel Lib. 167tl, K. Russell. 167tr, S. Maze/ Corbis UK Ltd. 167b, R. Duaso/ Vision Photo. 168, K. Russell. 169, AA Photo Lib./M. Jourdan. 170, K. Russell. 171t, AA Photo Lib./M. Jourdan. 171b, AA Photo Lib./M. Jourdan. 172, AA Photo Lib./S. Day. 173t, K. Russell. 173b, AA Photo Lib./S. Day. 174, Gettyone/Stone. 175, A. Blomqvist/The Seeing Eye. 176, Zooid Pictures. 177, Archivo Gallen/ Godo-Foto. 178, M. Chaplow/ Andalucia Slide Lib. 180, A. Guinart/ Vision Photo. 181, M. Chaplow/AA Photo Lib. 182, M. Chaplow/ Andalucia Slide Lib. 183, M. Chaplow/Andalucia Slide Lib. 184, Sipa Press/Rex Features. 185t, Vision Photo. 185b, James Davis Worldwide: Work by Salvador Dali, ©Kingdom of Spain, universal heir of Salvador Dali/DACS 2001. 186/187, M. Alavedra/Fototext. 187, A. Guinart/Vision Photo. 188, J. M. Escofet/Vision Photo. 189, R. Duaso/ Vision Photo. 191, G. Milverton/ Impact Photos. 192, James Davis Worldwide. 193, Kord Photographics/ Images Colour Lib. 194, R. Manent/ Corbis UK Ltd. 194/195, M.

Alavedra/ Fototext. 196t, F. Dunlop. 196b, M. Alavedra/Fototext. 197, M. Alavedra/ Fototext. 198, M. Alavedra/Fototext. 199, Eye Ubiquitous. 200, A. Guinart/ Vision Photo. 202, A. Guinart/Vision Photo. 203, A. Guinart/Vision Photo. 204, Age Fotostock. 205, D. Waugh/ Gettyone/Stone. 206, A. Guinart/ Vision Photo. 207, AA Photo Lib./M. Chaplow 208, Age Fotostock. 209, P.A. Thompson/ Index Stock Photography Inc. 211, H. G. Schmidt/Travel Lib. 212, Godo-Foto. 213, F. Dunlop. 214, Age Fotostock. 215, R. Vanni/Corbis UK Ltd. 216/217, A. Guinart/Vision Photo. 218/219, H.G. Schmidt/Travel Lib. 220, Index Stock Photography Inc. 221, R. Richardson/Travel Lib. 222, M. Busselle/Corbis UK Ltd. 223, Travel Lib. 224, Index Stock Photography Inc. 225, R. Richardson/Travel Lib. 226, A. Guinart/Vision Photo. 227, A. Guinart/Vision Photo. 228, F. Dunlop. 229, Index Stock Photo-graphy Inc. 230, Age Fotostock. 231, J. Miller/Robert Harding Picture Lib. 232, A. Guinart/Vision Photo. 233, B. Barbey/Magnum Photos. 235, M. Henley/Impact Photos. 236, J. Cornish/Gettyone/Stone. 237, Age Fotostock. 238, Salvador Dali, El Quijote, 1945, © Kingdom of Spain, universal heir of Salvador Dali/DACS 2001. 238/239, C. Penn/Impact Photos. 241, N. Egerton/Travel Ink. 242, M. Busselle/Corbis UK Ltd. 243, Godo-Foto. 244, James Davis Worldwide. 246, R. Frerck/Odyssey/ Chicago/Robert Harding Picture Lib. 247, G. M. Azumendi/Vision Photo. 248, Robert Harding Picture Lib. 249, F. Dunlop. 250/251, Robert Harding Picture Lib. 251, Age Fotostock. 252, H. Gruyaert/Magnum Photos. 253t, Private Collection/Bridgeman Art Lib., London. 253b, A. Guinart/Vision Photo. 254/255, A. Guinart/Vision Photo. 255, A. Guinart/Vision Photo. 256, Age Fotostock. 256/257, H. Gruyaert/Magnum Photos. 258, Age Fotostock. 259, C. Coe/Axiom. 262/263, M. Alavedra/Fototext. 264/265, C. Caldicott/Axiom. 265, C. Coe/Axiom. 266, P. Seheult/Eye Ubiquitous. 267, AA Photo Lib./A. Molyneux. 268, C. Caldicott/Axiom. 269t, H. Sitton/Gettyone/Stone. 269c, C. Coe/Axiom. 269bl, M. Chaplow/ Andalucia Slide Lib. 269br, Iranzo/ Index Fototeca. 270, Godo-Foto. 271, M. Chaplow/Andalucia Slide Lib. 272, A. Williams/Axiom. 273t, S. Greenland/Eye Ubiquitous. 273bl, M. Chaplow/Andalucia Slide Lib. 273br. M. Chaplow/Andalucia Slide Lib. 274, R. & J. Kemp/Oxford Scientific Films. 275, P. Enticknap/Travel Lib. 276/277, M. Alavedra/Fototext. 277, A. Guinart/Vision Photo. 278, A. Guinart/Vision Photo. 279, S. Black/Travel Lib. 280, B. Battersby/ Eye Ubiquitous. 281, C. Caldicott/ Axiom. 282, M. Chaplow/Andalucia Slide Lib. 283, AA Photo Lib./J. Tims. 284, AA Photo Library/M. Chaplon. 285, Travel Lib. 286/287, M. Chaplow/Andalucia Slide Lib. 288/289, D. Codina/Fototext. 289, M.

Chaplow/ Andalucia Slide Lib. 290, P. Ward/ Corbis UK Ltd. 291, M. Chaplow/ Andalucia Slide Lib. 292, AA Photo Lib./D. Robertson. 293, H. G. Schmidt/Travel Lib. 294, M. Chaplow/Andalucia Slide Lib. 295, M. Chaplow/Andalucia Slide Lib. 296/297, A. Guinart/Vision Photo. 298, F. Dunlop. 299, R. Duaso/ Fototext. 300t, L. Miles/Eye Ubiquitous. 300b, Godo-Foto. 301, L. Miles/Eye Ubiquitous. 302, R. Westlake/Travel Ink. 303, A. Blomqvist/The Seeing Eye. 304, James Davis Worldwide. 304/305, Age Fotostock. 306, L. Miles/Eye Ubiquitous. 308, M. Chaplow/ Andalucia Slide Lib. 309, M. Chaplow/Andalucia Slide Lib. 310, F. Dunlop. 311, M. Chaplow/Andalucia Slide Lib. 312, D. Contantine/Axiom. 313, F. Alda/Corbis UK Ltd. 314, Ch. Hermes/Travel Lib. 315, T. Mata/ Vision Photo. 316, T. Mata/Vision Photo. 318/319, M. Rubio/James Davis Worldwide. 319, A. Guinart/ Vision Photo. 320, M. Chaplow/ Andalucia Slide Lib. 321, M. Chaplow/Andalucia Slide Lib. 322, M. Chaplow/Andalucia Slide Lib. 323, S. Benbow/Axiom. 324, J. Balanya/ Vision Photo. 326/327, Ch. Hermes/ Travel Lib. 328/329, AA Photo Lib./K. Paterson. 330, James Davis World-wide. 331, S. Benbow/Axiom. 332, Age Fotostock. 333, AA Photo Lib./J. Tims. 334, S. Black/Travel Lib. 336, S. Black/Travel Lib. 337, AA Photo Lib./R. Moore. 338, AA Photo Lib./J. Tims. 339, AA Photo Lib./C. Sawyer. 340, D. Robertson/Travel Lib. 341, A. Arzoz/Axiom.

The world's largest nonprofit scientific and educational organization, the National Geographic Society was founded in 1888 "for the increase and diffusion of geographic knowledge." Since then it has supported scientific exploration and spread information to its more than 9 million members worldwide.

The National Geographic Society educates and inspires millions every day through magazines, books, television programs, videos, maps and atlases, research grants, the National Geographic Bee, teacher workshops, and innovative classroom materials.

The Society is supported through membership dues, charitable gifts, and income from the sale of its educational products. Members receive NATIONAL GEOGRAPHIC magazine— the Society's official journal—discounts on Society products, and other benefits.

For more information about the National Geographic Society, its educational programs, publications, or how to support its work, call 1-800-NGS-LINE (647-5463), or write to: National Geographic Society, 1145 17th Street, N.W., Washington, D.C. 20036 U.S.A.
Printed in the U.S.A.

Published by the National Geographic Society

John M. Fahey, Jr., *President and Chief Executive Officer*
Gilbert M. Grosvenor, *Chairman of the Board*
Nina D. Hoffman, *Executive Vice President,*
President, Books and School Publishing
William R. Gray, *Vice President and Director, Book Division*
Elizabeth L. Newhouse, *Director of Travel Publishing*
Barbara A. Noe, *Senior Editor and Project Manager*
Cinda Rose, *Art Director*
Caroline Hickey, *Senior Researcher*
Carl Mehler, *Director of Maps*
Joe Ochlak, *Map Coordinator*
Lise Sajewski, *Editorial Consultant*
Gary Colbert, *Production Director*
Ric Wain, *Production Project Manager*
Keith R. Moore, *Contributor*
Larry Porges, *Editorial Coordinator*

Edited and designed by AA Publishing (a trading name of Automobile Association Developments Limited, whose registered office is Norfolk House, Priestley Road, Basingstoke, Hampshire, England RG24 9NY. Registered number: 1878835).
Rachel Alder, Marilynne Lanng, *Project Managers*
David Austin, *Senior Art Editor*
Betty Sheldrick, *Senior Editor*
Keith Russell, *Designer*
Inna Nogeste, *Senior Cartographic Editor*
Richard Firth, *Production Director*
Steve Gilchrist, *Prepress Production Controller*
Cartography by AA Cartographic Production
Picture Research by Zooid Pictures Ltd. and Liz Wells, AA Photo Library
Drive maps drawn by Chris Orr Associates, Southampton, England
Cutaway illustrations drawn by Maltings Partnership, Derby, England

Library of Congress Cataloging-in- Publication Data
Dunlop, Fiona, 1952-
    The National Geographic traveler. Spain / Fiona Dunlop.
      p. cm.
    Includes index.
    ISBN 0-7922-7922-2
    1. Spain--Guidebooks. I. Title: Spain. II. Title.

    DP14 .D86 2001
    914.604'83--dc21   00-052681

Printed and bound by R.R. Donnelley & Sons, Willard, Ohio.
Color separations by Leo Reprographic Ltd., Hong Kong
Cover separations by L.C. Repro, Aldermaston, U.K.
Cover printed by Miken Inc., Cheektowaga, New York.

Visit the society's Web site at http://www.nationalgeographic.com

THE NATIONAL GEOGRAPHIC TRAVELER

A Century of Travel Expertise in Every Guide

- **Australia** ISBN: 0-7922-7431-8
- **Boston & Environs** ISBN: 0-7922-7926-3
- **California** ISBN: 0-7922-7564-0
- **Canada** ISBN: 0-7922-7427-X
- **The Caribbean** ISBN: 0-7922-7434-2
- **China** ISBN: 0-7922-7921-2
- **Costa Rica** ISBN: 0-7922-7946-8
- **Florence & Tuscany** ISBN: 0-7922-7924-7
- **Florida** ISBN: 0-7922-7432-6
- **France** ISBN: 0-7922-7426-1
- **Great Britain** ISBN: 0-7922-7425-3
- **Greece** ISBN: 0-7922-7923-9
- **Hawaii** ISBN: 0-7922-7944-1

- **Italy** ISBN: 0-7922-7562-4
- **Japan** ISBN: 0-7922-7563-2
- **London** ISBN: 0-7922-7428-8
- **Los Angeles** ISBN: 0-7922-7947-6
- **Miami and the Keys** ISBN: 0-7922-7433-4
- **New Orleans** ISBN: 0-7922-7948-4
- **New York** ISBN: 0-7922-7430-X
- **Paris** ISBN: 0-7922-7429-6
- **Rome** ISBN: 0-7922-7566-7
- **San Francisco** ISBN: 0-7922-7565-9
- **Spain** ISBN: 0-7922-7922-0
- **Sydney** ISBN: 0-7922-7435-0
- **Thailand** ISBN: 0-7922-7943-3

AVAILABLE WHEREVER BOOKS ARE SOLD